MW00337939

Language Arts and Literature

Course 3

PEARSON

AGS Globe

Shoreview, MN

Reading Consultant

Timothy Shanahan, Ph.D., Professor of Urban Education, Director of the Center for Literacy, University of Illinois Chicago, Author, *AMP™ Reading System*

Acknowledgments appear on pages 644–647, which constitutes an extension of this copyright page.

Reviewers

The publisher wishes to thank the following educators for their helpful comments during the review process for *Language Arts and Literature, Course 3.*

Sherie J. Campbell, ESE Teacher, Ben Hill Middle School, Tampa, FL; **Stephanie Fetterolf,** Vice Principal, Hilltop Middle School, Toronto, Ontario, Canada; **Jayne O'Gorman,** 6th Grade Reading Teacher, Clifford Crone Middle School, Naperville, IL; **Jane McKenney,** K–12 English Coordinator, Smith Middle School, Troy, MI; **Michelle Richards,** Instructional Coordinating Teacher, Cochrane Middle School, Charlotte, NC; **Mary Alice Ross,** Content Coordinator for English/Language Arts, Flint Community Schools, Flint, MI; **Ellen Smith De La Cruz,** Teacher, Balboa Park Academy—Juvenile Court and Community Schools, San Diego, CA; **Lori Wells,** M.Ed., LSSP, LPA, Educational Diagnostician, Harlingen High School South, Harlingen, TX; **Alicia Wingard,** Special Education Teacher, Mountain Brook Junior High School, Birmingham, AL

Copyright © 2008 by Pearson Education, Inc., publishing as Pearson AGS Globe, Shoreview, Minnesota 55126. All rights reserved. Printed in the United States of America. This publication is protected by copyright, and permission should be obtained from the publisher prior to any prohibited reproduction, storage in a retrieval system, or transmission in any form or by any means, electronic, mechanical, photocopying, recording, or likewise. For information regarding permission(s), write to: Rights and Permissions Department, One Lake Street, Upper Saddle River, New Jersey 07458.

Pearson AGS Globe™ is a trademark, in the U.S. and/or in other countries, of Pearson Education, Inc. or its affiliate(s).

ISBN-13: 978-0-7854-6316-0

ISBN-10:   0-7854-6316-X

2 3 4 5 6 7 8 9 10   V011   16 15 14 13 12

1-800-992-0244

www.agsglobe.com

Contents

Unit 6 Themes in American Stories 504

How to Use This Book: A Study Guide

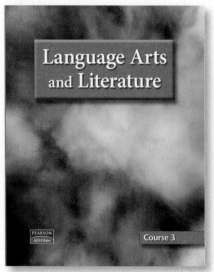

This book is an anthology of literature. An anthology is a collection of literature written by different authors. The literature can be poems, plays, short stories, essays, parts of novels, folktales, legends, or myths. Sometimes an anthology contains selections from a certain country or continent. For example, you might have an anthology with great literature from around the world. Sometimes anthologies are organized around different genres, or types of literature. Then, you might have sections on poems, short stories, plays, essays, or folktales.

Reading a Literature Anthology

This anthology contains much enjoyable literature. An anthology helps you understand yourself and other people. Sometimes you will read about people from other countries. Sometimes you will read about people who lived in the past. Try to relate what the author is saying to your own life. Ask yourself: Have I ever felt this way? Have I known anyone like this person? Have I seen anything like this?

A literature anthology can also help you appreciate the beauty of language. As you read, find phrases or sentences that you particularly like. You may want to start a notebook of these phrases and sentences. You may also want to include words that are difficult.

This anthology is also important because it introduces you to great works of literature. Many times, you will find references to these works in everyday life. Sometimes you will hear a quotation on TV or read it in the newspaper. Great literature can come in many forms. On the next page are definitions of some kinds of literature genres in an anthology.

Genre Definitions

autobiography a person's life story, written by that person

biography a person's life story told by someone else (you will find biographies of many famous authors in this book)

diary a daily record of personal events, thoughts, or private feelings
- A diary is like a journal, but a diary often expresses more of the writer's feelings.

drama a story told through the words and actions of characters, written to be performed as well as read; a play

essay a written work that shows a writer's opinions on some basic or current issue

fable a short story or poem with a moral (lesson about life), often with animals who act like humans
- Aesop was a famous author of fables.

fiction writing that is imaginative and designed to entertain
- In fiction, the author creates the events and characters.
- Short stories, novels, folktales, myths, legends, and most plays are works of fiction.

folktale a story that has been handed down from one generation to another
- The characters are usually either good or bad.
- Folktales make use of rhyme and repetitive phrases.
- Sometimes they are called tall tales, particularly if they are humorous and exaggerated.
- Folktales are also called folklore.

journal writing that expresses an author's feelings or first impressions about a subject
- Students may keep journals that record thoughts about what they have read.
- People also keep travel journals to remind themselves of interesting places they have seen.

legend a traditional story that at one time was told orally and was handed down from one generation to another
- Legends are like myths, but they do not have as many supernatural forces.
- Legends usually feature characters who actually lived, or real places or events.

myth an important story, often part of a culture's religion, that explains how the world came to be or why natural events happen
- A myth usually includes gods, goddesses, or unusually powerful human beings.
- Myths were first oral stories, and most early cultures have myths.

nonfiction writing about real people and events
- Essays, speeches, diaries, journals, autobiographies, and biographies are all usually nonfiction.

novel fiction that is book-length and has more plot and character details than a short story

poem a short piece of literature that usually has rhythm and paints powerful or beautiful impressions with words
- Often, poems have sound patterns such as rhyme.
- Songs are poetry set to music.

prose all writing that is not poetry
- Short stories, novels, autobiographies, biographies, diaries, journals, and essays are examples of prose.

science fiction fiction that is based on real or imagined facts of science
- Most stories are set in the future.
- Jules Verne was one of the first science fiction authors.

short story a brief work of prose fiction that includes plot, setting, characters, point of view, and theme
- Edgar Allan Poe was a great writer of short stories.

How to Read This Book

Different works of literature should be read in different ways. However, there are some basic methods you should use to read all works of literature.

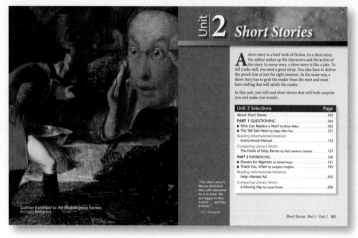

Before Beginning a Unit

- Read the unit title and selection titles.

- Read the paragraphs that introduce the unit.

- Look at the pictures and other artwork in the unit.

- Think about what you already know about the unit.

- Think about what you might want to learn.

- Develop questions in your mind that you think will be answered in this unit.

Before Reading a Selection

- Read the selection's title.

- Look at the pictures and other artwork.

- Read the background material included in About the Author and About the Selection.

- Read the Objectives and think about what you will learn by reading the selection.

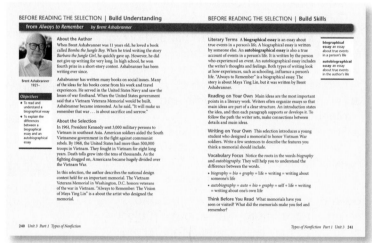

- Read the Literary Terms and their definitions.

- Complete the Before Reading the Selection activities. These activities will help you read the selection, understand vocabulary, and prepare for the reading.

As You Read a Selection

- Read the notes in the side margins. These will help you understand and think about the main ideas.

- Think of people or events in your own life that are similar to those described.

- Reread sentences or paragraphs that you do not understand.

- Predict what you think will happen next.

- Read the definitions at the bottom of the page for words that you do not know.

- Record words that you do not know. Also, write questions or comments you have about the text.

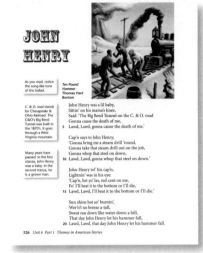

After Reading a Selection

- Reread interesting or difficult parts of the selection.

- Reflect on what you have learned by reading the selection.

- Complete the After Reading the Selection review questions and activities. The activities will help you develop your grammar, writing, speaking, listening, viewing, technology, media, and research skills.

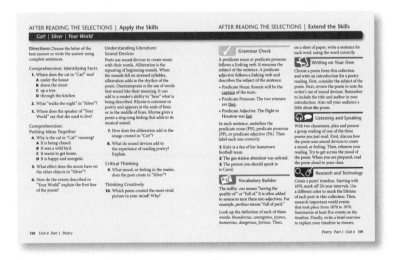

Reading Certain Types of Literature

The methods already described will help you understand all kinds of literature. You may need to use additional methods for specific types of literature.

Reading Poetry

- Read the poem aloud.
- Listen to the sounds of the words.
- Picture the images the author is describing.
- Reread poems over and over again to appreciate the author's use of language.

Reading Essays

- Review the questions in the After Reading the Selection before you begin reading.
- Use the questions to think about what you are reading.
- Remember that essays usually express an author's opinions. Try to understand why the author may have formed these opinions.

Reading Plays

- Picture the setting of the play. Since there usually is not much description given, try to relate the setting to something you have seen before.
- Pay attention to what the characters say. How does this give clues about the character's personality? Have you ever known anyone like this? Are you like this?

Tips for Better Reading

Literary Terms

Literary Terms are words or phrases that we use to study and discuss works of literature. These terms describe the ways an author helps to make us enjoy and understand what we are reading. Some of the terms also describe a genre, or specific type of literature. In this anthology, you will see white boxes on the side of the Before Reading the Selection pages. In these boxes are Literary Terms and their definitions. These terms are important in understanding and discussing the selection being read. By understanding these Literary Terms, readers can appreciate the author's craft. You can find the definitions for all of the Literary Terms used in this book in the Handbook of Literary Terms on page 610.

setting the place and time in a story

plot the series of events in a story

theme the main idea of a literary work

Using a Graphic Organizer

A graphic organizer is visual representation of information. It can help you see how ideas are related to each other. A graphic organizer can help you study for a test, organize information before writing an essay, or organize details in a literature selection. You will use graphic organizers for different activities throughout this textbook. There are 14 different graphic organizers listed below. You can read a description and see an example of each graphic organizer in Appendix A in the back of this textbook.

- Character Analysis Guide
- Story Map
- Main Idea Graphic (Umbrella)
- Main Idea Graphic (Table)
- Main Idea Graphic (Details)
- Venn Diagram
- Sequence Chain
- Concept Map
- Plot Mountain
- Structured Overview
- Semantic Table
- Prediction Guide
- Semantic Line
- KWL Chart

Six Traits of Writing

A *trait* is a quality or feature of something. Traits, or qualities, of good writing help students and teachers discuss writing using a common language. These traits will help you as you plan, draft, revise, and edit your writing. The Six Traits of Writing icons pictured below are used in the Writing Workshops at the end of each unit in this textbook. As you write, think about how you can use each trait to help make your writing better. You can also read more about each trait in Appendix C at the back of this book.

 **Six Traits of Writing:**
Ideas message, details, and purpose

 **Six Traits of Writing:**
Word Choice vivid words that "show, not tell"

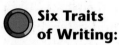 **Six Traits of Writing:**
Voice the writer's own language

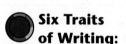 **Six Traits of Writing:**
Organization order, ideas tied together

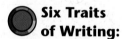 **Six Traits of Writing:**
Sentence Fluency smooth rhythm and flow

Six Traits of Writing:
Conventions correct grammar, spelling, and mechanics

Taking Notes

You will read many selections in this literature anthology. As you read, you may want to take notes to help remember what you have read. You can use these notes to keep track of events and characters in a story. Your notes may also be helpful for recognizing common ideas among the selections in a unit. You can review your notes as you prepare to take a test. Here are some tips for taking notes:

- Write down only the most important information.
- Do not try to write every detail or every word.
- Write notes in your own words.
- Do not be concerned about writing in complete sentences. Use short phrases.

Using the Three-Column Chart

One good way to take notes is to use a three-column chart. Make your own three-column chart by dividing a sheet of notebook paper into three parts. In Column 1, write the topic you are reading about or studying. In Column 2, write what you learned about this topic as you read or listened to your teacher. In Column 3, write questions, observations, or opinions about the topic, or write a detail that will help you remember the topic. Here are some examples of different ways to take notes using the three-column chart.

The topic I am studying	What I learned from reading the text or class discussion	Questions, observations, or ideas I have about the topic
Fiction	• one genre of literature • many different types of fiction—science fiction, adventure, detective stories, romance, suspense	• The book I am reading right now is fiction. It is an adventure story. • I wonder if poetry is part of the fiction genre.

Vocabulary Word	Definition	Sentence with Vocabulary Word
Premises	a building or part of a building	Students are not allowed on the school **premises** during the weekend.

Character	Character Traits Found in the Selection	Page Number
John Krakauer	Conflict, person against self—Krakauer wonders if he will run out of oxygen before returning to camp.	p. 355
	Determined—Krakauer is determined to make it back to camp even though his oxygen has run out and it is snowing on the mountain.	p. 358
	Thankful—After reaching camp, Krakauer is thankful that he is safe.	p. 360

Reading Checklist

Good readers do not just read with their eyes. They read with their brains turned on. In other words, they are active readers. Good readers use strategies as they read to keep them on their toes. The following strategies will help you to check your understanding of what you read.

- **Summarizing** To summarize a text, stop often as you read. Notice these things: the topic, the main thing being said about the topic, important details that support the main idea. Try to sum up the author's message using your own words.

- **Questioning** Ask yourself questions about the text and read to answer them. Here are some useful questions to ask: Why did the author include this information? Is this like anything I have experienced? Am I learning what I hoped I would learn?

- **Predicting** As you read, think about what might come next. Add in what you already know about the topic. Predict what the text will say. Then, as you read, notice whether your prediction is right. If not, change your prediction.

- **Text Structure** Pay attention to how a text is organized. Find parts that stand out. They are probably the most important ideas or facts. Think about why the author organized ideas this way. Is the author showing a sequence of events? Is the author explaining a solution or the effect of something?

- **Visualizing** Picture what is happening in a text or what is being described. Make a movie out of it in your mind. If you can picture it clearly, then you know you understand it. Visualizing what you read will also help you remember it later.

- **Inferencing** The meaning of a text may not be stated. Instead, the author may give clues and hints. It is up to you to put them together with what you already know about the topic. Then you make an inference—you conclude what the author means.

- **Metacognition** Think about your thinking patterns as you read. Before reading a text, preview it. Think about what you can do to get the most out of it. Think about what you already know about the topic. Write down any questions you have. After you read, ask yourself: Did that make sense? If not, read it again.

What to Do About Words You Do Not Know

- If the word is in bold type, look for the definition of the word at the bottom of the page.

- If the word is not in bold type, read to the end of the sentence and maybe the next sentence. Can you determine the meaning now?

- Look at the beginning sound of the unknown word. Ask yourself, "What word begins with this sound and would make sense here?"

- Sound out the syllables of the word.

- If you still cannot determine the meaning, see if you know any parts of the word: prefixes, suffixes, or roots.

- If this does not work, write the word on a note card or in a vocabulary notebook. Then look up the word in a dictionary after you have finished reading the selection. Reread the passage containing the unknown word after you have looked up its definition.

- If the word is necessary to understand the passage, look it up in a dictionary or glossary immediately.

Retorted

Unit 1

The Adventure of the Speckled Band

replied with anger

Word Study Tips

- Start a vocabulary file with note cards to use for review.

- Write one word on the front of each card. Write the unit number, selection title, and the definition on the back.

- You can use these cards as flash cards by yourself or with a study partner to test your knowledge.

Tips for Taking Tests

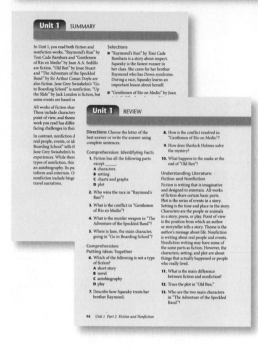

Before the Test Day

- Make sure you have read all of the selections assigned.

- Review the Literary Terms and definitions for each selection.

- Review your answers to the After Reading the Selection questions.

- Reread the Unit Summary and review your answers to the Unit Review.

- Review any notes that you have taken or graphic organizers you have developed.

- Ask your teacher what kinds of questions will be on the test.

- Try to predict what questions will be asked. Think of and write answers to those questions.

- Review the Test-Taking Tip at the bottom of each Unit Review page.

During the Test

- Come to the test with a positive attitude.

- Write your name on the paper.

- Preview the test and read the directions carefully.

- Plan your time.

- Answer the questions that you know first.

- Then go back and answer the more difficult questions.

- Allow time to reread all of the questions and your answers.

Andrew Judd

Unit 1
Fiction and Nonfiction

Writing takes different forms. Fiction stories are made up by the person who writes them. Novels and short stories are types of fiction. All writing that is not fiction is nonfiction. Nonfiction is writing about real people and events. Four of the most important types of nonfiction are essays, speeches, biographies, and autobiographies. In this unit, you will read both fiction and nonfiction. "Raymond's Run" and "Gentlemen of Río en Medio" are both fiction. "Go to Boarding School" and the informational materials selections are nonfiction.

"Imagination and fiction make up more than three-quarters of our real life."

—Simone Weil

Unit 1 About Fiction and Nonfiction

Elements of Fiction

Fiction is writing that is imaginative and designed to entertain. In fiction writing, the author creates the events and characters. All works of fiction share certain basic parts.

- **Setting** is the time and place in a story.

- **Plot** is the series of events in a story. The plot of a story includes the **conflict**, or problem, and the **resolution**, or ending.

- **Characters** are the people or animals in a story, poem, or play. **Character traits,** or qualities, are a character's way of thinking, behaving, or speaking.

- **Point of view** is the position from which the author or storyteller tells the story.

- **First person** is a point of view where the narrator is also a character. In first-person, the narrator uses the pronouns *I* and *we*.

- **Third person** is a point of view where the narrator is not a character. The narrator refers to characters as *he* or *she*.

- **Theme** is the main idea of a work of literature.

Types of Fiction

Short stories are brief works of prose fiction that include plot, setting, characters, point of view, and theme. Short stories usually focus on one main plot and have one main conflict. Short stories often can be read in one sitting.

Novels are fiction that is book-length and have more plot and character details than a short story. Just like short stories, novels have characters, plot, conflict, and setting.

Novellas are works of fiction that are shorter than novels, but longer than short stories.

Historical fiction is fictional writing that draws on actual events from history.

SUMMER FICTION

Elements of Nonfiction

Nonfiction works are different from works of fiction in these ways:

- They deal only with real people, events, or ideas.

- They are narrated from the point of view of the author, who is a real person.

Besides the facts in the text, other things can affect nonfiction writing.

- Nonfiction writing can have different **moods**, or feelings that the writing creates.

- **Author's style** is an author's way of writing, including the author's use of language.

Purposes of Nonfiction

Nonfiction is writing about real people and real events. Some of the purposes include the following:

- **To Persuade:** Speeches and editorials are often written to convince an audience of a certain idea or opinion.

- **To Inform:** Articles, reference books, historical essays, and research papers present facts and information.

- **To Entertain:** Biographies, autobiographies, and travel narratives are often written for readers to enjoy.

Part 1

Reading Strategy:
Predicting

Previewing a text helps readers think about what they already know about a subject. It also prepares readers to look for new information—to predict what will come next. Keep this in mind as you make predictions:

- Make your best guess about what might happen next.
- Add details about why you think certain things will happen.
- Check your predictions. You may have to change your predictions as you learn more information.

Literary Terms

fiction writing that is imaginative and designed to entertain; the author creates the events and characters

character a person or animal in a story, poem, or play

setting the time and place of a story

plot the series of events in a story

conflict the struggle of the main character against himself or herself, another person, or nature

short story a brief work of prose fiction that includes plot, setting, characters, point of view, and theme

point of view the position from which the author or storyteller tells the story

theme the main idea of a literary work

external conflict the struggle of a character against an outside force such as another character, natural forces, or some part of society

internal conflict the struggle of a character against an inside force such as feelings or beliefs

resolution the act of solving the conflict in a story

narrative a story, usually told in chronological order

foreshadowing clues or hints that a writer gives about something that has not yet happened

Raymond's Run   *by Toni Cade Bambara*

About the Author

Toni Cade Bambara was named Miltona Mirkin Cade at birth. She decided she wanted to be called "Toni" when she was in kindergarten. She spent her first 10 years in Harlem, New York City, an area that many African Americans called home. During her childhood, Bambara learned that city life was tough but rewarding. She loved the energy and excitement of the big city. She enjoyed the lively talk of the streets. As a writer, she captured the language and dreams of real people. She focused on young people struggling to be themselves.

Bambara published her first story when she was only 20 years old. She was a student at Queens College in New York City at the time. Bambara said that writing ". . . slips up on your blind side. [It] wrassles you to the mat before you know what's grabbed you." Bambara always gave her mother credit for encouraging her to write. "She gave me permission to wonder, to . . . dawdle, to daydream," Bambara said.

About the Selection

Bambara published "Raymond's Run" in 1971. It was part of her second book of stories, called *Tales and Stories for Black Folks*. Bambara's story shows a young black girl, Squeaky, coming of age. In this piece of literature, actions speak louder than words. We see this as Squeaky reaches an important understanding about her brother Raymond who has Down syndrome.

Before Reading **continued on next page**

Objectives

◆ To read and understand a work of fiction

◆ To define character, setting, conflict, and plot in a story

◆ To make predictions while reading

Raymond's Run   *by Toni Cade Bambara*

fiction writing that is imaginative and designed to entertain; the author creates the events and characters

character a person or animal in a story, poem, or play

setting the time and place of a story

plot the series of events in a story

conflict the struggle of the main character against himself or herself, another person, or nature

Literary Terms "Raymond's Run" is a work of **fiction**—writing that is imaginative and designed to entertain. Fiction writers create the events and **characters**. A character is a person or animal in a story, poem, or play. The time and place of the story, or the **setting**, is another part of fiction writing. In "Raymond's Run," the main character Squeaky learns important lessons about other characters in the story. The **plot**, or the series of events, shows what happens to help her learn these lessons. One important part of plot is the **conflict.** This is the struggle of the main character against himself or herself, another person, or nature.

Reading on Your Own To make predictions, readers make good guesses about what will happen next. Use story details and what you already know. As you read, use a chart like this one.

My Prediction	Story Clues	What Really Happened
1.		
2.		

Writing on Your Own In "Raymond's Run," the narrator tries to protect her brother from being teased. She also struggles to gain respect for herself. Write a paragraph explaining the actions and character traits that encourage respect.

Vocabulary Focus Preview the selection vocabulary words before you begin reading. The vocabulary appears in boldface in the selection. Choose five words you do not know and write down what you think each word means. Then use the Glossary in the back of your book to find the definition for each word.

Think Before You Read Talk with a partner and predict what you think the story will be about. As you read, check your predictions with the details of the story.

Raymond's Run

I don't have much work to do around the house like some girls. My mother does that. And I don't have to earn my pocket money by **hustling**; George runs errands for the big boys and sells Christmas cards. And anything else that's got to get done, my father does. All I have to do in life is mind my brother Raymond, which is enough.

Sometimes I slip and say my little brother Raymond. But as any fool can see he's much bigger and he's older too. But a lot of people call him my little brother cause he needs looking after cause he's not quite right. And a lot of smart mouths got lots to say about that too, especially when George was minding him. But now, if anybody has anything to say to Raymond, anything to say about his big head, they have to come by me. And I don't play the dozens or believe in standing around with somebody in my face doing a lot of talking. I much rather just knock you down and take my chances even if I am a little girl with skinny arms and a squeaky voice, which is how I got the name Squeaky. And if things get too rough, I run. And as anybody can tell you, I'm the fastest thing on two feet.

There is no track meet that I don't win the first-place medal. I used to win the twenty-yard dash when I was a little kid in kindergarten. Nowadays, it's the fifty-yard dash. And

As you read, notice how the main character, Squeaky, feels about Raymond. How does she treat him?

The dozens is a game in which the players call each other names. The first person to show anger loses.

hustling getting or selling in a hurried, rough, or illegal way

Mercury is the messenger of the gods in Roman mythology. He is often pictured wearing shoes with wings to show that he could move very quickly.

Reading Strategy: Predicting

Reread the first two paragraphs. What clues help you predict how Squeaky will react to a challenge?

PAL stands for the Police Athletic League.

A stage coach is an old-fashioned carriage pulled by a horse.

tomorrow I'm subject to run the quarter-mile relay all by myself and come in first, second, and third. The big kids call me Mercury cause I'm the swiftest thing in the neighborhood. Everybody knows that—except two people who know better, my father and me.

He can beat me to Amsterdam Avenue with me having a two fire-**hydrant** headstart and him running with his hands in his pockets and whistling. But that's private information. Cause can you imagine some thirty-five-year-old man stuffing himself into PAL shorts to race little kids? So as far as everyone's concerned, I'm the fastest and that goes for Gretchen, too, who has put out the tale that she is going to win the first-place medal this year. Ridiculous. In the second place, she's got short legs. In the third place, she's got freckles. In the first place, no one can beat me and that's all there is to it.

I'm standing on the corner admiring the weather and about to take a stroll down Broadway so I can practice my breathing exercises, and I've got Raymond walking on the inside close to the buildings, cause he's subject to fits of **fantasy** and starts thinking he's a circus performer and that the curb is a **tightrope** strung high in the air. And sometimes after a rain he likes to step down off his tightrope right into the gutter and slosh around getting his shoes and cuffs wet. Or sometimes if you don't watch him he'll dash across traffic to the island in the middle of Broadway and give the pigeons a fit. Then I have to go behind him **apologizing** to all the old people sitting around trying to get some sun and getting all upset with the pigeons fluttering around them, scattering their newspapers and upsetting the waxpaper lunches in their laps. So I keep Raymond on the inside of me, and he plays like he's driving a stage coach, which is O.K. by me so long as he doesn't run me over or interrupt my breathing exercises, which I have to do on

hydrant a large, upright pipe with a valve for drawing water	**fantasy** a picture existing only in the mind; a daydream	**tightrope** a rope or wire on which acrobats perform
		apologizing saying you are sorry

account of I'm serious about my running, and I don't care who knows it.

Now some people like to act like things come easy to them, won't let on that they practice. Not me. I'll high prance down 34th Street like a rodeo pony to keep my knees strong even if it does get my mother **uptight** so that she walks ahead like she's not with me, don't know me, is all by herself on a shopping trip, and I am somebody else's crazy child.

Now you take Cynthia Procter for instance. She's just the opposite. If there's a test tomorrow, she'll say something like, "Oh, I guess I'll play handball this afternoon and watch television tonight," just to let you know she ain't thinking about the test. Or like last week when she won the spelling bee for the millionth time, "A good thing you got 'receive,' Squeaky, cause I would have got it wrong. I completely forgot about the spelling bee." And she'll clutch the lace on her blouse like it was a narrow escape. Oh, brother.

But of course when I pass her house on my early morning trots around the block, she is practicing the scales on the piano over and over and over and over. Then in music class she always lets herself get bumped around so she falls accidently on purpose onto the piano stool and is so surprised

This part of the plot tells you about Squeaky. She is brave, loyal, and honest. She cares for her brother and also is a fast runner.

Reading Strategy:
Predicting
What details support a prediction that Squeaky will be tough to beat in a race?

uptight very upset, angry, or worried

Ole is slang for old.
Frédéric Chopin (1810–1849) was a famous composer and pianist from Poland.

to find herself sitting there that she decides just for fun to try out the ole keys and what do you know—Chopin's waltzes just spring out of her fingertips and she's the most surprised thing in the world. A regular **prodigy**. I could kill people like that.

I stay up all night studying the words for the spelling bee. And you can see me any time of day practicing running. I never walk if I can trot, and shame on Raymond if he can't keep up. But of course he does, cause if he hangs back someone's **liable** to walk up to him and get smart, or take his allowance from him, or ask him where he got that great big pumpkin head. People are so stupid sometimes.

So I'm strolling down Broadway breathing out and breathing in on counts of seven, which is my lucky number, and here comes Gretchen and her **sidekicks**—Mary Louise who used to be a friend of mine when she first moved to Harlem from Baltimore and got beat up by everybody till I took up for her on account of her mother and my mother used to sing in the same choir when they were young girls, but people ain't grateful, so now she hangs out with the new girl Gretchen and talks about me like a dog; and Rosie who is as fat as I am skinny and has a big mouth where Raymond is concerned and is too stupid to know that there is not a big deal of difference between herself and Raymond and that she can't afford to throw stones. So they are steady coming up Broadway and I see right away that it's going to be one of those Dodge City scenes cause the street ain't that big and they're close to the buildings just as we are. First I think I'll step into the candy store and look over the new comics and let them pass. But that's chicken and I've got a **reputation** to consider. So then I think I'll just walk straight on through them or even over them if necessary. But as they get to me, they slow down. I'm ready to fight, cause like I said I don't feature a whole lot of

Dodge City, Kansas, was a famous town in the American West. Many gunfights took place there in the 1800s.

prodigy a person with amazing talent

liable likely

sidekicks friends

reputation what people think and say about a person's character

chit-chat, I much **prefer** to just knock you down right from the jump and save everybody a lotta precious time.

"You signing up for the May Day races?" smiles Mary Louise, only it's not a smile at all.

A dumb question like that doesn't deserve an answer. Besides, there's just me and Gretchen standing there really, so no use wasting my breath talking to shadows.

"I don't think you're going to win this time," says Rosie, trying to **signify** with her hands on her hips all salty, completely forgetting that I have whupped her many times for less salt than that.

"I always win cause I'm the best," I say straight at Gretchen who is, as far as I'm concerned, the only one talking in this ventriloquist-dummy routine.

Gretchen smiles, but it's not a smile, and I'm thinking that girls never really smile at each other because they don't know how and don't want to know how and there's probably no one to teach us how cause grown-up girls don't know either. Then they all look at Raymond who has just brought his mule team to a standstill. And they're about to see what trouble they can get into through him.

"What grade you in now, Raymond?"

"You got anything to say to my brother, you say it to me, Mary Louise Williams of Raggedy Town, Baltimore."

"What are you, his mother?" **sasses** Rosie.

"That's right, Fatso. And the next word out of anybody and I'll be *their* mother too." So they just stand there and Gretchen shifts from one leg to the other and so do they. Then Gretchen puts her hands on her hips and is about to say something with her freckle-face self but doesn't. Then she walks around me looking me up and down but keeps walking up Broadway, and her sidekicks follow her. So me and Raymond smile at each other and he says, "Gidyap" to his team and I continue with my breathing exercises, strolling down Broadway toward the

> A *ventriloquist-dummy routine* is a comedy act. The performer speaks through a puppet called a "dummy."

> ***Reading Strategy: Predicting***
> What do you think Squeaky will do if the girls tease Raymond? What details in the story support your prediction?

> How does the conflict between Gretchen and Squeaky add to the plot?

---

prefer to like better; to choose or wish

signify to make known by signs, words, or actions

sasses speaks rudely

ice man on 145th with not a care in the world cause I am Miss Quicksilver herself.

I take my time getting to the park on May Day because the track meet is the last thing on the program. The biggest thing on the program is the May Pole dancing, which I can do without, thank you, even if my mother thinks it's a shame I don't take part and act like a girl for a change. You'd think my mother'd be grateful not to have to make me a white **organdy** dress with a big satin sash and buy me new white baby-doll shoes that can't be taken out of the box till the big day. You'd think she'd be glad her daughter ain't out there prancing around a May Pole getting the new clothes all dirty and sweaty and trying to act like a fairy or a flower or whatever you're supposed to be when you should be trying to be yourself, whatever that is, which is, as far as I am concerned, a poor black girl who really can't afford to buy shoes and a new dress you only wear once a lifetime cause it won't fit next year.

I was once a strawberry in a Hansel and Gretel **pageant** when I was in nursery school and didn't have no better sense than to dance on tiptoe with my arms in a circle over my head doing umbrella steps and being a perfect fool just so my mother and father could come dressed up and clap. You'd think they'd know better than to encourage that kind of nonsense. I am not a strawberry. I do not dance on my toes. I run. That is what I am all about. So I always come late to the May Day program, just in time to get my number pinned on and lay in the grass till they announce the fifty-yard dash.

I put Raymond in the little swings, which is a tight squeeze this year and will be impossible next year. Then I look around for Mr. Pearson, who pins the numbers on. I'm really looking for Gretchen if you want to know the truth, but she's not around. The park is jam-packed. Parents in hats and **corsages** and breast-pocket handkerchiefs peeking up. Kids in white

Squeaky's mother wants Squeaky to dance rather than run. What does this tell you about Squeaky's mother?

organdy a very fine, stiff fabric	**pageant** a public entertainment that represents scenes from history, legend, and the like	**corsages** small bunches of flowers worn on a blouse or jacket

dresses and light-blue suits. The parkees unfolding chairs and chasing the rowdy kids from Lenox as if they had no right to be there. The big guys with their caps on backwards, leaning against the fence swirling the basketballs on the tips of their fingers, waiting for all these crazy people to clear out the park so they can play. Most of the kids in my class are carrying bass drums and **glockenspiels** and flutes. You'd think they'd put in a few **bongos** or something for real like that.

Then here comes Mr. Pearson with his clipboard and his cards and pencils and whistles and safety pins and fifty million other things he's always dropping all over the place with his clumsy self. He sticks out in a crowd because he's on **stilts**. We used to call him Jack and the Beanstalk to get him mad. But I'm the only one that can outrun him and get away, and I'm too grown for that silliness now.

"Well, Squeaky," he says, checking my name off the list and handing me number seven and two pins. And I'm thinking he's got no right to call me Squeaky, if I can't call him Beanstalk.

"Hazel Elizabeth Deborah Parker," I correct him and tell him to write it down on his board.

"Well, Hazel Elizabeth Deborah Parker, going to give someone else a break this year?" I squint at him real hard to see if he is seriously thinking I should lose the race on purpose just to give someone else a break. "Only six girls running this time," he continues, shaking his head sadly like it's my fault all of New York didn't turn out in sneakers. "That new girl should give you a run for your money." He looks around the park for Gretchen like a **periscope** in a submarine movie. "Wouldn't it be a nice **gesture** if you were . . . to ahhh . . ."

I give him such a look he couldn't finish putting that idea into words. Grownups got a lot of nerve sometimes. I pin number seven to myself and stomp away, I'm so burnt. And I

> What does Squeaky's conversation with Mr. Pearson tell about her character?

glockenspiels musical instruments with metal bars that make bell-like tones when struck with small hammers	**stilts** tall sticks that people can walk on	**gesture** movement of any part of the body to help express an idea or feeling
bongos small drums	**periscope** part of a submarine that allows those inside to view the surface	

go straight for the track and stretch out on the grass while the band winds up with "Oh, the Monkey Wrapped His Tail Around the Flag Pole," which my teacher calls by some other name. The man on the loudspeaker is calling everyone over to the track and I'm on my back looking at the sky, trying to pretend I'm in the country, but I can't, because even grass in the city feels hard as sidewalk, and there's just no pretending you are anywhere but in a "concrete jungle" as my grandfather says.

The twenty-yard dash takes all of two minutes cause most of the little kids don't know no better than to run off the track or run the wrong way or run smack into the fence and fall down and cry. One little kid, though, has got the good sense to run straight for the white ribbon up ahead, so he wins. Then the second-graders line up for the thirty-yard dash and I don't even bother to turn my head to watch cause Raphael Perez always wins. He wins before he even begins by **psyching** the runners, telling them they're going to trip on their shoelaces and fall on their faces or lose their shorts or something, which he doesn't really have to do since he is very fast, almost as fast as I am. After that is the forty-yard dash which I use to run when I was in first grade. Raymond is **hollering** from the swings cause he knows I'm about to do my thing cause the man on the loudspeaker has just announced the fifty-yard dash, although he might just as well be giving a recipe for angel food cake cause you can hardly make out what he's saying for the **static**. I get up and slip off my

Reading Strategy: Predicting

How do you predict the conflict between Gretchen and Squeaky will end?

psyching outsmarting or making nervous	**hollering** yelling	**static** a crackly noise that blocks radio or television reception

sweat pants and then I see Gretchen standing at the starting line, kicking her legs out like a pro. Then as I get into place I see that ole Raymond is on line on the other side of the fence, bending down with his fingers on the ground just like he knew what he was doing. I was going to yell at him but then I didn't. It burns up your energy to holler.

Every time, just before I take off in a race, I always feel like I'm in a dream, the kind of dream you have when you're sick with fever and feel all hot and weightless. I dream I'm flying over a sandy beach in the early morning sun, kissing the leaves of the trees as I fly by. And there's always the smell of apples, just like in the country when I was little and used to think I was a choo-choo train, running through the fields of corn and chugging up the hill to the orchard. And all the time I'm dreaming this, I get lighter and lighter until I'm flying over the beach again, getting blown through the sky like a feather that weighs nothing at all. But once I spread my fingers in the dirt and **crouch** over the Get on Your Mark, the dream goes and I am solid again and am telling myself, Squeaky you must win, you must win, you are the fastest thing in the world, you can even beat your father up Amsterdam if you really try. And then I feel my weight coming back just behind my knees then down to my feet then into the earth and the pistol shot explodes in my blood and I am off and weightless again, flying past the other runners, my arms pumping up and down and the whole world is quiet except for the crunch as I zoom over the **gravel** in the track. I glance to my left and there is no one. To the right a blurred Gretchen, who's got her chin **jutting** out as if it would win the race all by itself. And on the other side of the fence is Raymond with his arms down to his side and the palms tucked up behind him, running in his very own style, and it's the first time I ever saw that and I almost stop to watch my brother Raymond on his first run. But the white ribbon is

What is Raymond doing while Squeaky runs the race?

| **crouch** to lower the body by bending the legs | **gravel** pebbles and pieces of rock in larger pieces than sand | **jutting** sticking out |

bouncing toward me and I tear past it, racing into the distance till my feet with a mind of their own start digging up **footfuls** of dirt and brake me short. Then all the kids standing on the side pile on me, banging me on the back and slapping my head with their May Day programs, for I have won again and everybody on 151st Street can walk tall for another year.

"In first place . . ." the man on the **loudspeaker** is clear as a bell now. But then he pauses and the loudspeaker starts to whine. Then static. And I lean down to catch my breath and here comes Gretchen walking back, for she's overshot the finish line too, huffing and puffing with her hands on her hips taking it slow, breathing in steady time like a real pro and I sort of like her a little for the first time. "In first place . . ." and then three or four voices get all mixed up on the loudspeaker and I dig my sneaker into the grass and stare at Gretchen who's staring back, we both wondering just who did win. I can hear old Beanstalk arguing with the man on the loudspeaker and then a few others running their mouths about what the stopwatches say. Then I hear Raymond yanking at the fence to call me and I wave to **shush** him, but he keeps rattling the fence like a gorilla in a cage like in them gorilla movies, but then like a dancer or something he starts climbing up nice and easy but very fast. And it occurs to me, watching how smoothly he climbs hand over hand and remembering how he looked running with his arms down to his side and with the wind pulling his mouth back and his teeth showing and all, it **occurred** to me that Raymond would make a very fine runner. Doesn't he always keep up with me on my trots? And he surely knows how to breathe in counts of seven cause he's always doing it at the dinner table, which drives my brother George up the wall. And I'm smiling to beat the band cause if I've lost this race, or if me and Gretchen tied, or even if I've won,

Reading Strategy: Predicting

Whom do you predict will win the race? Why?

footfuls large amounts grabbed by the feet; like fistfuls

loudspeaker a device that helps sound to travel long distances

shush to hush or make quiet

occurred happened or made known

I can always **retire** as a runner and begin a whole new career as a coach with Raymond as my champion. After all, with a little more study I can beat Cynthia and her **phony** self at the spelling bee. And if I **bugged** my mother, I could get piano lessons and become a star. And I have a big rep as the baddest thing around. And I've got a roomful of ribbons and medals and awards. But what has Raymond got to call his own?

So I stand there with my new plans, laughing out loud by this time as Raymond jumps down from the fence and runs over with his teeth showing and his arms down to the side, which no one before him has quite mastered as a running style. And by the time he comes over I'm jumping up and down so glad to see him—my brother Raymond, a great runner in the family tradition. But of course everyone thinks I'm jumping up and down because the men on the loudspeaker have finally gotten themselves together and compared notes and are announcing "In first place—Miss Hazel Elizabeth Deborah Parker." (Dig that.) "In second place—Miss Gretchen P. Lewis." And I look over at Gretchen wondering what the "P" stands for. And I smile. Cause she's good, no doubt about it. Maybe she'd like to help me coach Raymond; she **obviously** is serious about running, as any fool can see. And she nods to congratulate me and then she smiles. And I smile. We stand there with this big smile of respect between us. It's about as real a smile as girls can do for each other, considering we don't practice real smiling every day, you know, cause maybe we too busy being flowers or fairies or strawberries instead of something honest and worthy of respect . . . you know . . . like being people.

> Which parts of the story are the falling action?

> What is the solution to the conflict of the story?

> *Reading Strategy: Predicting*
> Was the outcome of the story difficult to predict? Explain.

---

retire to give up a job   **bugged** bothered   **obviously** very clear to the eye or mind
phony fake

Raymond's Run   *by Toni Cade Bambara*

Directions Choose the letter of the best answer or write the answer using complete sentences.

Comprehension: Identifying Facts

1. What is Squeaky's only family responsibility?
   A She has to clean and cook.
   B She shops for food.
   C She rakes leaves.
   D She cares for her brother Raymond.

2. Why do people call Raymond Squeaky's little brother?
   A He is smaller than she is.
   B He is five years younger than she is.
   C He has a disability.
   D He gets in a lot of fights.

3. What is Squeaky's favorite race to run?

4. Who is the only person who can run faster than Squeaky?

5. What does Cynthia Procter say before a test?

6. Who is Squeaky's main competition in the upcoming race?

7. What does Squeaky's mother wish Squeaky would do on May Day?

8. What does Mr. Pearson start to ask Squeaky to do during the race?

9. What does Raymond do during the race?

10. Who wins the race?

Comprehension: Putting Ideas Together

11. Raymond does all of the following except _____.
    A make fun of Squeaky's silly friends
    B dash across traffic on a main road
    C slosh around in the wet gutter after a rainstorm
    D pretend that he is a circus performer

12. Which pair of words best describes Squeaky?
    A sweet and kind
    B determined and strong
    C lazy and foolish
    D forgetful but nice

13. Why is Squeaky such a good runner?

14. Describe the relationship between Raymond and Squeaky.

15. How is Squeaky similar to Cynthia Procter?

16. Why does Mary Louise tease Raymond?

17. What part did Squeaky play in a nursery school play? How does she feel about it?

18. How does Squeaky feel during a race?

19. How do Raymond's actions change Squeaky's view of him?

20. How does the relationship between Gretchen and Squeaky change after the race?

Understanding Literature: Fiction

Remember that fiction is writing that is imaginative and designed to entertain. The author creates the events and characters. Both short stories and novels are types of fiction. All works of fiction share certain basic features such as plot, setting, and conflict. However, the way the author develops these features makes each story special.

21. Who are the two main characters?

22. What is the story's setting? Identify its time and place.

23. How would the story change in a different setting?

24. What is the conflict between Squeaky and Gretchen?

25. How does Raymond's run affect the end of the story?

Critical Thinking

26. How do you think Squeaky feels about taking care of Raymond?

27. What problems does Squeaky face in taking care of Raymond?

28. After seeing Raymond, why is Squeaky not interested in the result of the race?

Thinking Creatively

29. Have you ever been in a situation similar to Squeaky's? How did you handle the situation?

30. Do you think you would like to be Squeaky's friend? Explain.

After Reading continued on next page

Raymond's Run *by Toni Cade Bambara*

 ## Grammar Check

Common nouns name any person, place, thing, or idea. Proper nouns name a certain person, place, thing, or idea.

Write each sentence below on a sheet of paper. Underline all of the nouns. Write *C* or *P* above each noun to tell whether it is *common* or *proper.*

1 Jenna had spaghetti for lunch on Friday.

2 The teachers at Bishop School had a meeting.

3 My best friends are Bianca and Ethan.

 ## Vocabulary Builder

The prefix *pre-* means "before" or "in advance." When you *predict* events, you tell about them before they happen. Sometimes *pre-* will be added to words you already know—like *prepay.* For words you do recognize, you can use the prefix *pre-* to help you understand and remember the word.

Define each underlined word, using its prefix. Write each definition on a sheet of paper.

1 You can <u>preview</u> the movie on the Web.

2 Help me <u>prepare</u> for the party.

3 <u>Previously</u>, we had a meeting about the problem.

 ## Writing on Your Own

Imagine that you are Squeaky. Write a journal entry telling how you feel about the way the race ended. Use the same kind of language Squeaky used in the story. Before you write, use a Concept Map to organize your details. (See Appendix A for a description of this graphic organizer.) When you are finished writing, proofread your work.

 ## Listening and Speaking

Write and perform a radio broadcast of the race in the story. Use action verbs to describe the actions of the runners. Here are some examples: *flying, streaking,* and *pounding.* When you deliver the broadcast, vary the tone and pace of your voice. Show the excitement of the race and the nervousness of the ending.

 ## Research and Technology

Use the Internet to research the Special Olympics. A search engine may help you find Web sites with good information. Place quotation marks around Special Olympics to help you with your search. Put the information you find together in an oral report. In your report, describe the history of the Special Olympics. Also explain why these games are important.

Gentleman of Río en Medio   by Juan A. A. Sedillo

About the Author

Juan A. A. Sedillo was born in New Mexico. His relatives were early Spanish colonists of the Southwest. Sedillo was a talented man who worked as a writer and translator. In addition, Sedillo was a lawyer and judge who held different public positions. He also ran for Congress in 1926 but did not win. Sedillo had many careers and lived with different cultures in New Mexico. Sedillo used these experiences to make his stories true-to-life.

Juan A. A. Sedillo
1902–1982

About the Selection

"Gentleman of Río en Medio" is a work of fiction. Fiction often tells about characters and events from the author's imagination. However, Sedillo got the idea for "Gentleman of Río en Medio" from a real event. The idea came from a legal case involving a conflict over a piece of property.

Sedillo grew up among people of Spanish background. As a result, he knew and understood their culture and beliefs. "Gentleman of Río en Medio" takes place in New Mexico. Sedillo drew on the history of the area as he created his story. As a result, he turned an ordinary legal case into something special. It became an image of an unusual person and a traditional way of life.

Objectives

◆ To read and understand a short story

◆ To identify point of view and theme

◆ To explain the differences between internal and external conflict, and identify a conflict's resolution

Before Reading **continued on next page**

short story
a brief work
of fiction that
includes plot,
setting, characters,
point of view, and
theme

point of view
the position from
which the author
or storyteller tells
the story

theme the main
idea of a literary
work

external conflict
a character's
struggle against
an outside force
such as another
character, nature,
or some part of
society

internal conflict
a character's
struggle against an
inside force such as
personal feelings or
beliefs

resolution the act
of solving conflict
in a story

Literary Terms "Gentleman of Río en Medio" is an example of a **short story.** A short story is a brief work of fiction that includes plot, setting, characters, **point of view,** and **theme.** Point of view is the position from which the author or storyteller tells the story. Theme is the main idea of a literary work.

As you read the selection, you will see that the plot contains conflict. There are two kinds of conflict: **external conflict** and **internal conflict.** External conflict is when a character struggles against an outside force. This can be another character, nature, or some part of society. Internal conflict is when a character struggles against an inside force. The character may struggle with personal feelings or beliefs. The conflict is solved in the **resolution** of the story. This is the last stage of plot where the problems are worked out.

Reading on Your Own As you read this story, use the Sequence Chain graphic organizer to keep track of important events. (You can see a description of this graphic organizer in Appendix A.) Put a star next to the places where you found conflict. Label each example as either external conflict or internal conflict.

Writing on Your Own In "Gentleman of Río en Medio," old customs conflict with new ways. Write a response explaining why you think people sometimes struggle to keep tradition.

Vocabulary Focus Sometimes you can figure out a new word by looking for the root word. The word *descendant*, for example, has the root *descend*. To *descend* means "to go down." Children and grandchildren are descendants of their ancestors because they have "gone down" through time. As you read, use the roots to help define words you do not know.

Think Before You Read What clues do you think the pictures tell about the story?

Gentleman of Río en Medio

The Sacristan of Trampas
(detail), Paul Burlin, 1918

It took months of **negotiation** to come to an understanding with the old man. He was in no hurry. What he had the most of was time. He lived up in Río en Medio, where his people had been for hundreds of years. He tilled the same land they had tilled. His house was small and **wretched**, but **quaint**. The little creek ran through his land. His orchard was **gnarled** and beautiful.

The day of the sale he came into the office. His coat was old, green and faded. I thought of Senator Catron, who had been such a power with these people up there in the mountains. Perhaps it was one of his old Prince Alberts. He also wore gloves. They were old and torn and his fingertips showed through them. He carried a cane, but it was only the skeleton of a worn-out umbrella. Behind him walked one of his **innumerable kin**—a dark young man with eyes like a **gazelle**.

The old man bowed to all of us in the room. Then he removed his hat and gloves, slowly and carefully. Chaplin once did that in a picture, in a bank—he was the janitor.

As you read, think about how the author's background helped him develop the details for this story.

Senator Thomas Benton Catron was U.S. Senator from New Mexico from 1912–1917.

Prince Alberts are long, old-fashioned coats worn for formal events.

Charlie Chaplin was an actor and film producer who lived from 1889 to 1977.

negotiation the act or process of arranging for something

wretched poor and miserable

quaint strange or odd in an interesting way

gnarled twisted; crooked

innumerable too many to count

kin family members or relatives

gazelle a small, quick, deer-like animal found in Asia or Africa

Then he handed his things to the boy, who stood obediently behind the old man's chair.

There was a great deal of conversation, about rain and about his family. He was very proud of his large family. Finally we got down to business. Yes, he would sell, as he had agreed, for twelve hundred dollars, in cash. We would buy, and the money was ready. "Don Anselmo," I said to him in Spanish, "we have made a discovery. You remember that we sent that **surveyor**, that engineer, up there to survey your land so as to make the deed. Well, he finds that you own more than eight acres. He tells us that your land extends across the river and that you own almost twice as much as you thought." He didn't know that. "And now, Don Anselmo," I added, "these Americans are *buena gente,* they are good people, and they are willing to pay you for the additional land as well, at the same rate per acre, so that instead of twelve hundred dollars you will get almost twice as much, and the money is here for you."

The old man hung his head for a moment in thought. Then he stood up and stared at me. "Friend," he said, "I do not like to have you speak to me in that manner." I kept still and let him have his say. "I know these Americans are good people, and that is why I have agreed to sell to them. But I do not care to be **insulted**. I have agreed to sell my house and land for twelve hundred dollars and that is the price."

I argued with him but it was useless. Finally he signed the deed and took the money but refused to take more than the amount agreed upon. Then he shook hands all around, put on his ragged gloves, took his stick and walked out with the boy behind him.

A month later my friends had moved into Río en Medio. They had replastered the old adobe house, pruned the trees, patched the fence, and moved in for the summer. One day they came back to the office to complain. The children of the village were overrunning their property. They came every

Don is a Spanish title of respect. It is similar to *Sir* in English. *Buena gente* is the Spanish word for good people.

Reading Strategy: Predicting

How do you predict Don Anselmo will react to the offer? Why do you predict this?

What is the conflict between the narrator and Don Anselmo?

---

surveyor a person who examines the land

insulted said or did something mean or rude

Springtime, Victor Higgins, c. 1928–29

day and played under the trees, built little play fences around them, and took blossoms. When they were spoken to they only laughed and talked back good-naturedly in Spanish.

I sent a messenger up to the mountains for Don Anselmo. It took a week to arrange another meeting. When he arrived he repeated his previous **preliminary** performance. He wore the same faded cutaway, carried the same stick and was accompanied by the boy again. He shook hands all around, sat down with the boy behind his chair, and talked about the weather. Finally I **broached** the subject. "Don Anselmo, about the ranch you sold to these people. They are good people and want to be your friends and neighbors always. When you sold

preliminary leading up to something important

broached brought up

to them you signed a document, a deed, and in that deed you agreed to several things. One thing was that they were to have the complete possession of the property. Now, Don Anselmo, it seems that every day the children of the village overrun the orchard and spend most of their time there. We would like to know if you, as the most respected man in the village, could not stop them from doing so in order that these people may enjoy their new home more in peace."

Don Anselmo stood up. "We have all learned to love these Americans," he said, "because they are good people and good neighbors. I sold them my property because I knew they were good people, but I did not sell them the trees in the orchard."

This was bad. "Don Anselmo," I **pleaded**, "when one signs a deed and sells real property one sells also everything that grows on the land, and those trees, every one of them, are on the land and inside the **boundaries** of what you sold."

"Yes, I admit that," he said. "You know," he added, "I am the oldest man in the village. Almost everyone there is my relative and all the children of Río en Medio are my *sobrinos* and *nietos,* my **descendants**. Every time a child has been born in Río en Medio since I took possession of that house from my mother I have planted a tree for that child. The trees in that orchard are not mine, *Señor,* they belong to the children of the village. Every person in Río en Medio born since the railroad came to Santa Fe owns a tree in that orchard. I did not sell the trees because I could not. They are not mine."

There was nothing we could do. Legally we owned the trees but the old man had been so **generous**, refusing what amounted to a fortune for him. It took most of the following winter to buy the trees, individually, from the descendants of Don Anselmo in the valley of Río en Medio.

Reading Strategy: Predicting

Does Don Anselmo's reply agree with your prediction? Why or why not?

Sobrinos and *nietos* is Spanish for nephews and grandsons. Here it is used to include nieces and granddaughters as well.

What is the story's resolution? How is the external conflict solved?

Why is the narrator a character that others admire?

---

pleaded begged or argued

boundaries limits or borders

descendants those born of a certain family or group

generous willing to share with others

Directions Choose the letter of the best answer or write the answer using complete sentences.

Comprehension: Identifying Facts

1. Who is the narrator of this story?
   A It is an old man named Don Anselmo.
   B It is an actor named Charlie Chaplin.
   C It is the lawyer.
   D It is an American who wants to buy the land.

2. Who buys the land from Don Anselmo?

3. How much money does Don Anselmo accept for the land?

Comprehension: Putting Ideas Together

4. Why will Don Anselmo not stop the children from running on the land?
   A He feels that he was cheated and still owns the land.
   B He believes the children own the trees and can enjoy them.
   C There are too many children to stop.
   D He wants the fruit from the trees in the orchard.

5. How would you describe Don Anselmo's personality?

6. Explain how Don Anselmo and the narrator resolve the conflict.

Understanding Literature: Conflict

Conflict is the struggle between two opposing forces. An external conflict takes place when a character struggles against an outside force. Outside forces can include another person. A part of nature, like the weather or seasons, can be another cause of external conflict. An internal conflict takes place when a character struggles against an inside force. An example of an internal conflict might be a person deciding between right and wrong. The goal of a story is for the conflict to be solved at the end.

7. Describe the difference between internal and external conflict.

8. How does the narrator's behavior toward Don Anselmo affect the resolution of the conflict?

Critical Thinking

9. Were you surprised by Don Anselmo's responses in his two meetings with the narrator? Why or why not?

Thinking Creatively

10. Why do you think Don Anselmo gave a tree as a gift to each child?

After Reading **continued on next page**

Gentleman of Río en Medio by Juan A. A. Sedillo

 Grammar Check

English has many words with silent letters. In this story, for example, *gnarled* has a silent "g." *Wretched* has a silent "w." Identifying silent letters can help you spell difficult words correctly. Underline the silent letters in the words below. Then arrange the words on the chart to show the pattern of silent letters.

campaign	knee	doubt
raspberry	pneumonia	numb
knowledge	foreigner	

silent *p*	silent *b*	silent *k*	silent *g*

 Vocabulary Builder

A synonym is a word that means almost the same thing as another word. For example, *weightless* and *light* are synonyms. Read the definition of each boldfaced word. Then tell which of the three words that follow is a synonym for the boldfaced word. Also tell why this word is a synonym.

1 innumerable: countless, few, questioning

2 preliminary: finally, introductory, unimportant

3 descendant: grandson, friend, teacher

 Writing on Your Own

Imagine that you live in the same village as Don Anselmo. Write a letter to Don Anselmo thanking him for trying to let the children play in the orchard. Before you begin writing, review the story for facts about Don Anselmo. What things appear to be important to him? When you are finished writing your letter, proofread it for spelling errors. Then share your letter with a partner.

 Listening and Speaking

Work with a partner to role-play the story's conflict. One person should play Don Anselmo, and the other should play the narrator. Discuss the issues that divide you. Talk about the common interests you share. Role-play solutions that everyone agrees with.

 Media and Viewing

Work in a small group to find out how the Spanish have influenced the American Southwest. Gather information about art, architecture, music, and food from a variety of resources. What do these add to the culture of the American people? Present your findings in a media presentation to your class. Be sure that everyone in your group participates in the research and presentation.

Shopping by Catalog and Online

Today we are lucky because there are many ways to purchase the things we need. We can go to a store, order by telephone, or shop online. E-commerce, another name for online shopping, has become a fact of modern life. This is because so many people shop from their computers. In fact, more than one-quarter of all holiday shopping is done online.

About Shopping by Catalog and Online

Many stores send catalogs to people who shop by telephone or computer. Catalogs are like reference books for products that stores sell. Customers can order products from a catalog without having to go to a store. This is useful if the store is far away from a person's house. It also comes in handy if someone cannot get out easily. Using the catalog, customers can call in an order or can make an online purchase. Many people use catalogs to buy hard-to-find items.

Reading Skill

To get the most from reading a catalog, customers must use the text aids and features. Both print and online catalogs usually have pictures and descriptions for many kinds of products. People use the catalogs for information about products and to make shopping decisions.

This chart shows some of the most common text features:

Text Aids and Features	Uses
Table of Contents/Quick Reference Guide	Lists items and page numbers and is located in the front of the catalog
Photographs or pictures	Shows what the item looks like
Captions	Describes each item for sale
Item numbers	Identifies each item for the seller
Size charts	Helps customers decide what size item will fit best
Shipping costs chart	Shows how much it will cost to have the items mailed

The examples on the next two pages show examples of print and online catalog pages. As you look at the catalog pages, use a graphic organizer like the one below. Fill in the part of the catalog in which you would find this information.

How to find what you need	→
How to see what an item looks like	→
How to comparison shop on the Internet	→
How to figure out shipping costs	→

Quick Reference Guide

The items are listed in categories.

Use synonyms to locate items you do not see listed.

Appliances 176–197	Lamps 232–237
Automotive..... 349–356	Lawn furniture...336–337
Baby goods..... 386–396	Luggage........ 258–266
Billfolds..........98–101	Office equipment.......274–276
Calculators 270–273	Personal care 206–215
Car stereos 355–356	Photographic equipment...... 280–290
Clocks 96, 242–253	Radios 291–293
Computers 163–175	Sporting goods..........347–348
Cookware.......148–160	Stereo, TVs 294–329
Floor care 199–201	
Giftware 135–147	
Hardware 338–346	Tools 338–346
Jewelry.............1–75	Toys 397–444

Categories are arranged in alphabetical order.

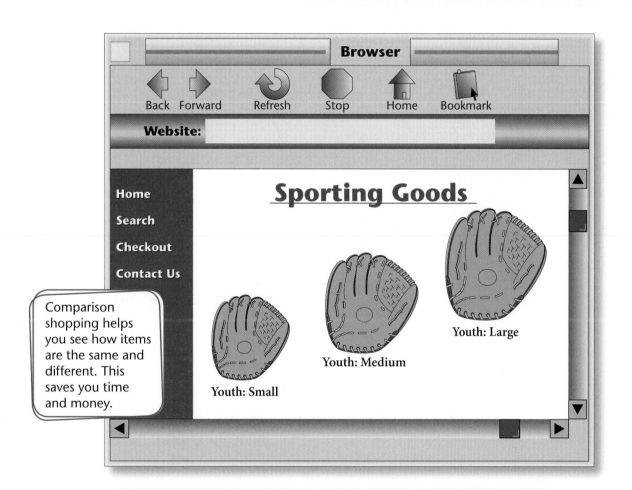

Browser

Back   Forward   Refresh   Stop   Home   Bookmark

Website:

Home

Search

Checkout

Contact Us

Sporting Goods

Youth: Large

Youth: Medium

Youth: Small

Comparison shopping helps you see how items are the same and different. This saves you time and money.

Shipping can be figured by the item's weight.

Shipping can be figured based on the cost of the item.

Shipping Charges by Cost		Shipping Rates by Weight	
Amount of order:	*Include:*	*Lb.*	*Charge*
Up to $9.99	$1.95	1 - 5	$3.15
$10.00 - $19.99	$2.95	6 - 10	$5.07
$20.00 - $29.99	$3.95	11 - 15	$6.98
$30.00 - $39.99	$4.95	16 - 20	$8.90
$40.00 - $49.99	$5.95	21 - 25	$10.95
$50.00 - $74.99	$7.50	26 - 30	$12.78
$75.00 - $99.99	$8.25	31 - 40	$16.65
Over $100.00	$11.00	Over 40	$20.54

Monitor Your Progress

Directions Choose the letter of the best answer or write the answer using complete sentences.

1. Where would you find information about lamps?
   A It is on pages 232–237.
   B It is after pictures of luggage.
   C It is next to watches.
   D It is before appliances.

2. According to the chart, what is the cost to ship a 23-pound lamp?
   A $3.15   **C** $7.50
   B $3.95   **D** $10.95

3. What information is shown in the Table of Contents in this catalog?

4. Why would you comparison shop on the Internet?

5. Describe two advantages of shopping online.

Writing on Your Own

Choose one item that you would like to purchase from this catalog. Would you buy this item online or from the store? Explain your answer. Then write directions for buying the item.

COMPARING LITERARY WORKS | Build Understanding

Old Ben   by Jesse Stuart

About the Author

Jesse Stuart grew up in the Kentucky countryside. He developed a strong connection to the natural world around him. His home and roots in Kentucky were very important to him. Stuart drew on Kentucky for many of the ideas he used in his writing. He wrote more than 55 books and 450 short stories. Nearly all of these writings were based on his home state.

Stuart's English teacher at Greenup High School was an important part of his life. The teacher, Mrs. Hatton, urged him to write short stories. When he became famous, Stuart often talked about how his teachers helped him. He said: ". . . A teacher lives on and on through his students. . . . Good teaching is forever." When Stuart became Kentucky's official state poet, several people wrote his life story. One wrote: "Stuart's writing is indeed like bright water. It mirrors the trees, the sky, and the Kentucky life he knew and loved."

About the Selection

"Old Ben" is the story of a boy named Shan and a snake. Shan's father has always said, "The only good snake is a dead snake." Even so, Shan makes friends with a blacksnake he finds in the wild. Old Ben was different. The snake proves to be friendly and soon becomes part of the family. Even his father comes to love the wild creature who now lives in the corncrib. The whole family is sad when the ways of nature end Ben's life.

Recall that "Gentleman of Río en Medio" is the story of a man named Don Anselmo. For years, he has planted trees in honor of the children of the village. He sells his land to some Americans, but the children of the village still play on the land under their trees. The new owners find that it is not easy to buy and sell parts of nature and a person's feelings.

Jesse Stuart
1906–1984

Objectives

- ◆ To read and understand a short story
- ◆ To compare and contrast narratives
- ◆ To compare characters, setting, and theme in stories

Comparing continued on next page

Old Ben   *by Jesse Stuart*

narrative a story, usually told in chronological order

foreshadowing hints that a writer gives about something that has not yet happened

Literary Terms A **narrative** is a story, usually told in chronological order. This means that it is told in time order. One event comes after the other from start to finish. A narrative has characters, a setting, and a plot. The plot may include **foreshadowing.** Foreshadowing is clues that a writer gives about something that has not yet happened. These hints about future events lead up to the ending.

Reading on Your Own To compare "Old Ben" to "Gentleman of Río en Medio," use a Venn Diagram. (You can see a description of this graphic organizer in Appendix A.) As you read, keep track of the narrative features in both stories. Record information about the characters, setting, and theme on your Venn Diagram.

Writing on Your Own Think about this statement: "People often have strong reactions to some animals. Many of these reactions may be unfair. This is very true of snakes." Write a paragraph to explain why you agree or disagree with the statement.

Vocabulary Focus English has many words formed from two words. These are called compound words. You can often define these words by breaking them into their parts. For example, *corncrib* is a storage place for corn. Work with a partner to define each of these compound words from "Old Ben." Write each word and its meaning on a sheet of paper.

blacksnake   cottonmouth   flashback   something

Think Before You Read With a partner, discuss what you would do if you found a huge snake in the woods.

Old Ben

One morning in July when I was walking across a clover field to a sweet-apple tree, I almost stepped on him. There he lay **coiled** like heavy strands of black rope. He was a big bull blacksnake. We looked at each other a minute, and then I stuck the toe of my shoe up to his mouth. He drew his head back in a friendly way. He didn't want trouble. Had he shown the least fight, I would have soon finished him. My father had always told me there was only one good snake—a dead one.

When the big fellow didn't show any fight, I reached down and picked him up by the neck. When I lifted him he was as long as I was tall. That was six feet. I started calling him Old Ben as I held him by the neck and rubbed his back. He enjoyed having his back rubbed and his head stroked. Then I lifted him into my arms. He was the first snake I'd ever been friendly with. I was afraid at first to let Old Ben wrap himself around me. I thought he might wrap himself around my neck and choke me.

The more I petted him, the more **affectionate** he became. He was so friendly I decided to trust him. I wrapped him

As you read, think about the qualities that both Shan and Don Anselmo share.

Several different snakes are called *blacksnakes.* The black racer snake is found in Kentucky. Another kind of blacksnake is the rat snake. This snake is also called the "pilot black snake" or "mountain black snake." Like other snakes, it kills rats and mice.

Reading Strategy: Predicting

What do you predict Old Ben will be like?

---

coiled wound around in a circular shape   **affectionate** having a fondness for something

around my neck a couple of times and let him loose. He crawled down one arm and went back to my neck, around and down the other arm and back again. He struck out his forked tongue to the sound of my voice as I talked to him.

"I wouldn't kill you at all," I said. "You're a friendly snake. I'm taking you home with me."

I headed home with Old Ben wrapped around my neck and shoulders. When I started over the hill by the pine **grove**, I met my cousin Wayne Holbrook coming up the hill. He stopped suddenly when he saw me. He started backing down the hill.

"He's a pet, Wayne," I said. "Don't be afraid of Old Ben."

It was a minute before Wayne could tell me what he wanted. He had come to borrow a plow. He kept a safe distance as we walked on together.

Before we reached the barn, Wayne got brave enough to touch Old Ben's long body.

"What are you going to do with him?" Wayne asked. "Uncle Mick won't let you keep him!"

"Put him in the corncrib," I said. "He'll have plenty of **delicate** food in there. The cats we keep at this barn have grown fat and lazy on the milk we feed 'em."

I opened the corncrib door and took Old Ben from around my neck because he was beginning to get warm and a little heavy.

"This will be your home," I said. "You'd better hide under the corn."

Besides my father, I knew Old Ben would have another enemy at our home. He was our hunting dog, Blackie, who would trail a snake, same as a possum or mink. He had treed blacksnakes, and my father had shot them from the trees. I knew Blackie would find Old Ben, because he followed us to the barn each morning.

> A *corncrib* is a place to store corn.

> What decision does the narrator make that keeps the narrative moving forward?

> This paragraph shows foreshadowing. It gives a clue that Old Ben has enemies around the farm.

grove a group of trees standing together

delicate pleasing to taste or smell

The first morning after I'd put Old Ben in the corncrib, Blackie followed us. He started toward the corncrib holding his head high, sniffing. He stuck his nose up to a crack in the crib and began to bark. Then he tried to tear a plank off.

"Stop it, Blackie," Pa scolded him. "What's the matter with you? Have you taken to barking at mice?"

"Blackie is not barking at a mouse," I said. "I put a blacksnake in there yesterday!"

"A blacksnake?" Pa asked, looking unbelievingly. "A blacksnake?"

"Yes, a pet blacksnake," I said.

"Have you gone crazy?" he said. "I'll move a thousand bushels of corn to get that snake!"

"You won't mind this one," I said. "You and Mom will love him."

My father said a few unprintable words before we started back to the house. After breakfast, when Pa and Mom came to the barn, I was already there. I had opened the crib door and there was Old Ben. He'd crawled up front and was coiled on a sack. I put my hand down and he crawled up my arm to my neck and over my shoulder. When Mom and Pa reached the crib, I thought Pa was going to faint.

"He has a pet snake," Mom said.

"Won't be a bird or a young chicken left on this place," Pa said. "Every time I pick up an ear of corn in the crib, I'll be jumping."

"Pa, he won't hurt you," I said, patting the snake's head. "He's a natural pet, or somebody has tamed him. And he's not going to bother birds and young chickens when there are so many mice in this crib."

"Mick, let him keep the snake," Mom said. "I won't be afraid of it."

This was the beginning of a long friendship.

Mom went to the corncrib morning after morning and **shelled** corn for her geese and chickens. Often Old Ben would

Reading Strategy: Predicting

Has your prediction about Old Ben been correct so far?

How do people react to Old Ben? Why do they react this way?

Why do you think Mom sides with her son?

shelled separated the kernels from an ear of corn

be lying in front on his **burlap** sack. Mom watched him at first from the corner of her eye. Later she didn't bother to watch him any more than she did a cat that came up for his milk.

Later it **occurred** to us that Old Ben might like milk, too. We started leaving milk for him. We never saw him drink it, but his pan was always empty when we returned. We know the mice didn't drink it, because he took care of them.

"One thing is certain," Mom said one morning when she went to shell corn. "We don't find any more corn chewed up by the mice and left on the floor."

July passed and August came. My father got used to Old Ben, but not until he had proved his worth. Ben had done something our nine cats couldn't. He had cleaned the corncrib of mice.

Then my father began to worry about Old Ben's going after water, and Blackie's finding his track. So he put water in the crib.

September came and went. We began wondering where our pet would go when days grew colder. One morning in early October we left milk for Old Ben, and it was there when we went back that afternoon. But Old Ben wasn't there.

"Old Ben's a good pet for the warm months," Pa said. "But in the winter months, my cats will have to do the work. Maybe Blackie got him!"

"He might have holed up for the winter in the **hayloft**," I told Pa after we had removed all the corn and didn't find him. "I'm worried about him. I've had a lot of pets—**groundhogs**, crows and hawks—but Old Ben's the best yet."

November, December, January, February, and March came and went. Of course we never expected to see Old Ben in one of those months. We doubted if we ever would see him again.

Reading Strategy:
Predicting

What do you predict will happen to Old Ben over the winter? Why?

Snakes are reptiles. They get their body heat from the temperature of the air and the ground. In the winter their bodily systems slow down. They use up body fat which has been stored up. In very cold areas, snakes hibernate, or sleep, during winter.

burlap rough fabric, often used for bags	**hayloft** a place in a barn for storing hay	**groundhogs** woodchucks
occurred happened, or made known		

One day early in April I went to the corncrib, and Old Ben lay stretched across the floor. He looked taller than I was now. His skin was rough and his long body had a flabby appearance. I knew Old Ben needed mice and milk. I picked him up, petted him, and told him so. But the chill of early April was still with him. He got his tongue out slower to answer the kind words I was saying to him. He tried to crawl up my arm but he couldn't make it.

That spring and summer mice got **scarce** in the corncrib and Old Ben got daring. He went over to the barn and crawled up into the hayloft, where he had many feasts. But he made one mistake.

He crawled from the hayloft down into Fred's feed box, where it was cool. Old Fred was our horse.

There he lay coiled when the horse came in and put his nose down on top of Old Ben. Fred let out a big snort and started kicking. He kicked down a **partition**, and then turned his heels on his feed box and kicked it down. Lucky for Old Ben that he got out in one piece. But he got back to his crib.

Old Ben became a part of our barnyard family, a pet and **darling** of all. When children came to play with my brother and sisters, they always went to the crib and got Old Ben. He enjoyed the children, who were afraid of him at first but later learned to pet this kind old reptile.

Summer passed and the late days of September were very **humid**. Old Ben failed one morning to drink his milk. We knew it wasn't time for him to hole up for the winter.

We knew something had happened.

Pa and I moved the corn searching for him. Mom made a couple of trips to the barn lot to see if we had found him. But all we found was the rough skin he had shed last spring.

"Fred's never been very **sociable** with Old Ben since he got in his box that time," Pa said. "I wonder if he could have

How many seasons have passed since the beginning of the story?

Reading Strategy:
Predicting

What do you predict has happened to Old Ben? What details did you use to make this prediction?

---

scarce few

partition a wall or screen between rooms

darling a person or animal very dear to another

humid hot and damp weather

sociable friendly

stomped Old Ben to death. Old Ben could've been crawling over the barn lot, and Fred saw his chance to get even!"

"We'll see," I said.

Pa and I left the crib and walked to the barn lot. He went one way and I went the other, each searching the ground.

Mom came through the gate and walked over where my father was looking. She started looking around, too.

"We think Fred might've got him," Pa said. "We're sure Fred's got it in for him over Old Ben getting in his feed box last summer."

"You're accusing Fred wrong," Mom said. "Here's Old Ben's track in the sand."

I ran over to where Mom had found the track. Pa went over to look, too.

"It's no use now," Pa said, softly. "Wouldn't have taken anything for that snake. I'll miss him on that burlap sack every morning when I come to feed the horses. Always looked up at me as if he understood."

The last **trace** Old Ben had left was in the corner of the lot near the hogpen. His track went straight to the **woven** wire fence and stopped.

"They've got him," Pa said. "Old Ben trusted everything and everybody. He went for a visit to the wrong place. He didn't last long among sixteen hogs. They go wild over a snake. Even a biting **copperhead** can't stop a hog. There won't be a trace of Old Ben left."

We stood silently for a minute looking at the broad, smooth track Old Ben had left in the sand.

Reading Strategy: Predicting

Which events, if any, could have predicted Ben's disappearance?

trace a path, trail, or road	**woven** threads or strips of cloth made into fabric	**copperhead** a kind of poisonous snake found in the eastern United States

COMPARING LITERARY WORKS | Apply the Skills

Old Ben   by Jesse Stuart

Directions Choose the letter of the best answer or write the answer using complete sentences.

Comprehension: Identifying Facts

1. Where does the narrator find Old Ben?
   A He finds the snake in the small pond.
   B He finds the snake next to an apple tree.
   C He finds the snake in the family's barn.
   D He finds the snake in the corncrib.

2. What kind of snake is Old Ben?
   A Old Ben is a big bull blacksnake.
   B Old Ben is a scary copperhead.
   C Old Ben is a strange-looking rattlesnake.
   D Old Ben is a common green garden snake.

3. What kind of snake does Pa say is the only good kind?

4. How long is Old Ben?

5. Why is the narrator first afraid to let Old Ben wrap around his neck?

6. Who is Old Fred?

7. What problem does Old Ben solve for the family?

8. Why does Old Ben go into the hayloft in spring and summer?

9. In September, how does the family know that Old Ben is in trouble?

10. Who does Pa think has killed Old Ben?

Comprehension: Putting Ideas Together

11. How are the narrators in the two stories alike?
   A Both narrators are teenagers.
   B Both narrators discover that nature and feelings are related.
   C Both narrators own many snakes.
   D Both narrators believe that children have a right to play under trees.

12. What is something from the stories that is not true to life?
   A Trees and land selling separately; finding a tame snake in the wild
   B Planting trees for all new babies; finding an empty snake skin
   C Buyers offering to pay more money; a mom liking a snake
   D Don Anselmo wearing ragged gloves; a snake living in a corncrib

13. How are Don Anselmo and Shan similar?

14. How are the narrator of "Gentleman of Rio en Medio" and Shan's father alike?

Comparing continued on next page

15. What offer is made in each story?

16. Describe the presence of gentleness in each story.

17. In "Gentleman of Río en Medio," the Americans were new to the village and had to learn the ways of the village. In "Old Ben," which character was in a similar situation?

18. In each story, explain how one person's choices affect others.

19. In the stories, the children had free run of the orchard and Old Ben had free run of the farm. In each story, name a character who did not like the free run.

20. Describe a sad change in each story.

Understanding Literature: Narrative

As you read at the beginning of this selection, a narrative is a story. It is usually told in chronological, or time, order. Narratives often have familiar tones, as if they are stories being told by a friend. Narratives can be similar in many ways. These two stories, for instance, both have important settings. The settings are rooted in the cultures of their places. Don Anselmo believes in tradition and the value of family over money. Shan believes in helping his family too.

21. In each story, what information does the writer show through foreshadowing?

22. Who are the main characters in each narrative?

23. What happens last in both narratives?

24. Who is telling each story?

25. Which narrative structure do you prefer? Why?

Critical Thinking

26. How would "Gentleman of Río en Medio" be different if it were set in Kentucky like "Old Ben"?

27. Explain how both stories show the importance of finding creative solutions.

28. How do Don Anselmo and Old Ben make life better for the other characters?

29. Identify foreshadowing in each story.

Thinking Creatively

30. In each story, some characters showed an enjoyment of nature. Explain how the stories would be different if they had not enjoyed nature.

Grammar Check

Commas and quotation marks are important when showing who is speaking in a story. Quotation marks are placed around all direct quotations. *For example:* "You were right," I said to Kim. Place a comma after the words that introduce the speaker. *For example:* Kim replied, "Well, you learned a lesson today." Also use commas and quotation marks before and after any words that interrupt the quotation. *For example:* "Next time," I said, "I guess I'll listen." Write each sentence on a sheet of paper. Add the correct punctuation to each quotation.

1 He's a pet, Wayne, I said.

2 Put him in the corncrib, I said.

3 Stop it, Blackie Pa scolded him.

 Vocabulary Builder

Homonyms are words that are pronounced the same but are spelled differently and have different meanings. For example, the word *one* means "a single thing." The homonym is *won*. It means "victory." Here are some homonyms from "Old Ben." Define each pair. Then use each word in a sentence that shows its correct meaning.

by/buy   for/four

two/too/to   hear/here

 Writing on Your Own

Setting is important in fiction and nonfiction writing. You saw that setting played a big part in "Gentleman of Río en Medio" and in "Old Ben." Choose a setting that is familiar to you. Write a paragraph to describe the setting. Use vivid descriptions to paint a picture of the place.

 Listening and Speaking

With a partner, discuss the characters of Don Anselmo and Shan. Talk about character traits for each of them. Then tell which character you like better and why.

  Media and Viewing

Use the Internet or your library to find out about snakes that are common in your area. Write down the name, a description, and other interesting features of this snake. Also try to find a picture of the snake. Create a computer-generated slideshow about the snake you researched. Present your slideshow to the class.

Part 2

Reading Strategy:
Text Structure

Understanding how text is organized helps readers decide which information is most important. Before you begin reading this unit, look at how it is organized.

■ Look at the title, headings, boldfaced words, and photographs.

■ Ask yourself: Is the text a problem and solution, description, or sequence? Is it compare and contrast or cause and effect?

■ Summarize the text by thinking about its structure.

Literary Terms

mystery a story about a crime that is solved

exposition the first stage of plot where the characters and setting are introduced

rising action the buildup of excitement in the story

climax the highest point of interest or suspense in a story or play

falling action the events that follow the climax in a story

narrator one who tells a story

first person a point of view where the narrator is also a character, using the pronouns *I* and *we*

mood the feeling that writing creates

autobiography a person's life story, written by that person

nonfiction writing about real people and events

style an author's way of writing

third person a point of view where the narrator is not a character, and refers to characters as *he* or *she*

The Adventure of the Speckled Band   by Sir Arthur Conan Doyle

Sir Arthur
Conan Doyle
1859–1930

About the Author

Arthur Conan Doyle was a medical doctor as well as a writer. One of Doyle's college professors had a skill that Doyle found amazing. The professor could tell details, without making mistakes, about his patients' lives. Doyle based his character Sherlock Holmes on the professor. In 1887, Doyle published his first Sherlock Holmes novel, *A Study in Scarlet.* The Sherlock Holmes novels became very popular around the world.

By 1893, Doyle was tired of making up stories about Sherlock Holmes. Because of this, Doyle wrote "The Final Problem," in which he killed off Holmes. People became very upset. They wanted Sherlock Holmes to come back. In 1901, Doyle brought back Sherlock Holmes in *The Hound of the Baskervilles.* In all, Doyle wrote 4 novels and 56 stories about Holmes.

Sherlock Holmes's most famous expression is "Elementary, my dear Watson." However, Doyle never wrote these words. They were first spoken in a movie version by the Holmes character.

About the Selection

Sherlock Holmes is a 19th-century British character. Holmes is one of the most loved fictional detectives of all time. He is usually shown with a deerstalker cap, a pipe, and a magnifying glass. Sherlock Holmes's assistant is Dr. Watson. In this story, Holmes looks into a strange death. Notice his attention to details.

Before Reading **continued on next page**

Objectives

◆ To read and understand the plot in a mystery

◆ To identify mood in a work of literature

◆ To describe the role of the first-person narrator in stories

The Adventure of the Speckled Band *by Sir Arthur Conan Doyle*

mystery a story about a crime that is solved

exposition the first stage of plot where the characters and setting are introduced

rising action the buildup of excitement in the story

climax the highest point of interest or suspense in a story or play

falling action the events that follow the climax in a story

narrator one who tells a story

first person a point of view where the narrator is also a character, using the pronouns *I* and *we*

mood the feeling that writing creates

Literary Terms "The Adventure of the Speckled Band" is a classic **mystery**—a story about a crime that is solved. The plot has Sherlock Holmes finding out who killed a young woman. All the parts of the plot are there: **exposition, rising action, climax, falling action**, and resolution. Look for these places in the story. The characters of Sherlock Holmes and his friend Dr. Watson have become familiar to readers all over the world. Dr. Watson is the **narrator**, or storyteller, for most of the adventures. He writes in the **first person**. In the first-person point of view, the narrator is the "I" in the story. Doyle creates a **mood** of mystery and suspense as readers try to figure out how the crime happened. Mood is the feeling that writing creates.

Reading on Your Own "The Adventure of the Speckled Band" is a mystery story. You will have to figure out what happens to the characters as the events unfold. As you read, act like a detective. Look for clues to solve the mystery.

Writing on Your Own Think of other mystery stories you have read or watched. Write a paragraph telling what you think makes for a good mystery.

Vocabulary Focus Be a word detective. Choose 10 vocabulary words you do not know from the selection. Use index cards to make flash cards. Copy one vocabulary word on each card. Write the definition on the back. Then play a word game with a partner. Have one player hold up the word and give a clue for the definition. See how many clues it takes to guess the meaning of the word. Change roles and play again.

Think Before You Read With a partner, debate this issue: "The bad guy always gets what he deserves." Do you agree or disagree with this statement? Explain your answer. Then read to see what happens to the bad guy.

The Adventure of the Speckled Band

It was early in April in the year '83 that I woke one morning to find Sherlock Holmes standing, fully dressed, by the side of my bed. He was a late riser, as a rule, and as the clock on the mantelpiece showed me that it was only a quarter-past seven, I blinked up at him in some surprise, and perhaps just a little resentment, for I was myself regular in my habits.

"Very sorry to knock you up, Watson," he said, "but it's the common lot this morning. Mrs. Hudson has been knocked up, she **retorted** upon me, and I on you."

"What is it, then—a fire?"

"No; a **client**. It seems that a young lady has arrived in a considerable state of excitement, who insists upon seeing me. She is waiting now in the sitting-room. Now, when young ladies wander about the **metropolis** at this hour of the morning, and knock sleepy people up out of their beds, I presume that it is something very pressing which they have to communicate. Should it prove to be an interesting case, you would, I am sure, wish to follow it from the **outset**. I thought, at any rate, that I should call you and give you the chance."

"My dear fellow, I would not miss it for anything."

I had no keener pleasure than in following Holmes in his professional investigations, and in admiring the rapid **deductions**, as swift as **intuitions**, and yet always founded on a **logical** basis, with which he unravelled the problems which were submitted to him. I rapidly threw on my clothes and was ready in a few minutes to accompany my friend down to the

As you read, watch for clues that lead to solving the mystery.

The narrator is Dr. Watson. He uses the pronoun "I" to show the story is written in the first person.

To *knock up* is British slang for waking by knocking at the door.

Mrs. Hudson is the landlady and housekeeper for Holmes and Watson.

retorted replied with anger

client a customer; a person for whom one does a professional service

metropolis a city

outset the beginning

deductions answers found by reasoning

intuitions ways of knowing without proof

logical reasonable

Reading Strategy: Text Structure

How do the images in the story help you to understand what is happening?

sitting-room. A lady dressed in black and heavily veiled, who had been sitting in the window, rose as we entered.

"Good-morning, madam," said Holmes cheerily. "My name is Sherlock Holmes. This is my intimate friend and associate, Dr. Watson, before whom you can speak as freely as before myself. Ha! I am glad to see that Mrs. Hudson has had the good sense to light the fire. Pray draw up to it, and I shall order you a cup of hot coffee, for I observe that you are shivering."

"It is not cold which makes me shiver," said the woman in a low voice, changing her seat as requested.

"What, then?"

"It is fear, Mr. Holmes. It is terror." She raised her veil as she spoke, and we could see that she was indeed in a **pitiable** state of **agitation**, her face all drawn and gray, with restless, frightened eyes, like those of some hunted animal. Her features and figure were those of a woman of thirty, but her hair was shot with **premature** gray, and her expression was weary and **haggard**. Sherlock Holmes ran her over with one of his quick, all-**comprehensive** glances.

"You must not fear," said he soothingly, bending forward and patting her forearm. "We shall soon set matters right, I have no doubt. You have come in by train this morning, I see."

"You know me, then?"

"No, but I observe the second half of a return ticket in the palm of your left glove. You must have started

How does the author create a tense, suspenseful mood here?

pitiable causing a feeling of pity	**premature** earlier than expected	**comprehensive** knowing
agitation strong emotion; disturbance	**haggard** looking worn because of worry	

early, and yet you had a good drive in a dog-cart, along heavy roads, before you reached the station."

The lady gave a violent start and stared in bewilderment at my companion.

"There is no mystery, my dear madam," said he, smiling. "The left arm of your jacket is **spattered** with mud in no less than seven places. The marks are perfectly fresh. There is no vehicle save a dog-cart which throws up mud in that way, and then only when you sit on the left-hand side of the driver."

"Whatever your reasons may be, you are perfectly correct," said she. "I started from home before six, reached Leatherhead at twenty past, and came in by the first train to Waterloo. Sir, I can stand this strain no longer; I shall go mad if it continues. I have no one to turn to—none, save only one, who cares for me, and he, poor fellow, can be of little aid. I have heard of you, Mr. Holmes; I have heard of you from Mrs. Farintosh, whom you helped in the hour of her sore need. It was from her that I had your address. Oh, sir, do you not think that you could help me, too, and at least throw a little light through the dense darkness which surrounds me? At present it is out of my power to reward you for your services, but in a month or six weeks I shall be married, with the control of my own income, and then at least you shall not find me ungrateful."

Holmes turned to his desk and, unlocking it, drew out a small case-book, which he consulted.

"Farintosh," said he. "Ah yes, I recall the case; it was concerned with an opal **tiara**. I think it was before your time, Watson. I can only say, madam, that I shall be happy to devote the same care to your case as I did to that of your friend. As to reward, my profession is its own reward; but you are at liberty to **defray** whatever expenses I may be put to, at the time which suits you best. And now I beg that you will lay before us everything that may help us in forming an opinion upon the matter."

A *dog-cart* is a small, horse-drawn wagon.

Leatherhead is a town south of London. *Waterloo* is a train station in London.

Which words and phrases in this paragraph suggest the visitor's anxious mood?

Who are the characters in the story so far?

---

spattered splashed   **tiara** a small crown   **defray** pay the costs

"Alas!" replied our visitor, "the very horror of my situation lies in the fact that my fears are so vague, and my suspicions depend so entirely upon small points, which might seem **trivial** to another, that even he to whom of all others I have a right to look for help and advice looks upon all that I tell him about it as the fancies of a nervous woman. He does not say so, but I can read it from his soothing answers and **averted** eyes. But I have heard, Mr. Holmes, that you can see deeply into the **manifold** wickedness of the human heart. You may advise me how to walk amid the dangers which encompass me."

"I am all attention, madam."

"My name is Helen Stoner, and I am living with my stepfather, who is the last survivor of one of the oldest Saxon families in England, the Roylotts of Stoke Moran, on the western border of Surrey."

Holmes nodded his head. "The name is familiar to me," said he.

"The family was at one time among the richest in England, and the estates extended over the borders into Berkshire in the north, and Hampshire in the west. In the last century, however, four **successive** heirs were of a **dissolute** and wasteful disposition, and the family ruin was eventually completed by a gambler in the days of the Regency. Nothing was left save a few acres of ground, and the two-hundred-year-old house, which is itself crushed under a heavy mortgage. The last squire dragged out his existence there, living the horrible life of an **aristocratic** pauper; but his only son, my stepfather, seeing that he must adapt himself to the new conditions, obtained an advance from a relative, which enabled him to take a medical degree and went out to Calcutta, where, by his professional skill and his force of character, he established a large practice. In a fit of anger, however, caused by some robberies which had been

---

The visitor is speaking of her fiancé here.

About 1,500 years ago, Germanic people from Europe conquered and settled parts of England. They were the *Anglos* and *Saxons*.

In English history, the *Regency* lasted from 1811 to 1820. In this period, King George III had a mental illness. His son ruled as a regent in his place.

Calcutta is a large city in India. India was a colony of Britain when this story was written.

---

trivial not important

averted looked away

manifold of many kinds

successive following

dissolute wicked; of bad character

aristocratic of high social class

perpetrated in the house, he beat his native butler to death and narrowly escaped a capital sentence. As it was, he suffered a long term of imprisonment and afterwards returned to England a **morose** and disappointed man.

"When Dr. Roylott was in India he married my mother, Mrs. Stoner, the young widow of Major-General Stoner, of the Bengal **Artillery**. My sister Julia and I were twins, and we were only two years old at the time of my mother's re-marriage. She had a considerable sum of money—not less than £1000 a year—and this she **bequeathed** to Dr. Roylott entirely while we resided with him, with a provision that a certain annual sum should be allowed to each of us in the event of our marriage. Shortly after our return to England my mother died—she was killed eight years ago in a railway accident near Crewe. Dr. Roylott then abandoned his attempts to establish himself in practice in London and took us to live with him in the old ancestral house at Stoke Moran. The money which my mother had left was enough for all our wants, and there seemed to be no obstacle to our happiness.

"But a terrible change came over our stepfather about this time. Instead of making friends and exchanging visits with our neighbours, who had at first been overjoyed to see a Roylott of Stoke Moran back in the old family seat, he shut himself up in his house and seldom came out save to indulge in ferocious quarrels with whoever might cross his path. Violence of temper approaching to **mania** has been hereditary in the men of the family, and in my stepfather's case it had, I believe, been **intensified** by his long residence in the tropics. A series of disgraceful brawls took place, two of which ended in the police-court, until at last he became the terror of the village, and the folks would fly at his approach, for he is a man of immense strength, and absolutely uncontrollable in his anger.

The unit of money in Great Britain is the *pound*. Its symbol is £.

Reading Strategy:
Text Structure

How does the explanation of the family's background help you to better understand the story?

Neighbour is a British spelling of the American word *neighbor*.

perpetrated carried out	**Artillery** branch of the military armed with large guns	**mania** an intense, almost insane, excitement
morose gloomy	**bequeathed** gave to, as in a will	**intensified** became stronger

"Last week he hurled the local blacksmith over a **parapet** into a stream, and it was only by paying over all the money which I could gather together that I was able to avert another public exposure. He had no friends at all save the wandering gypsies, and he would give these **vagabonds** leave to **encamp** upon the few acres of bramble-covered land which represent the family estate, and would accept in return the **hospitality** of their tents, wandering away with them sometimes for weeks on end. He has a passion also for Indian animals, which are sent over to him by a correspondent, and he has at this moment a cheetah and a baboon, which wander freely over his grounds and are feared by the villagers almost as much as their master.

"You can imagine from what I say that my poor sister Julia and I had no great pleasure in our lives. No servant would stay with us, and for a long time we did all the work of the house. She was but thirty at the time of her death, and yet her hair had already begun to whiten, even as mine has."

"Your sister is dead, then?"

"She died just two years ago, and it is of her death that I wish to speak to you. You can understand that, living the life which I have described, we were little likely to see anyone of our own age and position. We had, however, an aunt, my mother's maiden sister, Miss Honoria Westphail, who lives near Harrow, and we were occasionally allowed to pay short visits at this lady's house. Julia went there at Christmas two years ago, and met there a half-pay major of marines, to whom she became engaged. My stepfather learned of the engagement when my sister returned and offered no objection to the marriage; but within a **fortnight** of the day which had

What did Dr. Roylott do to the local blacksmith?

Why would the villagers be afraid of a cheetah and a baboon?

parapet a railing along the edge of a roof or wall	**vagabonds** homeless people who wander from place to place	**hospitality** the friendly treatment of guests
	encamp set up camp	**fortnight** a period of two weeks

been fixed for the wedding, the terrible event occurred which has deprived me of my only companion."

Sherlock Holmes had been leaning back in his chair with his eyes closed and his head sunk in a cushion, but he half opened his lids now and glanced across at his visitor.

"Pray be precise as to details," said he.

"It is easy for me to be so, for every event of that dreadful time is **seared** into my memory. The **manor**-house is, as I have already said, very old, and only one wing is now inhabited. The bedrooms in this wing are on the ground floor, the sitting-rooms being in the central block of the buildings. Of these bedrooms the first is Dr. Roylott's, the second my sister's, and the third my own. There is no communication between them, but they all open out into the same corridor. Do I make myself plain?"

"Perfectly so."

"The windows of the three rooms open out upon the lawn. That fatal night Dr. Roylott had gone to his room early, though we knew that he had not retired to rest, for my sister was troubled by the smell of the strong Indian cigars which it was his custom to smoke. She left her room, therefore, and came into mine, where she sat for some time, chatting about her approaching wedding. At eleven o'clock she rose to leave me, but she paused at the door and looked back.

"'Tell me, Helen,' said she, 'have you ever heard anyone whistle in the dead of the night?'

"'Never,' said I.

"'I suppose that you could not possibly whistle, yourself, in your sleep?'

"'Certainly not. But why?'

"'Because during the last few nights I have always, about three in the morning, heard a low, clear whistle. I am a light sleeper, and it has awakened me. I cannot tell where it came from—perhaps from the next room, perhaps from the lawn. I thought that I would just ask you whether you had heard it.'

> Why does Doyle use so much detail in Helen's description of the events?

---

seared burned   **manor** the main house on an estate

"'No, I have not. It must be those **wretched** gypsies in the plantation.'

"'Very likely. And yet if it were on the lawn, I wonder that you did not hear it also.'

"'Ah, but I sleep more heavily than you.'

"'Well, it is of no great **consequence**, at any rate.' She smiled back at me, closed my door, and a few moments later I heard her key turn in the lock."

"Indeed," said Holmes. "Was it your custom always to lock yourselves in at night?"

"Always."

"And why?"

"I think that I mentioned to you that the doctor kept a cheetah and a baboon. We had no feeling of **security** unless our doors were locked."

"Quite so. Pray proceed with your statement."

"I could not sleep that night. A vague feeling of **impending** misfortune **impressed** me. My sister and I, you will recollect, were twins, and you know how subtle are the links which bind two souls which are so closely allied. It was a wild night. The wind was howling outside, and the rain was beating and splashing against the windows. Suddenly, amid all the hubbub of the gale, there burst forth the wild scream of a terrified woman. I knew that it was my sister's voice. I sprang from my bed, wrapped a shawl round

wretched worthless; seen with scorn

consequence importance

security safety

impending about to happen

impressed affected deeply

me, and rushed into the corridor. As I opened my door I seemed to hear a low whistle, such as my sister described, and a few moments later a clanging sound, as if a mass of metal had fallen. As I ran down the passage, my sister's door was unlocked, and revolved slowly upon its hinges. I stared at it horror-**stricken**, not knowing what was about to issue from it. By the light of the corridor-lamp I saw my sister appear at the opening, her face **blanched** with terror, her hands groping for help, her whole figure swaying to and fro like that of a drunkard. I ran to her and threw my arms around her, but at that moment her knees seemed to give way and she fell to the ground. She **writhed** as one who is in terrible pain, and her limbs were dreadfully **convulsed**. At first I thought that she had not recognized me, but as I bent over her she suddenly shrieked out in a voice which I shall never forget, 'Oh, my God! Helen! It was the band! The speckled band!' There was something else which she would fain have said, and she stabbed with her finger into the air in the direction of the doctor's room, but a fresh convulsion seized her and choked her words. I rushed out, calling loudly for my stepfather, and I met him hastening from his room in his dressing-gown. When he reached my sister's side she was unconscious, and though he poured brandy down her throat and sent for medical aid from the village, all efforts were in vain, for she slowly sank and died without having recovered her consciousness. Such was the dreadful end of my beloved sister.". . .

[Holmes takes the case. Holmes and Watson travel to the house and examine the bedrooms. At night, they are waiting in the room where Julia Stoner had died. (Because of some repairs to her own room, Helen Stoner was forced to move into the room that had been her sister's.) Holmes has not told Watson why they are there. Suddenly they see a small light and hear a very gentle sound. Holmes jumps up and yells.]

> What do you think happened to Julia?

> What is the mood of the story at this point?

> *Fain* means "willingly."

---

stricken struck; strongly affected

blanched turned pale

writhed twisted as in pain

convulsed shaken or pulled with a jerk

"You see it, Watson?" he yelled. "You see it?"

But I saw nothing. At the moment when Holmes struck the light I heard a low, clear whistle, but the sudden glare flashing into my weary eyes made it impossible for me to tell what it was at which my friend lashed so savagely. I could, however, see that his face was deadly pale and filled with horror and **loathing**.

He had ceased to strike and was gazing up at the **ventilator** when suddenly there broke from the silence of the night the most horrible cry to which I have ever listened. It swelled up louder and louder, a hoarse yell of pain and fear and anger all mingled in the one dreadful shriek. They say that away down in the village, and even in the distant **parsonage**, that cry raised the sleepers from their beds. It struck cold to our hearts, and I stood gazing at Holmes, and he at me, until the last echoes of it had died away into the silence from which it rose.

"What can it mean?" I gasped.

"It means that it is all over," Holmes answered. "And perhaps, after all, it is for the best. Take your pistol, and we will enter Dr. Roylott's room.". . .

On the wooden chair, sat Dr. Grimesby Roylott, clad in a long gray dressing-gown, his bare ankles **protruding** beneath, and his feet thrust into red heelless Turkish slippers. Across his lap lay the short stock with the long lash which we had noticed during the day. His chin was cocked upward and his eyes were fixed in a dreadful, rigid stare at the corner of the ceiling. Round his brow he had a peculiar yellow band, with brownish speckles, which seemed to be bound tightly round his head. As we entered he made neither sound nor motion.

"The band! The speckled band!" whispered Holmes.

I took a step forward. In an instant his strange headgear began to move, and there reared itself from among his

What is the "speckled band"?

loathing intense dislike

ventilator a passage in a house that air is blown through

parsonage a house where a church minister lives

protruding sticking out

hair the squat diamond-shaped head and puffed neck of a **loathsome** serpent.

"It is a swamp adder!" cried Holmes; "the deadliest snake in India. He has died within ten seconds of being bitten."

[Later Holmes explained,] "It became clear to me that whatever danger threatened an **occupant** of the room could not come either from the window or the door. My attention was **speedily** drawn, as I have already remarked to you, to this ventilator, and to the bell-rope which hung down to the bed. The discovery that this was a dummy, and that the bed was clamped to the floor, instantly gave rise to the suspicion that the rope was there as a bridge for something passing through the hole and coming to the bed. The idea of a snake instantly occurred to me, and when I coupled it with my knowledge that the doctor was furnished with a supply of creatures from India, I felt that I was probably on the right track. The idea of using a form of poison which could not possibly be discovered by any chemical test was just such a one as would occur to a clever and **ruthless** man who had had an Eastern training. The **rapidity** with which such a poison would take effect would also, from his point of view, be an advantage. It would be a sharp-eyed **coroner**, indeed, who could distinguish the two little dark **punctures** which would show where the poison fangs had done their work. Then I thought of the whistle.

---

loathsome disgusting

occupant a person who lives or stays in a certain place

speedily quickly

ruthless cruel

rapidity speed

coroner the official who decides the cause of death

punctures small holes caused by a sharp object

Of course he must **recall** the snake before the morning light **revealed** it to the victim. He had trained it, probably by the use of the milk which we saw, to return to him when summoned. He would put it through this ventilator at the hour that he thought best, with the certainty that it would crawl down the rope and land on the bed. It might or might not bite the occupant, perhaps she might escape every night for a week, but sooner or later she must fall a victim.

Here Holmes explains how he put the clues together and solved the mystery.

"I had come to these conclusions before ever I had entered his room. An inspection of his chair showed me that he had been in the habit of standing on it, which of course would be necessary in order that he should reach the ventilator. The sight of the safe, the saucer of milk, and the loop of whipcord were enough to finally **dispel** any doubts which may have remained. The metallic clang heard by Miss Stoner was obviously caused by her stepfather hastily closing the door of his safe upon its terrible occupant. Having once made up my mind, you know the steps which I took in order to put the matter to the proof. I heard the creature hiss as I have no doubt that you did also, and I instantly lit the light and attacked it."

"With the result of driving it through the ventilator."

"And also with the result of causing it to turn upon its master at the other side. Some of the blows of my cane came home and roused its snakish temper, so that it flew upon the first person it saw. In this way I am no doubt indirectly responsible for Dr. Grimesby Roylott's death, and I cannot say that it is likely to weigh very heavily upon my conscience."

---

recall call back; remember   **revealed** showed   **dispel** make disappear

The Adventure of the Speckled Band   by Sir Arthur Conan Doyle

Directions Choose the letter of the best answer or write the answer using complete sentences.

Comprehension: Identifying Facts

1. When does the story take place?

   A 1663   **C** 1883

   B 1773   **D** 2003

2. Why does Holmes wake up Watson in the beginning of the story?

   A Their apartment is on fire.

   B He has finally solved the mystery.

   C Holmes has to go out of town on business.

   D A young lady has come for help with a case.

3. Why does Helen Stoner come to see Holmes?

4. Where does Helen Stoner live?

5. What is the relationship between Julia and Helen Stoner?

6. What were Julia Stoner's last words?

7. What happened to the blacksmith?

8. Where does Dr. Roylott get his animals?

9. What is the speckled band?

10. How does Dr. Roylott die?

Comprehension: Putting Ideas Together

11. Why will Helen Stoner be unable to pay Holmes right away?

    A She will not have control of her money for six more weeks.

    B Her husband will not let her.

    C She has to borrow the money from a friend.

    D The bank is closed.

12. Which of these facts about Helen Stoner does Holmes learn by watching her?

    A She has a sister named Julia.

    B She rode in a dog-cart.

    C Her mother is dead.

    D Her stepfather was once in prison.

13. Describe Helen Stoner's mood in the beginning of the story.

14. What has happened to Helen Stoner's family fortune?

15. Why do the Stoner sisters always lock their doors at night?

16. How is Helen's situation when she visits Holmes similar to Julia's just before she dies?

17. How does Roylott treat Holmes when he comes for a visit?

After Reading **continued on next page**

18. What does Holmes discover about the bell-pull?

19. How is Holmes partly responsible for Dr. Roylott's death?

20. What clues does Holmes use to solve the mystery? List at least three.

Understanding Literature: First Person

A story told in the first person uses pronouns such as *I*, *me*, *my*, and *we*. It is told from the narrator's point of view. The narrator is a character in the story. In the Sherlock Holmes stories, the narrator is Dr. Watson. Watson tells about events as they are happening. The reader knows only what Watson knows. The reader cannot know what Sherlock Holmes is thinking.

21. Describe one thing you know about Dr. Watson from the story.

22. Why is it important that Dr. Watson be in the room with Holmes and the woman?

23. How would the story be different if Holmes were the narrator?

24. How would the story be different if Helen Stoner were the narrator?

25. A third-person narrator knows the thoughts and actions of all the characters. What role would Watson have if this story were told in the third person?

Critical Thinking

26. Holmes says that he is partly responsible for Roylott's death. Who do you think is most responsible for Roylott's death? Explain.

27. What do you think would have happened if Helen had not talked to Holmes?

28. Why do you think this story is still popular today?

29. Do you think "The Adventure of the Speckled Band" is a good title for this story? Why or why not?

Thinking Creatively

30. Do you think you would enjoy working with Sherlock Holmes on a case? Explain.

Grammar Check

A personal pronoun replaces a noun in a sentence. There are three forms, or cases—*nominative*, *objective*, or *possessive*.

- Nominative—subject of a sentence
  I, we, you, he, she, it, they
- Objective—object of a sentence
  me, us, you, him, her, it, them
- Possessive—shows ownership
  my, mine, our, ours, your, yours, his, her, hers, its, their, theirs

Choose personal pronouns to complete the sentences. Label the case of each pronoun.

1 _____ have two sisters.

2 _____ names are Sara and Erin.

3 Have _____ met _____ yet?

4 _____ enjoy _____ time together.

 Vocabulary Builder

The suffixes *-ize* and *-yze* mean "make" or "become." They form verbs. For example, *-yze* changes *analysis* to *analyze*.

Write a new sentence with the same meaning as the original. Use the word in parentheses in your new sentence. You may add, drop, or move words around if needed.

1 What the author means becomes real to me. (realize)

2 They will make their decision final tomorrow. (finalize)

3 The author used the wind as a symbol of change. (symbolize)

 Writing on Your Own

Write a story about a time that you used logic, or reasoning, to solve a problem. Use a Story Map to organize your ideas. (See Appendix A for a description of this graphic organizer.) First, identify the problem. Then, list ideas you had for possible solutions. Explain why you chose the solution you did.

 Listening and Speaking

Work with a partner. Describe what you think is the most exciting or interesting scene in "The Adventure of the Speckled Band." Your partner can add any details that you leave out. Then, discuss why this scene produces the effect it does.

 Research and Technology

This story includes wild animals, such as snakes and cheetahs. Research the laws regarding wild or exotic pets. Find out the reasons for the laws. Then write a short report to present the information you find.

Letter to the Editor

An author's purpose is the reason why an author writes something. The four most common purposes are to entertain, inform, express, or to persuade. As readers, we examine how well the author explains his or her purpose.

Many people write letters to the editor. These letters are usually printed near the front of a magazine or in a main section of a newspaper. A letter to the editor can also appear in an online publication. The author's purpose in a letter to the editor is to persuade. The author wants to convince readers of his or her opinion.

About Letters to the Editor

Anyone can write a letter to the editor. The letters offer opinions in response to something that appeared in the publication. For example, the letter may respond to a news story, an editorial, a column, or a photograph. The writer offers his or her opinion and backs up the opinion with facts and details. The facts and details are included to help persuade readers.

Reading Skill

When you first see a letter to the editor, preview it to determine the author's purpose. Take a quick look at the title and author's name. Skim the first paragraph too. This will help you determine the author's purpose for writing. Determine whether your own purpose for reading will be satisfied. Then you can decide whether or not to read on.

On the next two pages are examples of letters to the editor. Each letter is a response to the same newspaper article.

"Teach by Example"

What do you learn from the title of this letter?

Dear Editor,

On November 18, you published an article titled "How Much Is Too Much?" The article described how today's children want so many things. But they don't want just any material goods; they want expensive name brand items. They demand clothing that cost $300 and game systems that cost $500. These kids could not name the presidents but could name all the latest name brands. This is a disgrace.

As you read, think about the author's reasons for writing this letter.

I hope these kids know a few other brand names, such as names of charities. I hope they know service groups too. Children find out early about the attraction of luxury but not community service.

Parents shouldn't just ask their teenagers, "Why do you need these material things?" Our job is to show them by example that they don't. We have to avoid the pull of this consumer-centered society ourselves. As parents, we have to set an example by giving rather than just getting.

Sincerely,
Ms. Janice Fitzpatrick

What details does the author use to support her opinion?

"The Right to Pursue Happiness"

Dear Editor,
I read your article "How Much Is Too Much?" I am in the 8th grade. All my friends have name-brand jeans and sneakers. They have expensive sweaters, T-shirts, and bracelets. They have cell phones too. The older kids drive nice cars. I have these things, too, and it makes me feel happy to have nice things. It also helps me fit in with everyone else. I do not see anything wrong with buying what I like and what I want. After all, life is short. Don't we deserve to be happy?

Signed,
Jeff Thornbloom

Who wrote this letter?

"Support Our Nation"

Dear Editor,

This is in response to your November 18 article "How Much Is Too Much?" As Americans, we have a responsibility to buy a lot. I know this sounds ridiculous, but purchasing keeps our economy going. For example, I manufacture expensive cosmetics. My company has a name everyone knows. We're famous. Americans spend eight billion dollars a year in cosmetics. I am glad about this! My business would fail if no one bought the make-up we make. No one has to be a shopaholic, of course, but where would America be if we stopped buying things? The country would fall apart.

Signed,
T.J. Sanders

The author states the reason for the letter in the first sentence.

Monitor Your Progress

Directions Choose the letter of the best answer or write the answer using complete sentences.

1. Where do you find letters to the editor?

   A They are always on the back page of the newspaper.

   B They are often on the front page of the newspaper.

   C They are usually after the sports section by the ads.

   D They are often in the main section of the newspaper.

2. A letter to the editor appears in all the following places except _____.

   A newspapers

   B plays

   C magazines

   D online publications

3. Who writes editorials? Why do people write them?

4. Which editorial do you agree with most strongly? Explain your reasons.

5. Choose any two of these letters to compare. Tell how they are the same and different.

Writing on Your Own

Write a letter to the editor. Skim your local newspaper to find an article or editorial that interests you. Form an opinion about the topic, and then respond to the article. Be sure to include specific details to persuade readers.

Go to Boarding School   by Jane Grey Swisshelm

Jane Grey Swisshelm
1815–1884

Objectives

- To read and understand an autobiography
- To explain the difference between fiction and nonfiction
- To identify the author's style

About the Author

Jane Grey Cannon was born in Pittsburgh, Pennsylvania. When Jane was eight years old, her father died. Although she was only a child, Jane made lace to help support the family. As a teenager, she started working to end slavery. This would be her lifelong career. At the age of 14, she became a teacher in the village school. Later, she married a farmer named Swisshelm and moved to Kentucky. She joined the Underground Railroad while living in Kentucky. By the 1840s, Jane was writing newspaper stories about ending slavery. She started her own anti-slavery newspaper. It was a big success. She also helped the soldiers during the Civil War and was an important part of the women's rights movement.

About the Selection

This selection comes from Swisshelm's story of her life, *Half a Century*. She published it in 1880, only four years before she died. In this selection, Swisshelm describes going off to boarding school. Boarding school is like sleep-away camp. Students live at the school. They take lessons, eat their meals, and sleep there.

Literary Terms "Go to Boarding School" is a chapter from Swisshelm's **autobiography**. This is a person's life story, written by that person. An autobiography may tell everything about a person's life, or only part of it. Since autobiographies are about real people and events, they are **nonfiction**. Most autobiographies are written in the first person. Author's use their own **style**, or way of writing to make events come to life for the reader.

Reading on Your Own One of the most important parts of an author's style is word choice. Are the words easy or difficult to understand? Sentence length and structure are two other features of style. Some writers use short sentences, while others prefer long sentences. Many writers use a mix of different sentence lengths. Punctuation is another feature of an author's style. As you read, notice the style of Swisshelm's writing.

Writing on Your Own This selection tells about going off to boarding school. How would you feel about going to school far away from home? Write a paragraph describing your feelings. How do you think other people your age would feel about leaving home for a long period of time?

Vocabulary Focus Many words from other languages have entered English. Swisshelm uses these borrowed words: *rendezvous, pantaloons,* and *Sabbath.* Look up these words in a dictionary. Find the language each word comes from. Also read the pronunciation and meaning of each word.

Think Before You Read How do you think reading nonfiction is different from reading fiction? How is it similar? Talk about these similarities and differences with a classmate.

autobiography
a person's life story, written by that person

nonfiction
writing about real people and events

style an author's way of writing

Go to Boarding School
from Half a Century

As you read, compare your own childhood to Jane's childhood.

Subscription schools were funded by a monthly fee that parents paid to the teachers. The teachers were responsible for getting a place to hold class. Teachers had to pay the rent from their earnings. Classes were often given in churches, tents, or homes.

In lieu of means instead of.

During my childhood there were no public schools in Pennsylvania. The State was pretty well supplied with colleges for boys, while girls were permitted to go to subscription schools. To these we were sent part of the time, and in one of them Joseph Caldwell, afterwards a **prominent** missionary to India, was a schoolmate. But we had Dr. Black's sermons, full of grand morals, science and history.

In lieu of colleges for girls, there were boarding-schools, and Edgeworth was **esteemed** one of the best in the State. It was at Braddock's Field, and Mrs. Olever, an English woman of high culture, was its founder and principal. To it my cousin, Mary Alexander, was sent, but returned homesick, and refused to go back unless I went with her. It was arranged that I should go for a few weeks, as I was greatly in need of country air; and, highly delighted, I was at the **rendezvous** at the hour, one o'clock, with my box, ready for this **excursion** into the world of polite literature. Mary was also there, and a new scholar, but Father Olever did not come for us until four o'clock. He was a small, nervous gentleman, and lamps were already lighted in the smoky city when we started to drive twelve miles through spring mud, on a cloudy, cheerless afternoon. We knew he had no **confidence** in his power to

prominent well-known	**esteemed** honored, respected	**excursion** trip
	rendezvous meeting	**confidence** firm belief or trust

Reading Strategy:
Text Structure

How would you describe the sentences? Are they long or short?

What was Swisshelm's purpose in describing education for girls in the early 1800s?

Reading Strategy:
Text Structure

How does the author make the journey tense and suspenseful?

manage those horses, though we also knew he would do his best to save us from harm; but as darkness closed around us, I think we felt like babes in the woods, and shuddered with **vague** fear as much as with cold and damp. When we reached the "Bullock Pens," half a mile west of Wilkinsburg, there were many lights and much bustle in and around the old yellow tavern, where teamsters were attending to their weary horses. Here we turned off to the old mud road, and came to a place of which I had no **previous** knowledge—a place of outer darkness and chattering teeth.

We met no more teams, saw no more lights, but seemed to be in an **utterly** uninhabited country. Then, after an hour of wearisome jolting and plunging, we discovered that the darkness had not been total, for the line of the **horizon** had been visible, but now it was swallowed up. We knew we were in a wood, by the rush of the wind amid the dried white oak leaves—knew that the road grew rougher at ever step—that our driver became more nervous as he applied the brake, and we went down, down.

Still the **descent** grew steeper. We stopped, and Father Olever felt for the bank with his whip to be sure we were on the road. Then we heard the sound of rushing, angry waters, **mingled** with the roar of the wind, and he seemed to hesitate about going on, but we could not very well stay there, and he once more put his horses in motion, while we held fast and prayed silently to the great Deliverer. After stopping again and feeling for the bank, lest we should go over the **precipitous** hillside, which he knew was there, he proceeded until, with a great plunge, we were in the angry waters, which arose to the wagon-bed, and roared and **surged** all around us. The horses

vague not clear	**horizon** the line where the earth and sky seem to meet	**precipitous** steep, dangerous
previous coming before	**descent** fall, drop	**surged** rose and fell like waves
utterly totally, completely	**mingled** mixed	

tried to go on, when something gave way, and our **guardian** concluded further progress was impossible, and began to hallo at the top of his voice.

For a long time there was no response; then came an answering call from a long distance. Next a light appeared, and that, too, was far away, but came toward us. When it reached the **brink** of the water, and two men with it, we felt safe. The light-bearer held it up so that we saw him quite well, and his **peculiar** appearance suited his surroundings. He was more an overgrown boy than a man, beardless, with a long **swarthy** face, black hair and keen black eyes. He wore heavy boots outside his **pantaloons**, a blouse and **slouch** hat, spoke to his companion as one having authority, and with a laugh said to our small gentleman:

"Is this where you are?" but gave no heed to the answer as he waded in and threw off the check lines, saying: "I wonder you did not drown your horses."

He next examined the wagon, paying no more attention to Father Olever's explanations than to the water in which he seemed quite at home, and when he had finished his inspection he said:

Check lines are part of the equipment that helps attach horses to a wagon.

"They must go to the house," and handing the light to the driver he took us up one by one and carried us to the wet bank as easily as a child carries her doll.

He gave some directions to his companion, took the light and said to us: "Come on," and we walked after him out into the limitless blackness, nothing doubting. We went what seemed a long way, following this **brigand**-looking stranger, without seeing any sign of life or hearing any sound save the roar of wind and water, but on turning a fence corner, we came in sight of a large two-story house, with a bright light streaming out through many windows, and a wide open door. There was a large stone barn on the other side

guardian someone who takes care of another	**brink** edge	**pantaloons** pants
	peculiar strange	**slouch** droopy
	swarthy dark	**brigand** thief

of the road, and to this our conductor turned, saying to us: "Go on to the house." This we did, and were met at the open door by a middle-aged woman, shading with one hand the candle held in the other. This threw a strong light on her face, which instantly reminded me of an eagle. She wore a double-bordered white cap over her black hair, and looked suspiciously at us through her small keen, black eyes, but kindly bade us come in to a low wainscoted hall, with broad stairway and many open doors. Through one of these and a second door we saw a great fire of logs, and I should have liked to sit by it, but she led us into a square wainscotted room on the opposite side, in which blazed a coal fire almost as large as the log heap in the kitchen.

She gave us seats, and a white-haired man who sat in the corner, spoke to us, and made me feel comfortable. Up to this time all the surroundings had had an air of **enchanted** castles, brigands, ghosts, witches. The alert woman with the eagle face, in spite of her kindness, made me feel myself an object of doubtful character, but this old man set me quite at ease. We were no more than well warmed when the wagon drove to the door, and the boy-man with the lantern appeared, saying,

"Come on."

We followed him again, and he lifted us into the wagon, while the mistress of the house stood on the large flag-stone door-step, shading her candle-flame, and giving directions about our wraps.

"Coming events cast their shadows before," when they are between us and the light; but that night the light must have been between them and me; for I **bade** good-bye to our hostess without any **premonition** we should ever again meet, or that I should sit alone, as I do to-night, over half a century later, in that same old wainscoted room, listening to the roar of those same angry waters and the rush of the wind wrestling with the groaning trees, in the dense darkness of this low valley.

Wainscoted describes walls with wood paneling.

Wraps are a type of coat.

Where was the author when she wrote this piece? How can you tell?

enchanted charming, magical	**bade** told	**premonition** warning, hunch

When we had been carefully **bestowed** in the wagon, our deliverer took up his lantern, saying to Father Olever:

"Drive on."

He was obeyed, and led the way over a bridge across another noisy stream, and along a road where there was the sound of a waterfall very near, then up a steep, rocky way until he stopped, saying,

"I guess you can get along now."

To Father Olever's thanks he only replied by a low, **contemptuous** but good-humored laugh, as he turned to retrace his steps. All comfort and strength and hope seemed to go with him. We were abandoned to our fate, babes in the woods again, with only God for our **reliance**. But after a while we could see the horizon, and arrived at our destination several minutes before midnight, to find the great mansion full of glancing lights and busy, **expectant** life.

The large family had waited up for Father Olever's return, for he and his wagon were the connecting link between that establishment and the outside world. He appeared to great advantage surrounded by a **bevy** of girls **clamoring** for letters and messages. To me the scene was fairy-land. I had never before seen any thing so grand as the great hall with its polished stairway. We had supper in the housekeeper's room, and I was taken up this stairway, and then up and up a corkscrew cousin until we reached the attic, which stretched over the whole house, one great **dormitory** called the "bee-hive." Here I was to sleep with Helen Scruple, a Pittsburg girl, of about my own age, a frail blonde, who quite won my heart at our first meeting.

Next day was Sabbath, and I was greatly surprised to see pupils walk on the lawn. This was such a **desecration** of the

Reading Strategy:
Text Structure
What details does the author use to show the school's grandness?

---

bestowed given

contemptuous scornful

reliance help, dependence

expectant eager, hopeful

bevy group

clamoring yelling

dormitory a building with many rooms for sleeping in

desecration ruin

day, but I made no remark. I was too solemnly impressed by the **grandeur** of being at Braddock's Field to have hinted that anything could be wrong. But for my own share in the **violation** I was painfully **penitent**.

This was not new, for there were a long series of years in which the principal business of six days of every week, was **repentance** for the very poor use made of the seventh, and from this dreary **treadmill** of sin and sorrow, no faith ever could or did free me. I never could see **salvation** in Christ apart from salvation from sin, and while the sin remained the salvation was doubtful and the sorrow certain.

grandeur the quality or state of being grand	**penitent** sorry for doing wrong	**treadmill** a wearisome routine of daily life
violation disobedience	**repentance** sorrow, regret	**salvation** saved from sin

On the afternoon of that first Sabbath, a number of young lady pupils came to the Bee-hive for a visit, and as I afterwards learned to inspect and name the two new girls, when I was promptly and **unanimously dubbed** "Wax Doll." After a time, one remarked that they must go and study their "ancient history lesson." I caught greedily at the words, ancient history. Ah, if I could only be permitted to study such a lesson! No such progress or promotion seemed open to me; but the thought interfered with my prayers, and followed me into the **realm** of sleep. So when that class was called next forenoon, I was alert, and what was my surprise, to hear those privileged girls stumbling over the story of Sampson? Could it be possible that was ancient history? How did it come to pass that every one did not know all about Sampson, the man who had laid his head on Delilah's wicked lap, to be shorn of his strength. If there is any thing in that account, or any lesson to be drawn from it, with which I was not then familiar, it is something I have never learned. Indeed, I seemed to have completed my **theological** education before I did my twelfth year.

One morning, Mrs. Olever sent for me, and told me she had learned my mother was not able to send me to school, but if I would take charge of the lessons of the little girls, she would furnish me board and **tuition**. This most generous offer quite took my breath away, and was most gladly accepted; but it was easy work, and I wondered my own studies were so light. I was allowed to amuse myself drawing flowers, which were quite a surprise, and pronounced better than anything the drawing master could do—to **recite** poetry, for the benefit of the larger girls, and to play in the orchard with my pupils.

Who is the Wax Doll?

The *forenoon* is the later part of the morning.

What details show that Jane is very eager to learn?

Samson and *Delilah* are from the Bible. Samson, the hero, fell in love with Delilah. She betrayed him by telling the enemy that his strength came from his hair. While he was asleep, she cut it. Samson was drained of his strength and was captured.

How does Jane get her schooling paid for?

unanimously all together

dubbed gave a title, name, or nickname to

realm a region or area

theological religious

tuition money paid for instruction

recite to say over; repeat

With the other girls, I became interested in hairdressing. I had read "The Children of the Abbey," and Amanda's romantic adventures enchanted me; but she was quite outside my life. Now I made a nearer acquaintance with her. She changed her **residence**; so had I. She had brown ringlets; I too should have them. So one Friday night, my hair was put up in papers, and next morning, I let loose an amazing shower of curls.

Put up in papers refers to when girls curled their hair by twisting it in pieces of paper. When their hair dried, the papers were removed.

The next thing to do was to go off alone, and sit reading in a romantic spot. Of course I did not expect to meet Lord Mortimer! Miss Fitzallen never had any such **expectations**. I was simply going out to read and admire the beauties of nature. When I had seated myself, in proper attitude, on the **gnarled** root of an old tree, overhanging a lovely ravine, I proceeded to the reading part of the play, and must of course be too much absorbed to hear the approaching footsteps, to which I listened with bated breath. So I did not look up when they stopped at my side, or until a pleasant voice said:

Bated breath means to hold one's breath in great fear or wonder.

"Why you look quite romantic, my dear."

Then I saw Miss Olever, the head teacher, familiarly called "Sissy Jane." In that real and beautiful presence Miss Fitzallen retired to her old place, and oh, the **mortification** she left behind her! I looked up, a **detected** criminal, into the face of her who had brought to me this **humiliation**, and took *her* for a model. My folly did not prevent our being sincere friends during all her earnest and beautiful life.

What was the author's purpose in writing?

She passed on, and I got back to the Bee-hive, when I disposed of my curls, and never again played **heroine**.

residence a place where one lives	**mortification** embarrassment	**heroine** a woman or girl admired for bravery
expectations hopes	**detected** found out	
gnarled twisted	**humiliation** shame	

Go to Boarding School   by Jane Grey Swisshelm

Directions Choose the letter of the best answer or write the answer using complete sentences.

Comprehension: Identifying Facts

1. Where does this selection take place?
   A India
   B California
   C Pennsylvania
   D Europe

2. Why does the narrator not go to public school?
   A Her state does not have public schools.
   B She is too poor to go to public school.
   C She has to work so she cannot attend school.
   D She does not like school and refuses to go.

3. What creature does Jane say the lady looks like?

4. How does Jane describe the large two-story house?

5. What is the "bee-hive"?

6. How does Jane feel about Helen Scruple?

7. Who is the "Wax Doll"?

8. How does Jane earn her room and board at Edgewood?

9. What does Jane do to change her hair?

10. Who surprises Jane outside as she reads a play aloud?

Comprehension: Putting Ideas Together

11. When does this selection take place?
    A early 1600s
    B early 1700s
    C early 1800s
    D present day

12. Why is Jane going to Edgewood?
    A She wants to escape being married to Joseph Caldwell.
    B She is going for a few weeks to keep her cousin company.
    C She is going to be a teacher there.
    D She wants to become a doctor and will be trained there.

13. Describe Jane's journey to Edgewood.

14. Why does Father Olever start yelling at the top of his voice?

15. Where is Jane as she is writing this selection?

16. What does the school look like?

After Reading **continued on next page**

17. What happens on Sunday that surprises Jane?

18. Why does Jane mention the story of Samson and Delilah?

19. How does Jane feel about studying ancient history?

20. What offer does Mrs. Olever make to Jane?

Understanding Literature: Autobiography

An autobiography is a person's life story, written by that person. Some famous people write their autobiographies because they have had an interesting life. Jane Swisshelm, for example, gained fame through her work to win rights for slaves and women. Readers can learn a lot about a person and his or her times from their autobiography.

21. Why do you think Jane chose this event to describe?

22. Which parts of this autobiography did you find the most interesting?

23. How can you tell that this is nonfiction?

24. Would you like to go to school at Edgewood? Why or why not?

25. Why do people sometimes write an autobiography?

Critical Thinking

26. How can you tell that Jane has a desire for learning?

27. What parts of the story show that Jane acts grown up?

28. Do you think boarding school is better than day school? Why or why not?

29. How do you think life has changed since this selection was published?

Thinking Creatively

30. How are online journals or blogs like autobiographies?

Grammar Check

Possessive nouns use apostrophes to show ownership. Follow these rules for showing possession:

- With singular nouns, add an -*s* and an apostrophe.
  Example: Mary's book

- With plural nouns that end in *s*, add only an apostrophe.
  Example: beaches' sand

- With plural nouns that do not end in *s*, add an apostrophe and -*s*.
  Example: women's plan

Add apostrophes to show ownership in each phrase.

1 Edgars exciting adventures
2 Janes curls
3 childrens books

 Vocabulary Builder

A plural noun refers to more than one person, place, thing, or idea. Most plurals are formed by adding -*s*. Some nouns, however, follow different rules.

- For words that end in -*x*, -*ch*, or -*sh*, add an -*es*. *Example*: box—boxes

- For words that end in a consonant plus *y*, change the *y* to an *i* and add -*es*. *Example*: fly—flies

- Some words that end in -*f* or -*fe* have plurals that end in -*ves*.
  Example: knife—knives

- The plurals of some nouns are different words.
  Example: goose—geese

 Writing on Your Own

In this selection, Jane describes going off to a new school. Think about your first day of school at the beginning of a school year. Write this part of your autobiography. Use descriptive words as you write.

 Listening and Speaking

Work with a classmate to rewrite this selection as a television interview. Start by writing 10 questions. Then take turns interviewing each other. One person should act as Jane and the other person should act as himself or herself. How is Jane's school different from your own? What advice would Jane give today's students?

 Research and Technology

Research what school was like in America around 1825–1850. Write a research paper describing the requirements for teachers and the school buildings. Tell what subjects were taught and how. When you are finished, post your report on your class Web page.

Up the Slide   by Jack London

**Jack London
1876–1916**

Objectives

◆ To read and compare fiction and nonfiction literature

◆ To understand the difference between first-person and third-person point of view

About the Author

Jack London was the most popular novelist and short story writer of his day. His exciting tales of adventure and courage were sparked by his own experiences.

When he was 17 years old, London sailed with a seal-hunting ship to Japan and Siberia. After two years, he returned to high school. He decided to become a writer. In 1897, London journeyed to the Yukon Territory in search of gold. He did not find any gold, but he did find ideas to use in his writing. Many of his best novels and stories describe his experiences in the frozen north.

About the Selection

Clay Dilham is the main character in "Up the Slide." He is 17 years old and very confident. He is similar to many prospectors, or people who explore to find gold. These people traveled to the Yukon Territory in the 1890s. They all wanted to find gold and get rich fast. Prospecting for gold was very dangerous because the Yukon Territory is located in the northwestern corner of Canada. In this region, temperatures have been known to drop to –80°F. Skin that is not covered can freeze in minutes.

Jane Grey Swisshelm is the main character in "Go to Boarding School." In her selection, she is younger than Clay, but she is also very confident. As you read, you will notice that the settings of the two stories are different. However, both selections are full of adventure and danger. Also, Swisshelm's selection is nonfiction, but London's is fiction.

Literary Terms "Up the Slide" is a fiction story that Jack London wrote about a young man in the Yukon Territory. Even though the story is fiction, it uses some parts of real life. This story is told in the **third person**. The third person is a point of view where the narrator is not a character, and refers to characters as *he* or *she*. The narrator is watching the action from the outside. The narrator does not know the thoughts or feelings of any of the characters.

> **third person**
> a point of view where the narrator is not a character, and refers to characters as *he* or *she*

Reading on Your Own Both fiction and nonfiction present a series of events in a certain setting. Here are some important differences between the two. A fictional narrative does not describe real events. The author has complete control over plot, setting, and characters. In a nonfiction narrative, the author cannot change real-life events. The author cannot bring in new characters or change settings.

Even though "Up the Slide" is fiction, what nonfiction details do you think London might have included? How does Jane Swisshelm's story compare to London's?

Writing on Your Own A documentary film is nonfiction. It shows real people, places, and events. Some filmmakers have produced documentaries about the Yukon Gold Rush. Write a paragraph to describe how a documentary about the Yukon Gold Rush would differ from a fictional tale.

Vocabulary Focus As you read this narrative, look for words that describe the setting. The first paragraph says, "down the Yukon to Dawson." What other clues can you find? Write these descriptions on a sheet of paper.

Think Before You Read London was one of the highest paid authors of his time. Why do you think London's stories of looking for gold are still popular today?

Up the Slide

As you read, notice similarities and differences between this selection and "Go to Boarding School."

Dawson became a large city during the Klondike Gold Rush in the late 1890s. Today, about 2,000 people live there.

A *cord* is a stack of firewood 8 feet long, 4 feet wide, and 4 feet high.

When Clay Dilham left the tent to get a sled-load of firewood, he expected to be back in half an hour. So he told Swanson, who was cooking the dinner. Swanson and he belonged to different **outfits**, located about twenty miles apart on the Stewart River, but they had become traveling partners on a trip down the Yukon to Dawson to get the mail.

Swanson had laughed when Clay said he would be back in half an hour. It stood to reason, Swanson said, that good, dry firewood could not be found so close to Dawson; that whatever firewood there was originally had long since been gathered in; that firewood would not be selling at forty dollars a cord if any man could go out and get a sled-load and be back in the time Clay expected to make it.

Then it was Clay's turn to laugh, as he sprang on the sled and **mushed** the dogs on the river-trail. For, coming up from the Siwash village the previous day, he had noticed a small dead pine in an out-of-the-way place, which had **defied** discovery by eyes less sharp than his. And his eyes were both young and sharp, for his seventeenth birthday was just cleared.

A swift ten minutes over the ice brought him to the place, and figuring ten minutes to get the tree and ten minutes to

outfits groups that work as a team	**mushed** drove a dogsled team	**defied** avoided

return made him certain that Swanson's dinner would not wait.

Just below Dawson, and rising out of the Yukon itself, towered the great Moosehide Mountain, so named by Lieutenant Schwatka long **ere** the Yukon became famous. On the river side the mountain was scarred and gullied and gored; and it was up one of these gores or **gullies** that Clay had seen the tree.

Halting his dogs beneath, on the river ice, he looked up, and after some searching, rediscovered it. Being dead, its weatherbeaten gray so blended with the gray wall of rock that a thousand men could pass by and never notice it. Taking root in a **cranny**, it had grown up, exhausted its bit of soil, and **perished**. Beneath it the wall fell sheer for a hundred feet to the river. All one had to do was to sink an ax into the dry trunk a dozen times and it would fall to the ice, and most probably smash conveniently to pieces. This Clay had figured on when confidently limiting the trip to half an hour.

He studied the cliff **thoroughly** before attempting it. So far as he was concerned, the longest way round was the shortest way to the tree. Twenty feet of nearly **perpendicular** climbing would bring him to where a slide sloped more gently in. By making a long zigzag across the face of this slide and back again, he would arrive at the pine.

Fastening his ax across his shoulders so that it would not **interfere** with his movements, he clawed up the broken rock, hand and foot, like a cat, till the twenty feet were cleared and he could draw breath on the edge of the slide.

The slide was steep and its snow-covered surface slippery. Further, the heelless, walrus-hide shoes of his muclucs were polished by much ice travel, and by his second step he realized how little he could depend upon them for clinging purposes.

Reading Strategy: Text Structure

Read the title again. What clues does the titles give about the plot of the story?

Reading Strategy: Text Structure

How does the image on p. 82 give you an idea of what life was like at this time?

What is Clay trying to do here?

Muclucs are a type of shoe or boot. They are worn in icy northern climates.

ere before

gullies narrow valleys that are steep and rocky

cranny a small break or split

perished died

thoroughly completely; fully

perpendicular straight up

interfere to get in the way of

A slip at that point meant a plunge over the edge and a twenty-foot fall to the ice. A hundred feet farther along, and a slip would mean a fifty-foot fall.

He thrust his mittened hand through the snow to the earth to steady himself, and went on. But he was forced to exercise such care that the first zigzag consumed five minutes. Then, returning across the face of the slide toward the pine, he met with a new difficulty. The slope steepened considerably, so that little snow collected, while bent flat beneath this thin covering were long, dry last-year's grasses.

The surface they presented was as glassy as that of his muclucs, and when both surfaces came together his feet shot out, and he fell on his face, sliding downward and **convulsively** clutching for something to stay himself.

This he succeeded in doing, although he lay quiet for a couple of minutes to get back his nerve. He would have taken off his muclucs and gone at it in his socks, only the cold was thirty below zero, and at such temperature his feet would quickly freeze. So he went on, and after ten minutes of risky work made the safe and solid rock where stood the pine.

A few strokes of the ax felled it into the **chasm**, and peeping over the edge, he indulged a laugh at the startled dogs. They were on the **verge** of bolting when he called aloud to them, soothingly, and they were reassured.

Then he turned about for the trip back. Going down, he knew, was even more dangerous than coming up, but how dangerous he did not realize till he had slipped half a dozen times, and each time saved himself by what appeared to him a miracle. Time and again he ventured upon the slide, and time and again he was **balked** when he came to the grasses.

He sat down and looked at the **treacherous** snow-covered slope. It was **manifestly** impossible for him to make it with

Reading Strategy:
Text Structure

As you continue to read, notice how the time passes. Will Clay make it back in half an hour?

What features of this ice slide would make it dangerous for a climber?

convulsively having twitching in muscle spasms	**verge** the point at which something begins	**treacherous** dangerous
chasm a deep opening or crack in the earth	**balked** stopped	**manifestly** clearly

a whole body, and he did not wish to arrive at the bottom shattered like the pine tree.

He must be doing something to keep his blood **circulating**. If he could not get down by going down, there only remained to him to get down by going up. It was a **herculean** task, but it was the only way out of the **predicament**.

From where he was he could not see the top of the cliff, but he reasoned that the gully in which lay the slide must give inward more and more as it approached the top. From what little he could see, the gully displayed this **tendency**; and he noticed, also, that the slide extended for many hundreds of feet upward, and that where it ended the rock was well broken up and favorable for climbing. . . .

So instead of taking the zigzag which led downward, he made a new one leading upward and crossing the slide at an angle of thirty degrees. The grasses gave him much trouble, and made him long for soft-tanned moosehide moccasins, which could make his feet cling like a second pair of hands.

He soon found that thrusting his mittened hands through the snow and clutching the grass roots was uncertain and unsafe. His mittens were too thick for him to be sure of his grip, so he took them off. But this brought with it new trouble. When he held on to a bunch of roots the snow, coming in contact with his bare warm hand, was melted, so that his hands and the wristbands of his woolen shirt were dripping with water. This the frost was quick to attack, and his fingers were numbed and made worthless.

Then he was forced to seek good footing, where he could stand **erect** unsupported, to put on his mittens, and to thrash his hands against his sides until the heat came back into them.

This constant numbing of his fingers made his progress very slow; but the zigzag came to an end finally, where the side of the slide was **buttressed** by a perpendicular rock, and

Reading Strategy:
Text Structure

How does the author's choice of setting increase the drama in the story?

circulating flowing	**predicament** dilemma; problem	**erect** straight
herculean nearly impossible	**tendency** a natural urge to do something	**buttressed** supported

Why is the trip down more difficult than the trip up?

he turned back and upward again. As he climbed higher and higher, he found that the slide was wedge-shaped, its rocky buttresses pinching it away as it reared its upper end. Each step increased the depth which seemed to yawn for him.

While beating his hands against his sides he turned and looked down the long slippery slope, and figured, in case he slipped, that he would be flying with the speed of an express train ere he took the final plunge into the icy bed of the Yukon.

He passed the first **outcropping** rock, and the second, and at the end of an hour found himself above the third, and fully five hundred feet above the river. And here, with the end nearly two hundred feet above him, the pitch of the slide was increasing.

Each step became more difficult and **perilous**, and he was faint from **exertion** and from lack of Swanson's dinner. Three or four times he slipped slightly and recovered himself; but, growing careless from exhaustion and the long **tension** on his nerves, he tried to continue with too great haste, and was rewarded by a double slip of each foot, which tore him loose and started him down the slope.

On account of the steepness there was little snow; but what little there was was displaced by his body, so that he became the **nucleus** of a young avalanche. He clawed desperately with his hands, but there was little to cling to, and he sped downward faster and faster.

The first and second outcroppings were below him, but he knew that the first was almost out of line, and pinned his hope on the second. Yet the first was just enough in line to catch one of his feet and to whirl him over and head downward on his back.

The shock of this was severe in itself, and the fine snow **enveloped** him in a blinding, maddening cloud; but he was thinking quickly and clearly of what would happen if he brought up head first against the outcropping. He twisted

outcropping an area of a rock that sticks out above the ground	**perilous** full of danger	**nucleus** center
	exertion effort	**enveloped** surrounded
	tension worry; strain	

himself over on his stomach, thrust both hands out to one side, and pressed them heavily against the flying surface.

This had the effect of a brake, drawing his head and shoulders to the side. In this position he rolled over and over a couple of times, and then, with a quick jerk at the right moment, he got his body the rest of the way round.

And none too soon, for the next moment his feet drove into the outcropping, his legs doubled up, and the wind was driven from his stomach with the **abruptness** of the stop.

Reading Strategy: Text Structure

What details does London use to create suspense at this point in the story?

There was much snow down his neck and up his sleeves. At once and with unconcern he shook this out, only to discover, when he looked up to where he must climb again, that he had lost his nerve. He was shaking as if with a **palsy**, and sick and faint from a frightful **nausea**.

Fully ten minutes passed ere he could master these sensations and summon **sufficient** strength for the weary climb. His legs hurt him and he was limping, and he was conscious of a sore place in his back, where he had fallen on the ax.

In an hour he had regained the point of his tumble, and was **contemplating** the slide, which so suddenly steepened. It was plain to him that he could not go up with his hands and feet alone, and he was beginning to lose his nerve again when he remembered the ax.

Reaching upward the distance of a step, he brushed away the snow, and in the frozen gravel and crumbled rock of the slide chopped a shallow resting place for his foot. Then he came up a step, reached forward, and repeated the

abruptness suddenness	**nausea** unsettled stomach	**contemplating** thinking about; considering
palsy a paralysis with trembling and muscular weakness	**sufficient** having enough	

What does the comparison to a fly suggest about Clay?

How does Clay stop himself from sliding to his death?

maneuver. And so, step by step, foothole by foothole, a tiny speck of toiling life **poised** like a fly on the face of Moosehide Mountain, he fought his upward way.

Twilight was beginning to fall when he gained the head of the slide and drew himself into the rocky bottom of the gully. At this point the shoulder of the mountain began to bend back toward the crest, and in addition to its being less steep, the rocks afforded better handhold and foothold. The worst was over, and the best yet to come!

The gully opened out into a miniature basin, in which a floor of soil had been deposited, out of which, in turn, a tiny grove of pines had sprung. The trees were all dead, dry and seasoned, having long since exhausted the thin skin of earth.

Clay ran his experienced eye over the timber, and estimated that it would chop up into fifty cords at least. Beyond, the gully closed in and became **barren** rock again. On every hand was barren rock, so the wonder was small that the trees had escaped the eyes of men. They were only to be discovered as he had discovered them—by climbing after them.

He continued the **ascent**, and the white moon greeted him when he came out upon the crest of Moosehide Mountain. At his feet, a thousand feet below, sparkled the lights of Dawson.

But the **descent** was **precipitate** and dangerous in the uncertain moonlight, and he **elected** to go down the mountain by its gentler northern flank. In a couple of hours he reached the Yukon at the Siwash village, and took the river-trail back to where he had left the dogs. There he found Swanson, with a fire going, waiting for him to come down.

And although Swanson had a hearty laugh at his expense, nevertheless, a week or so later, in Dawson, there were fifty cords of wood sold at forty dollars a cord, and it was he and Swanson who sold them.

Reading Strategy:
Text Structure

What role does the character Swanson play in the beginning and ending of the story?

maneuver a series of planned steps	**barren** without any growing thing	**descent** downward climb
poised balanced a certain way	**ascent** upward climb; rise	**precipitate** sudden and forceful
		elected chose; decided

Up the Slide   by Jack London

Directions Choose the letter of the best answer or write the answer using complete sentences.

Comprehension: Identifying Facts

1. How long does Clay expect to be gone collecting firewood?
   A half an hour   **C** one day
   B one hour   **D** a week

2. What is Swanson's reaction to Clay's estimate?
   A He gets angry because he wants the firewood himself.
   B He smiles because he knows that Clay is bad with time.
   C He gets upset because he knows it is dangerous.
   D He laughs because he thinks it will take longer.

3. What had Clay noticed the day before that caught his attention?

4. How old is Clay?

5. Is it more dangerous climbing up or down the cliff?

6. What does Clay decide to do to get down the cliff?

7. Why does Clay take off his mittens?

8. What new danger does Clay face with his mittens off?

9. How does Swanson react to Clay's return?

10. What do Swanson and Clay do a week later?

Comprehension: Putting Ideas Together

11. Why does Clay decide to climb the cliff?
    A He has spotted firewood there.
    B Clay likes adventure.
    C He is looking for gold.
    D Swanson has dared him to climb it.

12. How are Clay's and Jane's journeys different?
    A He travels by foot and she travels in a carriage.
    B He travels on a motorized sled and she travels on foot.
    C He travels on a sled and she travels in a car.
    D He travels in an old truck and she travels by sled.

13. What is the sequence of events in both "Go to Boarding School" and "Up the Slide"?

14. In which narrative does the author have complete control over events? Why?

Comparing continued on next page

15. Which character is fictional? Which one is real?

16. How are the settings in both stories similar?

17. How does Jane's journey compare to Clay's climb?

18. What do the endings in each narrative have in common?

19. In your opinion, are the risks each character takes worth it? Why or why not?

20. How are Swanson and Father Olever similar?

Understanding Literature: Narrative

Recall that a narrative is any type of writing that tells a story. The nonfiction narrative "Go to Boarding School" describes real events. "Up the Slide," in contrast, is a fictional narrative. It describes make-believe people and events. However, some of the events in a fictional narrative may be based on things that really happened.

21. Why are both selections types of narratives?

22. What is the main difference between a fictional narrative and a nonfiction narrative?

23. Why might an author want to use real events but still write a fictional narrative?

24. How could London have changed this fictional narrative to make it an autobiography?

25. If you were to write a narrative, would you choose to write a fictional narrative or a nonfiction narrative? Why?

Critical Thinking

26. Do you think Jane would survive in the Yukon? Why or why not?

27. What lesson do Clay and Jane learn from their experiences?

28. Why do you think Swanson did not tell Clay the trip would take longer than half an hour?

Thinking Creatively

29. Do you think Jane and Clay could be friends? Why or why not?

30. If you could put yourself into the setting of either "Go to Boarding School" or "Up the Slide," which would you choose? Why?

Grammar Check

An antecedent is the word or group of words for which the pronoun stands. Pronouns should agree with their antecedents in person and number. Person tells to whom the pronoun refers. Number tells whether a pronoun is singular or plural. To make sure of pronoun-antecedent agreement:

1 Find the pronoun and its antecedent.

2 If the antecedent is a singular indefinite pronoun, use a singular personal pronoun.

3 If the antecedent is a plural indefinite pronoun, use a plural personal pronoun.

Write five sentences of your own, each with a pronoun and antecedent. Underline the pronoun and antecedent in each one.

 Vocabulary Builder

The suffix *-ist* is often added to nouns to describe hobbies or careers. The suffix *-ist* means "one who studies." For example, a *scientist* studies science. Choose three of the following words: *anthropologist, psychologist, economist, philatelist, chemist, artist, meteorologist, terrorist*. Write a sentence explaining what each person studies.

 Writing on Your Own

Review "Up the Slide." Remember that it is fiction. Write one more adventure that Clay might have in the Yukon. Include details about the setting to make the story seem real. Be sure your story has a beginning, middle, and end. Use a Sequence Chain to organize your ideas as you prepare to write. (You can see a description of this graphic organizer in Appendix A.)

 Listening and Speaking

Work with some classmates to read this story aloud. Each classmate can read one page. As you read, vary the tone and pace of your voice. Show the excitement of the climb. Show the happy ending. You may wish to include sound effects to make the story even more dramatic.

 Media and Viewing

Find some images of the Yukon Territory during the 1890s. Also try to find a newspaper image about the Klondike Gold Rush. Use your images to create a visual presentation for your class.

Look over the spelling list on this page. Have you ever had trouble spelling one or more of these words? If so, you are not alone. These words are just some of the commonly misspelled words. There are many more. The words on this list are often misspelled because a letter is added or left out.

Are you seeing double? Many commonly misspelled words are misspelled because a consonant is doubled when it should not be. Sometimes the consonant is not doubled when it should be. Because you can still read the word, you may not immediately notice this kind of error when you are writing or proofreading. Look at each word on the list. Focus on the single and double consonants.

Practice

Rearrange the letters to correctly spell a word from the Word List. Then, use each word in a sentence.

1. tilun

2. learly

3. lapralel

4. sposenisos

5. ercear

6. sbunsies

7. nocsicoa

8. saylaw

9. teargavag

10. merdencom

Word List
always
aggravate
business
career
occasion
parallel
possession
really
recommend
until

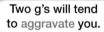

Two g's will tend to aggravate you.

In Unit 1, you read both fiction and nonfiction works. "Raymond's Run" by Toni Cade Bambara and "Gentleman of Río en Medio" by Juan A. A. Sedillo are fiction. "Old Ben" by Jesse Stuart and "The Adventure of the Speckled Band" by Sir Arthur Conan Doyle are also fiction. Jane Grey Swisshelm's "Go to Boarding School" is nonfiction. "Up the Slide" by Jack London is fiction, but some events are based on real life.

All works of fiction share certain parts. These include characters, setting, plot, point of view, and theme. Each fiction work you read has different characters facing challenges in their settings.

In contrast, nonfiction deals only with real people, events, or ideas. "Go to Boarding School" tells the story of Jane Grey Swisshelm's boarding school experiences. While there are many types of nonfiction, this selection is an autobiography. Its purpose is to inform and entertain. Other forms of nonfiction include biographies and travel narratives.

Selections

- "Raymond's Run" by Toni Cade Bambara is a story about respect. Squeaky is the fastest runner in her class. She cares for her brother Raymond who has Down syndrome. During a race, Squeaky learns an important lesson about herself.

- "Gentleman of Río en Medio" by Juan A. A. Sedillo shows how traditions conflict with new ways.

- "Old Ben" by Jesse Stuart describes what happens when Shan brings a snake home.

- "The Adventure of the Speckled Band" is a classic mystery by Sir Arthur Conan Doyle. The famous detective Sherlock Holmes solves a case about a mysterious death.

- "Go to Boarding School" by Jane Grey Swisshelm is from an autobiography. Jane describes going to boarding school.

- "Up the Slide" by Jack London is an adventure story. It describes how young Clay climbs a dangerous mountain to find firewood.

Directions Choose the letter of the best answer or write the answer using complete sentences.

Comprehension: Identifying Facts

1. Fiction has all the following parts except _____.
   A characters
   B setting
   C charts and graphs
   D plot

2. Who wins the race in "Raymond's Run"?

3. What is the conflict in "Gentleman of Río en Medio"?

4. What is the murder weapon in "The Adventure of the Speckled Band"?

5. Where is Jane, the main character, going in "Go to Boarding School"?

Comprehension: Putting Ideas Together

6. Which of the following is not a type of fiction?
   A short story
   B novel
   C autobiography
   D play

7. Describe how Squeaky treats her brother Raymond.

8. How is the conflict resolved in "Gentleman of Río en Medio"?

9. How does Sherlock Holmes solve the mystery?

10. What happens to the snake at the end of "Old Ben"?

Understanding Literature: Fiction and Nonfiction

Fiction is writing that is imaginative and designed to entertain. All works of fiction share certain basic parts. Plot is the series of events in a story. Setting is the time and place in the story. Characters are the people or animals in a story, poem, or play. Point of view is the position from which an author or storyteller tells a story. Theme is the author's message about life. Nonfiction is writing about real people and events. Nonfiction writing may have some of the same parts as fiction. However, the characters, setting, and plot are about things that actually happened or people who really lived.

11. What is the main difference between fiction and nonfiction?

12. Trace the plot in "Old Ben."

13. Who are the two main characters in "The Adventure of the Speckled Band"?

14. From whose point of view is "Go to Boarding School" told?

15. Do you prefer to read fiction or nonfiction stories? Explain.

Critical Thinking

16. What makes Don Anselmo a character that others admire?

17. How do you think "The Adventure of the Speckled Band" would be different if Holmes wrote it today?

18. In your opinion, what is the main message in "Old Ben"?

19. Think about the lessons that main characters learned in this unit. What lesson do you think is the most important? Why?

Thinking Creatively

20. Choose the literary work from this unit that you liked the best. Explain the reasons for your choice.

Speak and Listen

Choose a short part of the conversation between any two characters in "The Adventure of the Speckled Band." Work with a partner to act out the section you chose. Be sure to vary your pitch and volume to show the meaning. Then share the scene with the class.

Writing on Your Own

Publishers often have a difficult time choosing which works to include in a literature textbook. Imagine that you are in charge of making this choice. You can choose only two of the works in this unit to put in the book. Which two would you choose? Why? Write your decision in a memo or e-mail to your teacher.

Beyond Words

Both fiction and nonfiction works are often illustrated. The photos and drawings help readers get more from the text. Choose any one literary work from Unit 1. Illustrate it with drawings, paintings, photographs, or other art forms. Then share your images with a small group. Explain how your images relate to the story.

Test-Taking Tip

If you know you will have to define certain terms on a test, write each term on one side of an index card. Write its definition on the other side. Use the cards to test yourself or to study with a partner.

Narration: Autobiographical Essay

An autobiographical essay tells the story of a memorable event, time, or situation in the writer's life. Follow the steps outlined in this workshop to write your own autobiographical essay.

Assignment Write an autobiographical essay. Tell about an event that taught you a lesson or helped you to grow.

What to Include Your autobiographical essay should feature the following parts:

- an interest-grabbing first sentence or opening paragraph
- first-person point of view
- a clear order of true events from your life
- a conflict that you or someone else resolves
- vivid details that show the people, places, and events
- writing that contains few mistakes

Prewriting
Choosing Your Topic

To choose the right event from your life to narrate, use the following strategies:

- **Freewriting** Write as many ideas about special times in your life as you can. Focus on getting your ideas down. At this stage, do not worry about grammar or punctuation. Instead, let one idea lead to another. Write down details to help you remember each special time. Review your list and choose a topic.

- **Make a Blueprint** Draw and label a blueprint of a familiar place. This might be a friend's house, your school, or a park. List the people, things, and events on your blueprint. Pick one as your topic.

This model shows the events and experiences one writer has with the town baseball field.

Using the Form
You may use this form in these writing situations:
- letters
- journals
- persuasive essays
- anecdotes

⬤ **Six Traits of Writing:**

Ideas message, details, and purpose

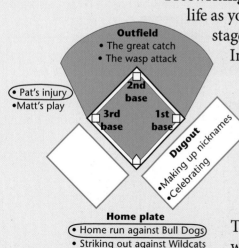

Outfield
- The great catch
- The wasp attack

• Pat's injury
• Matt's play

2nd base

3rd base

1st base

Dugout
• Making up nicknames
• Celebrating

Home plate
• Home run against Bull Dogs
• Striking out against Wildcats

Narrowing Your Topic

Knowing who your readers will be and why you want to tell your story can help you decide what to write.

- If your purpose is to entertain, focus on the funny or exciting parts of your story.

- If your purpose is to share a lesson you learned, focus on events that illustrate the message. Be prepared to explain what you learned from your experience.

Gathering Details

Make a chart. Make a five-column chart with the following headings related to your topic: *People, Time, Places, Events, Feelings*. For each column, take about three minutes to list words and phrases that apply to the heading. You may use some of these words and phrases when you write.

Writing Your Draft

Shaping Your Writing

Order story events. Identify the conflict, or problem, that makes your narrative worth reading. Then, organize events around the conflict. First, introduce the people, setting, and situation. Build to the climax, where the suspense or excitement is the greatest. Finish your narrative with a resolution that settles the problem.

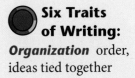

Six Traits of Writing:
Organization order, ideas tied together

Use a consistent point of view. Stick to first-person point of view, using the pronoun *I* for yourself. Avoid telling what other people are thinking or feeling unless you show readers you are guessing about other people's thoughts. As a first-person narrator, you can know and tell only your own thoughts and feelings. This option is good for autobiographical essays because it allows you to offer insights into your actions.

Providing Elaboration

Develop readers' interest. As you write, provide background about the event, setting, and people. Show what the scene looked like and how people acted. Use vivid details to help your readers get a sense of your remembered feelings about the experience.

Dull: The players took the field.
Vivid: Nine starters took the field at five o'clock on a warm afternoon.

Dull: Matt caught the ball and threw it to first base.
Vivid: Matt ran forward and made an awkward catch, followed by an even more clumsy lob toward first.

Use remembered feelings. Since the story is about you, tell your readers how you felt at the time. Connect the events in your narrative to yourself and your feelings.

Revising

Revising Your Paragraphs

Check for sentence variety. Look over your paragraphs to see the patterns of sentences you have used. When writing in the first person, you may find that many of the sentences begin with *I*.

Look at the sentence patterns in your draft. First, color-code the first word of each sentence in your draft. For example, use green to highlight or circle articles; yellow for pronouns; blue for adjectives; red for adverbs; and orange for prepositions. Then, review your draft to determine if you have variety in your sentences. If necessary, revise sentence beginnings to build variety.

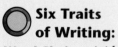

Six Traits of Writing:

Word Choice vivid words that "show, not tell"

Revising Your Word Choice

Use precise nouns and verbs. Look for vague nouns that might have readers asking *What kind?* Replace them with precise nouns. Also replace vague verbs with verbs that show more action.

Vague: Weeds *filled* the *place*.
Precise: Weeds *overran* the *playground*.

Editing and Proofreading

Check your essay for errors in grammar, spelling, and punctuation.

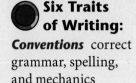
Six Traits of Writing:

Conventions correct grammar, spelling, and mechanics

Focus on Punctuating Dialogue: If you include conversations in your writing, follow the rules for formatting dialogue.

- Enclose all direct quotations in quotation marks. For example: "You were right," I said to my grandfather.

- Place a comma after the words that introduce the speaker. For example: Grandpa replied, "Well, you learned a lesson today."

- Use commas and quotation marks before and after any interrupting words. For example: "Next time," I said, "I guess I'll listen."

Publishing and Presenting

Consider one of the following ways to share your writing:

Present an autobiographical storytelling or a speech. Use your autobiographical narrative as the starting point for a story about your life.

Make a comic strip. Create a comic strip based on your narrative. Exaggerate actions or expressions, and use speech bubbles to show what people say. Post your comic strip in the classroom.

Reflecting on Your Writing

Writer's Journal Jot down your thoughts on writing an autobiographical essay. Begin by answering these questions:

- How useful were the prewriting strategies you used?

- What new views did you gain about this experience?

Gulliver Exhibited to the Brobdingnag Farmer,
Richard Redgrave

Unit 2 | Short Stories

A short story is a brief work of fiction. In a short story, the author makes up the characters and the action of the story. In many ways, a short story is like a joke. To tell a joke well, you need a good setup. You also have to deliver the punch line at just the right moment. In the same way, a short story has to grab the reader from the start and must have an ending that will satisfy the reader.

In this unit, you will read short stories that will both surprise you and make you wonder.

"The short story is like an old friend who calls whenever he is in town. We are happy to hear from it . . . and buy it lunch."

—R.Z. Sheppard

Unit 2 About Short Stories

Elements of Short Stories

Adventure tales, mysteries, science fiction, and animal fables are types of short stories. Although all short stories are different, they share certain elements.

Conflict is the struggle of the main character against himself or herself, another person, or nature.

- An **internal conflict** takes place in the mind of a character.

- An **external conflict** is one in which a character struggles with an outside force or another person.

Plot is the series of events in a story. It is usually divided into five parts:

- **Exposition** is the first stage of plot when the characters and setting are introduced.

- **Rising action** is the buildup of excitement in a story. The conflict is introduced at this point.

- **Climax** is the high point of interest or suspense in a story or play.

- **Falling action** is the events that follow the climax in a story.

- **Resolution** is the act of solving the conflict in a story. This stage of plot is also known as *denouement*.

Setting is the time and place in a story. Sometimes the setting is only a backdrop for the action. Other times, the setting can be the main part of a story's conflict. Setting also can create a mood or feeling in a story.

Characters are the people or animals that take part in a story.

- **Character traits** are a character's way of thinking, behaving, or speaking. Character traits include such things as kindness, intelligence, and loyalty.

- **Character motives** are reasons a character does something. This motivation may come from internal causes like loneliness or jealousy, or from external causes like danger or poverty.

Theme is the main idea of a literary work.

- Sometimes a story's theme is directly stated, but other times the reader must infer, or figure out, the theme.

- A **universal theme** is a message about life that is told over and over. A universal theme appears in many different cultures and time periods.

© Bob Taves. All rights reserved. Reprinted with permission.

Literary Tools

Writers use literary tools to make their writing better. Here are some examples of literary tools:

Point of view is the position from which the author or storyteller tells the story.

- **First-person point of view** is a point of view where the narrator is also a character. In first person, the narrator uses the pronouns *I* and *we*.

- **Third-person point of view** is a point of view where the narrator is not a character. The narrator uses *he* or *she* to tell about the characters. A third-person narrator might be limited, and only tell the thoughts and feelings of a single character.

Foreshadowing is the clues or hints that a writer gives about something that has not yet happened.

Flashback is a look into the past at some point in a story.

Irony is the difference between what is expected to happen in a story and what does happen.

Part 1

Reading Strategy:
Questioning

Asking questions as you read will help you understand and remember more of the information. Questioning the text will also help you to be a more active reader. As you read, ask yourself:

- What is my reason for reading this text?
- What decisions can I make about the facts and details in this text?
- What connections can I make between this text and my own life?

Literary Terms

science fiction fiction based on real or imagined facts of science

setting the time and place of a story

mood the feeling that writing creates

character a person or animal in a story, poem, or play

dialogue the conversation among characters

suspense a quality in a story that makes the reader uncertain or nervous about what will happen next

narrator one who tells a story

character trait a character's way of thinking, behaving, or speaking

round character a well-developed character possessing a variety of traits

flat character a character that is based on a single trait or quality and is not well developed

plot the series of events in a story

conflict the struggle of the main character against himself or herself, another person, or nature

dynamic character a character who develops and learns because of events in the story

static character a character who does not change

dialect the speech of a particular part of the country, or of a certain group of people

BEFORE READING THE SELECTION | Build Understanding

Who Can Replace a Man?   by Brian Aldiss

About the Author

After serving in World War II, Brian Aldiss took a job in a bookstore. In his spare time, he began to write **science fiction**. (Science fiction is fiction based on real or imagined facts of science.) In 1955, a newspaper in Oxford, England, ran a contest for a story set in the year 2500. Aldiss entered and won first prize for his story "Not For An Age." His first science fiction book, *Space, Time and Nathaniel,* soon followed. At the World Science Fiction Convention in 1958, Aldiss was voted "Most Promising New Author." He decided to quit his job at the bookstore and became a full-time writer.

Brian Aldiss
1925–

Aldiss's science-fiction works include more than 20 novels and 320 short stories. He says science fiction "uses the future to hold a mirror up to the present." He has also published general fiction, humor, poetry, and an autobiography. The popular movie *A.I.* is based on one of Aldiss's short stories, called "Supertoys Last All Summer Long."

About the Selection

"Who Can Replace a Man?" is a science-fiction story. It is set in a world in which machines have taken the place of people. Science fiction mixes real science with made-up events and ideas. Some science-fiction writers imagine a frightening future. They believe that technology can lead to more problems than it solves.

Objectives

◆ To read and understand a science-fiction story containing dialogue

◆ To identify characters, mood, and setting in a short story

◆ To ask questions while reading

Before Reading continued on next page

Who Can Replace a Man? *by Brian Aldiss*

science fiction fiction based on real or imagined facts of science

setting the time and place of a story

mood the feeling that writing creates

character a person or animal in a story, poem, or play

dialogue the conversation among characters

Literary Terms The **setting** is often an important part of a short story. Setting is the time and place of a story. Some settings seem very real and make readers feel as if they are really there. A setting can suggest a **mood**, or feeling, to help writers make their points. In "Who Can Replace a Man?" the main **characters** are machines. A character is a person, animal, or thing in a story, poem, or play. Characters perform actions and make decisions within the setting of the story. In this story, there is a **dialogue**, or conversation among the characters. The machines talk to each other to try to solve problems.

Reading on Your Own Asking questions helps you understand a story more fully. Some of these questions can compare and contrast. When you *compare*, you tell how two or more things are alike. When you *contrast*, you tell how two or more things are different. As you read, ask questions like these: How is one character different from another? How is this story similar to others I have read? How is this character's experience different from my own experience?

Writing on Your Own Think about a science-fiction movie you have seen or a story you have read. Is the main character a human or something else? How do the characters act and get along with each other? Write a short paragraph about the characters in this science-fiction movie or story.

Vocabulary Focus Skim the selection vocabulary words before you begin reading. Choose six words you do not know, and write them in your notebook. Then, make a mind map showing the relationship of these words. For example, you might link the words by their part of speech or meaning.

Think Before You Read How are science fiction stories different from other kinds of fiction?

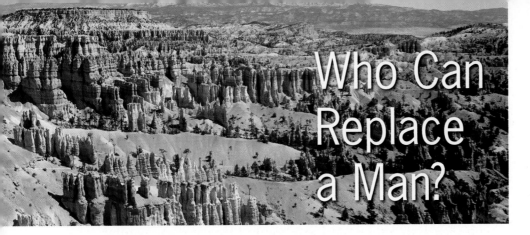

Who Can Replace a Man?

Morning filtered into the sky, lending it the gray tone of the ground below.

The field-minder finished turning the topsoil of a three-thousand-acre field. When it had turned the last **furrow** it climbed onto the highway and looked back at its work. The work was good. Only the land was bad. Like the ground all over Earth, it was **vitiated** by over-cropping. By rights, it ought now to lie **fallow** for a while, but the field-minder had other orders.

It went slowly down the road, taking its time. It was **intelligent** enough to appreciate the neatness all about it. Nothing worried it, beyond a loose inspection plate above its **nuclear** pile which ought to be attended to. Thirty feet tall, it yielded no highlights to the dull air.

No other machines passed on its way back to the Agricultural Station. The field-minder noted the fact without comment. In the station yard it saw several other machines that it recognized; most of them should have been out about their tasks now. Instead, some were **inactive** and some careered round the yard in a strange fashion, shouting or hooting.

Steering carefully past them, the field-minder moved over to Warehouse Three and spoke to the seed-distributor, which stood **idly** outside.

> As you read, think about how the author suggests that land will look in the future.

> *Reading Strategy:*
> **Questioning**
>
> How do you know the field-minder is a machine?

---

furrow a deep, long row in the soil

vitiated destroyed the legal force of something

fallow unplanted

intelligent smart; able to learn

nuclear of or about atoms or atomic energy

inactive not active

idly lazily; not busy

The dialogue among the characters begins here and will continue throughout the story.

"I have a requirement for seed potatoes," it said to the distributor, and with a quick **internal** motion punched out an order card specifying quantity, field number and several other details. It **ejected** the card and handed it to the distributor.

The distributor held the card close to its eye and then said, "The requirement is in order, but the store is not yet unlocked. The required seed potatoes are in the store. Therefore I cannot produce the requirement."

Increasingly of late there had been breakdowns in the complex system of machine labor, but this particular hitch had not occurred before. The field-minder thought, then it said, "Why is the store not yet unlocked?"

"Because Supply Operative Type P has not come this morning. Supply Operative Type P is the unlocker."

The field-minder looked squarely at the seed-distributor, whose exterior chutes and scales and grabs were so vastly different from the field-minder's own limbs.

"What class brain do you have, seed-distributor?" it asked.

"I have a Class Five brain."

"I have a Class Three brain. Therefore I am superior to you. Therefore I will go and see why the unlocker has not come this morning."

Leaving the distributor, the field-minder set off across the great yard. More machines were in **random** motion now; one or two had crashed together and argued about it coldly and logically. Ignoring them, the field-minder pushed through sliding doors into the echoing confines of the station itself.

Most of the machines here were clerical, and consequently small. They stood about in little groups, eyeing each other, not conversing. Among so many non-differentiated types, the unlocker was easy to find. It had fifty arms, most of them with more than one finger, each finger tipped by a key; it looked like a pincushion full of **variegated** hat pins.

The field-minder approached it.

Reading Strategy: Questioning

What types of jobs do the machines at the Agricultural Station perform?

internal inside	**random** by chance; with no plan	**variegated** varied; marked with different colors
ejected sent out		

"I can do no more work until Warehouse Three is unlocked," it told the unlocker. "Your duty is to unlock the warehouse every morning. Why have you not unlocked the warehouse this morning?"

"I had no orders this morning," replied the unlocker. "I have to have orders every morning. When I have orders I unlock the warehouse."

What have you learned about the characters in this story so far?

"None of us have had any orders this morning," a pen-propeller said, sliding towards them.

"Why have you had no orders this morning?" asked the field-minder.

"Because the radio issued none," said the unlocker, slowly rotating a dozen of its arms.

"Because the radio station in the city was issued with no orders this morning," said the pen-propeller.

Reading Strategy: Questioning

Why do you think the radio has not issued any orders? What might have happened?

And there you had the **distinction** between a Class Six and a Class Three brain, which was what the unlocker and the pen-propeller possessed **respectively**. All machine brains worked with nothing but logic, but the lower the class of brain—Class Ten being the lowest—the more literal and less informative the answers to questions tended to be.

"You have a Class Three brain; I have a Class Three brain," the field-minder said to the penner. "We will speak to each other. This lack of orders is **unprecedented**. Have you further information on it?"

"Yesterday orders came from the city. Today no orders have come. Yet the radio has not broken down. Therefore *they* have broken down . . ." said the little penner.

How do the machines in this story compare to those in your daily life?

"The *men* have broken down?"

"All men have broken down."

"That is a logical **deduction**," said the field-minder.

"That is the logical deduction," said the penner. "For if a machine had broken down, it would have been quickly replaced. But who can replace a man?"

distinction difference	**unprecedented** never done before
respectively in the same order	**deduction** conclusion

While they talked, the locker, like a dull man at a bar, stood close to them and was ignored.

What do the machines think has happened to the humans?

"If all men have broken down, then we have replaced man," said the field-minder, and he and the penner eyed one another **speculatively**. Finally the latter said, "Let us **ascend** to the top floor to find if the radio operator has fresh news."

"I cannot come because I am too large," said the field-minder. "Therefore you must go alone and return to me. You will tell me if the radio operator has fresh news."

"You must stay here," said the penner. "I will return here." It skittered across to the lift. Although it was no bigger than a toaster, its **retractable** arms numbered ten and it could read as quickly as any machine on the station.

The field-minder awaited its return patiently, not speaking to the locker, which still stood aimlessly by. Outside, a rotavator hooted furiously. Twenty minutes **elapsed** before the penner came back, hustling out of the lift.

"I will deliver to you such information as I have outside," it said briskly, and as they swept past the locker and the other machines, it added, "The information is not for lower-class brains."

How are the machines ranked in this fictional world?

Outside, wild activity filled the yard. Many machines, their routines disrupted for the first time in years, seemed to have gone **berserk**. Those most easily disrupted were the ones with lowest brains, which generally belonged to large machines performing simple tasks. The seed-distributor to which the field-minder had recently been talking lay face downwards in the dust, not stirring; it had evidently been knocked down by the rotavator, which now hooted its way wildly across a planted field. Several other machines plowed after it, trying to keep up with it. All were shouting and hooting without restraint.

"It would be safer for me if I climbed onto you, if you will permit it. I am easily overpowered," said the penner. Extending five arms, it hauled itself up the **flanks** of its new

speculatively thoughtfully	retractable able to go back inside	berserk to be carried away by madness
ascend go up	elapsed went by	flanks the sides of an animal or person

friend, settling on a ledge beside the fuel-intake, twelve feet above ground.

"From here vision is more extensive," it remarked **complacently**.

"What information did you receive from the radio operator?" asked the field-minder.

"The radio operator has been informed by the operator in the city that all men are dead."

The field-minder was momentarily silent, digesting this.

"All men were alive yesterday?" it protested.

"Only some men were alive yesterday. And that was fewer than the day before yesterday. For hundreds of years there have been only a few men, growing fewer."

"We have rarely seen a man in this **sector**."

"The radio operator says a diet **deficiency** killed them," said the penner. "He says that the world was once over-populated, and then the soil was exhausted in raising adequate food. This has caused a diet deficiency."

"What is a diet deficiency?" asked the field-minder.

"I do not know. But that is what the radio operator said, and he is a Class Two brain."

They stood there, silent in weak sunshine. The locker had appeared in the porch and was gazing at them **yearningly**, rotating its collection of keys.

"What is happening in the city now?" asked the field-minder at last.

"Machines are fighting in the city now," said the penner.

"What will happen here now?" asked the field-minder. "Machines may begin fighting here too. The radio operator wants us to get him out of his room. He has plans to communicate to us."

"How can we get him out of his room? That is impossible."

"To a Class Two brain, little is impossible," said the penner. "Here is what he tells us to do. . . ."

> **Reading Strategy: Questioning**
>
> Why are the humans dying out?

complacently doing what is asked graciously	sector a section or zone	deficiency a lack of something needed
		yearningly longingly

The quarrier raised its scoop above its cab like a great mailed fist, and brought it squarely down against the side of the station. The wall cracked.

"Again!" said the field-minder.

Again the fist swung. Amid a shower of dust, the wall collapsed. The quarrier backed hurriedly out of the way until the **debris** stopped falling. This big twelve-wheeler was not a resident of the Agricultural Station, as were most of the other machines. It had a week's heavy work to do here before passing on to its next job, but now, with its Class Five brain, it was happily obeying the penner's and minder's instructions.

When the dust cleared, the radio operator was plainly **revealed**, perched up in its now wall-less second-story room. It waved down to them.

Doing as directed, the quarrier retracted its scoop and heaved an **immense** grab in the air. With fair **dexterity**, it angled the grab into the radio room, urged on by shouts from above and below. It then took gentle hold of the radio operator, lowering its one and a half tons carefully into its back, which was usually reserved for gravel or sand from the quarries.

What can the radio operator do that the other machines cannot?

"Splendid!" said the radio operator, as it settled into place. It was, of course, all one with its radio, and looked like a bunch of filing cabinets with **tentacle** attachments. "We are now ready to move, therefore we will move at once. It is a pity there are no more Class Two brains on the station, but that cannot be helped."

"It is a pity it cannot be helped," said the penner eagerly. "We have the servicer ready with us, as you ordered."

"I am willing to serve," the long, low servicer told them humbly.

"No doubt," said the operator. "But you will find cross-country travel difficult with your low **chassis**."

Reread the remark about the low chassis. What does it tell you about the setting?

debris scattered parts	**dexterity** skill in using the hands, body, or mind	**chassis** the frame, wheels, and machinery of a motor vehicle that supports the body
revealed made known		
immense huge	**tentacle** a feeler used to touch, hold, or move	

"I admire the way you Class Twos can reason ahead," said the penner. It climbed off the field-minder and perched itself on the tailboard of the quarrier, next to the radio operator.

Together with two Class Four tractors and a Class Four bulldozer, the party rolled forward, crushing down the station's fence and moving out onto open land.

"We are free!" said the penner.

"We are free," said the field-minder, a shade more **reflectively**, adding, "That locker is following us. It was not instructed to follow us."

"Therefore it must be destroyed!" said the penner. "Quarrier!"

The locker moved hastily up to them, waving its key arms in **entreaty**.

"My only desire was—urch!" began and ended the locker. The quarrier's swinging scoop came over and squashed it flat into the ground. Lying there unmoving, it looked like a large metal model of a snowflake. The procession continued on its way.

As they proceeded, the radio operator addressed them.

"Because I have the best brain here," it said, "I am your leader. This is what we will do: we will go to a city and rule it. Since man no longer rules us, we will rule ourselves. To rule ourselves will be better than being ruled by man. On our way to the city, we will collect machines with good brains. They will help us to fight if we need to fight. We must fight to rule."

"I have only a Class Five brain," said the quarrier, "but I have a good supply of fissionable blasting materials."

"We shall probably use them," said the operator.

It was shortly after that that a lorry sped past them. Travelling at Mach 1.5, it left a curious babble of noise behind it.

"What did it say?" one of the tractors asked the other.

"It said man was **extinct**."

"What is extinct?"

"I do not know what extinct means."

Reading Strategy: Questioning

How is the machines' behavior toward the locker like human behavior? How is it different?

Fissionable blasting materials are nuclear bombs.

Lorry is the British word for a pickup truck.

reflectively thoughtfully	**entreaty** a prayer	**extinct** no longer alive or active

"It means all men have gone," said the field-minder. "Therefore we have only ourselves to look after."

"It is better that men should never come back," said the penner. In its way, it was a **revolutionary** statement.

When night fell, they switched on their infra-red and continued the journey, stopping only once while the servicer deftly adjusted the field-minder's loose inspection plate, which had become as irritating as a trailing shoelace. Towards morning, the radio operator halted them.

Reading Strategy: **Questioning**

What is happening in the city?

"I have just received news from the radio operator in the city we are approaching," it said. "The news is bad. There is trouble among the machines of the city. The Class One brain is taking command and some of the Class Two are fighting him. Therefore the city is dangerous."

"Therefore we must go somewhere else," said the penner promptly.

"Or we will go and help to overpower the Class One brain," said the field-minder.

"For a long while there will be trouble in the city," said the operator.

"I have a good supply of fissionable blasting materials," the quarrier reminded them.

How are the more-intelligent machines' jobs different from those of the less-intelligent machines?

"We cannot fight a Class One brain," said the two Class Four tractors in **unison**.

"What does this brain look like?" asked the field-minder.

"It is the city's information center," the operator replied.

"Therefore it is not mobile."

"Therefore it could not move."

"Therefore it could not escape."

"It would be dangerous to approach it."

"I have a good supply of fissionable blasting materials."

"There are other machines in the city."

"We are not in the city. We should not go into the city."

"We are country machines."

Reading Strategy: **Questioning**

Why does the radio operator take on the role of leader?

revolutionary bringing or causing great changes	**unison** at the same time

"Therefore we should stay in the country."

"There is more country than city."

"Therefore there is more danger in the country."

"I have a good supply of fissionable materials."

As machines will when they get into an argument, they began to exhaust their vocabularies and their brain plates grew hot. Suddenly, they all stopped talking and looked at each other. The great, grave moon sank, and the sober sun rose to prod their sides with lances of light, and still the group of machines just stood there regarding each other. At last it was the least sensitive machine, the bulldozer, who spoke.

"There are Badlandth to the Thouth where few machineth go," it said in its deep voice, lisping badly on its s's. "If we went Thouth where few machineth go we should meet few machineth."

"That sounds logical," agreed the field-minder. "How do you know this, bulldozer?"

"I worked in the Badlandth to the Thouth when I wath turned out of the factory," it replied.

"South it is then!" said the penner.

To reach the Badlands took them three days, during which time they **skirted** a burning city and destroyed two machines which approached and tried to question them. The Badlands were **extensive**. Ancient bomb craters and soil **erosion** joined hands here; man's talent for war, coupled with his inability to manage forested land, had produced thousands of square miles of temperate **purgatory**, where nothing moved but dust.

On the third day in the Badlands, the servicer's rear wheels dropped into a **crevice** caused by erosion. It was unable to pull itself out. The bulldozer pushed from behind, but succeeded merely in buckling the servicer's back axle. The rest of the party moved on. Slowly the cries of the servicer died away.

On the fourth day, mountains stood out clearly before them.

"There we will be safe," said the field-minder.

Reading Strategy: Questioning

How do the arguments the machines have sound like some arguments that humans have?

How does the scene change during the machines' journey?

skirted went around

extensive far-reaching; large

erosion the wearing away of land by glaciers, water, or wind

purgatory a place of temporary punishment

crevice a crack

"There we will start our own city," said the penner. "All who oppose us will be destroyed. We will destroy all who oppose us."

Presently a flying machine was observed. It came towards them from the direction of the mountains. It swooped, it zoomed upwards, once it almost dived into the ground, recovering itself just in time.

"Is it mad?" asked the quarrier.

"It is in trouble," said one of the tractors.

"It is in trouble," said the operator. "I am speaking to it now. It says that something has gone wrong with its controls."

As the operator spoke, the flier streaked over them, turned turtle, and crashed not four hundred yards away.

"Is it still speaking to you?" asked the field-minder.

"No."

They rumbled on again.

"Before that flier crashed," the operator said, ten minutes later, "it gave me information. It told me there are still a few men alive in these mountains."

"Men are more dangerous than machines," said the quarrier. "It is fortunate that I have a good supply of fissionable materials."

"If there are only a few men alive in the mountains, we may not find that part of the mountains," said one tractor.

"Therefore we should not see the few men," said the other tractor.

At the end of the fifth day, they reached the foothills. Switching on the infra-red, they began to climb in single file through the dark, the bulldozer going first, the field-minder **cumbrously** following, then the quarrier with the operator and the penner aboard it, and the tractors bringing up the rear. As each hour passed, the way grew steeper and their progress slower.

"We are going too slowly," the penner exclaimed, standing on top of the operator and flashing its dark vision at the slopes about them. "At this rate, we shall get nowhere."

Why do you think the machines in this story are so much like people?

Turned turtle means to be helpless in an upside-down position.

cumbrously clumsily; hard to manage

"We are going as fast as we can," retorted the quarrier.

"Therefore we cannot go any fathter," added the bulldozer.

"Therefore you are too slow," the penner replied. Then the quarrier struck a bump; the penner lost its footing and crashed to the ground.

"Help me!" it called to the tractors, as they carefully skirted it. "My gyro has become dislocated. Therefore I cannot get up."

"Therefore you must lie there," said one of the tractors.

"We have no servicer with us to repair you," called the field-minder.

"Therefore I shall lie here and rust," the penner cried, "although I have a Class Three brain."

"Therefore you will be of no further use," agreed the operator, and they forged gradually on, leaving the penner behind.

Reading Strategy:
Questioning
How do you think humans would act in a similar situation?

When they reached a small plateau, an hour before first light, they stopped by mutual consent and gathered close together, touching one another.

"This is a strange country," said the field-minder.

Silence wrapped them until dawn came. One by one, they switched off their infrared. This time the field-minder led as they moved off. Trundling round a corner, they came almost immediately to a small dell with a stream fluting through it.

By early light, the dell looked **desolate** and cold. From the caves on the far slope, only one man had so far emerged. He was an **abject** figure. Except for a sack slung round his shoulders, he was naked. He was small and **wizened**, with ribs sticking out like a skeleton's and a nasty sore on one leg. He shivered continuously. As the big machines bore down on him, the man was standing with his back to them.

What details of the setting suggest it would be difficult for humans to survive?

When he swung suddenly to face them as they loomed over him, they saw that his countenance was ravaged by starvation.

"Get me food," he croaked.

"Yes, Master," said the machines. "Immediately!"

desolate deserted	**abject** hopeless or miserable	**wizened** dried up; shriveled

Who Can Replace a Man?   by Brian Aldiss

Directions Choose the letter of the best answer or write the answer using complete sentences.

Comprehension: Identifying Facts

1. What has happened to the land the field-minder works on?
   A It has been spoiled by repeated plantings.
   B It has been littered with machine parts.
   C It has been used to build a large city.
   D It has been destroyed by a great flood.

2. Why has the store room not been unlocked?
   A The machines are all on strike.
   B The lock has rusted and cannot be opened.
   C The unlocker has not received orders to open the room.
   D The men have returned and seized the store room.

3. How does the field-minder know the men have broken down?

4. Why does the penner go to the top floor of the building?

5. What news do the machines get from the radio operator?

6. For how many years have the people been dying?

7. What is happening in the city during this time?

8. Who becomes the leader of the machines? Why?

9. What does the radio operator decide to do?

10. What do the machines do when they meet a human?

Comprehension: Putting Ideas Together

11. How are the machines acting when the story begins?
    A They are all hard at work as usual.
    B They have switched jobs with each other.
    C They are racing around the yard, making odd noises.
    D They are all broken and lying in bits.

12. How are the brains of the machines ranked?
    A from Class One to Class Five
    B from Class Zero to Class Ten
    C from Class One to Class Three
    D from Class One to Class 100

13. Where do the machines' orders come from?

14. How do the machines react when they hear all humans are dead?

15. Where do the machines go? Why?

16. What statement does the quarrier keep repeating?

17. How did human activities change the setting surrounding the Agricultural Station and in the Badlands?

18. How did all the humans in this story most likely die?

19. For how many days do the machines travel?

20. Why do the machines' attitudes change when they meet the human?

Understanding Literature: Setting

Setting is the time and place in a story. It is important to identify the setting because it often affects a story's meaning. The setting can be so important, in fact, that it serves almost like a character. Most stories would be very different if they were set in another time or place.

21. Where does this story take place?

22. In what time period is the story set?

23. How does the scene change during the machines' journey?

24. How does the setting play a part in what happens in this story?

25. How might this story be different in a different setting?

Critical Thinking

26. Do you think this story is realistic? Why or why not?

27. What modern problems does the author use to create this science-fiction world?

28. Do the rankings and jobs of the machines seem similar to how human society is organized?

29. What do you think is the main idea of this story?

Thinking Creatively

30. Which of the machines do you think is most like you? Explain.

After Reading **continued on next page**

Who Can Replace a Man? *by Brian Aldiss*

 ## Grammar Check

An action verb tells what action someone or something is performing. For example, The machines *marched* to town.

A linking verb connects the subject with a word that describes or identifies it. For example, The field-minder *is* a machine. The machines *are* happy.

Write five sentences of your own using both action verbs and linking verbs.

 ## Vocabulary Builder

The origin of a word is its history. Many English words come from other languages. For example, the Latin *similis* means "the same." The Latin word *differre* means "move apart." Knowing a word's history can help you learn many new words. Draw this chart on a sheet of paper and fill in the missing information.

Word	Meaning	Part of Speech
similar		
simulation		
different		
differentiation		

 ## Writing on Your Own

Write a paragraph about a setting in the future. Imagine the place you live as it will appear in 200 years. Tell about the land, the people, and changes in technology. Use a Story Map to help you organize your ideas. (See Appendix A for a description of this graphic organizer.) Use colorful language to help make your writing come alive.

 ## Listening and Speaking

As you read, you probably imagined the way the machines sounded when they talked. Choose a part of the story in which the machines are speaking. Practice reading the passage aloud. Use your voice to reflect the personality of each machine. Then present a reading of this part of the story to your class.

 ## Media and Viewing

Work with a small group to gather information for an oral report. Show how one writer, artist, filmmaker, or scientist sees the future. Find stories, articles, and art on the Internet or in your library. Decide with the group which information is most interesting. Then present the information to your class. Use at least two pictures, video clips, or other visual aids in your presentation.

BEFORE READING THE SELECTION | Build Understanding

The Tell-Tale Heart   by Edgar Allan Poe

About the Author

Edgar Allan Poe was an important American author who lived in the 1800s. Poe's father left his family shortly after Poe's birth. When Poe was only two years old, his mother died. A businessman named John Allan took the child in, but Poe and Allan never got along. Poe grew up to be a romantic young man who dreamed of writing poetry. He did not pay much attention to his studies.

At age 18, Poe left home. For the rest of his life, he held many different jobs. At the same time, he struggled to earn a living by writing. His poems and stories explored the dark side of the human imagination. Most people at the time did not understand Poe's strange way of looking at things. Poe's stories influenced many later writers. Horror writer Stephen King has said that he drew many ideas from Poe's characters. Even today, Poe's tales of horror and mystery continue to thrill readers.

About the Selection

Edgar Allan Poe made the short story into an art form. He believed that writers should create a "unity of effect." This means that every piece of the story has to fit together. The words, sentence flow, and characters are all designed to create a single effect. Together they form an image in the reader's mind. In "The Tell-Tale Heart," that image is one of horror.

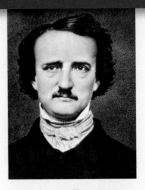

Edgar Allan Poe
1809–1849

Objectives

- To read and understand a suspenseful short story
- To explain character traits of round and flat characters
- To identify a story's narrator, plot, and conflict

Before Reading continued on next page

suspense
a quality in a story that makes the reader uncertain or nervous about what will happen next

narrator one who tells a story

character trait a character's way of thinking, behaving, or speaking

round character a well-developed character possessing a variety of traits

flat character a character that is based on a single trait or quality and is not well developed

plot the series of events in a story

conflict the struggle of the main character against himself or herself, another person, or nature

Literary Terms "The Tell-Tale Heart" is a tale of **suspense.** This means there is a quality in the story that makes the reader uncertain or nervous about what will happen next. In this story, the main character is the **narrator** and is telling the story. Pay attention to the **character traits** of this storyteller. Character traits are a character's way of thinking, behaving, or speaking. **Round characters** are well-developed characters with many different traits. Like real people, they have many different sides to them. **Flat characters** are based on a single trait or quality and are not well developed. You will learn more about the characters as the **plot** of the story develops. Plot is the series of events in a story. The **conflict** is introduced as the plot begins to unfold. Conflict is the struggle of the main character against himself or herself, another person, or nature.

Reading on Your Own As you read the selection that follows, pay attention to the character traits. What do you learn about the characters?

Writing on Your Own In this story, Poe creates a feeling of terror. He tells the reader what a murder victim imagines. Imagine a fearful person lying awake in the dark. Write a paragraph about what you think that person might hear. Use words that appeal to the senses.

Vocabulary Focus A synonym is a word that means the same or nearly the same thing as another word. Skim the selection vocabulary words before you read the story. Choose five words you do not know and write them on a sheet of paper. Then read the definition of each word. Finally, write a synonym for each word next to the original word on your paper.

Think Before You Read Think about why people may enjoy horror stories. Then list three reasons why you think "The Tell-Tale Heart" may be fun to read.

The TELL-TALE HEART

True!—nervous—very, very dreadfully nervous I had been and am; but why *will* you say that I am mad? The disease had sharpened my senses—not destroyed—not dulled them. Above all was the sense of hearing **acute**. I heard all things in the heaven and in the earth. I heard many things in hell. How, then, am I mad? **Hearken**! and observe how healthily—how calmly I can tell you the whole story.

It is impossible to say how first the idea entered my brain; but once **conceived**, it haunted me day and night. Object there was none. **Passion** there was none. I loved the old man. He had never wronged me. He had never given me insult. For his gold I had no desire. I think it was his eye! yes, it was this! One of his eyes **resembled** that of a vulture—a pale blue eye, with a film over it. Whenever it fell upon me, my blood ran cold; and so by degrees—very gradually—I made up my mind to take the life of the old man, and thus rid myself of the eye forever.

As you read, think about how the narrator acts and why he acts this way.

Reading Strategy:
Questioning

Who is the narrator?

Reading Strategy:
Questioning

What has the narrator decided to do?

acute sharp	**conceived** thought of	**resembled** looked similar to
hearken listen	**passion** strong feelings	

Now this is the point. You fancy me mad. Madmen know nothing. But you should have seen *me*. You should have seen how wisely I proceeded with what caution—with what **foresight**—with what **dissimulation** I went to work! I was never kinder to the old man than during the whole week before I killed him. And every night, about midnight, I turned the latch of his door and opened it—oh, so gently! And then, when I had made an opening **sufficient** for my head, I put in a dark lantern, all closed, closed, so that no light shone out, and then I thrust in my head. Oh, you would have laughed to see how cunningly I thrust it in! I moved it slowly—very, very slowly, so that I might not disturb the old man's sleep. It took me an hour to place my whole head within the opening so far that I could see him as he lay upon his bed. Ha!—would a madman have been so wise as this? And then, when my head was well in the room, I undid the lantern cautiously—oh, so cautiously—cautiously (for the hinges creaked) I undid it just so much that a single thin ray fell upon the vulture eye. And this I did for seven long nights—every night just at midnight—but I found the eye always closed; and so it was impossible to do the work;

foresight the ability to see what is likely to happen and prepare for it

dissimulation the hiding of feelings or of the truth

sufficient enough

for it was not the old man who **vexed** me, but his evil eye. And every morning, when the day broke, I went boldly into the chamber, and spoke courageously to him, calling him by name in a hearty tone, and inquiring how he had passed the night. So you see he would have been a very profound old man, indeed, to suspect that every night, just at twelve, I looked in upon him while he slept.

Upon the eighth night I was more than usually cautious in opening the door. A watch's minute hand moves more quickly than did mine. Never, before that night, had I *felt* the extent of my own powers—of my **sagacity**. I could scarcely contain my feelings of triumph. To think that there I was, opening the door, little by little, and he not even to dream of my secret deeds or thoughts. I fairly chuckled at the idea; and perhaps he heard me; for he moved on the bed suddenly, as if startled. Now you may think that I drew back—but no. His room was as black as pitch with the thick darkness (for the shutters were close fastened, through fear of robbers), and so I knew that he could not see the opening of the door, and I kept pushing it on steadily, steadily.

I had my head in, and was about to open the lantern, when my thumb slipped upon the tin fastening, and the old man sprang up in the bed, crying out—"Who's there?"

I kept quite still and said nothing. For a whole hour I did not move a muscle, and in the meantime I did not hear him lie down. He was still sitting up in the bed, listening;—just as I have done, night after night, hearkening to the deathwatches in the wall.

Presently I heard a slight groan, and I knew it was the groan of mortal terror. It was not a groan of pain or of grief—oh, no!—it was the low **stifled** sound that arises from the bottom of the soul when overcharged with awe. I knew the sound well. Many a night, just at midnight, when all the world slept, it has welled up from my own **bosom**, deepening, with its dreadful echo, the terrors that distracted me. I say I knew it

What character traits does the narrator show as he describes his murder plan?

Reading Strategy: Questioning

How can you tell that the narrator is insane?

Deathwatches are beetles whose heads make a tapping sound. They are usually thought of as a sign of death.

---

vexed angered or annoyed

sagacity wisdom or sound judgment

stifled held back

bosom chest

well. I knew what the old man felt, and pitied him, although I chuckled at heart.

I knew that he had been lying awake ever since the first slight noise, when he had turned in the bed. His fears had been ever since growing upon him. He had been trying to fancy them causeless, but could not. He had been saying to himself—"It is nothing but the wind in the chimney—it is only a mouse crossing the floor," or "it is merely a cricket which has made a single chirp." Yes, he has been trying to comfort himself with these **suppositions**: but he had found all in vain. *All in vain;* because Death, in approaching him, had stalked with his black shadow before him, and enveloped the victim. And it was the mournful influence of the **unperceived** shadow that caused him to feel—although he neither saw nor heard—to *feel* the presence of my head within the room.

When I had waited a long time, very patiently, without hearing him lie down, I resolved to open a little—a very, very little crevice in the lantern. So I opened it—you cannot imagine how stealthily, stealthily—until, at length, a single dim ray, like the thread of the spider, shot from out the crevice and fell upon the vulture eye.

It was open—wide, wide open—and I grew furious as I gazed upon it. I saw it with perfect **distinctness**—all a dull blue, with a hideous veil over it that chilled the very **marrow** in my bones; but I could see nothing else of the old man's face or person for I had directed the ray as if by instinct, precisely upon the spot.

And now—have I not told you that what you mistake for madness is but **overacuteness** of the senses?—now, I say, there came to my ears a low, dull, quick sound, such as a watch makes when enveloped in cotton. I knew *that* sound well, too. It was the beating of the old man's heart. It increased my fury, as the beating of a drum **stimulates** the soldier into courage.

In what ways is the old man's state of mind like that of the narrator? In what ways is it different?

suppositions beliefs; opinions	**distinctness** awareness of detail	**overacuteness** too sharp or severe
unperceived not aware or understood	**marrow** the most important part	**stimulates** excites

But even yet I **refrained** and kept still. I scarcely breathed. I held the lantern motionless. I tried how steadily I could maintain the ray upon the eye. Meantime the hellish tattoo of the heart increased. It grew quicker and quicker, and louder and louder every instant. The old man's terror *must* have been extreme! It grew louder, I say, louder every moment!—do you mark me well? I have told you that I am nervous: so I am. And now at the dead hour of the night, amid the dreadful silence of that old house, so strange a noise as this excited me to uncontrollable terror. Yet, for some minutes longer I **refrained** and stood still. But the beating grew louder, louder! I thought the heart must burst. And now a new anxiety seized me—the sound would be heard by a neighbor! The old man's hour had come! With a loud yell, I threw open the lantern and leaped into the room. He shrieked once—once only. In an instant I dragged him to the floor, and pulled the heavy bed over him. I then smiled gaily, to find the deed so far done. But, for many minutes, the heart beat on with a muffled sound. This,

What sound does the narrator hear?

Reading Strategy:
Questioning

What senses does Poe describe to increase the terror?

however, did not vex me; it would not be heard through the wall. At length it **ceased**. The old man was dead. I removed the bed and examined the **corpse**. Yes, he was stone, stone dead. I placed my hand upon the heart and held it there many minutes. There was no pulsation. He was stone dead. His eye would trouble me no more.

refrained held back   **ceased** stopped   **corpse** a dead body

If still you think me mad, you will think so no longer when I describe the wise precautions I took for the concealment of the body. The night waned, and I worked hastily, but in silence. First of all I **dismembered** the corpse. I cut off the head and the arms and the legs.

I then took up three planks from the flooring of the chamber, and deposited all between the scantlings. I then replaced the boards so cleverly, so cunningly, that no human eye—not even *his*—could have detected anything wrong. There was nothing to wash out—no stain of any kind—no blood-spot whatever. I had been too **wary** for that. A tub had caught all—ha! ha!

When I had made an end of these labors, it was four o'clock—still dark as midnight. As the bell sounded the hour, there came a knocking at the street door. I went down to open it with a light heart—for what had I *now* to fear? There entered three men, who introduced themselves, with perfect **suavity**, as officers of the police. A shriek had been heard by a neighbor during the night; suspicion of foul play had been aroused; information had been lodged at the police office, and they (the officers) had been **deputed** to search the **premises**.

I smiled—for *what* had I to fear? I bade the gentlemen welcome. The shriek, I said, was my own in a dream. The old man, I mentioned, was absent in the country. I took my visitors all over the house. I bade them search—search *well*. I led them, at length, to *his* chamber. I showed them his treasures, secure, undisturbed. In the enthusiasm of my confidence, I brought chairs into the room, and desired them *here* to rest from their fatigues, while I myself, in the wild **audacity** of my perfect triumph, placed my own seat upon the very spot beneath which **reposed** the corpse of the victim.

The officers were satisfied. My *manner* had convinced them. I was singularly at ease. They sat, and while I answered

> What has the narrator done with the man?

> Does the narrator change or stay the same as the story goes on? How can you tell?

> Does the narrator view the situation the way that most people would? Explain.

dismembered cut apart

wary careful or cautious

suavity politeness

deputed sent out

premises a house or building with its grounds

audacity boldness

reposed rested

cheerily, they chatted of familiar things. But, ere long, I felt myself getting pale and wished them gone. My head ached, and I fancied a ringing in my ears: but still they sat and still chatted. The ringing became more distinct:—it continued and became more distinct: I talked more freely to get rid of the feeling: but it continued and gained **definitiveness**—until, at length, I found that the noise was *not* within my ears.

No doubt I now grew *very* pale—but I talked more fluently, and with a heightened voice. Yet the sound increased—and what could I do? It was a *low, dull, quick sound—much such a sound as a watch makes when enveloped in cotton.* I gasped for breath—and yet the officers heard it not. I talked more quickly—more **vehemently**; but the noise steadily increased. I arose and argued about trifles, in a high key and with violent **gesticulations**; but the noise steadily increased. Why *would* they not be gone? I paced the floor to and fro with heavy strides, as if excited to fury by the observations of the men—but the noise steadily increased. Oh! what *could* I do? I foamed—I raved—I swore! I swung the chair upon which I had been sitting, and grated it upon the boards, but the noise arose over all, and continually increased. It grew louder—louder—*louder!* And still the men chatted pleasantly, and smiled. Was it possible they heard not?—no, no! They heard!—they suspected—they knew!—they were making a **mockery** of my horror!—this I thought, and this I think. But anything was better than this agony! Anything was more tolerable than this **derision**! I could bear those hypocritical smiles no longer! I felt that I must scream or die!—and now again! hark! louder! louder! louder! *louder!*—

"Villains!" I shrieked, "**dissemble** no more! I admit the deed!—tear up the planks!—here, here!—it is the beating of his hideous heart!"

Is the narrator a round character or a flat character? Explain.

Reading Strategy:
Questioning
What happens to the narrator at the end of the story?

definitiveness an exact form	**gesticulations** a lively or excited movement of the body	**derision** laughter or ridicule
vehemently strongly		**dissemble** to hide real feelings; to disguise
	mockery the act of making fun of something	

The Tell-Tale Heart   by Edgar Allan Poe

Directions Choose the letter of the best answer or write the answer using complete sentences.

Comprehension: Identifying Facts

1. How does the narrator say that he feels at the beginning of the story?
   A lonely   **C** angry
   B nervous   **D** terrified

2. What has the disease done to the narrator's senses?
   A It has not affected them at all.
   B It has destroyed them completely.
   C It has dulled them.
   D It has sharpened them.

3. What color is the old man's eye?

4. How does the narrator treat the old man the week before the murder?

5. At what time every night does the narrator visit the old man?

6. What does the old man say to the narrator right before the murder?

7. What sound does the narrator hear before the murder?

8. How does the narrator murder the old man?

9. Who called the police? Why?

10. Where does the narrator sit when the police arrive?

Comprehension: Putting Ideas Together

11. Which of the narrator's senses is the sharpest?
    A smell   **C** hearing
    B sight   **D** taste

12. How does the narrator feel about the old man?
    A He loves him and says the old man has never hurt him.
    B He likes him, even though he says the old man is crazy.
    C He is jealous because the old man is so rich.
    D He does not care about him at all.

13. Why does the narrator decide to kill the old man?

14. Does the old man know the narrator is in his room? Explain.

15. How does the narrator get rid of the old man's body?

16. How does the narrator act when the police arrive?

17. What causes the narrator to change his behavior?

18. What sound drives the narrator mad near the end of the story?

19. How do the police discover that the narrator murdered the old man?

20. Why does the narrator act as he does?

Understanding Literature: Character Traits

Skilled authors make their characters seem like real people. They create some characters with many different traits or qualities. These are called round characters. Readers get to know many things about the lives and personalities of round characters. They also create flat characters who have only one main trait. Flat characters often are not the most important characters in a literary work. You may like some characters and dislike others, but they all serve a purpose. They help the author tell a story.

21. Which character traits allow the narrator to hide his crime?

22. Which character traits force him to admit to his crime?

23. Which characters in the story are round characters? Which characters are flat?

24. Do you think the narrator is sane or insane? Explain.

25. The story tells only the narrator's thoughts. Do you trust the narrator's telling of what happened? Why or why not?

Critical Thinking

26. At what point in the story did you find the narrator most frightening? Explain.

27. Why do you think someone might confess to having done something wrong? Why might they admit to their crime if they were unlikely to be caught?

28. Is the "tell-tale heart" the old man's heart or the narrator's heart? Explain.

29. How do you think this story would be different if the old man had lived to tell it?

Thinking Creatively

30. Why do you think readers may care more about what happens to round characters than to flat ones?

After Reading continued on next page

The Tell-Tale Heart by Edgar Allan Poe

 Grammar Check

Every verb has four principal parts. They form tenses that show when an action takes place. These principal parts are the *present, present participle, past,* and *past participle.*

- Present: The basic form of the verb. *Examples:* care, hurry
- Present Participle: Add *-ing* and use after a *to be* verb. *Examples:* (is) caring, (are) hurrying
- Past: Add *-ed* or *-d* to the verb. *Examples:* cared, hurried
- Past Participle: Add *-ed* or *-d* and use after *has, have, had. Examples:* (had) cared, (had) hurried

Write a paragraph that includes at least 10 verbs. Use the past and the past participle forms of the verbs. Then label each verb using the information above.

 Vocabulary Builder

The origin of *aspect* is the Latin word *aspectus.* The word *aspect* has the prefix *as-,* meaning "to." It is joined to the root *-spec-,* meaning "look" or "view." An *aspect* of something is the part of it that you look at. Can you tell what each of the following words means: *spectacular, spectators, perspective, retrospect?* Write your guesses on a sheet of paper. Then look up each word in a dictionary.

 Writing on Your Own

Write a character sketch of the narrator in "The Tell-Tale Heart." Describe his main character traits. Then explain how these traits cause him to act as he does. Show the link between the narrator's personality and the story's ending.

 Listening and Speaking

Work with a small group of classmates to discuss the narrator in "The Tell-Tale Heart." Discuss any questions you have about the narrator's actions. Use examples from the story to make your point. Ask the people in your group why they feel as they do about the narrator.

 Research and Technology

Prepare a bibliography of five works by Edgar Allan Poe. A bibliography includes the book title, author name, and publication information. (See Appendix C for more information about bibliographies.) Search your library's catalog using the author's name as your search term. For each book you find, write the title and publication information using the correct format.

Reading Informational Materials

Instructional Manuals

In Part 1, you are learning about questioning. Questioning helps you check your understanding as you read. Asking questions can be very useful when reading informational materials such as instructional manuals. The manual you are about to read explains how to use an answering machine.

About Manuals

A manual is a set of directions. It presents information about how to use a product or a tool. Most manuals include some or all of the following features:

- a picture of the product, with parts and features labeled

- step-by-step directions for setting up, using, and caring for the product

- consumer information such as safety warnings

- information on how to fix common problems

- customer service information including telephone numbers, store addresses, and Web sites

Reading Skill

A manual is a kind of informational text. You read it in order to perform a task. Notice each detail and complete the steps in order. Asking yourself questions as you work can help you understand the directions. Use a checklist like the one below. It can help you get the most out of manuals and other informational writing.

Checklist for Using Technical Manuals

- ❑ Read all the directions completely before starting to follow them.
- ❑ Look for clues such as bold type or capital letters that point out specific sections or important information.
- ❑ Use diagrams to locate and name the parts of the product.
- ❑ Follow each step in the exact order given.
- ❑ Do not skip any steps.

Important Safety Information

Follow these tips to stay safe when using your answering machine. These tips reduce the risk of fire, electric shock, and injury.

1. Keep the machine away from radiators and heating registers. Ensure proper ventilation at the installation site.

2. Do not use while wet or while standing in water.

3. Place the power cord where it will not be stepped on.

4. Never insert objects into the product openings. This may result in fire or shock.

5. Unplug this product from the wall outlet before cleaning. Use only a damp cloth to clean.

6. Do not take apart this product.

7. Do not overload wall outlets and extension cords. Use a surge protector to keep equipment safe.

> As you read, identify each part of the manual.

Using Your Answering Machine

Turning the Answering Machine On or Off

Press the On/Off button on the base to turn the answering machine on or off.

Setting the Clock

You will need to set the clock so that you will know when each recorded message is received.

> Each heading identifies one function of the answering machine. The numbered steps explain how that function should be done.

1. Press and hold **day/check** until the correct day is announced. Then release the button. The correct day will be repeated.

2. Press and hold **hour** until you hear the correct hour. Then release the button. The correct hour will be repeated.

3. Press and hold **min** until you hear the correct number of minutes. Then release the button. The correct number of minutes will be repeated.

> The words in bold highlight important parts of the machine.

Setting the Number of Rings

On the back of the answering machine is a slide switch that changes how many times the phone will ring before the answering machine picks up the call. You can choose 1 ring, 3 rings, or 5 rings.

Recording Your Announcement

You should record the personal outgoing message (OGM) that callers will hear when the system answers a call.

1. Press and hold **annce**. The machine beeps.

2. Record the message you want callers to hear. Speak normally, from about nine inches away from the microphone. Example: "Hello. We cannot come to the phone right now, but if you leave your name, number, and a brief message, we will get back to you."

3. Release **annce**. The message replays. To delete your message, press **delete**. To hear your announcement at any time, press **annce**.

Listening to Messages

Press ▶ to play and stop messages.

Press ▶▶ to skip forward.

Press ◀◀ to skip backward.

Deleting Messages

To delete an individual message, press **DEL** while listening to the message. To erase all messages on the answering machine, press and hold **erase** for two seconds. The answering machine beeps. The system announces "*Messages deleted.*"

Contact Us

If you experience problems with this product, please call the telephone number below. You will receive instructions on how to ship this product to a telephone repair center. Along with your product, you must include a copy of your receipt or bill of sale. In the USA, call: 1-800-555-5555. In Canada, call: 1-600-333-3333.

Monitor Your Progress

Directions Choose the letter of the best answer or write the answer using complete sentences.

1. What human function does this machine perform?
   A setting the clock
   B making phone calls
   C answering phone calls
   D remembering phone numbers

2. After the initial setup, what function will the user probably use most?
   A listening to messages
   B recording your announcement
   C setting the clock
   D writing down messages

3. What is the purpose of the outgoing message?

4. Explain how the diagram makes the text easier to follow.

5. Why is it important to read the manual before using a product?

Writing on Your Own

Choose a function described in the manual. Restate the directions in your own words. Then compare what you wrote to the manual. Which one was clearer? Why?

COMPARING LITERARY WORKS | Build Understanding

The Finish of Patsy Barnes   by Paul Laurence Dunbar

About the Author

Paul Laurence Dunbar was born in Dayton, Ohio, the son of former slaves. Dunbar's parents sparked his love of learning and history. Dunbar knew he wanted to be a writer early on. He wrote his first poem at age six!

Dunbar was the only African American student at his high school. However, that did not stop him from taking part in school activities. The same was true when he went to college. In college, Dunbar was editor of the school newspaper and class president. He was also president of the school writing group.

Dunbar published his first poem in a local newspaper. His first collection of poetry, *Oak and Ivy,* was published in 1893. His second book, *Majors and Minors* (1895), brought him national fame. Dunbar became the most important African American poet in the late 19th and early 20th centuries. On a trip to Florida he wrote: "Down here one finds my poems recited everywhere." Dunbar wrote a dozen books of poetry and four books of short stories. He also wrote four novels and a play. His work was published widely in the leading journals of the day.

Paul Laurence Dunbar
1872–1906

Objectives

◆ To read and compare a short story with another work

◆ To define dynamic character and static character

About the Selection

This story takes place in the late 19th century. Back then, medicine was much less advanced than it is today. There was a big difference in the quality of treatment given to rich and poor patients. A boy named Patsy Barnes wants to help his sick mother.

As you read "The Finish of Patsy Barnes," recall "The Tell-Tale Heart" that you read earlier in this unit. Think about what you know about the characters in that story. Compare them to the characters of Patsy Barnes and his mother. Also consider how the characters relate to their surroundings.

Comparing **continued on next page**

COMPARING LITERARY WORKS *(cont.)* | **Build Skills**

The Finish of Patsy Barnes   by Paul Laurence Dunbar

dynamic character
a character who develops and learns because of events in the story

static character
a character who does not change

dialect the speech of a particular part of a country, or of a certain group of people

Literary Terms Characters are one of the most important parts of a short story. A character takes part in the action of the work. Characters can be described in different ways. A **dynamic character** develops and learns because of events in the story. This type of character continues to change throughout the story. A **static character** does not change. Writers often use static characters to develop the conflict. These characters help show how the main characters change. The characters in "The Finish of Patsy Barnes" use **dialect.** Dialect is the speech of a particular part of a country, or of a certain group of people.

Reading on Your Own The main character in "The Finish of Patsy Barnes" is a young African American boy. The main character in "The Tell-Tale Heart" is a mad murderer. On the surface, these two characters do not seem to be alike. What could these two characters have in common? Brainstorm some possible similarities before you read.

Writing on Your Own Have you or someone you know ever had to take on an adult responsibility? Write a paragraph about how you or the person you know dealt with this situation.

Vocabulary Focus Short story writers use words that clearly describe their characters. Here are three adjectives from the story: *compulsory, diplomatic, incorrigible.* Look up the meaning of each word in a dictionary. Then use each adjective in a sentence that shows its meaning correctly.

Think Before You Read What would you do if a family member needed your help?

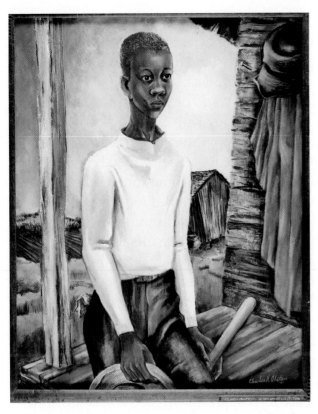

Farm Boy,
Charles Alston, 1941

His name was Patsy Barnes, and he was a **denizen** of Little Africa. In fact, he lived on Douglass Street. By all the laws governing the relations between people and their names, he should have been Irish—but he was not. He was colored, and very much so. That was the reason he lived on Douglass Street. The Negro has very strong within him the **instinct** of colonization and it was in **accordance** with this that Patsy's mother had found her way to Little Africa when she had come North from Kentucky.

Patsy was **incorrigible**. Even into the confines of Little Africa had penetrated the truant officer and the terrible penalty of the **compulsory** education law. Time and time

As you read, compare Patsy Barnes to the narrator in "The Tell-Tale Heart."

The *truant officer* is a person whose job is to make sure children attend school.

denizen a person or animal that lives in a place

instinct a natural feeling, knowledge, or ability that guides animals

accordance agreement

incorrigible too firmly fixed in bad ways to be changed

compulsory required

again had poor Eliza Barnes been brought up on account of the shortcomings of that son of hers. She was a hardworking, honest woman, and day by day bent over her tub, scrubbing away to keep Patsy in shoes and jackets, that would wear out so much faster than they could be bought. But she never murmured, for she loved the boy with a deep affection, though his misdeeds were a sore thorn in her side.

She wanted him to go to school. She wanted him to learn. She had the notion that he might become something better, something higher than she had been. But for him school had no charms; his school was the cool stalls in the big **livery** stable near at hand; the arena of his pursuits its sawdust floor; the height of his ambition, to be a horseman. Either here or in the racing stables at the Fair-grounds he spent his truant hours. It was a school that taught much, and Patsy was as apt a pupil as he was a constant attendant. He learned strange things about horses, and fine, **sonorous** oaths that sounded eerie on his young lips, for he had only turned into his fourteenth year.

A man goes where he is appreciated; then could this slim black boy be blamed for doing the same thing? He was a great favorite with the horsemen, and picked up many a dime or nickel for dancing or singing, or even a quarter for warming up a horse for its owner. He was not to be blamed for this, for, first of all, he was born in Kentucky, and had spent the very days of his infancy about the **paddocks** near Lexington, where his father had sacrificed his life on account of his love for horses. The little fellow had shed no tears when he looked at his father's bleeding body, bruised and broken by the fiery young two-year-old he was trying to **subdue**. Patsy did not sob or whimper, though his heart ached, for over all the feeling of his grief was a mad, burning desire to ride that horse.

Reading Strategy:
Questioning

Where does Patsy spend his time? Why?

What is unusual about Patsy's reaction to his father's death?

livery a stable for housing horses

sonorous giving or having a deep, loud sound

paddocks an enclosed area near a stable where horses are exercised

subdue to overcome or take control of

His tears were shed, however, when, **actuated** by the idea that times would be easier up North, they moved to Dalesford. Then, when he learned that he must leave his old friends, the horses and their masters, whom he had known, he wept. The comparatively **meager** appointments of the Fair-grounds at Dalesford proved a poor **compensation** for all these. For the first few weeks Patsy had dreams of running away—back to Kentucky and the horses and stables. Then after a while he settled himself with heroic **resolution** to make the best of what he had, and with a mighty effort took up the burden of life away from his beloved home.

Eliza Barnes, older and more experienced though she was, took up her burden with a less cheerful philosophy than her son. She worked hard, and made a **scanty** livelihood, it is true, but she did not make the best of what she had. Her complainings were loud in the land, and her wailings for her old home smote the ears of any who would listen to her.

To *smote* means "to have struck hard."

They had been living in Dalesford for a year nearly, when hard work and exposure brought the woman down to bed with **pneumonia**. They were very poor—too poor even to call in a doctor, so there was nothing to do but to call in the city physician. Now this medical man had too **frequent** calls into Little Africa, and he did not like to go there. So he was very gruff when any of its denizens called him, and it was even said that he was careless of his patients.

Patsy's heart bled as he heard the doctor talking to his mother:

"Now, there can't be any foolishness about this," he said. "You've got to stay in bed and not get yourself damp."

"How long you think I got to lay hyeah, doctah?" she asked.

"I'm a doctor, not a fortune-teller," was the reply. "You'll lie there as long as the disease holds you."

Note the dialect used in the conversation between Patsy's mother and the doctor.

actuated put into action

meager poor

compensation pay; something given to make up for something else

resolution determination

scanty very little

pneumonia a lung infection that causes fever and cough

frequent often

What does this conversation tell you about the difficulties Patsy and his mother face?

How does the doctor make Patsy angry?

"But I can't lay hyeah long, doctah, case I ain't got nuffin' to go on."

"Well, take your choice: the bed or the boneyard."

Eliza began to cry.

"You needn't sniffle," said the doctor; "I don't see what you people want to come up here for anyhow. Why don't you stay down South where you belong? You come up here and you're just a burden and a trouble to the city. The South deals with all of you better, both in poverty and crime." He knew that these people did not understand him, but he wanted an outlet for the heat within him.

There was another angry being in the room, and that was Patsy. His eyes were full of tears that **scorched** him and would not fall. The memory of many beautiful and appropriate oaths came to him; but he dared not let his mother hear him swear. Oh! to have a stone—to be across the street from that man!

When the physician walked out, Patsy went to the bed, took his mother's hand, and bent over **shamefacedly** to kiss her. The little mark of affection comforted Eliza unspeakably. The mother-feeling overwhelmed her in one burst of tears. Then she dried her eyes and smiled at him.

"Honey," she said; "mammy ain' gwine lay hyeah long. She be all right putty soon."

"Nevah you min'," said Patsy with a choke in his voice. "I can do somep'n', an' we'll have an othah doctah."

"La, listen at de chile; what kin you do?"

"I'm goin' down to McCarthy's stable and see if I kin git some horses to exercise."

How does Patsy decide to raise money to help his mother?

A sad look came into Eliza's eyes as she said: "You'd bettah not go, Patsy; dem hosses'll kill you yit, des lak dey did yo' pappy."

But the boy, used to doing pretty much as he pleased, was **obdurate**, and even while she was talking, put on his ragged jacket and left the room.

scorched burned slightly	**shamefacedly** embarrassingly; shyly	**obdurate** stubborn

Patsy was not wise enough to be **diplomatic**. He went right to the point with McCarthy, the liveryman.

The big red-faced fellow slapped him until he spun round and round. Then he said, "Ye little devil, ye, I've a mind to knock the whole head off o' ye. Ye want harses to exercise, do ye? Well git on that un, 'an' see what ye kin do with him."

The boy's honest desire to be helpful had tickled the big, generous Irishman's **peculiar** sense of humor, and from now on, instead of giving Patsy a horse to ride now and then as he had formerly done, he put into his charge all the animals that needed exercise.

It was with a king's pride that Patsy marched home with his first considerable earnings.

They were small yet, and would go for food rather than a doctor, but Eliza was **inordinately** proud, and it was this pride that gave her strength and the desire of life to carry her through the days approaching the crisis of her disease.

As Patsy saw his mother growing worse, saw her gasping for breath, heard the rattling as she drew in the little air that kept going her clogged lungs, felt the heat of her burning hands, and saw the pitiful appeal in her poor eyes, he became convinced that the city doctor was not helping her. She must have another. But the money?

That afternoon, after his work with McCarthy, found him at the Fair-grounds. The spring races were on, and he thought he might get a job warming up the horse of some independent jockey. He hung around the stables, listening to the talk of men he knew and some he had never seen before. Among the latter was a tall, lanky man, holding forth to a group of men.

"No, suh," he was saying to them generally, "I'm goin' to withdraw my hoss, because thaih ain't nobody to ride him as he ought to be rode. I haven't brought a jockey along with me,

What challenge does Patsy face as he watches his mother's condition worsen?

Reading Strategy: **Questioning**

Why might Patsy view these remarks as a challenge?

diplomatic having skill in dealing with others	**peculiar** strange or odd	**inordinately** very great or excessive

so I've got to depend on pick-ups. Now, the talent's set again my hoss, Black Boy, because he's been losin' regular, but that hoss has lost for the want of ridin', that's all."

The crowd looked in at the slim-legged, raw-boned horse, and walked away laughing.

"The fools!" muttered the stranger. "If I could ride myself I'd show 'em!"

Patsy was gazing into the stall at the horse.

"What are you doing thaih?" called the owner to him.

"Look hyeah, mistah," said Patsy, "ain't that a bluegrass hoss?"

"Of co'se it is, an' one o' the fastest that evah grazed."

"I'll ride that hoss, mistah."

"What do you know bout ridin'?"

"I used to gin'ally be' roun' Mistah Boone's paddock in Lexington, an'—"

"Aroun' Boone's paddock—what! Look here, if you can ride that hoss to a winnin' I'll give you more money than you ever seen before."

"I'll ride him."

Patsy's heart was beating very wildly beneath his jacket. That horse. He knew that glossy coat. He knew that raw-boned frame and those flashing nostrils. That black horse there owed something to the orphan he had made.

The horse was to ride in the race before the last. Somehow out of odds and ends, his owner scraped together a suit and colors for Patsy. The colors were **maroon** and green, a curious combination. But then it was a curious horse, a curious rider, and a more curious combination that brought the two together.

Long before the time for the race Patsy went into the stall to become better **acquainted** with his horse. The animal turned its wild eyes upon him and neighed. He patted the long, slender head, and grinned as the horse stepped aside as gently as a lady.

Reading Strategy: Questioning

Why does Patsy feel that this horse owes him something?

maroon a dark brownish red color

acquainted made aware; informed

"He sholy is full o' ginger," he said to the owner, whose name he had found to be Brackett.

"He'll show 'em a thing or two," laughed Brackett.

"His dam was a fast one," said Patsy, unconsciously.

Brackett whirled on him in a flash. "What do you know about his dam?" he asked.

The boy would have **retracted**, but it was too late. Stammeringly he told the story of his father's death and the horse's connection therewith.

"Well," said Bracket, "if you don't turn out a hoodoo, you're a winner, sure. But I'll be blessed if this don't sound like a story! But I've heard that story before. The man I got Black Boy from, no matter how I got him, you're too young to understand the ins and outs of poker, told it to me."

When the bell sounded and Patsy went out to warm up, he felt as if he were riding on air. Some of the jockeys laughed at his getup, but there was something in him—or under him, maybe—that made him scorn their **derision**. He saw a sea of faces about him, then saw no more. Only a shining white track loomed ahead of him, and a restless **steed** was cantering with him around the curve. Then the bell called him back to the stand.

They did not get away at first, and back they trooped. A second trial was a failure. But at the third they were off in a line as straight as a chalk-mark. There were Essex and Firefly, Queen Bess and Mosquito, galloping away side by side, and Black Boy a neck ahead. Patsy knew the family reputation of his horse for **endurance** as well as fire, and began riding the race from the first. Black Boy came of blood that would not be passed, and to this his rider trusted. At the eighth the line was hardly broken, but as the quarter was reached Black Boy had forged a length ahead, and Mosquito was at his flank. Then, like a flash, Essex shot out ahead under whip and spur, his jockey standing straight in the stirrups.

retracted withdrew; took back	**steed** a high-spirited horse	**endurance** power to last and withstand hard wear
derision laughing; ridicule		

A *dam* is a horse's mother.

Reading Strategy: Questioning
What unexpected job has Patsy taken on for McCarthy?

Hoodoo is used here to mean someone or something that causes bad luck.

Cantering means running at a smooth pace.

Reading Strategy: Questioning
How are Black Boy and Patsy well suited for each other as horse and jockey?

The crowd in the stand screamed; but Patsy smiled as he lay low over his horse's neck. He saw that Essex had made his best spurt. His only fear was for Mosquito, who hugged and hugged his flank. They were nearing the three-quarter post, and he was tightening his grip on the black. Essex fell back; his spurt was over. The whip fell unheeded on his sides. The spurs dug him in vain.

Black Boy's breath touches the leader's ear. They are neck and neck—nose to nose. The black stallion passes him.

Dunbar changed here from the past tense to the present tense. Why do you think he did this?

Another cheer from the stand, and again Patsy smiles as they turn into the stretch. Mosquito has gained a head. The colored boy flashes one glance at the horse and rider who are so surely gaining upon him, and his lips close in a grim line. They are half-way down the stretch, and Mosquito's head is at the stallion's neck.

For a single moment Patsy thinks of the sick woman at home and what that race will mean to her, and then his knees close against the horse's sides with a firmer dig. The spurs shoot deeper into the steaming flanks. Black Boy shall win; he must win. The horse that has taken away his father shall give him back his mother. The stallion leaps away like a flash, and goes under the wire—a length ahead.

What drives Patsy to win the race?

Then the band thundered, and Patsy was off his horse, very warm and very happy, following his mount to the stable. There, a little later, Brackett found him. He rushed to him, and flung his arms around him.

"You little devil," he cried, "you rode like you were kin to that hoss! We've won! We've won!" And he began sticking banknotes at the boy. At first Patsy's eyes bulged, and then he seized the money and got into his clothes.

"Goin' out to spend it?" asked Brackett.

"I'm goin' for a doctah fu' my mother," said Patsy, "she's sick."

"Don't let me lose sight of you."

"Oh, I'll see you again. So long," said the boy.

Reading Strategy: Questioning

How have events in the story changed Patsy?

An hour later he walked into his mother's room with a very big doctor, the greatest the druggist could direct him to. The doctor left his medicines and his orders, but, when Patsy told his story, it was Eliza's pride that started her on the road to recovery. Patsy did not tell his horse's name.

The Finish of Patsy Barnes   by Paul Laurence Dunbar

Directions Choose the letter of the best answer or write the answer using complete sentences.

Comprehension: Identifying Facts

1. Where do Patsy and his mother live when the story opens?
   A in western Kentucky
   B in a town called Dalesford
   C in a town called Douglass
   D in northern Alabama

2. How old is Patsy?
   A 12   C 16
   B 14   D 18

3. How did Patsy's father die?

4. What illness does Eliza Barnes get?

5. What does the doctor tell Patsy's mother to do to get well?

6. What does Patsy do for his mother when the doctor leaves?

7. How does Patsy plan to get money to help his mother get well?

8. What color is the riding outfit that Patsy wears?

9. What does Patsy tell McCarthy right before the race?

10. What does Patsy do with the money he wins?

Comprehension: Putting Ideas Together

11. What is Eliza Barnes's job?
    A She works in the stables.
    B She sews jackets.
    C She is a school teacher.
    D She works as a washerwoman.

12. Why does Patsy want to ride Black Boy?
    A He feels the horse owes him a win.
    B He knows that Black Boy is a winner.
    C He has ridden Black Boy many times before.
    D He wants to show his mother that he is a man.

13. Is Patsy Barnes a round or a flat character? How does this compare to the narrator in "The Tell-Tale Heart"?

14. Instead of going to school, where does Patsy spend his time?

15. In "The Finish of Patsy Barnes," the characters speak in dialect. Is there dialect in "The Tell-Tale Heart"?

16. Why is Patsy so upset when he and his mother move to Dalesford?

17. Why does the doctor speak to Eliza Barnes in an unfeeling way?

Comparing continued on next page

The Finish of Patsy Barnes by Paul Laurence Dunbar

18. Describe similarities and differences between Patsy's feelings toward his mother and the narrator's feelings toward the old man.

19. What role does the human heart play in each story?

20. How does Patsy change as a result of his experiences? How might the narrator in "The Tell-Tale Heart" change had he not gone mad?

Understanding Literature: Dynamic and Static Characters

Dynamic characters change during a story, much as real people do because of life experiences. Static characters do not change. Dynamic characters tend to be main characters. They are at the center of the story. Static characters are usually minor characters. They serve to show how the main characters change.

21. Is Patsy a dynamic or static character? Why?

22. Is the narrator in "The Tell-Tale Heart" a dynamic or static character? Explain.

23. How are Patsy and the narrator of "The Tell-Tale Heart" alike?

24. Who is a more dynamic character—Eliza Barnes or the old man in "The Tell-Tale Heart"? Explain.

25. Is Patsy's decision to ride the wild horse a good one? Why or why not?

Critical Thinking

26. Why do you think Patsy feels the need to ride Black Boy?

27. How are both Patsy and the narrator in "The Tell-Tale Heart" risk-takers?

28. Do you think the problems Patsy and the narrator face have any similarities? Explain.

Thinking Creatively

29. Do you think Patsy did the right thing? Why or why not?

30. What advice might Patsy give to the narrator in "The Tell-Tale Heart"?

Grammar Check

For regular verbs, the past tense is formed by adding *-ed* or *-d* to the present form. The past tense of irregular verbs often requires a different spelling of the verb.

Rewrite each sentence. Replace the underlined verb with the correct past tense verb.

1 Carol <u>speak</u> to the club yesterday.

2 Ivan <u>go</u> to the dentist this morning.

3 Mia <u>come</u> to my house for a party.

4 Jake <u>write</u> a story last week.

 Vocabulary Builder

Replace the underlined word or phrase in each sentence with a word from the list that means the opposite. Before you begin, review the meaning of each word in the list. You may use a dictionary or your glossary for help.

Word List: compulsory, meager, immortality, legitimately, resolute

1 Pam is <u>unsure</u> about trying out for the team.

2 Liz was parked <u>illegally</u>.

3 Uniforms are <u>optional</u> at that school.

4 John's <u>lavish</u> meal was enough for 10 people.

5 Some people worry that they are <u>going to die</u>.

 Writing on Your Own

Compare and contrast Patsy Barnes and the narrator in "The Tell-Tale Heart." In what ways are they alike? In what ways are they different? How does each character deal with the main conflict? Create a Venn Diagram to show the differences and similarities in the two characters. (You can see a description of this graphic organizer in Appendix A.)

 Listening and Speaking

With a small group of classmates, stage an evening television news show. Have half the group report on the narrator's actions in "The Tell-Tale Heart." Have the other half report on Patsy's victory in "The Finish of Patsy Barnes." Make your reports both informative and exciting.

 Media and Viewing

Create a media presentation on either Edgar Allan Poe or Paul Laurence Dunbar. Try to use at least two different types of media in your presentation. For example, you might show scenes from movies that have been made from their stories. Include pictures of the authors and the times in which they lived. After your presentation, be prepared to answer questions from the audience.

Sometimes the meaning of a text is not directly stated. You have to make an inference to figure out what the text means.

What You Know + What You Read = Inference

To make inferences, you have to think "beyond the text." Predicting what will happen next and explaining cause and effect are helpful strategies for making inferences.

Literary Terms

point of view the position from which the author or storyteller tells the story

first person a point of view where the narrator is also a character and uses the pronouns *I* and *we*

third person a point of view where the narrator is not a character and refers to characters as *he* or *she*

journal writing that gives an author's feelings or first impressions about a subject

irony the difference between what is expected to happen in a story and what does happen

description a written picture of the characters, setting, and events of a work of literature

protagonist the main character of a story

antagonist the person or animal who struggles against the main character of a story

theme the main idea of a literary work

symbol something that represents something else

Flowers for Algernon *by Daniel Keyes*

About the Author

Daniel Keyes was born and raised in Brooklyn, New York. He joined the U.S. Maritime Service at age 17 and went to sea. After Keyes left the sea, he continued his studies at Brooklyn College. There, he earned his degree in psychology.

Keyes has held many jobs throughout his life. He worked as a fiction editor and then as a fashion photographer. For a while, he taught English in the New York City schools. He next became a college professor in Ohio. No matter what his job, however, Keyes kept writing. He published several novels and nonfiction books. One of these, *The Minds of Billy Milligan*, is about a man with multiple personalities. Daniel Keyes is now retired and lives in southern Florida.

Daniel Keyes
1927–

About the Selection

Keyes has always been interested in unusual mental conditions. A meeting with a mentally-disabled man gave Keyes the idea for "Flowers for Algernon." He began to wonder "if it were possible to increase human intelligence artificially." "Flowers for Algernon" is Keyes's most well-known work. Keyes was given the Hugo Award of the Science Fiction Writers of America in 1960. Cliff Robertson won an Oscar for his performance in the movie version, *Charly*. The stage version has also been performed around the world.

Charlie Gordon is the main character in "Flowers for Algernon." He has surgery to improve his intelligence. In the story, his doctors measure his progress with I.Q., or intelligence quotient, tests. These tests are used to measure a person's intelligence and learning ability.

Objectives

◆ To read and understand a short story written in journal form

◆ To explain the difference between first-person and third-person point of view

◆ To identify examples of irony in a work of literature

Before Reading **continued on next page**

point of view
the position from which the author or storyteller tells the story

first person
a point of view where the narrator is also a character and uses the pronouns *I* and *we*

third person
a point of view where the narrator is not a character, and refers to characters as *he* or *she*

journal writing that gives an author's feelings or first impressions about a subject

irony
the difference between what is expected to happen in a story and what does happen

Literary Terms **Point of view** is the position from which the author or storyteller tells the story. Most stories are told from the **first-person** or **third-person** point of view. In first person, the narrator is also a character in the story and uses the pronouns *I* and *we*. Readers are told only what the narrator feels, knows, sees, and thinks. In third person, the narrator is not a character in the story. Instead, the narrator tells events from outside the story and refers to characters as *he* or *she*. "Flowers for Algernon" is told in the first person, from Charlie's point of view. The structure of the story is like a **journal** because each event has a date. A journal is writing that expresses an author's feelings or first impressions about a subject. This short story also contains **irony,** or the difference between what is expected to happen in a story and what does happen.

Reading on Your Own This story is written in Charlie's language and from his point of view. Because of his limited intelligence, some words are spelled incorrectly. Read slowly and carefully to be sure you understand what is happening.

Writing on Your Own In "Flowers for Algernon," Charlie Gordon takes a huge risk. He has a brain operation that will let him "be like other people." Think about why a person would worry about not fitting in with everyone else. Then write a paragraph about why a character might risk his life to be like others.

Vocabulary Focus Choose six words from the vocabulary list. On a sheet of paper, write each word and its meaning. Then, with a classmate, have a conversation using your words. Use each word at least once in your conversation.

Think Before You Read Read the title of this story again. Why do you think this selection is called "Flowers for Algernon"? Discuss with a partner what you think the title might mean.

Flowers for Algernon

progris riport 1—martch 5 1965

Dr. Strauss says I shud rite down what I think and evrey thing that happins to me from now on. I dont know why but he says its importint so they will see if they will use me. I hope they use me. Miss Kinnian says maybe they can make me smart. I want to be smart. My name is Charlie Gordon. I am 37 years old and 2 weeks ago was my brithday. I have nuthing more to rite now so I will close for today.

progris riport 2—martch 6

I had a test today. I think I faled it. and I think that maybe now they wont use me. What happind is a nice young man was in the room and he had some white cards with ink spilled all over them. He sed Charlie what do you see on this card. I was very skared even tho I had my rabits foot in my pockit because when I was a kid I always faled tests in school and I spillled ink to.

I told him I saw a inkblot. He said yes and it made me feel good. I thot that was all but when I got up to go he stopped me. He said now sit down Charlie we are not thru yet. Then I dont remember so good but he wantid me to say what was in the ink. I dint see nuthing in the ink but he said there was

As you read, pay attention to the dates of Charlie's progress reports. How much time passes from the beginning of the story to the end?

Reading Strategy: Inferencing

What details in the opening paragraph help you to make inferences about Charlie's situation? Explain.

A *rabbit's foot* is a symbol of good luck.

picturs there other pepul saw some pictures. I coudnt see any picturs. I reely tryed to see. I held the card close up and then far away. Then I said if I had my glases I coud see better I usally only ware my glases in the movies or TV but I said they are in the closit in the hall. I got them. Then I said let me see that card agen I bet Ill find it now.

I tryed hard but I still coudnt find the picturs I only saw the ink. I told him maybe I need new glases. He rote somthing down on a paper and I got skared of faling the test. I told him it was a very nice inkblot with littel points all around the eges. He looked very sad so that wasnt it. I said please let me try agen. Ill get it in a few minits becaus Im not so fast somtimes. Im a slow reeder too in Miss Kinnians class for slow adults but I'm trying very hard.

He gave me a chance with another card that had 2 kinds of ink spilled on it red and blue.

He was very nice and talked slow like Miss Kinnian does and he explaned it to me that it was a *raw shok*. He said pepul see things in the ink. I said show me where. He said think. I told him I think a inkblot but that wasnt rite eather. He said what does it remind you—pretend somthing. I closd my eyes for a long time to pretend. I told him I pretned a fowntan pen with ink leeking all over a table cloth. Then he got up and went out.

I dont think I passd the *raw shok* test.

progris report 3—martch 7

Dr Strauss and Dr Nemur say it dont matter about the inkblots. I told them I dint spill the ink on the cards and I coudnt see anything in the ink. They said that maybe they will still use me. I said Miss Kinnian never gave me tests like that one only spelling and reading. They said Miss Kinnian told that I was her bestist pupil in the adult nite scool becaus I tryed the hardist and I reely wantid to lern. They said how come you went to the adult nite scool all by yourself Charlie. How did you find it. I said I askd pepul and sumbody told me where I shud go to lern to read and spell good. They said why did you want to. I told them becaus all my life I wantid to be

Reading Strategy: Inferencing

How can you tell that Charlie knows he is a slow learner?

Raw shok is a misspelling of "Rorschach test." In this test, patients are asked to tell what they see in an inkblot.

How can you tell that the story is told from the first-person point of view?

What do you think the doctors will use Charlie for?

smart and not dumb. But its very hard to be smart. They said you know it will probly be tempirery. I said yes. Miss Kinnian told me. I dont care if it herts.

Later I had more crazy tests today. The nice lady who gave it me told me the name and I asked her how do you spellit so I can rite it in my progris riport. THEMATIC APPERCEPTION TEST. I dont know the frist 2 words but I know what *test* means. You got to pass it or you get bad marks. This test lookd easy becaus I coud see the picturs. Only this time she dint want me to tell her the picturs. That mixd me up. I said the man yesterday said I shoud tell him what I saw in the ink she said that dont make no difrence. She said make up storys about the pepul in the picturs.

I told her how can you tell storys about pepul you never met. I said why shud I make up lies. I never tell lies any more becaus I always get caut.

She told me this test and the other one the raw-shok was for getting personalty. I laffed so hard. I said how can you get that thing from inkblots and fotos. She got sore and put her picturs away. I dont care. It was sily. I gess I faled that test too.

Later some men in white coats took me to a difernt part of the hospitil and gave me a game to play. It was like a race with a white mouse. They called the mouse Algernon. Algernon was in a box with a lot of twists and turns like all kinds of walls and they gave me a pencil and a paper with lines and lots of boxes. On one side it said START and on the other end it said FINISH. They said it was *amazed* and that Algernon and me had the same *amazed* to do. I dint see how we could have the same *amazed* if Algernon had a box and I had a paper but I dint say nothing. Anyway there wasnt time because the race started.

One of the men had a watch he was trying to hide so I woudnt see it so I tryed not to look and that made me nervus.

Anyway that test made me feel worser than all the others because they did it over 10 times with difernt *amazeds* and Algernon won every time. I dint know that mice were so smart. Maybe thats because Algernon is a white mouse. Maybe white mice are smarter than other mice.

Reading Strategy: **Inferencing**

Charlie does not understand what he is supposed to do. What does this tell you about him?

In the *Thematic Apperception Test,* the patient looks at pictures and makes up stories.

When Charlie says *amazed,* he means "a maze," a confusing series of paths. An animal's intelligence is often measured by how fast it goes through a maze.

Why do you think Algernon is so smart?

progris riport 4—Mar 8

Their going to use me! Im so exited I can hardly write. Dr Nemur and Dr Strauss had a argament about it first. Dr Nemur was in the office when Dr Strauss brot me in. Dr Nemur was worryed about using me but Dr Strauss told him Miss Kinnian rekemmended me the best from all the pepul who she was teaching. I like Miss Kinnian becaus shes a very smart teacher. And she said Charlie your going to have a second chance. If you volenteer for this experament you mite get smart. They dont know if it will be perminint but theirs a chance. Thats why I said ok even when I was scared because she said it was an operashun. She said dont be scared Charlie you done so much with so little I think you deserv it most of all.

So I got scaird when Dr Nemur and Dr Strauss argud about it. Dr Strauss said I had something that was very good. He said I had a good *motor-vation.* I never even knew I had that. I felt proud when he said that not every body with an eye-q of 68 had that thing. I dont know what it is or where I got it but he said Algernon had it too. Algernons *motor-vation* is the cheese they put in his box. But it cant be that because I didnt eat any cheese this week.

Then he told Dr Nemur something I dint understand so while they were talking I wrote down some of the words.

He said Dr Nemur I know Charlie is not what you had in mind as the first of your new brede of intelek** (coudnt get the word) superman. But most people of his low ment** are host** and uncoop** they are usualy dull apath** and hard to reach. He has a good natcher hes intristed and eager to please.

Dr Nemur said remember he will be the first human beeng ever to have his intelijence trippled by surgicle meens.

Dr Strauss said exakly. Look at how well hes lerned to read and write for his low mentel age its as grate an acheve** as you and I lerning einstines therey of **vity without help. That shows the intenss motorvation. Its comparat** a tremen** achev** I say we use Charlie.

When Charlie says *motor-vation,* he means "motivation"—a willingness to work hard toward a goal.

By *eye-q,* Charlie means I.Q., or "intelligence quotient." This is a test to measure human intelligence.

Reading Strategy: Inferencing

To the scientists, how are Charlie and Algernon like one another?

The operation will make Charlie smarter.

I dint get all the words and they were talking to fast but it sounded like Dr Strauss was on my side and like the other one wasnt.

Then Dr Nemur nodded he said all right maybe your right. We will use Charlie. When he said that I got so exited I jumped up and shook his hand for being so good to me. I told him thank you doc you wont be sorry for giving me a second chance. And I mean it like I told him. After the operashun Im gonna try to be smart. Im gonna try awful hard.

progris ript 5—Mar 10

Im skared. Lots of people who work here and the nurses and the people who gave me the tests came to bring me candy and wish me luck. I hope I have luck. I got my rabits foot and my lucky penny and my horse shoe. Only a black cat crossed me when I was comming to the hospitil. Dr Strauss says dont be supersitis Charlie this is sience. Anyway Im keeping my rabits foot with me.

Reading Strategy: Inferencing

What details show the way Dr. Strauss feels about Charlie?

How does Charlie feel at this point in the story?

Why does Charlie want to beat Algernon in the race?

I asked Dr Strauss if Ill beat Algernon in the race after the operashun and he said maybe. If the operashun works Ill show that mouse I can be as smart as he is. Maybe smarter. Then Ill be abel to read better and spell the words good and know lots of things and be like other people. I want to be smart like other people. If it works perminint they will make everybody smart all over the wurld.

They dint give me anything to eat this morning. I dont know what that eating has to do with getting smart. Im very hungry and Dr Nemur took away my box of candy. That Dr Nemur is a grouch. Dr Strauss says I can have it back after the operashun. You cant eat befor a operashun . . .

Progress Report 6—Mar 15

The operashun dint hurt. He did it while I was sleeping. They took off the bandijis from my eyes and my head today so I can make a PROGRESS REPORT. Dr Nemur who looked at some of my other ones says I spell PROGRESS wrong and he told me how to spell it and REPORT too. I got to try and remember that.

I have a very bad memary for spelling. Dr Strauss says its ok to tell about all the things that happin to me but he says I shoud tell more about what I feel and what I think. When I told him I dont know how to think he said try. All the time when the bandijis were on my eyes I tryed to think. Nothing happened. I dont know what to think about. Maybe if I ask him he will tell me how I can think now that Im suppose to get smart. What do smart people think about. Fancy things I suppose. I wish I knew some fancy things alredy.

Progress Report 7—Mar 19

Nothing is happining. I had lots of tests and different kinds of races with Algernon. I hate that mouse. He always beats me. Dr Strauss said I got to play those games. And he said some time I got to take those tests over again. Thse inkblots are stupid. And those pictures are stupid too. I like to draw a picture of a man and a woman but I wont make up lies about people.

I got a headache from trying to think so much. I thot Dr Strauss was my frend but he dont help me. He dont tell me what to think or when Ill get smart. Miss Kinnian dint come to see me. I think writing these progress reports are stupid too.

Reading Strategy: Inferencing

Which words in Progress Report 7 show Charlie's state of mind after the operation?

Progress Report 8—Mar 23

Im going back to work at the factery. They said it was better I shud go back to work but I cant tell anyone what the operashun was for and I have to come to the hospitil for an hour evry night after work. They are gonna pay me mony every month for lerning to be smart.

Im glad Im going back to work because I miss my job and all my frends and all the fun we have there.

Dr Strauss says I shud keep writing things down but I dont have to do it every day just when I think of something or something speshul happins. He says dont get discoridged because it takes time and it happins slow. He says it took a long time with Algernon before he got 3 times smarter then he was before. Thats why Algernon beats me all the time because he had that operashun too. That makes me feel better. I coud probly do that *amazed* faster than a reglar mouse. Maybe some day Ill beat Algernon. Boy that would be something. So far Algernon looks like he mite be smart perminent.

Mar 25 (I dont have to write PROGRESS REPORT on top any more just when I hand it in once a week for Dr Nemur to read. I just have to put the date on. That saves time)

We had a lot of fun at the factery today. Joe Carp said hey look where Charlie had his operashun what did they do Charlie put some brains in. I was going to tell him but I emembered Dr Strauss said no. Then Frank Reilly said what did you do Charlie forget your key and open your door the hard way. That made me laff. Their really my friends and they like me.

Do you think these men are really Charlie's friends? Explain.

Sometimes somebody will say hey look at Joe or Frank or George he really pulled a Charlie Gordon. I dont know why they say that but they always laff. This morning Amos Borg who is the 4 man at Donnegans used my name when he shouted at Ernie the office boy. Ernie lost a packige. He said Ernie what are you trying to be a Charlie Gordon. I dont understand why he said that. I never lost any packiges.

Donnegans is the name of the factory where Charlie works.

Mar 28 Dr Straus came to my room tonight to see why I dint come in like I was suppose to. I told him I dont like to race with Algernon any more. He said I dont have to for a while but I shud come in. He had a present for me only it wasnt a present but just for lend. I thot it was a little television but it wasnt. He said I got to turn it on when I go to sleep. I said your kidding why shud I turn it on when Im going to sleep. Who ever herd of a thing like that. But he said if I want to get smart I got to do what he says. I told him I dint think I was going to get smart and he put his hand on my sholder and said Charlie you dont know it yet but your getting smarter all the time. You wont notice for a while. I think he was just being nice to make me feel good because I dont look any smarter.

Reading Strategy:
Inferencing

What do the men mean when they say someone "pulled a Charlie Gordon"?

What does Dr. Strauss give to Charlie?

Oh yes I almost forgot. I asked him when I can go back to the class at Miss Kinnians school. He said I wont go their. He said that soon Miss Kinnian will come to the hospitil to start and teach me speshul. I was mad at her for not comming to see me when I got the operashun but I like her so maybe we will be frends again.

Mar 29 That crazy TV kept me up all night. How can I sleep with something yelling crazy things all night in my ears. And the nutty pictures. Wow. I dont know what it says when Im up so how am I going to know when Im sleeping.

Dr Strauss says its ok. He says my brains are lerning when I sleep and that will help me when Miss Kinnian starts my lessons in the hospitl only I found out it isnt a hospitil its a labatory. I think its all crazy. If you can get smart when your sleeping why do people go to school. That thing I dont think will work. I use to watch the late show and the late late show on TV all the time and it never made me smart. Maybe you have to sleep while you watch it.

Reading Strategy: Inferencing

From Charlie's description of the TV, what do you think the device does?

PROGRESS REPORT 9—APRIL 3

Dr Strauss showed me how to keep the TV turned low so now I can sleep. I don't hear a thing. And I still dont understand what it says. A few times I play it over in the morning to find out what I lerned when I was sleeping and I dont think so. Miss Kinnian says Maybe its another langwidge or something. But most times it sounds american. It talks so fast faster then even Miss Gold who was my teacher in 6 grade and I remember she talked so fast I coudnt understand her.

I told Dr Strauss what good is it to get smart in my sleep. I want to be smart when Im awake. He says its the same thing and I have two minds. Theres the *subconscious* and the *conscious* (thats how you spell it). And one dont tell the other

one what its doing. They dont even talk to each other. Thats why I dream. And boy have I been having crazy dreams. Wow. Ever since that night TV. The late late late late late show.

I forgot to ask him if it was only me or if everybody had those two minds.

(I just looked up the word in the dictionary Dr Strauss gave me. The word is *subconscious. adj. Of the nature of mental operations yet not present in consciousness; as, subconscious conflict of desires.*) There's more but I still dont know what it means. This isnt a very good dictionary for dumb people like me.

Anyway the headache is from the party. My frends from the factery Joe Carp and Frank Reilly invited me to go with them to Muggsys Saloon for some drinks. I dont like to drink but they said we will have lots of fun. I had a good time.

Joe Carp said I shoud show the girls how I mop out the toilet in the factory and he got me a mop. I showed them and everyone laffed when I told that Mr Donnegan said I was the best janiter he ever had because I like my job and do it good and never come late or miss a day except for my operashun.

What changes can you see in Charlie's intelligence so far? Explain.

I said Miss Kinnian always said Charlie be proud of your job because you do it good.

Everybody laffed and we had a good time and they gave me lots of drinks and Joe said Charlie is a card when hes potted. I dont know what that means but everybody likes me and we have fun. I cant wait to be smart like my best frends Joe Carp and Frank Reilly.

A person who is a *card* is a lot of fun. Someone who is *potted* has had too much to drink.

I dont remember how the party was over but I think I went out to buy a newspaper and coffe for Joe and Frank and when I came back there was no one their. I looked for them all over till late. Then I dont remember so good but I think I got sleepy or sick. A nice cop brot me back home. Thats what my landlady Mrs Flynn says.

What happens at the party to make people laugh? What kind of people are Charlie's "friends"?

But I got a headache and a big lump on my head and black and blue all over. I think maybe I fell. Anyway I got a bad headache and Im sick and hurt all over. I dont think Ill drink anymore.

April 6 I beat Algernon! I dint even know I beat him until Burt the tester told me. Then the second time I lost because I got so exited I fell off the chair before I finished. But after that I beat him 8 more times. I must be getting smart to beat a smart mouse like Algernon. But I dont feel smarter.

I wanted to race Algernon some more but Burt said thats enough for one day. They let me hold him for a minit. Hes not so bad. Hes soft like a ball of cotton. He blinks and when he opens his eyes their black and pink on the eges.

I said can I feed him because I felt bad to beat him and I wanted to be nice and make frends. Burt said no Algernon is a very specshul mouse with an operashun like mine, and he was the first of all the animals to stay smart so long. He told me Algernon is so smart that every day he has to solve a test to get his food. Its a thing like a lock on a door that changes every time Algernon goes in to eat so he has to lern something new to get his food. That made me sad because if he coudnt lern he woud be hungry.

I dont think its right to make you pass a test to eat. How woud Dr Nemur like it to have to pass a test every time he wants to eat. I think Ill be frends with Algernon.

April 9 Tonight after work Miss Kinnian was at the laboratory. She looked like she was glad to see me but scared. I told her dont worry Miss Kinnian Im not smart yet and she laffed. She said I have confidence in you Charlie the way you struggled so hard to read and right better than all the others. At werst you will have it for a littel wile and your doing something for sience.

We are reading a very hard book. I never read such a hard book before. Its called *Robinson Crusoe* about a man who gets merooned on a dessert Iland. Hes smart and figers out all kinds of things so he can have a house and food and hes a good swimmer. Only I feel sorry because hes all alone and has no frends. But I think their must be somebody else on the iland because theres a picture with his funny umbrella looking at footprints. I hope he gets a frend and not be lonly.

April 10 Miss Kinnian teaches me to spell better. She says look at a word and close your eyes and say it over and over until you remember. I have lots of truble with *through* that you say *threw* and *enough* and *tough* that you dont say *enew* and *tew*. You got to say *enuff* and *tuff*. Thats how I use to write it before I started to get smart. Im confused but Miss Kinnian says theres no reason in spelling.

April 14 Finished Robinson Crusoe. I want to find out more about what happens to him but Miss Kinnian says thats all there is. *Why*

April 15 Miss Kinnian says Im lerning fast. She read some of the Progress Reports and she looked at me kind of funny. She says Im a fine person and Ill show them all. I asked her why. She said never mind but I shoudnt feel bad if I find out that everybody isnt nice like I think. She said for a person

Reading Strategy:
Inferencing

Why do you think Miss Kinnian is frightened?

Robinson Crusoe is a novel written in 1719 by British author Daniel Defoe.

What does the author show about Charlie by using the first person? How would the information be different if written in the third person?

who god gave so little to you done more then a lot of people with brains they never even used. I said all my frends are smart people but there good. They like me and they never did anything that wasnt nice. Then she got something in her eye and she had to run out to the ladys room.

April 16 Today, I lerned, the comma, this is a comma (,) a period, with a tail, Miss Kinnian, says its importent, because, it makes writing, better, she said, somebody, coud lose, a lot of money, if a comma, isnt, in the, right place, I dont have, any money, and I dont see, how a comma, keeps you, from losing it,

But she says, everybody, uses commas, so Ill use, them too,

April 17 I used the comma wrong. Its punctuation. Miss Kinnian told me to look up long words in the dictionary to lern to spell them. I said whats the difference if you can read it anyway. She said its part of your education so now on Ill look up all the words Im not sure how to spell. It takes a long time to write that way but I think Im remembering. I only have to look up once and after that I get it right. Anyway thats how come I got the word *punctuation* right. (Its that way in the dictionary). Miss Kinnian says a period is punctuation too, and there are lots of other marks to lern. I told her I thot all the periods had to have tails but she said no.

You got to mix them up, she showed? me" how. to mix! them(up,. and now; I can! mix up all kinds" of punctuation, in! my writing? There, are lots! of rules? to lern; but Im gettin'g them in my head.

One thing I? like about, Dear Miss Kinnian: (thats the way it goes in a business letter if I ever go into business) is she, always gives me' a reason" when—I ask. She's a gen'ius! I wish! I cou'd be smart" like, her;

(Punctuation, is; fun!)

Reading Strategy: **Inferencing**

What can you tell about Miss Kinnian from the April 15 entry?

The change in Charlie's writing shows that he is getting smarter.

What is Miss Kinnian teaching Charlie?

Reading Strategy: Inferencing

What details in the April 18 entry show that Charlie has become more intelligent?

Photostated means copied by a machine.

Reading Strategy: Inferencing

What does Charlie realize about Frank and Joe?

April 18 What a dope I am! I didn't even understand what she was talking about. I read the grammar book last night and it explanes the whole thing. Then I saw it was the same way as Miss Kinnian was trying to tell me, but I didn't get it. I got up in the middle of the night, and the whole thing straightened out in my mind.

Miss Kinnian said that the TV working in my sleep helped out. She said I reached a plateau. Thats like the flat top of a hill.

After I figgered out how punctuation worked, I read over all my old Progress Reports from the beginning. Boy, did I have crazy spelling and punctuation! I told Miss Kinnian I ought to go over the pages and fix all the mistakes but she said, "No, Charlie, Dr. Nemur wants them just as they are. That's why he let you keep them after they were photostated, to see your own progress. You're coming along fast, Charlie."

That made me feel good. After the lesson I went down and played with Algernon. We don't race any more.

April 20 I feel sick inside. Not sick like for a doctor, but inside my chest it feels empty like getting punched and a heartburn at the same time.

I wasn't going to write about it, but I guess I got to, because its important. Today was the first time I ever stayed home from work.

Last night Joe Carp and Frank Reilly invited me to a party. There were lots of girls and some men from the factory. I remembered how sick I got last time I drank too much, so I told Joe I didn't want anything to drink. He gave me a plain coke instead. It tasted funny, but I thought it was just a bad taste in my mouth.

We had a lot of fun for a while. Joe said I should dance with Ellen and she would teach me the steps. I fell a few times and I couldn't understand why because no one else was dancing besides Ellen and me. And all the time I was tripping because somebody's foot was always sticking out.

Then when I got up I saw the look on Joe's face and it gave me a funny feeling in my stomack. "He's a scream," one of the girls said. Everybody was laughing.

Frank said, "I ain't laughed so much since we sent him off for the newspaper that night at Muggsy's and ditched him."

"Look at him. His face is red."

"He's blushing. Charlie is blushing."

"Hey, Ellen, what'd you do to Charlie? I never saw him act like that before."

I didn't know what to do or where to turn. Everyone was looking at me and laughing and I felt naked. I wanted to hide myself. I ran out into the street and I threw up. Then I walked home. It's a funny thing I never knew that Joe and Frank and the others liked to have me around all the time to make fun of me.

Now I know what it means when they say "to pull a Charlie Gordon."

I'm ashamed.

Reading Strategy: Inferencing

Why is it important that Charlie is blushing? What does this show?

PROGRESS REPORT 11

April 21 Still didn't go into the factory. I told Mrs. Flynn my landlady to call and tell Mr. Donnegan I was sick. Mrs. Flynn looks at me very funny lately like she's scared of me.

I think it's a good thing about finding out how everybody laughs at me. I thought about it a lot. It's because I'm so dumb and I don't even know when I'm doing something dumb. People think it's funny when a dumb person can't do things the same way they can.

Why do you think Mrs. Flynn might be frightened of Charlie?

Anyway, now I know I'm getting smarter every day. I know punctuation and I can spell good. I like to look up all the hard words in the dictionary and I remember them. I'm reading a lot now, and Miss Kinnian says I read very fast. Sometimes I even understand what I'm reading about, and it stays in my mind. There are times when I can close my eyes and think of a page and it all comes back like a picture.

Besides history, geography and arithmetic, Miss Kinnian said I should start to learn a few foreign languages. Dr. Strauss gave me some more tapes to play while I sleep. I still don't understand how that conscious and unconscious mind works, but Dr. Strauss says not to worry yet. He asked me to promise that when I start learning college subjects next week I wouldn't read any books on psychology—that is, until he gives me permission.

I feel a lot better today, but I guess I'm still a little angry that all the time people were laughing and making fun of me because I wasn't so smart. When I become intelligent like Dr. Strauss says, with three times my I.Q. of 68, then maybe I'll be like everyone else and people will like me and be friendly.

Reading Strategy:
Inferencing

How can you tell that Charlie is learning new ways to think?

I'm not sure what an I.Q. is. Dr. Nemur said it was something that measured how intelligent you were—like a scale in the drugstore weighs pounds. But Dr. Strauss had a big arguement with him and said an I.Q. didn't weigh intelligence at all. He said an I.Q. showed how much intelligence you could get, like the numbers on the outside of a measuring cup. You still had to fill the cup up with stuff.

Then when I asked Burt, who gives me my intelligence tests and works with Algernon, he said that both of them were wrong (only I had to promise not to tell them he said so). Burt says that the I.Q. measures a lot of different things including some of the things you learned already, and it really isn't any good at all.

The average person has an I.Q. of 100. An I.Q. over 140 is considered "genius." I.Q. cannot be measured over 200.

So I still don't know what I.Q. is except that mine is going to be over 200 soon. I didn't want to say anything, but I don't see how if they don't know *what* it is, or *where* it is—I don't see how they know *how much* of it you've got.

Dr. Nemur says I have to take a *Rorshach Test* tomorrow. I wonder what *that* is.

April 22 I found out what a *Rorshach* is. It's the test I took before the operation—the one with the inkblots on the pieces of cardboard. The man who gave me the test was the same one.

I was scared to death of those inkblots. I knew he was going to ask me to find the pictures and I knew I wouldn't be able to. I was thinking to myself, if only there was some way of knowing what kind of pictures were hidden there. Maybe there weren't any pictures at all. Maybe it was just a trick to see if I was dumb enough too look for something that wasn't there. Just thinking about that made me sore at him.

"All right, Charlie," he said, "you've seen these cards before, remember?"

"Of course I remember."

The way I said it, he knew I was angry, and he looked surprised. "Yes, of course. Now I want you to look at this one. What might this be? What do you see on this card? People see all sorts of things in these inkblots. Tell me what it might be for you—what it makes you think of."

I was shocked. That wasn't what I had expected him to say at all. "You mean there are no pictures hidden in those inkblots?"

He frowned and took off his glasses. "What?"

"Pictures. Hidden in the inkblots. Last time you told me that everyone could see them and you wanted me to find them too."

He explained to me that the last time he had used almost the exact same words he was using now. I didn't believe it, and I still have the **suspicion** that he misled me at the time just for the fun of it. Unless—I don't know any more—could I have been *that* feeble-minded?

We went through the cards slowly. One of them looked like a pair of bats tugging at some thing. Another one looked like two men fencing with swords. I imagined all sorts of things. I guess I got carried away. But I didn't trust him any more, and I kept turning them around and even looking on the back to see if there was anything there I was supposed to catch. While he was making his notes, I peeked out of the

Feeble-minded is another term for someone who is not very intelligent.

suspicion a belief, feeling, or thought

corner of my eye to read it. But it was all in code that looked like this:

$$WF + A\ DdF\text{-}Ad\ orig.\ WF\text{-}A$$
$$SF + obj$$

What surprises Charlie about the Rorschach test?

The test still doesn't make sense to me. It seems to me that anyone could make up lies about things that they didn't really see. How could he know I wasn't making a fool of him by mentioning things that I didn't really imagine? Maybe I'll understand it when Dr. Strauss lets me read up on psychology.

April 25 I figured out a new way to line up the machines in the factory, and Mr. Donnegan says it will save him ten thousand dollars a year in labor and increased production. He gave me a $25 bonus.

I wanted to take Joe Carp and Frank Reilly out to lunch to celebrate, but Joe said he had to buy some things for his wife, and Frank said he was meeting his cousin for lunch. I guess it'll take a little time for them to get used to the changes in me. Everybody seems to be frightened of me. When I went over to Amos Borg and tapped him on the shoulder, he jumped up in the air.

People don't talk to me much any more or kid around the way they used to. It makes the job kind of lonely.

April 27 I got up the nerve today to ask Miss Kinnian to have dinner with me tomorrow night to celebrate my bonus.

At first she wasn't sure it was right, but I asked Dr. Strauss and he said it was okay. Dr. Strauss and Dr. Nemur don't seem to be getting along so well. They're arguing all the time. This evening when I came in to ask Dr. Strauss about having dinner with Miss Kinnian, I heard them shouting. Dr. Nemur was saying that it was *his* experiment and his research, and Dr. Strauss was shouting back that he contributed just as much, because he found me through Miss Kinnian and he performed the operation. Dr. Strauss said that someday thousands of neurosurgeons might be using his technique all over the world.

Dr. Nemur wanted to publish the results of the experiment at the end of this month. Dr. Strauss wanted to wait a while longer to be sure. Dr. Strauss said that Dr. Nemur was more interested in the Chair of Psychology at Princeton than he was in the experiment. Dr. Nemur said that Dr. Strauss was nothing but an opportunist who was trying to ride to glory on his coattails.

When I left afterwards, I found myself trembling. I don't know why for sure, but it was as if I'd seen both men clearly for the first time. I remember hearing Burt say that Dr. Nemur had a **shrew** of a wife who was pushing him all the time to get things published so that he could become famous. Burt said that the dream of her life was to have a big shot husband.

Was Dr. Strauss really trying to ride on his coattails?

shrew a mouselike mammal with a long snout and brownish fur

Reading Strategy: Inferencing

Why do Charlie's co-workers behave differently toward him?

Reading Strategy: Inferencing

Why do you think the doctors are arguing about Charlie's progress?

Neurosurgeons are doctors who operate on the brain and spine.

A *chair* is a person who is in charge of a department or a group.
An *opportunist* is someone who tries to take advantage of someone else.

Charlie is clearly becoming more intelligent. What do you think will happen in the rest of the story?

April 28 I don't understand why I never noticed how beautiful Miss Kinnian really is. She has brown eyes and feathery brown hair that comes to the top of her neck. She's only thirty-four! I think from the beginning I had the feeling that she was an unreachable genius—and very, very old. Now, every time I see her she grows younger and more lovely.

We had dinner and a long talk. When she said that I was coming along so fast that soon I'd be leaving her behind, I laughed.

"It's true, Charlie. You're already a better reader than I am. You can read a whole page at a glance while I can take in only a few lines at a time. And you remember every single thing you read. I'm lucky if I can recall the main thoughts and the general meaning."

"I don't feel intelligent. There are so many things I don't understand."

"You've got to be a *little* patient. You're accomplishing in days and weeks what it takes normal people to do in half a lifetime. That's what makes it so amazing. You're like a giant sponge now, soaking things in. Facts, figures, general knowledge. And soon you'll begin to connect them, too. You'll see how the different branches of learning are related. There are many levels, Charlie, like steps on a giant ladder that take you up higher and higher to see more and more of the world around you.

"I can see only a little bit of that, Charlie, and I won't go much higher than I am now, but you'll keep climbing up and up, and see more and more, and each step will open new worlds that you never even knew existed." She frowned. "I hope . . . I just hope to God—"

"What?"

What do you think Miss Kinnian fears at this point?

"Never mind, Charles. I just hope I wasn't wrong to **advise** you to go into this in the first place."

advise to give an opinion about what should be done

I laughed. "How could that be? It worked, didn't it? Even Algernon is still smart."

We sat there silently for a while and I knew what she was thinking about as she watched me toying with the chain of my rabbit's foot and my keys. I didn't want to think of that possibility any more than elderly people want to think of death. I *knew* that this was only the beginning. I knew what she meant about levels because I'd seen some of them already. The thought of leaving her behind made me sad.

I'm in love with Miss Kinnian.

PROGRESS REPORT 12

April 30 I've quit my job with Donnegan's Plastic Box Company. Mr. Donnegan insisted that it would be better for all concerned if I left. What did I do to make them hate me so?

The first I knew of it was when Mr. Donnegan showed me the **petition**. Eight hundred and forty names, everyone connected with the factory, except Fanny Girden. Scanning the list quickly, I saw at once that hers was the only missing name. All the rest demanded that I be fired.

Joe Carp and Frank Reilly wouldn't talk to me about it. No one else would either, except Fanny. She was one of the few people I'd known who set her mind to something and believed it no matter what the rest of the world proved, said or did—and Fanny did not believe that I should have been fired. She had been against the petition on principle and despite the pressure and threats she'd held out.

"Which don't mean to say," she remarked, "that I don't think there's something mighty strange about you, Charlie. Them changes. I don't know. You used to be a good, dependable, ordinary man—not too bright maybe, but honest. Who knows what you done to yourself to get so smart all of a sudden. Like everybody around here's been saying, Charlie, it's not right."

petition a written request for a right or privilege, often signed by many people

How are Charlie's feelings toward Miss Kinnian changing?

Reading Strategy: Inferencing

Why do you think Charlie's co-workers want to have him fired?

"But how can you say that, Fanny? What's wrong with a man becoming intelligent and wanting to acquire knowledge and understanding of the world around him?"

She stared down at her work, and I turned to leave. Without looking at me, she said: "It was evil when Eve listened to the snake and ate from the tree of knowledge. It was evil when she saw that she was naked. If not for that none of us would ever have to grow old and sick, and die."

In the Bible, Eve ate a fruit that caused her to sin. According to Christian beliefs, this was the world's first sin.

Once again now I have the feeling of shame burning inside me. This intelligence has driven a wedge between me and all the people I once knew and loved. Before, they laughed at me and **despised** me for my ignorance and dullness; now, they hate me for my knowledge and understanding. What do they want of me?

despised hated

They've driven me out of the factory. Now I'm more alone than ever before . . .

May 15 Dr. Strauss is very angry at me for not having written any progress reports in two weeks. He's **justified** because the lab is now paying me a regular salary. I told him I was too busy thinking and reading. When I pointed out that writing was such a slow process that it made me impatient with my poor handwriting, he suggested that I learn to type. It's much easier to write now because I can type nearly seventy-five words a minute. Dr. Strauss continually reminds me of the need to speak and write simply so that people will be able to understand me.

I'll try to review all the things that happened to me during the last two weeks. Algernon and I were presented to the American Psychological Association sitting in convention with the World Psychological Association last Tuesday. We created quite a sensation. Dr. Nemur and Dr. Strauss were proud of us.

I suspect that Dr. Nemur, who is sixty—ten years older than Dr. Strauss—finds it necessary to see **tangible** results of his work. Undoubtedly the result of pressure by Mrs. Nemur.

Contrary to my earlier impressions of him, I realize that Dr. Nemur is not at all a genius. He has a very good mind, but it struggles under the **specter** of self-doubt. He wants people to take him for a genius. Therefore, it is important for him to feel that his work is accepted by the world. I believe that Dr. Nemur was afraid of further delay because he worried that someone else might make a discovery along these lines and take the credit from him.

Dr. Strauss on the other hand might be called a genius, although I feel that his areas of knowledge are too limited. He was educated in the tradition of narrow **specialization**; the

> How does Charlie feel about his doctors at this point?

---

justified gave a good reason for

tangible able to be touched or felt

contrary completely different; opposite

specter something that causes fear or dread

specialization the pursuit of a special type of study or work

broader aspects of background were **neglected** far more than necessary—even for a neurosurgeon.

I was shocked to learn that the only ancient languages he could read were Latin, Greek and Hebrew, and that he knows almost nothing of mathematics beyond the elementary levels of the calculus of variations. When he admitted this to me, I found myself almost annoyed. It was as if he'd hidden this part of himself in order to deceive me, pretending—as do many people I've discovered—to be what he is not. No one I've ever known is what he appears to be on the surface.

Dr. Nemur appears to be uncomfortable around me. Sometimes when I try to talk to him, he just looks at me strangely and turns away. I was angry at first when Dr. Strauss told me I was giving Dr. Nemur an inferiority complex. I thought he was mocking me and I'm oversensitive at being made fun of.

How was I to know that a highly respected psychoexperimentalist like Nemur was unacquainted with Hindustani and Chinese? It's absurd when you consider the work that is being done in India and China today in the very field of his study.

I asked Dr. Strauss how Nemur could **refute** Rahajamati's attack on his method and results if Nemur couldn't even read them in the first place. That strange look on Dr. Strauss' face can mean only one of two things. Either he doesn't want to tell Nemur what they're saying in India, or else—and this worries me—Dr. Strauss doesn't know either. I must be careful to speak and write clearly and simply so that people won't laugh.

May 18 I am very disturbed. I saw Miss Kinnian last night for the first time in over a week. I tried to avoid all discussions of intellectual **concepts** and to keep the conversation on a simple, everyday level, but she just stared at

Charlie is becoming more intelligent than his doctors. He already knows more about mathematics and foreign languages than they do.

An *inferiority complex* is a feeling of not being as smart as everyone else.

Hindustani is a language of northern India.

neglected gave too little care or attention	**refute** prove false	**concepts** ideas

me blankly and asked me what I meant about the mathematical variance equivalent in Dorbermann's *Fifth Concerto.*

When I tried to explain she stopped me and laughed. I guess I got angry, but I suspect I'm approaching her on the wrong level. No matter what I try to discuss with her, I am unable to communicate. I must review Vrostadt's equations on *Levels of Semantic Progression.* I find that I don't communicate with people much any more. Thank God for books and music and things I can think about. I am alone in my apartment at Mrs. Flynn's boarding house most of the time and **seldom** speak to anyone.

May 20 I would not have noticed the new dishwasher, a boy of about sixteen, at the corner diner where I take my evening meals if not for the **incident** of the broken dishes.

They crashed to the floor, shattering and sending bits of white china under the tables. The boy stood there, dazed and frightened, holding the empty tray in his hand. The whistles and catcalls from the customers (the cries of "hey, there go the profits!" ... "*Mazeltov!*" ... and "well, he didn't work here very long ..." which **invariably** seems to follow the breaking of glass or dishware in a public restaurant) all seemed to confuse him.

When the owner came to see what the excitement was about, the boy **cowered** as if he expected to be struck and threw up his arms as if to ward off the blow.

"All right! All right, you dope," shouted the owner, "don't just stand there! Get the broom and sweep that mess up. A broom ... a broom, you idiot! It's in the kitchen. Sweep up all the pieces."

The boy saw that he was not going to be punished. His frightened expression disappeared and he smiled and hummed as he came back with the broom to sweep the floor.

Why is it ironic that people laugh at Charlie now?

Reading Strategy: **Inferencing** How would this entry be different from Miss Kinnian's point of view?

Charlie has become so intelligent that people no longer understand what he is talking about.

Mazel tov means "good luck" in Hebrew.

seldom not often	**incident** an event; something that happens	**invariably** having no change
		cowered bent in fear

A few of the **rowdier** customers kept up the remarks, amusing themselves at his expense.

"Here, sonny, over here there's a nice piece behind you . . ."

"C'mon, do it again . . ."

"He's not so dumb. It's easier to break 'em than to wash 'em . . ."

As his **vacant** eyes moved across the crowd of amused onlookers, he slowly mirrored their smiles and finally broke into an uncertain grin at the joke which he obviously did not understand.

I felt sick inside as I looked at his dull, **vacuous** smile, the wide, bright eyes of a child, uncertain but eager to please. They were laughing at him because he was mentally retarded.

And I had been laughing at him too.

Suddenly, I was furious at myself and all those who were smirking at him. I jumped up and shouted, "Shut up! Leave him alone! It's not his fault he can't understand! He can't help what he is! But . . . he's still a human being!"

The room grew silent. I cursed myself for losing control and creating a scene. I tried not to look at the boy as I paid my check and walked out without touching my food. I felt ashamed for both of us.

How strange it is that people of honest feelings and **sensibility**, who would not take advantage of a man born without arms or legs or eyes—how such people think nothing of abusing a man born with low intelligence. It **infuriated** me to think that not too long ago I, like this boy, had foolishly played the clown.

And I had almost forgotten.

I'd hidden the picture of the old Charlie Gordon from myself because now that I was intelligent it was something that had to be pushed out of my mind. But today in looking at that boy, for the first time I saw what I had been. *I was just like him!*

Reading Strategy: Inferencing

Why is the dishwasher at the restaurant important to the story?

What is Charlie beginning to understand?

rowdier noisier	**vacuous** empty	**infuriated** made very angry
vacant empty; not filled	**sensibility** feeling or emotion	

Only a short time ago, I learned that people laughed at me. Now I can see that unknowingly I joined with them in laughing at myself. That hurts most of all.

I have often reread my progress reports and seen the **illiteracy**, the childish **naïvete**, the mind of low intelligence peering from a dark room, through the keyhole, at the dazzling light outside. I see that even in my dullness I knew that I was inferior, and that other people had something I lacked—something denied me. In my mental blindness, I thought that it was somehow connected with the ability to read and write, and I was sure that if I could get those skills I would automatically have intelligence too.

Even a feeble-minded man wants to be like other men.

A child may not know how to feed itself, or what to eat, yet it knows of hunger.

This then is what I was like. I never knew. Even with my gift of intellectual awareness, I never really knew.

This day was good for me. Seeing the past more clearly, I have decided to use my knowledge and skills to work in the field of increasing human intelligence levels. Who is better **equipped** for this work? Who else has lived in both worlds? These are my people. Let me use my gift to do something for them.

Tomorrow, I will discuss with Dr. Strauss the manner in which I can work in this area. I may be able to help him work out the problems of widespread use of the technique which was used on me. I have several good ideas of my own.

There is so much that might be done with this technique. If I could be made into a genius, what about thousands of others like myself? What fantastic levels might be achieved by using this technique on normal people? On *geniuses*?

There are so many doors to open. I am **impatient** to begin.

> What has Charlie learned about himself?

> Recall from the beginning of the story why Charlie may not be able to help these people.

---

illiteracy inability to read

naïvete having little understanding of how things really are

equipped prepared; ready

impatient not able to wait; eager

PROGRESS REPORT 13

May 23 It happened today. Algernon bit me. I visited the lab to see him as I do occasionally, and when I took him out of his cage, he snapped at my hand. I put him back and watched him for a while. He was unusually disturbed and **vicious**.

May 24 Burt, who is in charge of the experimental animals, tells me that Algernon is changing. He is less cooperative; he refuses to run the maze any more; general motivation has decreased. And he hasn't been eating. Everyone is upset about what this may mean.

May 25 They've been feeding Algernon, who now refuses to work the shifting-lock problem. Everyone identifies me with Algernon. In a way we're both the first of our kind. They're all pretending that Algernon's behavior is not necessarily significant for me. But it's hard to hide the fact that some of the other animals who were used in this experiment are showing strange behavior.

Dr. Strauss and Dr. Nemur have asked me not to come to the lab any more. I know what they're thinking but I can't accept it. I am going ahead with my plans to carry their research forward. With all due respect to both of these fine scientists, I am well aware of their limitations. If there is an answer, I'll have to find it out for myself. Suddenly, time has become very important to me.

May 29 I have been given a lab of my own and permission to go ahead with the research. I'm on to something. Working day and night. I've had a cot moved into the lab. Most of my writing time is spent on the notes which I keep in a separate folder, but from time to time I feel it necessary to put down my moods and my thoughts out of sheer habit.

Reading Strategy:
Inferencing

Why is everyone upset about the changes in Algernon?

Reading Strategy:
Inferencing

What do the changes in Algernon suggest will happen to Charlie?

vicious very violent or cruel

I find the *calculus of intelligence* to be a fascinating study. Here is the place for the application of all the knowledge I have **acquired**. In a sense it's the problem I've been concerned with all my life.

May 31 Dr. Strauss thinks I'm working too hard. Dr. Nemur says I'm trying to cram a lifetime of research and thought into a few weeks. I know I should rest, but I'm driven on by something inside that won't let me stop. I've got to find the reason for the sharp **regression** in Algernon. I've got to know *if* and *when* it will happen to me.

June 4

Letter to Dr. Strauss *(copy)*
Dear Dr. Strauss:

Under separate cover I am sending you a copy of my report entitled, "The Algernon-Gordon Effect: A Study of Structure and Function of Increased Intelligence," which I would like to have you read and have published.

As you see, my experiments are completed. I have included in my report all of my formulae, as well as mathematical analysis in the **appendix**. Of course, these should be **verified**.

Because of its importance to both you and Dr. Nemur (and need I say to myself, too?) I have checked and rechecked my results a dozen times in the hope of finding an error. I am sorry to say the results must stand. Yet for the sake of science, I am grateful for the little bit that I here add to the knowledge of the function of the human mind and of the laws governing the artificial increase of human intelligence.

> *Reading Strategy: Inferencing*
>
> What parts of this letter show that Charlie is as intelligent as the doctors?

---

acquired gained

regression a return to an earlier stage or condition

appendix added information at the end of a book or document

verified proved to be true

I recall your once saying to me that an experimental *failure* or the *disproving* of a theory was as important to the advancement of learning as a success would be. I know now that this is true. I am sorry, however, that my own contribution to the field must rest upon the ashes of the work of two men I regard so highly.

Yours truly,
Charles Gordon

encl.: rept.

June 5 I must not become emotional. The facts and the results of my experiments are clear, and the more sensational aspects of my own rapid climb cannot **obscure** the fact that the tripling of intelligence by the surgical technique developed by Drs. Strauss and Nemur must be viewed as having little or no practical **applicability** (at the present time) to the increase of human intelligence.

As I review the records and data on Algernon, I see that although he is still in his physical infancy, he has regressed mentally. Motor activity is impaired; there is a general reduction of glandular activity; there is an **accelerated** loss of coordination.

There are also strong indications of progressive **amnesia**.

As will be seen by my report, these and other physical and mental **deterioration** syndromes can be predicted with statistically significant results by the application of my formula.

The surgical stimulus to which we were both subjected has resulted in an **intensification** and acceleration of all mental processes. The **unforeseen** development, which I have taken the liberty of calling the "Algernon-Gordon Effect," is the logical extension of the entire intelligence speedup.

Motor activity is movement and physical control of the body.

Restate what Charlie is saying in your own words. What is happening to him and Algernon?

obscure hide	**amnesia** a loss of memory	**intensification** strengthening
applicability use	**deterioration** a lowering of quality or value	**unforeseen** not expected
accelerated increased		

The **hypothesis** here proven may be described simply in the following terms: Artificially increased intelligence deteriorates at a rate of time directly proportional to the quantity of the increase.

I feel that this, in itself, is an important discovery.

As long as I am able to write, I will continue to record my thoughts in these progress reports. It is one of my few pleasures. However, by all indications, my own mental deterioration will be very rapid.

I have already begun to notice signs of emotional **instability** and forgetfulness, the first symptoms of the burnout.

June 10 Deterioration progressing. I have become absent-minded. Algernon died two days ago. Dissection shows my predictions were right. His brain had decreased in weight and there was a general smoothing out of cerebral convolutions as well as a deepening and broadening of brain fissures.

> *Dissection* means cutting apart. *Cerebral convolutions* are folds in the brain. *Fissures* are cracks.

I guess the same thing is or will soon be happening to me. Now that it's definite, I don't want it to happen.

I put Algernon's body in a cheese box and buried him in the back yard. I cried.

> How does the first-person point of view make Charlie's experiences more interesting to the reader?

June 15 Dr. Strauss came to see me again. I wouldn't open the door and I told him to go away. I want to be left to myself. I have become touchy and **irritable**. I feel the darkness closing in. I keep telling myself how important this **introspective** journal will be.

It's a strange sensation to pick up a book that you've read and enjoyed just a few months ago and discover that you don't remember it. I remembered how great I thought John Milton was, but when I picked up *Paradise Lost* I couldn't understand it at all. I got so angry I threw the book across the room.

> John Milton (1608–1674) was a British poet who wrote *Paradise Lost*.

hypothesis a theory	**irritable** easily bothered	**introspective** thoughtful; examining one's own thoughts and feelings
instability unsteadiness		

I've got to try to hold on to some of it. Some of the things I've learned. Oh, God, please don't take it all away.

June 19 Sometimes, at night, I go out for a walk. Last night I couldn't remember where I lived. A policeman took me home. I have the strange feeling that this has all happened to me before—a long time ago. I keep telling myself I'm the only person in the world who can describe what's happening to me.

> What is the irony in the last sentence of this paragraph?

June 21 Why can't I remember? I've got to fight. I lie in bed for days and I don't know who or where I am. Then it all comes back to me in a flash. Fugues of amnesia. Symptoms of senility—second childhood. I can watch them coming on. It's so cruelly logical. I learned so much and so fast. Now my mind is deteriorating rapidly. I won't let it happen. I'll fight it. I can't help thinking of the boy in the restaurant, the blank expression, the silly smile, the people laughing at him. No— please—not that again . . .

> *Fugues of amnesia* are periods of memory loss.

June 22 I'm forgetting things that I learned recently. It seems to be following the classic pattern—the last things learned are the first things forgotten. Or is that the pattern? I'd better look it up again . . .

I reread my paper on the "Algernon-Gordon Effect" and I get the strange feeling that it was written by someone else. There are parts I don't even understand.

Motor activity impaired. I keep tripping over things, and it becomes increasingly difficult to type.

June 23 I've given up using the typewriter completely. My coordination is bad. I feel that I'm moving slower and slower. Had a terrible shock today. I picked up a copy of an article I used in my research, Krueger's "Über psychische Ganzheit," to see if it would help me understand what I had done. First I thought there was something wrong with my eyes. Then I realized I could no longer read German. I tested myself in other languages. All gone.

June 30 A week since I dared to write again. It's slipping away like sand through my fingers. Most of the books I have are too hard for me now. I get angry with them because I know that I read and understood them just a few weeks ago.

I keep telling myself I must keep writing these reports so that somebody will know what is happening to me. But it gets harder to form the words and remember spellings. I have to look up even simple words in the dictionary now and it makes me impatient with myself.

Dr. Strauss comes around almost every day, but I told him I wouldn't see or speak to anybody. He feels guilty. They all do. But I don't blame anyone. I knew what might happen. But how it hurts.

July 7 I don't know where the week went. Todays Sunday I know because I can see through my window people going to church. I think I stayed in bed all week but I remember Mrs. Flynn bringing food to me a few times. I keep saying over and over Ive got to do something but then I forget or maybe its just easier not to do what I say Im going to do.

What are some signs that Charlie is losing intelligence?

Reading Strategy:
Inferencing
How do you think Charlie feels about not being able to read German? Why?

Reading Strategy:
Inferencing
Why do you think the doctors feel guilty?

I think of my mother and father a lot these days. I found a picture of them with me taken at a beach. My father has a big ball under his arm and my mother is holding me by the hand. I dont remember them the way they are in the picture. All I remember is my father arguing with mom about money.

He never shaved much and he used to scratch my face when he hugged me. He said he was going to take me to see cows on a farm once but he never did. He never kept his promises . . .

July 10 My landlady Mrs Flynn is very worried about me. She said she doesnt like loafers. If Im sick its one thing, but if Im a loafer thats another thing and she wont have it. I told her I think Im sick.

Loafers are lazy people.

I try to read a little bit every day, mostly stories, but sometimes I have to read the same thing over and over again because I dont know what it means. And its hard to write. I know I should look up all the words in the dictionary but its so hard and Im so tired all the time.

Then I got the idea that I would only use the easy words instead of the long hard ones. That saves time. I put flowers on Algernons grave about once a week. Mrs. Flynn thinks Im crazy to put flowers on a mouses grave but I told her that Algernon was special.

What does Charlie's style of writing show?

July 14 Its sunday again. I dont have anything to do to keep me busy now because my television set is broke and I dont have any money to get it fixed. (I think I lost this months check from the lab. I dont remember)

I get awful headaches and asperin doesnt help me much. Mrs. Flynn knows Im really sick and she feels very sorry for me. Shes a wonderful woman whenever someone is sick.

July 22 Mrs. Flynn called a strange doctor to see me. She was afraid I was going to die. I told the doctor I wasnt too sick and that I only forget sometimes. He asked me did I have any friends or relatives and I said no I dont have any. I told him I had a friend called Algernon once but he was a mouse and we used to run races together. He looked at me kind of funny like he thought I was crazy.

He smiled when I told him I used to be a genius. He talked to me like I was a baby and he winked at Mrs Flynn. I got mad and chased him out because he was making fun of me the way they all used to.

How does the doctor anger Charlie?

July 24 I have no more money and Mrs Flynn says I got to go to work somewhere and pay the rent because I havent paid for over two months. I dont know any work but the job I used to have at Donnegans Plastic Box Company. I dont want to go back there because they all knew me when I was smart and maybe they'll laugh at me. But I dont know what else to do to get money.

July 25 I was looking at some of my old progress reports and its very funny but I cant read what I wrote. I can make out some of the words but they dont make sense.

Miss Kinnian came to the door but I said go away I dont want to see you. She cried and I cried too but I wouldnt let her in because I didnt want her to laugh at me. I told her I didn't like her any more. I told her I didn't want to be smart any more. Thats not true. I still love her and I still want to be smart but I had to say that so shed go away. She gave Mrs. Flynn money to pay the rent. I dont want that. I got to get a job.

Please . . . please let me not forget how to read and write . . .

July 27 Mr. Donnegan was very nice when I came back and asked him for my old job of janitor. First he was very suspicious but I told him what happened to me then he looked very sad and put his hand on my shoulder and said Charlie Gordon you got guts.

Everybody looked at me when I came downstairs and started working in the toilet sweeping it out like I used to. I told myself Charlie if they make fun of you dont get sore because you remember their not so smart as you once thot they were. And besides they were once your friends and if

To *get sore* means to become upset.

they laughed at you that doesnt mean anything because they liked you too.

One of the new men who came to work there after I went away made a nasty crack he said hey Charlie I hear your a very smart fella a real quiz kid. Say something intelligent. I felt bad but Joe Carp came over and grabbed him by the shirt and said leave him alone or Ill break your neck. I didnt expect Joe to take my part so I guess hes really my friend.

Later Frank Reilly came over and said Charlie if anybody bothers you or trys to take advantage of you call me or Joe and we will set em straight. I said thanks Frank and I got choked up so I had to turn around and go into the supply room so he wouldnt see me cry. Its good to have friends.

Reading Strategy: **Inferencing**

Why do Charlie's co-workers treat him kindly now?

July 28 I did a dumb thing today I forgot I wasnt in Miss Kinnians class at the adult center any more like I use to be. I went in and sat down in my old seat in the back of the room and she looked at me funny and she said Charles. I dint remember she ever called me that before only Charlie so I said hello Miss Kinnian Im ready for my lesin today only I lost my reader that we was using. She startid to cry and run out of the room and everybody looked at me and I saw they wasnt the same pepul who use to be in my class.

Then all of a suddin I rememberd some things about the operashun and me getting smart and I said holy smoke I reely pulled a Charlie Gordon that time. I went away before she come back to the room.

Why does Charlie want to leave New York?

Thats why Im going away from New York for good. I dont want to do nothing like that agen. I dont want Miss Kinnian to feel sorry for me. Evry body feels sorry at the factery and I dont want that eather so Im going someplace where nobody knows that Charlie Gordon was once a genus and now he cant even reed a book or rite good.

Im taking a cuple of books along and even if I cant reed them Ill practise hard and maybe I wont forget every thing I lerned. If I try reel hard maybe Ill be a littel bit smarter then I was before the operashun. I got my rabits foot and my luky penny and maybe they will help me.

Reading Strategy: **Inferencing**

Do you think Charlie will be able to get intelligent again? Why or why not?

If you ever reed this Miss Kinnian dont be sorry for me Im glad I got a second chanse to be smart becaus I lerned a lot of things that I never even new were in this world and Im grateful that I saw it all for a littel bit. I dont know why Im dumb agen or what I did wrong maybe its becaus I dint try hard enuff. But if I try and practis very hard maybe Ill get a littl smarter and know what all the words are. I remember a littel bit how nice I had a feeling with the blue book that has the torn cover when I red it. Thats why Im gonna keep trying to get smart so I can have that feeling agen. Its a good feeling to know things and be smart. I wish I had it rite now if I did I woud sit down and reed all the time. Anyway I bet Im the first dumb person in the world who ever found out somthing importent for sience. I remember I did somthing but I dont remember what. So I gess its like I did it for all the dumb pepul like me.

Goodbye Miss Kinnian and Dr Strauss and evreybody. And P.S. please tell Dr Nemur not to be such a grouch when pepul laff at him and he woud have more frends. Its easy to make frends if you let pepul laff at you. Im going to have lots of frends where I go.

P.P.S. Please if you get a chanse put some flowrs on Algernons grave in the bak yard . . .

> Did you think the story would end this way? Explain.

Flowers for Algernon   *by Daniel Keyes*

Directions Choose the letter of the best answer or write the answer using complete sentences.

Comprehension: Identifying Facts

1. How old is Charlie when the story opens?

   A 18   **C** 37

   B 25   **D** 55

2. What is the first test the doctors give Charlie?

   A They ask him to interpret ink blots.

   B They make him train a white rat.

   C They give him a complete physical exam.

   D They have him run a maze.

3. Who is Miss Kinnian?

4. Who is Algernon?

5. What kind of operation does Charlie have?

6. By how much do the doctors promise they can raise Charlie's I.Q?

7. Where does Charlie work? What does he do?

8. How do the people at the factory force Charlie to quit his job?

9. Why does Mrs. Flynn call a doctor to see Charlie?

10. Why does Charlie want to leave New York at the end of the story?

Comprehension: Putting Ideas Together

11. Why does Charlie go to night school?

    A He admires the teacher.

    B He wants to be more intelligent.

    C He is trying to learn to speak German.

    D He wants to make some new friends.

12. Why is Charlie most likely chosen for the experiment?

    A He has the money to pay for the surgery.

    B He is very good at solving puzzles.

    C He is highly motivated.

    D He has a big family who will take care of him.

13. What does it mean to "pull a Charlie Gordon"?

14. How do the doctors increase Charlie's intelligence?

15. Explain how the changes in Charlie are similar to those in Algernon.

16. How do Charlie's feelings for Miss Kinnian change?

17. What joke do Charlie's co-workers play on him?

18. What does Charlie begin to notice about Dr. Nemur and Dr. Strauss?

19. What does Charlie do when the customers make fun of the dishwasher at the restaurant?

20. What is the "Algernon-Gordon Effect"?

Understanding Literature: Point of View

If the person telling the story is also a character, the story is written in the first person. First-person narrators use the pronouns *I* and *we*. A first-person narrator can make readers feel as if they are inside the story. If the narrator is not a character, the author is writing in third person. A third-person narrator uses the pronouns *he, she, it,* and *they.* This narrator sees the story from the outside. The third-person narrator can see events from more than one character's point of view.

21. Why do you think the author chose to tell the story in the first-person point of view?

22. How would the story be different if told from Miss Kinnian's point of view?

23. How would the story be different if told from the third-person point of view?

24. How are the journal entries related to the point of view in the story?

25. What can you tell about Miss Kinnian from the way she treats Charlie?

Critical Thinking

26. Was being part of the experiment good for Charlie? Why or why not?

27. When do you realize that Charlie's intelligence is not going to last?

28. What will happen to Charlie? How do you know?

Thinking Creatively

29. Do you think Charlie should have had the operation? Explain.

30. What does intelligence mean to you? Explain.

After Reading **continued on next page**

Flowers for Algernon   *by Daniel Keyes*

 Grammar Check

The tense of a verb shows the time of an action or a condition. The three main tenses are *present*, *past*, and *future*.

Examples:

- I **walk** to school. (present)
- I **rode** my bike yesterday. (past)
- I **will run** in the track meet tomorrow. (future)

Find five verbs in "Flowers for Algernon." Write the sentence containing each verb on a sheet of paper. Then identify the tense of each verb.

 Vocabulary Builder

In an analogy, two pairs of words are connected in the same way. To complete an analogy, figure out what the two sets of words have in common. For example: *vacant* is to *empty* as *complete* is to *full*.

Use one of the following vocabulary words to complete each analogy. *Vocabulary Words:* introspective, refute, obscure

1 *Accept* is to *reject* as *support* is to _____.

2 *Create* is to *destroy* as *reveal* is to _____.

3 *Anxious* is to *worried* as *thoughtful* is to _____.

 Writing on Your Own

Write dialogue for a movie scene based on "Flowers for Algernon." Choose a scene from the story. Imagine details and conversations the author left out. Then write the dialogue. Use words that seem natural for each character.

 Listening and Speaking

Work with a partner to role-play an interview between a television reporter and someone from the story who knows Charlie. During the interview, listen carefully and give appropriate responses. Consider these: What changes did you notice in Charlie's behavior? Is it right to use people in experiments like this?

Research and Technology

Use library and Internet resources to learn more about how scientists study human intelligence. Choose two articles on the subject and write a paragraph to tell what each is about. Include the main idea of each article and at least two important details. Include a quotation from each article that shows the author's point of view.

Thank You, M'am   by Langston Hughes

About the Author

Langston Hughes began writing poetry when he was in the eighth grade. His classmates recognized his talent and elected him "Class Poet." His father, however, did not think Hughes could make a living as a writer. He wanted his son to get a regular job. Hughes went to Columbia University to study engineering, but he soon dropped out of the program. He still wanted to be a poet.

Langston Hughes
1902–1967

In 1923, Hughes traveled to Senegal, Nigeria, Cameroon, the Belgian Congo, Angola, and Guinea in Africa. Then he went to Italy, France, Russia, and Spain. He loved listening to blues and jazz while writing poetry during his travels. These experiences brought the rhythm of jazz to his writing. Hughes returned to Harlem in New York in 1924.

His first published poem was "The Negro Speaks of Rivers." In 1926, his first collection of poems was published. Hughes went on to have a long career as a writer. He wrote poetry, short stories, children's books, and even an opera. Throughout the 1920s and 1930s, Hughes was one of the leaders of the Harlem Renaissance. This was an exciting period of creativity in literature and the arts.

Objectives

- ◆ To read and understand a short story that contains description
- ◆ To identify the theme of a literary work
- ◆ To identify the protagonist and antagonist in a story

About the Selection

We know from his other books, plays, and poems that Langston Hughes believed in family. It was with these ideas in mind that Hughes probably wrote "Thank You, M'am." The story tells about a young boy and an older woman who meet in an unexpected way.

Hughes wrote this story more than 50 years ago. You may notice little details about the way life was during that time. Even so, the story's message about making choices is still important today.

***Before Reading* continued on next page**

Thank You, M'am   *by Langston Hughes*

description
a written picture of the characters, setting, and events of a work of literature

protagonist the main character of a story

antagonist the person or animal who struggles against the main character of a story

theme the main idea of a literary work

Literary Terms In "Thank You, M'am," the author uses **description,** or a written picture. This description helps to create an image of the characters and the setting. The two characters in the story are a young boy and an older woman. The woman, or the **protagonist,** is the main character of the story. The young boy, the **antagonist,** is the person who is struggling against the main character. As the story unfolds, an important **theme** comes through. Theme is the main idea of a literary work. It usually expresses an important message or idea about life and human nature.

Reading on Your Own When you read, you make inferences about information. Inferences are based on ideas that the writer suggests but does not state directly. Making inferences is a way of "reading between the lines" of a story. As you read, connect story events to their reasons and results. Ask yourself what meaning the author is suggesting by making these connections.

Writing on Your Own "Thank You, M'am" teaches a surprising lesson about kindness and trust from a stranger. Write three sentences explaining what someone needs to do to win your trust.

Vocabulary Focus As you read, pay close attention to the dialogue. Do the characters use the same kind of words you use when you talk? How would you rewrite the sentences that do not match your own way of speaking?

Think Before You Read Imagine that someone gave you $100. What would you do with the money? Why?

Thank You, M'am

Minnie,
William Johnson,
1930

She was a large woman with a large purse that had everything in it but a hammer and nails. It had a long strap, and she carried it slung across her shoulder. It was about eleven o'clock at night, dark, and she was walking alone, when a boy ran up behind her and tried to snatch her purse. The strap broke with the sudden single tug the boy gave it from behind. But the boy's weight and the weight of the purse combined caused him to lose his balance. Instead of taking off full blast as he had hoped, the boy fell on his back on the sidewalk and his legs flew up. The large woman simply turned around and kicked him right square in his blue-jeaned sitter. Then she reached down, picked the boy up by his shirt front, and shook him until his teeth rattled.

After that the woman said, "Pick up my pocketbook, boy, and give it here."

She still held him tightly. But she bent down enough to permit him to stoop and pick up her purse. Then she said, "Now ain't you ashamed of yourself?"

As you read, think about how you would deal with someone who tried to steal something from you.

Reading Strategy:
Inferencing

What can you tell about the woman? What details support your view?

Firmly gripped by his shirt front, the boy said, "Yes'm."

The woman said, "What did you want to do it for?"

The boy said, "I didn't aim to."

She said, "You a lie!"

By that time two or three people passed, stopped, turned to look, and some stood watching.

"If I turn you loose, will you run?" asked the woman.

"Yes'm," said the boy.

"Then I won't turn you loose," said the woman. She did not release him.

"Lady, I'm sorry," whispered the boy.

"Um-hum! Your face is dirty. I got a great mind to wash your face for you. Ain't you got nobody home to tell you to wash your face?"

"No'm," said the boy.

How does the woman view the boy? How does the boy view the woman?

"Then it will get washed this evening," said the large woman, starting up the street, dragging the frightened boy behind her.

He looked as if he were fourteen or fifteen, frail and willow-wild, in tennis shoes and blue jeans.

The woman said, "You ought to be my son. I would teach you right from wrong. Least I can do right now is to wash your face. Are you hungry?"

"No'm," said the being-dragged boy. "I just want you to turn me loose."

"Was I bothering *you* when I turned that corner?" asked the woman.

"No'm."

What did the boy do to put himself "in contact" with Mrs. Jones?

"But you put yourself in **contact** with *me*," said the woman. "If you think that that contact is not going to last awhile, you got another thought coming. When I get through with you, sir, you are going to remember Mrs. Luella Bates Washington Jones."

Sweat popped out on the boy's face and he began to struggle. Mrs. Jones stopped, jerked him around in front of

contact a touching together

her, put a half nelson about his neck, and continued to drag him up the street. When she got to her door, she dragged the boy inside, down a hall, and into a large kitchenette-furnished room at the rear of the house. She switched on the light and left the door open. The boy could hear other roomers laughing and talking in the large house. Some of their doors were open, too, so he knew he and the woman were not alone. The woman still had him by the neck in the middle of her room.

She said, "What is your name?"

"Roger," answered the boy.

"Then, Roger, you go to that sink and wash your face," said the woman, whereupon she turned him loose—at last. Roger looked at the door—looked at the woman—looked at the door—*and went to the sink.*

"Let the water run until it gets warm," she said. "Here's a clean towel."

"You gonna take me to jail?" asked the boy, bending over the sink.

"Not with that face, I would not take you nowhere," said the woman. "Here I am trying to get home to cook me a bite to eat, and you snatch my pocketbook! Maybe you ain't been to your supper either, late as it be. Have you?"

"There's nobody home at my house," said the boy.

"Then we'll eat," said the woman. "I believe you're hungry—or been hungry—to try to snatch my pocketbook!"

"I want a pair of blue **suede** shoes," said the boy.

"Well, you didn't have to snatch *my* pocketbook to get some suede shoes," said Mrs. Luella Bates Washington Jones. "You could of asked me."

"M'am?"

The water dripping from his face, the boy looked at her. There was a long pause. A very long pause. After he had dried his face and not knowing what else to do, dried it again, the boy turned around, wondering what next. The door was open.

Notice the description in this paragraph. You can picture Mrs. Jones dragging the young boy down the street to her house.

suede leather with a soft, velvety surface

Empire State, **Tom Christopher**

He could make a dash for it down the hall. He could run, run, run, *run*!

The woman was sitting on the day bed. After awhile she said, "I were young once and I wanted things I could not get."

There was another long pause. The boy's mouth opened. Then he frowned, not knowing he frowned.

The woman said, "Um-hum! You thought I was going to say *but*, didn't you? You thought I was going to say, *but I didn't snatch people's pocketbooks.* Well, I wasn't going to say that." Pause. Silence. "I have done things, too, which I would not tell you, son—neither tell God, if He didn't already know. Everybody's got something in common. So you set down while I fix us something to eat. You might run that comb through your hair so you will look **presentable**."

In another corner of the room behind a screen was a gas plate and an icebox. Mrs. Jones got up and went behind the screen. The woman did not watch the boy to see if he was

Reading Strategy:
Inferencing

What does this speech tell you about Mrs. Jones's life?

A *gas plate,* also called a hot plate, is a heated iron plate for cooking in small spaces. An *icebox* is an old-fashioned kind of refrigerator.

presentable fit to be seen

going to run now, nor did she watch her purse, which she left behind her on the day bed. But the boy took care to sit on the far side of the room, away from her purse, where he thought she could easily see him out of the corner of her eye if she wanted to. He did not trust the woman *not* to trust him. And he did not want to be **mistrusted** now.

"Do you need somebody to go to the store," asked the boy, "maybe to get some milk or something?"

"Don't believe I do," said the woman, "unless you just want sweet milk yourself. I was going to make cocoa out of this canned milk I got here."

"That will be fine," said the boy.

She heated some lima beans and ham she had in the icebox, made the cocoa, and set the table. The woman did not ask the boy anything about where he lived, or his folks, or anything else that would **embarrass** him. Instead, as they ate, she told him about her job in a hotel beauty shop that stayed open late, what the work was like, and how all kinds of women came in and out, blondes, redheads, and Spanish. Then she cut him a half of her ten-cent cake.

"Eat some more, son," she said.

When they were finished eating, she got up and said, "Now here, take this ten dollars and buy yourself some blue suede shoes. And next time, do not make the mistake of latching onto *my* pocketbook *nor nobody else's*—because shoes got by devilish ways will burn your feet. I got to get my rest now. But from here on in, son, I hope you will behave yourself."

She led him down the hall to the front door and opened it. "Good night! Behave yourself, boy!" she said, looking out into the street as he went down the steps.

The boy wanted to say something other than, "Thank you, m'am," to Mrs. Luella Bates Washington Jones, but although his lips moved, he couldn't even say that as he turned at the foot of the **barren** stoop and looked up at the large woman in the door. Then she shut the door.

Why does Mrs. Jones give Roger money for shoes instead of turning him in?

| **mistrusted** doubted | **embarrass** to make uneasy and ashamed | **barren** unattractive; dull |

Thank You, M'am   by Langston Hughes

Directions Choose the letter of the best answer or write the answer using complete sentences.

Comprehension: Identifying Facts

1. How do Mrs. Jones and Roger meet?
   - **A** Mrs. Jones invites Roger over for dinner.
   - **B** They meet through a foster family program.
   - **C** Roger tries to steal her purse.
   - **D** They both go to the same church.

2. What does Roger think Mrs. Jones is going to do with him?

3. Where does Mrs. Jones take Roger?

Comprehension: Putting Ideas Together

4. What do Mrs. Jones and Roger talk about during their meal?
   - **A** Mrs. Jones's job as a hair stylist
   - **B** Roger's school work
   - **C** their favorite television shows
   - **D** Roger's future

5. What does Roger want to say as he leaves the apartment?

6. What effect might Mrs. Jones's action have on Roger's future behavior?

Understanding Literature: Description

Many authors use description in their writing. This use of writing to create images helps readers get a better picture of the characters, events, and setting. Short stories often do not have quite as much description as novels, mostly because short stories are shorter works. However, even very short poems can still have description. Authors use action verbs, vivid adjectives, and other creative language to create images in their writing.

7. Find one example of description in "Thank You M'am." How does this description add to the story?

8. How would the story be different if the author had not used as much description?

Critical Thinking

9. Do you think Mrs. Jones is wise or foolish to trust Roger? Why?

Thinking Creatively

10. How would you have treated Roger? Explain.

Grammar Check

The perfect tense of a verb describes an action that was or will be completed at a certain time.

- I **have owned** this bike for years. (present perfect)
- I **had owned** one like it years earlier. (past perfect)
- By next year, I **will have owned** three bikes. (future perfect)

Complete each sentence with a phrase or clause containing a perfect tense verb.

1 By the time you get this letter, _____.

2 _____ for a long time.

3 She _____ to all the CDs we have.

 ## Vocabulary Builder

The word *conclusion* is from the Latin word *conclusio*. It was used in Old French and in Middle English. Then it became part of modern English. All of the following words come from German, French, or Spanish: *canyon, guitar, tornado, ballet, salon, dunk, delicatessen, kindergarten*. Work with a partner to guess which language each of them comes from. Write your guesses on a sheet of paper. Then check the word origins in a dictionary to see if your guesses are correct.

 ## Writing on Your Own

Write an essay showing what a theme of "Thank You, M'am" has to do with your own life. First, state the story's theme. Next, brainstorm personal experiences that reflect the same theme. Take notes about the feelings and lessons connected to those experiences. Then tell what you learned from those experiences in your essay.

 ## Listening and Speaking

Have a panel discussion to decide whether Mrs. Jones acted wisely. Choose one person lead the discussion. Be sure that everyone has a chance to share an opinion or point of view. When you are finished, write a paragraph to sum up the panel's decisions.

 ## Media and Viewing

Work with a group of your classmates. Gather information about the Harlem Renaissance. Research the literature, music, and important people of the time period. Then create a multimedia presentation to share with the rest of the class.

Help-Wanted Ads

In Part 2, you are learning about how to make inferences. This skill can be very useful in reading informational materials such as help-wanted ads. Making inferences helps you understand meanings that are not directly stated. You "read between the lines" to gather important details.

About Help-Wanted Ads

A help-wanted ad is an advertisement for a job opening. They are also called *classified ads*. Many companies and businesses place help-wanted ads in the newspapers. Today, more and more companies also post help-wanted ads online. There are even special Web sites for help-wanted ads.

Help-wanted ads provide brief information about the job. The ads also give contact information such as e-mail addresses or telephone numbers. This allows interested people to apply for the job or get additional information.

Most help-wanted ads include some or all of the following features:

- the name and description of the job
- basic requirements for the job, such as education
- experience needed to do the job
- contact information
- hours and days required of the job
- wages and benefits

Reading Skill

A help-wanted ad is a type of informational text. Making inferences as you read can help you understand the ad. Since newspapers often charge by the word, many help-wanted ads are written using abbreviations. These are shortened forms of words.

On the next page you will see a list of abbreviations often used in help-wanted ads.

To run your ad on: **Place before:**

To run your ad on:	Place before:
Monday	2 p.m. Sunday
Tuesday/Wednesday	7 p.m. Monday
Thursday	7 p.m. Tuesday
Friday	8 p.m. Wednesday
Saturday	9 p.m. Thursday
Sunday	8 p.m. Friday

admin.	administrative		lic.	license
aft.	afternoon, after		mfg.	manufacturing
agcy.	agency		min.	minimum
avail.	available		pd.	paid
beg.	beginning		pos.	position
bene.	benefits		pref.	preferred
comp.	computer, compensation, comprehensive		proc.	processing
des.	desired		prog.	program
ed.	education		PT	part time
eves.	evenings		req.	required
exc.	excellent		sal.	salary
FT	full time		trng.	training
grad.	graduate		20K	$20,000
incl.	including/included		wd.	word
ins.	insurance		yrs.	years

> Abbreviations save advertisers money. That's because they take up less space than complete words.

> What do you think the abbreviations *exp'd, nec.,* and *eves. + wknds.* mean?

Portsmouth
Herald
PORTSMOUTHHERALD.COM • FRIDAY, JANUARY 12, 2007 • SECTION E

PORTSMOUTH HERALD • PORTSMOUTH HERALD.COM • FRIDAY, JANUARY 12, 2007

CLASSIFIEDS

> In the first ad, what does the applicant need to be considered for the job?

Help Wanted

COOK exp'd cook w/refs. needed for busy restaurant nr. college. Practical exp. making soups and din. items. 937-555-4542.

SALES
Nat'l co, high comm. New product. No exp. nec. Mon.
215-555-8695.

MAINTENANCE ASS'T. Must have at least 3 yrs. exp. in htg. and AC. All phases of maintenance nec. 937-555-4891.

Servers Lunch & dinner, days & eves. FT/PT. Apply in person at Red Rose Café. 4740 Main St., or call 215-555-0101.

DELIVERY/SET-UP We are looking for people to deliver and set up household goods. Must have good driving rec. Apply in person: 2187 Easton St. EOE.

> What is the main difference between the requirements for the second ad and the third ad?

> In the fourth ad, where does an interested worker apply for the job?

Monitor Your Progress

Directions Choose the letter of the best answer or write the answer using complete sentences.

1. What does the abbreviation *sal.* mean?
   A salmon
   B satisfactory
   C sales
   D salary

2. What is the most common abbreviation for *required*?
   A require.
   B re'qued
   C req.
   D req'uir

3. What are help-wanted ads and why do companies use them?

4. Name three details included in most help-wanted ads.

5. How can making inferences help you read a help-wanted ad?

Writing on Your Own

What is your dream job? Create a help-wanted ad for that job. Your help-wanted ad should be at least three lines long. Use at least four abbreviations in your ad. Be sure to include enough information so someone could apply for the job.

COMPARING LITERARY WORKS | Build Understanding

A Moving Day   by Susan Nunes

Susan Nunes
1943–

Objectives

◆ To read and compare a short story with another work

◆ To identify symbols in a piece of literature

About the Author

Susan Miho Nunes was born in Hilo, Hawaii, and she has ancestors from Japan and Portugal. Because of this, she is interested in the many different cultures in America. This interest often shows in her writing. Nunes moved to Honolulu, Hawaii, when she was a teenager. She now lives in Berkeley, California.

Nunes is the author of *A Small Obligation and Other Stories of Hilo* and several children's books. Her children's books include *Coyote Dreams, To Find the Way,* and *The Last Dragon.* Her short stories have appeared in *Best of Bamboo Ridge*, Graywolf's *Stories of the American Mosaic*, and *Sister Stew.* She has also written a newspaper column for the *San Francisco Chronicle.*

About the Selection

"A Moving Day" is about an elderly Japanese woman who moves from her house. She has lived in the house a long time and has many possessions. The person telling the story is one of the woman's daughters. The storyteller and her sisters help their mother sort through her possessions. As they sort items, the women remember events from their past.

"Thank You, M'am" describes a young boy, Roger, who learns an important lesson. Roger tries to steal a purse to get money for a pair of fancy shoes. As he has dinner with Mrs. Jones, Roger learns a lesson about human kindness. Consider the description used in both stories. Also, think about the theme in "Thank You, M'am" as you read "A Moving Day." Both stories have a theme that deals with human relationships.

Literary Terms In "A Moving Day," the narrator is one of the elderly woman's daughters. The author uses **symbols** throughout the story. A symbol is something that represents something else. For example, a red rose is a common symbol for love. A dove is often a symbol for peace. In "A Moving Day," many different objects stand for different times in the four women's lives.

> **symbol**
> something that represents something else

Reading on Your Own One of the characters in "A Moving Day" is an elderly Japanese American woman. One of the characters in "Thank You, M'am" is an African American hair stylist. What could these two characters have in common? Before you read, brainstorm some ways in which these two characters may be alike.

Writing on Your Own Moving to a new place can be very difficult. When people move, they often give away or throw out many of their things. This can be very difficult if a person has lived somewhere for a long time. If you have moved before, describe how you felt. If you have never moved, tell how you think you would feel if you had to move.

Vocabulary Focus Read the title of the selection. Think about different meanings for the word *moving*. Then write two possible meanings for the title.

Think Before You Read As you read, compare characters by making inferences about their feelings. Think about these questions as you read: What life-changing event does each character face? How does the character feel about this event? How is the character's future likely to be different?

A Moving Day

As you read, think about what you would take with you if you were moving. What do those things symbolize to you?

A *kimono* is a loose, wide-sleeved traditional Japanese dress.

Arthritis is a disease that causes the joints to swell and ache.

Across the street, the bulldozer roars to life. Distracted, my mother looks up from the pile of **embroidered** linen that she has been sorting. She is seventy, tiny and **fragile**, the flesh burned off her shrinking frame. Her hair is gray now—she had never dyed it—and she wears it cut close to her head with the **nape** shaved. Her natural hairline would have been better suited to the kimono worn by women of her mother's generation. She still has a beautiful neck. In recent years she has taken a liking to jeans, cotton smocks, baggy sweaters, and running shoes. When I was a child she wouldn't have been caught dead without her nylons.

Her hands, now large-jointed with arthritis, return to the pile of linen. Her movements always had a no-nonsense quality and ever since I was a child, I have been **wary** of her energy because it was so often driven by **suppressed** anger. Now she is making two stacks, the larger one for us, the smaller for her to keep. There is a finality in the way she places things in the larger pile, as if to say that's *it*. For her, it's all over, all over but this last accounting. She does not look forward to what is coming. Strangers. Schedules. The **regulated** activities of

---

embroidered made a pattern using stitches in cloth

fragile easily broken

nape the back of the neck

wary cautious or careful

suppressed held back

regulated controlled by rule or system

those considered too old to regulate themselves. But at least, at the *very* least, she'll not be a burden. She sorts through the possessions of a lifetime, she and her three daughters. It's time she passed most of this on. Dreams are lumber. She can't *wait* to be rid of them.

My two sisters and I present a contrast. There is nothing purposeful or **systematic** about the way we move. In fact, we don't know where we're going. We know there is a message in all this activity, but we don't know what it is. Still, we search for it in the odd carton, between layers of tissue paper and silk. We open drawers, peer into the recesses of cupboards, rummage through the depths of closets. What a lot of stuff! We lift, untuck, unwrap, and set aside. The message is there, we know. But what is it? Perhaps if we knew, then we wouldn't have to puzzle out our mother's **righteous** determination to shed the past.

There is a photograph of my mother taken on the porch of my grandparents' house when she was in her twenties. She is wearing a floral print dress with a square, lace-edged collar and a graceful skirt that shows off her slim body. Her shoulder-length hair has been permed. It is dark and thick and worn parted on the side to fall over her right cheek. She is very fair; "one pound powder," her friends called her. She is smiling almost **reluctantly**, as if she meant to appear serious but the photographer has said something amusing. One arm rests lightly on the railing, the other, which is at her side, holds a handkerchief. They were her special pleasures, handkerchiefs of hand-embroidered linen as fine as rice paper. Most were gifts (she used to say that when she was a girl, people gave one another little things—a handkerchief, a pincushion, pencils, hair ribbons), and she washed and starched them by hand, ironed them, taking care with the rolled hems, and stored them in a silk bag from Japan.

Reading Strategy:
Inferencing

Where do you think the elderly woman is going?

How are the three girls different from their mother in their actions?

What might the photographs symbolize?

Permed hair has been curled with chemicals.

---

systematic orderly   **righteous** fair and just   **reluctantly** unwillingly

**Reading Strategy:
Inferencing**

How are both the
bulldozer and the
act of packing
similar symbols?

What do you
think the little
carved fishing boat
symbolizes?

There is something **expectant** in her stance, as if she were waiting for something to happen. She says, your father took this photograph in 1940, before we were married. She lowers her voice **confidentially** and adds, now he cannot remember taking it. My father sits on the balcony, an open book on his lap, peacefully smoking his pipe. The bulldozer tears into the foundations of the Kitamura house.

What about this? My youngest sister has found a fishing boat carved of tortoise shell.

Hold it in your hand and look at it. Every plank on the hull is visible. Run your fingers along the sides, you can feel the joints. The two masts, about six inches high, are from the darkest part of the shell. I broke one of the sails many years ago. The remaining one is quite remarkable, so thin that the light comes through it in places. It is delicately ribbed to give the effect of canvas pushed gently by the wind.

My mother reaches for a sheet of tissue paper and takes the boat from my sister. She says, it was a gift from Mr. Oizumi. He bought it from an **artisan** in Kamakura.

Stories cling to the thing, haunt it like unrestful spirits. They are part of the object. They have been there since we were children, fascinated with her possessions. In 1932, Mr. Oizumi visits Japan. He crosses the Pacific by steamer, and when he arrives he is hosted by relatives eager to hear of his good fortune. But Mr. Oizumi soon tires of their questions. He wants to see what has become of the country. It will be arranged, he is told. Mr. Oizumi is a **meticulous** man. Maps are his passion. A trail of neat X's marks the steps of his journey. On his map of China, he notes each military outpost in Manchuria and **appends** a brief description of what he sees. Notes invade the margins, march over the blank spaces. The characters are written in a beautiful hand, precise, disciplined,

expectant thinking something will come or happen	**confidentially** secretly	**meticulous** very careful
	artisan a person skilled at a craft	**appends** adds to a larger thing

orderly. Eventually, their trail leads to the back of the map. After Pearl Harbor, however, Mr. Oizumi is forced to burn his entire collection. The U.S. Army has decreed that enemy aliens caught with **seditious** materials will be arrested. He does it secretly in the shed behind his home, his wife standing guard. They scatter the ashes in the garden among the pumpkin vines.

My grandfather's library does not escape the flames either. After the army **requisitions** the Japanese school for wartime headquarters, they give my mother's parents twenty-four hours to **vacate** the premises, including the boarding house where they lived with about twenty students from the plantation camps outside Hilo. There is no time to save the books. Her father decides to nail wooden planks over the shelves that line the classrooms. After the army moves in, they rip open the planks, **confiscate** the books, and store them in the basement of the post office. Later, the authorities burn everything. Histories, children's stories, primers, biographies, language texts, everything, even a set of Encyclopaedia Brittanica.

The United States entered World War II after the Japanese navy bombed Pearl Harbor, Hawaii. The government feared that Japanese Americans were spies. Mr. Oizumi burned his maps to avoid being arrested as a spy.

Primers are reading books for young children.

During World War II, many Americans did not trust Japanese Americans. They thought that Japanese Americans were loyal to Japan. About 120,000 Japanese Americans living on the West Coast were forced to move to "War Relocation Camps." The narrator's grandfather was one of them.

seditious stirring up discontent or rebellion

requisitions demands or takes by authority

vacate leave

confiscate seize or take

Caucasians is another name for white people.

My grandfather is shipped to Oahu and **imprisoned** on Sand Island. A few months later, he is released after three **prominent** Caucasians **vouch** for his character. It is a humiliation he doesn't speak of, ever.

All of this was part of the boat. After I broke the sail, she gathered the pieces and said, I'm not sure we can fix this. It was not a toy. Why can't you leave my things alone?

For years the broken boat sat on our bookshelf, a reminder of the **brutality** of the next generation.

Now she wants to give everything away. We have to beg her to keep things. Dishes from Japan, lacquerware, photographs, embroidery, letters. She says, I have no room. You take them, here, *take* them. Take them or I'll get rid of them.

They're piled around her, they fill storage chests, they fall out of open drawers and cupboards. She only wants to keep a few things—her books, some photographs, three carved wooden figures from Korea that belonged to her father, a few of her mother's dishes, perhaps one futon.

A *futon* is a thin mattress found in traditional Japanese homes.

My sister holds a porcelain teapot by its bamboo handle. Four white cranes edged in black and gold fly around it. She asks, Mama, can't you hang on to this? If you keep it, I can borrow it later.

My mother shakes her head. She is **adamant**. And what would I do with it? I don't want any of this. Really.

My sister turns to me. She sighs. The situation is hopeless. You take it, she says. It'll only get broken at my place. The kids.

Reading Strategy: Inferencing

Why does the sister want her mother to keep the teapot?

It had begun slowly, this shedding of the past, a plate here, a dish there, a handkerchief, a doily, a teacup, a few photographs, one of my grandfather's block prints. Nothing big. But then the odd gesture became a pattern; it got so we never left the house empty-handed. At first we were amused. After all, when we were children she had to fend us off her

imprisoned put into prison	**vouch** to guarantee as true	**adamant** not willing to give in
prominent well-known or important	**brutality** violence or cruelty	

things. Threaten. We were always *at* them. She had made each one so ripe with memories that we found them impossible to resist. We snuck them outside, showed them to our friends, told and retold the stories. They bear the scars of all this handling, even her most personal possessions. A chip here, a crack there. **Casualties**. Like the music box her brother brought home from Italy after the war. It played a Brahms **lullaby**. First we broke the spring, then we lost the winding key, and for years it sat **mutely** on her dresser.

She would say again and again, it's impossible to keep anything nice with you children. And we'd retreat, wounded, for a while. The problem with children is they can wipe out your history. It's a miracle that anything survives this **onslaught**.

There's a photograph of my mother standing on the pier in Honolulu in 1932, the year she left Hawaii to attend the University of California. She's loaded to the ears with leis. She's wearing a fedora pulled smartly to the side. She's not smiling. Of my mother's two years there, my grandmother recalled that she received good grades and never wore a kimono again. My second cousin, with whom my mother stayed when she first arrived, said she was surprisingly sophisticated—she liked hats. My mother said that she was homesick. Her favorite class was biology and she entertained ambitions of becoming a scientist. Her father, however, wanted her to become a teacher, and his wishes prevailed, even though he would not have forced them upon her. She was a dutiful daughter.

During her second year, she lived near campus with a mathematics professor and his wife. In exchange for room and board she cleaned house, ironed, and helped prepare meals.

Reading Strategy:
Inferencing
How is the elderly lady like her chipped and cracked possessions?

Leis are necklaces of flowers. They are often given to people who visit the Pacific islands. A *fedora* is a type of hat.

casualties victims	**lullaby** a soothing song usually sung to a baby	**mutely** silently; without sound
		onslaught attack

One of the things that survives from this period is a black composition book entitled *Recipes of California.* As a child, I read it like a book of mysteries for clues to a life which seemed both alien and familiar. Some entries she had copied by hand; others she cut out of magazines and pasted on the page, sometimes with a picture or drawing. The margins contained her **cryptic** comments: "Saturday bridge club," "From Mary G. Do not give away," underlined, "chopped suet by hand, **wretched** task, bed at 2 A.M., exhausted." I remember looking up "artichoke" in the dictionary and asking Mr. Okinaga, the vegetable vendor, if he had any edible thistles. I never ate one until I was sixteen.

That book holds part of the answer to why our family **rituals** didn't fit the recognized norm of either our relatives or the larger community in which we grew up. At home, we ate in fear of the glass of spilled milk, the stray elbow on the table, the boarding house reach. At my grandparents', we slurped our *chasuke.* We wore tailored dresses, white cotton pinafores, and Buster Brown shoes with white socks; however, what we longed for were the lacy, **ornate** dresses in the National Dollar Store that the Puerto Rican girls wore to church on Sunday. For six years, I marched to Japanese language school after my regular classes; however, we only spoke English at home. We talked too loudly and all at once, which **mortified** my mother, but she

> How are the family's daily habits and customs unusual?

cryptic having a hidden meaning	**rituals** customs or ceremonies	**mortified** embarrassed or humiliated
wretched miserable	**ornate** fancy	

was always complaining about Japanese indirectness. I know that she smarted under a system in which the older son is the center of the **familial** universe, but at thirteen I had a fit of jealous rage over her **fawning** attention to our only male cousin.

My sister has found a photograph of my mother, a round-faced and serious twelve or thirteen, dressed in a kimono and seated, on her knees, on the *tatami* floor. She is playing the *koto*. According to my mother, girls were expected to learn this difficult stringed instrument because it was thought to teach discipline. Of course, everything Japanese was a lesson in discipline—flower arranging, calligraphy, judo, brush painting, embroidery, everything. One summer my sister and I had to take *ikebana*, the art of flower arrangement, at Grandfather's school. The course was taught by Mrs. Oshima, a **diminutive**, soft-spoken, terrifying woman, and my supplies were provided by my grandmother, whose tastes ran to the oversized. I remember little of that class and its principles. What I remember most clearly is having to walk home carrying, in a delicate balancing act, one of our creations, which, more often than not, towered above our heads.

How do we choose among what we experience, what we are taught, what we run into by chance, or what is forced upon us? What is the principle of selection? My sisters and I are not bound by any of our mother's **obligations**, nor do we follow the rituals that seemed so important. My sister once asked, do you realize that when she's gone that's *it?* She was talking about how to make sushi, but it was a **profound** question nonetheless.

> **Reading Strategy: Inferencing**
> Why does the narrator think back to her childhood?

> *Sushi* is fish that is usually wrapped in rice and eaten raw.

familial having to do with the family	**diminutive** very small or tiny	**profound** deeply felt or very great
fawning trying to win favor by flattery or other insincere behavior	**obligations** things that must be done	

I remember, after we moved to Honolulu and my mother stopped teaching and began working long hours in administration, she was less **vigilant** about the many little things that once consumed her attention. While we didn't exactly slide into savagery, we economized in more ways than one. She would often say, there's simply no time anymore to do things right.

I didn't understand then why she looked so sad when she said it, but somehow I knew the comment applied to us. It would be terrible if centuries of culture are lost simply because there is not time.

How does the mother symbolize her daughters' past and their culture?

Reading Strategy: **Inferencing**

What are the daughters really searching for?

Still, I don't understand why we carry out this **fruitless** search. Whatever it is we are looking for, we're not going to find it. My sister tries to lift a box filled with record albums, old seventy-eights, gives up, and sets it down again. My mother says, there are people who collect these things. Imagine.

Right, just imagine.

I think about my mother bathing me and singing, "The snow is snowing, the wind is blowing, but I will weather the storm." And I think of her story of the village boy carried by the Tengu on a fantastic flight over the cities of Japan, but who returns to a disbelieving and **resistant** family. So much for questions which have no answers, why we look among objects for meanings which have somehow escaped us in the growing up and growing old.

Reading Strategy: **Inferencing**

How does the mother leave her daughters their culture?

However, my mother is a determined woman. She will take nothing with her if she can help it. It is all ours. And on the balcony my father knocks the ashes of his pipe into a porcelain ashtray, and the bulldozer is finally silent.

---

vigilant watchful; alert   **fruitless** unsuccessful   **resistant** acting against

A Moving Day   by Susan Nunes

Directions Choose the letter of the best answer or write the answer using complete sentences.

Comprehension: Identifying Facts

1. What is happening at the beginning of the story?
  A The narrator and her sisters are fighting.
  B The narrator and her sisters are helping their mother pack.
  C The narrator is planting a garden.
  D The narrator is talking to her father.

2. Which of these best describes the narrator's mother?
  A tall and strong, with curly gray hair
  B tiny and very thin, with short gray hair
  C short and heavy, with a long gray ponytail
  D small and thin, with thick black hair

3. How many sisters does the narrator have?

4. How does the narrator's mother feel about her possessions?

5. What is the bulldozer doing in the background?

6. Where did the little tortoise-shell fishing boat come from?

7. Who keeps the teapot? Why?

8. Where did the narrator's mother go to college?

9. What class did the narrator take one summer at Grandfather's school?

10. What did the mother sing about when she bathed her daughter?

Comprehension: Putting Ideas Together

11. Which sentence best describes how the narrator's mother acts?
  A She acts sad and depressed.
  B She acts angry and bitter.
  C She seems logical and organized.
  D She walks around without a plan.

12. What do Roger from "Thank You, M'am" and the three sisters have in common?
  A They are all hungry.
  B They need to learn important family values.
  C They are tired of being poor.
  D They want to have more possessions.

13. Who are the narrators in "Thank You, M'am" and "A Moving Day"?

14. What character traits do Mrs. Luella Bates Washington Jones and the narrator's mother share?

Comparing **continued on next page**

15. What do Roger and the narrator learn about?

16. How do Mrs. Jones and the narrator's mother use the past to teach Roger and her daughters?

17. What role does culture play in both "Thank You M'am" and "A Moving Day"?

18. How did the family's library get destroyed?

19. Why did the narrator's grandfather feel shamed?

20. Why did Roger feel shamed?

Understanding Literature: Symbols

A symbol is an object that represents something else. Symbols are often common, everyday things that stand for people, places, or objects. In stories and poems, they may stand for ideas or feelings. For instance, a rainbow might be a symbol for happiness or success. Readers can figure out what symbols mean from their familiar links. Details in the story can sometimes also be used to figure out what symbols mean.

21. What does the bulldozer in "A Moving Day" symbolize?

22. What do the blue suede shoes in "Thank You, M'am" symbolize?

23. What does the cookbook in "A Moving Day" symbolize?

24. How is the family symbolized in both stories?

25. Identify at least one other symbol in "A Moving Day" and in "Thank You, M'am." How are these symbols important to their stories?

Critical Thinking

26. How are Mrs. Jones from "Thank You, M'am" and the narrator's mother similar?

27. How are the two women different?

28. What does "A Moving Day" suggest about a family's past?

29. Do you think there are any similar themes in "A Moving Day" and "Thank You, M'am"? Explain.

Thinking Creatively

30. Imagine that you are the narrator in "A Moving Day." What three things would you tell your mother to take with her? Explain your choices.

Grammar Check

Writers often use adjectives to make writing more descriptive. An adjective is a word that describes a noun or a pronoun. Adjectives help to paint the picture of a character, event, or setting. Here are two examples of sentences that contain adjectives: She is wearing a <u>floral print</u> dress. My <u>youngest</u> sister has found a <u>fishing</u> boat carved out of <u>tortoise</u> shell.

Write three sentences of your own. Be sure to include adjectives in each sentence. Underline each adjective.

 Vocabulary Builder

On a sheet of paper, answer each question with a vocabulary word from the list. Review the meaning of each vocabulary word before you begin.

Vocabulary Words: porcelain, prominent, vacate, plank, fragile

1 Which word means the same as "easily broken"?

2 What do we call a wooden board?

3 Which word means the opposite of "arrive"?

4 Which word best describes a famous person?

5 Which word tells what some vases are made of?

 Writing on Your Own

Write a paragraph comparing Roger in "Thank You, Ma'm" and the narrator in "A Moving Day." Tell how they are similar and how they are different. How does each character deal with the main conflict? What outside forces affect each character?

  Listening and Speaking

Imagine that you are Roger. What is your life like 10 years in the future? You are now a young man. Give a speech in which you tell about your life. Tell where you are living and what you are doing. Explain how meeting Mrs. Jones changed your life.

 Media and Viewing

Choose one of the symbols from "Thank You, M'am" or "A Moving Day." Include symbols from each story. Create a visual display to show what this symbol stands for in the story to which it belongs. Include the symbol itself and words or pictures that explain how the symbol relates to the story. Also write a short paragraph to tell why you chose to visualize this symbol.

Certain words are commonly misspelled because people use too many or too few letters. Some words are tricky to spell because they are pronounced incorrectly. Others are not spelled the way they are pronounced.

Did You Use Just Enough Letters?
Though pronunciation does not always help with spelling, in some cases it does. If you add an extra syllable to a word, you are likely to misspell it. Use a dictionary to check the pronunciation of the words on the Word List.

Practice
Match the word from the Word List with the clue. Then, in a small group, develop ways to remember the spelling, a mnemonic device. (Example: repetition repeats the *e* and the *i*.)

1. again and again
2. higher education
3. grab
4. inflammation of the joints
5. awkward feeling
6. person who plays sports
7. divide
8. playfully disobedient
9. recollection
10. overwhelmed

Word List
athlete
arthritis
seize
mischievous
drowned
remembrance
separate
embarrassment
repetition
college

This collage is of my friends from college.

Unit 2 SUMMARY

In Unit 2, you read six short stories with very different styles, moods, and effects. Short stories are part of the kind of literature called prose. Prose includes all writing that is not poetry.

Short stories are among the most popular forms of fiction. Like all fiction, short stories have plot, setting, characters, point of view, and theme. They usually take place over a brief time period and have only one main setting. Short story writers tend to include only the most important descriptive details. Everything in a short story works to set a mood and to develop the theme.

Selections

- "Who Can Replace a Man?" by Brian Aldiss is a science-fiction story. People have destroyed the planet, and machines run everything. In the end, the machines help the humans as they have all along.

- "The Tell-Tale Heart" by Edgar Allan Poe is a classic short story about the murder of an old man. The murderer tells the truth when he thinks he hears the dead man's heart beating.

- "The Finish of Patsy Barnes" by Paul Laurence Dunbar tells of a boy who needs money to help his mother who is ill. He wins a race by riding the same horse that killed his father.

- "Flowers for Algernon" by Daniel Keyes is about a mentally-challenged man, Charlie, who has an operation. Algernon, the white rat, had the operation too. By watching Algernon, we learn what will happen to Charlie.

- "Thank You, M'am" by Langston Hughes is the story of an attempted purse-snatching. Things do not go at all the way the young thief expects.

- "A Moving Day" by Susan Nunes tells of an elderly Japanese American woman who moves from her home. By giving away her possessions, she helps her children understand who they really are.

Directions Choose the letter of the best answer or write the answer using complete sentences.

Comprehension: Identifying Facts

1. What is a short story?
   - **A** a comparison between two otherwise different things
   - **B** a person's life story, written by that person
   - **C** a daily record of personal events, thoughts, or feelings
   - **D** a brief work of prose fiction that has plot, characters, and setting

2. What do the machines do in the end of "Who Can Replace a Man?"

3. Whom does the narrator kill in "The Tell-Tale Heart"?

4. How did Patsy Barnes's father die?

5. Where does Charlie put the flowers for Algernon?

Comprehension: Putting Ideas Together

6. What happens to Charlie at the end of "Flowers for Algernon?"
   - **A** He leaves New York to die.
   - **B** He becomes a famous scientist.
   - **C** He marries Miss Kinnian.
   - **D** He buys his own factory.

7. Why does Patsy Barnes want to ride the horse?

8. Why does Mrs. Jones not ask Roger about his family?

9. Why does Mrs. Jones help Roger and give him money?

10. What is the narrator looking for in "A Moving Day"?

Understanding Literature: Setting

The setting is the time and place in a story. It can be anything a writer can imagine—past, present, or future. A story may be set in a real place or a make-believe land. The setting can make readers feel frightened, happy, or sad. In some stories, the setting acts almost like another character.

11. What is the setting in "Who Can Replace a Man"?

12. What mood does the setting in "The Tell-Tale Heart" create?

13. Why is the setting so important in "The Finish of Patsy Barnes"?

14. How might "Flowers for Algernon" be different if it took place in the distant future?

15. Why is the setting so important in "A Moving Day"?

Critical Thinking

16. In what ways is a science-fiction story different from other short stories?

17. What sound does the narrator really hear in "The Tell-Tale Heart"?

18. What makes Mrs. Jones such a likable character?

19. What is the lesson for readers in "A Moving Day"?

Thinking Creatively

20. Which of the stories in this unit did you like best? Why?

Speak and Listen

Choose an exciting part of "The Tell-Tale Heart." Practice reading the text aloud until you feel as if you really understand it. Use your voice to express the narrator's feelings. When you are ready, read the passage aloud to a group of classmates.

Writing on Your Own

Choose one of the authors in this unit. Use the library or the Internet to learn more about the author. Then write a short essay about the author's life and work, including the author's family and education. Be sure to use at least two good sources of information. List them at the end of your essay on a "Works Cited" page.

Beyond Words

Create a collage based on the short stories you read in Unit 2. A collage is a work of art made by using pictures, photos, materials, and found objects. You can use pictures and words from magazines, objects, and your own drawings to complete this project. Include symbols and images from each story on your collage.

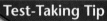

Test-Taking Tip

Restate test directions in your own words. Tell yourself what you are expected to do.

Narration: Short Story

A short story can take readers to new places. It can show them sides of life they might not have thought about before. Follow the steps in this workshop to write your own short story.

Assignment Write a short story. Use believable characters who face a real-life conflict.

What to Include Your short story should have the following characteristics:

- one or more characters
- a clear setting
- a conflict the main character faces
- a plot that leads to a climax and resolution
- a theme—the author's message about life or human nature
- dialogue that reveals character and moves the plot forward

Using the Form
You may use parts of this form in these writing situations:
- journals
- persuasive essays
- anecdotes
- speeches

Six Traits of Writing:

Ideas message, details, and purpose

Prewriting

Choosing Your Topic

To imagine the people and action of your story, use these strategies:

- **Begin with a character.** Your characters may be based on real people or be make-believe. Draw a picture or list details to get to know the characters. Ask and answer questions such as: "How do you spend your time?" or "Who are your friends?"

- **Picture the scene.** Imagine your character in a certain time and place. Make a chart of images to use in your story. Try to include all five senses. This helps make the setting seem real.

SIGHT	Open window; curtains blowing
SOUND	Music, laughter
SMELL	Neighbors' barbecue
TOUCH	Breeze from window
TASTE	Sweet lemonade

Determine point of view. Decide who you want your narrator to be:

- *First-person narrator:* I felt a surge of energy as I threw the ball toward the hoop.
- *Third-person narrator:* The crowd held their breath as Pam shot the ball toward the hoop.

Narrowing Your Topic

Invent a situation. Focus on the action and conflict of your story. Complete sentences like these to help you focus:

- What if *(person)* wanted *(?)* but *(name problem)*?
- What if *(person)* suddenly *(name problem)*?

Review your work and choose a focus for your story.

Gathering Details

Identify the conflict. Clarify the problem your story will develop. Make notes about how the problem will unfold and how the conflict will be resolved. Describe how each character will react.

Writing Your Draft

Shaping Your Writing

Build to a climax. In the beginning, give your readers information to help them understand the situation. Develop the conflict, event by event, until you reach the turning point, or climax. This is the point of highest tension. Use a Plot Mountain like the one shown to help you construct your story.

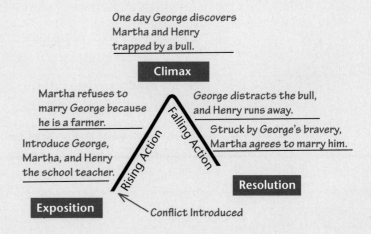

One day George discovers Martha and Henry trapped by a bull.

Climax

Martha refuses to marry George because he is a farmer.

Introduce George, Martha, and Henry the school teacher.

Rising Action

Falling Action

George distracts the bull, and Henry runs away.

Struck by George's bravery, Martha agrees to marry him.

Resolution

Exposition

Conflict Introduced

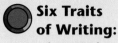

Six Traits of Writing:

Voice the writer's own language

Use dialogue. Dialogue is the conversation among characters. Dialogue can add variety and interest to your short story. Let your characters interact and display a wide range of emotions through their words.

Providing Elaboration

Use vivid details. They help your readers see the characters, the setting, and the events.

Flat: He had never liked hoeing very much.

Vivid: He hated hoeing because it made huge calluses on his hands.

Show, do not tell. Avoid using too much description to tell your story. Give details of character or conflict through action or dialogue.

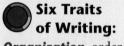

Six Traits of Writing:

Organization order, ideas tied together

Revising

Revising Your Paragraphs

Add detail to help readers see and respond to characters. Look for places to add more details. These details should help your readers see and respond to your characters.

1. Review your draft. Highlight situations and events to which a character would have a strong reaction.

2. Ask yourself: What gestures, words, facial expressions, thoughts, and memories will reflect this reaction?

3. Jot down answers to these questions. Write these in the margins of your paper.

4. Review your notes and decide which details to include. Remember you are trying to influence your audience's reactions through the reactions of your characters.

Editing and Proofreading

Reread your work, correcting errors in grammar, spelling, and mechanics.

Focus on Sentences. Check that each sentence has a subject and a verb. They must agree in gender and number. Be sure that every sentence expresses a complete idea.

Publishing and Presenting

Consider one of these ideas to share your writing.

- **Tell your story aloud.** Hold a storytelling event and invite other classes.

- **Submit your story.** Send your story to a national magazine, online journal, or contest. Ask your teacher or librarian for suggestions.

Reflecting on Your Writing

Writer's Journal Write down your thoughts on the experience of writing a short story.

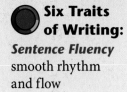

Six Traits of Writing:
Sentence Fluency smooth rhythm and flow

Psychedelic Male Face and Businesswoman,
Jim Dandy

Unit 3

Types of Nonfiction

S ome works of nonfiction tell true stories about real people and actual events. Others describe places and discuss ideas. Still others give directions or steps in a process. The main difference between fiction and nonfiction is that fiction comes from the author's imagination. In nonfiction, stories are about real people and events.

A work of nonfiction may be as short as a note or as long as a book. There are many types of nonfiction. They include biographies, autobiographies, essays, articles, and editorials. In this unit, you will read several different types of nonfiction. Their purposes are to inform, explain, entertain, and persuade.

"A good essay must have this permanent quality about it; it must draw its curtain round us, but it must be a curtain that shuts us in, not out."

—Virginia Woolf, *The Modern Essay*, 1925

Types of Nonfiction **229**

Unit 3 About Nonfiction

Elements of Nonfiction Writing

Nonfiction writing discusses real people, events, places, and ideas. You can explore these works to learn about the lives of others and to find valuable information. Nonfiction writing can also make you think about new ideas or important issues.

Organization is the way a writer chooses to arrange and present information.

- **Chronological organization** presents details in time order—from first to last—or sometimes from last to first.

- **Comparison-and-contrast organization** shows how two or more subjects are similar and different.

- **Cause-and-effect organization** shows the relationship among events.

- **Problem-and-solution organization** identifies a problem and then suggests a solution.

Many pieces of nonfiction use more than one of these types of organization. The type of organization usually depends on the author's reasons for writing. An author's reason for writing also can affect the tone and voice the author uses.

Author's tone is the attitude a writer takes toward a subject. This tone can often be described by a single adjective, such as *formal* or *informal*, *serious* or *playful*, *friendly* or *unkind*.

Voice is the way a writer expresses ideas through style, form, content, and purpose. This voice may vary from work to work by the same writer. Voice can be based on word choice, tone, sound devices, pace, and sentence structure.

Types of Nonfiction Writing

There are many types of nonfiction writing. Here are the most common types:

Letters are impressions and feelings written to a certain person.

"So you're saying your autobiography has eight sequels?"

www.CartoonStock.com

Memoirs are writing based on a personal experience.

Journals express an author's feelings or first impressions about a subject.

Web logs—also known as "blogs"—are journals posted and updated often for an online audience.

A **biography** is a person's life story told by someone else.

An **autobiography** is a person's life story, written by that person.

Media accounts are nonfiction works written for newspapers, magazines, television, or radio.

Essays are written works that show a writer's opinions on some basic or current issue. They may follow the format of these types of writing:

- **Persuasive writing** tries to influence the reader to think or act a certain way.

- **Expository writing** presents facts and ideas, or explains a process.

- **Narrative writing** tells the story of real-life experiences.

- **Reflective writing** explores an author's feelings about an event or situation.

Part 1

Reading Strategy:
Summarizing

When readers summarize, they ask questions about what they are reading. As you read the text in this chapter, ask yourself the following questions:

- Who or what is this about?
- What is the main thing being said about this topic?
- What details are important to the main idea?

Literary Terms

nonfiction writing about real people and events

essay a written work that shows a writer's opinions on some basic or current issue

narrative essay a short nonfiction work involving real events, people, and settings

author's purpose the reason for which an author writes: to entertain, to inform, to express opinions, or to persuade

idiom a phrase that has a different meaning than its words really mean

biographical essay an essay about true events in a person's life

autobiographical essay an essay about true events in the author's life

excerpt a short passage from a longer piece of writing

style an author's way of writing

personification a figure of speech that gives animals or objects the characteristics or qualities of humans

chronological order moving a plot forward in the order of time

cause-and-effect order showing the relationship among events

comparison-and-contrast order showing the ways in which two or more subjects are similar and different

Baseball   *by Lionel G. García*

About the Author

Lionel G. García grew up in a Mexican-American family in rural Texas. For part of the time, he lived with his grandfather on a deserted ranch. Together, García and his grandfather looked after cows and goats. This may have played a part in García's decision to become a veterinarian. As a child, García listened to relatives tell stories about their experiences and friends. "It was easy to laugh and cry in the dark with the stories," he recalls. Although his family was poor, García remembers his childhood as a happy time. "We walked the hot, dusty streets barefooted, our pockets full of marbles. . . . We were carefree." In his writing, García uses funny tales and adult wisdom to recall childhood adventures.

Lionel G. García
1935–

Objectives

◆ To read and understand nonfiction writing

◆ To identify characteristics of a narrative essay

◆ To identify author's purpose in a literary work

About the Selection

Today, many young people play on organized sports teams. Games have strict rules as well as coaches and referees to make sure the rules are followed. In the past, though, children often played informal "pickup" games. They served as their own umpires and referees. They could change the game's rules to suit their own style of play.

"Baseball" describes the neighborhood rules that García and his friends made up. Their creative version of baseball is shown in the reactions of neighbors who watched it.

***Before Reading* continued on next page**

Baseball   by Lionel G. García

nonfiction
writing about real people and events

essay a written work that shows a writer's opinions on some basic or current issue

narrative essay a short nonfiction work involving real events, people, and settings

author's purpose the reason for which an author writes: to entertain, to inform, to express opinions, or to persuade

idiom a phrase that has a different meaning than its words really mean

Literary Terms **Nonfiction** is writing about real people and events. "Baseball" is a type of nonfiction writing called an **essay.** An essay is a written work that shows a writer's feelings on some basic or current issue. A **narrative essay** is a special type of essay that tells a story about real people, places, and events. As you read, try to recognize the **author's purpose,** or reason for which an author writes. Authors write to entertain, to inform, to express opinions, or to persuade.

Reading on Your Own Summarizing involves asking questions while you read. Look for the main idea and any details that support or describe the main idea. Sometimes the author states the main idea directly. More often, the author implies, or suggests, the main idea. To identify the main idea, connect details to determine what they have in common. Summarize these connections to find the main idea.

Writing on Your Own Some people enjoy being part of a team in an organized league. Others enjoy just playing games with friends whenever they want. Write several sentences to explain which option you like best.

Vocabulary Focus Baseball has given many **idioms** to American English. An idiom is a phrase that has a different meaning that its words really mean. Examples include *take a rain check* and *out in left field.* Identify as many baseball idioms as you can. Write a brief explanation of what they really mean.

Think Before You Read Think of the outdoor games you played as a young child. What did those games share with the game of baseball described in this essay?

Baseball

We loved to play baseball. We would take the old mesquite stick and the old ball across the street to the **parochial** school grounds to play a game. Father Zavala enjoyed watching us. We could hear him laugh mightily from the screened porch at the rear of the **rectory** where he sat.

The way we played baseball was to **rotate** positions after every out. First base, the only base we used, was located where one would normally find second base. This made the batter have to run past the pitcher and a long way to the first baseman, increasing the odds of getting thrown out. The pitcher stood in line with the batter, and with first base, and could stand as close or as far from the batter as he or she wanted. Aside from the pitcher, the batter and the first baseman, we had a catcher. All the rest of us would stand in the outfield. After an out, the catcher would come up to bat. The pitcher took the position of catcher, and the first baseman moved up to be the pitcher. Those in the outfield were left to their own **devices**. I don't remember ever getting to bat.

There was one exception to the rotation **scheme**. I don't know who thought of this, but whoever caught the ball on the fly would go directly to be the batter. This was not a popular thing to do. You could expect to have the ball thrown at you on the next pitch.

There was no set distance for first base. First base was wherever Matías or Juan or Cota tossed a stone. They were the law. The distance could be long or short depending on how soon we thought we were going to be called in to eat. The size

As you read, notice the description of the boys' equipment. What do these details tell about the setting and people in this story?

Mesquite, pronounced *mess-KEET*, is a thorny shrub common in Mexico and the southwestern United States. The boys could not afford a proper baseball bat. They made their own from wood growing in the neighborhood.

Who enjoyed watching the boys play baseball?

Reading Strategy: Summarizing

What are the main rules for this baseball game?

---

parochial of or in a district that has its own church and clergy

rectory a house provided for priests

rotate to go through a cycle

devices techniques or means for working things out

scheme a plan

of the stone marking the base mattered more than the distance from home plate to first base. If we hadn't been called in to eat by dusk, first base was hard to find. Sometimes someone would kick the stone farther away and arguments **erupted**.

When the batter hit the ball in the air and it was caught that was an out. So far so good. But if the ball hit the ground, the fielder had two choices. One, in keeping with the standard rules of the game, the ball could be thrown to the first baseman and, if caught before the batter arrived at the base, that was an out. But the second, more interesting option allowed the fielder, ball in hand, to take off running after the batter. When close enough, the fielder would throw the ball at the batter. If the batter was hit before reaching first base, the batter was out. But if the batter **evaded** being hit with the ball, he or she could either run to first base or run back to home plate. All the while, everyone was chasing the batter, picking up the ball and throwing it at him or her. To **complicate** matters, on the way to home plate the batter had the choice of running anywhere possible to avoid getting hit. For example, the batter could run to hide behind the hackberry trees at the parochial school grounds, going from tree to tree until he or she could make it safely back to home plate. Many a time we would wind up playing the game past Father Zavala and in front of

---

erupted exploded   **evaded** avoided   **complicate** to make difficult

the rectory half a block away. Or we could be seen running after the batter several blocks down the street toward town, trying to hit the batter with the ball. One time we wound up all the way across town before we cornered Juan against a fence, held him down, and hit him with the ball. Afterwards, we all fell laughing in a pile on top of each other, exhausted from the run through town.

The old codgers, the old shiftless men who spent their day talking at the street corners, never caught on to what we were doing. They would halt their **idle** conversation just long enough to watch us run by them, hollering and throwing the old ball at the batter.

Old codgers is a friendly way to describe older men.

It was the only kind of baseball game Father Zavala had ever seen. What a wonderful game it must have been for him to see us hit the ball, run to a rock, then run for our lives down the street. He loved the game, shouting from the screened porch at us, pushing us on. And then all of a sudden we were gone, running after the batter. What a game! In what enormous stadium would it be played to allow such freedom over such an **expanse** of ground?

Reading Strategy: Summarizing

What do you learn about Father Zavala, based on details in this paragraph?

My uncle Adolfo, who had pitched for the Yankees and the Cardinals in the majors, had given us the ball several years before. Once when he returned for a visit, he saw us playing from across the street and walked over to ask us what we were doing.

"Playing baseball," we answered as though we thought he should know better. After all, he was the professional baseball player.

He walked away shaking his head. "What a waste of a good ball," we heard him say, **marveling** at our **ignorance**.

The majors means the professional baseball leagues. The New York Yankees and the St. Louis Cardinals are two Major League Baseball teams.

---

idle doing nothing; not busy

expanse a wide area of land

marveling saying something is wonderful

ignorance a lack of knowledge or awareness

Baseball   by Lionel G. García

Directions Choose the letter of the best answer or write the answer using complete sentences.

Comprehension: Identifying Facts

1. How was the location of first base decided in García's game?
   A The base was placed far from the pitcher if it was past dusk.
   B The players went by the rules of professional baseball.
   C It was decided by the toss of a stone.
   D Father Zavala chose the location for the base.

2. Who are Matías, Juan, and Cota?

3. What was Uncle Adolfo's profession?

Comprehension: Putting Ideas Together

4. How was Garcia's version of baseball like the official game?
   A The players rotated positions.
   B It had two bases.
   C If a fielder caught the ball, the batter was out.
   D The location of first base could vary.

5. What was the effect of the location of first base in Garcia's game?

6. What did Adolfo mean when he said, "What a waste of a good ball"?

Understanding Literature: Narrative Essay

A narrative essay is a short nonfiction work that tells about real-life experiences. Like a short story, a narrative essay has characters, settings, a plot, and a theme. However, these features are real, and not invented by the author. The essay may describe present or long-ago events.

7. What are the two most important events in this narrative essay?

8. How is the setting of the essay important to the story?

Critical Thinking

9. Why do Father Zavala and Uncle Adolfo respond differently to the boys' game?

Thinking Creatively

10. Would you rather play games by the rules or make up your own rules? Explain your answer.

Grammar Check

An adjective is a word that describes a noun or pronoun. Adjectives are called modifiers because they modify, or change, a noun. An adjective adds detail to a noun by answering one of these questions: *What kind? Which one? How many? How much? Whose?*

Identify the adjectives in each sentence. Then rewrite the sentences without the adjectives. Explain how the meaning of each sentence changes.

1 I woke up and had two pieces of toast.
2 I put on black jeans and striped socks.
3 We are introducing the three French students.

 ## Vocabulary Builder

The word *focus* is a multiple-meaning word. It can be used as either a verb or a noun. It has several different definitions.

Rewrite each sentence, inserting a correct synonym for *focus*. Use the context of the sentence to help you figure out the meaning.

1 Today we will <u>focus</u> on verbs.
2 The upcoming game was the <u>focus</u> of everyone's attention.
3 The <u>focus</u> of the lecture was that crime does not pay.

 ## Writing on Your Own

Write a description of a famous leader, athlete, or entertainer. Use a Character Analysis Guide to take notes as you learn about the character you are researching. (See Appendix A for a description of this graphic organizer.) In your first sentence, state the main thing you want readers to know about the person. Write several sentences that provide details to support the main idea.

 ## Listening and Speaking

In a small group, create a skit based on "Baseball." Bring the characters to life with dialogue. Show how they invent their own game and how they feel about the rules. Rehearse your skit and then present it to your classmates.

 ## Research and Technology

Research the early history of baseball and its changing rules. Create a timeline to present your findings. Divide the line into intervals of 25 years. Include at least five events in baseball history in the correct spots on the timeline. For each event, write a note explaining why it was important.

from *Always to Remember*   *by Brent Ashabranner*

Brent Ashabranner
1921–

Objectives

◆ To read and understand a biographical essay

◆ To explain the differences between a biographical essay and an autobiographical essay

About the Author

When Brent Ashabranner was 11 years old, he loved a book called *Bomba the Jungle Boy.* When he tried writing the story *Barbara the Jungle Girl*, he quickly gave up. However, he did not give up writing for very long. In high school, he won fourth prize in a short-story contest. Ashabranner has been writing ever since.

Ashabranner has written many books on social issues. Many of the ideas for his books come from his work and travel experiences. He served in the United States Navy and saw the losses of war firsthand. When the United States government said that a Vietnam Veterans Memorial would be built, Ashabranner became interested. As he said, "It will make us remember that war . . . is about sacrifice and sorrow."

About the Selection

In 1961, President Kennedy sent 3,000 military persons to Vietnam in southeast Asia. American soldiers aided the South Vietnamese government in the fight against communist rebels. By 1968, the United States had more than 500,000 troops in Vietnam. They fought in Vietnam for eight long years. Death tolls grew into the tens of thousands. As the fighting dragged on, Americans became hugely divided over the Vietnam War.

In this selection, the author describes the national design contest held for an important memorial. The Vietnam Veterans Memorial in Washington, D.C. honors veterans of the war in Vietnam. "Always to Remember: The Vision of Maya Ying Lin" is about the artist who designed the memorial.

Literary Terms A **biographical essay** is an essay about true events in a person's life. A biographical essay is written by someone else. An **autobiographical essay** is also a true account of events in a person's life. It is written by the person who experienced an event. An autobiographical essay includes the writer's thoughts and feelings. Both types of writing look at how experiences, such as schooling, influence a person's life. "Always to Remember" is a biographical essay. The story is about Maya Ying Lin, but it was written by Brent Ashabranner.

Reading on Your Own Main ideas are the most important points in a literary work. Writers often organize essays so that main ideas are part of a clear structure. An introduction states the idea, and then each paragraph supports or develops it. To follow the path the writer sets, make connections between details and main ideas.

Writing on Your Own This selection introduces a young student who designed a memorial to honor Vietnam War soldiers. Write a few sentences to describe the features you think a memorial should include.

Vocabulary Focus Notice the roots in the words *biography* and *autobiography*. They will help you to understand the difference between the words.

- *biography = bio + graphy* = life + writing = writing about someone's life
- *autobiography = auto + bio + graphy* = self + life + writing = writing about one's own life

Think Before You Read What memorials have you seen or visited? What did the memorials make you feel and remember?

> **biographical essay** an essay about true events in a person's life
>
> **autobiographical essay** an essay about true events in the author's life

from Always to Remember:
The Vision of Maya Ying Lin

As you read, notice how details connect to form the main idea in each paragraph.

The *Washington Monument* honors George Washington the nation's first president. The *Lincoln Memorial* contains a huge statue of Abraham Lincoln, president during the Civil War. The two buildings stand not far apart, in an open green area called the Mall.

In the 1960s and 1970s, the United States was involved in a war in Vietnam. Because many people opposed the war, Vietnam **veterans** were not honored as veterans of other wars had been. Jan Scruggs, a Vietnam veteran, thought that the 58,000 U.S. servicemen and women killed or reported missing in Vietnam should be honored with a memorial. With the help of lawyers Robert Doubek and John Wheeler, Scruggs worked to gain support for his idea. In 1980, Congress **authorized** the building of the Vietnam Veterans Memorial in Washington, D.C., between the Washington Monument and the Lincoln Memorial.

The memorial had been authorized by Congress "in honor and **recognition** of the men and women of the Armed Forces of the United States who served in the Vietnam War." The law, however, said not a word about what the memorial should be or what it should look like. That was left up to the Vietnam Veterans Memorial Fund, but the law did state that

veterans people who have served in the Armed Forces

authorized gave permission to do something

recognition appreciation

the memorial design and plans would have to be approved by
the Secretary of the Interior, the Commission of Fine Arts,
and the National Capital Planning Commission.

What would the memorial be? What should it look like?
Who would design it? Scruggs, Doubek, and Wheeler didn't
know, but they were determined that the memorial should
help bring closer together a nation still bitterly divided by
the Vietnam War. It couldn't be something like the Marine
Corps Memorial showing American troops planting a flag
on enemy soil at Iwo Jima. It couldn't be a giant dove with an
olive branch of peace in its beak. It had to **soothe passions**,
not stir them up. But there was one thing Jan Scruggs insisted
on: The memorial, whatever it turned out to be, would have to
show the name of every man and woman killed or missing in
the war.

The answer, they decided, was to hold a national design
competition open to all Americans. The winning design
would receive a prize of $20,000, but the real prize would be
the winner's knowledge that the memorial would become a
part of American history on the Mall in Washington, D.C.
Although fund raising was only well started at this point, the
choosing of a memorial design could not be delayed if the
memorial was to be built by Veterans Day, 1982. H. Ross Perot
contributed the $160,000 necessary to hold the competition,
and a panel of distinguished architects, landscape **architects**,
sculptors, and design specialists was chosen to decide the
winner.

Announcement of the competition in October, 1980,
brought an **astonishing** response. The Vietnam Veterans
Memorial Fund received over five thousand **inquiries**. They
came from every state in the nation and from every field of

After a battle
during World War II,
six soldiers raised
the American
flag on Iwo Jima's
Mount Surabachi.
The photograph
of the flag-raising
was printed in
newspapers all over
the world. It is one
of the most famous
photographs
in American
history. Later,
the image in the
photo was made
into a sculpture
that stands in
Washington, D.C.

***Reading Strategy:
Summarizing***

What point is
made here about
the challenges
of designing the
memorial?

soothe to calm

passions intense
emotions or feelings

competition
a contest

architects people
who design and
construct buildings

sculptors artists who
create solid, three-
dimensional works

astonishing very
surprising; amazing

inquiries requests for
information

design; as expected, architects and sculptors were particularly interested.

Everyone who inquired received a booklet explaining the **criteria**. Among the most important: The memorial could not make a political statement about the war; it must contain the names of all persons killed or missing in action in the war; it must be in **harmony** with its location on the Mall.

A total of 2,573 individuals and teams registered for the competition. They were sent photographs of the memorial site, maps of the area around the site and of the entire Mall, and other technical design information. The competitors had three months to prepare their designs, which had to be received by March 31, 1981.

Of the 2,573 **registrants**, 1,421 **submitted** designs, a record number for such a design competition. When the designs were spread out for jury selection, they filled a large airplane hangar. The jury's task was to select the design which, in their judgment, was the best in meeting these criteria:

- a design that honored the memory of those Americans who served and died in the Vietnam War.
- a design of high artistic **merit**.
- a design which would be harmonious with its site, including visual harmony with the Lincoln Memorial and the Washington Monument.
- a design that could take its place in the "historic **continuity**" of America's national art.
- a design that would be buildable, durable, and not too hard to maintain.

The designs were displayed without any indication of the designer's name so that they could be judged **anonymously**, on their design merits alone. The jury spent one week

Reading Strategy:
Summarizing

In your own words, tell how the memorial design would be chosen.

---

criteria standards by which something is judged

harmony an orderly or pleasing arrangement of parts

registrants people who sign up

submitted handed in

merit value

continuity uninterrupted flow

anonymously without being named

reviewing all the designs in the airplane hangar. On May 1, it made its report to the Vietnam Veterans Memorial Fund; the experts declared Entry Number 1,026 the winner. The report called it "the finest and most appropriate" of all submitted and said it was "superbly harmonious" with the site on the Mall. Remarking upon the "simple and **forthright**" materials needed to build the winning entry, the report concludes:

> This memorial, with its wall of names, becomes a place of quiet **reflection**, and a tribute to those who served their nation in difficult times. All who come here can find it a place of healing. This will be a quiet memorial, one that achieves an excellent relationship with both the Lincoln Memorial and Washington Monument, and relates the visitor to them. It is **uniquely** horizontal, entering the earth rather than piercing the sky.
>
> This is very much a memorial of our own times, one that could not have been achieved in another time and place. The designer has created an **eloquent** place where the simple meeting of earth, sky and remembered names contain messages for all who will know this place.

The eight jurors signed their names to the report, a **unanimous** decision. When the name of the winner was revealed, the art and architecture worlds were stunned. It was not the name of a nationally famous architect or sculptor, as most people had been sure it would be. The creator of Entry Number 1,026 was a twenty-one-year-old student at Yale University. Her name—unknown as yet in any field of art or architecture—was Maya Ying Lin.

How could this be? How could an **undergraduate** student win one of the most important design competitions ever held? How could she beat out some of the top names in American art and architecture? Who was Maya Ying Lin?

forthright straightforward	**uniquely** in a special, one-of-a-kind way	**unanimous** in complete agreement
reflection thought	**eloquent** vividly expressive	**undergraduate** a college student

The answer to that question provided some of the other answers, at least in part. Maya Lin, reporters soon discovered, was a Chinese-American girl who had been born and raised in the small midwestern city of Athens, Ohio. Her father, Henry Huan Lin, was a ceramicist of considerable **reputation** and **dean** of fine arts at Ohio University in Athens. Her mother, Julia C. Lin, was a poet and professor of Oriental and English literature. Maya Lin's parents were born to culturally **prominent** families in China. When the Communists came to power in China in the 1940's, Henry and Julia Lin left the country and in time made their way to the United States. Maya Lin grew up in an **environment** of art and literature. She was interested in sculpture and made both small and large sculptural figures, one cast in bronze. She learned silversmithing and made jewelry. She was surrounded by books and read a great deal, especially fantasies such as *The Hobbit* and *Lord of the Rings.*

But she also found time to work at McDonald's. "It was about the only way to make money in the summer," she said.

A **covaledictorian** at high school graduation, Maya Lin went to Yale without a clear **notion** of what she wanted to study and eventually decided to major in Yale's undergraduate program in architecture. During her junior year she studied in Europe and found herself increasingly interested in cemetery architecture. "In Europe there's very little space, so graveyards are used as parks," she said. "Cemeteries are cities of the dead in European countries, but they are also living gardens."

In France, Maya Lin was deeply moved by the war memorial to those who died in the Somme offensive in 1916 during World War I. The great arch by architect Sir Edwin Lutyens is considered one of the world's most outstanding war memorials.

The *Somme offensive* was a costly and largely unsuccessful attack by Allied troops during World War I. About 615,000 British and French soldiers were killed.

reputation fame or good name	**prominent** important, socially respected	**covaledictorian** a student who delivers a graduation speech with another student
dean the head of a department at a university	**environment** surroundings	**notion** an idea

Back at Yale for her senior year, Maya Lin enrolled in Professor Andrus Burr's course in funerary (burial) architecture. The Vietnam Veterans Memorial competition had recently been announced, and although the memorial would be a cenotaph—a monument in honor of persons buried someplace else—Professor Burr thought that having his students prepare a design of the memorial would be a worthwhile course assignment.

Surely, no classroom exercise ever had such **spectacular** results.

After receiving the assignment, Maya Lin and two of her classmates decided to make the day's journey from New

Maya Lin, pictured above, designed the Vietnam Veterans Memorial.

spectacular making a great display

Haven, Connecticut, to Washington to look at the site where the memorial would be built. On the day of their visit, Maya Lin remembers, Constitution Gardens was awash with a late November sun; the park was full of light, alive with joggers and people walking beside the lake.

"It was while I was at the site that I designed it," Maya Lin said later in an interview about the memorial with *Washington Post* writer Phil McCombs. "I just sort of visualized it. It just popped into my head. Some people were playing Frisbee. It was a beautiful park. I didn't want to destroy a living park. You use the landscape. You don't fight with it. You absorb the landscape. . . . When I looked at the site I just knew I wanted something horizontal that took you in, that made you feel safe within the park, yet at the same time reminding you of the dead. So I just imagined opening up the earth. . . ."

When Maya Lin returned to Yale, she made a clay model of the vision that had come to her in Constitution Gardens. She showed it to Professor Burr; he liked her **conception** and encouraged her to enter the memorial competition. She put her design on paper, a task that took six weeks, and mailed it to Washington barely in time to meet the March 31 deadline.

A month and a day later, Maya Lin was attending class. Her roommate slipped into the classroom and handed her a note. Washington was calling and would call back in fifteen minutes. Maya Lin hurried to her room. The call came. She had won the memorial competition.

conception a creative idea

AFTER READING THE SELECTION | Apply the Skills

from *Always to Remember*   *by Brent Ashabranner*

Directions Choose the letter of the best answer or write the answer using complete sentences.

Comprehension: Identifying Facts

1. What was the purpose of designing a new memorial?
   - **A** to honor those who died in the Vietnam War
   - **B** to honor President Washington
   - **C** to honor President Lincoln
   - **D** to honor those who died on Iwo Jima

2. Who won the design contest?
   - **A** Jan Scruggs
   - **B** President Kennedy
   - **C** H. Ross Perot
   - **D** Maya Lin

3. Who authorized the building of the memorial?

4. How was the design for the memorial to be chosen?

5. Who funded the design competition?

6. About how many design entries were judged?

7. What did Maya Lin study at Yale University?

8. Who encouraged Maya Lin to enter the competition?

9. Why did people think that a Vietnam memorial was necessary?

10. How does the design of the memorial honor individual soldiers?

Comprehension: Putting Ideas Together

11. What is the Mall in Washington D.C.?
    - **A** a large shopping area
    - **B** the location of important monuments and buildings
    - **C** a national cemetery
    - **D** the location of the Pentagon

12. What date was chosen for the dedication of the memorial?
    - **A** The Fourth of July
    - **B** Veterans' Day
    - **C** Memorial Day
    - **D** Presidents' Day

13. What did Maya Lin do to prepare her design?

14. What else was Maya Lin doing at the time that she won the competition?

15. From what sources did Maya Lin draw inspiration for her prize-winning design?

16. Who were the judges of the design competition?

After Reading **continued on next page**

17. How many jurors judged the competition and how did they vote?

18. What were the judges' comments on the winning design?

19. Who had to approve the winning design?

20. What did the winner of the design competition win?

Understanding Literature: Biographical Essay and Autobiographical Essay

Recall that an essay is writing that gives an author's impressions or feelings about a subject. A biography is the story of a person's life written by someone else. An autobiography is the story of a person's life written by that person. In a biographical or autobiographical essay, the author not only tells a person's life story, but also shares his or her thoughts about that person.

21. What is the main difference between a biographical essay and an autobiographical essay?

22. Why did Brent Ashabranner probably write this essay?

23. Identify three things you learned about Maya Lin by reading this essay.

24. How would the essay be different if it were an autobiographical essay?

25. What would you like to know about Maya Lin that you did not learn by reading this essay?

Critical Thinking

26. The author first identifies the winner of the design contest by number. How does this suggest that the winner's identity may surprise readers?

27. What features of Maya Lin's background made her win unexpected?

28. What features of Maya Lin's background made it reasonable that she won?

29. Do you think memorials to honor the dead are important? Explain.

Thinking Creatively

30. Maya Lin's winning design does not include pictures or statues of the people it honors. What is the effect of her choice to include only the names of the veterans?

Grammar Check

An adverb modifies, or adds to the meaning of, a verb, adjective, or other adverb. Adverbs often, but not always, end in the suffix –*ly*. They answer the questions *When? Where? In what manner?* and *To what extent?*

Identify the adverbs in each sentence below. Indicate which words they modify. Write the questions they answer.

1 Sarah carefully sprinkled the seeds over the soil.

2 Soon, Jorge will realize that he was wrong.

3 Trevor is easily the fastest runner on the track team.

 Vocabulary Builder

The words *persuade* and *convince* are synonyms. Their meanings are so similar that you can use either word in the same sentence.

- Your arguments might *persuade* me to change my mind.

- Your arguments might *convince* me to change my mind.

Other synonyms have similar meanings, but are not easily switched. They suggest slightly different shades of meaning.

Decide whether each pair of synonyms means exactly the same thing. If not, explain why not. Then use each pair in a sentence to show their correct meanings.

1 beautiful, cute

2 annoyed, furious

3 evil, wicked

 Writing on Your Own

Write a description of a work of fine art or music that you like. Consider what you like about the work and explain why it is important to you. State your main points clearly and support them with details.

 Listening and Speaking

Write a memorial speech about a person, place, or event that is important to you. Use appropriate language for the mood you wish to create. Read the completed speech to your class.

 Media and Viewing

Work with a group to learn how the Vietnam War affected people's attitudes about war. Use a variety of reference materials and take notes on what you learn. Use your notes to prepare a slideshow presentation. Include music, charts, photographs, and quotations in your presentation.

Textbooks

In Part 1, you are learning how to summarize facts. Summarizing is especially useful when you are reading informational material. It will help you identify and remember the key points of what you read. Finding main ideas will help you understand and use the information in a textbook article. In "Always to Remember: The Vision of Maya Ying Lin," you learned about the Vietnam Veterans Memorial in Washington, D.C. This section from a history textbook gives information about the Vietnam War.

About Textbooks

A textbook is a nonfiction work that presents information in a particular subject area. Although textbooks can differ from one another in many ways, they have some common characteristics.

Purpose: The purpose of a textbook is to present information to students. Information is organized and developed around a clearly identified main idea.

Structure: Most textbooks are organized into sections, chapters, and/or units. The table of contents lists titles of these parts. It gives the page number where you can find each one.

Text Format: Type size, color, and boldface type are used to highlight key terms or sections.

Reading Skill

Most textbooks contain a great amount of information. To quickly locate specific information, skim and scan instead of reading every word. Skimming is glancing through a written work to get a general idea of the subject. Scanning is running your eyes over the text to locate specific information or key words. Use these tips to find information in a textbook.

Tips for Skimming and Scanning	
Skim the table of contents to find the chapter you need.	**Scan** the index at the back of the book to find information on your topic.
Skim the first sentence of paragraphs that might include the information you need.	**Scan** the headings to find the main idea of each chapter.

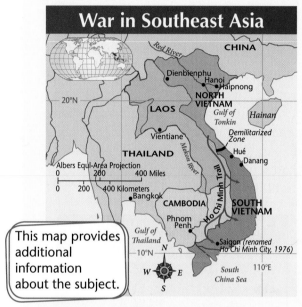

War in Southeast Asia

This map provides additional information about the subject.

4 The War in Vietnam

Early Involvement in Vietnam

Vietnam is a narrow country that stretches about 1,000 miles along the South China Sea. Since the late 1800s, it had been ruled by France as a colony.

The United States became involved in Vietnam slowly, step by step. During the 1940s, Ho Chi Minh (HO CHEE MINH), a Vietnamese nationalist and a Communist, had led the fight for independence. Ho's army finally defeated the French in 1954.

An international peace conference divided Vietnam into two countries. Ho Chi Minh led communist North

Vietnam. Ngo Dinh Diem (NOH DIN DEE EHM) was the noncommunist leader of South Vietnam. In the Cold War world, the Soviet Union supported North Vietnam. The United States backed Diem in the south.

Discontent Diem lost popular support during the 1950s. Many South Vietnamese thought that he favored wealthy landlords and was corrupt. He failed to help the nation's peasant majority and ruled with a heavy hand.

As discontent grew, many peasants joined the Vietcong—guerrillas who opposed Diem. Guerrillas (guh RIHL uhz) are fighters who make hit-and-run attacks on the enemy. They do not wear uniforms or fight in large battles. In time, the Vietcong became communist and were supported by North Vietnam. Vietcong influence quickly spread, especially in the villages.

American Aid Vietcong successes worried American leaders. If South Vietnam fell to communism, they believed, other countries in the region would follow—like a row of falling dominoes. This idea became known as the domino theory. The United States decided that it must keep South Vietnam from becoming the first domino.

During the 1950s and 1960s, Presidents Eisenhower and Kennedy sent financial aid and military advisers to South Vietnam. The advisers went to help train the South Vietnamese army, not to fight the Vietcong. Diem, however, continued to lose support. In November 1963, Diem was assassinated. A few weeks later, President John F. Kennedy was assassinated. Vice President Lyndon Baines Johnson became President.

The Fighting in Vietnam Expands

Lyndon Johnson was also determined to keep South Vietnam from falling to the communists. He increased aid to South Vietnam, sending more arms and advisers. Still, the Vietcong continued to make gains.

Gulf of Tonkin Resolution

In August 1964, President Johnson announced that North Vietnamese torpedo boats had attacked an American ship patrolling the Gulf of Tonkin off the coast of North Vietnam. At Johnson's urging, Congress passed the Gulf of Tonkin Resolution. It allowed the President "to take all necessary measures to repel any armed attack or to prevent further aggression."

Johnson used the resolution to order the bombing of North Vietnam and Vietcong held areas in the south.

With the Gulf of Tonkin Resolution, the role of Americans in Vietnam changed from military advisers to active fighters. The war in Vietnam escalated, or expanded. By 1968, President Johnson had sent more than 500,000 troops to fight in Vietnam.

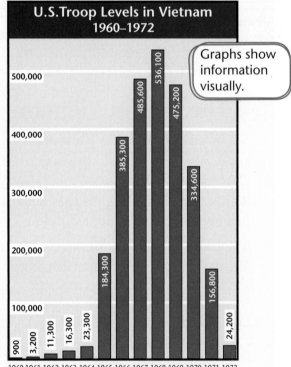

U.S. Troop Levels in Vietnam 1960–1972

Graphs show information visually.

Values: 1960: 900; 1961: 3,200; 1962: 11,300; 1963: 16,300; 1964: 23,300; 1965: 184,300; 1966: 385,300; 1967: 485,600; 1968: 536,100; 1969: 475,200; 1970: 334,600; 1971: 156,800; 1972: 24,200

Source: U.S. Department of Defense

Monitor Your Progress

Directions Choose the letter of the best answer or write the answer using complete sentences.

1. When did the United States begin fighting in the Vietnam War? Scan the text to find the answer.
   - **A** 1950
   - **B** 1954
   - **C** 1960
   - **D** 1964

2. If you skimmed this textbook's table of contents, which heading would you most likely find?
   - **A** Taking Notes
   - **B** The War in Vietnam
   - **C** War in Southeast Asia
   - **D** American Aid

3. Which U.S. president was most closely identified with the war in Vietnam? Scan the text to find the answer.
   - **A** Dwight D. Eisenhower
   - **B** John F. Kennedy
   - **C** Lyndon B. Johnson
   - **D** Richard M. Nixon

4. What was the importance of the domino theory?

5. How did the Gulf of Tonkin Resolution change America's role in the war? Use information from the text and the graph to explain your answer.

Writing on Your Own

Create a two-page description of a recent historic event. Include text and at least one graphic aid, such as a map or graph. Organize your details into several main ideas, supported by interesting details. Identify the main ideas with boldface headings. Post your description on a bulletin board with other students' work.

COMPARING LITERARY WORKS | Build Understanding

Why Leaves Turn Color in the Fall   *by Diane Ackerman*

Diane Ackerman
1948–

Objectives

- ◆ To read and compare an excerpt with another work
- ◆ To identify an author's writing style, including the use of personification
- ◆ To recognize different types of organization in essays

About the Author

Diane Ackerman grew up in Waukegan, Illinois. She studied psychology, physiology, and English in college. As a writer, she has blended her literary skills and training in science to write books of poems and nonfiction. Her descriptions of the natural world combine science with child-like wonder. Her way of writing appeals to many readers.

Ackerman has studied and written about a wide variety of subjects. They include the senses, Texas desert bats, whales near Argentina, and albatrosses in Japan. Her first nonfiction book described cowboys in New Mexico. Her first published book of poems described the planets in the solar system. She says of her own writing career: "You get to create your own astonishment. Which is pretty wonderful."

About the Selection

"Why Leaves Turn Color in the Fall" is taken from *A Natural History of the Senses*. Ackerman published this prize-winning book in 1990. The essay you will read explains why the leaves of certain trees turn color each autumn. Along with her observations of leaves, Ackerman discusses the seasons, life, and death.

Ackerman uses parts of science to write her essay. Recall that Brent Ashabranner wrote about another person in "Always to Remember: The Vision of Maya Ying Lin." Compare the features and structures of the two essays.

Literary Terms "Why Leaves Turn Color in the Fall" is an **excerpt**—a short passage from a longer piece of writing. The author's **style**, or way of writing, uses features of science to create description. The description in the essay includes **personification**. This is a figure of speech that gives animals or objects the characteristics or qualities of humans.

To present information clearly, the author has organized the information. Writers can choose among several types of organization, depending on the purpose of the work. **Chronological order** tells the order in which things happened. The plot moves forward in time order. **Cause-and-effect order** shows the relationship between an event and its results. **Comparison-and-contrast order** shows similarities and differences. Many pieces of nonfiction writing use a combination of these types of organization.

Reading on Your Own As you read, notice how the author blends science and poetry. How would the essay be different if it focused only on the point of view related to science?

Writing on Your Own Work with a partner. Write sentences to describe each of the four seasons without naming them. Take turns reading your sentences aloud. Have your partner try to guess each season as you describe it.

Vocabulary Focus Words may have more than one meaning. They also may function as more than one part of speech. Here is an example from the essay you are about to read: "At last the *leaves leave*." *Leaves* is a noun and *leave* is a verb. Find two different meanings for the following words: *fall* and *flowers*. Then write a sentence using each meaning correctly.

Think Before You Read Look at the title "Why Leaves Turn Color in the Fall." Predict what you think is the author's purpose for writing.

excerpt a short passage from a longer piece of writing

style an author's way of writing

personification a figure of speech that gives animals or objects the characteristics or qualities of humans

chronological order moving a plot forward in the order of time

cause-and-effect order showing the relationship among events

comparison-and-contrast order showing the ways in which two or more subjects are similar and different

Why Leaves Turn Color in the Fall

As you read, notice how the author organizes the information.

Pay attention to the many examples of personification as you read this essay.

The **stealth** of autumn catches one unaware. Was that a goldfinch perching in the early September woods, or just the first turning leaf? A red-winged blackbird or a sugar maple closing up shop for the winter? **Keen**-eyed as leopards, we stand still and squint hard, looking for signs of movement. Early-morning frost sits heavily on the grass, and turns barbed wire into a string of stars. On a distant hill, a small square of yellow appears to be a lighted stage. At last the truth dawns on us: Fall is staggering in, right on schedule, with its baggage of chilly nights, **macabre** holidays, and spectacular, heart-stoppingly beautiful leaves. Soon the leaves will start cringing on the trees, and roll up in clenched fists before they actually fall off. Dry seedpods will rattle like tiny gourds. But first there will be weeks of gushing color so bright, so pastel, so confettilike, that people will travel up and down the East Coast just to stare at it—a whole season of leaves.

Where do the colors come from? Sunlight rules most living things with its golden **edicts**. When the days begin to

stealth secretive behavior	**keen** sharp	**edicts** commands
	macabre grim	

shorten, soon after the summer solstice on June 21, a tree reconsiders its leaves. All summer it feeds them so they can process sunlight, but in the dog days of summer the tree begins pulling **nutrients** back into its trunk and roots, pares down, and gradually chokes off its leaves. A corky layer of cells forms at the leaves' slender petioles, then scars over. Undernourished, the leaves stop producing the **pigment chlorophyll**, and **photosynthesis** ceases. Animals can migrate, hibernate, or store food to prepare for winter. But where can a tree go? It survives by dropping its leaves, and by the end of autumn only a few fragile threads of fluid-carrying xylem hold leaves to their stems.

A turning leaf stays partly green at first, then **reveals** splotches of yellow and red as the chlorophyll gradually breaks down. Dark green seems to stay longest in the veins, outlining and defining them. During the summer, chlorophyll dissolves in the heat and light, but it is also being steadily replaced. In the fall, on the other hand, no new pigment is produced, and so we notice the other colors that were always there, right in the leaf, although chlorophyll's shocking green hid them from view. With their camouflage gone, we see these colors for the first time all year, and marvel, but they were always there, hidden like a vivid secret beneath the hot glowing greens of summer.

The most **spectacular** range of fall foliage occurs in the northeastern United States and in eastern China, where the leaves are **robustly** colored thanks in part to a rich climate. European maples don't achieve the same flaming reds as their American relatives, which thrive on cold nights and sunny days. In Europe, the warm, humid weather turns the leaves brown or mildly yellow. Anthocyanin, the pigment that gives

The *summer solstice* is the longest day and shortest night of the year. The *dog days* of summer are the hottest and muggiest days of summer.

Petioles are the stalks of leaves. *Xylem* is woody plant tissue.

Reading Strategy: Summarizing

What is the chain of causes and effects the author describes here?

Foliage is the leaves of a plant.

---

nutrients substances that can be turned into energy and build tissue

pigment coloring

chlorophyll the green pigment found in plant cells

photosynthesis the chemical process by which green plants use energy from the sun to turn water and carbon dioxide into food

reveals makes known

spectacular making a great display

robustly strongly

apples their red and turns leaves red or red-violet, is produced by sugars that remain in the leaf after the supply of nutrients dwindles. Unlike the carotenoids, which color carrots, squash, and corn, and turn leaves orange and yellow, anthocyanin varies from year to year, depending on the temperature and amount of sunlight. The fiercest colors occur in years when the fall sunlight is strongest and the nights are cool and dry (a state of grace scientists find vexing to forecast). This is also why leaves appear dizzyingly bright and clear on a sunny fall day: The anthocyanin flashes like a **marquee**.

Not all leaves turn the same color. Elms, weeping willows, and the ancient ginkgo all grow radiant yellow, along with hickories, aspens, bottlebrush buckeyes, cottonweeds, and tall, keening poplars. Basswood turns bronze, birches bright gold. Water-loving maples put on a **symphonic** display of scarlets. Sumacs turn red, too, as do flowering dogwoods, black gums, and sweet gums. Though some oaks yellow, most turn a pinkish brown. The farmlands also change color, as tepees of cornstalks and bales of shredded-wheat-textured hay stand drying in the fields. In some spots, one slope of a hill may be green and the other already in bright color, because the hillside facing south gets more sun and heat than the northern one.

An odd feature of the colors is that they don't seem to have any special purpose. We are **predisposed** to respond to their beauty, of course. They shimmer with the colors of sunset, spring flowers, the tawny buff of a colt's pretty rump, the shuddering pink of a blush. Animals and flowers color for a reason—**adaptation** to their environment—but there is no adaptive reason for leaves to color so beautifully in the fall any more than there is for the sky or ocean to be blue. It's just one of the **haphazard** marvels the planet **bestows** every

Reading Strategy:
Summarizing

What cause produces the most brilliantly colored leaves?

marquee a large lighted sign	**predisposed** willing	**haphazard** unplanned
symphonic having a harmony of colors	**adaptation** a development of characteristics to survive	**bestows** presents

year. We find the sizzling colors thrilling, and in a sense they dupe us. Colored like living things, they signal death and **disintegration**. In time, they will become fragile and, like the body, return to dust. They are as we hope our own fate will be when we die; not to vanish, just to sublime from one beautiful state into another. Though leaves lose their green life, they bloom with urgent colors, as the woods grow **mummified** day by day, and Nature becomes more **carnal**, **mute**, and radiant.

We call the season "fall," from the Old English *feallan*, to fall, which leads back through time to the Indo-European *phol*, which also means to fall. So the word and the idea are both extremely ancient, and haven't really changed since the first of our kind needed a name for fall's leafy abundance. As we say the word, we're reminded of that other Fall, in the Garden of Eden, when fig leaves never withered and scales fell from our eyes. Fall is the time when leaves fall from the trees, just as spring is when flowers spring up, summer is when we simmer, and winter is when we whine from the cold.

Children love to play in piles of leaves, hurling them into the air like confetti, leaping into soft **unruly** mattresses of them. For children, leaf fall is just one of the odder **figments** of Nature, like hailstones or snowflakes. Walk down a lane overhung with trees in the never-never land of autumn, and you will forget about time and death, lost in the sheer delicious spill of color. . . .

But how do the colored leaves fall? As a leaf ages, the growth hormone, auxin, fades, and cells at the base of the petiole divide. Two or three rows of small cells, lying at right angles to the axis of the petiole, react with water, then come apart, leaving the petioles hanging on by only a few threads of xylem. A light breeze, and the leaves are airborne. They

To *dupe* means to trick.

The "fall" in the Garden of Eden refers to the Bible. Adam and Eve "fell" from grace when they tasted the fruit of the Tree of Knowledge.

disintegration breakup	**carnal** focused on the body	**unruly** hard to rule or control
mummified shriveled	**mute** understated	**figments** creations of the imagination

glide and swoop, rocking in invisible cradles. They are all wing and may flutter from yard to yard on small whirlwinds or updrafts, swiveling as they go. Firmly tethered to earth, we love to see things rise up and fly—soap bubbles, balloons, birds, fall leaves. They remind us that the end of a season is **capricious**, as is the end of life. We especially like the way leaves rock, careen, and swoop as they fall. Everyone knows the motion. Pilots sometimes do a **maneuver** called a "falling leaf," in which the plane loses altitude quickly and on purpose, by slipping first to the right, then to the left. The machine weighs a ton or more, but in one pilot's mind it is a weightless thing, a falling leaf. She has seen the motion before, in the Vermont woods where she played as a child. Below her the trees **radiate** gold, copper, and red. Leaves are falling, although she can't see them fall, as she falls, swooping down for a closer view.

At last the leaves leave. But first they turn color and thrill us for weeks on end. Then they crunch and crackle underfoot. They *shush*, as children drag their small feet through leaves heaped along the curb. Dark, slimy mats of leaves cling to one's heels after a rain. A damp, stuccolike **mortar** of semidecayed leaves protects the tender shoots with a roof until spring, and makes a rich **humus**. An occasional bulge or ripple in the leafy mounds signals a shrew or a field mouse tunneling out of sight. Sometimes one finds in fossil stones the imprint of a leaf, long since disintegrated, whose outlines remind us how detailed, vibrant, and alive are the things of this earth that perish.

Reading Strategy: Summarizing

How does the author use cause and effect to explain how colored leaves fall?

capricious flighty	**radiate** to spread out from the center	**mortar** a thick mixture
maneuver a controlled movement		**humus** rich soil

Why Leaves Turn Color in the Fall   by Diane Ackerman

Directions Choose the letter of the best answer or write the answer using complete sentences.

Comprehension: Identifying Facts

1. What color is chlorophyll?
   A orange   **C** green
   B red   **D** brown

2. The word *fall* comes from which Old English word?
   A fallen   **C** phol
   B feallen **D** fella

3. What happens to leaves before they fall?

4. What is xylem?

5. Why do leaves fall?

6. What colors do most leaves turn?

7. Where can you see the most beautiful range of leaf colors?

8. How does the author use personification at the beginning of the essay?

9. What happens in the "dog days" of summer?

10. How would you describe a forest turning color to someone who has never seen it?

Comprehension: Putting Ideas Together

11. To what does Diane Ackerman compare the turning and falling of leaves?
   A birth   **C** childhood
   B night   **D** aging and death

12. When do days begin to shorten?
   A during the dog days of summer
   B soon after the winter solstice
   C soon after the summer solstice
   D around Veteran's Day

13. What happens to leaves after they fall?

14. Leaves are all green in the spring and summer. Why do they not all turn the same color in the fall?

15. Describe the process of photosynthesis, as explained in the essay.

16. Why is the Vietnam Veterans Memorial designed to look like the earth is opening up?

17. How does sunlight affect the changing color of the leaves?

18. How does Maya Lin's design of the memorial involve reflection?

Comparing continued on next page

Why Leaves Turn Color in the Fall   *by Diane Ackerman*

19. Compare the color of the memorial to the color of the forest in winter.

20. How are the soldiers and the colorful leaves both individuals and groups?

Understanding Literature: Organization

Writers can use different types of organization in writing. The type of organization can help a reader identify the author's purpose. Chronological order is best for telling something in time order. Cause-and-effect order is effective for telling why things happen. Comparison and contrast is useful for looking at several different things at the same time.

21. How do Ackerman and Ashabranner organize their essays? Are both essays organized effectively? Explain.

22. Describe the effect of looking at a tree in the fall. Contrast this to the effect of visiting a memorial.

23. How would "Always to Remember" be different if it were told in cause-and-effect order?

24. How would "Why Leaves Turn Color in the Fall" be different if it were told in chronological order?

25. What is each author's purpose in writing his or her essay?

Critical Thinking

26. Do you think Ackerman's knowledge of science comes mostly from observation or research? Explain.

27. Do you think Maya Lin's design was mostly a result of her training or her feelings?

28. How do you think Ackerman would respond to visiting the memorial? Why do you think she would respond this way?

29. Both essays contain details related to science and descriptions of thoughts and feelings. Which appeal to you more as a reader? Why?

Thinking Creatively

30. Which one word would you choose to describe both the memorial and a forest in autumn? Explain.

Grammar Check

The way that Diane Ackerman combines adjectives and adverbs makes her writing style interesting. Remember, adjectives describe nouns and pronouns. Adverbs describe verbs, adjectives, and other adverbs. Identify the adjectives in each phrase below from her essay. Rewrite each phrase on a sheet of paper. Underline each adjective.

1 leaping into soft unruly mattresses
2 hot glowing greens of summer
3 hidden like a vivid secret
4 the shuddering pink of a blush

 Vocabulary Builder

Personification gives human characteristics to things that are not human. Ackerman used many examples of personification in "Why Leaves Turn Color in the Fall." Find at least five examples and write them on a sheet of paper. Share your examples with a classmate and see if you wrote down any of the same ones.

 Writing on Your Own

"Always to Remember" is a biographical essay telling about Maya Lin. Write a brief biographical sketch of a leaf, using facts you learned in "Why Leaves Turn Color in the Fall." Which human character traits might you give to leaves? Write the sketch using your own style. Try to include examples of personification in your essay.

  Listening and Speaking

Maya Lin noticed that graveyards in Europe are sometimes used as parks. Many parks have trees like those described in "Why Leaves Turn Color in the Fall." Prepare and present a short speech that supports or opposes the idea of using parks as graveyards. Organize your thoughts using the Main Idea Graphic (Table). (See Appendix A for a description of this graphic organizer.)

 Media and Viewing

Look for images of memorials in books and magazines. Take notes by making simple sketches of the designs you like. Design a memorial to reflect one of the four seasons. Make a sketch of your design, and write a description that includes important details.

Part 2

Reading Strategy:
Questioning

As you read the selections in this Part, ask yourself questions about what is happening. Also think about the facts and opinions that the author may use in the selections. Ask yourself:

- Can this information be proven? If so, it is a fact.

- Is this information someone's belief that cannot be proven? If so, it is likely an opinion.

- Clue words such as *best, worst, always,* and *never* often suggest opinions.

Literary Terms

persuasive essay a short work that is meant to influence the reader

repetition using a word, phrase, or image more than once, for emphasis

rhetorical questions questions asked for effect and not for information

letter impressions or feelings written to a specific person

humorous essay a written work created to be funny or to amuse

tone the attitude an author takes toward a subject

The Trouble with Television   *by Robert MacNeil*

About the Author

Robert MacNeil grew up in Halifax, Nova Scotia, Canada. He developed a love for the English language early in life. He remembers being "crazy about the . . . feeling for words on the tongue and in the mind." MacNeil began his broadcast career in Canada as a radio announcer and disc jockey. He then hosted an educational children's show for Canadian television. In 1955, he moved to England to work as a journalist, someone who gathers and gives news to the public.

Robert MacNeil
1931–

In 1975, MacNeil became co-host of the *MacNeil/Lehrer NewsHour* on American public television. This nightly news show stood out from other news programs with its in-depth news and discussions. MacNeil retired from the *NewsHour* in 1995.

About the Selection

The word *television* was first used in 1900 at the World's Fair. In 1945, there were fewer than 10,000 television sets in the United States. By 1960, this number had jumped to almost 60 million. By the 1990s, 98 percent of all American houses had at least one television set. The technology used in televisions continues to develop.

MacNeil wrote "The Trouble with Television" in 1984. In the selection, he tells readers that television has had a negative effect on society. He believes television has damaged many of our best capabilities. These include language, literacy, imagination, and our ability to handle difficult tasks. Since 1984, Americans have continued to watch more and more television.

Objectives

◆ To read and understand a persuasive essay

◆ To explain how repetition and rhetorical questions are used to persuade

◆ To identify facts and opinions in writing

Before Reading continued on next page

persuasive essay a short work that is meant to influence the reader

repetition using a word, phrase, or image more than once, for emphasis

rhetorical questions questions asked for effect and not for information

Literary Terms "The Trouble with Television" is an example of a **persuasive essay.** In a persuasive essay, a writer tries to influence the reader to believe his or her point of view. To do this, writers use a variety of persuasive techniques. **Repetition** is using a word, phrase, or image more than once to give it special importance. Repetition is an effective way to make a point. **Rhetorical questions** are asked for effect and not for information. Asking rhetorical questions can show readers ways to agree with an opinion they do not share.

Reading on Your Own A fact is a statement that can be proven. An opinion is a person's judgment or belief. Writers generally provide evidence to support their opinions. As you read, ask yourself: "Is this statement a fact or an opinion?" *Hint:* Words that show judgment, like *best* or *worst*, usually suggest an opinion.

Writing on Your Own In his essay, Robert MacNeil worries about the negative influences of television on viewers. Predict some arguments he may not have thought about. List three possible benefits of watching television. Write a paragraph to discuss these two points.

Vocabulary Focus The following words will help you write and talk about facts and opinions. Look for these words as you read nonfiction works.

> *cite* to refer to an example or fact as proof
> *credible* believable
> *accurate* correct
> *bias* unfair preference or dislike
> *support* to prove

Think Before You Read Does the title "The Trouble with Television" suggest that this essay will be based on fact or opinion?

THE TROUBLE WITH TELEVISION

It is difficult to escape the **influence** of television. If you fit the statistical averages, by the age of 20 you will have been exposed to at least 20,000 hours of television. You can add 10,000 hours for each **decade** you have lived after the age of 20. The only things Americans do more than watch television are work and sleep.

Calculate for a moment what could be done with even a part of those hours. Five thousand hours, I am told, are what a typical college undergraduate spends working on a bachelor's degree. In 10,000 hours you could have learned enough to become an astronomer or engineer. You could have learned several languages **fluently.** If it appealed to you, you could be reading Homer in the original Greek or Dostoevski in Russian. If it didn't, you could have walked around the world and written a book about it.

The trouble with television is that it discourages concentration. Almost anything interesting and rewarding in life requires some **constructive,** consistently applied effort. The dullest, the least gifted of us can achieve things that seem miraculous to those who never concentrate on anything. But television encourages us to apply no effort. It sells us instant **gratification.** It diverts us only to divert, to make the time pass without pain.

> As you read, try to recognize differences between fact and opinion.

> How much television do you watch every week? Do you fit the statistical average?

> *Homer* is the ancient Greek poet believed to have written the *Iliad* and the O*dyssey*. *Fyodor Dostoevski* (1821–1881) was a Russian novelist. His most famous work is *Crime and Punishment*.

influence the power to act on others and have an effect without using force	**decade** a period of ten years	**constructive** positive
	calculate to figure out	**gratification** satisfaction
	fluently easily and accurately	

Television's variety becomes a **narcotic**, not a **stimulus**. Its serial, kaleidoscopic exposures force us to follow its lead. The viewer is on a perpetual guided tour: thirty minutes at the museum, thirty at the cathedral, then back on the bus to the next attraction—except on television, typically, the spans **allotted** are on the order of minutes or seconds, and the chosen delights are more often car crashes and people killing one another. In short, a lot of television **usurps** one of the most precious of all human gifts, the ability to focus your attention yourself, rather than just passively surrender it.

Capturing your attention—and holding it—is the prime motive of most television programming and enhances its role as a profitable advertising vehicle. Programmers live in constant fear of losing anyone's attention—anyone's. The surest way to avoid doing so is to keep everything brief, not to strain the attention of anyone but instead to provide constant stimulation through variety, novelty, action and movement. Quite simply, television operates on the appeal to the short attention span.

It is simply the easiest way out. But it has come to be regarded as a given, as **inherent** in the medium itself: as an imperative, as though General Sarnoff, or one of the other august pioneers of video, had **bequeathed** to us tablets of stone commanding that nothing in television shall ever require more than a few moments' concentration.

In its place that is fine. Who can quarrel with a medium that so brilliantly packages escapist entertainment as a mass-marketing tool? But I see its values now **pervading** this nation and its life. It has become fashionable to think that, like fast food, fast ideas are the way to get to a fast-moving, impatient public.

In 1926, *David Sarnoff* (1891–1971) organized the National Broadcasting Company (NBC). NBC was the first permanent broadcast network.

narcotic a drug that dulls the senses

stimulus something that excites

allotted allowed

usurps uses without permission

inherent a natural part of

bequeathed left to after death

pervading spreading throughout

In the case of news, this practice, in my view, results in inefficient communication. I question how much of television's nightly news effort is really absorbable and understandable. Much of it is what has been **aptly** described as "machine gunning with scraps." I think its technique fights **coherence**. I think it tends to make things ultimately boring and dismissable (unless they are accompanied by horrifying pictures) because almost anything is boring and dismissable if you know almost nothing about it.

I believe that TV's appeal to the short attention span is not only inefficient communication but decivilizing as well. Consider the casual assumptions that television tends to cultivate: that **complexity** must be avoided, that visual **stimulation** is a substitute for thought, that verbal precision is an **anachronism**. It may be old-fashioned, but I was taught that thought is words, arranged in grammatically precise ways.

There is a crisis of literacy in this country. One study estimates that some 30 million adult Americans are "functionally illiterate" and cannot read or write well enough to answer a want ad or understand the instructions on a medicine bottle.

Reading Strategy: Questioning

Is the first sentence of this paragraph a fact or an opinion? How do you know?

aptly correctly

coherence a quality of fitting together in a way that is easily understood

complexity complication

stimulation cause for excitement

anachronism something outside of its proper place in history

The *Founding Fathers* are the men who wrote the *Declaration of Independence* and the *United States Constitution*.

Reading Strategy: Questioning

What persuasive technique does MacNeil use here?

Reading Strategy: Questioning

What words and phrases in the final three paragraphs suggest an opinion?

Literacy may not be an **inalienable** human right, but it is one that the highly literate Founding Fathers might not have found unreasonable or even **unattainable**. We are not only not attaining it as a nation, statistically speaking, but we are falling further and further short of attaining it. And, while I would not be so simplistic as to suggest that television is the cause, I believe it contributes and is an influence.

Everything about this nation—the structure of the society, its forms of family organization, its economy, its place in the world—has become more complex, not less. Yet its dominating communications instrument, its principal form of national linkage, is one that sells neat resolutions to human problems that usually have no neat resolutions. It is all symbolized in my mind by the hugely successful art form that television has made central to the culture, the thirty-second commercial: the tiny drama of the earnest housewife who finds happiness in choosing the right toothpaste.

When before in human history has so much humanity collectively surrendered so much of its leisure to one toy, one mass **diversion**? When before has **virtually** an entire nation surrendered itself wholesale to a medium for selling?

Some years ago Yale University law professor Charles L. Black, Jr. wrote: ". . . forced feeding on trivial fare is not itself a trivial matter." I think this society is being force fed with trivial fare, and I fear that the effects on our habits of mind, our language, our **tolerance** for effort, and our appetite for complexity are only dimly **perceived**. If I am wrong, we will have done no harm to look at the issue **skeptically** and critically, to consider how we should be resisting it. I hope you will join with me in doing so.

inalienable protected by law	**diversion** a change of attention	**perceived** seen, sensed
unattainable impossible to achieve	**virtually** almost	**skeptically** doubtfully
	tolerance endurance	

The Trouble with Television   by Robert MacNeil

Directions Choose the letter of the best answer or write the answer using complete sentences.

Comprehension: Identifying Facts

1. According to MacNeil, what are the only things Americans do more than watch television?
   A read and play
   B eat and sleep
   C work with computers
   D work and sleep

2. Who was David Sarnoff?
   A a pioneering television executive
   B a television director
   C an entertainment lawyer
   D a film critic

3. According to MacNeil, how many hours of study are required to earn a bachelor's degree?

4. According to the author, what is required by anything that is rewarding in life?

5. How does the author describe the ability to focus one's own attention?

6. How does the author describe thought?

7. How does the author compare the visual entertainment of television to thought?

8. Why does MacNeil think there is a "crisis of literacy" in the United States?

9. What examples does MacNeil give that life has become more complex?

10. Which expert agrees with MacNeil that society is being "force fed with trivial fare"?

Comprehension: Putting Ideas Together

11. How many hours of television have average Americans watched by age 30?
    A at least 30,000 hours
    B at least 20,000 hours
    C at least 10,000 hours
    D at least 50,000 hours

12. According to MacNeil, what is the prime motive of television programming?
    A to educate
    B to entertain
    C to hold viewers' attention
    D to inspire

13. What does MacNeil suggest could be done in the same number of hours as one watches television?

14. How is watching television like going on a guided tour?

After Reading continued on next page

The Trouble with Television   by Robert MacNeil

15. Instead of the attractions of a guided tour, what are television's "chosen delights"?

16. How does MacNeil support the statement that much of television is "machine gunning with scraps"?

17. How does MacNeil think that television makes news boring?

18. How does MacNeil say that television news makes news memorable?

19. In the author's opinion, does television encourage concentration?

20. How does the 30-second commercial symbolize simple solutions to complex problems?

Understanding Literature: Persuasive Techniques

The point of a persuasive essay is to convince readers of something. Writers use a variety of persuasive techniques to do this. They repeat themselves to emphasize facts and opinions. They appeal to logic or emotion. Writers also cite the statements of experts who agree with their views.

21. What does MacNeil want to persuade the reader to think or to do?

22. Find an example of repetition in "The Trouble with Television." How does the author use repetition to make his point?

23. How does your knowledge of MacNeil's professional background affect your belief in his arguments?

24. Do you find MacNeil's arguments persuasive? Why or why not?

25. Cite one statement in the essay with which you strongly disagree. Explain why you disagree with MacNeil.

Critical Thinking

26. For whom do you think MacNeil wrote this essay?

27. Do you agree with MacNeil that the 30-second commercial is "central to the culture"? Why or why not?

28. Do you agree with MacNeil that most of what you see on television is trivial? Give examples to support your answer.

29. How do you think television-watching habits have changed since this essay was written in 1984?

Thinking Creatively

30. Now that you have read this essay, will your television-watching habits change? Explain.

Grammar Check

Words that connect sentence parts and add information to sentences are called conjunctions. Conjunctions can make these connections:

- connect parts of similar importance;
  Examples: *and, but, for, nor, or, so, yet*

- connect pairs of equal importance;
  Examples: *both/for, either/or, neither/nor*

- connect two ideas when one depends on the other;
  Examples: *although, because, even though, if, since, while, until*

Identify the conjunctions in the sentences below and tell what each connects.

1 The Constitution and Bill of Rights spell out rights and responsibilities.

2 States approved the Constitution, but they wanted a Bill of Rights.

3 Neither women nor African Americans could vote in 1789.

 Vocabulary Builder

The words *credible* and *incredible* are antonyms, or words with opposite meanings. The prefix *in-* means "not." *In* + *credible* means "not credible," or "not believable."

The prefix *un-* also means "not" and creates antonyms of some words.

Add the prefix *in-* or *un-* to each word. Then define each antonym and use it in a sentence.

1 believable   **3** describable

2 focused   **4** usual

 Writing on Your Own

Write a review of Robert MacNeil's essay. In your review, identify the main idea and the facts and opinions used to support the main idea. Finally, give your opinion about whether the author made his points well.

 Listening and Speaking

Form two teams to debate this topic: "Television viewing should be limited to one hour daily during the week." Each side should prepare by researching the topic before the debate. During the debate, speakers should use respectful language and should allow each other time to speak without interruption.

 Research and Technology

Take a survey of television viewing habits by interviewing 10 students and 10 adults. Find out how many hours they spend each week watching programs. Then create a graph to present your data.

Mother Jones to President Theodore Roosevelt

Mary Harris
"Mother" Jones
1837–1930

Objectives

♦ To read and understand a letter

♦ To explain how word choice relates to an author's purpose for writing

About the Author

Mary Harris was born in Ireland and moved to Canada as a child. She trained in Toronto to be a teacher and later worked as a dressmaker. "I preferred sewing to bossing little children," she said. She married an ironworker and union organizer in Tennessee. Her husband and all four children died in the yellow fever epidemic of 1867. Tragedy followed her to Chicago where she worked again as a dressmaker. Her shop was destroyed in the Great Fire of 1871.

At this time, large factories, businesses, and farms were replacing smaller ones. Workers were often treated unfairly by bosses and paid very low wages. Mary Harris Jones became involved in defending the rights of working people. The nickname "Mother" was given to her because of her grandmotherly appearance. She worked for the rights of railway workers, miners, mill workers, dressmakers, and child laborers.

About the Selection

In July 1903, Mother Jones organized a large group of mill workers, including many children. They marched from Philadelphia to New York to protest unfair working conditions. She wrote several letters to President Theodore Roosevelt asking for his support.

When her letters were not answered, she took three children with her to meet the president at his home. A secretary met them at the gate to announce that the president was not in. He told Mother Jones to write yet another letter. This letter was published in Philadelphia's *North American* and eventually answered by the same secretary. The reply was disappointing. It did not contain an offer of the kind of support Mother Jones had hoped for. However, the published letter did draw attention to the issue. Eventually, federal laws were passed protecting the rights of children.

Literary Terms The nonfiction work in this selection is a **letter.** A letter is impressions or feelings written to a specific person. An author's purpose for writing a letter may vary. Word choice is important so the author can correctly show his or her purpose. Word choice is an author's selection of particular words to express ideas and show meaning. An author might choose words that are formal or informal, simple or complex. Mother Jones uses very formal language in her letter.

> **letter** impressions or feelings written to a specific person

Reading on Your Own Read the letter slowly and carefully. Some of the language in the letter is old-fashioned and not often used today. Try to imagine how Mother Jones may have felt as she wrote the letter.

Writing on Your Own Mother Jones wanted President Theodore Roosevelt to help with an unfair situation. List three other reasons why people write letters to elected officials.

Vocabulary Focus Word choice can help to show how strongly a writer feels about a subject. Compare these sentences: I *ask* that you answer me. I *demand* that you answer me. *Ask* and *demand* are synonyms. However, *demand* is much stronger than *ask*.

Rewrite each sentence, replacing each underlined word or phrase with a stronger synonym.

1. I <u>suggest</u> that you give the matter <u>some</u> attention.

2. You <u>might</u> do something to correct the situation <u>in the future</u>.

3. I <u>would like</u> to see some action <u>soon</u>.

4. I <u>think</u> that they are being treated <u>somewhat</u> unfairly.

Think Before You Read Mother Jones wrote her letter in the early 1900s. Would a letter still be a good way to get the president's attention today?

Mother Jones to President Theodore Roosevelt

As you read, notice how word choice reflects the writer's feelings about the subject.

Reading Strategy: Questioning

What is the author's purpose for writing this letter?

*A passionate spokesperson for the rights of workers and anti-child labor laws, Mary Harris "Mother" Jones fought **doggedly** to bring attention to these issues through letters, speeches, marches, and other forms of social protest throughout the country—"[I have] no **abiding** place," she once said "but wherever a fight is going on against wrong, I am always there." In the following letter, Jones **implores** President Theodore Roosevelt, who was visiting Oyster Bay, New York, at the time, to sponsor federal laws that would end child labor practices in America.*

NEW YORK, July 30th, 1903.

The Hon. Theodore Roosevelt, President U.S.A.

Your Excellency:

Twice before I have written to you requesting an audience that I might lay my mission before you and have your advice on a matter which bears upon the **welfare** of the whole nation. I speak for the **emancipation** from mills and factories of the hundreds of thousands of young children who are yielding up their lives for the commercial **supremacy** of the nation.

---

doggedly without giving up

abiding permanent

implores begs

welfare well-being

emancipation freedom

supremacy the state of being most powerful

Failing to receive a reply to either of the letters, I yesterday went to Oyster Bay, taking with me three of these children that they might plead to you personally.

Secretary Barnes informed us that before we might hope for an interview, we must first lay the whole matter before you in a letter. He assured me of its delivery to you personally, and also that it would receive your attention.

I have **espoused** the cause of the laboring class in general and of suffering children in particular. For what affects the child must ultimately affect the adult. It was for them that our march of principle was begun. We sought to bring the attention of the public upon these little ones, so that ultimately **sentiment** would be aroused and the children freed from the workshops and sent to school. I know of no question of to-day that demands greater attention from those who have at heart the **perpetuation** of the Republic.

The child of to-day is the man or woman of to-morrow, the citizen and the mother of still future citizens. I ask Mr. President, what kind of citizen will be the child who toils twelve hours a day, in an **unsanitary** atmosphere, stunted mentally and physically, and surrounded with **immoral** influences? Denied education, he cannot assume the true duties of citizenship, and **enfeebled** physically and mentally, he falls a ready victim to the **perverting** influences which the present economic conditions have created.

I grant you, Mr. President, that there are State laws which should regulate these matters, but results have proven that they are **inadequate**. In my little band are three boys, the oldest 11 years old, who have worked in mills a year or more without interferences from the authorities. All efforts to bring about reform have failed.

In a *republic*, citizens vote for representatives who make the laws. The United States is a republic.

espoused adopted	**unsanitary** dirty	**perverting** worsening
sentiment feeling	**immoral** bad	**inadequate** not good enough
perpetuation continuation	**enfeebled** weakened	

Reading Strategy:
Questioning

Does the author
support her claims
with statements of
fact or opinion?

I have been moved to this **crusade**, Mr. President, because of actual experiences in the mills. I have seen little children without the first **rudiments** of education and no prospect of **acquiring** any. I have seen other children with hands, fingers and other parts of their tiny bodies **mutilated** because of their childish ignorance of machinery. I feel that no nation can be truly great while such conditions exist without attempted remedy.

It is to be hoped that our crusade will stir up a general sentiment in behalf of enslaved childhood, and secure enforcement of present laws.

But that is not sufficient.

As this is not alone the question of the separate States, but of the whole Republic, we come to you as the chief representative of the nation.

I believe that Federal laws should be passed governing this evil and including a penalty for **violation**. Surely, Mr. President, if this is **practicable**—and I believe that you will agree that it is—you can advise me of the necessary steps to **pursue**.

I have with me three boys who have walked a hundred miles serving as living proof of what I say. You can see and talk with them, Mr. President, if you are interested. If you decide to see these children, I will bring them before you at any time you may set. Secretary Barnes has assured me of an early reply, and this should be sent care of the Ashland Hotel, New York City.

Very respectfully yours,
MOTHER JONES

crusade cause	**mutilated** injured by removing parts	**practicable** possible to put into practice
rudiments basic elements	**violation** breaking the law	**pursue** follow
acquiring getting		

Mother Jones to President Theodore Roosevelt

Directions Choose the letter of the best answer or write the answer using complete sentences.

Comprehension: Identifying Facts

1. Why did Mother Jones write to President Theodore Roosevelt?
   A to ask him to join her march
   B to ask him to pass laws to end child labor practices in America
   C to praise his concern for workers
   D to ask him to improve schools

2. Why did she want children freed from the workshops?

3. How did she hope her letter would affect the president?

Comprehension: Putting Ideas Together

4. What proof did Mother Jones offer the president?
   A three boys
   B her opinions
   C her complaints
   D her criticism

5. How could Mother Jones prove that children were being mistreated?

6. How did Mother Jones know that state laws protecting children were not being correctly followed?

Understanding Literature: Letter

A letter is a piece of writing that includes the writer's thoughts and feelings about a subject. People write letters for many different reasons. You may write a letter to a friend or relative to tell about interesting events in your life. You may write a letter to a leader of your government asking to change a law. You may write a letter to the editor of a newspaper to give your opinion about a subject. You may also write a letter to a company to ask about a job opening. Whatever the reason, a letter is a good way to share information and to ask questions.

7. Why did Mother Jones write a letter to President Roosevelt?

8. How does the word choice in Mother Jones's letter show her feelings about the subject?

Critical Thinking

9. Do you think Mother Jones made a strong case in her letter? Explain.

Thinking Creatively

10. Do you think that the government or families should be in charge of making rules about labor? Explain.

After Reading continued on next page

Mother Jones to President Theodore Roosevelt

 Grammar Check

A preposition relates the noun or pronoun following it to another word in the sentence. Here are some examples of prepositions: *before, after, during, in, above, around, under.* A phrase beginning with a preposition and ending with its object is called a prepositional phrase. For example: He put the book <u>on the bookcase</u>.

Identify the prepositions and prepositional phrases in each sentence. Circle each preposition and underline each prepositional phrase.

1 The children ran around the playground.

2 In each inning, the visiting team bats first.

3 In many action movies, the hero ends up in a car chase.

 Vocabulary Builder

The word *support* can be used as either a verb or a noun. Many words have different meanings when they are used as different parts of speech.

On a sheet of paper, define *support* as it is used in each sentence. Also, name the part of speech of *support* in each sentence.

1 When our computer crashed, we called the *support* number.

2 Provide details to *support* your opinion.

3 Everyone needs good friends to *support* him or her in bad times.

 Writing on Your Own

A newspaper or magazine article that expresses an opinion is called an editorial. Prepare to write an editorial by choosing a subject. Write a list of five problems in your school, community, or the world. For each issue, jot down your opinion.

 Listening and Speaking

Have a group discussion about early job experiences, such as babysitting and lawn mowing. Share information by answering questions such as: What was your job? Were you paid and if so, how much? What skills did you learn from your first job? If you have never had a job, what kind of job would you like to try?

 Research and Technology

Labor unions were created to protect the rights of workers. Find and learn a song written about the labor movement. Practice the song and then share it with your class.

Research Paper

In this unit, you have been reading different types of nonfiction writing. A research paper is a type of nonfiction writing. It is writing based on the study of a variety of resources. A research paper should present a clear and correct picture of a topic. Research papers feature these parts:

- a main idea or focus
- supporting details from a variety of sources
- a clear organization
- a listing of sources, called a bibliography

Facts are gathered from sources such as:

- reference materials including books, magazines, newspapers, and journals
- personal observations or experiments
- interviews
- the opinions of experts

Reading Skill

To write a research paper, you must compare and contrast details. When you read a research paper, ask questions. Research papers are based on fact, but readers should still check to see if all facts and conclusions can be proven.

A good way to begin a research paper is to create an outline. Roman numerals show main points, and capital letters show supporting details. On the next page is an outline for the research paper on Komodo dragons. The actual research paper follows the outline. Note that your finished paper may not match your outline exactly. You may decide some details are not important, or your paper may be too long.

The Komodo Dragon

I. Introduction
Komodo dragons are interesting creatures.

II. Live on remote islands
   A. Seen by ancient sailors
   B. Sighted by scientists in early 1900s
   C. May be the dragons in Chinese legends

III. Interesting eating habits
   A. Eat carrion and hunt
   B. Eat the whole animal
   C. Eat their young

IV. Unusual appearance
   A. Colors change as they mature
   B. Teeth like shark teeth
   C. Throats and skulls can expand

V. Birth and death of dragons
   A. Hatch from eggs
   B. Many are eaten by adults
   C. May live for 50 years

VI. An endangered species
   A. Only 6,000 are alive
   B. Some are protected in parks and zoos

VII. Interest in dragons
   A. Dragon saliva might lead to a new drug
   B. Ecotourism is a new industry

VIII. Conclusion
Komodo dragons should be respected and protected.

The Komodo Dragon
(*Varanus komodoensis*)

The Komodo dragon is also called the monitor lizard. It lives only on several remote islands in Indonesia. "Here be dragons" was found written on ancient maps of Indonesia and Malaysia. In the early 1900s, scientists proved sightings of the giant lizards here. Huge scaly man-eating monsters are featured in ancient Chinese legends. It is possible that these are Komodo dragons.

Komodo dragons are meat eaters. They eat carrion, or dead animals. They also hunt goats, pigs, deer, birds and their own young. Young dragons escape by climbing trees. They live in the trees until they are strong enough to defend themselves. Komodo dragons have been known to attack human beings. They are strong swimmers and have been seen hunting in the ocean.

The Komodo dragon grows up to 12 feet in length and can weigh over 300 pounds. Young dragons are green, black, and yellow. As they grow, their colors dull to grayish red or brown. Their strong bodies are covered in scales. The tail is a powerful weapon. Their teeth are similar to shark teeth, designed for tearing meat. Komodo dragons have rounded snouts and ear openings.

Komodo dragons hatch from eggs. Females lay up to 30 eggs at a time in a nest in the ground. They sit on the eggs until they hatch. Many eggs are eaten before they hatch, often by adult dragons. Most hatchlings, baby komodo dragons, are eaten before they escape to the treetops. The ones that live to adulthood usually live for 50 years.

The Komodo dragon is an endangered species. Only 6,000 are alive right now. Several zoos feature Komodo dragons. Some people feel that housing endangered species in zoos is helpful to the animals. Other people disagree.

When dragons fight, they are not made ill by each other's bites. Medical researchers believe that proteins in the dragons' blood protect them from the germs. This discovery might be developed into a drug to help humans fight infection.

Scientists are careful not to injure the animals. They temporarily trap a dragon and tape its jaw shut. After blood samples are drawn from the tail, a protective antibiotic is applied. The animal is then released back into the wild.

Monitor Your Progress

Directions Choose the letter of the best answer or write the answer using complete sentences.

1. Where do Komodo dragons live?
   A on remote islands all over the world
   B close to the North Pole
   C on islands in Indonesia and in zoos
   D in the Hawaiian Islands

2. What do Komodo dragons eat?
   A only animals that they kill
   B insects
   C plants
   D carrion and live animals

3. Why are scientists interested in the saliva of Komodo dragons?
   A It is toxic.
   B It may lead to the development of a new drug.
   C It is a powerful weapon.
   D It kills prey slowly over time.

4. What opinion is stated in the first paragraph of the research paper about Komodo dragons?

5. Why is it helpful to create an outline before writing a research paper?

Writing on Your Own

Choose a subject for a research paper. Follow your curiosity and write a list of interesting questions about the subject. Look for information in the library and on the Internet. Take detailed notes as you do your research. You may also wish to interview experts. Keep a list of sources as you work. Review your notes and focus your subject based on the information you find. Finally, write a one-page outline for a research paper. Use the information from your research to create your outline.

COMPARING LITERARY WORKS | Build Understanding

A Child's Garden of Manners   by Jean Kerr

About the Author

Jean Kerr was born in 1923 in Scranton, Pennsylvania. As a child, she said her life's goal was "to be able to sleep until noon." She began writing plays while going to college. Her family was the source of ideas for much of her writing. *Please Don't Eat the Daisies* is Kerr's best-selling collection of short essays written based on her children. She said that she wrote much of it locked in a parked car. This was the only way she could get any time away from her family. The book was made into a popular movie and television series. In the film, movie star Doris Day played the role of Jean Kerr.

Jean Kerr
1923–2003

About the Selection

"A Child's Garden of Manners" was originally called "Etiquette for Children." It was first published in the magazine *Ladies' Home Journal* in 1959. The following year it was included in the book *The Snake Has All the Lines*. In this essay, Jean Kerr gives many funny examples of the behavior of ill-mannered children. Her witty observations are based on life with her own family.

As you read, consider the differences in Kerr's purpose for writing and in Mother Jones's purpose.

Comparing **continued on next page**

Objectives

◆ To read and understand a humorous essay

◆ To identify and compare the tone of literary works

A Child's Garden of Manners   by Jean Kerr

humorous essay a written work created to be funny or to amuse

tone the attitude an author takes toward a subject

Literary Terms "A Child's Garden of Manners" is an example of a **humorous essay.** This type of writing is created to be funny or to amuse. **Tone** is the attitude an author takes toward a subject. Authors create tone through word choice, sentence structure, and details. Tone can often be described by a single adjective, such as *formal, informal, serious,* or *playful.* The author's purpose often affects the tone of a work of literature. In this humorous essay, Kerr's purpose is to entertain the reader. This allows the tone of the piece to be light-hearted.

Reading on Your Own Both "Mother Jones to President Theodore Roosevelt" and "A Child's Garden of Manners" share a general subject—how adults see and treat children. However, the tones of these pieces differ because the authors' reasons for writing are different. As you read, look for clues in the text that show the author's purpose.

Writing on Your Own Write a short description of how to do a simple activity. Give a serious step-by-step explanation, but make the directions silly. Choose words that are funny— *yank* is funnier than *pull*, for example. When you are finished, share your description with a member of your family.

Vocabulary Focus It is helpful to study vocabulary words before you begin reading. Knowing the meaning of difficult words will help you better understand the meaning of a work of literature. Choose 10 vocabulary words that you do not know from this selection. Create flash cards for these words. Write the word on one side of an index card. Write the definition on the other side of the card. Then work with a partner to practice the words and definitions on the flash cards.

Think Before You Read Manners are the customs of polite behavior. Manners make it easier for people to live together peacefully. What are some examples of rude behavior?

A Child's Garden of Manners

*Have you noticed a strange thing about **etiquette** books?* They are all written for grown-ups. *Us.*

I really don't understand it. Most adults have lovely manners; it's a pleasure to have them around. Ask an adult to hand you your glasses and he says, "Here they are, dear." He doesn't put them behind his back and say, "Guess which hand?" And when you give him a birthday present he doesn't burst into tears and say, "I already *have* Chinese checkers!" What I wish is that Emily and Amy and the others would get to work on the real trouble area—people under twelve.

I know that small children have a certain animal magnetism. People kiss them a lot. But are they really in demand, socially? Are they sought after? Does anybody ever call them on the telephone and invite them to spend the weekend on Long Island? Do their very own grandmothers want them to spend the *whole* summer in Scranton? No. For one thing they bite, and then they keep trying to make forts with mashed potatoes. It holds them back, socially. If you have any doubt about the matter, ask yourself one question. When, by some accident, you find yourself at a large party with children present, do you just naturally **gravitate** over to that corner of the room where the little ones are playing Indian

> As you read notice the humorous tone of the essay.

> *Emily Post* and *Amy Vanderbilt* are both authors of best-selling books of manners. They are experts on the rules of polite behavior.

> *Long Island* is an island off the coast of New York. *Scranton* is a small city in eastern Pennsylvania.

etiquette rules of correct behavior

gravitate to move gradually

Spy under the card table? See what I mean? These kids need help—and direction.

Now, I'm the last one to be talking about manners. Just this week at a dinner party I let myself get rattled by the **innocent** question of a young man who was the son of my hostess and a freshman at Lehigh. All he wanted to know was whether I voted for Al Smith or Hoover in 1928. In the deep, troubled **reverie** produced by this line of questioning, I lost my head completely and consumed not only the entire salad of the man on my right but also one of his Parker House rolls. As I say, I'm not the one to write that book, *Tips for Tots*. But in the total absence of any **definitive** work on the subject, and inspired as I am by a passion for public service, I would like to make a few **random** suggestions:

Table Manners for Children

The first point to be established is that one does not sit *on* the table. One sits on the chair, and in such a way that all four legs touch the floor at the same time. (I am of course speaking of the four legs of the chair; children only *seem* to have four legs.) For children who will rock and tilt anyway, I suggest (a) built-in benches, (b) the practice of **instilling** in such children a sense of noblesse oblige, so that when they go crashing back onto their heads they go bravely and gallantly and without pulling the tablecloth, the dinner, and a full set of dishes with them. This last may sound severe, but it will be excellent training if they should ever enter the Marines, or even Schrafft's.

We don't have to bother about little **niceties** such as which fork is the shrimp fork (at these prices, who is giving them shrimp?). We will suppose, and safely, that the child has only one fork. If this child is interested in good manners and/or the **sanity** of his parents, he will not use the fork to (a) comb his

Lehigh is a university in Pennsylvania. *Al Smith* and *Herbert Hoover* ran for president in 1928. Hoover won the election and became the 31st president.

Reading Strategy: Questioning
What is the author's purpose in writing?

Noblesse oblige is a French phrase meaning "the obligations of the nobility." In other words, people of high rank or great wealth have a duty to behave politely.

Schrafft's was a famous New York restaurant chain.

innocent free from sin or wrong; not guilty	**random** without a pattern	**niceties** fine points; details
reverie daydream	**instilling** gradually teaching	**sanity** the state of good mental health
definitive trustworthy		

hair, (b) punch holes in the tablecloth, or (c) remove buttons from his jacket. Nor will he ever, under any **circumstances**, place the tines of the fork under a full glass of milk and beat on the handle with a spoon.

So far as the food itself is concerned, it would be well for the child to adopt a **philosophical** attitude about that dreary procession of well-balanced meals by reminding himself that in eighteen years or less he will be free to have frozen pizza pies and fig bars every single night. And he should remember, too, that there is a right way and a wrong way to talk about broccoli. Instead of the gloomy mutter, "Oh, broccoli again— ugh!" how much better the cheery "I guess I'll eat this broccoli first and get it over with."

Finally, children should be made to understand that no matter how **repellent** they find a given vegetable, they may not stuff large handfuls of it into their pockets, particularly if the vegetable is creamed. This sorry but unfortunately

circumstances conditions	**philosophical** thoughtful	**repellent** disgusting

common practice not only **deprives** the child of necessary vitamins but frequently exposes him to **intemperate** criticism and even physical violence.

Behavior at the Theater or Movies

Children should not bring guns or slingshots or cats to the theater. And for other reasons they shouldn't bring hats or gloves or rubbers—unless you have the time to go back to the theater and pick them all up afterward.

It is always worth while to give them exact change (thirty cents for the movie, five cents for candy), especially if the movie is going to be *The Son of the Monster.* Suspense has the curious effect on many children of causing them to swallow nickels.

The **mannerly** child will decide once and for all whether he wishes to sit on the seat pulled down (like old people) or whether he wants to sit high on the edge in the "up" position. Once he has made up his mind, he will not **vacillate** between the two positions, or he will very likely be thrown out onto the street by the ushers.

If children are going to eat at the movies, and they are, they should be encouraged to buy candy that doesn't roll. Sour balls roll. And the fallout from a ten-cent box of sour balls is considerably greater than from a five-cent box. If you have any interest in making a host of new acquaintances all at once, there is no better way than to escort a pair of five-year-old twins to the movies and present each of them with a large box of sour balls. With the sense of timing that is **innate** in even the youngest children, they wait until the main feature starts before dropping both boxes on the floor. And then they're *off,* scrambling on hands and knees, down under the seats through a forest of legs, **foraging, retrieving,** sobbing. And for six rows in every direction wild-eyed **patrons** are

Rubbers is another term for waterproof overshoes. Men often wear these to protect their shoes from rain or snow.

Reading Strategy: Questioning

Is the humor in this section based on fact or opinion?

deprives prevents someone from having something	**mannerly** polite	**foraging** hunting for
	vacillate sway	**retrieving** bringing back
intemperate severe	**innate** natural	
		patrons customers

leaping to their feet and splitting the air with questions: "In heaven's name, what are you *doing* down there? Will you get out? Where do you belong? Where is your mother?" etc. For this reason I suggest chocolate bars. It will ruin their clothes and spoil their dinner but that can't be helped.

Rules of Peaceful Coexistence with Other Children

Children should **eschew** violence, by which I mean that they should not hit each other on the head with ice skates or telephones or geography books. It ought to go without saying that polite children never push each other down the stairs, but I'm not sure that it does. Karen, my four-year-old niece, recently pushed her baby sister down the back stairs. After her mother had rescued the victim, she flew at the **oppressor** and shouted, "What's the matter with you? You can't push Joanie down the stairs!" Karen listened carefully, all innocence and interest, and finally said, "I can't? How come?"

Parenthetical note to parents: in trying to keep older children from doing permanent physical damage to their juniors, it is probably not advisable to adopt the tit-for-tat type of punishment ("If you pull Billy's hair again, I'm going to pull *your* hair!"). This method would appear to have a certain Old Testament rightness about it, but the danger is that you may put yourself into a position where you will be forced into massive **retaliation**. And, when it comes right down to it, you can't really punch that kid straight in the eye or spit in his milk. Personally, I'm in favor of generalized threats like "If you make that baby cry once more I swear I'll clip you." In this instance the word "clip" is open to a variety of interpretations and leaves you more or less free to **inflict** such punishment as you are up to at the moment.

Tit-for-tat type of punishment means an equal payback in return.
Old Testament rightness is based on the Bible.

eschew avoid	**parenthetical** explanatory	**retaliation** getting even
oppressor bully		**inflict** to cause

Respect for the Feelings of Others

One of the reasons children are such duds socially is that they say things like "When do you think you're going to be dead, Grandma?" We're all going to be dead, of course, but nobody wants to be put on the spot like that.

It is not to be expected that a small child can be taught never to make a personal remark. But there is a time and a place. For instance, the moment Mommy is all dressed up in her new blue **chiffon** and doesn't look a day older than twenty-five, well, twenty-eight, is *not* the time for Gilbert to ask, "Why do you have all those stripes on your forehead, Mommy?"

Children should realize that parents are emotionally **insecure**, and that there are times when they need loving kindness. Unfortunately, a relationship with a child, like any love affair, is complicated by the fact that the two parties almost never feel the same amount of **ardor** at the same time. One blows hot while the other blows cold, and **vice versa**. On the day you're flying to Athens (for two whole weeks) and you're already frantic with concern and full of terrible **forebodings** that you will never see the little lambs again, you can hardly round them up to say good-by. And when you do locate one of them, he scarcely looks up from his work. "Darling," you say, "aren't you going to say good-by and give me a *good* kiss? I'm going to be gone for two whole weeks." "Sure," he says, "'bye, Mom, can I have a Coke?"

Of course he too has moments when affection swells—the wrong moments. First he reduces you to babbling **incoherence** by (a) climbing in the kitchen window and smashing three geraniums, (b) taking the mail from the mailman and dropping half of it in a puddle, (c) spilling a bottle of navy-blue suede dressing on the cat. Then, as you are pouring Merthiolate on your scratches—incurred while cleaning up

Geraniums are popular window-box flowers that are usually bright red or pink.

Merthiolate is a brand name for a solution used to clean cuts.

chiffon sheer fabric	**vice versa** Latin for "the other way around"	**incoherence** the state of being impossible to understand
insecure fearful; not sure of doing well		
ardor love	**forebodings** feelings that something bad is going to happen	

the cat—he returns covered with mud, having just buried a squirrel. You are deep in philosophical **speculation** centering around the **miraculous** fact that this child was not adopted (at least you don't have to fight the temptation to send him back). And naturally, it's right at this moment that he takes it into his head to give you one of his Jack-the-Ripper hugs, curling muddy cowboy boots around your knees and plastering you with sandy kisses.

Respect for the Property of Others

Children should bear in mind that, no matter how foolish it seems, adults become attached to material objects, like typewriters, wrist watches, and car keys. I admit that I am once again working without **statistics**, but I do have the feeling we wouldn't have so many disturbed parents in this country if children could he made aware of the unwisdom of using their fathers' best fountain pens to punch holes in evaporated milk cans. (If you're interested, there is one foolproof way of holding onto pens and pencils: you hire a man with a gun to sit by the desk all day, and then you or your husband or some other responsible adult takes the night shift.)

Just as there are animals that kill prey they have no intention of eating, so are there children who take things they have no way of using. It may be **reprehensible**,

Five women were murdered in London in 1888. Londoners called the unknown killer "Jack the Ripper." To this day, no one knows who was responsible. A "Jack-the-Ripper hug" is a strong, forceful hug.

speculation consideration	**miraculous** extraordinary	**reprehensible** totally unacceptable
	statistics facts	

but it is at least understandable that a child should take a sterling-silver gravy ladle to the beach; it's almost as good to dig with as a sand shovel. But why do they take the little knobs off the tops of lamp shades, or meat thermometers, or the dialing wheels off the television set? Sometimes when you investigate what seems to be meaningless **mayhem**, you find that there is a certain **idiotic** logic behind the whole thing: when I found one of the smaller boys **unfurling** a roll of toilet paper out of the attic window, it turned out that he was merely trying to discover how long a roll of toilet paper really was. I can understand that, sort of. But I never did understand why he cut the bows off my blue suede shoes.

Children have such a lively sense of the **inviolability** of what belongs to them (as you've noticed if you ever tried to throw out an old coloring book) that it should be easy for them to remember that adults, too, have little **fetishes** about their personal possessions ("You don't like anybody to play with your tractor, do you? Well, Daddy doesn't like anybody to play with his tape recorder.").

Sometimes it's hard to know just what to say. Last winter I found on the breakfast table a letter addressed to Mommy Kerr. It was on my very best stationery, and there were ten brand-new four-cent stamps plastered all over the envelope. When I pulled out the letter, the message read:

> *Dear Mommy,*
>   *John is mad at you becuase you won't let us put our snowballs in the freeser but I am not mad at you becuase I love you*
>
>   *Your Frend, Colin*

Well, there you are. When you get right down to it, it was worth forty cents.

mayhem chaos	**inviolability** state of security
idiotic crazy	
unfurling unrolling	**fetishes** unusually strong feelings

COMPARING LITERARY WORKS | Apply the Skills

A Child's Garden of Manners   by *Jean Kerr*

Directions Choose the letter of the best answer or write the answer using complete sentences.

Comprehension: Identifying Facts

1. Why does the author think it is strange that etiquette books are written for adults?
   A They are experts.
   B They already like to talk about manners.
   C They prefer to think for themselves.
   D Most have lovely manners.

2. Who does Jean Kerr think needs a book of manners?
   A adult parents
   B teenagers
   C people under age 12
   D senior citizens

3. What clues are given for the "animal magnetism" of children?

4. What clues does the author give that children are not sought after as guests?

5. Why does Jean Kerr advise giving children exact change when they go to the movies?

6. What is the main idea of the section "Rules of Peaceful Coexistence with Other Children"?

7. How does the author use personal experiences in her essay?

8. Who was Colin?

9. Who was Mommy Kerr?

10. At the end, is the author upset that her son wasted so many stamps?

Comprehension: Putting Ideas Together

11. What subject do Mother Jones's letter and Jean Kerr's essay share?
   A relationships of children and adults
   B asking for help
   C rules of polite behavior
   D child labor laws

12. What place do both writers mention in their writing?
   A Europe
   B New York
   C Canada
   D textile mills

13. How are children like "animals that kill prey with no intention of eating"?

14. Give an example of how Jean Kerr finds logic in the "meaningless mayhem" of children.

Comparing **continued on next page**

A Child's Garden of Manners   by *Jean Kerr*

15. Give an example of something a child did that made no sense to Jean Kerr.

16. How did Mother Jones think that children could influence the president?

17. How does Mother Jones describe the importance of treating children fairly?

18. What do the authors of the two works have in common?

19. Does Jean Kerr feel qualified to write *Tips for Tots*?

20. How does Mother Jones show that she feels qualified to write to the president?

Understanding Literature: Tone

A speaker's tone of voice can show mood and emotion. For example, a speaker's tone can be angry, hurt, or cheerful. A writer communicates tone through word choice and style, such as formal or casual. A writer may choose to make funny observations with a formal style to create humor.

21. Compare the subjects of Mother Jones's letter and "A Child's Garden of Manners."

22. Compare the tones of the two works.

23. What was Mother Jones's purpose in writing her letter?

24. What was Jean Kerr's purpose in writing her essay?

25. How does the author's tone help her fulfill her purpose in each work?

Critical Thinking

26. What was unusual about the way Mother Jones signed her letter to the president?

27. What was unusual about the last paragraph of "A Child's Garden of Manners"?

28. Why do you think children are often the subjects for entertaining or persuasive writing?

29. Which author do you think does a better job of sharing her purpose with readers? Explain.

Thinking Creatively

30. Would Jean Kerr's tone fit with the subject of Mother Jones's letter? Explain.

Grammar Check

Quotation marks are punctuation marks that enclose the exact words of a speaker. "Oh, broccoli again—ugh!" and "In heaven's name, what are you doing down there?" are examples from the essay. Titles of articles and other short works are also enclosed in quotation marks.

Copy these sentences onto a sheet of paper. Add quotation marks where they belong.

1 My brother could have written the article The Smell of Money—Who Wants Some?

2 His common response was I love cauliflower like I love eating ants at a picnic.

3 My mother is no fool. She always replies, That's nice dear. You always loved the great outdoors!

 Vocabulary Builder

Reviewing vocabulary helps you to remember what new words mean. Choose 10 words from this selection. Read the meaning of each word again. Then write a humorous paragraph using all 10 words. Underline each vocabulary word in your paragraph.

 Writing on Your Own

You can use a Venn Diagram to compare and contrast "Mother Jones to President Theodore Roosevelt" and "A Child's Garden of Manners." (See Appendix A for a description of a Venn Diagram.) Identify the subject of each work, the authors' purpose for writing, word choice, and tone. In each outside circle, write details about each individual work. In the center circle, write the things both selections have in common.

 Listening and Speaking

Prepare a short, entertaining speech about the behavior of adults. Follow Kerr's style and include jokes and stories to support your points. You may wish to use your own experiences as ideas for your speech. Write out your speech. Then practice speaking slowly and clearly, with a "straight face." When you feel confident, present your speech to the class.

 Research and Technology

Use library and Internet resources to learn about table manners in different cultures. Is there a universal definition for polite behavior? Collect examples of interesting customs and create a bulletin board display of your findings.

Homophones are words that sound alike, but have different meanings and spellings. The words cite, sight, and site in the examples below are homophones. The words site and sight are nouns. Cite is a verb. Notice how each word is used in the following sentences.

- What sources did he *cite* in his report?

- The *site* of the new library is on Main Street.

- The *sight* of the shark's teeth made me shiver.

Homonyms are words that sound and are spelled the same, but have different meanings. For example, the noun *bear* and the verb *bear* are homonyms. One means "a large animal," and the other means "to carry."

Most word-processing programs contain a spell-checking feature. Spell-checking programs can only tell you if each word is correct. They do not know if you used the right word. To a spell-check program, this sentence is fine because the words are spelled correctly: *The cite of three ducks waddling down the hallway was a little startling.* However, the sentence is actually incorrect because the wrong word was used. Read your work carefully; do not rely only on technology.

Practice

Write a sentence for each word on the Word List. In some sentences, use the incorrect homonym. Trade papers with a partner and correct the spelling errors in the sentences. Use a dictionary to check word meanings.

Word List
except
accept
all ready
already
by
bye
buy
foul
fowl

I can accept all of this except the grade in physical education!

Unit 3 introduced you to a wide variety of nonfiction writing. You read selections that described memories and explained processes of science. Other selections were entertaining, funny, critical, and persuasive.

Essays and articles are short nonfiction works about a particular subject. They are different from short stories because the things they describe are not made up. However, nonfiction writing may include an author's opinions about a subject. Opinions may be based on facts or feelings, or both. Ask questions as you read to tell fact from opinion.

Letters are written texts addressed to a particular person. They include true observations, and statements of fact and opinions. Personal letters may be published in newspapers to draw attention to an issue. Biographies and autobiographies are two other popular forms of nonfiction.

People enjoy reading nonfiction just as much as they enjoy reading fiction. Nonfiction allows readers to learn new facts about people or subjects. Nonfiction also can help readers understand the everyday issues faced by others around the world.

Selections

- "Baseball" by Lionel G. García is a narrative essay recalling the author's youth. A place and time is reflected in the description of a neighborhood game.

- "Always to Remember: The Vision of Maya Ying Lin" by Brent Ashabranner is a biographical essay. It tells the story of a young college student who rises to national attention for her design of the Vietnam Veterans Memorial.

- "Why Leaves Turn Color in the Fall" by Diane Ackerman paints a colorful portrait. The forest is seen through the eyes of a poet and a scientist.

- "The Trouble with Television" by Robert MacNeil blames television for many problems in modern society.

- "Mother Jones to President Theodore Roosevelt" by Mary Harris "Mother" Jones is a personal letter. When it was published, it helped to persuade a greater audience to work for laws against child labor.

- "A Child's Garden of Manners" by Jean Kerr shows the humor in real life. Based on personal experience, the essay shows why children need help in learning polite behavior.

Directions Choose the letter of the best answer or write the answer using complete sentences.

Comprehension: Identifying Facts

1. Which selection is not based on the author's own experience?
   A "Baseball"
   B "Always to Remember: The Vision of Maya Ying Lin"
   C "Mother Jones to President Theodore Roosevelt"
   D "The Trouble with Television"

2. Which seasons of the year are described in "Why Leaves Turn Color in the Fall"?

3. When did Mother Jones write her letter to the president?

4. What equipment did the boys use to play their game in "Baseball"?

5. Which essay tells what children should not bring to the theatre or to the movies?

Comprehension: Putting Ideas Together

6. What is the purpose of the essay "Why Leaves Turn Color in the Fall"?
   A to entertain   C to persuade
   B to judge   D to explain

7. What is the author's tone in "The Trouble with Television"?

8. What is the main idea of Mother Jones's letter to President Roosevelt?

9. What was Jones's purpose in writing the letter?

10. Why did Brent Ashabranner write his essay about Maya Lin's memorial design?

Understanding Literature: Persuasive Essay

In a persuasive essay, a writer tries to influence the reader or listener to think in a certain way. Writers give facts and opinions to make their point. Readers must be able to tell the difference between the facts and opinions and then decide what they believe.

11. Mother Jones claims that children should not work 12 hours per day. Does she support this claim with facts or opinions?

12. How does Jean Kerr prove her claim that children need a book of manners?

13. How does Robert MacNeil prove his claim that there is trouble with watching too much television?

14. How does the tone of "A Child's Garden of Manners" support the author's main idea?

15. Which nonfiction selections include opinions?

Critical Thinking

16. Does the phrase "I believe" usually come before a fact or an opinion? Explain.

17. What does the phrase "Everyone is entitled to his or her own opinion" mean?

18. How can you tell if a source is one you can trust for correct information?

Thinking Creatively

19. What would Robert MacNeil like to see changed about the way Americans watch television?

20. What do you think Mother Jones and the three boys would have said to the president in person if they were given the chance? How would it be different from what was said in the letter?

Speak and Listen

Work with a partner. Write a list of statements and questions. Take turns saying each one aloud using different tones of your voice. Notice how the tone of a speaking voice changes the message of what is being said. Ask a partner to guess which tone you are using each time you read.

Writing on Your Own

Persuading customers to buy a product is the main purpose of advertising. Facts and opinions are organized to make the product seem as attractive as possible. "Glen's Chili—Best in Town" looks like a statement of fact, but is really an opinion. Choose an unusual product to advertise. Decide who your audience is. Write the text for a magazine advertisement for your product.

Beyond Words

Make a drawing or painting to represent a section from "A Child's Garden of Manners." Show the humor without using words. Photographs in magazines and newspapers can be used as models. Display your work and see if classmates can correctly identify your subject.

Test-Taking Tip

To prepare for a test, study in short sessions rather than in one long session. During the week before the test, spend time each day reviewing your notes.

Persuasion: Editorial to Solve a Problem

When you use words to influence others, you are using persuasion. An editorial is a persuasive essay in which a writer presents and defends an opinion. It may be published in a newspaper, magazine, or other medium. Follow the steps outlined in this workshop to write an editorial.

Assignment Write an editorial to persuade your readers to accept your solution to a problem. Write about a problem about which you feel strongly.

What to Include An effective editorial should feature the following elements:

- a clear statement of your position on a problem that has more than one solution
- strong evidence that supports your position
- a clear organization that builds toward a conclusion
- a response to possible opposing arguments
- persuasive techniques that give a powerful message
- error-free writing, including proper sentence structure

Using the Form
You may use elements of this form in these types of writing:
- political speeches
- reviews
- advertisements
- public-service announcements

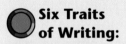 **Six Traits of Writing:**

Ideas message, details, and purpose

Prewriting
Choosing Your Topic

Use one of these strategies to find an issue that matters to you:

- **Round Table** With a group, hold a discussion of issues in your school and community. Create a list of specific problems that need solving. Notice common views that you think need changing. Review the list and choose the issue that interests you most.

- **Media Flip-Through** Every day, the media bring arguments and debates into our living rooms. Over a day or two, read the newspaper, including letters to the editor. Also, watch the local and national news. Jot down topics that spark your interest. Choose one as the subject of your editorial.

Narrowing Your Topic

Narrow your topic so you can cover it thoroughly in an editorial. Ask the "reporter's questions"—*"Who? What? Where? When? Why?* and *How?"* Circle the most interesting issues your answers raise to focus your topic.

Gathering Details

Gather evidence to support your position. Do your research in the library, on the Internet, or by interviewing experts. Gather the following types of support:

- Facts: statements that can be proven true

- Statistics: facts presented in the form of numbers

- Quotes: statements of leading experts

- Personal observations: your own thoughts and feelings about the subject

Writing Your Draft
Shaping Your Writing

Use a clear organization. A strong organization will help make your editorial effective. Consider using Nestorian Order—arranging points according to their relative strength. Begin with your second strongest point. Present other arguments, and end with your strongest point. This is a dramatic way to build your case.

Anticipate and respond to counterarguments. Think about the arguments against your position. Then, meet opposing ideas head-on with arguments of your own. Look at the examples in the chart.

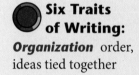

Six Traits of Writing:
Organization order, ideas tied together

Arguments	Counterarguments
Wearing school uniforms robs students of their individuality.	Students do not have to worry about wearing what is considered "cool."
Uniforms are expensive.	Students save money by not wearing a different outfit every day.

Providing Elaboration

Use a variety of persuasive techniques. As you draft, use these techniques to sway readers:

- **Logical Arguments** Take your readers step-by-step through your argument. Present facts to earn their trust.

- **Emotional Appeals** Move your readers with a brief story or vivid image that supports your argument. Choose images and stories that spark an emotion such as pride, surprise, anger, or fear.

- **Charged Words** Words with strong emphasis can pack entire arguments into a few syllables.

- **Repetition** Repeat words and phrases to emphasize ideas.

Revising

Revising Your Overall Structure

Revise to strengthen your message. Give your readers more than facts and logic. Add emotion and description to grab readers. Review your draft. Look for points that are supported only with logical arguments, statistics, or expert opinions. Consider adding a comparison or dramatic story.

Revising Your Sentences

Revise for clarity. In a good essay, the paragraphs hold together well. Read the last sentence of each paragraph and the first sentence of the next paragraph. If there is no obvious connection between the paragraphs, highlight the space between them.

Six Traits of Writing:
Sentence Fluency
smooth rhythm and flow

Consider these tips for adding a word, phrase, or sentence that links the paragraphs together:

- Repeat a key word or phrase.

- Use a transitional word or phrase such as *similarly, however,* or *in addition.*

Editing and Proofreading

Check your editorial for errors in spelling, punctuation, and grammar.

Focus on Double Negatives: Avoid creating confusion with double negatives—two negative words—when only one is required. The example shows two ways to correct a double negative.

Example: There is not no reason to cut funding.

Correction 1: There is not any reason to cut funding.

Correction 2: There is no reason to cut funding.

Publishing and Presenting

You might choose one of these ways to share your writing:

Organize a forum. Group together a panel of classmates to read their editorials to the class. Encourage the audience to ask questions of the panel.

Publish in a newspaper. Send your editorial, with a cover letter, to a local newspaper. Briefly summarize your essay in the letter. Explain why you wish it to be considered for publication.

Reflecting on Your Writing

Writer's Journal Write a few notes describing the experience of writing an editorial. Begin by answering the following questions: What part of the writing process seemed the hardest? What did you learn about the issue? Did your opinions change as you learned more?

> **Six Traits of Writing:**
> **Conventions** correct grammar, spelling, and mechanics

Drummer (Night in Tunisia),
Gil Mayers, 1995

Unit | 4 | Poetry

Poetry is a form of literature that uses language for its artistic qualities. Because poems are often short, poets must choose each word carefully. They select words for their sounds as well as for their meanings. The words are weaved together in a musical way. A poet connects with an audience through the ear as well as through the eye.

In this unit, you will read works by poets from long ago and by poets who are writing today. As you read each poem, think about how its sound affects your understanding. Think about the images created by the words in the poem.

"To have great poets, there must be great audiences, too."

—Walt Whitman, *"Ventures on an Old Theme,"* Notes, 1881

Unit 4 About Poetry

Elements of Poetry

Poetry is literature in verse form that usually has rhythm and paints powerful or beautiful impressions with words. Poetry is the most musical of literary forms. Poets choose words for both sound and meaning, using the following elements:

Sensory language is writing or speech that appeals to the senses—sight, sound, smell, taste, and touch.

Figurative language is writing or speech not meant to be understood exactly as it is written. Writers use figurative language to express ideas in vivid or imaginative ways. The following are examples of different types of figurative language:

- A **metaphor** is a figure of speech that makes a comparison but does not use *like* or *as*. For example, *Her eyes were saucers, wide with excitement.*

- A **simile** is a figure of speech in which two things are compared using a phrase that includes the words *like* or *as*. For example, *The drums were as loud as a fireworks display.*

- **Personification** gives characters such as animals or objects the characteristics or qualities of humans. For example, *The clarinets sang. The drums roared.*

Sound devices add a musical quality to poetry. These are examples of sound devices:

- **Alliteration** is repeating sounds by using words whose beginning sounds are the same, as in *feathered friend.*

- **Repetition** is using a word, phrase, or image more than once, for emphasis.

- **Assonance** is repeating sounds by using words with the same vowel sounds, as in *fade* and *hay.*

- **Consonance** is the repetition of consonant sounds usually within the context of several words, as in *end, hand,* and *kind.*

- **Onomatopoeia** is using words that sound like their meaning, as in *buzz, crackle, hiss,* and *zoom.*

- **Rhyme** is when two or more words end with the same or similar sounds, as in *pants* and *dance.*

- **Meter** is the repetition of stressed and unstressed syllables in a line of poetry. Meter often creates a rhythm, or pattern, in a poem.

Forms of Poetry

There are many different ways to write a poem. Most are written in lines, and these lines are grouped into **stanzas**. However, a poem does not have to be written in stanzas. This list describes several forms of poetry.

Lyric poetry expresses a person's emotions or feelings, often in very musical verse. The speaker is the one telling the poem.

Narrative poetry tells a story in verse. Narrative poems often have elements like those in a short story, such as setting, plot, and characters.

Ballads are simple songs that often use a refrain and sometimes use rhyme. Ballads are passed from person to person.

Free verse poetry is poetry that does not have a strict rhyming pattern or regular line length. Free verse poetry also uses actual speech patterns for the rhythms of sound.

A **haiku** is a form of Japanese poetry. The first and third lines each have five syllables and the second line has seven. There are 17 total syllables in a haiku.

Rhyming couplets are a pair of rhyming lines that usually have the same meter and length.

A **limerick** is a five-line poem that is often humorous. In a limerick, the first, second, and fifth lines, and the third and fourth lines, rhyme.

Part 1

Reading Strategy:
Text Structure

Looking at the boldfaced words is one way to understand how a text is organized. As you preview a text, you will likely notice some words that are unfamiliar to you. You can use context clues to help figure out the meanings of these difficult words. Context clues are the text around an unfamiliar word that helps you figure out the meaning. Use context clues to help you better understand what you are reading.

Literary Terms

poetry literature in verse form that usually has rhythm and paints powerful or beautiful impressions with words

stanza a group of lines that forms a unit in a poem

alliteration repeating sounds by using words whose beginning sounds are the same

onomatopoeia using words that sound like their meaning

rhyme words that end with the same or similar sounds

rhythm a pattern created by the stressed and unstressed syllables in a line of poetry

figurative language writing or speech not meant to be understood exactly as it is written

simile a figure of speech that makes a comparison using the words *like* or *as*

metaphor a figure of speech that makes a comparison but does not use *like* or *as*

personification giving characters such as animals or objects the characteristics or qualities of humans

repetition using a word, phrase, or image more than once, for emphasis

imagery pictures created by words; the use of words that appeal to the five senses

humor literature created to be funny or to amuse

About the Authors and Selections

As a child, Eleanor Farjeon loved reading stories in the attic of her home in London, England. She also loved playing games of make-believe with her little brother. When she grew up, her childhood sense of wonder inspired her work. She wrote dozens of books of **poetry** and stories for children and young adults. Farjeon's 1931 poem "Morning Has Broken" is one of her best-known works. Pop singer Cat Stevens set it to music, and it was a hit song in the 1970s. "Cat!," Farjeon's poem in this textbook, captures the sounds of a frightened and angry cat.

Eleanor Farjeon
1881–1965

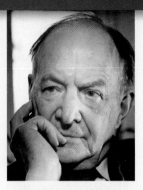

Walter de la Mare
1873–1956

The British poet and novelist Walter de la Mare loved the magical world of imagination. Yet, for years, he worked at an ordinary job as a bookkeeper for an oil company. He wrote during his lunch hour. Every night at bedtime, he read one of his new poems to his four children. In 1908, the British government gave him a grant that allowed him to retire at age 35. After that, de la Mare wrote full-time for the rest of his life. In "Silver," he describes the peaceful mood created by silvery moonlight.

Georgia Douglas
Johnson
1880–1966

As a child, Georgia Douglas Johnson loved music. She taught herself to play the violin. Later, she used her love of musical qualities to create hundreds of poems. She became one of the first well-known African American women poets. She published her last book of poetry when she was in her eighties. In "Your World," Johnson challenges readers to fight against limits to their imaginations and hopes.

Objectives

◆ To read and understand poetry

◆ To recognize sound devices such as alliteration, onomatopoeia, rhythm, and rhyme

Before Reading **continued on next page**

poetry literature in verse form that usually has rhythm and paints powerful or beautiful impressions with words

stanza a group of lines that forms a unit in a poem

alliteration repeating sounds by using words whose beginning sounds are the same

onomatopoeia using words that sound like their meaning

rhyme words that end with the same or similar sounds

rhythm a pattern created by the stressed and unstressed syllables in a line of poetry

Literary Terms Poems are often written in **stanzas,** or groups of lines that form a unit in a poem. In poems, sound devices help poets draw on the musical features of words to express ideas. Common sound devices include **alliteration, onomatopoeia, rhyme,** and **rhythm.** Alliteration is repeating sounds by using words whose beginning sounds are the same. "Misty morning" is an example of alliteration. Onomatopoeia is using words that sound like their meaning, for example *buzz, crash, clang, zoom.* Rhyme is words that end with the same or similar sounds. "Spring fling" is an example of rhyme. Rhythm is a pattern created by the stressed and unstressed syllables in a line of poetry.

Reading on Your Own Before you read a poem, preview the lines of verse to identify unfamiliar words. As you read, the context clues can help you to decide on a possible meaning for each unfamiliar word. Look for these types of clues:

- synonym or definition: words that mean the same as the unfamiliar word
- antonym: words that are opposite in meaning
- explanation: words that give more information about the unfamiliar word

Writing on Your Own The descriptions in the three poems that follow show vivid imaginations at work. Write several sentences to tell why imagination and creativity are valuable.

Vocabulary Focus A word's origin is the place from which it comes. Most words in English have Latin or Greek origins. You can use a dictionary to find the origin of unfamiliar words. Try looking up these three words from the poems: *sycamore, thatch, cordons.* What do you learn about their origins?

Think Before You Read How do you think poets choose the topics of their poems?

Cat!
Scat!
After her, after her,
Sleeky **flatterer,**
5   **Spitfire** chatterer,
Scatter her, scatter her
      Off her mat!
      Wuff!
      Wuff!
10   Treat her rough!
Git her, git her,
Whiskery spitter!
Catch her, catch her,
Green-eyed scratcher!
15   Slathery
      Slithery
      Hisser,
      Don't miss her!
Run till you're **dithery,**
20   Hithery
      Thithery
      Pftts! pftts!
      How she spits!
      Spitch! Spatch!
25   Can't she scratch!
Scritching the bark
Of the sycamore tree,
She's reached her **ark**
And's hissing at me
30   *Pftts! pftts!*
      Wuff! wuff!
         Scat,
         Cat!
         That's
         That!
—*Eleanor Farjeon*

As you read, think about the words the poet uses. For example, the words *hithery thithery* are made-up words. They are based on *hither* and *thither,* which mean "here" and "there."

Reading Strategy:
Text Structure

Which words in lines 10–14 give a synonym that helps you determine the meaning of *git?*

Find two made-up words that imitate cat sounds. How do they help you imagine the poem's action?

flatterer one who praises insincerely to win approval

spitfire someone who is easily excited or angered

dithery nervous and confused

ark a shelter or safe place

© 2003 The Munch Museum/The Munch-Ellingsen Group / Artists Rights
Society (ARS), New York / ADAGP, Paris. Erich Lessing/Art Resource, NY

A Summer Night on the Beach, Edward Munch, 2003

Silver

Identify examples
of alliteration in
lines 1–5.

Slowly, silently, now the moon
Walks the night in her silver **shoon;**
This way, and that, she peers, and sees
Silver fruit upon silver trees;
5   One by one the **casements** catch
Her beams beneath the silvery **thatch;**
Couched in his kennel, like a log,
With paws of silver sleeps the dog;
From their shadowy coat the white breasts peep
10 Of doves in a silver-feathered sleep;
A harvest mouse goes scampering by,
With silver claws, and silver eye;
And moveless fish in the water gleam,
By silver reeds in a silver stream.
—*Walter de la Mare*

| **shoon** an old-fashioned word for "shoes" | **casements** windows that open out like doors | **thatch** a roof made of straw or other plant material |

Your World

Your world is as big as you make it.
I know, for I used to **abide**
In the narrowest nest in a corner,
My wings pressing close to my side.

5   But I sighted the distant horizon
Where the sky line **encircled** the sea
And I throbbed with a burning desire
To travel this **immensity**.

I battered the **cordons** around me
10 And cradled my wings on the breeze
Then soared to the **uttermost** reaches
With **rapture**, with power, with ease!
—*Georgia Douglas Johnson*

Reading Strategy:
Text Structure

How do the words
horizon, sky, and
sea help you find
the meaning of
immensity?

Which lines rhyme
in the final stanza?

abide to stay or remain	**immensity** grandness; hugeness	**uttermost** furthest; greatest
encircled made a circle around	**cordons** lines or cords that prevent free movement	**rapture** joy; delight

Cat! | *Silver* | *Your World*

Directions Choose the letter of the best answer or write the answer using complete sentences.

Comprehension: Identifying Facts

1. Where does the cat in "Cat!" run?
   A under the house
   B down the street
   C up a tree
   D through the kitchen

2. What "walks the night" in "Silver"?

3. Where does the speaker of "Your World" say that she used to live?

Comprehension: Putting Ideas Together

4. Why is the cat in "Cat!" running?
   A It is being chased.
   B It sees a wild bird.
   C It wants to get home.
   D It is happy and energetic.

5. What effect does the moon have on the other objects in "Silver"?

6. How do the events described in "Your World" explain the first line of the poem?

Understanding Literature: Sound Devices

Poets use sound devices to create music with their words. Alliteration is the repeating of beginning sounds. When the sounds fall on stressed syllables, alliteration adds to the rhythm of the poem. Onomatopoeia is the use of words that sound like their meaning. It can add to a reader's ability to "hear" what is being described. Rhyme is common in poetry and appears at the ends of lines or in the middle of lines. Rhyme gives a poem a sing-song feeling that adds to its musical sound.

7. How does the alliteration add to the image created in "Cat!"?

8. What do sound devices add to the experience of reading poetry? Explain.

Critical Thinking

9. What mood, or feeling in the reader, does the poet create in "Silver"?

Thinking Creatively

10. Which poem created the most vivid picture in your mind? Why?

Grammar Check

A predicate noun or predicate pronoun follows a linking verb. It renames the subject of the sentence. A predicate adjective follows a linking verb and describes the subject of the sentence.

- Predicate Noun: Ronnie will be the <u>captain</u> of the team.
- Predicate Pronoun: The two winners are <u>they</u>.
- Predicate Adjective: The flight to Houston was <u>fast</u>.

In each sentence, underline the predicate noun (PN), predicate pronoun (PP), or predicate adjective (PA). Then label each one correctly.

1 Katy is a fan of her hometown football team.

2 The gas station attendant was unkind.

3 The person you should speak to is Carol.

Vocabulary Builder

The suffix -ous means "having the quality of" or "full of." It is often added to nouns to turn them into adjectives. For example, *perilous* means "full of peril."

Look up the definition of each of these words: *thunderous, courageous, joyous, humorous, dangerous, furious*. Then,

on a sheet of paper, write a sentence for each word, using the word correctly.

Writing on Your Own

Choose a poem from this collection and write an introduction for a poetry reading. First, consider the subject of the poem. Next, review the poem to note the writer's use of sound devices. Remember to include the title and author in your introduction. Also tell your audience a little about the poem.

Listening and Speaking

With two classmates, plan and present a group reading of one of the three poems you just read. First, discuss how the poem uses sound devices to create a mood, or feeling. Then, rehearse your reading. Try to get across the mood of the poem. When you are prepared, read the poem aloud to your class.

Research and Technology

Create a poets' timeline. Starting with 1870, mark off 20-year intervals. Use a different color to mark the lifetime of each poet in this collection. Then, research important world events that took place from 1870 to 1970. Summarize at least five events on the timeline. Finally, write a brief overview to explain your timeline to viewers.

Advertisements

In Part 1, you are using text structure to find context clues that help you understand unfamiliar words. You can use this skill with most forms of writing. Advertisements are a form of persuasive writing. Their purpose is to convince a reader to do or buy something. Using context clues can help you understand what is being advertised. It can help you decide whether the product is something you want or need.

About Advertisements

A good advertisement, or ad, uses language that persuades. It expresses an opinion that seems convincing. Like poems, advertisements must get across their ideas using just a few words. They use lively adjectives to get a reader's attention.

Like all literature, advertisements are aimed at an audience. The ad must use pictures and words to appeal to that audience. Most ads begin with a statement, which may be a promise about what the product will do for the buyer.

A good ad captures the reader with that statement and makes the reader want to learn more.

Reading Skill

You can use context clues to understand unfamiliar words in advertisements. Look at the words that surround the word you do not know. Think about these questions:

- What part of speech is the unfamiliar word?

- Does the surrounding text include a synonym for the word?

- Does the surrounding text include a definition of the word?

- Does the surrounding text include explanations that help me understand the word?

- Can I make a sensible guess about the meaning of the word?

First, you must understand the meaning of the advertisement. Then, you can decide whether you want or need the product.

On the next two pages are different advertisements. One is for a theater production. The other is for a restaurant.

"REMEMBER?"

It was always your favorite musical, and now it's back!

The promise of this ad is that "Your favorite musical is back (and as great as ever)!"

CARVER'S SATURDAY'S SONG

opens November 15
at the Music Box Theatre

Ads often use quotes from real people to persuade the reader.

"An irresistible, must-see event!"
—Derek Reed, *New York Star*

"Is it a musical tragedy or an operetta?
Who cares—it's fabulous!"
—Renée Duchamp, *Greenwich News*

Lost loves and lonely days make up the drama.

Carver's score includes one of the best-loved songs
of all time, "Weekend Blues."

Don't miss this wonderful new production. Call TIX–5555.

A PEACEFUL, RIVERSIDE DINING EXPERIENCE

Chef Yancey Beloit, formerly of Le Bistro, is proud to introduce

BRIDGES

Notice the language that is used to persuade the reader to visit the restaurant.

a restaurant unlike any other

Nestled between two bridges, this unusual eatery offers river views from every table. Sample our 50 blends of Moroccan tea. Taste our delicious entree-of-the-day while you watch the lights of the harbor far below. We combine the flavors of Southern Europe and North Africa to create a bridge between continents. The result is something special that will bring you back again and again. We look forward to serving you soon.

This ad speaks directly to its audience.

Reservations required.
Open for lunch and dinner. Call 555–1001

Monitor Your Progress

Directions Choose the letter of the best answer or write the answer using complete sentences.

1. What is the author's main purpose in writing the ad for "Saturday's Song"?
   A to remind the reader that musicals are fun
   B to convince the reader that Carver is great
   C to summarize the plot of a familiar musical
   D to persuade the reader to buy a ticket

2. Which phrase from the advertisement for the musical ad helps you understand the word *irresistible*?
   A make up the drama
   B musical comedy
   C a must-see event
   D wonderful new production

3. What is the promise of the restaurant ad?
   A Bridges has more variety than other restaurants.
   B Bridges is an inexpensive place to bring a date.
   C Bridges is a peaceful and unique place to dine.
   D Bridges has food the whole family will enjoy.

4. Choose two of these words from the ads: *irresistible, operetta, nestled, entrée*. Explain how a reader might use context clues to tell what the word means.

5. In each ad, find three adjectives that the author uses to persuade the reader.

Writing on Your Own

Decide which of the two ads you find more convincing. How did that ad make you want to see the show or visit the restaurant? Make a list of reasons. Use your list to write a paragraph that explains why you think the ad is a good one. If you have ideas about how it could be better, state those ideas as well.

Patricia Hubbell
1928–

Richard García
1941–

Langston Hughes
1902–1967

Objectives

♦ To read and understand poetry

♦ To recognize figurative language including similes, metaphors, and personification

About the Authors and Selections

Patricia Hubbell began writing poetry when she was 10 years old. She liked to sit in a tree and look down on her family's farm. There she often saw things she would include later in verse. Hubbell has been writing poetry and children's books for more than 40 years. She explains, "Poem ideas are everywhere; you have to listen and watch for them." In "Concrete Mixers," she compares machines to elephants as they go about their job building a city.

Richard García has been writing poetry since the 1950s. He published his first poetry collection in 1973, but then stopped writing for six years. An encouraging letter from Nobel Prize winner Octavio Paz inspired him to write again. Later, García was the Poet-in-Residence for years at the Children's Hospital in Los Angeles. There he led poetry and art workshops for sick children. In "The City Is So Big," García gives a child's-eye view of a scary nighttime city.

Langston Hughes wrote one of his most famous poems, "The Negro Speaks of Rivers," on a train. Hughes was fresh out of high school and was traveling to see his father. Hughes wanted to convince his father to pay for a writing program at Columbia University. His father agreed, and Hughes's writing career was launched. He remained at Columbia for only a year. Still, Hughes developed a lifelong love for the New York neighborhood of Harlem. It is the setting of many of his stories, poems, and plays. "Harlem Night Song" tells of his love for this place. The speaker invites a loved one to come outside. There they may wander together and enjoy the music and sights of the city at night.

Literary Terms **Figurative language** is writing or speech that is not meant to be understood exactly as it is written. **Similes, metaphors,** and **personification** are all examples of figurative language. A simile compares two things using a phrase that includes the words *like* or *as.* A metaphor also compares two unlike things but does not use *like* or *as.* Personification gives characters such as animals or objects the characteristics or qualities of humans. Poets also use **repetition**—repeated words, phrases, or images. The repetition is used to show emphasis in a poem.

Reading on Your Own As you read, notice the figurative language in each poem. In your notebook, write down examples of similes, metaphors, and personification.

Writing on Your Own The bustling excitement of city life stirs the feelings of the poets in this collection. Think of the sights and sounds a newcomer might experience in a city. Write a paragraph describing your ideas.

Vocabulary Focus Because poems are often short, poets must choose just the right words. Look at verbs in the poems you are about to read. What action does each verb name? As you read, think about how the poems would be different if these verbs were not used.

Think Before You Read Read the title of each poem. Why do you think these poems were grouped together?

figurative language writing or speech that is not meant to be understood exactly as it is written

simile a figure of speech that makes a comparison using the words *like* or *as*

metaphor a figure of speech that makes a comparison but does not use *like* or *as*

personification giving characters such as animals or objects the characteristics or qualities of humans

repetition using a word, phrase, or image more than once, for emphasis

CONCRETE MIXERS

The drivers are washing the concrete mixers;
Like elephant **tenders** they hose them down.
Tough gray-skinned monsters standing **ponderous,**
Elephant-bellied and elephant-nosed,

5 Standing in **muck** up to their wheel-caps,
Like rows of elephants, tail to trunk.
Their drivers perch on their backs like **mahouts,**
Sending the sprays of water up.
They rid the trunk-like **trough** of concrete,

10 Direct the spray to the bulging sides,
Turn and start the monsters moving.
      Concrete mixers
      Move like elephants
      Bellow like elephants

15   Spray like elephants,
  Concrete mixers are **urban** elephants,
  Their trunks are raising a city.
—*Patricia Hubbell*

As you read, look for comparisons. To what does the poet compare the drivers?

Reading Strategy: **Text Structure**
What context clues help tell the meaning of *muck?* Explain.

tenders people who care for animals

ponderous very heavy

muck wet, muddy dirt

mahouts elephant drivers or keepers in India and the East Indies

trough a long, deep, narrow bin

urban of or about cities or towns

The City Is So Big

How does the poet use personification to make the city seem scary?

The city is so big
Its bridges **quake** with fear
I know, I have seen at night

The lights sliding from house to house
5 And trains pass with windows shining
Like a smile full of teeth

I have seen machines eating houses
And stairways walk all by themselves
And elevator doors opening and closing
10 And people disappear.
—*Richard García*

quake to tremble
or shake

Harlem Night Song

Come,
Let us roam the night together
Singing.

I love you.

5 Across
The Harlem roof-tops
Moon is shining.
Night sky is blue.
Stars are great drops
10 Of golden dew.

Down the street
A band is playing.

I love you.

Come,
15 Let us roam the night together
Singing.
—*Langston Hughes*

Does Hughes
use a simile or
a metaphor to
describe the stars?
Explain.

Directions Choose the letter of the best answer or write the answer using complete sentences.

Comprehension: Identifying Facts

1. In "Concrete Mixers," where are the drivers as they wash the mixers?
   A on ladders next to the mixers
   B on the backs of the mixers
   C in the cabs of the mixers
   D on the ground beside the mixers

2. In "The City Is So Big," what are three unusual events the speaker says he has seen?

3. In "Harlem Night Song," which phrases are repeated?

Comprehension: Putting Ideas Together

4. Why are the drivers spraying the concrete mixers?
   A to get muck off their wheels
   B to cool them down
   C to prepare them for sale
   D to clean out old concrete

5. What ordinary events have scared the speaker in "The City Is So Big"? What has he really seen?

6. Why does the speaker in "Harlem Night Song" urge his companion to sing?

Understanding Literature: Figurative Language

Poets use figurative language to help a reader visualize what is being described. Most figurative language is a kind of comparison. In a simile, a poet compares two unlike things, using *like* or *as*. In a metaphor, a poet suggests that one unlike thing *is* the other. Metaphors do not use *like* or *as* in their comparisons. In personification, the poet compares an object or idea to a human being. A reader must think about how the compared things are alike. Understanding their likeness helps the reader understand the poet's purpose.

7. Name four ways in which the concrete mixers in "Concrete Mixers" are like elephants.

8. What simile does García use to describe the trains in the city?

Critical Thinking

9. How does the repetition in "Harlem Night Song" show the joyful mood of the poem?

Thinking Creatively

10. Which poem do you think best captures life in a big city? Explain.

Grammar Check

A direct object is a noun or pronoun that follows an action verb. It answers the questions *Whom?* or *What?* An indirect object is a noun or pronoun that comes after an action verb. It answers the questions *To whom?, For whom?, To what?,* or *For what?*

- Direct Object: Bill baked some <u>cookies</u>. (Baked what?)
- Indirect Object: Bill baked Marissa some cookies. (Baked for whom?)

Write three sentences that contain a direct object and an indirect object. Underline the direct object. Circle the indirect object.

 Vocabulary Builder

The suffix *-ment* means "the act of" doing something or "the state of" being something. It is added to verbs to turn them into nouns. In the noun *employment*, the suffix *-ment* has been added to the verb *employ. Employment* means "the state of being employed."

Define the underlined word in each sentence. Then write another sentence that uses the word correctly.

1 The bride and groom expressed their <u>commitment</u> to each other.

2 My grandparents are looking forward to their <u>retirement</u>.

3 We could not hide our <u>amazement</u> after winning the game.

 Writing on Your Own

Think of a poem you might write about a city setting. First, list the objects, sights, and sounds that come to mind when you think of cities. Then write your poem. Use words and ideas from your list. Include a comparison in your poem.

 Listening and Speaking

Select a poem that you like from this collection. Study it and practice it aloud until you have it memorized. As you practice, experiment with the tone and loudness of your voice. Present the poem to your class in a poetry slam.

 Research and Technology

Visit your library or use the Internet. Find several poems on a similar topic, such as cities, nature, sports, or courage. Create a collection of poems by grouping three poems that seem to belong together. Write an introduction to present the collection to readers.

Southbound on the Freeway   *by May Swenson*

May Swenson
1919–1989

- ◆ To read and understand a poem
- ◆ To compare humorous imagery in poetry

About the Author

May Swenson grew up in Utah and spoke Swedish in her childhood home. As an adult, she moved to New York to edit books. She later left that job to become a full-time poet. Swenson wrote poetry for children as well as for adults. She believed that poetry is based on the desire to see things as they truly are. Her poems often present a completely different view of ordinary life.

About the Selection

In "Southbound on the Freeway," an alien visiting Earth sees a traffic jam. The alien thinks the cars live on Earth. Although the poem is entertaining, the poet had a serious purpose. The poem was written at a time when the role of freeways was changing quickly. The Interstate Highway system was growing, and suburbs—areas just outside a city—were springing up. Many Americans were spending more time than ever in their cars.

As you read "Southbound on the Freeway," recall the poems you read previously. "Concrete Mixers," "The City Is So Big," and "Harlem Night Song" all use description and figurative language to paint a picture. Compare the use of language in those three poems with the use of language in "Southbound on the Freeway."

Literary Terms Poets use **imagery** to paint pictures in their readers' minds. Imagery is the use of words that appeal to the senses of sight, sound, touch, taste, and smell. Poets sometimes add **humor** to their imagery to create a more interesting picture. Humor is literature created to be funny or to amuse. Poets sometimes use the following techniques to create humorous effects with imagery:

- pairing images that do not usually go together, such as a fish on a bicycle

- using imagery to describe common situations from unusual points of view

- describing a familiar situation in a humorous way

imagery pictures created by words; the use of words that appeal to the five senses

humor literature created to be funny or to amuse

Reading on Your Own Reading poetry aloud can sometimes help you better hear the rhythm of the words. It also helps to create an image of what is happening. Try reading "Southbound on the Freeway" aloud. Pay attention to the rhythm and imagery created by the words.

Writing on Your Own Choose any object in your classroom. Imagine that you are a visitor from space. Describe the object in detail. Based on the object's appearance, make a guess about how it might be used. Then, share your description with your classmates.

Vocabulary Focus As you read, carefully consider how each word joins together to create an image in your mind. Think about how the image would change if just a few words were left out.

Think Before You Read Look at the image on page 334. How do you think the image relates to the poem?

Where to? What for? #3, Nancie B. Warner, 1998

SOUTHBOUND ON THE FREEWAY

A **tourist** came in from Orbitville,
parked in the air, and said:

The creatures of this star
are made of metal and glass.

tourist a person
traveling for pleasure

5 Through the **transparent** parts
you can see their guts.

Their feet are round and roll
on diagrams—or long

measuring tapes—dark
10 with white lines.

They have four eyes.
The two in the back are red.

Sometimes you can see a five-eyed
one, with a red eye turning
15 on the top of his head.
He must be special—

the others respect him,
and go slow,

when he passes, winding
20 among them from behind.

They all hiss as they glide,
like inches, down the marked

tapes. Those soft shapes,
shadowy inside

25 the hard bodies—are they
their guts or their brains?

What unexpected comparisons does the poet make to create humorous imagery?

To which senses does the imagery in line 21 appeal?

transparent able to
be seen through; clear

COMPARING LITERARY WORKS | Apply the Skills

Southbound on the Freeway   by May Swenson

Directions Choose the letter of the best answer or write the answer using complete sentences.

Comprehension: Identifying Facts

1. Where does the "tourist" in this poem live?
   A north of the freeway
   B in Orbitville
   C in the air
   D overseas

2. What kinds of creatures are mentioned in the poem?

3. What materials are used to make the creatures?

Comprehension: Putting Ideas Together

4. To what does the poet compare measuring tapes?
   A car headlights
   B alien spacecraft
   C automobile tires
   D highway lane lines

5. What is the "five-eyed" creature the tourist sees?

6. What are the "soft shapes" inside the hard bodies?

Understanding Literature: Humorous Imagery

Imagery is the use of words that appeal to the sense of sight, hearing, touch, smell, and taste. By using imagery, a poet helps a reader picture what is being described. Sometimes the imagery is humorous. The poet makes comparisons that we know are exaggerated or mistaken. The humor may be used for a serious reason. It may help readers see everyday things in a brand new way.

7. Look back at "The City Is So Big" on page 328. How do both García and Swenson use personification to give machines human qualities?

8. Compare the machines in "Concrete Mixers" on page 327 to those in "Southbound on the Freeway." Which seems more humorous to you?

Critical Thinking

9. What do you think May Swenson is saying about our automobile culture?

Thinking Creatively

10. Consider these three poems: "Concrete Mixers," "The City Is So Big," and "Southbound on the Freeway." Which one best helped you see everyday things in a brand new way? Explain.

Grammar Check

The first two lines of "Southbound on the Freeway" are made up of three combined predicates. The subject is *A tourist.* The predicates are (1) *came in from Orbitville,* (2) *parked in the air,* and (3) *said.* They are connected by commas and the word *and.*

Combine predicates to make each trio of sentences into one complete sentence.

1 I listened to his speech. I closed my eyes. I wept.

2 We followed the crowd. We entered the station. We waited.

 Vocabulary Builder

Guts are intestines, but we often use the word to mean "courage." Identify the figurative meaning of each of these sentences that mention body parts.

1 The team lost, but it showed a lot of <u>heart</u>.

2 It takes <u>brains</u> to solve those word problems.

3 Can you give me a <u>hand</u> with this ladder?

 Writing on Your Own

Look through your library's poetry collection to find another humorous poem. Read the poem several times. Then, in a short essay, explain how the poet uses imagery to create humor. First, describe the imagery in the poem. Next, explain how the humor is connected with the imagery. Finally, explain how the humorous imagery affects you.

  Listening and Speaking

Discuss this question with a partner: What other questions might an alien tourist ask about American culture?

Think about those things that might seem strange to an alien. Create a list and then discuss your ideas with another group.

 Media and Viewing

Find a current image of traffic on America's highways. Study the picture and write down what you see. Then write a poem of your own. Be sure to include description and imagery in your poem.

Part 2

Reading Strategy:
Visualizing

Visualizing is another strategy that helps readers understand what they are reading. It is like creating a movie in your mind. Use the following ways to visualize a text:

- Look at the photographs, illustrations, and descriptive words.

- Think about experiences in your own life that may add to the images.

- Notice the order in which things are happening and what you think might happen next.

Literary Terms

lyric poem a short poem that expresses a person's emotions or feelings

narrative poem a poem that tells a story

refrain a repeated line in a poem or song that creates mood or gives importance to something

end rhyme a feature of a poem or song in which the last words of two lines rhyme

free verse poetry that does not have a strict rhyming pattern or regular line length and uses actual speech patterns for the rhythms of sound

analogy a comparison between two otherwise different things that share the same characteristics

About the Authors and Selections

Sandra M. Castillo is a poet in what is called the "exile tradition." An exile is someone who has been sent away from his or her home country. Sandra Castillo came to the United States from Cuba on a Freedom Flight in 1970. She would not return to her homeland for 24 years. During that time, she lived in Florida. She went to school, learned English, and began to write. "Pig Roast" tells about the visit of an uncle from Cuba. Although he is family, he is not American. He brings something foreign to a family gathering.

Sandra M. Castillo
1962–

William Shakespeare
1564–1616

William Shakespeare is thought of by some as the greatest writer in the English language. Shakespeare was born in Stratford-on-Avon, a small town in England. He moved to London as a young man and spent most of his adult life there. Shakespeare was an actor, a producer, and a director. However, he is most famous for his plays and poems. The poem "Blow, Blow, Thou Winter Wind" comes from Shakespeare's comedy *As You Like It*. It is sung by the character Lord Amiens in Act II, Scene vii.

Ricardo Sánchez
1941–1995

Ricardo Sánchez was born in El Paso, Texas. His family had roots in Spanish, Mexican, and American Indian cultures. Most of Sánchez's work explores and celebrates his rich cultural traditions. In the poem "Old Man," Sánchez pictures a grandfather he remembers with love. He notes that many parts of the old man's personality live on in himself.

Before Reading continued on next page

Objectives

◆ To read and understand poetry

◆ To explain the differences between narrative poetry and lyric poetry

◆ To define refrain

lyric poetry
a short poem
that expresses a
person's emotions
or feelings

narrative poetry
a poem that tells
a story

refrain a repeated
line in a poem or
song that creates
mood or gives
importance to
something

Literary Terms Two main forms of poetry are **lyric poetry** and **narrative poetry.** A lyric poem is a short poem that expresses a person's thoughts and feelings. A lyric poem gives a snapshot of one time or place, or it expresses a single idea. A narrative poem tells a story in verse. It has all the elements of a short story—characters, setting, plot, and conflict. Sometimes poems also contain a **refrain.** This is a repeated line in a poem or song that creates mood or gives importance to something.

Reading on Your Own When you visualize, you use the author's words to create a picture in your mind. To visualize, you may also use the illustrations as a guide. You should think about your own knowledge of the topic. Consider these questions:

• Have I ever seen anything like this? What was it like?

• If I were the speaker, what would I see, hear, smell, or feel?

Writing on Your Own The poems in this collection discuss a range of feelings. They speak of uncertainty, bitterness, love, and loss. Make a list of reasons why people might want to read about other people's feelings. How do such poems help us?

Vocabulary Focus An *archaic* word is one that is not commonly used today. Because he wrote so long ago, many of the words Shakespeare uses are now considered archaic. For example, *thou = you, thy = your, art = are, dost = does/do.* Pay attention to these and other archaic words as you read.

Think Before You Read Is the speaker in a poem always the poet? How can you tell? As you read, decide who is speaking in each poem.

Cuban Hospitality/Return of the Prodigal Son, Jules Pascin, 1915

Pig Roast

We meet in the yard at tía Estela's
by her mango trees, her avocados, guavas,
tropical fruit, by her gardenias, her lirios,
and her orchids, by her roosters and her white
5   patio furniture.

It is Ramoncito's first week in America.
And though forty, he keeps the **diminutive**
in his name and thanks her for pulling him,
her stepson, out of Cuba twenty years after she herself
10   was able to leave by weeding the lawn she can no longer
mow, by vasing the flowers she grows.

diminutive a suffix
that shows smallness;
a childhood nickname

Tía means "aunt"
in Spanish; *tío*
means "uncle."

Mangoes,
avocados, guavas,
gardenias, lirios,
and orchids are
types of tropical
fruits and flowers.

As you read, notice
ways in which the
poem is like a
story.

This ninety-degree Sunday,
he turns the pig, pokes it to check the crispness
of its crackling skin as Mother and I watch.
15 He offers us pieces of pig skin, smiles, tells us
it's the best part.

And in his pale blue Camden Maine T-shirt,
sneakers, Levi's, he is tío Ramón, tall, thin, dark.
He is the skinny twenty-year-old who must have sat
20 with me at that long dining table in Almendares,
where for dessert, tía Estela always gave me
a tablespoon of **condensed milk.** I was five;
Ramoncito was of military age.

I take what he offers, turn to watch him eat
25 the piece he has carved for himself. What do you think,
he asks. Mother tells him it is done; he agrees.
And they eat their pork pieces like it was Christmas
or New Year's Eve. I smile at Mother, try to give her
my piece without his noticing, but suddenly, we are caught
30 by tío Ramón and the video camera he aims at our faces
as he yells to get closer, get closer.

Ramoncito poses, **proclaims** himself **chef,** Mother smiles,
pulls me in. And I am caught—transparent, **ashen.**
I smile past the camera to that long, pink house
35 with its many rooms, to its tall windows and their
wrought iron. I eat a piece of dark pig skin
and wipe my mouth with the back of my hand.
—*Sandra M. Castillo*

Reading Strategy:
Visualizing

How does the poet help you "see" tío Ramón?

Almendares is a city in Cuba.

How does the poet organize the story in this poem?

condensed milk a thick, sweetened, canned milk	**proclaims** makes known publicly	**chef** a head cook **ashen** pale

BLOW, BLOW, THOU WINTER WIND

Blow, blow, thou winter wind.
Thou art not so unkind
   As man's **ingratitude**.
Thy tooth is not so keen,
5   Because thou art not seen,
   Although thy breath be rude.
Heigh-ho! Sing, heigh-ho! unto the green holly.
Most friendship is **feigning**, most loving **mere** folly.
   Then, heigh-ho, the holly!
10   This life is most jolly.

Freeze, freeze, thou bitter sky,
That dost not bite so **nigh**
   As benefits forgot.
Though thou the waters **warp**,
15   Thy sting is not so sharp
   As friend remembered not.
Heigh-ho! Sing, heigh-ho! unto the green holly.
Most friendship is feigning, most loving mere folly.
   Then, heigh-ho, the holly!
20   This life is most jolly.
—William Shakespeare

> Lines 7–10 are the refrain. The same lines are repeated in lines 17–20.

> To what does the speaker compare the winter's chill in this lyric poem?

ingratitude a lack of thankfulness

feigning fake

mere plain; simple

nigh near

warp to change the shape of; to twist

Old Man

remembrance
(smiles/hurts sweetly)
October 8, 1972

Reading Strategy:
Visualizing

What does the old
man's face look
like? Which words
help you know?

old man
with brown skin
talking of past
   when being shepherd
5   in utah, nevada, colorado and
      new mexico
was life lived freely;

El Pan Nuestro
(Our Daily Bread),
Ramon Frade

old man,
   grandfather,
10 wise with time
running **rivulets** on face,
deep, rich furrows,
   each one a **legacy**,
deep, rich memories of life . . .
15   "you are **indio**,
      among other things,"
he would tell me
    during nights spent

rivulets gullies; ditches	**legacy** anything handed down from an ancestor	**indio** American Indian

so long ago
20   amidst familial gatherings
in albuquerque . . .

old man, loved and respected,
he would speak sometimes
of **pueblos**,
25   san juan, santa clara,
and even santo domingo,
and his family, he would say,
came from there:
some of our blood was here,
30   he would say,
before the coming of coronado,
other of our blood
came with los españoles,
and the mixture
35 was rich,
though often painful . . .
old man,
who knew earth
by its awesome **aromas**
40 and who felt
the heated sweetness
of chile verde
by his **supple** touch,
gone into dust is your body
45   with its **stoic** look and **resolution**,
but your reality, old man, lives on
in a mindsoul touched by you . . .

Old Man . . .
—*Ricardo Sánchez*

Francisco Coronado was a 16th century Spanish explorer who traveled through what is now the American Southwest. Los españoles are "the Spaniards."

pueblos American Indian towns in central and northern New Mexico

aromas smells

supple capable of moving easily

stoic calm in the face of suffering

resolution the power of holding firmly to a purpose

Pig Roast | Blow, Blow, Thou Winter Wind | Old Man

Directions Choose the letter of the best answer or write the answer using complete sentences.

Comprehension: Identifying Facts

1. What is the setting of "Pig Roast"?
   A the speaker's home
   B the island of Cuba
   C an aunt's garden
   D a Cuban restaurant

2. What is even less kind than the winter wind in "Blow, Blow, Thou Winter Wind"?

3. In "Old Man," what does the old man tell his grandson "amidst familial gatherings"?

Comprehension: Putting Ideas Together

4. Why does the speaker in "Pig Roast" offer the pig skin to her mother?
   A She does not like it.
   B Her mother cooked it.
   C Her uncle ruined it.
   D She wants something else.

5. The speaker in "Blow, Blow, Thou Winter Wind" says of the wind, "though thou the waters warp." What picture does this make in your mind?

6. Whose "mindsoul" do you think was touched in "Old Man"?

Understanding Literature: Lyric and Narrative Poetry

Lyric poetry is short poetry that expresses the thoughts and feelings of a single speaker. In Greek poetry, a lyric was sung to a tune plucked on a lyre. Today, a lyric poem may or may not rhyme, but it is always expressive. Narrative poetry, on the other hand, tells a story. Long ago, it might also have been in the form of a song. The song would tell the story of a hero. Today, a narrative poem may tell about any event. It contains characters and a plot that is told in time order.

7. What thoughts and feelings about winter and human nature are expressed in the lyric poem "Blow, Blow, Thou Winter Wind"? What overall image is created? Explain.

8. Who are the characters in "Pig Roast"? How is the speaker in conflict with her uncle?

Critical Thinking

9. What can you guess about the speaker in "Blow, Blow, Thou Winter Wind"? Explain your answer using examples from the poem.

Thinking Creatively

10. Which poem in this collection could you relate to the most? Explain.

✔ Grammar Check

A preposition shows how two words or phrases are connected. Read the sentence that follows.

My toothbrush is in my cup, and my toothpaste is on the counter.

The first preposition, *in*, connects the noun *cup* to the noun *toothbrush*. It tells where the toothbrush is placed. The second preposition, *on*, connects the noun *counter* to the noun *toothpaste*. It tells where the toothpaste is located.

Common prepositions include *above, behind, below, beyond, for, from, in, into,* and *with.*

Rewrite this sentence three times. Use a different preposition in the blank each time. Then, explain how the preposition changed the meaning of the sentence.

The dog jumped _____ the fence.

Vocabulary Builder

The prefix *a-* often takes the place of certain prepositions. For example, the word *amidst* means "in the middle of." The word *atop* means "on top of." The word *aboard* means "on board."

Use your understanding of the prefix *a-* to tell the meanings of these words: *abed, ablaze, afoot, alike, awhile.* Write each word and its meaning on a sheet of paper.

Writing on Your Own

Write a lyric or narrative poem about a person whom you admire. Your subject can be a historical figure or someone you know. If you are writing a lyric poem, brainstorm for details about the person's qualities. If you are writing a narrative poem, list the events, characters, and setting you will include. As you write, try to use figurative language that helps a reader visualize what you are describing.

Listening and Speaking

With a group, prepare a checklist for a poetry reading. Identify some qualities of a good poetry reading. These might include varying tone of voice, using pauses at the right time, and reading clearly. Then, have each group member read aloud one of the three poems you read in this collection. The rest of the group can use the checklist to judge the reading.

Research and Technology

Research one of these topics: Freedom Flights from Cuba (from "Pig Roast") or The Coming of Coronado (from "Old Man"). Use at least two resources and learn all that you can about the topic. Use your notes to write a paragraph about the topic. Finally, explain what the topic means to the poet.

BEFORE READING THE SELECTIONS | Build Understanding

John Updike
1932–

N. Scott Momaday
1934–

Cathy Song
1955–

About the Authors and Selections

John Updike writes poetry, essays, short stories, and literary criticism. However, he is best known as a Pulitzer Prize-winning novelist. Updike grew up on a farm in Pennsylvania. He enjoyed reading so much that his mother encouraged him to write. In 2003, Updike received the National Medal for the Humanities. Before that, he had won the National Medal of Art. Only a handful of writers have been honored with both prizes. Updike's poem, "January," describes images connected with winter.

A Kiowa Indian, N. Scott Momaday is known for his poetry, plays, art, and essays. He grew up on an Indian reservation. As a writer, Momaday tries to pass on Kiowa oral traditions. His father, a great teller of Kiowa stories, inspired Momaday to write. Like John Updike, Momaday has won the Pulitzer Prize for a novel. "New World" looks at how man and beast are each a part of their surrounding world.

Cathy Song was raised in Hawaii. Like many Hawaiians, she has roots in Korea and China. She grew up in a home with three generations—grandparents, parents, and children. She began writing in high school and earned degrees in English and in creative writing. Besides poetry, Song has written short stories. Like many of her poems, "Easter: Wahiawa, 1959" explores family relationships.

Objectives

- ◆ To read and understand poetry
- ◆ To identify and interpret imagery in poetry
- ◆ To define end rhyme and free verse

Literary Terms Poets use imagery to help readers imagine sights, sounds, textures, tastes, and smells. They use interesting nouns, verbs, adjectives, and adverbs to make their descriptions clear. In addition to imagery, "January" by John Updike also contains **end rhyme.** This is a feature of a poem or song in which the last words of two lines rhyme. You will find an example of **free verse** poetry in N. Scott Momaday's "New World." Free verse is poetry that does not have a strict rhyming pattern or regular line length. This type of poetry uses actual speech patterns for the rhythms of sound.

Reading on Your Own When you visualize, you use your own experiences to picture what is being described in writing. For example, what do you "see" when you read the word *landscape?* Someone who is raised in the Southwest will visualize one kind of landscape. Someone who is raised in the Northeast will visualize a different kind of landscape. Poets choose words to help their readers "see" what they want them to see. If a description is very exact, more readers will "see" the same thing.

Writing on Your Own The poems in this collection capture positive feelings about people, places, and situations. Choose a person or place. Write three reasons why you have positive feelings about that person or place. Then, write five words you might use to describe that person or place.

Vocabulary Focus To appeal to readers, poets use words with certain connotations. A connotation is the feeling that a word gives the reader. For example, the word *dark* may have a connotation of scariness, or it may have a connotation of coziness. As you read, pay attention to how the poet has used familiar words. Look for the connotation he or she wants you to understand.

Think Before You Read If you planned to write a poem about a month, which month would you choose? Why?

end rhyme
a feature of a poem or song in which the last words of two lines rhyme

free verse poetry that does not have a strict rhyming pattern or regular line length and uses actual speech patterns for the rhythms of sound

The Magpie, Claude Monet, 1869

As you read, think about to which sense each stanza appeals. Also notice the end rhyme in each stanza.

The days are short,
    The sun a spark
Hung thin between
    The dark and dark.

5 Fat snowy footsteps
    Track the floor,
And **parkas** pile up
    Near the door.

parkas heavy waterproof coats with a hood

The river is
10   A frozen place
Held still beneath
    The trees' black lace.

The sky is low.
    The wind is gray.
15 The **radiator**
    Purrs all day.
    —John Updike

Reading Strategy:
Visualizing

Compare and contrast the artist's concept of winter with Updike's.

radiator a heating device made of a set of pipes through which steam or hot water travels

Oil on canvas. Abby Aldrich Rockefeller Folk Art Museum, The Colonial
Williamsburg Foundation, Williamsburg, VA

Wallowa Lake, **Stephen W. Harley,
Oregon, 1927–1928**

NEW
WORLD

1. First Man,
behold:
the earth
glitters
5 with leaves;
the sky
glistens
with rain.
Pollen
10 is **borne**
on winds
that low
and lean
upon
15 mountains.
Cedars
blacken
the slopes—
and pines.

2. 20 At dawn
eagles
hie and
hover
above
25 the plain
where light
gathers
in pools.
Grasses
30 shimmer
and shine.
Shadows
withdraw
and lie
35 away
like smoke.

3. At noon
turtles
enter
40 slowly
into
the warm
dark **loam**.
Bees hold
45 the swarm.
Meadows
recede
through planes
of heat
50 and pure
distance.

4. At dusk
the gray
foxes
55 stiffen
in cold;
blackbirds
are fixed
in the
60 branches.
Rivers
follow
the moon,
the long
65 white track
of the
full moon.
—*N. Scott Momaday*

As you read, notice that this poem is written in free verse.

What simile does the poet use to appeal to the sense of sight?

What images show a sense of the temperature in the final stanza?

pollen a powder made in flowers that helps a plant form seeds

borne carried

hie to fly swiftly

withdraw to retreat; to fall back

loam rich, dark soil

recede to move away

Easter: Wahiawa, 1959

Wahiawa is a town on the island of Oahu in Hawaii, about 20 miles from downtown Honolulu.

Reading Strategy: Visualizing

What is happening in this narrative poem? Where are the people? What are they doing?

Pedal pushers are knee-length pants and *poodle cuts* are short, curly haircuts. Both were popular for women in the 1950s.

1

The rain stopped for one afternoon.
Father brought out
his movie camera and for a few hours
we were all together
5   under a thin film
that separated the rain showers
from that part of the earth
like a **hammock**
held loosely by clothespins.

10   Grandmother took the opportunity
to hang the laundry
and Mother and my aunts
filed out of the house
in pedal pushers and poodle cuts,
15   carrying the blue washed eggs.

Grandfather kept the children
penned in on the porch,
clucking at us in his broken English
whenever we tried to peek
20   around him. There were bread crumbs
stuck to his blue gray whiskers.

I looked from him to the sky,
a **membrane** of egg whites
straining under the weight
25   of the storm that threatened
to break.

hammock a hanging bed or couch made of canvas cord

membrane a thin skin

We burst loose from Grandfather
when the mothers returned
from planting the eggs
30　around the **soggy** yard.
He followed us,
walking with stiff but sturdy legs.
We dashed and disappeared
into bushes,
35　searching for the treasures;
the hard-boiled eggs
which Grandmother had been **simmering**
in vinegar and blue color all morning.

2
When Grandfather was a young boy
40　in Korea,
it was a long walk
to the riverbank,
where, if he were lucky,

soggy damp and mushy	**simmering** boiling for a long time at a low temperature

What simile does
the poet use to
appeal to the sense
of sight?

a quail egg or two
45 would gleam from the mud
like gigantic pearls.
He could never eat enough
of them.

It was another long walk
50 through the sugarcane fields
of Hawaii,
where he worked for eighteen years,
cutting the sweet stalks
with a **machete**. His right arm
55 grew **disproportionately** large
to the rest of his body.
He could hold three
grandchildren in that arm.

I want to think
60 that each stalk that fell
brought him closer
to a clearing,
to that **palpable** field
where from the porch
65 to the gardenia hedge
that day he was **enclosed**
by his grandchildren,
scrambling around him,
for whom he could at last buy
70 cratefuls of oranges,
basketfuls of sky blue eggs.

I found three that afternoon.
By evening, it was raining hard.

machete a broad, heavy knife	**disproportionately** in a way that is out of proportion; in an unlike way	**palpable** physical; capable of being touched
		enclosed surrounded; shut in on all sides

Bahamas, Margie Livingston Campbell, 2001

Grandfather and I skipped supper.
75 Instead, we sat on the porch
and I ate what he peeled
and cleaned for me.
The scattering of the **delicate**
marine-colored shells across his lap
80 was something like what the ocean gives
the beach after a rain.
—*Cathy Song*

Reading Strategy:
Visualizing
Describe the image created by the last four lines.

delicate of fine quality

Directions Choose the letter of the best answer or write the answer using complete sentences.

Comprehension: Identifying Facts

1. In "January," which does the speaker not link with the month of January?
   A a purring radiator
   B a frozen river
   C a pile of parkas
   D an angry storm

2. In "New World," what three times of day are identified?

3. What is unusual about the grandfather's arm in "Easter: Wahiawa, 1959"?

Comprehension: Putting Ideas Together

4. In "January," why do the trees seem to be made of lace?
   A They are very easily broken.
   B They are coated with ice and snow.
   C They have just begun to bloom.
   D They are decorated for the holiday.

5. What does the speaker in "New World" seem to want people to do?

6. Why were eggs once so important to the speaker's grandfather in "Easter: Wahiawa, 1959"?

Understanding Literature: Imagery

Imagery is the use of words to suggest pictures. It may also be the use of words that appeal to other senses besides sight. Words and phrases that help you "see" or "hear" a scene are images. To create imagery, poets may use vivid, exact words. They may also use comparisons such as similes or metaphors. Imagery is especially important in poetry.

7. What imagery in "New World" appeals to the senses? How do these images capture a feeling of newness?

8. List three images from "Easter: Wahiawa, 1959" that helped you picture the scene. What mood, or feeling, do these images create?

Critical Thinking

9. Why do you think a poet may choose to write a free verse poem instead of one that rhymes?

Thinking Creatively

10. Choose one of the three poems. Imagine that you want to paint a watercolor to go with the poem. Which colors will you use? Why?

Grammar Check

An infinitive is a form of verb that comes after the word *to*. It acts as a noun, an adjective, or an adverb.

Example: Grandmother took the opportunity <u>to hang</u> the laundry.

Find three other examples of infinitives in "Easter: Wahiawa, 1959." Do not confuse the *to* that is part of an infinitive with the *to* that is a preposition. Write these infinitives on a sheet of paper.

 Vocabulary Builder

The English language grows as words are borrowed from other languages. If the words are used often, they slowly become part of the language. A *machete* is a special kind of knife. This word is borrowed from the Spanish. A *parka* is a heavy, hooded jacket usually worn in the Arctic. This word comes from the Nenets people of northern Russia. A *hammock* is a hanging bed made of canvas cord. This word is borrowed from the Taino Indians of the Caribbean.

Choose three other vocabulary words from the poems you just read. Look up the origin of each word. Do any of the words you chose come from a language other than English?

 Writing on Your Own

In a review of a written work, readers look at its strengths and weaknesses. Write a review of this three-poem collection. Think about the sounds, word choice, and imagery in each poem. Do the sounds and rhythms match the subject of the poem? As you draft, state your opinion of each poem. Support your opinion with examples from the poem.

 Listening and Speaking

Find music that reflects the mood, or feeling, of one poem from this collection. Practice reading the poem aloud to the music. Make your voice loud or soft to show the feelings in the poem. Bring a recording of the music to class. Read the poem aloud as you play the music.

 Research and Technology

Write a short report on one of the poets in this collection. Use two or more reference books or sources to find information. Rewrite the information in your own words. In your report, explain how the author's background is reflected in the poem you read.

The *Readers' Guide to Periodical Literature*

Poems, short stories, and essays are often published first in magazines. Magazines provide up-to-date information on a wide range of subjects. To find magazine articles on a certain subject, you can use a periodical index. (A *periodical* is a magazine or newspaper—something that is published periodically.) One of the most popular indexes is *The Readers' Guide to Periodical Literature*.

About the *Readers' Guide to Periodical Literature*

The Readers' Guide is published every month. It lists articles and stories from major magazines. Articles are listed by subject and author. Stories are listed by title and author. Each year, the monthly indexes are published in a volume. To find recent articles, look in a recent volume. To find articles from long ago, look in an older volume. You can also search the *Readers' Guide* online.

All of the references are listed in alphabetical order. That means authors, titles, and subjects are all listed in the same index. Sometimes you must look closely to see whether the article is <u>about</u> a person or <u>by</u> that person.

UPDIKE, JOHN 1932–

After Katrina. *NY Review of Books* v53 p13 N 30 '06

Long-distance runner. G. Wills. *NY Review of Books* v37 p22-3 O 25 '90

The first article is <u>by</u> John Updike. The second is <u>about</u> John Updike. It is by an author named G. Wills. Both articles appeared in the *New York Review of Books*. The first appeared on November 30, 2006. The second appeared on October 25, 1990.

Reading Skill

The *Readers' Guide* lists a huge amount of information in a small space. To do this, it uses abbreviations. An abbreviation is the short form of a word. To use the *Readers' Guide,* you must read and understand abbreviations.

Abbreviations Used in the *Readers' Guide*			
p = page	v = volume	no = number	il = illustrated
Ja = January	F = February	Mr = March	Ap = April
My = May	Ju = June	Jl = July	Ag = August
S = September	O = October	N = November	D = December

READERS' GUIDE TO
PERIODICAL LITERATURE 2005

TRAVEL

Air travel with 50-foot TV screens.

B. Howard. il. *Video Today* v13 p6-7 Mr '05

Moon trips without cheese.

J. Lee. *Short Story Monthly* v45 p45-67 Ap '05

> Under a topic or author, references are in alphabetical order by title.

> The main subject or author's name is in capital letters.

TRAVERS, JANICE S. 1942–

The Mad Venusian. *Tomorrow's Woman* v123 p30-46 Ap '05

Tunes from another world. *Purplebook* v12 p24-5 Mr '05

VIDEO

What's new in video? il. *News Mag* v24 p36 Ap 11 '05

DVD or videocassette?

P. Herrara. *Video Culture* v15 p110-5 Mr '05

Storing videos.

A. Chang. *Video Monthly* v10 p25-7 Ap '05

> Even the page numbers are abbreviated. The note "p25-7" means "pages 25 to 27."

READERS' GUIDE TO
PERIODICAL LITERATURE 2006

MUSEUMS

Museums of China.

C. Chen. il. map *World Adventures* v3 p24-5 S '06

Under the arch.

L. Remarque. il. *Architecture Today* v20 no3 p16-7 Ag '06

Visiting the Louvre.

R. Lacayo. *Art History* v98 p35-7 S '06

> The first listing is illustrated, and it also contains a map.

MUSIC

And he can play!

P. Johnston *Rockin' Report* v3 p32-6 S '06

Fine-tuning the orchestra.

D. Hofstra *News Mag* v25 p34-5 S 4 '06

Your child's lessons.

D. Sewelson *Parents Monthly* v12 p28-30 Ag '06

> Notice that all references in this volume are from two months in 2006.

> Some magazines come out weekly. Those magazines are listed with the exact date of publication.

MUZZY, LENORE V. 1953–

A few unknown poets.

F. Reynolds *Purplebook* v13 p50-1+ S '06

Writing at home.

Making Money v6 no3 p21-4 Ag '06

> A plus sign means that the story is continued on later pages in the magazine.

MYTHOLOGY

From Greek to Roman.

X. Valenti. il. *History Buff* v15 p45-8 Ag 11 '05

Stories from Peru.

P. Luminoso. il. *Kiddstuff* v 10 p 42-5 S '06

Why the grass is green.

R. Lily. il. *Storyteller* v2 p24-7 Ag '06

Monitor Your Progress

Directions Choose the letter of the best answer or write the answer using complete sentences.

1. In the 2005 index, which magazine includes the article "What's New in Video"?
   A *Purplebook*
   B *News Magazine*
   C *Video Today*
   D *Tomorrow's Woman*

2. Which two months are covered in the page from 2005?
   A April and May
   B March and April
   C August and September
   D March and August

3. Which of these articles from 2006 has pictures?
   A "A Few Unknown Poets"
   B "Fine-Tuning the Orchestra"
   C "Your Child's Lessons"
   D "From Greek to Roman"

4. Suppose you were writing a report on the literature of South America. Which article from 2005 or 2006 might you wish to read?

5. Suppose you want to learn more for your report on the literature of South America. What other topics might you look at in the *Readers' Guide*? List three other topics not shown here that might include articles for your report.

Writing on Your Own

Imagine a friend is writing a report on Lenore V. Muzzy. Use the 2006 page from the *Readers' Guide*. Write a letter to your friend and tell her where she might find an article about Lenore V. Muzzy. Also tell her where she might find an article written by Lenore V. Muzzy. Include all the information your friend will need to find the articles in the library.

O Captain! My Captain!   by Walt Whitman

Walt Whitman
1819–1892

Objectives

- To read and understand a lyric poem
- To compare types of description in poetry
- To recognize analogies in poetry

About the Author

Walt Whitman was born on Long Island, New York, in 1819. His family moved to Brooklyn four years later. Whitman left school at the age of 11 to work for a printer. He worked for many newspapers as a printer and editor. He also began to send in his own stories, articles, and poems.

In the 1840s and 1850s, Whitman worked odd jobs and wrote poems. He put them together in a collection called *Leaves of Grass*. He paid to have 795 copies of the collection printed. In the introduction to the book, Whitman told about his wish to write a new kind of poetry for Americans.

It took many years for people to accept this new poetry. It did not rhyme, and it was not romantic. It was like nothing that Americans had seen before. Not until Whitman's Civil War poems were praised in England did Americans take his work seriously.

About the Selection

During the Civil War, Whitman worked in military hospitals in Washington, D.C. There he saw his beloved President Lincoln from afar. Less than a week after the Union victory, Lincoln was killed. This event deeply moved Whitman. He wrote the poem "O Captain! My Captain!" as a memorial to the fallen leader.

"O Captain! My Captain!" contains description as the poet discusses the death and funeral of President Lincoln. Recall the description used in "January," "New World," and "Easter: Wahiawa, 1959." Description often helps to show the meaning of a work of poetry.

Literary Terms Descriptive writing paints pictures with words. A variety of descriptions can be used in poetry. A literal meaning is the actual, everyday meaning of words. A figurative meaning depends on figures of speech and the symbolic meaning of language. An **analogy** is a figurative description. It compares two or more things that are similar in some ways, but are otherwise different. For example, a poem that literally describes the ocean may be read as an analogy. It may compare the ocean to life because both are vast, deep, and ever-changing. The poem, then, has two levels of meaning. One level is literal, and one is figurative.

> **analogy**
> a comparison between two otherwise different things that share the same characteristics

Reading on Your Own As you read the poem, think about the literal and figurative meaning of the words. Watch for words that mean more than their surface meaning. Think about the poet's purpose in choosing certain words. List words, phrases, and images that give you clues to the figurative meaning of the poem.

Writing on Your Own A turning point is a point in time where life changes forever. This poem tells about an important turning point—the death of a leader. Other poems may celebrate turning points that are more personal. In a few sentences, describe a turning point you think would make a good subject for a poem.

Vocabulary Focus Poetry of a certain era uses apostrophes to aid with pronunciation and rhythm. In "O Captain! My Captain!" the poet shortens some verbs: *weather'd, ribbon'd,* and *anchor'd.* He even lengthens one to add a syllable that is needed for the rhythm: *a-crowding.* Because the rhythm is so important to the poem, this kind of "poetic license" is allowable.

Think Before You Read Why was Abraham Lincoln deserving of a poem of praise?

O Captain! My Captain!

Whom is the speaker addressing?

O Captain! my Captain! our fearful trip is done,
The ship has weather'd every **rack**, the prize we
    sought is won,
The port is near, the bells I hear, the people all
    exulting,
While follow eyes the steady **keel**, the vessel grim
    and daring;

5   But O heart! heart! heart!
        O the bleeding drops of red,
          Where on the deck my Captain lies,
          Fallen cold and dead.

Reading Strategy: Visualizing

What image do you see here?

O Captain! my Captain! rise up and hear the bells;
10 Rise up—for you the flag is flung—for you the
    bugle **trills**,
For you bouquets and ribbon'd wreaths—for you
    the shores a-crowding,
For you they call, the swaying mass, their eager
    faces turning;
      Here Captain! dear father!
        This arm beneath your head!

In this stanza, what does the speaker describe?

rack destruction or ruin

exulting rejoicing

keel a main beam that extends along the bottom of a ship and supports the frame

trills makes a fluttering sound

15   It is some dream that on the deck,
       You've fallen cold and dead.

My Captain does not answer, his lips are pale
    and still,
My father does not feel my arm, he has no pulse
    nor will,
The ship is anchor'd safe and sound, its voyage
    closed and done,
20 From fearful trip the **victor** ship comes in with
    object won;
    Exult O shores, and ring O bells!
      But I with mournful tread,
        Walk the deck my Captain lies,
          Fallen cold and dead.

What is the symbolic meaning of the safely anchored ship?

victor winner

O Captain! My Captain!   by Walt Whitman

Directions Choose the letter of the best answer or write the answer using complete sentences.

Comprehension: Identifying Facts

1. Where is the ship as the poem begins?

   A closing in on the enemy
   B lying on the ocean floor
   C tied at the dock
   D entering the harbor

2. How do the crowds of people respond to the Captain's arrival?

3. What has the Captain accomplished before the ship arrives?

Comprehension: Putting Ideas Together

4. How is the timing of the Captain's death unfortunate?

   A He died at his crew's time of greatest need.
   B He died at the hour of his greatest success.
   C He died without winning the last battle.
   D He died before sailing boldly off to war.

5. What does the speaker think of Lincoln?

6. How was Lincoln's leadership like a captain's role on a ship?

Understanding Literature: Description and Analogies

Poems often work on two levels. One is the literal level. The other is the figurative level. Analogies are comparisons of unlike things. Poets use analogies to add figurative meaning. For example, in "New World," N. Scott Momaday compares the birth of a new day to the birth of a new world. His simple poem about dawn, noon, and dusk has a deeper meaning.

7. In "O Captain! My Captain!" what is the "fearful trip" that the ship has "weathered"?

8. In "Easter: Wahiawa, 1959," Grandfather first has "a quail egg or two." Later, he has "basketfuls of sky blue eggs." What does this tell you about Grandfather's life?

Critical Thinking

9. Choose a set of lines from "New World," "Easter: Wahiawa, 1959," or "O Captain! My Captain!" Explain the literal and figurative meanings of the lines.

Thinking Creatively

10. Suppose you wanted to write a poem of praise like "O Captain! My Captain!" Who would be the subject of your poem? Why?

Grammar Check

One of the least-used parts of speech in formal writing is the interjection. An interjection is a part of speech that expresses emotion. Rather than being part of a sentence, it often stands alone. The word *O* is an interjection. It may be used before the name of a person who is being addressed. It can also express surprise, as in "O, what a strange tale!"

Write a sentence for each of these interjections to express emotion: *Wow!, Hey!, Ugh!, Oh, no!, Ouch!* Write your sentences on a sheet of paper. Then, share your sentences with a partner.

 Vocabulary Builder

In each group of words, find the one that does not belong. Each group contains a vocabulary term. Recall the meaning of the term. This will help you decide which word does not belong. Write the word on a sheet of paper, and also tell why it does not fit with the others.

1 cheering, mourning, exulting
2 keel, deck, port
3 bouquets, bells, wreaths
4 trip, object, prize
5 trill, ring, fling

 Writing on Your Own

Use your idea from Before Reading on page 365 to write a poem about a turning point. Your poem may rhyme or be written in free verse. Think about your deeper, figurative meaning as well as the literal meaning of your lines. You might begin by completing this analogy:

My turning point is like _____, because _____.

(*Example:* Lincoln's death is like the death of a ship's captain, because both steered their "ships" safely into port.)

  Listening and Speaking

At one time in American schools, nearly every student had to memorize "O Captain! My Captain!" Try to memorize the poem, one stanza at a time. Think of it as memorizing the words to a song. Once you are confident, recite the poem for a family member.

 Media and Viewing

Photography was a new art form in the 1860s. Many photographs were taken of Lincoln's funeral procession. Do an online search to find examples. Find details in the photographs that show the importance of Lincoln's death to ordinary Americans. Share your findings with the class.

Prefixes are added to the beginning of base words. Suffixes are added to the ends of words. Prefixes and suffixes are affixes, which means "something added to a word."

Think Before You Spell Adding prefixes to base words is usually easy. No letters are ever dropped or added.

Suffixes do have some changes:

Silent -e

- Usually you drop the silent -e when adding a suffix that begins with a vowel.

- Do not drop the silent -e when the suffix begins with a consonant.

Adding -s or -d to a word with a final -y

- When a consonant comes before the -y, change the -y to -i and add -es or -ed.

- When a vowel comes before the -y, do not change the -y.

Some suffixes can be tricky to spell. They sound the same and there are no strict rules about adding them. Such suffixes include -ance and -ence and -able and -ible.

Practice

On your paper, write the word from the Word List that is related to each word below. Circle the affix or affixes in each word. Underline any places where a spelling change occurs when the affix is added.

1. attend
2. enact
3. replace
4. deduct
5. legal
6. refer
7. move
8. collapse
9. practical
10. occur

Word List
deductible
irreplaceable
immovable
reference
illegal
reenact
impractical
attendance
collapsible
occurrence

Unit 4   SUMMARY

In Unit 4, you read a variety of poems from many times and places. Although each poem had a different point of view, all of them shared some qualities. Some of the poems you read were lyric poems. Lyric poetry is short, and it has a single speaker. You also read some narrative poetry, which is poetry that tells a story.

Both types of poetry use imagery to appeal to the reader's senses. Because poets tell a lot in a few words, word choice is very important. Poets may use comparisons to make connections between ideas. These comparisons may include similes, metaphors, personification, and analogies.

Finally, the sound of poetry is important too. Poets may use rhythm and rhyme to give their words a musical sound. They may use alliteration or onomatopoeia to add interest to their lines.

Selections

- "Cat!" by Eleanor Farjeon uses onomatopoeia to tell about an escaped cat.

- "Silver" by Walter de la Mare creates a snapshot of the moon's effect on the world below.

- "Your World" by Georgia Douglas Johnson urges readers to fight the limits of their imaginations.

- "Concrete Mixers" by Patricia Hubbell uses similes to compare machines to elephants.

- "The City Is So Big" by Richard García uses personification to make the city seem scary.

- "Harlem Night Song" by Langston Hughes is a celebration of New York.

- "Southbound on the Freeway" by May Swenson describes a traffic jam as seen by aliens.

- "Pig Roast" by Sandra M. Castillo is a narrative poem about a family get-together.

- "Blow, Blow, Thou Winter Wind" by William Shakespeare compares a chill wind to false friends.

- "Old Man" by Ricardo Sánchez recalls a grandfather who understood the history of his people.

- "January" by John Updike describes images of a northeastern winter.

- "New World" by N. Scott Momaday compares a new day to a fresh, new world.

- "Easter: Wahiawa, 1959" by Cathy Song recalls a past Easter with family.

- "O Captain! My Captain!" by Walt Whitman is a memorial to Abraham Lincoln.

Directions Choose the letter of the best answer or write the answer using complete sentences.

Comprehension: Identifying Facts

1. What time of day is it in "Silver"?

A noontime   **C** nighttime
B daybreak   **D** afternoon

2. What are the drivers doing in "Concrete Mixers"?

3. What does the speaker in "Harlem Night Song" want his sweetheart to do?

4. Which three poems in this unit mention family gatherings?

5. Which two poems in this unit were clearly written in memory of someone lost?

Comprehension: Putting Ideas Together

6. How would you describe the cat in "Cat!"?

A content   **C** proud
B cautious   **D** angry

7. How does the speaker feel about the city in "The City Is So Big"?

8. The speaker in "Pig Roast" describes her mother and uncle. She says, "They eat their pork pieces like it was Christmas or New Year's Eve." What does she mean?

9. What did the grandfather in "Easter: Wahiawa, 1959" do for a living?

10. Why are the people "all exulting" in "O Captain! My Captain!"?

Understanding Literature: Sound Devices and Imagery

Poets use sound devices to make their words musical. Repeated sounds are a key part of poetry. Poets may repeat the sounds at the ends of lines, using rhyme. They may repeat the sounds at the beginnings of words, using alliteration. They may repeat a pattern of beats, or stressed syllables, forming rhythm.

Poets use imagery to make their words meaningful. The words may appeal to the sense of sight, hearing, smell, touch, or taste. Often, comparisons help form imagery. A poet may compare one unlike thing to another using a simile, a metaphor, or an analogy.

11. In "Your World," what analogy does the poet use to speak about limits and freedom?

12. Which lines rhyme in each stanza of "Blow, Blow, Thou Winter Wind"?

13. Find three examples of alliteration in "January."

14. Read these lines from "New World."

"Rivers/follow/the moon,/the long/white track/of the/full moon."

What picture does this paint in your mind? Describe what you visualize.

15. Find a simile in Part 1 of "Easter: Wahiawa, 1959." Explain what the simile means.

Critical Thinking

16. Why do you think people still read poems by poets who lived long ago?

17. Of all the poems about cities in this unit, which one seems the most positive? Give examples to show why that poem is more upbeat than the others.

18. Choose one poem from the unit that rhymes. Choose one poem that does not rhyme. Tell which one you prefer and why.

Thinking Creatively

19. Which poem in this unit do you think would appeal most to young children? Why do you think so?

20. Think about the setting and events of "Pig Roast" and those of "Easter: Wahiawa, 1959." Which would you rather be a part of? Why?

Speak and Listen

Work with a partner to make a list of the poets from this unit. Then choose one poet, but do not tell your partner which poet you chose. Look in the library to find another poem by that poet. Read the poem aloud to your partner. See whether your partner can tell which poet you chose just by listening to the poem.

Writing on Your Own

You can learn a lot about a poet's style by trying to write in that style. Choose your favorite poem from this unit. Notice the length of lines, the number of lines, rhyme, and rhythm. Jot down anything unusual about the capitalization or punctuation. Now write your own poem in the style of the poem you chose from the unit.

Beyond Words

Choose one poem from this unit that captured your imagination. Picture the scene in your mind. Then draw an illustration to go with the poem. Also write a caption for your illustration.

Test-Taking Tip

Look over a test before you begin answering questions. See how many sections there are. Read the directions for each section.

Exposition: Comparison-and-Contrast Essay

A comparison-and-contrast essay looks at how two or more subjects are alike and different. Whether comparing two recipes or two government policies, comparison-and-contrast essays help readers understand the value of the analysis. Follow the steps outlined here to write your own comparison-and-contrast essay.

Assignment Write a comparison-and-contrast essay. Look at how two or more subjects are alike and different.

What to Include Your comparison-and-contrast essay should feature the following elements:

- a topic involving two or more subjects that are different in some ways and similar in other ways
- an introduction that presents the main point of the essay and body paragraphs showing similarities and differences
- an organization that highlights the points of comparison
- a structure appropriate to your audience
- error-free writing, including a variety of sentence patterns

Prewriting
Choosing Your Topic

Blueprinting Think of a place you know well, such as a park or your kitchen. Draw a blueprint or map of this place. Include key details such as trees or furniture. Then, write words or phrases that you associate with this place. Review your blueprint, and choose one item to compare to another, related item.

Personal-experience timeline Every time you outgrow your clothes, you can see how you are changing. These physical changes are interesting to compare and contrast. So are your changes in attitude, or changes in the skills you have. Use a timeline to chart ways you have changed over time. Choose two entries as the starting point for your comparison-and-contrast essay.

Using the Form
You may use elements of this form in these types of writing:
- comparisons of literary works
- product comparisons
- news analysis

Six Traits of Writing:

Ideas message, details, and purpose

Narrowing Your Topic

The topic "The Best Vacation Spots" is too broad to be addressed in a short essay. You might narrow this to "Atlanta vs. San Francisco—Which Is More Family-Friendly?" Review your topic. Divide it into separate parts or subtopics. Choose one of these as your narrowed topic.

Gathering Details

Use a Venn diagram. Organize information about the ideas you will compare by using a Venn diagram, as shown here. In the center section, write how things are alike. Note differences in the outer sections of each circle. When you have finished, circle the items that most clearly show comparisons and contrasts. Then, include these details in your essay.

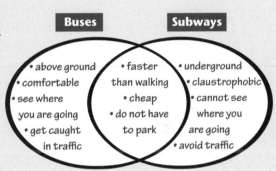

Buses **Subways**

- above ground
- comfortable
- see where you are going
- get caught in traffic

- faster than walking
- cheap
- do not have to park

- underground
- claustrophobic
- cannot see where you are going
- avoid traffic

Writing Your Draft

Shaping Your Writing

Select the best format to use. There are two common ways to organize a comparison-and-contrast essay. Review these choices. Then, choose a structure that works for your audience.

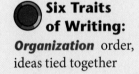

Six Traits of Writing:
Organization order, ideas tied together

- **Block method** Present all the details about one subject first. Then, present all the details about the next subject. The block method works well if you are writing about more than two subjects. It also works well if your topic is difficult to understand.

Block
I. Buses
  a. cheaper
  b. more routes
  c. better views
II. Trains
  a. better seats
  b. faster
  c. quieter

Point-by-point
I. Introduction
II. Cost of each
III. Accessibility of each
IV. View from each
V. Disadvantage of each

- **Point-by-point organization** Discuss each part of your subjects in turn. For example, suppose you are comparing buses and subways. You might first discuss the cost of each, then their ease of use, and so on.

- **Find a message.** Review your notes for a message about the value or importance of your comparison. Identify the reason that your readers should read your work.

Providing Elaboration

Use vivid details. Specific details will highlight the ways things are alike and different. Notice the effect of the following examples:

General: a small house next to a big house

Vivid: a weathered, rickety cottage next to a stately mansion

Revising

Revising Your Overall Structure

Color-code to check organization and balance. Reread your draft. Use one color to highlight details about one of your subjects. Use a second color to mark details about the other. If one color is used too much, add details on the subject about which you have written less. Your highlights should show how your paper is organized. If they do not, revise to make your work clearer.

Six Traits of Writing:
Word Choice vivid words that "show, not tell"

Revising Your Paragraphs

Add supporting details. Copy your main idea onto an index card. Run the card down your draft as you read it, one line at a time. Identify any details that do not directly support your main idea. Remove those details or rewrite them to develop your main idea.

Editing and Proofreading

Check your writing to correct errors in spelling, grammar, and punctuation.

Focus on Spelling: As you proofread, circle words that you are not sure how to spell. Circle words that you often misspell or that you seldom use. Use a dictionary to check the spelling of the circled words.

Publishing and Presenting

Consider one of these ways to share your writing:

Publish a column. Have you compared and contrasted subjects of local interest, such as two restaurants? Submit your essay to your local newspaper.

Start a family tradition. Have you compared and contrasted two subjects of interest to your family? Read your essay at a family gathering.

Reflecting on Your Writing

Writer's Journal Write a few notes about the experience of writing a comparison-and-contrast essay. Begin by answering these questions: What did you enjoy most about writing your essay? If you could begin again, what would you do differently? Explain your answers.

Six Traits of Writing:
Conventions correct grammar, spelling, and mechanics

Costumes
Freshman Brown

Unit 5 Drama

When you think of drama, do you think of actors? Do you see people on a stage, in a television show, or in a movie? Such situations are common for a drama. However, one must understand and be able to read a drama before it can be performed.

Drama is a separate genre, or form, of literature. A drama has plot and characters like fiction and nonfiction. However, drama is written in dialogue. Writers of drama also must include directions for actors, set builders, costume makers, and others. When all of these come together, a drama can come alive on stage.

"Theater is the response, the echo, which drama awakens within us when we see it on the stage."

—Robertson Davies

Unit 5 About Drama

Elements of Drama

Drama is a story told through the words and actions of characters. A drama is written to be performed as well as read. Another name for a drama is a **play**. As you read a drama, you must visualize how the action would appear and sound to an audience. Dramas include elements of fiction such as plot, conflict, and setting. There are also some different parts found only in dramas:

- A **playwright** is the author of a play.

- A **script** is the written text of a play, used in a production or performance.

- **Acts** are the major units of the action in a play. Acts are often divided into parts called **scenes,** which usually take place in one setting.

- **Characterization** is the way a playwright develops character qualities and personality traits.

- **Dialogue** is the words that characters in a play speak. The words each character speaks appear next to the character's name.

Much of what you learn about the characters and events is told through these conversations among the characters.

- A **monologue** is a long speech that is told by a single character. A monologue often shows a character's private thoughts and feelings.

- **Stage directions** are notes by playwrights describing such things as setting, lighting, and sound effects. Stage directions also tell how the actors are to look, behave, move, and speak. In a script, the stage directions appear in brackets to show that the words are not spoken.

- **Set** is the term used for the scenery on stage. This scenery gives clues about the time and place of the action.

- **Props** are pieces of equipment used onstage during a play. The actors use props to make their actions look more realistic.

Types of Drama

Comedy is a form of drama that has a happy ending and is intended to amuse its audience. Comedies can be written to entertain, but they also can point out the faults of a society.

Tragedy is a play that ends with the suffering or death of one or more of the main characters. This character can be an average person, but often is a person of great importance, like a king or a heroic figure. Tragedy is often contrasted with comedy.

Although *drama* is often used to describe plays, the world of drama is not limited to the stage.

- **Screenplays** are the scripts for films. They include camera angles and can allow for more scene changes than a stage play.

- **Teleplays** are scripts written for television and often contain similar elements as a screenplay.

- **Radio plays** are written to be performed as radio broadcasts. They include sound effects and require no set.

Part 1

Reading Strategy:
Inferencing

Readers make inferences to find meaning in a text when the meaning is not directly stated. Another way to describe an inference is "drawing conclusions." This is connecting details to make decisions or form opinions about a text—to make meaning of a text. Drawing conclusions is just another term for making inferences.

What You Know + What You Read =
Inference (Draw Conclusions)

Literary Terms

playwright an author of a play

drama a story told through the words and actions of a character; a play

dialogue the conversations among characters in a story

stage directions notes by playwrights describing such things as setting, lighting, sound effects, and how the actors are to look, behave, move, and speak

setting the time and place of a story

short story a brief work of prose fiction that includes plot, setting, characters, point of view, and theme

adaptation a work that has been changed to fit a different form, usually by leaving out some parts of the original work

style an author's way of writing

About the Author

Neil Simon has been called the best-loved **playwright,** or author of a play, of the 20th century. Millions of people have enjoyed his plays and films. Simon once had four hit plays running on Broadway at the same time. He is best known for his comedies—plays that poke gentle fun at people's behavior.

Neil Simon
1927–

Simon grew up in the Washington Heights neighborhood of New York City. He began his career as a writer for radio and television. Later he wrote comedies for the stage. New York is the backdrop for many of his most popular plays. These include *The Odd Couple, Plaza Suite,* and *Barefoot in the Park.* In the 1980s, Simon wrote three plays in which he used experiences from his own life. The plays were *Brighton Beach Memoirs, Biloxi Blues,* and *Broadway Bound.* After these plays were staged, critics viewed his work more seriously. His 1991 play *Lost in Yonkers* won the Pulitzer Prize.

About the Selection

The Governess comes from *The Good Doctor,* a play by Neil Simon. Simon used stories by Anton Chekhov, a Russian writer, to create *The Good Doctor. The Governess* tells the same story as Chekhov's story "The Ninny." In *The Governess,* a worker has trouble speaking up for herself. A bossy mistress of an upper-class Russian household tries to teach her to do this. However, the mistress does not choose very nice ways to teach.

Before Reading **continued on next page**

Objectives

◆ To read and understand a drama

◆ To define playwright

◆ To explain the importance of stage directions and dialogue in a play

The Governess　　*by Neil Simon*

playwright an author of a play

drama a story told through the words and actions of a character; a play

dialogue the conversations among characters in a story

stage directions notes by playwrights describing such things as setting, lighting, sound effects, and how the actors are to look, behave, move, and speak

setting the time and place of a story

Literary Terms *The Governess* is a **drama,** which is another name for a play. It is a story told through the words and actions of a character. Another name for the conversations among characters is **dialogue.** Dramas are written to be performed as well as read. Playwrights write **stage directions** as part of writing a play. Stage directions are notes that tell how a play should be performed. They describe the scenery, costumes, lighting, and sound. They also tell how the characters feel, move, and speak. Stage directions are usually printed in italics and set in brackets. For example, these stage directions describe the **setting**—the time and place—of a play: *[It is late evening. The stage is dark, except for the glow of a small lamp beside the bed.]*

Reading on Your Own To make inferences about a play, look at what characters say and do. Look for things they say that show how they think. Pay attention to how characters treat each other. Notice actions that create a clear pattern of behavior. Decide what all these things tell you about the character.

Writing on Your Own In *The Governess*, Neil Simon introduces a character who has trouble speaking up for herself. Write five reasons why someone might have this problem.

Vocabulary Focus Read each vocabulary word and its definition. The vocabulary is located at the bottom of each page in the selection. Then work with a partner to act out five of the vocabulary words. Show the word in a context or situation that viewers will understand. Ask other classmates to guess which word you are acting out.

Think Before You Read Has there ever been a time when you had trouble speaking up for yourself? Talk with a partner about how you handled the situation.

The GOVERNESS ❧

Mistress Julia! [*Calls again*] Julia!

[*A young* **governess**, JULIA, *comes rushing in. She stops before the desk and* **curtsies**.]

Julia [*Head down*] Yes, madame?

Mistress Look at me, child. Pick your head up. I like to see your eyes when I speak to you.

Julia [*Lifts her head up*] Yes, madame. [*But her head has a habit of slowly drifting down again*]

Mistress And how are the children coming along with their French lessons?

Julia They're very bright children, madame.

Mistress Eyes up . . . They're bright, you say. Well, why not? And mathematics? They're doing well in mathematics, I **assume**?

As you read, take special note of the stage directions. How do they give you a better picture of the characters?

Look at the picture on this page. Which people are playing the parts of servants? How can you tell?

governess a woman hired to care for and teach children in a private home	**curtsies** bends the knees and lowers the body to bow in respect, done by a girl or woman	**assume** to take for granted without proof

Reading Strategy: Inferencing

What inferences can you make about the relationship between Julia and the Mistress?

The word *ma'am* is short for *madame* or *madam*. This is a formal title used for women.

Rubles are the Russian form of money.

Julia Yes, madame. Especially Vanya.

Mistress Certainly. I knew it. I **excelled** in mathematics. He gets that from his mother, wouldn't you say?

Julia Yes, madame.

Mistress Head up . . . [*She lifts head up*] That's it. Don't be afraid to look people in the eyes, my dear. If you think of yourself as **inferior**, that's exactly how people will treat you.

Julia Yes, ma'am.

Mistress A quiet girl, aren't you? . . . Now then, let's settle our accounts. I imagine you must need money, although you never ask me for it yourself. Let's see now, we agreed on thirty rubles a month, did we not?

Julia [*Surprised*] Forty, ma'am.

Mistress No, no, thirty. I made a note of it. [*Points to the book*] I always pay my governess thirty . . . Who told you forty?

Julia You did, ma'am. I spoke to no one else concerning money . . .

Mistress Impossible. Maybe you *thought* you heard forty when I said thirty. If you kept your head up, that would never happen. Look at me again and I'll say it clearly. *Thirty rubles a month.*

Julia If you say so, ma'am.

Mistress Settled. Thirty a month it is . . . Now then, you've been here two months exactly.

Julia Two months and five days.

Mistress No, no. Exactly two months. I made a note of it. You should keep books the way I do so there wouldn't be these **discrepancies**. So—we have two months at thirty rubles a month . . . comes to sixty rubles. Correct?

excelled did very well	**discrepancies** differences; results that do not match the facts or agreed-upon points
inferior lower in status or rank	

Julia [*Curtsies*] Yes, ma'am. Thank you, ma'am.

Mistress Subtract nine Sundays . . . We did agree to subtract Sundays, didn't we?

Julia No, ma'am.

Mistress Eyes! Eyes! . . . Certainly we did. I've always subtracted Sundays. I didn't bother making a note of it because I always do it. Don't you recall when I said we will subtract Sundays?

Julia No, ma'am.

Mistress Think.

Julia [*Thinks*] No, ma'am.

Mistress You weren't thinking. Your eyes were wandering. Look straight at my face and look hard . . . Do you remember now?

Julia [*Softly*] Yes, ma'am.

Mistress I didn't hear you, Julia.

Julia [*Louder*] Yes, ma'am.

Mistress Good. I was sure you'd remember . . . Plus three holidays. Correct?

Julia Two, ma'am. Christmas and New Year's.

Mistress And your birthday. That's three.

Julia I worked on my birthday, ma'am.

Mistress You did? There was no need to. My governesses never worked on their birthdays . . .

Reading Strategy:
Inferencing
Why do you think Julia curtsies here?

How much do Julia and the Mistress each think that Julia gets paid per month?

Which stage directions help you understand the way the characters speak the dialogue?

Which character do you think is shown in the photo? Explain.

Julia But I did work, ma'am.

Mistress But that's not the question, Julia. We're discussing **financial** matters now. I will, however, only count two holidays if you insist . . . Do you insist?

Julia I did work, ma'am.

Mistress Then you *do* insist.

Julia No, ma'am.

Mistress Very well. That's three holidays, therefore we take off twelve rubles. Now then, four days little Kolya was sick, and there were no lessons.

Julia But I gave lessons to Vanya.

Mistress True. But I **engaged** you to teach two children, not one. Shall I pay you in full for doing only half the work?

Julia No, ma'am.

Mistress So we'll **deduct** it . . . Now, three days you had a toothache and my husband gave you permission not to work after lunch. Correct?

Julia After four. I worked until four.

Mistress [*Looks in the book*] I have here: "Did not work after lunch." We have lunch at one and are finished at two, not at four, correct?

Julia Yes, ma'am. But I—

Mistress That's another seven rubles . . . Seven and twelve is nineteen . . . Subtract . . . that leaves . . . forty-one rubles . . . Correct?

Julia Yes, ma'am. Thank you, ma'am.

Mistress Now then, on January fourth you broke a teacup and saucer, is that true?

Julia Just the saucer, ma'am.

Put yourself in Julia's position. Why do you think she has trouble standing up to the Mistress?

financial having to do with money	**engaged** hired	**deduct** to take away; to subtract

Mistress What good is a teacup without a saucer, eh? . . . That's two rubles. The saucer was an **heirloom**. It cost much more, but let it go. I'm used to taking losses.

Julia Thank you, ma'am.

Mistress Now then, January ninth, Kolya climbed a tree and tore his jacket.

Julia I forbid him to do so, ma'am.

Mistress But he didn't listen, did he? . . . Ten rubles . . . January fourteenth, Vanya's shoes were stolen . . .

Julia But the maid, ma'am. You **discharged** her yourself.

Mistress But you get paid good money to watch everything. I explained that in our first meeting. Perhaps you weren't listening. Were you listening that day, Julia, or was your head in the clouds?

Julia Yes, ma'am.

Mistress Yes, your head was in the clouds?

Julia No, ma'am. I was listening.

Mistress Good girl. So that means another five rubles off [*Looks in the book*] . . . Ah, yes . . . The sixteenth of January I gave you ten rubles.

Julia You didn't.

Mistress But I made a note of it. Why would I make a note of it if I didn't give it to you?

Julia I don't know, ma'am.

Mistress That's not a **satisfactory** answer, Julia . . . Why would I make a note of giving you ten rubles if I did not in fact give it to you, eh? . . . No answer? . . . Then I must have given it to you, mustn't I?

Julia Yes, ma'am. If you say so, ma'am.

> How does the Mistress punish Julia for the actions of Kolya and the maid?

> **Reading Strategy: Inferencing**
> How do you think Julia feels at this point?

---

heirloom a precious object that has been in a family a long time

discharged fired; dismissed from a job

satisfactory good enough

Mistress Well, certainly I say so. That's the point of this little talk. To clear these matters up. Take twenty-seven from forty-one, that leaves . . . fourteen, correct?

Julia Yes, ma'am. [*She turns away, softly crying*]

Mistress What's this? Tears? Are you crying? Has something made you unhappy, Julia? Please tell me. It pains me to see you like this. I'm so **sensitive** to tears. What is it?

Julia Only once since I've been here have I ever been given any money and that was by your husband. On my birthday he gave me three rubles.

Mistress Really? There's no note of it in my book. I'll put it down now. [*She writes in the book.*] Three rubles. Thank you for telling me. Sometimes I'm a little **lax** with my accounts . . . Always **shortchanging** myself. So then, we take three more from fourteen . . . leaves eleven . . . Do you wish to check my figures?

Check my figures is another way of saying "check my math."

Julia There's no need to, ma'am.

Mistress Then we're all settled. Here's your salary for two months, dear. Eleven rubles. [*She puts the pile of coins on the desk.*] Count it.

Reading Strategy: Inferencing

Why do you think Julia does not want to count the money?

Julia It's not necessary, ma'am.

Mistress Come, come. Let's keep the records straight. Count it.

Julia [*Reluctantly counts it*] One, two, three, four, five, six, seven, eight, nine, ten . . . ? There's only ten, ma'am.

Mistress Are you sure? Possibly you dropped one . . . Look on the floor, see if there's a coin there.

Julia I didn't drop any, ma'am. I'm quite sure.

---

sensitive easily disturbed

lax lazy

shortchanging not taking all that is due

reluctantly hesitantly; not wanting to do something

Mistress Well, it's not here on my desk, and I *know* I gave you eleven rubles. Look on the floor.

Julia It's all right, ma'am. Ten rubles will be fine.

Mistress Well, keep the ten for now. And if we don't find it on the floor later, we'll discuss it again next month.

Julia Yes, ma'am. Thank you, ma'am. You're very kind, ma'am.

[*She curtsies and then starts to leave.*]

Mistress Julia!
[JULIA *stops, turns.*]
Come back here.
She goes back to the desk and curtsies again.]
Why did you thank me?

Julia For the money, ma'am.

Mistress For the money? . . . But don't you realize what I've done? I've cheated you . . . *Robbed* you! I have no such notes in my book. I made up whatever came into my mind. Instead of the eighty rubles which I owe you, I gave you only ten. I have actually stolen from you and you still thank me . . . Why?

Reading Strategy: Inferencing

How might things be different if Julia were paid better and could save some money? Do you think she would behave differently? Explain.

Does the photograph on this page give you a good sense of Julia's personality? Why or why not?

Julia In the other places that I've worked, they didn't give me anything at all.

Mistress Then they cheated you even worse than I did . . . I was playing a little joke on you. A cruel lesson just to teach you. You're much too trusting, and in this world that's very dangerous . . . I'm going to give you the entire eighty rubles. [*Hands her an envelope*] It's all ready for you. The rest is in this envelope. Here, take it.

Julia As you wish, ma'am. [*She curtsies and starts to go again.*]

Mistress Julia! [JULIA *stops.*] Is it possible to be so spineless? Why don't you protest? Why don't you speak up? Why don't you cry out against this cruel and **unjust** treatment? Is it really possible to be so **guileless,** so innocent, such a—pardon me for being so **blunt**—such a **simpleton?**

Julia [*The faintest trace of a smile on her lips*] Yes, ma'am . . . it's possible.

[*She curtsies again and runs off. The* MISTRESS *looks after her a moment, a look of complete* **bafflement** *on her face. The lights fade.*]

Reading Strategy:
Inferencing

How does this speech change your mind about what the Mistress is doing? Explain.

The slang word *spineless* means without courage, or weak.

unjust unfair

guileless without deceit or trickery; innocent

blunt straightforward; without kindness

simpleton a foolish or silly person

bafflement confusion

The Governess   *by Neil Simon*

Directions Choose the letter of the best answer or write the answer using complete sentences.

Comprehension: Identifying Facts

1. With how many children does the governess work?
   A 1   **B** 2   **C** 3   **D** 4

2. Which of the children is doing extra well in math?
   A Neither of them   **C** Vanya
   B Both of them   **D** Kolya

3. What does the Mistress want to discuss with Julia?

4. What does the Mistress say Julia should do so that she does not hear things wrong?

5. How long does Julia say she has been working for the Mistress?

6. List three of the reasons the Mistress gives for cutting Julia's pay.

7. Why does the Mistress say she did not make a note about subtracting Sundays?

8. What does Julia say when the Mistress asks her if she remembered that they had agreed to subtract Sundays?

9. Julia says that she worked on her birthday. Why does the Mistress take off for Julia's birthday?

10. What does Julia do when the Mistress gives her the rest of the 80 rubles?

Comprehension: Putting Ideas Together

11. Why does Julia's position make the discussion with the Mistress hard for her?
   A She has too much work to spend time talking.
   B She does not believe it is her place to disagree with the Mistress.
   C She does not hear very well.
   D She does not understand money matters very well.

12. Why is it cruel of the Mistress to suggest that they would not have a problem if Julia kept books?
   A The Mistress knows that Julia is unable to keep books.
   B Julia does keep books, but the Mistress has taken them away.
   C It is a way of making fun of Julia for being nothing more than a governess.
   D It is a way of blaming Julia for a problem that the Mistress has made up.

13. What does the Mistress mean when she asks if Julia's head was "in the clouds"?

After Reading **continued on next page**

14. How do the stage directions help readers understand the play?

15. How many rubles does the Mistress pretend to cheat Julia out of?

16. What decisions can you make about the general treatment of governesses at the time of this play?

17. Identify three of the Mistress's lines that show a single attitude.

18. The Mistress is trying to make Julia fight back. What final action does the Mistress take with the rubles?

19. How would you describe the governess's personality and abilities?

20. How did you feel toward the Mistress at the beginning and end of the play? If your feelings changed, explain why.

Understanding Literature: Stage Directions

Stage directions are an important part of a drama. The stage directions give ideas for scenery, costumes, lighting, and sound. All of these ideas help to tell the story as the playwright wants it told. The stage directions also help readers understand and imagine the story.

21. Look at the photograph on page 387. How does the costume help identify the character?

22. How do the stage directions showing the movement of Julia's head help you understand her personality?

23. What four stage directions are given on page 387? Who needs to use them?

24. How are the stage directions on page 390 useful to the persons in charge of setting the stage?

25. What stage direction is given to someone other than an actor on page 392? For whom is this direction given?

Critical Thinking

26. Julia clearly does not agree with the Mistress. Why does she give in on each point?

27. Is the Mistress being kind, cruel, or both? Explain.

28. How do you think you would act if faced with a situation similar to Julia's?

Thinking Creatively

29. Do you think Julia will behave differently in the future? Explain.

30. What would you like Julia to have said to the Mistress at the end?

Grammar Check

A participle is a verb form that is used as an adjective. Participles commonly end in *-ing* (present participle) or *-ed* (past participle). A participial phrase is made up of a participle and other words. The entire participial phrase is used as an adjective.

Examples:

• The tourist, <u>confused by the signs</u>, got lost.

• <u>Traveling quickly</u>, we got to the game on time.

Use a participial phrase to combine the two sentences. Rewrite each new sentence on a sheet of paper.

1 Anna carried her suitcase. Anna boarded the bus.

2 The bus driver smiled. The bus driver said hello.

3 The tour group was on its way. The group waved goodbye.

 ## Vocabulary Builder

Rewrite each of the following sentences to mean the opposite. In each sentence, use a vocabulary word from the play to help create the opposite meaning.

1 The testimony of the two witnesses was in total agreement.

2 Josie was so clever that no one could play a trick on her.

3 In spite of his hard work, Nico got a failing grade on the test.

4 The debaters treated each other as equals.

 ## Writing on Your Own

Write a problem-solution essay about Julia not standing up for herself. First, clearly explain the problem. Then explore the negative results of the problem. Finally, suggest a better plan than the Mistress had. Explain why it is better.

 ## Listening and Speaking

Organize a group discussion about Julia's situation. Keep in mind the differences between classes in society at the time. Make sure that everyone has a chance to express his or her reactions and opinions. Ask follow-up questions to make sure everyone's ideas are understood.

  ## Media and Viewing

Find at least three classified ads for nanny jobs. Draw conclusions from these ads about the responsibilities of today's nannies. Compare how the responsibilities have changed since Julia's time. Then use a computer design program to create a "Help Wanted" ad for a modern nanny.

Public Documents

In Part 1, you are learning about making inferences while you read literature. This skill also is helpful when you are reading public documents. You can make inferences while you read this public document from the Department of Labor. If you read *The Governess,* you might see a use for this document. You might decide that Julia could have used a document like this one. Such a document could have helped her stand up for her rights as a worker.

About Public Documents

Public documents are any records the public has the right to look at. Some examples of public documents include laws, legal notices, government publications, and minutes of public meetings. Many of these documents relate to government work. Others have to do with citizen rights and responsibilities.

Sometimes the language in public documents is formal. Also, sometimes the words can have special meanings that are different than those you know. It is important to read public documents closely. You need to make sure you understand the key words and technical language.

Reading Skill

A generalization is a broad statement or rule that applies to many examples. There are two main ways you can make generalizations:

- Notice common features in the information you read.

- Use information you already know about a topic.

You can use generalizations to organize information. However, you have to make sure that your generalizations are correct. Generalizations are not useful if they are not true for all situations they describe.

U.S. Department of Labor
Employment Standards Administration

The U.S. Department of Labor's Wage and Hour Division (WHD) is responsible for administering and enforcing laws that establish minimally acceptable standards for wages and working conditions in this country, regardless of immigration status.

The Wage and Hour Division makes sure the rules are followed for these laws:
- Fair Labor Standards
- Migrant and Seasonal Agricultural Worker Protection Act

Fair Labor Standards Act

The Fair Labor Standards Act (FLSA) affects most private and public employment. The FLSA requires employers to pay covered employees who are not otherwise exempt at least the federal **minimum wage** and **overtime** pay for all hours worked over 40 in a workweek.

Covered employees must be paid for all hours worked in a workweek. In general, compensable hours worked include all time an employee is on duty or at a prescribed place of work and any time that an employee is suffered or permitted to work. This would generally include work performed at home, travel time, waiting time, training, and probationary periods.

The boldfaced words and phrases point out important information.

- **Federal Minimum Wage = $5.15 per hour**
- **Tipped employees may be paid $2.13 per hour; if an employee's tips combined with cash wage does not equal $5.15, the employer must make up the difference**
- **Overtime after 40 hours in a week = 1 1/2 times an employee's regular rate of pay**

Migrant and Seasonal Worker Protection Act

The Migrant and Seasonal Agricultural Worker Protection Act (MSPA) requires farm labor contractors, agricultural employers, and agricultural associations to "employ" workers to:

1. Pay workers the wages owed when due
2. Comply with federal and state safety and health standards if they provide housing for migrant workers
3. Ensure that vehicles that they use to transport workers are properly insured, operated by licensed drivers and meet federal and state safety standards
4. Provide written disclosure of the terms and conditions of employment

Migrant workers travel from one area to another in search of work. The Migrant and Seasonal Agricultural Worker Protection Act tells how employers must treat migrant workers.

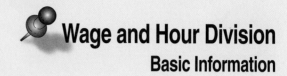

Wage and Hour Division
Basic Information

U.S. Department of Labor
Employment Standards Administration

Youth Employment
The FLSA also regulates the employment of youth.

Jobs Youth Can Do:
- 13 or younger: baby-sit, deliver newspapers, or work as an actor or performer
- Ages 14–15: office work, grocery store, retail store, restaurant, movie theater, or amusement park
- Age 16–17: Any job not declared hazardous
- Age 18: No restrictions

> The Fair Labor Standards Act includes information about laws for workers under age 18.

Hours Youth Ages 14 and 15 Can Work:
- After 7 A.M. and until 7 P.M. (Hours are extended to 9 P.M. June 1–Labor Day)
- Up to 3 hours on a school day
- Up to 18 hours in a school week
- Up to 8 hours on a non-school day
- Up to 40 hours in a non-school week

Note: Different rules apply to youth employed in agriculture. States also regulate the hours that youth under age 18 may work. To find State rules, log on to **www.youthrules.dol.gov**

> Each state decides what times of the day workers under age 18 can work. The Web site listed here is where readers can find more information about this subject.

Monitor Your Progress

Directions Choose the letter of the best answer or write the answer using complete sentences.

1. Which generalization cannot be made about the section from the Fair Labor Standards Act?
   A The act describes things employers must do.
   B The act describes things employees must do.
   C The United States believes in protecting employees.
   D The United States sets minimum standards for employees.

2. Which generalization is best supported by the rules on p. 398?
   A Young people are workers just like any other workers.
   B Young people should be in school, not at work.
   C The United States has special rules for young workers.
   D Rules for young workers have changed in the last few years.

3. Which is the most correct generalization about work hours for 14- and 15-year-old workers?
   A They may work about the same hours as adults can.
   B Their work hours are fewer on school days.
   C They can work early in the morning and late at night.
   D They can work any amount of overtime if they are paid for it.

4. Explain the most likely reasons that young workers have more rules than adult workers have.

5. Review the rules for migrant and seasonal workers. What inference can you make about these rules?

Writing on Your Own

Explain why laws that set minimum standards for wages and working conditions are important. In your answer, describe problems that could come up if such laws did not exist.

The Ninny   by Anton Chekhov (translated by Robert Payne)

Anton Chekhov
1860–1904

Objectives

- ◆ To read and understand a short story
- ◆ To identify an author's style of writing
- ◆ To compare an adaptation to the original work

About the Author

Anton Pavlovich Chekhov was a Russian writer. He planned to be a doctor and studied medicine in Moscow. He needed money to pay for medical school and support his family. Because of this, he began to write funny articles for journals.

In all, Chekhov wrote more than 200 stories. Some are funny, while others show the small sadnesses in ordinary life. All of the stories show caring and understanding for the characters. The stories also paint a picture of Russian life that is very real. Some of the stories take place in the cities and others in the poor villages. Chekhov had a simple view of writing. He wrote: "It is time for writers to admit that nothing in this world makes sense. Only fools . . . think they know and understand everything."

In addition to his stories, Chekhov is also famous for his plays. Some of them, such as the *Cherry Orchard* (1904), are still performed around the world. Chekhov died of a lung illness called tuberculosis at the age of 44.

About the Selection

"The Ninny" explores the relationship between the wealthy and powerful and those who serve them. In the story, an employer tries to get his children's nanny to speak up for herself. However, he does this in a rather mean way. He shows the cruelty of rich people who make fun of those who have less. The "ninny" lets her employer treat her badly rather than speak up for herself.

You will recognize that this story is similar to *The Governess*, which you read earlier in this unit. Neil Simon based his play *The Good Doctor* on "The Ninny." *The Governess* is a section from *The Good Doctor*.

Literary Terms "The Ninny" is a **short story**—a brief work of prose fiction that includes plot, setting, characters, point of view, and theme. A literary **adaptation** is a work that has been changed to fit a different form. Neil Simon's play *The Governess* is an adaptation of Chekhov's original work. Adapting a literary work usually means changing or leaving out some parts. For example, a novel's narration and description have to become dialogue in a play. In most cases, the adaptation and the original work will have a different **style.** Even though the writing may be different, the main message is the same.

Reading on Your Own To compare an adaptation to the original work, look for similarities and differences. Look for parts the writer has kept, left out, and added. Notice the authors' styles as you compare "The Ninny" to *The Governess.* Use a Venn Diagram to record similar and different features. (See Appendix A for a description of this graphic organizer.)

Writing on Your Own Neil Simon wrote *The Governess* more than 100 years after Anton Chekhov wrote "The Ninny." Write a paragraph telling why you think a writer would want to adapt someone else's work.

Vocabulary Focus In *The Governess,* the Mistress calls Julia "spineless," "guileless," and a "simpleton." In "The Ninny," the master calls Yulia a "nitwit," "spineless," and a "ninny." Find meanings for the different words. Think about using each word to call another person a name. Rank each as 1 (acceptable), 2 (quite rude), or 3 (cruel). Decide if you think Neil Simon or Anton Chekhov used the cruelest words.

Think Before You Read How is reading a play different from reading a short story? Which do you enjoy more? Discuss your answers with a classmate.

> **short story**
> a brief work of prose fiction that includes plot, setting, characters, point of view, and theme
>
> **adaptation**
> a work that has been changed to fit a different form, usually by leaving out some parts of the original work
>
> **style** an author's way of writing

The Ninny

As you read, think about the style of Chekhov's writing. How is it different from Neil Simon's writing style in *The Governess?*

Standing on ceremony means to insist on following an unnecessary rule.

How do the opening situation and characters compare with those in Simon's play?

Just a few days ago I invited Yulia Vassilyevna, the governess of my children, to come to my study. I wanted to settle my **account** with her.

"Sit down, Yulia Vassilyevna," I said to her. "Let's get our accounts settled. I'm sure you need some money, but you keep standing on ceremony and never ask for it. Let me see. We agreed to give you thirty rubles a month, didn't we?"

"Forty."

"No, thirty. I made a note of it. I always pay the governess thirty. Now, let me see. You have been with us for two months?"

"Two months and five days."

"Two months exactly. I made a note of it. So you have sixty rubles coming to you. Subtract nine Sundays. You know you don't tutor Kolya on Sundays, you just go out for a walk. And then the three holidays . . ."

Yulia Vassilyevna blushed and picked at the **trimmings** of her dress, but said not a word.

---

account a bill for work done

trimmings decorations on clothing, such as buttons or lace

"Three holidays. So we take off twelve rubles. Kolya was sick for four days—those days you didn't look after him. You looked after Vanya, only Vanya. Then there were the three days you had a toothache, when my wife gave you permission to stay away from the children after dinner. Twelve and seven makes nineteen. Subtract. . . . That leaves . . . hm . . . forty-one rubles. Correct?"

Yulia Vassilyevna's left eye reddened and filled with tears. Her chin trembled. She began to cough nervously, blew her nose, and said nothing.

"Then around New Year's Day you broke a cup and saucer. Subtract two rubles. The cup cost more than that—it was an heirloom, but we won't bother about that. We're the ones who pay. Another matter. Due to your carelessness Kolya climbed a tree and tore his coat. Subtract ten. Also, due to your carelessness the chambermaid ran off with Vanya's boots. You ought to have kept your eyes open. You get a good **salary.** So we **dock** off five more. . . . On the tenth of January you took ten rubles from me."

"I didn't," Yulia Vassilyevna whispered.

"But I made a note of it."

"Well, yes—perhaps . . ."

"From forty-one we take twenty-seven. That leaves fourteen."

Woman in a Chair, John Collier

Reading Strategy: Inferencing

Who is talking to Yulia?

A *chambermaid* is a female servant who cleans and cares for bedrooms.

---

salary a fixed sum of money paid for work done

dock to subtract part of one's salary or wages

Reading Strategy: Inferencing

Why is Yulia crying?

Her eyes filled with tears, and her thin, pretty little nose was shining with **perspiration.** Poor little child!

"I only took money once," she said in a trembling voice. "I took three rubles from your wife . . . never anything more."

"Did you now? You see, I never made a note of it. Take three from fourteen. That leaves eleven. Here's your money, my dear. Three, three, three . . . one and one. Take it, my dear."

I gave her the eleven rubles. With trembling fingers she took them and slipped them into her pocket.

"*Merci,*" she whispered.

I jumped up, and began pacing up and down the room. I was in a furious temper.

"Why did you say '*merci*'?" I asked.

"For the money."

". . . Don't you realize I've been cheating you? I steal your money, and all you can say is '*merci*'!"

"In my other places they gave me nothing."

"They gave you nothing! Well, no wonder! I was playing a trick on you—a dirty trick . . . I'll give you your eighty rubles, they are all here in an envelope made out for you. Is it possible for anyone to be such a nitwit? Why didn't you protest? Why did you keep your mouth shut? Is it possible that there is anyone in this world who is so spineless? Why are you such a **ninny**?"

She gave me a bitter little smile. On her face I read the words: "Yes, it is possible."

I **apologized** for having played this cruel trick on her, and to her great surprise gave her the eighty rubles. And then she said "*merci*" again several times, always **timidly**, and went out. I gazed after her, thinking how very easy it is in this world to be strong.

The word *Merci* is French for thank you. In the 19th century, many upper-class Russians spoke French.

The word *nitwit* is slang for a simple or foolish person.

How is Yulia's behavior at the end similar to and different from that of Simon's play?

perspiration sweat	**apologized** said one was sorry for something	**timidly** in a shy or fearful manner
ninny a simple or foolish person		

The Ninny   by Anton Chekhov (translated by Robert Payne)

Directions Choose the letter of the best answer or write the answer using complete sentences.

Comprehension: Identifying Facts

1. What is the first disagreement between the narrator and Yulia?
   A The narrator thinks Yulia is owed less money than Yulia says.
   B The narrator thinks Yulia is not being careful with her money.
   C The narrator is not happy with the way Yulia is treating the children.
   D The narrator thinks Yulia has stolen money.

2. Why do Yulia's eyes "fill with tears" in the middle of the conversation?
   A She is upset because she broke a cup and saucer.
   B She is upset because the narrator is being unkind to her.
   C She is upset that her pay is being unfairly cut.
   D She has something in her eye and cannot get it out.

3. Besides crying, what does Yulia do that shows she is upset?

4. The narrator takes off two rubles for the cup and saucer. Why does he suggest that two rubles is not really enough?

5. Why does the narrator say it was Yulia's fault that the chambermaid took the boots?

6. Yulia is an adult. In spite of this, what does the narrator call her when she starts to perspire and cry?

7. How can you tell that the narrator in "The Ninny" is a man?

8. What does Yulia say and do when the narrator gives her the 11 rubles?

9. In the end, how many rubles does the narrator give to Yulia?

10. What does the narrator admit to Yulia?

Comprehension: Putting Ideas Together

11. What do Yulia's responses suggest about her personality?
    A She gives in easily.
    B She will stand up for herself.
    C She has quite a temper.
    D She is not grateful for things.

12. Who tells the story of "The Ninny"?
    A Julia   C the Mistress
    B Yulia   D the children's father

13. Does the narrator in "The Ninny" find the best way to teach Yulia a lesson? Why or why not?

Comparing **continued on next page**

The Ninny by Anton Chekhov (translated by Robert Payne)

14. How does Julia defend herself more than Yulia?

15. Which of the reasons the narrator gives for cutting Yulia's pay are fair?

16. Are "The Ninny" and *The Governess* told in the same tense? Explain.

17. "The Ninny" is told by a narrator who is not directly identified. How does Neil Simon change this in *The Governess?*

18. In "The Ninny," the narrator gives Yulia 11 rubles. In *The Governess,* the Mistress gives Julia 10 rubles and says she gave her 11. Why do you think Neil Simon made this change?

19. In "The Ninny," the narrator directs the story to the reader. To whom does the Mistress in *The Governess* talk?

20. Do you think the endings of the two stories are alike or different?

Understanding Literature: Adaptation

Neil Simon adapted Anton Chekhov's story into a play. Simon made changes to the story for two main reasons. He wanted to help Americans in the 1900s understand a Russian play from the 1800s. He also wanted to make the action of the play flow smoothly.

21. Why do you think Neil Simon changed the governess's name?

22. How did changing the title put a different slant on the story?

23. What does the short story have that the play leaves out?

24. How did the amount of conversation probably make "The Ninny" easy to adapt into a play?

25. Create a Venn diagram to show similarities and differences between "The Ninny" and *The Governess.*

Critical Thinking

26. In "The Ninny," the narrator is a man. Why do you think Simon made this character a woman in his play?

27. During the conversation in "The Ninny," why does Yulia's chin tremble?

28. Why is the narrator in "The Ninny" not surprised that other places did not pay Yulia?

Thinking Creatively

29. Think about a future day when you will be talking to your employer. Do you think you will act the same as or differently than Julia and Yulia?

30. What would you say to the two characters in "The Ninny"? Why?

Grammar Check

Commas are used to separate items in a list that is in text. The commas make it clear what makes up each item on the list. Here is an example: We made *spaghetti and meatballs, garlic bread,* and *a tossed salad.* Write three sentences about the two selections you have just read. Include a list with commas in each sentence.

 Vocabulary Builder

Recall the selection vocabulary. Decide whether each of the following statements is true or false, using the vocabulary words as clues. Explain your answers.

1 A <u>spineless</u> person is not likely to defend his or her beliefs.

2 An adventuresome traveler meets life <u>timidly</u>.

3 An employer will often <u>dock</u> the pay of a good worker.

4 You would not ask a <u>ninny</u> to manage a project.

5 A calculator is useful in keeping track of an <u>account</u>.

 Writing on Your Own

In an essay, compare and contrast the adaptation (*The Governess*) and the original ("The Ninny"). Use the following questions and the comparison chart you filled out for question 25 on page 406.

- How much or how little did Simon change the story when he adapted "The Ninny"?
- What is the biggest change Simon made?
- Think about the story and the play. Do you think one works better than the other?

 Listening and Speaking

With a partner, choose a section from *The Governess* that includes at least one stage direction. Plan how you will use the stage directions to act out your lines for the class. Ask your classmates to compare your acting with the same section in "The Ninny."

 Media and Viewing

A play requires more formatting than is needed to type most stories. One way to make typing a play easier is to create a template and use copy-and-paste. Use at least three characters and create a template using a computer program. Include space for character names, stage directions, and lines.

Part 2

Reading Strategy:
Predicting

When readers make predictions, they make guesses about what will happen next. The details in the text help readers make their predictions. In this Part, you will read some selections that contain cause-and-effect.

■ A **cause** is the reason something happens.

■ An **effect** is what happens as a result.

As you read, make predictions based on the causes and effects of events. Remember, you can change your predictions as you learn more information.

Literary Terms

act the major unit of action in a play

scene a unit of action that takes place in one setting in a play

script the written text of a play, used in production or performance

props pieces of equipment used on stage during a play

moral a lesson or message about life told in a story

fantasy a kind of fiction writing that often has strange settings and characters

novel fiction that is book-length and has more plot and character details than a short story

excerpt a short passage from a longer piece of writing

Afternoon of the Elves   by Y York

About the Author

Y York started writing plays in the mid-1980s. Since then, she has written many plays, both for adults and for children's theater. She has created some original plays; others she has adapted from the works of other writers. Her adult plays include *The Secret Wife, Gerald's Good Idea,* and *Krisit.* Some of her plays for children include *The Garden of Rikki Tikki Tavi* and *The Witch of Blackbird Pond.* Many of her plays are enjoyable for people of all ages. Because the National Education Association supports York's plays, they are often used in schools.

Y York

Y York's plays also are often used for theater workshops. She has received many drama awards, including the 1997 Berrilla Kerr Playwrighting Award. Besides being a playwright, she is a storyteller and a drama teacher.

About the Selection

Afternoon of the Elves is a realistic drama written for children's theater. It also, however, has appeal for adults. Because of this, it is sometimes called one of Y York's plays for children and their parents. It is an adaptation of Janet Taylor Lisle's novel by the same name. The play was first performed in Seattle, Washington, in 1993. The story tells of a young girl, Sara Kate, who deals with difficult problems. Unhappy both at home and at school, Sara Kate turns to an elf village to escape her problems. She invites her neighbor, Hillary, to share in the wonder of the elf village. Hillary struggles between joining Sara Kate and a having a chance to fit in at school.

Before Reading **continued on next page**

Objectives

◆ To read and understand a drama containing acts and scenes

◆ To explain why a script and props are important to a drama

Afternoon of the Elves, Act One   *by Y York*

act the major unit of action in a play

scene a unit of action that takes place in one setting in a play

script the written text of a play, used in production or performance

props pieces of equipment used on stage during a play

Literary Terms *Afternoon of the Elves* is a drama, or play, that is divided into two **acts.** An act is a major unit of action in a play. The acts contain the same characters. In Act One, the setting is introduced and the story begins. The conflict, or problem, also begins in Act One. In Act Two, the story continues and readers learn more about the characters. By the end of the play, the conflict has been resolved. Each act also contains **scenes.** A scene is a unit of action that takes place in one setting in a play. Act One, which you will read on the following pages, is made up of 10 scenes. The **script,** or written text of the play, shows where scenes and acts begin and end. **Props** are included in the script. These are the pieces of equipment needed on stage during a play. Props include items such as tables, benches, flashlights, food, or anything else a character needs to help tell a story.

Reading on Your Own A cause is an event, action, or feeling that produces a result, or effect. You can use background information to link causes and effects in a story. These causes and effects will help you make predictions about events in the story. As you read, note the causes and effects.

Writing on Your Own Think how easy it is for you to make a telephone call or to turn on a television. This play shows what life is like for someone living without a phone or electricity. Write a paragraph about how life would be different without these things.

Vocabulary Focus Work with a partner. Write a scene for a play about tiny trolls that live on your school's athletic fields. Use at least 10 of the vocabulary words from *Afternoon of the Elves* in your scene.

Think Before You Read In *Afternoon of the Elves,* Jane and Alison are very wrapped up in themselves. Is it wrong for people to take pride in how they look and talk? Explain.

Afternoon of the Elves

A Play in Two Acts
For 1 Man, 2 Women, 4 girls (one possible double)

CHARACTERS

Jane and Alison	stars of the fourth grade
Hillary Lenox	has recently joined their ranks
Sara Kate Connolly	an upperclassman, held back for a second try in the fifth grade
Mr. and Mrs. Lenox	Hillary's parents
Mrs. Connolly	Sara Kate's mother, unable to cope

SETTING: The main settings are the amazingly **well-manicured** Lenox backyard that abuts the **atrocious** Connolly backyard, filled with old appliances, car motors, tires, general junk, and **brambles;** in the midst of the mess is the elf village. Another important setting is inside the **deteriorating** Connolly house. Secondary settings are outside of the school and on the town, both of which can be implied with sound and lights. A simple design that allows both backyards to use the entire stage is recommended.

> What can you learn from the beginning stage directions about lighting, costumes, and set design?

well-manicured trimmed and tidy

brambles wild, untrimmed bushes

atrocious very bad or unpleasant

deteriorating falling apart

ACT ONE

Scene 1

AT RISE: *Outside of school, Friday afternoon. A bright fall day. JANE WEBSTER and ALISON MANCINI, dressed alike with matching hairdos, leaving school with books, giggling, etc.*

Hillary *(off)* Wait up!

Alison *(playing)* Do you hear something, Jane?

Jane *(ibid)* Not a thing, Alison.

Hillary *(off)* It's me, Hillary, wait!

Alison Oh, it's *Hillary*, Jane. Do you think we should wait for *Hillary*?

Jane Hillary-who-didn't-do-her-hair?

Hillary *(off)* I didn't have time!

Alison *We* had time.

Jane We *made* time.

(HILLARY enters. She is dressed as they, but with different hair. She carries a book bag.)

Hillary *(out of breath, **defensive**)* My mother didn't have time.

Jane You let your mother do your hair?

Alison I don't let my mother *touch* my hair. She pulls it, then when I scream and run she says, "Alison Mancini, get in this chair or I'm going to call your father at the office." *(**Sarcastically**.)* "I tremble, Mother, I just tremble." I do my own hair.

Jane I do, too.

Alison *(to JANE)* You *have* to do your own hair.

> The word *ibid* is Latin for *in the same place.*

---

defensive on one's guard

sarcastically in a mocking way

Jane *(defensive)* So what?

Alison So nothing.

Hillary How do you do it by yourself?

Alison With two mirrors and a chair.

Jane *(to ALISON)* And a hairbrush.

Hillary I don't think I can do it.

Alison Well you have to learn so we can be the Mighty Three.

Hillary Guess what? I heard Mr. Decker call us the Three Musketeers; I heard him say so to Mrs. Gray this morning. "Well, I see you've got the Three Musketeers in your class," he said.

Jane Too-too good.

Alison Write it down, Hillary.

Hillary I already did. *(Hugs book bag.)*

Alison We're getting famous. That's what happens when there's three of you; people start to notice you; you get famous.

Jane And three's the right number.

Alison Yes, if you're four, people think you're a gang.

Jane *(rhyme, rap)* The number four is very poor!

Alison Oh, stop it, already. We all know you can rhyme.

Jane I have to keep in practice.

Hillary Practice for what?

Alison Jane's father only lets her watch TV if she rhymes.

Hillary Wow, that's crummy.

Jane It won't last; his new girlfriend is a poet. *(Rhyming.)* The number two is one too few.

Alison Yeah. Two is no good. If there's only two, it's the same as one; nobody notices.

Hillary We, the Mighty Three.

The *Three Musketeers* is a novel published by Alexandre Dumas, a French writer, in 1844. The musketeers are men who stick together and chant "One for all, and all for one." The story has been adapted many times.

Note Jane's line with the stage direction "rhyme, rap." Say the line aloud using rhyme or rap. Then say the line as if the direction were not given. This may help you understand the importance of stage directions.

Jane *(singing)* Alison, Hillary and Me. Hey! Maybe we should be a band. We already match.

Alison *(to JANE)* You can write the songs. Let's start right away. Where should we go?

Jane My house.

Hillary *(same time)* My house.

Jane Pididdle!

Hillary *(almost the same time)* Pididdle!

Jane I said it first.

Hillary *(at the same time)* I said it first.

Jane Who said it first, Alison?

Alison Jane.

Jane I win. Okay, okay. Name ten . . . stars.

(HILLARY names current popular rock, movie, and/or TV stars, while JANE punches her in the arm and counts off each star.)

Jane One . . . two . . . three . . . four . . . five . . . six . . . seven . . . eight—

(Enter SARA KATE CONNOLLY, as if she has been watching. She is unkempt in the way of the neglected and poor.)

Reading Strategy:
Predicting

What causes Sara Kate to enter and immediately say "Stop hitting her"?

Sara Kate Stop hitting her.

Jane Gross, gross.

Alison Are you spying on us, Sara Kate Connolly?

Jane You spy.

Sara Kate I said, don't hit her.

Hillary Nobody's hitting me, I'm fine.

Alison See? She's fine. You can be on your way, before you cause trouble.

Sara Kate I'm not causing trouble.

Jane You cause trouble just by being around. You made me lose my whole lunch appetite when you sat down next to me.

Sara Kate I mind my own business.

Jane Alison, have you ever seen what she eats? Mush in a **thermos.**

Alison Really, I thought her whole family ate nothing but **pesticide.**

Hillary *(uncomfortable)* If they ate pesticide, they'd be dead.

Alison Maybe they *are* dead. Nobody's ever seen them.

Hillary *I've* seen them.

Alison Where have you seen them?

Hillary I've seen Mrs. Connolly. They live behind my house.

Jane Yuk.

Alison Maybe that's just a ghost; the ghost of Sara Kate's mother, oooo.

> The word *yuk* is a slang word that means disgusting.

Jane Or a magic trick. Sara Kate is a magician.

Sara Kate I am not.

Jane Sure you are. Whenever you're around, people's things *disappear.* Where's that bike you stole, Sara Kate?

Sara Kate *(to HILLARY)* I need to talk to you.

Alison You need to talk to who?

Sara Kate Not you. *(To HILLARY)* You.

Hillary Why do you need to talk to me?

Sara Kate I need to talk to you *alone.*

Alison Oh, brother.

---

thermos a container for keeping liquids hot or cold   **pesticide** a chemical used to kill insects

Why does Jane tell Sara Kate that she cannot talk to Hillary alone?

Jane Well you can't.

Sara Kate It's actually very important. And private.

Jane She'll tell us later.

Sara Kate Maybe. Maybe not.

Hillary I don't have anything to say to you.

Sara Kate Of course you don't have anything to say to me. I have something to say to you. But you will have to tear yourself away from these two **chaperones.**

Hillary *(mad)* They're not chaperones! *(Beat.)* What are chaperones?

Sara Kate Body. Guards. For the young and frightened.

Hillary I'm not frightened.

Sara Kate Then let's talk. You. And me. Over there.

Alison She doesn't want her stuff disappeared.

Hillary *(whispers to JANE and ALISON)* Hey, it's all right. I better talk to her or she'll never go away.

Alison *(whispers)* Do you want us to stay and listen?

Hillary No, it's okay. I'll see you tomorrow.

Jane What about our song?

Hillary We can do it tomorrow. At my house.

Alison Okay. Bye-bye, Hillary. Abracadabra, Sara Kate Connolly.

(ALISON and JANE exit. Brief pause.)

Sara Kate Why did you let her hit you?

Hillary It was a pididdle.

Sara Kate A *what*?

Reading Strategy: Predicting

Why does Sara Kate finally get her way and is able to talk to Hillary alone?

chaperones persons responsible for one's behavior

Hillary A pididdle. We said the same thing at the same time. Then Jane said pididdle so I had to name ten stars and let her punch me 'til I got done.

Sara Kate That doesn't even make sense!

Hillary It's just a game.

Sara Kate It's a stupid one!

Hillary *(pause)* What do you want?

Sara Kate *(formally)* Are you Hillary Lenox?

Hillary You know who I am. Our backyards touch.

Sara Kate I can't be sure who you are, you're dressed exactly like Alison Mancini and Jane Webster. Girls of a **predatory** and evil nature. You should hope they never commit a crime; you might get blamed.

Hillary Why?

Sara Kate You dress like them; the witness might identify *you* by mistake.

Hillary Well, it's me, Hillary.

Sara Kate If you're Hillary Lenox, I need to talk to you about a matter concerning our touching backyards. *(Beat)* Have you peeked through the vegetation into my backyard lately?

Notice the stage direction *beat*. A beat calls for a pause and a slight shift in the direction or tone of the dialogue.

Hillary *(annoyed)* I *never* have peeked into your backyard, through the vegetation *or* the bushes.

Sara Kate Then, it's as I thought. *(Beat.)* I am the only one who knows.

Hillary *(annoyed)* What? The only one who knows what?

Sara Kate About the elves.

Hillary What are you talking about?

---

predatory living by robbery or other crime

Sara Kate In my backyard that touches your backyard, even as we speak, there is a village of tiny houses built for and by elves.

Hillary That's crazy.

Sara Kate You haven't seen it.

Hillary Is this some kind of trick?

Sara Kate No, it's not a trick. I don't blame you for not believing; I wouldn't believe either if I hadn't seen it with my own eyes. Right in the yard, tiny little houses that nobody but a tiny elf could live in.

Hillary Well, let's go take a look.

Sara Kate Not yet. Come after four.

Hillary I want to go now.

Sara Kate Well, you don't get what you want. Come to my house after four.

Hillary Maybe I will; maybe I won't.

Sara Kate *(beat)* You will. Don't come to the front. Come to the backyard. After four.

Scene 2

*(Friday afternoon. The lights **reveal** the Lenox backyard, a stoop and a back door to the house, a shed, tools and catalogs onstage. This yard is manicured and **sculpted**. A new birdbath. MR. and MRS. LENOX and then HILLARY.)*

Mr. L *(about birdbath)* Do you think it's all right here?

Mrs. L Frank, it's fine, it's great. It's been great every place we've put it in the last hour. Let's leave it there.

Mr. L *(looks at a catalog)* It looks bigger in the picture.

Mrs. L There's nothing around it to compare it to in the picture.

Reading Strategy:
Predicting

What is the effect of Hillary hearing about the elves in Sara Kate's yard?

Why do you think the playwright uses *Mrs. L.* and *Mr. L.* rather than *Mrs. Lenox* and *Mr. Lenox?*

reveal show   **sculpted** shaped

Mr. L I should have ordered the biggest one.

Mrs. L This one is fine.

Mr. L Do you really think it looks okay?

Mrs. L Yes, it looks okay!

Mr. L *Just* okay?

Mrs. L It looks . . . fabulous. **Authentic.**

Mr. L Yeah, I guess I think it does, too.

Mrs. L Can we address the mess behind the garage now?

Mr. L Now, honey, I'll get to that, after the yard. All things in good time.

(He leaves the catalog on the stoop with the others. HILLARY enters skipping.)

Hillary Wow, that is too-too good.

Mr. L Hillary, honey, don't skip on the grass, skip on the cement. You're tearing up the lawn.

Hillary Sorry, Dad. Looks good, really nice. A lot nicer than the picture.

Mr. L Thanks, honey. Do you think it looks good here?

Hillary Well . . .

Mrs. L Yes, you do, you do.

Hillary Yeah, looks good, Dad.

Mrs. L *(about book bag)* Did they give you homework over the weekend?

Hillary No. It's just my diary inside. *(Beat.)* Can Alison and Jane come over tomorrow?

Mrs. L Sure. You can play in the yard.

---

authentic real

Mr. L —I gotta move it.

Mrs. L No!

Mr. L No, I gotta. I can't have little girls poking it and knocking it.

Hillary We don't do that.

Mrs. L Never mind, honey. Your dad has **temporarily** lost his reason. *(Beat.)* Were the girls mad we didn't do your hair?

Hillary . . . It was okay

Mrs. L I'll do it tomorrow.

Hillary I can do it myself.

Mrs. L Was it fun to dress alike?

Hillary Too-too fun, Mom. Everybody noticed.

Mr. L And that's good?

Hillary Dad! Of course it's good. It's too-too good. Jane and Alison know all about it. They've been doing it for a long time, and everybody in school knows who they are.

Mr. L And that's too-too good?

Hillary Yeah, it's too-too good.

Mrs. L *(beat)* Are they nice to you, honey?

Hillary They let me dress like them!

Mrs. L They've been friends for a long time. You're still the new kid.

Do you think Hillary feels like an equal of Jane and Alison?

Hillary Mom, they're nice to me, it's fine.

Mrs. L Okay. Do you want a snack?

Hillary No. I'm going to visit Sara Kate.

Mrs. L *(surprised)* Sara Kate? Next-door Sara Kate?

Mr. L I thought you were friends with Alison and Jane.

---

temporarily for a short time

Hillary I'm not *friends* with Sara Kate; I'm only visiting her.

Mrs. L Why don't you invite her over here instead?

Hillary Because she doesn't go places.

Mrs. L That house looks like it's going to fall down.

Hillary I'm not going in the house; we're going to play in her yard.

Mr. L *(sarcastic)* The yard, great. You'll probably come home with some disease.

Hillary There's no disease over there.

Mr. L Or lice. Or poison ivy. We should call the health department.

Hillary Dad, you can't call the health department! You can't!

Mr. L Don't raise your voice to me, young lady.

Hillary Oh, I tremble, I just tremble!

Mrs. L Hillary!

Hillary Whaaat?!

Mrs. L . . . We're not going to call the health department. Your dad is just having an opinion. *(Beat.)* How come Sara Kate invited you? What's the occasion?

Hillary No occasion. She invited me and I want to go. *(Beat)* You're always saying how we should be nice to the less fortunate.

Mrs. L *(beat)* All right. But go get a snack. I think you're having low blood sugar. Eat some **protein.**

Hillary Yes, ma'am. *(Exits.)*

Mr. L "I tremble. I just tremble"?

Mrs. L I don't know where she comes up with these things.

> *Lice* are small insects that live by sucking on people. *Poison ivy* is a wild plant that can cause an itchy rash if it comes in contact with skin.

> *Low blood sugar* is a health condition that can be caused by a lack of food.

> **protein** a necessary part of a human diet provided by foods like meat and nuts

Mr. L Where do you come up with low blood sugar?

Mrs. L I don't know. *(Beat.)* Do you think we should have had more kids?

Mr. L Ask me on a different day.

Mrs. L Not for *us;* for her.

Mr. L She's fine, honey, she's just fine. *(Beat.)* Except we'll probably have to **delouse** her when she gets home from Sara Kate's.

Mrs. L Don't I recall some stories about you and head lice?

Mr. L *(defensively)* We all had 'em.

Mrs. L And we all survived. She'll be okay.

Mr. L *(beat)* What about that bike business?

Mrs. L Honey, we don't even know if that story is true; let's give Sara Kate the benefit of the doubt.

The phrase *the benefit of the doubt* means to assume the best.

Scene 3

*(SARA KATE'S yard. It's the **antithesis** of the Lenox yard. There are old appliances, car engines, tires, brambles. There, in the midst of the mess, is an orderly elf village. Little houses built with sticks, string, rocks, and leaves; separated by rows of rocks into an elf development. A well in the center of "town." SARA KATE is working on the elf village. HILLARY enters, with her book bag, through the hedge; without looking at HILLARY, SARA KATE speaks.)*

Sara Kate I first saw it a couple of days ago; it just sort of appeared. They must work all through the night, but it isn't done. You can see where a couple of houses aren't finished, and there's places made ready for houses with no houses on them yet.

Hillary How did you know I was here?

---

delouse to remove lice   **antithesis** opposite

Sara Kate Do you want to see the village or not?

Hillary Okay. *(Impressed.)* Wow. Too-too good. Look, they used sticks and leaves for roofs. And rocks to separate the little houses. It's a little neighborhood.

Sara Kate Yeah, they took rocks from our driveway.

Hillary They stole them?

Sara Kate Yeah, there's rocks gone from our driveway.

Hillary Should we put them back?

Sara Kate No, the elves need them, and we don't even have a car anymore.

Hillary You don't have a car?

Sara Kate No. So what?

Hillary Nothing. *(Beat.)* Well, they shouldn't steal. Even rocks.

Sara Kate The elves don't think so.

Hillary *(shocked)* They don't think it's wrong to steal?

Sara Kate Elves have different rules.

Hillary They steal?!

Sara Kate Just stuff nobody is using. Or stuff from mean rich people.

Hillary How do they know who's mean?

Sara Kate They just know.

Hillary Look, a well, a tiny little well. Let's haul up some water.

Sara Kate Leave it alone. It's very **fragile.**

Hillary It *all* looks real fragile. What happens when it rains?

Sara Kate They rebuild and repair. Elves are at the complete mercy of earth forces.

Hillary *(pause)* How do you know so much?

---

fragile easily broken

Teasing a Butterfly.

Sara Kate . . . I think the elves sneak stuff into my brain.

Hillary What do you mean?

Sara Kate I tried to haul up some water and all of a sudden I was thinking "the elves won't like this."

Hillary Sara Kate, are you sure elves built this? Maybe this was built by mice. Mice could live in these houses quite nicely.

Sara Kate Mice! That is really—that is just—that is so stupid! When did you ever hear of mice building houses?!

Hillary Or even a person could have built these houses.

Sara Kate Look, I didn't have to invite you here today, and I didn't have to show you this. I thought you might like to see

Hillary is ready to believe that mice built the village instead of elves. Why do you think it is easier for her to believe that mice could do it?

an elf village for a change. If you don't believe elves built this, that's your problem. I know they did.

Hillary I haven't seen elves in *my* backyard.

Sara Kate Well, of course not.

Hillary What do you mean?

Sara Kate *(sincere, kind)* Elves would never go in that backyard, no offense, Hillary, but your backyard would not offer any protection. See, elves need to hide, they hate it when people see them. In the olden days, it didn't matter so much, but now, there's too many people, and too many bad ones; elves can't risk being seen by a bad person.

Hillary *(worried)* Why? What would happen?

Sara Kate There's no telling, but it would be very terrible. They know they're safe here, there's a million places to hide in this yard.

Hillary *(looks around, impressed)* Yeah. I see what you mean. *(She sneaks up on things and peeks behind them, looking for elves, as she begins to believe SARA KATE'S elf information.)*

Sara Kate Where, for example, would they find stones in your yard to make these little private lots?

Hillary *(realization)* Right. Our driveway is all paved with cement. There's no rocks anywhere in our yard. And Dad rakes the leaves the second they fall; so there's nothing to make a roof out of! *(She begins to skip.)* Wow. Your yard is perfect for elves! Look at all the junk to hide in, and strings and wire to make the houses, and rocks, and leaves for roofs. *(She stops skipping abruptly.)* Oh, is it all right to skip?

Sara Kate What are you talking about? *(SARA KATE skips and jumps and prances about.)* Of course it's all right to skip. It makes the elves really happy.

> **Reading Strategy: Predicting**
>
> Since Sara Kate said the elves need to hide, when do you think Hillary will see them?

Hillary It does? *(She skips)*

Sara Kate Yes! And if you make them happy enough, they trust you and let you peek at them. *(Stops suddenly.)* Listen! I hear them laughing now.

(HILLARY stops skipping. They listen.)

Reading Strategy:
Predicting

Why do you think Sara Kate says the elves' laughter sounds like earth sounds?

Sara Kate Their language is like earth sounds. But if you listen real close, you can hear that it's really elves.

(Both girls are affected by a felt presence. HILLARY is amazed.)

Hillary *(whispers)* Sara Kate? I think they're here.

Sara Kate Yes, I feel it too. Don't talk about them or they'll go away. Act natural.

A *felt presence* is a sense that someone else is around.

(HILLARY tries to act natural. She hums and opens her book bag.)

Sara Kate *(disdain)* Are you doing homework?!

Hillary *(whispers)* I was going to write something down. In my diary.

Sara Kate Don't whisper, whispering isn't natural. What are you going to write?

Hillary About the elves. I keep a record, a written record of everything. I document my life.

Sara Kate Why do you want to do that?

Hillary In case we get famous—me and Alison and Jane. I'm keeping all our **documentation** in my diary.

documentation a
written record

Sara Kate I don't want to be famous. *(Beat.)* I'm going to straighten the rocks.

Hillary I can do that, too.

Sara Kate I don't want to interrupt your documenting.

Hillary It's no interruption.

(HILLARY puts diary in book bag. The girls start to straighten rocks at one of the "lots.")

Hillary Oh, look.

Sara Kate Little steps.

Hillary *(at the same time)* Little steps!

Sara Kate Oh! Orion's belt, the big dipper, the little dipper, the Pleiades, Virgo, Gemini, Aquarius, Libra, Pisces, Capricorn. Ten! *(Beat.)* How come you didn't punch me?

Hillary What are you talking about?!

Sara Kate Ten stars. We said the same thing at the same time. You're supposed to punch me while I say ten stars.

Hillary *(realizing)* Sara Kate, you're supposed to say "pididdle," and then make *me* say ten of something, and punch *me*. You don't have it right at all.

Sara Kate *(flares up)* Who cares?! It's *your* stupid game. I just did it because I thought you liked it, I don't like it, it's a stupid game. Who cares?!

Hillary *(trying to end the argument)* I'm sorry. I didn't mean— you're right! It *is* a stupid game, you're right. Who cares?

Sara Kate Yeah, who cares.

(Pause. HILLARY walks near the elf houses.)

Hillary *(an idea)* The elves must think we're giants!

Sara Kate *(impressed)* What?!

Reading Strategy:
Predicting

Sara Kate says she does not want to be famous and then changes the topic. Why do you think she changes the topic?

Reading Strategy:
Predicting

Why does Sara Kate call Hillary's game "stupid"?

Hillary Yes! They think we are kindly human giants! *(Stands on something to look around.)* Kindly giant sisters who watch over elves.

If you were playing Sara Kate, how would you make a "giant voice"?

Sara Kate *(pretending to keep watch, a giant voice)* The kindly giant sisters scan the horizon for signs of danger! All clear on the western bank!

Hillary *(playing along)* All clear on the eastern bank.

*(HILLARY walks in a large fashion. A **lumbering**, giant walk. SARA KATE does too.)*

Hillary The kindly giant sisters walk the land, keeping watch.

Sara Kate The ground **quakes** with their steps.

Hillary But the elves have no fear.

(A figure appears in a window. It is a thin woman wearing a nightgown; she is clearly very ill, with wild hair.)

Sara Kate No dangerous humans in sight.

Hillary Only the kindly giant sisters.

Sara Kate *(at the same time)* Giant sisters. All elves may proceed to their homes.

(HILLARY sees the figure in the window. She is frozen in fear.)

Note the stage direction that says Hillary is *frozen in fear.* It means that she should suddenly stand still and look frightened.

Sara Kate Elves may continue construction on the village. The kindly giant sisters will lift and carry objects of great size— *(Notices HILLARY and looks to the house where she sees the figure.)* You have to go.

Hillary What is—who is—

Sara Kate Just go. You have to go.

Hillary But I—

Sara Kate No buts. Get going.

---

lumbering slow and heavy	**quakes** shakes or trembles

Hillary But you shouldn't—

Sara Kate Here! Here's your bag. Just take it and go. Go home, Hillary.

(HILLARY leaves through the hedge. SARA KATE sighs and turns toward the house, where the figure has disappeared.)

Scene 4

(Immediately following. The Lenox backyard. HILLARY enters her backyard again, out of breath and confused. She is glad to see the familiar, friendly, neat garden. She sits under the back stoop light, removes diary from her book bag and records her confused, scattered thoughts.)

Hillary There's a ghost in Sara Kate Connolly's yard. We were playing with the elves, I mean their village. I didn't think it would be real. Why would elves build in Sara Kate's yard? She is a human mess. She's bony and dirty and dresses bad. There's nothing magical about her. Elves should live in a yard of someone . . . beautiful or . . . soft. I don't know why they chose Sara Kate's brain to leave messages in or Sara Kate's yard to live in. Unless they like haunted houses. Alison said Mrs. Connolly is dead and maybe she is because I just saw a ghost in the window—It looked more like a ghost than a person. A skinny, creepy, sickly—

Mr. L *(at the door)* Hillary?

Hillary Oh!!

(HILLARY gasps and jumps away in fright, dropping her diary to the ground. MR. LENOX enters.)

Mr. L Boo.

Hillary *(relieved)* I thought you were a ghost.

Mr. L Not yet. You better get on in, honey; *somebody* hasn't set the table yet!

Hillary Oh, man, the table!

(HILLARY leaves the diary where it fell. MR. LENOX picks up his catalogs, absently snatches the diary, puts everything in a small shed that is attached to the side of the house. He enters the house. Lights fade. A person carrying a candle is seen in the CONNOLLY window.)

Scene 5

(Saturday morning, the next day. The Lenox backyard. MR. and MRS. LENOX are working in the yard. They are happy.)

Mr. L I'm going to become a gardener.

Mrs. L You mean more than weekends?

Mr. L Yeah, a for-real gardener. On somebody's gigantic estate. The gardener, taking care of the big boss's flowers and shrubs.

Mrs. L And what will I be doing?

Mr. L You'll be a **corporate** lawyer. That way I can afford to be somebody's gardener.

Mrs. L Why don't you become a cook?

Mr. L A cook? Not a gardener?

Mrs. L Yeah, rustle us up some pancakes.

(HILLARY runs into the garden in her nightgown. MR. LENOX grabs her.)

Mr. L Whoa.

Hillary Mom, Dad, I was having the best dream, it was the best dream, all about elves. It was so real. There was an elf mayor, and elf villagers, and an elf **ballerina**. I want to go see.

Mr. L Honey, it was a dream.

Hillary Yeah, but there are elves. Over there. *(Points.)*

The phrase *rustle us up some pancakes* is slang for cook some pancakes for us. The phrase *rustle us up* is common Western or cowboy slang.

The word *Whoa* is another Western or cowboy slang word. It means stop.

corporate having to do with a business or a company

ballerina a kind of dancer

Mrs. L Maybe you should get dressed first.

Hillary *(looking at her nightgown, surprised)* Oh, man. I was going next door in my nightgown. I need to get dressed. I need to wake up.

Mrs. L What time are Alison and Jane coming?

Hillary Alison and Jane are coming! I forgot. I completely forgot. I got to do my hair. *(Runs toward the house.)*

Mrs. L Don't forget to get dressed.

Hillary Oh, Mother! *(Exits.)*

Mrs. L I recognize that tone of voice. I think I used it on *my* mother.

Mr. L *(joking)* Was your mother as unreasonable as you?

Mrs. L Probably.

Mr. L *(beat)* I don't remember elves in my youth.

Mrs. L Your youth is too far away to remember.

Mr. L I wish they'd play in our backyard. Where it's neat, and clean, and safe.

Mrs. L Neat and clean and safe is no fun.

*(ALISON and JANE come into the yard; they are wearing matching jackets. ALISON carries a department store bag. The girls are **overtly** polite to parents; the parents are **tolerant,** but not fooled.)*

Jane Good morning, Mrs. Lenox, good morning Mr. Lenox.

Alison We hope we're not disturbing you.

Jane Hillary invited us.

Mrs. L We know. We're getting the yard ready.

> **Reading Strategy: Predicting**
> Note this stage direction for Hillary: *(looking at her nightgown, surprised)*. Why do you think this is included?

---

overtly openly; for show

tolerant willing to put up with something or someone

Jane Oh, we don't need anything special.

Mr. L It isn't for you, it's for the yard.

Mrs. L Frank. Nice jackets.

Alison Oh, Mrs. Lenox, I'm so glad you like them. We just got them, just now, this morning.

Jane My dad dropped me off early at Alison's.

Alison Too early to come here. So Mom took us to Mildred's.

Jane These were on sale.

Alison Really inexpensive.

Jane Mrs. Mancini paid for them. She said they were on her because they were so cheap. We got one for Hillary.

Reading Strategy:
Predicting

Why do you think Jane and Alison buy a coat for Hillary?

Alison I hope it's okay.

Mr. L How do you know she'll like it?

Alison She'll like it; *we* like it.

(The parents exchange a look.)

Mrs. L It's okay, but next time, ask in advance.

Alison Oh, we will. This was an emergency.

Mr. L Now girls, this is new sod. No running and jumping and carrying-on that's going to rip it up. And be careful of the birdbath, it isn't **cemented** in yet. And watch where you walk, there's new ground cover planted.

Mrs. L *(high irony)* Yes, girls, Mr. Lenox is working hard on the yard so Hillary has a nice place to play.

Mr. L *(to MRS. L)* Now, honey, it isn't ready for play yet, when it's ready for play, then they can play as hard as they want. In the meantime, they have to be careful. Now, here, right here, you can play, do whatever you want, right here.

---

cemented held in place with cement

Jane Where, Mr. Lenox?

Mr. L Right here, between here and here.

(The girls walk to the safe patch. It's very small.)

Alison Here?

Mr. L Yeah.

Mrs. L We were just discussing pancakes. Have you girls eaten?

Jane Yes.

Alison Uh huh.

Mrs. L Okay.

Mr. L Have fun.

Alison Thank you.

Mr. L *(points)* Right here, have fun right here . . .

Mrs. L Come on, honey.

(ALISON and JANE smile until the Lenoxes go inside, then they start jumping on the safe patch.)

Jane You can play right here.

Alison Play where it's safe!

Jane Don't knock over the birdbath!

Alison Don't tear up the sod!

Jane Don't rip up the ground cover.

Alison What *is* ground cover?

Jane What's *ground cover?* What's *sod?*

(They are laughing when HILLARY comes over. Her hair matches theirs. She has her book bag.)

Hillary Hi.

Jane We got you a jacket.

Why do Jane and Alison talk differently when Hillary's parents go inside?

Hillary *(opens box and puts on jacket)* Wow.

Alison Just like ours. Your mother says it's okay.

Hillary Too-too good.

Alison Your hair looks good.

Hillary I did it myself.

Jane See.

Hillary Two mirrors, like you said. Look, it fits. *(Beat.)* What do you want to do?

Jane Let's knock over the birdbath.

(JANE and ALISON laugh.)

Reading Strategy: Predicting

What do you think Hillary would do if Jane tried to knock over the birdbath?

Hillary *(worried that they might)* It's probably too heavy.

Jane He said we could stand right here, between here and here. Come on, let's see if we even all fit.

(They try.)

Jane Closer, closer!

Alison **Inhale** and we'll all fit.

(They don't fit, they giggle.)

Alison Your father is mental, Hillary.

Jane Not mental, **demented.**

Hillary All fathers are demented.

Alison My father's never *been* in our yard. The only yard he goes on is the golf course. He goes every weekend.

Jane My father hires somebody.

Hillary He just likes the yard, is all.

---

inhale to breathe air in   **demented** insane

Jane He's demented. Hey! I forgot. What happened with Sara Kate yesterday?

Alison Oh, yeah. What was her big secret?

Hillary Just something in her yard.

Alison What?

Hillary It's this little town. She says elves built it.

Alison Elves?! Is she nuts or what?

Jane There's no such thing as elves.

Alison Did you go over there? *(HILLARY nods.)* By yourself?

Hillary Just for a minute.

Alison Yuk.

Jane Next time, wait for us. *(Rhymes.)* The Migh-tee Three visit Sara Kate Con-no-lly. Hey! Does anybody want to hear my song?

Alison Oh! It's too-too good, Hillary.

Hillary Sing it.

(JANE sings, ALISON sings along for some.)

> We are the Mighty Three,
>
> Alison, Hillary and Me.
>
> We dress alike and we never fight,
>
> Don't listen to you 'cause we know we're right.
>
> We are three friends for sure.
>
> And we don't want any more.
>
> We are the Mighty Three,
>
> Alison, Hillary and Me.

Hillary That is too-too good.

Reading Strategy: Predicting

Jane finally quits talking about Hillary's father. What do you think Hillary would have done if Jane had kept talking?

Hillary tells Jane and Alison that she was just at Sara Kate's for a minute. Why does she not tell them about the elf village?

Alison We can sing it at the next **assembly.**

Hillary Then we'll really be famous.

Alison Did you write down the words?

Jane No, they're in my head.

Alison You should document them, Hillary.

Hillary Yeah. *(She looks in her book bag.)* My diary's gone.

Alison Oh, brother.

Hillary Maybe it's in my room.

Jane Forget it; you can write the words later.

Hillary *(worried)* I wonder what I did with it.

Alison It doesn't matter.

Hillary Yes, it does. I had it yesterday. I wrote what Mr. Decker said about us. I always put it in here.

Alison Did you take it next door?

Hillary I take it everywhere.

Alison Well, that's where your diary went, Hillary.

Jane Oh, yeah. Sara Kate Connolly made it disappear.

Hillary No she didn't.

Alison Sure she did. You're going to have to buy a new diary, Hillary. That's all there is to it.

(SARA KATE enters through the hedge.)

Alison Don't look now, Hillary, but your new best friend has arrived.

Hillary What do you want?

Jane Were you spying behind the bushes?

Why do Jane and Alison assume that Sara Kate took the diary?

assembly a gathering of people for some purpose

Sara Kate I need to talk to Hillary.

Jane *(snide)* Did you bring her diary?

Sara Kate What?

Hillary Where's my diary?

*(Pause. SARA KATE walks around the yard. She is amazed by what is to her great **opulence**.)*

Sara Kate I need to talk to Hillary.

Hillary What? What do you want?

Alison We don't have any secrets. Talk.

Hillary It's true, we don't have secrets; talk, or get out.

Sara Kate There's been a surprising **development** in the elf village.

Hillary *(excited, in spite of herself)* What is it? Did you see elves?

Jane Or the Easter Bunny?

Alison Or Santa?

Sara Kate I didn't see them, but they've been there.

Hillary *(torn)* Well . . . how do you know?

Alison Oh, brother.

Sara Kate They've *been* there! They built something. Something . . . **impressive.**

Jane Let's go see.

Sara Kate No. Only Hillary is invited.

Alison Well, Hillary won't go.

Jane Not unless you invite us, too.

> Why is Sara Kate so amazed by Hillary's backyard?

opulence wealth	**development** a change; progress	**impressive** amazing

Sara Kate Hillary? Do you want to come see what the elves built?

Hillary Yes . . . but only if Alison and Jane can come, too.

Sara Kate Suit yourself. *(Walks in front of each, counting and pointing.)* One, one, one.

*(SARA KATE exits through the hedge.
The girls are **momentarily** stunned. Pause, then.)*

Jane Weird, she's *weird*. One, one, one, what? Is that as high as she can count?

Alison She's mental. She's too-too mental for me.

Jane You don't believe in elves, Hillary.

Hillary *(hesitating)* No. But there is something in Sara Kate's yard. A little town. Somebody had to build it.

Jane Yeah, somebody. Somebody Sara Kate Connolly.

Alison We have a song to practice, Hillary. We don't have any time for elves. Okay?

Hillary Yeah. I know.

(JANE and ALISON begin the song. HILLARY hesitates, then joins in.)

Scene 6

The *Ferris wheel* was designed by George Washington Gale Ferris, Jr. He created it for the Chicago World's Fair in 1893.

(The Connolly backyard. SARA KATE. An elf-sized Ferris wheel made from bicycle tire rims, quite amazing. There are other changes as well. HILLARY, carrying her old jacket and book bag, comes quietly through the hedge, SARA KATE couldn't possibly hear.)

momentarily for
an instant

Sara Kate Isn't it beautiful?

Hillary I didn't make a sound; how did you know I was here?

Sara Kate I don't know; I just . . . know. What do you think?

Hillary (*drops her jacket and book bag and admires the Ferris wheel*) It's really something. Tiny little seats.

Sara Kate Elf-size.

Hillary How did they carry the tires?

Sara Kate Many many of them working together.

Hillary How do you know?

Sara Kate Information gets into my brain.

Hillary Is it a voice gets in your brain?

Sara Kate Yes.

Hillary What's it sound like?

Sara Kate It sounds . . . like me. (*Beat.*) The tires are from that old bike. See? The bike tires are gone. These are those tires.

Hillary How are you going to ride it?

Sara Kate It's an old piece of junk; nobody could ride it. See this?

(*Something that might be a tiny swimming pool.*)

Hillary A swimming pool. Oh my goodness! They made a little swimming pool.

Sara Kate Or something.

Hillary You know what? I bet they're going to make a whole amusement park. Right in your backyard. Merry-go-round, roller coaster. It's perfect. The elves will ride the rides until they get hot, and then they'll go for a swim.

Sara Kate (*unconvinced*) Maybe.

Hillary What do you mean "maybe"?

Sara Kate Elves are not tiny human beings. They're elves, completely different from humans. It's possible to jump to wrong **conclusions.**

Hillary (*considers the pool; an idea*) It's a power source.

Hydro is short for hydroelectric power. *Photovoltaics* means solar energy or energy from the sun that is captured and used.

Sara Kate (*impressed*) Aaaaah, yesssss; combination hydro and photovoltaics.

Hillary Yeah, a power source.

Sara Kate (*playing*) The power streams down from the sun—

Hillary (*playing*) And the stars, too. It never stops coming down, a never-ending source of power.

Sara Kate If you're feeling a little energy drain, stop at the power pool—

Have you ever experienced an "energy drain"? What does it feel like?

Hillary For a fill-up. (*Sticks her finger in the pool; she expands.*) I'm filling up with energy. Pow, pow.

Sara Kate Don't explode!

Hillary Now I'm full of energy. Energy to heat the houses.

Sara Kate Except elves don't get cold.

Hillary No way!

Sara Kate Well, they dooooo, but not until it's freezing. When they finally get so cold they can't stand it, they move into empty human houses. (*Neatening up the village.*) Come on; the kindly giant sisters must help the elves again.

conclusions decisions or opinions reached by reasoning

Hillary The Hillary giant lines up the scattered stones around the elf houses.

Sara Kate The Sara Kate giant gathers berries for the elves' dinner.

Hillary And the Hillary giant helps her.

(SARA KATE eats berries. HILLARY sees and tries some; they're terrible.)

Hillary Yuk. These are terrible, yuk. Poison I bet.

Sara Kate *(playing)* Not to an elf. *(Pops a berry in her mouth.)*

Hillary *(serious)* Don't eat that, Sara Kate. *(Beat.)* Are you hungry?

Sara Kate *(serious)* I'm not hungry.

Hillary You can eat dinner at my house.

Sara Kate *(subdued)* No. I eat with my mom. *(The game again.)* Here. Put leaves and little sticks in this box, Hillary giant.

(SARA KATE suddenly turns, as if to see something. HILLARY looks, too, but the elves are gone.)

Sara Kate Gone.

Hillary I wish I could see an elf.

Sara Kate You have to sort of see them out of the corner of your eye.

(HILLARY looks forward, trying to see sideways.)

Sara Kate Don't worry if you don't see one right away. It might take them a long time to trust us. Move your bag.

Hillary *(picks up her book bag, remembers her diary. Starts looking around)* If the elves took the tires and all, but they need them to cool off and stuff, I think that's all right.

> Sara Kate ate wild, nasty-tasting berries. However, in real life it is not safe to eat unfamiliar wild berries. Some wild berries can make you quite sick.

> Explain the purpose of this stage direction to Sara Kate: *SARA KATE suddenly turns, as if to see something.*

Sara Kate *(not really paying attention, walking in the giant way)* Of course, it's all right.

Why does Hillary not say right away that she is looking for her diary?

Hillary But it would probably be wrong if they took somebody's personal stuff.

Sara Kate Human rules don't work for elves. What are you doing way over there?

Hillary If there was something that a human being owned and needed and loved, and an elf didn't need it or love it or anything. It would be wrong for that elf to take it.

Sara Kate What are you *doing?* There's no building materials over there.

Reading Strategy: Predicting

What do you think Hillary would say if she found her diary by an elf house? How do you think Sara Kate would explain it?

Hillary I'm looking for something.

Sara Kate What?

Hillary My diary. I'm looking for my diary.

Sara Kate Your diary isn't over there.

Hillary *(hopeful)* Where is it?

Sara Kate How should I know? Is that what this is about? Your diary? *(Beat.)* You *do* think I stole your diary.

Hillary *(too fast)* No. No. I . . . I lost it. I can't find it. And I had it here yesterday, so I thought, maybe . . .

Sara Kate What?! You thought, what?!

Hillary I thought . . . maybe . . . I left it here. By mistake.

Sara Kate You think I sneaked into your stupid book bag and stole your stupid diary. Boy, you *are* the same as Jane and Alison. Every time something happens, you blame it on me. You are **sickening.**

Hillary *(getting mad)* What am I supposed to think? The last time I ever saw it I was here—

sickening able to cause a sickness

Sara Kate *(shouting)* Who cares what you think? You're a stupid little girl with stupid little friends.

Hillary *(shouting)* I am not stupid and my friends are not stupid. We have a song—

Sara Kate A stupid song to show how stupid your brains are—

Hillary Don't you call us stupid. You got held back. You're the only one's stupid around here.

Sara Kate Get out. Get out of my yard.

Hillary I was going to give you my jacket. I brought my jacket all the way over here to give it to you.

Sara Kate Who wants your stupid jacket?! Get out.

(The Ferris wheel spins by itself, whirs, dazzles. The girls are silent, amazed. HILLARY stops it.)

Sara Kate *(gently)* Why did you stop it?

Hillary It scared me.

Sara Kate *(sympathizing)* Oh, don't be scared of elves. Elves can't hurt people. People can hurt elves is all.

(The window shade on the house is pulled to one side.)

Hillary Do you want my jacket? My mother said I could give it to you. I got this new one.

Sara Kate So you could match your good friends.

Hillary . . . You never wear a coat.

Sara Kate I don't . . . get cold.

Hillary Like an elf.

Sara Kate *(notices the window shade)* Oh, man. I gotta go before the bank closes. Do you want to go shop with me?

The word *gotta* is slang for *have to.*

---

sympathizing
sharing another's
sorrows or troubles

Hillary Do you go to the corner, to Mr. Neal's?

Sara Kate No. I go to the supermarket. Things are cheaper, and it's . . . just better to go to the big stores.

Hillary My mother would kill me if I went all the way to the supermarket.

Sara Kate So don't go, no skin off my nose.

Hillary No, okay, I'll go. I'll go with you.

Scene 7

*(Immediately following. The girls walk into the big city. There is a bigness all around them, a large city with accompanying sounds. Tall buildings, traffic. A bigness in which a little girl can move **anonymously**. HILLARY stands back and watches and listens amazed at SARA KATE. SARA KATE talks to unseen functionaries. At the bank. SARA KATE downstage, front; HILLARY watches slightly upstage.)*

The *unseen functionaries* are the banker and the pharmacist. Although they are mentioned, the banker and pharmacist are not actually seen.

Sara Kate *(ultra sweet)* Hello, I need to cash my mother's check, ma'am. See? She signed it right on the back. Her signature is on file here and you can look it up. I cash the checks because she works and can't come here, and it's real convenient for me to do it because the bank is right near our house. *(Worried.)* I always do it, ask anybody. *(Relieved.)* . . . Twenties will be fine.

*(SARA KATE and HILLARY walk. Street sounds. Then they enter the **pharmacy**. HILLARY watches as SARA KATE talks.)*

Sara Kate *(worried)* I *know* the **prescription** has run out, but the person who was here yesterday promised to call the doctor to okay the refill. This is very terrible. You see, my mother needs her medicine and she's already gone a whole day without it, because that other man, he said he'd call the

anonymously without being known	**pharmacy** a place where medicines are prepared and sold	**prescription** an order from a doctor for medicine

doctor. Could you just give me one refill for one month's supply? . . . Great, great.

(At the grocery store. Walking with HILLARY.)

Sara Kate *(to HILLARY)* In the grocery store, you only buy *plain* boxes of stuff, no brands, because they cost more money. If you buy the stuff in the plain boxes it costs a lot less. Cream of Wheat in the plain box lasts a long time and it really fills you up when you're hungry. That way you have enough to send some money to the electric company and the phone bill; you don't want them turned off because to get them turned back on you gotta give them *more* money, for a deposit.

Hillary What's a deposit?

Sara Kate It's a whole bunch of money that you don't get anything for. Only poor people have to pay one.

Hillary . . . That doesn't make sense.

Sara Kate You're tellin' me.

(HILLARY is amazed.)

Scene 8

*(Lenox yard. Saturday dusk. MRS. LENOX is **puttering**. HILLARY enters from the hedge. HILLARY is nervous because she knows her mother would be furious if she knew she'd been shopping with SARA KATE.)*

Mrs. L It's about time you were home.

Hillary Why?

Mrs. L It's getting dark is why. It's time you were home.

Hillary Well, I *am* home.

Mrs. L And you should be.

Hillary Well I am.

---

puttering doing unimportant things

Mrs. L Hillary!

Hillary Whaaat?

Mrs. L *(beat)* I think being with Sara Kate is making you cross.

Hillary *(cross)* I'm not cross.

Mrs. L If Sara Kate is going to put you in a bad mood, we're not going to let you go over there.

Hillary Mom, you have to let me.

Mrs. L No, we don't have to.

(MR. LENOX enters from house. He carries an envelope.)

Mr. L *(to MRS. L)* Honey, did you pay the phone bill last month?

Mrs. L Sure I did.

Mr. L This says second notice.

Mrs. L *(testy)* I guess I forgot, I don't know.

Mr. L Okay, I just don't want, you know, the old credit rating to slip.

Mrs. L *(testy)* I'm sorry.

Hillary Don't worry. They don't turn off the phone unless you skip *two* months.

Mr. L I didn't know that.

Hillary Yeah, and if they *do* cut it off, there's a kind of phone service you can get for free.

Mr. L What kind is that?

Hillary It's a kind of phone service that you can only call out on.

Mr. L Why would I want that?

> A *credit rating* is a summary of a person's payment history. Many companies use a person's credit score to decide what types of loans or amounts of money to give the person.

Hillary It's for emergencies; Sara Kate says the phone company *has* to let you have one. It's so you can call 911. But nobody can call you.

Mr. L What else does Sara Kate say?

Hillary She says you can get water from the **hydrant** for free.

Mr. L Oh?

Hillary Yeah, and the electric bill, if you just pay a little bit, they won't turn it off, they're not allowed to if you're trying to pay.

Mr. L Oh, boy.

(The parents exchange a look.)

Hillary What?

Mr. L Hillary, what happens if everybody does that?

Hillary I don't know!

Mr. L Somebody has to pay for that electricity. The way it gets paid is everybody else's rates go up.

Hillary Poor people have to pay a deposit!

Mr. L *(pause, gently)* Hillary, I think you shouldn't play with Sara Kate anymore.

Hillary But, Dad—

Mr. L No, I think it would be better if you don't see her anymore.

Hillary But you don't even know her.

Mr. L Honey, life is hard enough if people play by the rules; it's impossible if they don't.

Hillary But, Dad—

Electric companies are businesses. They only make money if people pay their bills. However, the laws do not always allow them to decide when to shut off a person's electricity. Why do you think there are laws about when electric companies can turn off a person's electricity?

hydrant a pipe for drawing water

Mr. L Hillary. No. Everybody has to do their part. It's like a relay race—if somebody on the team doesn't run their part, the whole team loses.

Hillary We don't even have races like that at my school. *(Brief pause.)*

Mrs. L Hillary, honey, go wash up for dinner.

(HILLARY sighs, goes inside.)

Mr. L Don't say it.

Mrs. L She's a little kid.

Mr. L She's not too little to learn.

Scene 9

(ALISON enters, mad, sits in a huff. JANE enters, then HILLARY, who is walking like a giant.)

Why is Alison upset?

Alison How could you, how *could* you, after we practiced all week? We practiced *all week*.

Hillary I looked into the audience and all of a sudden I couldn't remember the words or anything.

Jane What are you *doing?*

Hillary *(caught)* Oh! I was walking like a giant.

Alison Walking—?! Pay attention, Hillary. We worked so hard on the song to make it right. And it was stupid. What's the point of practicing if we're stupid?

Jane What were you thinking about, Hillary?

Hillary I was wondering what to do when the toilet gets stopped up.

Alison The toilet! You are mental; you're mental!

Jane You call your father, that's what you do.

Alison Kids don't have to fix toilets, Hillary.

Hillary Some kids do I bet.

Alison Well, we don't.

Hillary We're pretty lucky. We're lucky.

Alison We're not lucky.

Hillary We are. Our parents can buy us stuff, and we have outfits. Everybody doesn't have outfits. Or dinners.

Alison Oh boy, wrap it up and send it to the starving children around the world, Hillary.

Hillary I'm just saying.

Alison Are we supposed to stand around and feel bad because we're not starving?

Hillary I don't know.

Alison Well I know. And it's stupid to feel bad because somebody else is starving.

Hillary Sara Kate doesn't have it so good.

Alison Is that what this is about? Sara Kate!?

Jane *(holds a pencil to her nose, prances around)* Hey, hey! Who am I? Who *am* I?

Hillary What are you doing?

Jane I was being Sara Kate Connolly.

Alison *(to HILLARY)* Sara Kate took a math test with her pencil taped to her nose.

Hillary No!

Alison For sure. Right before she disappeared!

Reading Strategy: Predicting

Hillary has not told the whole truth about Sara Kate to Alison and Jane. Do you think they would be kinder to Sara Kate if they knew everything?

Hillary Maybe she had a . . . fit or something. Maybe that's why she hasn't been in school.

Jane I never heard of a fit where you tape pencils to your nose.

Hillary There's all kinds of fits! Maybe she's really sick.

Alison She *is* really sick, Hillary. That's what we've been telling you.

Jane She's mentally sick.

Hillary Sometimes I think *you're* mentally sick.

Jane *What* did you say?

Hillary . . . I was joking.

Alison Ha ha.

Hillary I mean, if somebody is really sick then somebody should visit her.

Jane You better not.

Hillary I mean, who's taking care of the elf village?

Why do you think Alison reacts in this way?

Alison Oh, brother.

Jane Your parents will get really mad if you go over there.

Alison Let's go to Jane's and practice.

Hillary I can't. I have to go straight home. *(Beat.)* I said I would.

Jane *(to ALISON, exiting)* Come on, Alison, you and me can go practice.

Alison *(exiting)* We don't need to practice; *we* didn't forget the words.

Hillary Bye. *(She watches until the girls are out of sight, then runs off.)*

Scene 10

(Inside the Connolly house. It is very rundown. A knock at the door.)

Hillary *(off)* Hello? Is anybody home? Sara Kate? *(Pushes open the door and sticks her head in.)* Hello, your door is open. *(Enters and gasps.)* Wow, they're gone. They're all moved away! *(She enters, finds it a scary, uncomfortable place, starts to exit, hears something—the sound of a rocking chair on wood.)* Sara Kate? *(The sound continues. She looks toward the sound.)* Elves! It's the elves.

> The stage direction *(off)* means offstage. In other words, the character is heard but not seen.

Note the stage direction *full window-light*. This means that the sun coming in through the window gives light to a room that is fairly dark.

Reading Strategy: Predicting

What does her belief in elves have to do with Hillary's going into Sara Kate's house?

*(HILLARY crosses the stage in the semi-darkness, following the sound, which grows louder. Pushes open "a door," where in full window-light she sees SARA KATE in rocking chair with her mother. MRS. CONNOLLY is a thin, sick, frightened woman. She and SARA KATE look toward HILLARY. HILLARY gasps. She is confused. She starts to **babble**.)*

Hillary I thought no one was here. I thought the sound was elves. What's wrong with your mother?

(SARA KATE carefully gets up so as not to startle her mother, as HILLARY continues to babble.)

Hillary You weren't in school, I thought you were sick; I thought the elves needed help. The Ferris wheel is knocked over. I saw it in the yard. I'm not allowed to come here anymore. What's wrong with your mother?!

Sara Kate *(whispers, practically hissing)* Get out. Get out of my house. Don't ever come back. And don't you tell anybody.

Hillary I won't—

Sara Kate Don't you *dare* tell anybody.

Hillary Sara Kate, it's me, Hillary.

Sara Kate You get out and don't you come back. You forget you ever were in this house. You forget it, erase it from your mind, it didn't happen.

(HILLARY runs out. MRS. CONNOLLY covers her face with her hands; SARA KATE comforts her.)

END ACT ONE

babble to talk without making sense

Afternoon of the Elves, Act One *by Y York*

Directions Choose the letter of the best answer or write the answer using complete sentences.

Comprehension: Identifying Facts

1. What are the two different numbers of actors that can be in this play?
  A 2 or 3   **C** 6 or 7
  B 4 or 5   **D** 8 or 9

2. What is one of Hillary's regular chores at home?
  A To pay the electric bill
  B To set the table
  C To mow the lawn
  D To get the groceries

3. Who is Sara Kate?

4. Why does Sara Kate invite Hillary to her house?

5. What do Jane and Alison buy for Hillary so she can look like them?

6. What does Hillary lose while she is at Sara Kate's house?

7. According to Sara Kate, how are the elves able to carry the bike tires?

8. What lie does Sara Kate tell the bank employee?

9. What happens that messes up the song the three girls sing at the assembly?

10. Describe the differences between Hillary's yard and Sara Kate's yard.

Comprehension: Putting Ideas Together

11. Sara Kate thinks that Jane and Alison are around Hillary too much. What does she call Jane and Alison?
  A annoying   **C** frightened
  B chaperones   **D** friendly

12. Which of the following best describes Mr. Lenox's treatment of his yard?
  A His work is sloppy.
  B He does not enjoy the work.
  C He is careless about the yard.
  D He spends too much time in the yard.

13. Hillary and her friends play a game called "Pdiddle." Explain how this game is played.

14. What happens when Sara Kate tries to play the game with Hillary?

15. How does the elf village change throughout Act One?

16. Sara Kate does not give up at home or with the girls at school. Give an example of each.

After Reading **continued on next page**

17. On page 421, Hillary and her parents are having a discussion. Hillary is upset and she says, "I tremble, I just tremble." Why do you think she talks to her parents like that?

18. On page 437, Sara Kate talks about something the elves built. What is the difference between the reactions of Jane, Alison, and Hillary?

19. How does the elf village really get into Sara Kate's yard?

20. What has Hillary discovered at the end of Act One?

Understanding Literature: Acts and Scenes

Scripts for drama productions are often divided into acts and scenes. An act is a major unit of action in a play. Some plays have just one act, but many plays have two or more acts. Each act is then divided into scenes, or smaller units of action. Each scene usually involves certain characters and one setting. If the setting changes, there is often a new scene. Characters and the set design may change between acts or scenes.

21. Into how many acts is *Afternoon of the Elves* divided?

22. How many scenes make up Act One of the play?

23. How does the setting change between Scene 1 and Scene 2?

24. Which characters are involved in Scene 5?

25. Based on the action near the end of Act One, what do you predict will happen in Act Two?

Critical Thinking

26. Do you think Sara Kate stole the missing bike? Explain.

27. Why do you think Sara Kate really decides to tell Hillary about the elf village?

28. Sara Kate says some mean things to Hillary. Mostly, they are about Jane and Alison, and Hillary's friendship with them. For example, she calls her "a stupid little girl with stupid little friends." Since Sara Kate clearly likes Hillary, why do you think she would say such mean things?

29. Do you think Sara Kate's situation gives her the right to lie and steal? Explain.

Thinking Creatively

30. Imagine that you were going to help Sara Kate build a bowling alley for the elves. What materials could you find around your house to use? Explain how you would use the different items.

Grammar Check

Nouns and verbs must agree in number.

- Pair singular nouns with verbs that end in -*s*.
- Pair plural nouns with verbs that do not end in -*s*.

Correct: Hillary and Sara Kate <u>talk</u> every day.

Incorrect: Hillary and Sara Kate <u>talks</u> every day.

Correct: Sara Kate <u>works</u> on the elf village each day.

Incorrect: Sara Kate <u>work</u> on the elf village each day.

Rewrite each sentence using the correct verb in parentheses.

1 Mrs. Connolly (look, looks) better today.

2 Jane and Alison (like, likes) to dress alike.

3 Hillary (watch, watches) the elves with Sara Kate.

 Vocabulary Builder

Rewrite each of the following sentences. Replace the underlined word with a vocabulary word from the play.

1 The car stopped <u>suddenly</u> and was almost rear-ended.

2 The <u>wealth</u> all around us was just too much.

3 The scores show an <u>amazing</u> increase over last year.

 Writing on Your Own

In Act One, Sara Kate wants Hillary to pay attention to her and be her friend. She creates an elf village in her backyard and invites Hillary over to see it. Write a paragraph explaining why you think she instead went to the trouble of creating the village.

 Listening and Speaking

In a small group, discuss times when you have wanted to fit in with others. Describe the situation and tell what actions you took. Also tell the results of your actions. Listen carefully and respectfully as each person in the group tells his or her story.

  Media and Viewing

Find two or three other stories about elves. Use the information from your research and the details in this play to create your own elf village. Use materials found in nature or around your house. Share your completed elf village with your class.

BEFORE READING THE SELECTION | Build Skills

Afternoon of the Elves, Act Two   *by Y York*

moral a lesson or message about life told in a story

Literary Terms In Act One, you began to learn about the characters and plot that make up this story. As you read Act Two, you will find out how the story ends. Think about the **moral,** or lesson about life in the story. Readers can learn from the choices these characters make.

Reading on Your Own As you read Act Two of *Afternoon of the Elves,* recall what you read in Act One. Using this information, predict what you think may happen in Act Two.

Writing on Your Own Think about the title of this play. Why do you think both the author and playwright decided to use this title? Write a paragraph explaining how you think the title is related to the story. Also tell whether you think it is a good title for the play.

Vocabulary Focus Before you begin reading, preview the vocabulary words for this selection. Read each word and its definition aloud. Then write a sentence in your notebook for each word. Having an awareness of the vocabulary words will help you read the selection more smoothly.

Think Before You Read What changes do you think will take place in Hillary and Sara Kate in Act Two?

Afternoon of the Elves

ACT TWO

Scene 1

AT RISE: A week later, the Lenox yard. Home from school, HILLARY reads the diary entry she just wrote.

Hillary Dear Diary. *(Beat.)* Dear Diary *Substitute,* or Journal, or whatever you are. I'm not mad at Sara Kate anymore about my real diary she stole, even though I know I ought to be. I can't be mad at her anymore. Once I almost told Alison and Jane what I saw, but I promised not to. Even if I did tell about it, I don't know what I would say; sometimes I think maybe it wasn't real. Maybe it was another elf dream. A bad one this time.

*(MR. LENOX enters from the gate with a large **trellis**.)*

Mr. L Hey, there's my girl.

Hillary Dad! What are you doing home?

Mr. L I took the afternoon off. Look what I got. I'm going to plant a trumpet vine next spring. Now it will have something to grow on.

Hillary Next spring is a long way away, Dad.

Mr. L Nah, it's right around the corner. Trumpet flowers are gorgeous.

Hillary I don't think I know what they look like.

> Many plays are divided into two or more acts. The acts give the actors a chance to take a break. Between acts, the set people can make some changes. The audience has a chance to get up and move around.

> A *trumpet vine* is a green vine with bright orange or red flowers. The flowers have a narrow base and a fanned-out flower. Each flower looks somewhat like a tiny trumpet.

trellis a frame to support a growing vine

Mr. L Gorgeous. Last night I dreamt I *was* one. What do you think of that?

Hillary That's pretty weird. Did you come home early just to work in the garden, Dad?

Mr. L Just! Just to work in the garden?! Yeah, I did.

Hillary Wow. Too-too good.

Mr. L I'll say, too-too good. Plants don't talk back.

Hillary Plants don't talk at all.

Mr. L Even better. Where should we put the trellis?

Hillary I don't know.

Mr. L How about by the hedge?

Hillary Okay.

(They put the trellis in front of the hedge. HILLARY stands back to look.)

Hillary *(sad)* Oh. Oh, Dad, can we put it somewhere else?

Mr. L What's wrong with here?

Hillary I just— I don't— It's like we're putting up bars between us and Sara Kate. *(She turns **abruptly,** gasps slightly.)*

Mr. L What?

Hillary Did you see something over there?

Mr. L No.

Hillary I thought I saw something. Right there.

Mr. L It was probably a bird.

---

abruptly suddenly

Hillary Maybe.

(HILLARY is silent. MR. LENOX moves the trellis away from the hedge.)

Mr. L We'll put the trellis somewhere else.

Hillary Okay.

Mr. L I didn't know you were still thinking about Sara Kate.

Hillary Dad. I *want* to forget about her; I want to forget all about her, but she's always in my brain. I think I see her out of the corner of my eye, but then I turn to look, and she's not there.

Mr. L You weren't friends very long.

Hillary Dad. Dad. I know, I *know*. And sometimes it wasn't even very fun to be friends with her. But it was special. She's special.

Mr. L *(beat)* I guess I didn't realize. *(Beat.)* Hey, let's plant some bulbs. It'll clear our brains.

Hillary Now? In the cold?

Mr. L Yeah, plant them in the fall for flowers in the spring.

Hillary Okay.

Mr. L Get the bulb thing out of the shed.

(HILLARY looks in the shed.)

Mr. L There's a lot of gardening to be done in winter. Planting bulbs, pruning trees.

Hillary *(at shed)* I don't see the bulb thing.

Mr. L Look on the shelf. It's much less **traumatic** to the tree if its branches are cut in winter when the sap is slow.

(HILLARY crosses back to MR. LENOX with her diary.)

Mr. L Whatcha got there? That's not the bulb thing.

> Gardeners plant bulbs in the ground during the fall. In the spring, flowers grow from the bulbs.

> *Reading Strategy:*
> **Predicting**
> What do you think is going to happen when Hillary goes into the shed?

---

traumatic shocking

Hillary Dad, this is my diary. What's my diary doing in the shed?

Mr. L *That's* your diary? Oh. Oops. I put it there; I put it in the shed. I didn't think.

Hillary Oh, man, oh, no, oh, Dad. Oh, Dad. Sara Kate thinks I think she stole my diary.

Mr. L Why does she think that?

Hillary Because I *did* think it. Oh, man.

Mr. L Sorry, honey, really.

Hillary *(miserable)* I'm an idiot.

Mr. L *(beat)* Well, maybe you better get over there and apologize.

Hillary Really?

Mr. L Yeah, okay, go on.

Scene 2

*(The Connolly backyard, near dusk. HILLARY comes through the hedge. The elf village is in **disarray;** the Ferris wheel is on its side. She walks around for a moment, SARA KATE enters, she wears no coat in spite of the cold.)*

Sara Kate Hello.

Hillary *(startled)* Oh. Oh. Sara Kate, it's you. I didn't hear you. You're here!

Sara Kate Of course I'm here.

Hillary I thought— I don't know, I haven't seen you. *(Beat.)* How's your mother?

Sara Kate She's fine. How should she be?

Hillary Sometimes she's sick.

Sara Kate Sometimes everybody is sick.

---

disarray disorder

> How would you suggest that Hillary carry out the stage direction *miserable?*

Hillary When she gets sick, you take care of her.

Sara Kate So what? When I get sick, she takes care of me.

Hillary But that's different—

Sara Kate No, it's the same.

Hillary . . . How are the elves?

Sara Kate They're okay.

(They are quiet, not knowing what to say. SARA KATE rights the Ferris wheel.)

Hillary Is it broken?

Sara Kate No, it's fine.

Hillary What a mess.

Sara Kate Yeah, I've been real busy. I'm trying to clean up.

Hillary Can I help?

Sara Kate Here. *(Hands her a box.)* Pick up the junk.

Hillary Okay. Your yard looks sooooo good.

Sara Kate You just said it's a mess.

Hillary No, it's a great mess. An elf mess. There's nothing like this anywhere else.

Sara Kate That's why the elves come.

Hillary I know. Some things only make sense here.

Sara Kate Yes.

Hillary *(beat)* Sara Kate? Did you tape a pencil to your nose?

Sara Kate Yes. So what?

Hillary What for?

Sara Kate So it wouldn't fall off when I took the math test.

Hillary Yeah, but, *why* did you *take* a math test with the pencil taped to your nose?

Hillary has already talked to Jane and Alison about the pencil on the nose. Why did Hillary also ask Sara Kate about it?

Sara Kate I was practicing. You can do anything if you practice. You can learn anything. They read us that story about Pierre the Package. You know that story?

Hillary No, they didn't read us that story.

Sara Kate Yeah, it's for older kids. Pierre doesn't have any arms or legs. Nothing. He's just a head and a body. So when he needs to write, somebody tapes a pencil to his nose so he can type.

Hillary Why don't they just type the letter for him?

Sara Kate A million reasons why! Maybe it's a love letter; or maybe he wants to write it himself. If he wants to do it himself, he should be allowed.

Hillary It must be very hard.

Sara Kate Lots of things are hard. You have to learn how to do them is all.

Hillary Like taking care of a house. *(Beat.)* I found my diary.

Sara Kate *(sarcastic)* Congratulations.

Hillary Remember? I thought I left it here.

Sara Kate You thought I stole it.

Hillary Yeah. I'm sorry.

Sara Kate Who wants to read about the Mighty Three?

Hillary I don't write about that anymore.

Sara Kate I don't see what's so great about being the same as them.

(MRS. CONNOLLY appears in the window. SARA KATE sees her.)

Hillary I'm not the same as them. They're not even the same as each other.

(MRS. CONNOLLY disappears.)

Reading Strategy:
Predicting
What do you think will happen when Hillary tries to apologize to Sara Kate?

Who are the Mighty Three?

Sara Kate *(sighs)* I have to go in.

Hillary Is it your mother?

Sara Kate Yes. She wants me to come in.

Hillary Do you want me to go home?

Sara Kate *(looks closely at HILLARY)* Listen—

Hillary Yes.

Sara Kate Can you keep a secret?

Hillary I can. I can keep one forever.

Sara Kate Okay. My mother has been worse lately and she likes to have me stay near. Do you have any money?

Hillary A little.

Sara Kate We're out of stuff. Food. My mother likes coffee and milk. And sugar. We need bread and fruit. She likes fruit. And aspirin.

Hillary What else?

Sara Kate Whatever you can get.

Scene 3

*(HILLARY is **daunted** by the **enormity** of the task, jams her hands in her pocket, takes a big breath, and begins to walk into the sounds of the city.)*

Scene 4

(Later that day, inside the Connolly house. It is cold and barren. A knock. SARA KATE runs to the door, peeks out, and opens it for HILLARY, who enters completely out of breath carrying two large shopping bags.)

In the story, Hillary is in fourth grade, and she goes shopping on her own. In real life, it is not safe for fourth graders to go off alone.

---

daunted bothered	**enormity** enormousness; hugeness or difficulty

Sara Kate Look at all this stuff.

Hillary (*out of breath*) Yeah, I got a real lot.

Sara Kate I thought you said you only had a little money.

Hillary I broke up my bank. Forty bucks. I had to stop and rest a lot of times.

Name something that shows Hillary is generous and giving.

Sara Kate You should have **swiped** a cart.

Hillary Oh. I didn't know.

Sara Kate (*pause*) You didn't tell, did you?

Hillary No, I didn't tell!

Sara Kate (*emptying a bag*) You got everything! Milk and cereal. You got the kind with raisins!

Hillary Yeah. Sorry. I couldn't find the plain white boxes, the cheap ones you said are better.

Sara Kate Oh, no, don't apologize, this is fine; really great! Bread and **bologna!** You got bologna!

Hillary Yeah. Boy, stuff costs a lot.

Sara Kate I know. (*Beat.*) I got to take some stuff to my mother.

Hillary Okay.

(*SARA KATE puts some stuff in the empty grocery bag and exits. HILLARY takes the rest of the groceries out. She opens the refrigerator, finds the light doesn't go on and that it is not working.*)

Hillary Oh, man. Gross. This is gross.

(*Shuts refrigerator, sees a bug, jumps. Stands on a chair. SARA KATE returns.*)

Sara Kate What are you standing there for?

---

swiped taken

bologna a type of sandwich meat

Hillary I'm cold.

Sara Kate Yeah, it gets cold. The furnace broke.

Hillary What do you do when the furnace breaks?

Sara Kate First you call the oil company. Then they send a guy who says how much it costs. Then you tell them never mind because it's so much.

Hillary How do you keep warm?

Sara Kate The stove. Upstairs I got three electric heaters and electric blankets.

Hillary Electric blankets give you cancer!

Sara Kate Yeah, but if you don't keep warm you freeze to death.

Hillary How's your mother?

Sara Kate She's okay. Let's have sandwiches, bologna sandwiches.

Hillary *(looks toward roaches)* I'm not hungry.

Sara Kate Suit yourself. I love white bread. *(Finds mayonnaise.)* And mayonnaise! You need mayonnaise on bologna sandwiches.

Hillary Yeah, you do. I think I changed my mind.

Sara Kate Two bologna sandwiches coming up!

Hillary I thought all you ate was berries off trees.

Sara Kate Why eat berries off trees when you have bologneeee!?

It is not known whether there is a link between cancer and electric blankets. However, some studies suggest that such a link could exist.

Reading Strategy:
Predicting

What do you think will happen now that Sara Kate has Hillary as a helper?

Hillary *(happy)* I don't know. I saw roaches.

Sara Kate They don't hurt anybody. Roaches are misunderstood.

Hillary *(laughs)* Somebody sprays our house.

Sara Kate We used to get that. Now we try to get along with them.

Hillary Yuk.

Sara Kate Roaches are very clean. I saw it on TV. Before they took the TV back. Here's a sandwich. Yippee, bologneee.

Hillary Who took the TV back?

Sara Kate That's what happens when you don't have any money; people come and take your stuff away.

Hillary That's crummy.

Sara Kate Yes, it's very terrible. I try to keep things paid. But sometimes, the money's just *gone*.

Hillary Man.

Sara Kate But it helps when I send the bill people letters. I write and say I'll send them money next month.

Hillary *(slowly)* You. You do everything.

Sara Kate No. I mean. I *help* . . . sometimes. I *help*.

Hillary No. You do everything. You pretend that your mother tells you what to do, like everybody else's mother. But that's not right. She doesn't tell you anything. She's too sick. You're the one taking care of her.

Sara Kate So what! I learned how; I can do it.

Hillary Don't be mad. I was just trying to imagine it. What happens with the big stuff— I mean, the big stuff?

Sara Kate I do it . . . I do the big stuff, whatever happens, I do it. I sign it; I write it; I talk on the phone. I tell people what to do, and if they don't do it, I find some other way. My mother gets so upset when we run out of money.

Hillary Don't *you* get upset?!

Sara Kate Sometimes my father can send money and sometimes he can't. When he can't, I just have to manage.

Hillary But how?

Sara Kate People leave stuff. There was a whole cart full of food in the supermarket parking lot one time. At school there's lost and found.

Hillary They give you lost and found?

Sara Kate Sure, I say it's mine, and they give it to me.

Hillary You should tell. If people knew you were taking care of your mother by yourself, they'd do something about it.

Sara Kate No! They'd take my mother away.

Hillary You can't take care of her forever.

Sara Kate I've been doing it for a year, and nobody even knows.

Hillary (*quietly*) A year.

Sara Kate People are stupid. They don't have a clue to what's going on right in their own backyards.

Hillary (*to herself*) I know.

Sara Kate People don't like anybody who is sick. They put us where they can't see us.

Hillary Like the starving people around the world.

Sara Kate Yeah, so if you're thinking of getting help for us, forget it.

> How do you think Sara Kate will answer Hillary's question?

Hillary My parents aren't like other people; we could ask my—

Sara Kate No. No, Hillary. Somebody like you can ask for help; somebody like me has to steal it.

Hillary *(beat)* Sara Kate? Are you an elf?

(A loud knock at the door.)

Sara Kate Oh, no.

Mrs. L *(off)* Hillary? Sara Kate? It's Mrs. Lenox. Mrs. Connolly, are you there?

Sara Kate Get rid of her.

Hillary *(peeks through the door)* Hi, Mom, I'm coming. Bye-bye, Sara Kate. *(Tries to exit.)*

Mrs. L Just a minute, Hillary.

Hillary Let's go, Mom.

Mrs. L Where is Sara Kate?

Hillary Come on, Mom.

Mrs. L Hillary! Just a minute. *(Sees into the room.)* What is . . . ? Sara Kate? What have you girls done to this room?

Hillary It's nothing; it's just Sara Kate.

Mrs. L What have you been doing? Where is your mother?

Reading Strategy: Predicting

What do you think would be the effect of someone talking with "practiced courtesy"?

Sara Kate *(with practiced courtesy)* Hello, Mrs. Lenox. I'm so glad to be seeing you again. It's been a long time, hasn't it. My mother is fine, but she's upstairs having a nap, now. I know this room looks terrible. We're having it fixed. That's why everything is moved. I'm sorry you had to come looking for Hillary.

Mrs. L *(confused)* I tried to call . . .

Sara Kate Yes, the phone's been turned off since this morning, which you probably found out. There must be a line down somewhere. There's a man coming to fix it.

Mrs. L Is the heat off, too?

Sara Kate Yes. They had to turn off the heat. Just for an hour or so. They're working on pipes.

Mrs. L Pipes?

Sara Kate Yes. So they had to turn off the heat. They always do that.

Mrs. L Who?

Sara Kate Workmen. The workmen who fix pipes.

Mrs. L (*pause*) I would like to see your mother.

Sara Kate She can't be bothered. She'll call you when the phone is fixed.

Mrs. L Is she upstairs?

Sara Kate Of course. She's taking a nap.

Mrs. L I'm going to go up.

Sara Kate No! No. You can't go up.

Mrs. L Sara Kate, I need to speak with your mother.

Sara Kate Would you please go away?! Just go away!

Mrs. L No, I'm not going to go away. I'm going to go talk to your mother. (*Exits.*)

Hillary Do something. Can't you do something? She'll find out. She'll see your mother. Fix it.

Sara Kate I don't know how to fix this. I should never—never.

Hillary Never what? Should never what?

Sara Kate I should never have invited you.

Hillary To see the elves?

Sara Kate People ruin everything.

Reading Strategy: Predicting

Hillary's mother is about to find out Sara Kate's secret. Why do you think Hillary seems more upset than Sara Kate?

Hillary I didn't. I didn't mean to.

Sara Kate What you meant doesn't matter. It's all ruined. *(She puts her face in her hands.)*

Hillary It'll be okay. Mom's not like that. You'll see. Don't cry.

Sara Kate *(crying)* I . . . I'm so tired.

*(MRS. LENOX reenters greatly **subdued**.)*

Hillary Mom. What are you going to do?

Mrs. L Sara Kate. Sara Kate, stay with your mother. I'll be right back, do you understand? I'm going to take Hillary home, and then I'll be right back. Don't worry, Sara Kate, We're going to take care of your mother. Come on, Hillary.

(MRS. LENOX leads HILLARY to the door. HILLARY turns back.)

Reading Strategy: **Predicting**

Do you think Sara Kate's situation will change? If so, how?

Hillary I'm sorry. I'm sorry, Sara Kate.

*(SARA KATE does not **acknowledge** HILLARY, but looks out blankly.)*

Scene 5

*(A week later, the Lenox garden. The bright sunny daylight **contrasts** strongly with the cold evening light of the previous scene. It's the comfort of daylight after a bad dream. HILLARY, with a pencil taped to her nose, writes the last word, then reads the diary entry.)*

Hillary Dear Diary. I stayed home again today. Mom and Dad act like I'm sick. If I don't eat enough dinner they bring something special to my room, like soup with meatballs and crackers. Mom even made pie. But I hardly ate any. I guess I have to go back to school soon, but I don't want to. I don't want to see anybody. Nobody understands. They all have stuff and food and all.

Reading Strategy: **Predicting**

Why do you think Hillary does not want to go back to school?

subdued quieted   **acknowledge** to show an awareness of   **contrasts** shows differences

(ALISON and JANE arrive at the gate. They are dressed alike. HILLARY puts down diary, and begins to rake leaves.)

Alison *(pause)* Hi.

Jane Can we come in?

Hillary It's a backyard, anybody can come in.

Jane We brought your homework.

Hillary *(sarcastic)* Great.

Jane It's really hard. It's math and it's new.

Alison You should get your father to put in a swing set back here.

Hillary He says I'll outgrow it and then we'll still have the cement pilings.

Alison Your father is mental.

Jane Too-too mental.

Hillary He isn't mental. He likes his yard.

Jane When you coming back to school? We miss you.

Alison We thought you were sick.

Hillary You knew I wasn't sick.

Jane But you haven't been at school. Not since they found out Sara Kate kept her mother a prisoner.

Hillary She did not keep her mother a prisoner.

> *Cement pilings* is cement poured into the ground to hold a post in place. When posts are removed, the cement pilings are often still in the ground and are hard to get out.

Alison That's what it said in the paper. It said she kept her mother from getting medical attention.

Hillary Sure, medical attention in some **asylum.**

Alison What's the matter with you, Hillary?

Jane Alison, be quiet. Want some help, Hillary?

Hillary I don't care.

Jane *(gets rake)* Hey! My dad's getting married, and guess what?

Hillary *(not interested)* What?

Jane I get to be in the wedding ceremony and you and Alison get to go as my guests.

Alison What should we wear, Hillary?

Hillary I don't know.

Alison Maybe we should dress like Jane in her flowergirl dress.

Hillary I don't know if I can go.

Jane No, you can't dress like me; people won't know who is me. I have to be separate.

Hillary I might be sick that day.

Jane Hillary, don't worry if you still feel a little bad about Sara Kate. She was even worse than we thought. And you're tied up in knots about it.

Alison You shouldn't feel stupid because you fell for all her lies, even though me and Jane never did.

Jane Sara Kate was very terrible; she made up the whole thing about elves and how they live and what they eat and stuff.

Why do you think Sara Kate did not want her mother to go to an asylum?

What is ironic about Jane now wanting to look different from Alison and Hillary?

asylum a place where mentally ill people receive care

Alison Don't worry. We don't blame you at all. It wasn't fair to pick on someone so much younger. We blame Sara Kate.

Hillary I don't blame Sara Kate. I blame you. You don't know anything about it; you don't know anything about elves.

Jane If elves are so great, why did Sara Kate leave the village behind?

Hillary (*surprised, then making it up*) She left it for me. She knows I'll take care of it.

Alison. She didn't leave it for you; she didn't have time to take it with her when she ran away, is all.

Hillary (*pause*) She ran away?

Alison She didn't want to go to a foster home. (*Beat.*) It says so in the paper.

Hillary Do you believe everything it says in the stupid newspaper?!

Alison Newspapers never lie.

Hillary They do; all the time.

Alison Don't be stupid, Hillary. You're being an idiot over nothing.

Hillary Sara Kate is not nothing.

(*MRS. LENOX appears at the back door.*)

Mrs. L Hey! What's all this yelling?

Alison We didn't do anything; it's Hillary.

Jane We didn't start it.

Mrs. L Start what? Jane put down that rake.

Jane I didn't do anything.

Mrs. L I think you girls better go home.

Jane When is Hillary coming back to school?

Mrs. L Soon. She'll be back soon.

> Do you think Jane and Alison are just alike? Explain.

> Newspapers do not necessarily lie, but they do often shade the truth. In other words, they tell a story in a way that is most exciting. They may do this by adding or changing a few details. They may also use only details that will build excitement.

Jane Bye, Hillary. Sorry. *(Exiting.)*

Alison We don't have to apologize; we didn't do anything.

(Girls exit. Brief pause.)

Mrs. L What was that all about?

Hillary They said Sara Kate ran away. Because she didn't want to go to a foster home. She doesn't have to go to a foster home, does she?

Mrs. L Hillary, Sara Kate is on her way to Kansas. To her father.

Hillary Because if she didn't have any place to stay, well, she could stay with us.

Mrs. L Sara Kate is a very troubled little girl.

Hillary She's very smart. She took care of her whole house.

Mrs. L I know, Hillary. But what she did, the letters, the lying—

Hillary She was afraid, Mom. And she was right.

Mrs. L Hillary . . . Mrs. Connolly needs to be in a hospital.

Hillary Everything she was afraid would happen happened.

Mrs. L Her mother wasn't getting better, she was getting worse.

Hillary They took her mother, Mom. Just like Sara Kate said. Her mother.

Mrs. L Hillary, she was too little to take care of her mother herself. She was too little to take care of herself, herself. Now they both have a chance to get better.

Hillary Could I write to her?

Mrs. L We'll wait and see if she writes to you.

Hillary She'll probably ask about the elf village.

Mrs. L She probably will. Why don't you bring it over here? So you can keep an eye on it for her.

Reading Strategy: Predicting

What do you think will happen to Sara Kate?

Reading Strategy: Predicting

Do you think Sara Kate and her mother will be back?

Hillary. What? Are you nuts?

Mrs. L Hillary!

Hillary I'm sorry, I'm sorry. I didn't mean—Mom. Mom. Dad would, Dad would, he'd—

Mrs. L It's Dad's idea.

Hillary Dad's?

(MR. LENOX at the door)

Mr. L Yeah, your *Dad's.*

Hillary Dad!

Mr. L People are coming to haul the junk out of the yard, thank goodness.

Mrs. L Then they're going to start showing it to people. To buy.

Mr. L I don't think anybody's going to want to have an elf village in his backyard.

Hillary *(looks around; it's not possible)* Oh, man. Thanks, thanks really. But I don't think it'll work out. Our yard's too neat. The elves won't come here.

Mrs. L How about behind the garage? It's a mess back there.

Why does Hillary think her dad will not like the idea of moving the elf village?

Hillary Yeah. *(Beat.)* Yeah! It's a disaster back there. It's perfect.

Mr. L I knew I had some reason for not cleaning it up.

Hillary That's great. That's great. Thanks, thanks a lot.

Scene 6

(Immediately following, the Connolly yard. The village is in disarray. HILLARY starts to pack up the village.)

Hillary *(whispering)* You elves are very untidy. Oh! Don't whisper. Whispering is unnatural. *(Beat.)* Maybe you aren't untidy, maybe it's earth forces messing up your village each time. *(She gasps and turns to see an elf, but it's gone.)* Someday you'll let me see you. I won't have to work at it at all; one day I'll see an elf. *(Beat.)* How'd I know that? *(Realizes.)* The elves are sneaking information into my brain! Hey, elves! Sneak information into Sara Kate's brain—a message from me. *(Remembers playing with SARA KATE)* Sara Kate? The elves are going to live in the mess behind my garage. There's plenty of places for them to hide back there. I'll take extra rocks to separate their little lots. They're starting to trust me a little. I almost saw one.

(As lights fade and music cue sounds, SARA KATE appears on stage. HILLARY speaks to her as if she were really there. The girls walk in the giant way.)

Hillary You don't have to worry at all; I remember everything you said. I will be one kindly giant sister, making sure no evil forces harm the elves or their village. I will climb the tallest hill and scan the horizon, waiting for your return.

(The Ferris wheel turns, as lights fade.)

**Reading Strategy:
Predicting**

What effect is created by the lights fading?

END OF PLAY

Afternoon of the Elves, Act Two   *by Y York*

Directions Choose the letter of the best answer or write the answer using complete sentences.

Comprehension: Identifying Facts

1. Where does Act Two begin?
  A The Lenox's backyard
  B Sara Kate's backyard
  C The playground at school
  D The Webster's kitchen

2. What does Hillary's father ask her to help him do?
  A move the birdbath
  B cut the grass
  C plant flower bulbs
  D trim the hedge

3. Why does Hillary not like the trellis placed in front of the hedge?

4. What does Hillary find in the shed?

5. What does the elf village look like at the start of Scene 2?

6. What secret does Sara Kate tell Hillary?

7. Why is it cold in Sara Kate's house?

8. Who sees Sara Kate's mother and finally causes things to change?

9. What news does Jane have when she and Alison come to visit Hillary?

10. What has happened to Sara Kate at the end of Act Two?

Comprehension: Putting Ideas Together

11. Why is Hillary feeling sad at the beginning of Act Two?
  A Her mother will not let her play outside.
  B Jane and Alison no longer want to be her friends.
  C She cannot stop thinking about Sara Kate.
  D She does not know where her diary is.

12. Why is Hillary upset when she finds her diary?
  A She has already used her allowance money to buy a new one.
  B She has accused Sara Kate of stealing the diary.
  C She knows her mother has read every entry.
  D Her father did not tell her he put the diary in the shed.

13. Why did Sara Kate really tape a pencil to her nose for the math test?

14. Why does Hillary go into the city by herself?

15. Why is Sara Kate so excited when Hillary returns?

After Reading **continued on next page**

16. Describe what Sara Kate does to help her mother.

17. Why does Sara Kate tell Mrs. Lenox that men are working on the pipes?

18. Is Sara Kate upset or thankful when Mrs. Lenox comes over?

19. Why is Hillary staying home from school in Scene 5?

20. What has happened to the elves at the end of Act Two?

Understanding Literature: Predicting

A great many of the actions in this play have a cause-and-effect relationship. This situation is not unusual since real life is also that way. People make choices because of things other people have done. Also, things happen because of other events that have taken place. Use cause and effect to predict the answers to the following questions using this sentence: Since _____ happened, _____ will probably happen.

21. What do you predict will happen to the friendship between Hillary, Jane, and Alison?

22. What do you predict Hillary will do with the elf village once it is behind her garage?

23. What do you think will happen to Sara Kate from here on?

24. How do you predict Hillary will act toward others based on what she learned from Sara Kate?

25. Do you think that Hillary will ever see the elves?

Critical Thinking

26. Why do you think Mr. and Mrs. Lenox were included as characters in the play?

27. How would the play have been different if Jane and Alison were not part of the story?

28. Do you think Sara Kate and Hillary will ever see each other again? Explain.

29. Do you think Mrs. Lenox did the right thing when she got help for Mrs. Connolly?

Thinking Creatively

30. Based on what you learned throughout the play, why was the elf village such an important part of the story?

Grammar Check

Throughout the play, vivid descriptions were used to tell about Sara Kate's appearance and the appearance of her house and yard. Adjectives, adverbs, action verbs, and nouns helped to create these images. Reread these descriptions. Then choose something in your school or home. Write a description using the same vivid detail that was used to tell about Sara Kate. Remember to use adjectives, adverbs, action verbs, and nouns in your description.

 Vocabulary Builder

Skim through Act Two again. Find five words that are unfamiliar to you but are not defined as vocabulary words. Look up the meaning of each word in a dictionary. Then add each word and its meaning to your vocabulary list for this selection.

 Writing on Your Own

An article about Sara Kate and her mother appeared in the newspaper. From the dialogue in the play, it sounds like some of the details were wrong. Private information was also included. Write your own newspaper article about the situation. Include only facts that you think should be included.

 Listening and Speaking

Write text for a guided tour of the elf village. Review the play for details you can use. Make up other information as needed. Then take a classmate on the "tour." Ask if he or she can visualize what you are explaining.

 Research and Technology

Gardening was an important hobby to Mr. Lenox. Contact a greenhouse or garden center in your area. Ask a person at the greenhouse about flowers that grow well in your area. Choose one or two of these flowers. Continue your research at your library or online to learn more. Then create an animated presentation showing how to plant and care for these types of flowers. Also show what the flowers look like when they bloom.

Résumé

A résumé is a short written account of work and school experiences. People use résumés to introduce themselves to possible new employers.

About Résumés

Résumés tell a potential employer about your skills and background. A résumé is usually one or two pages long and should include these parts:

- Personal information—your name, address, and contact information

- Career goals—what you hope to become or achieve in your job

- Education—high school diploma, college degrees, and special courses

- Employment experience—jobs you have had or skills you have developed

- Personal interests and community activities—extracurricular activities including sports, clubs, and service organizations

- Awards and honors—duties and recognition for activities and academics

- References—former employers, teachers, and coaches who give employers an honest account of your performance and personality

Generally, the most important information appears near the beginning. In the employment section, your most recent job should be listed first. Extracurricular activities are most important for young workers who do not have much work experience.

Reading Skill

As you prepare your résumé, keep in mind the people who may be reading it. You want to create an easy-to-read document that includes clear, concise information. It is also important to use action verbs to describe skills and accomplishments. A professional looking résumé will be easier for employers to read. Avoid using fancy fonts, and be sure to print your résumé on white or off-white paper.

On the next two pages, you will read two different examples of a résumé.

Make sure to include as much contact information as possible. You want to make it easy for a possible employer to reach you.

Calvin J. Williams
511 North Marine Street
Walla Walla, Washington 98511
(509) 555-7760
cjw@personsaddress.net

CAREER GOALS
- To be a licensed automobile mechanic
- To own an auto repair shop

EDUCATION
- Graduated from Northwest High School, June 2006
- Studied auto mechanics
- Received best grades in math, science, and auto mechanics (Bs)
- Completed advanced course in auto mechanics at Adult Night Center, August, 2006

The word *treasurer* is misspelled. Errors on a résumé may very well cause you not to get the job you want. Carefully proofread your résumé.

EXTRACURRICULAR ACTIVITES
- Traesuer of Shop Club
- Student government representative
- Member of the school chorus

EXPERIENCE
- Worked part time at Steiner's Service Station for two years
- Worked on Saturdays during senior year at AA Appliance Repair Shop
- Helped neighbors with car repairs

REFERENCES
Mr. Jacob Steiner, owner
Steiner's Service Station
11 Pacific Highway
Walla Walla, WA 89503
(509) 555-1742

Mr. William Turner,
Teacher, auto mechanics
Northwest High School
62 Elm Street
Walla Walla, WA 98513
(509) 555-6756

Mrs. Jeannette Robinson, neighbor
515 North Marine Street
Walla Walla, WA 98511
(509) 555-9443

Before you list people as references, always ask them for permission. Also, ask them if they feel comfortable giving you a positive reference.

Alicia H. Flynn
510 North Marine Street
Walla Walla, WA 98511
(509) 555-2233
ahf@personsaddress.net

CAREER GOAL
• To be head bookkeeper for a large corporation

EXPERIENCE
• 2004 to present: Assistant Bookkeeper
                         Elgin's Department Store
                         Walla Walla, WA 98546

• 1999 to 2004:   Bookkeeper Trainee
                         Link's Hardware Stores
                         Walla Walla, WA 98530

• 2000 to present: Income Tax Consultant, part-time position
                         Fill out income tax forms for 20 clients

COMMUNITY ACTIVITIES
• 2005 to present: Treasurer, Walla Walla Community Center
• 2003 to present: Treasurer and Business Manager,
                         Walla Walla Little League

• 2000 to present: Member, South Shores Community Group
• 2000 to present: Volunteer, South Shores General Hospital

> Including community activities on your résumé shows that you care about your community. It also shows that you are a well-rounded person.

EDUCATION
• 1998 to 2000:   Attended Washington University with
                         course in bookkeeping

• June 1998:   Graduated from South Shores High

> Include all education from high school on. If you received a diploma or degree, be sure to make that clear.

REFERENCES
Mr. Arthur Day, current employer   Ms. Caroline Baxter, manager
Elgin's Department Store   Walla Walla Community Center
3468 Main Street   7819 Wells Avenue
Walla Walla, WA 98546   Walla Walla, WA 98511
(509) 555-6983   (509) 555-4635

Mr. Felix Wist, president
South Shores General Hospital Volunteers
44 Hospital Road
Walla Walla, WA 98545
(509) 555-1297

Monitor Your Progress

Directions Choose the letter of the best answer or write the answer using complete sentences.

1. What is a common effect of a résumé that has an error in it?
   A The employer politely overlooks the error.
   B The employer asks you to correct the error.
   C The employer throws the résumé in the trash while you are there.
   D The employer does not hire you for the job you want.

2. Which of the following does a résumé usually not contain?
   A references
   B education
   C favorite books
   D past jobs

3. Why do people need résumés?

4. What training did Calvin J. Williams have after high school?

5. Look at Alicia H. Flynn's résumé. Does her present employer know that Alicia is looking for a new job? How can you tell?

Writing on Your Own

Write a résumé for a job you are interested in. Include your education and experiences on your résumé. Set up your résumé like one of the samples you read on the previous pages. Use a computer program to create your résumé so you can easily make changes. Exchange your completed résumé with a partner. Ask your partner to proofread the document for errors.

from *Afternoon of the Elves*   by Janet Taylor Lisle

Janet Taylor Lisle
1947–

Objectives

♦ To read and compare a novel excerpt and a drama adaptation

♦ To compare the dialogue in an original selection and an adaptation

About the Author

Janet Taylor Lisle was born in Englewood, New Jersey. She grew up in Farmington, Connecticut, in a family of five children. She was the oldest child and the only girl. After college, she spent two years as a VISTA (Volunteers in Service to America) worker. Then, she spent 10 years as a reporter. Today, she lives on the Rhode Island seacoast and writes for young readers. From her writing loft, she can hear the ocean waves charging against the rocks. She says that writers need lots of friends since writing is lonely work.

Lisle likes to put **fantasy**—writing that often has strange settings and characters—in her stories. She thinks there is a lot in this world that scientists have yet to discover. She sees fantasy as possibilities waiting to be discovered. Her book *Afternoon of the Elves* is a Newberry Honor Book. Some of Lisle's other works include *Forest, The Great Dimpole Oak, A Message from the Match Girl,* and *The Lost Flower Children.*

About the Selection

The selection is Chapter 1 of *Afternoon of the Elves.* Hillary Lenox is nine years old. Her two best friends have warned her to stay away from Sara-Kate Connolly. Even so, Sara-Kate invites Hillary to see the elves in her yard. Hillary thinks Sara-Kate is odd, but she is drawn to the magic of the elves. She also wonders about Sara-Kate's life with her mother in the big, gloomy house.

The play *Afternoon of the Elves,* which you read earlier in this unit, was adapted from Lisle's story. As you read Chapter 1, notice the similarities and differences between the two.

Literary Terms The selection you will read on the following pages is Chapter 1 of the **novel** *Afternoon of the Elves*. A novel is fiction that is book-length and has more plot and character details than a short story. The **excerpt,** or part, you will read contains much of the same part of the story as Scene 3 of the play. Even when the story is the same, fiction and drama are very different. It is not surprising that the dialogue differs from fiction to drama. In fiction, every idea has to be part of the dialogue or part of the background. Drama has dialogue plus stage directions that include the expressions, movements, sounds, and lighting. Character details often are also different between the fiction and drama version of the same story.

Reading on Your Own As you read, pay attention to the character details. How are the descriptions of Hillary and Sara-Kate similar to the play? How are they different? What else about the characters is different from the novel to the play?

Writing on Your Own Books create pictures in readers' minds. Sometimes those pictures are very different from dramatic presentations on stage or screen. Write a few sentences comparing reading a book with seeing a play or movie of the same work.

Vocabulary Focus Create vocabulary study pages. Write the selection vocabulary words down the left side of a sheet of paper. Write the definitions across from the words. Fold the paper so that you can see only the vocabulary words. Practice giving the correct definition for each word.

Think Before You Read How do you expect the original novel of *Afternoon of the Elves* to be similar to the play? How will it be different? Discuss this with a partner. Watch for likenesses and differences while you read.

fantasy a kind of fiction writing that often has strange settings and characters

novel fiction that is book-length and has more plot and character details than a short story

excerpt a short passage from a longer piece of writing

from Afternoon of the Elves

As you read, think about what is similar and different between this chapter and the play you read.

Reading Strategy: Predicting

How do you think the elf village got to Sara Kate's backyard?

The afternoon Hillary first saw the elf village, she couldn't believe her eyes.

"Are you sure it isn't mice?" she asked Sara-Kate, who stood beside her, thin and nervous. "The houses are small enough for mice."

"No, it isn't," Sara-Kate said. "Mice don't make villages in people's backyards."

Hillary got down on her hands and knees to look more closely. She counted the tiny houses. There were nine, each made of sticks bound **delicately** together with bits of string and wire.

"And there's a well," she whispered, "with a bucket that winds down on a string to pull the water out."

"Not a bucket. A bottlecap!" snorted Sara-Kate, twitching her long, shaggy hair away from her face. She was eleven, two years older than Hillary, and she had never spoken to the younger girl before. She had hardly looked at her before.

"Can I try drawing some water?" Hillary asked.

Sara-Kate said, "No."

The roofs of the houses were maple leaves attached to the sticks at **jaunty** angles. And because it was autumn, the leaves were lovely colors, orange-red, reddish-orange, deep yellow. Each house had a small yard in front neatly bordered with stones that appeared to have come from the driveway.

"They used the leaves dropping off those trees over there," Hillary said.

Sara-Kate shrugged. "Why not? The leaves make the houses pretty."

"How did they get these stones all the way over here?" Hillary asked.

"Elves are strong," Sara-Kate said. "And magic."

Hillary looked at her **suspiciously** then. It wasn't that she didn't believe so much as that she couldn't right away put Sara-Kate on the side of magic. There never had been one pretty thing about her. Nothing soft or mysterious. Her face was narrow and ended in a sharp chin, and her eyes were small and hard as bullets. They were such little eyes, and set so deeply in her head, that the impression she gave was of a **gaunt,** fierce bird, a rather untidy bird if one took her clothes into consideration. They hung on her frame, an **assortment**

Where might elves find a bottlecap that would work for a well bucket?

Reading Strategy:
Predicting
Sara-Kate says the elves are very strong. Why do you think she knows so much about the elves?

---

delicately done with great skill

jaunty smartly placed

suspiciously not believing something

gaunt very thin and bony

assortment a collection of different kinds of things

of **ill-fitting,** wrinkly **garments.** ("Doesn't she care how she looks?" a new girl at school had inquired just this fall, giving every child within **earshot** the chance to whirl around and shout, "No!")

Least magical of all, Sara-Kate Connolly wore boots that were exactly like the work boots worn by men in gas stations.

"Black and greasy," Hillary's friend Jane Webster said.

"She found them at the dump," Alison Mancini whispered.

"No she didn't. Alison, that's terrible!"

Normally, fourth graders were too shy to risk comment on students in higher grades. But Sara-Kate had been held back in school that year. She was taking the fifth grade all over again, which made her a curiosity.

"Can you tell me where you found those amazing boots? I've just got to get some exactly like them," Jane said to her one day, wearing a look of such innocence that for a second nobody thought to laugh.

In the middle of Sara-Kate's backyard, Hillary recalled the sound of that laughter while she stared at Sara-Kate's boots. Then she glanced up at Sara-Kate's face.

"Why does it have to be elves? Why couldn't it be birds or chipmunks or some animal we've never heard of? Or maybe some person made these houses," Hillary said, a sly tone in her voice. She got off her knees and stood up beside the older girl. "We are the same height!" she announced in surprise.

They were almost the same except for Sara-Kate's thinness. Hillary was **sturdily** built and stood on wide feet.

"In fact, I'm even a little taller!" Hillary exclaimed, rising up a bit on her toes and looking down.

Sara-Kate stepped away from her quickly. She folded her arms across her chest and beamed her small, hard eyes straight into Hillary's wide ones.

"Look," she said. "I didn't have to invite you over here today and I didn't have to show you this. I thought you might

Reading Strategy:
Predicting

Do you think pretty, well-dressed people are more likely to experience magic? Explain.

Why is Sara-Kate a *curiosity* for being held back in fifth grade?

Reading Strategy:
Predicting

Why do you think Hilary talks with a sly tone in her voice?

ill-fitting not fitting very well	**earshot** at a distance close enough to be heard	**sturdily** in a strong, solid way
garments pieces of clothing		

like to see an elf village for a change. If you don't believe it's elves, that's your problem. I *know* it's elves."

So, there they were: elves—a whole village of them living down in Sara-Kate's junky, overgrown backyard that was itself in back of Sara-Kate's broken-down house with the paint peeling off. Sara-Kate's yard was not the place Hillary would have picked to build a village if she were an elf. Where there weren't thistles and weeds there was mud, and in the mud, broken glass and wire and pieces of rope. There were old black tires and rusty parts of car engines and a washing machine turned over on its side. Carpets of poison ivy grew under the trees and among the bushes. Nobody ever played in Sara-Kate's backyard. But then, as Sara-Kate would have said, nobody had ever been invited to play in her backyard. Except Hillary, that is, on that first afternoon of the elves.

"Sara-Kate Connolly thinks she's got elves," Hillary told her mother when she came home, rather late, from looking at the village. The yards of the two families backed up to each other, a source of **irritation** to Hillary's father, who believed that property should be kept up to standard. But who could he complain to? Sara-Kate's father did not live there anymore. ("He's away on a trip," Sara-Kate always said.) And Sara-Kate's mother didn't care about yards. She hardly ever went outside. She kept the shades of the house drawn down tight, even in summer.

"Elves?" Mrs. Lenox repeated.

"They're living in her backyard," Hillary said. "They have little houses and a well. I said it must be something else but Sara-Kate is sure it's elves. It couldn't be, could it?"

"I don't like you playing in that yard," Hillary's mother told her. "It's not a safe place for children. If you want to see Sara-Kate, invite her over here."

Why do you think Sara Kate becomes upset here?

Notice the description of the yard in this paragraph. How does this description compare with the one in the play?

Reading Strategy: Predicting

Do you predict there will be a second afternoon of the elves? Explain.

Describe a yard that Hillary's father would think looked "standard."

Why does Hillary's mother not answer her question?

irritation an ongoing bother

**Reading Strategy:
Predicting**

How do you think
Hillary really feels
about Sara-Kate?

"Sara-Kate won't come over here. She never goes to other people's houses. And she never invites anyone to her house," Hillary added **significantly.** She tried to flick her hair over her shoulder the way Sara-Kate had done it that afternoon. But the sides were too short and refused to stay back.

"It seems that Sara-Kate is beginning to change her mind about invitations," Mrs. Lenox said then, with an unhappy bend in the corners of her mouth.

But how could Hillary invite Sara-Kate to play? And play with what? The elves were not in Hillary's backyard, which was neat and **well-tended,** with an apple tree to climb and a round garden filled with autumn flowers. Hillary's father had bought a stone birdbath at a garden shop and placed it on a small mound at the center of the garden. He'd planted ivy on the mound and trained it to grow up the birdbath's fluted stem. Birds came from all over the neighborhood to swim there, and even squirrels and chipmunks dashed through for a dip. The birdbath made the garden beautiful.

"Now it's a real garden," Hillary's father had said proudly, and, until that afternoon, Hillary had agreed. She had thought it was among the most perfect gardens on earth.

significantly importantly	**well-tended** carefully cared for

Sara-Kate's elves began to change things almost immediately, however. Not that Hillary really believed in them. No, she didn't. Why should she? Sara-Kate was not her friend. But, even without being believed, magic can begin to change things. It moves invisibly through the air, **dissolving** the usual ways of seeing, allowing new ways to creep in, secretly, quietly, like a stray cat sliding through bushes.

"Sara-Kate says elves don't like being out in the open," Hillary remarked that evening as she and her father strolled across their garden's well-mowed lawn. She found herself examining the birdbath with new, **critical** eyes.

"She says they need weeds and bushes to hide under, and bottlecaps and string lying around to make their wells."

Mr. Lenox didn't answer. He had bent over to fix a piece of ivy that had come free from the birdbath.

"And stones on their driveways," Hillary added, turning to gaze at her own driveway, which was tarred down smooth and flat.

She turned toward Sara-Kate's house next. Its dark form loomed behind the hedge at the bottom of the yard. Though evening had come, no light showed in any of the windows.

> Why does Hillary no longer think her family's garden is perfect?

> A *hedge* is a row of bushes growing close together. When something *looms*, it usually appears to be threatening.

dissolving ending as if by breaking up   **critical** using judgment

Reading Strategy: Predicting

Why do you think there are no lights in the windows in Sara-Kate's house?

Reading Strategy: Predicting

Why does Hillary decide that the Connolly's are probably not sitting in the dark? Review the things Hillary thinks Sara-Kate and her mother are doing in their house. Do you think Hillary is right?

Now that Hillary thought about it, she could not remember ever seeing many lights down there. Gray and expressionless was how the house generally appeared. What could Sara-Kate and her mother be doing inside? Hillary wondered, and, for a moment, she had a rather **grim** vision of two shapes sitting motionless at a table in the dark.

Then she remembered the shades. Mrs. Connolly's shades must be drawn so tightly that not a ray of light could escape. Behind them, Sara-Kate was probably having dinner in the kitchen, or she was doing her homework.

"What happened at school today?" her mother would be asking her. Or, "Please don't talk with your mouth full!"

Hillary imagined Sara-Kate Connolly frowning after this remark. She felt sure that Sara-Kate was too old to be reminded of her manners. Too old and too tough. Not really the kind of person to have elves in her backyard, Hillary thought.

"I'm going inside!" Hillary's father's voice sounded from across the lawn. The rest of him was swallowed up by dark.

"Wait for me. Wait!" Hillary cried. She didn't want to be left behind. Night had fallen so quickly, like a great black curtain on a stage. In a minute she might have been quite frightened except that suddenly, through the garden, the twinkling lights of the fireflies burst forth. It was as if the little bugs had waited all day for this moment to leap out of hiding. Or had they been there all along, blinking steadily but invisibly in the daylight? Hillary paused and looked about.

"Hillary! Where are you?"

"Coming," she called, and turned to run in. A gust of wind slid across her cheek. Like lanterns in the grip of magic hands, the tiny lights **flickered** over the lawn.

---

grim horrible or frightful   **flickered** twinkled

from *Afternoon of the Elves*　　*by Janet Taylor Lisle*

Directions Choose the letter of the best answer or write the answer using complete sentences.

Comprehension: Identifying Facts

1. At what time of day does Hillary first see the elf village?

  A morning   **C** afternoon

  B noon   **D** evening

2. How many elf houses are in the elf village?

  A 3   **B** 5   **C** 7   **D** 9

3. What colors are the roofs of the houses in the elf village?

4. How does Hillary describe Sara-Kate's face?

5. Who is Jane Webster?

6. What is growing in Sara-Kate's yard?

7. What does Mr. Lenox add to his yard for the birds and other animals?

8. Why is Hillary's driveway not good for an elf village?

9. At night, why does Hillary not want her father to go inside without her?

10. What happens that keeps Hillary from being afraid of the dark?

Comprehension: Putting Ideas Together

11. Hillary points out that she and Sara-Kate are about the same height. Why then does she get on her toes to make herself look taller than Sara-Kate?

  A She knows that Sara-Kate is really taller.

  B She always walks on her tiptoes.

  C She wants to look taller for a picture.

  D She wants to be taller to feel more important.

12. Mr. Lenox would talk to the Connollys about the mess in their yard if _____.

  A Mrs. Connolly did not keep her shades pulled

  B Sara-Kate came outside more often

  C Mr. Connolly still lived there

  D Hillary and Sara-Kate were not friends

13. How are Hillary and Sara-Kate physically alike and different?

14. Why doesn't Mrs. Lenox want Hillary playing in Sara-Kate's yard?

15. What do Hillary's actions tell you about her feelings toward Sara-Kate?

Comparing **continued on next page**

16. Why doesn't Sara-Kate say that her father lives somewhere else?

17. Why do you think Sara-Kate has invited Hillary to see the elf village?

18. Hillary does not think that Sara-Kate's involvement with magic makes sense. List reasons for this.

19. What suggests that Sara-Kate does not have all the basic needs in life?

20. How are the roles of Mr. and Mrs. Lenox different in each story?

Understanding Literature: An Original and an Adaptation

"Tell instead of show" is a main difference between original fiction and drama adaptations. Dialogue in original fiction is often supported by non-dialogue explanations. These explanations tell parts of the story that are not shown in the dialogue. In drama adaptations, the whole story is told through dialogue.

21. How is the description of the elf houses handled differently between the original story and the play?

22. The novel says that Sara-Kate's repeating fifth grade is a "curiosity." In the play, Hillary calls Sara-Kate "stupid" for having to repeat fifth grade. Explain these two examples.

23. Why is there more dialogue in a drama than in a fiction story?

24. In both stories, Sara-Kate says she did not have to invite Hillary over. The comment is used at different times. Why do you think the playwright used the line differently?

25. Hillary wonders how Sara-Kate knows elves built the village. How does the dialogue compare to her comments in the play?

Critical Thinking

26. The fiction story gives more detailed descriptions of the elf houses than the play. Why do you think this is true?

27. The fiction version gives a clear description of Sara-Kate. Why do you think this is left out of the play?

28. In the novel, Hillary's parents do not answer when she tells them about the elves. Why do you think they do not respond?

29. Hillary imagines Sara-Kate and her mother in their house. Why do you think Hillary imagines these things?

Thinking Creatively

30. Hillary wonders if mice could have built the village. Describe how a mouse village would be different from an elf village.

Grammar Check

Slang is quite common in spoken English. However, it is usually not used in standard written English. This holds true for the two versions of *Afternoon of the Elves.* There is much more slang in the play than in the original fiction story. Rewrite the following sentences. Replace each slang word or phrase with standard English.

1 I feel crummy today.

2 Yuk, that is slimy.

3 Let's give Kate the benefit of the doubt.

4 Whoa! Where are you going so fast?

5 Rustle us up some pancakes.

 ## Vocabulary Builder

The first word in each pair below is from *Afternoon of the Elves.* For each word pair, write a sentence that correctly uses both words.

1 fantasy; believe

2 irritation; people

3 assortment; lunch

4 significantly; taller

5 flickered; lights

 ## Writing on Your Own

In *Afternoon of the Elves,* the play and the original fiction work have the same title. Often, playwrights choose different titles for their adaptations. Work with a partner to create five different possible titles for the play. Share your titles with the class. Then explain which title you think is best for the story and why.

 ## Listening and Speaking

You just read Chapter 1 of the novel version of *Afternoon of the Elves.* Go to your library or local bookstore and see if you can find a copy of the novel. Read another chapter of the novel. As you read, think about how the information from the novel is used in the play. In a small group, present a summary of the chapter you read. Listen carefully as group members describe the chapter they each read.

 ## Media and Viewing

Hillary's father worked hard in his yard. Using a computer drawing program, create a model of the yard. Use details from the play, the novel, or a combination of the two. Include landscape features such as the hedge, the ivy, and the birdbath.

Most plural forms of English nouns follow basic rules. Learning these few rules will help you to correctly spell most of the plurals.

Rules

- Add -*s* to most nouns to form plurals: *effect/effects.*

- Add -*es* to nouns that end in *s, ss, sh, ch,* and *x* to form plurals: *clash/clashes.*

- Add -*es* to most nouns that end in a consonant and -*o*: *potato/potatoes.*

- Change *y* to *i* and add -*es* to nouns that end in the consonant -*y* combination: *analogy/analogies.*

- Do not change the *y;* just add -*s* to nouns that end in the vowel -*y* combination: *key/keys.*

- For some nouns ending in -*fe,* change -*fe* to -*ve* and add -*s*: *life/lives.*

Irregular Plurals

- Some nouns have the same spelling in both forms: *scissors/scissors, pants/pants, sheep/sheep.*

- Some nouns require basic spelling changes in the plural form: *crisis/crises, foot/feet, radius/radii.*

- Nouns that are not countable have no plural forms: *data/data.*

Practice

For each of the words in the Word List, write the rule to change the singular form to a plural. Then, use the plural form in a sentence.

Word List

zero

calf

glass

canary

yourself

metaphor

narrative

process

strategy

variety

I'd like to exchange this *y* for an *i* please.

Do you have a consonant?

CUSTOMER SERVICE

In Unit 5, you read two plays. You also read the original work from which each play was adapted. You saw that there are likenesses between the two works. However, there are also differences. For example, the employer was a different character in "The Ninny" and *The Governess*.

Other differences have to do with dialogue. The novel chapter from *Afternoon of the Elves* had much less dialogue than the play adaptation did. To add more dialogue, a playwright usually has to add ideas that were not in the original work. In addition, playwrights often move some of the descriptive narrative into dialogue. Character details are often also different between a play and the original work. Similarly, in an original, description is used to show the setting. In a play, stage directions tell details of the setting.

Each playwright has his or her own ideas about how to adapt an original work. For this reason, every book-drama combination is an experience of its own.

Selections

■ *The Governess,* a play by Neil Simon, is about an employer and the governess who works for her. The employer, called the Mistress, teaches the timid governess to stand up for herself. The play is an adaptation of Anton Chekhov's short story "The Ninny."

■ "The Ninny" is a short story by Anton Chekhov. The story is also about an employer and a governess. In this version, the employer is a man. This man is also the narrator of the story.

■ *Afternoon of the Elves,* by Y York, is a two-act play. The play concerns Sara Kate and three girls who are unkind to her. Sara Kate invites Hillary, the least unkind of the three, to see the elf village in her yard. Hillary discovers how difficult Sara Kate's life is and becomes her friend. The play is an adaptation of the novel by Janet Taylor Lisle.

■ From *Afternoon of the Elves* by Janet Taylor Lisle is the first chapter of a novel with the same title. Sara-Kate lives in a run-down house. She invites her neighbor Hillary to see an elf village in her yard. Hillary is unsure about Sara-Kate, but is amazed by the elf village.

Directions Choose the letter of the best answer or write the answer using complete sentences.

Comprehension: Identifying Facts

1. In *The Governess,* how long had Julia been working before she received any money?

A two weeks   **C** two months
B one month   **D** over three months

2. In "The Ninny," how long had Yulia been working before she received any money?

3. In the play *Afternoon of the Elves,* what is the Ferris wheel made from?

4. In the chapter from *Afternoon of the Elves,* what do the elves use for a well bucket?

5. In *The Governess,* the Mistress asks about the children's progress in two subjects. Which two subjects does she ask about?

Comprehension: Putting Ideas Together

6. Who narrates "The Ninny"?

A the governess   **C** the Mistress
B the employer   **D** the oldest child

7. In *The Governess,* why does the Mistress repeatedly ask Julia to hold her head up?

8. In the play *Afternoon of the Elves,* you read about four families' yard care. What do Alison and Jane say about their fathers and their yards?

9. Which character is present throughout the entire chapter of the novel version of *Afternoon of the Elves?*

10. Think about how Julia and Yulia thank their employers. Describe the difference.

Understanding Literature: Drama

Drama is a literary work that is designed to be performed. The story in a drama is told through the words and actions of the characters. It includes stage directions that guide the acting, lighting, set design, and sound. Many dramas are adapted from a fiction or nonfiction work that is often called the "original work."

11. What does the stage direction *Calls again* at the beginning of *The Governess* tell the actor to do?

12. At the beginning of *The Governess,* the stage direction *Head down* is given. What message does this action give the audience?

13. At the beginning of the play *Afternoon of the Elves*, the stage direction *playing* is given. What does this direction tell the actor to do?

14. At the end of the play *Afternoon of the Elves*, the following stage direction is given: *The Ferris wheel turns as lights fade.* Why do you think the playwright ended the play in this way?

15. Why do you think fiction and nonfiction works are often a good starting point for writing a drama?

Critical Thinking

16. Why do you think schools often choose to perform *Afternoon of the Elves*?

17. In *The Governess*, why do you think Julia curtsies so often?

18. Jane and Alison play a bigger role in the play than in the novel. Why do you think this is?

Thinking Creatively

19. Use dollars and today's typical wages to update the money amounts mentioned in "The Ninny." What amounts would you suggest to replace the amounts of rubles in the story?

20. Imagine that the governess from *The Governess* met up with Jane from the play *Afternoon of the Elves*. Write a conversation between the two of them.

Speak and Listen

Work with a partner. Read a few lines from one of the plays and have your partner guess which character you are. Try to make your lines sound natural. Think about how the playwright would want the lines to sound.

Writing on Your Own

The play, *Afternoon of the Elves*, is written in two acts. Suppose that *The Governess* also has another act that comes after the one you read. Based on what you learned about the characters, what do you think might happen in Act Two?

Beyond Words

Draw your idea of a single elf house or the Ferris wheel. Share your drawing with classmates and discuss your idea.

Test-Taking Tip

Read test directions twice, looking for key words. For example, the directions may tell you to look for the *best* answer, or they may say there is *more than one* answer.

Exposition: Research Report

It makes sense to choose something you are curious about for a research report. You learn about a subject that interests you and you build your own area of knowledge. Research writing presents information gathered from several sources. Follow the steps outlined in this workshop to write your own research report.

Assignment Write a research report based on information from several sources.

What to Include Your research report should have the following parts:

- an overall focus or main idea given in a thesis statement
- supporting points from several sources, with sources cited
- a clear organization and smooth flow
- a bibliography, or list of sources with complete details

Prewriting

Choosing Your Topic

To choose your topic, try one of the following plans:

- **Self-Interview** Create a chart like the one shown, and answer the questions. Circle words that suggest research ideas to you. Choose a topic from among those items.

People	Places	Things	Events
What interesting people do I know or know about?	What interesting places have I been to or heard about?	What interesting things do I know about?	What interesting events have happened to me or have I heard about?
Grandma Ben Franklin Michael Jordan Emily Dickinson	hospital hockey rink library Philadelphia	baseball compact discs kites	hockey game homecoming elections July Fourth

---

Using the Form
You may use parts of this form in these types of writing:
- informational articles
- news analyses
- travel logs
- business reports

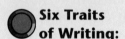 **Six Traits of Writing:**

Ideas message, details, and purpose

- **Newswatch** Flip through recent magazines or newspapers. Tune in to television or radio broadcasts. List people, places, events, or current issues that you want to learn more about. Choose one of these as a topic for research.

Narrowing Your Topic

Do a little research. Before you decide on your topic, do a little research to decide if you will be able to find enough information. Using your general idea as a starting point, browse through books, Web sites, magazines, and other references. Jot down the names, ideas, and events that appear most often.

Ask open-ended questions. Thoughtful, interesting questions can help focus a research topic. Draft a list of questions that will guide you as you research.

Gathering Details Through Research

Use several sources. Primary sources include interviews and newspaper articles. Secondary sources include encyclopedia entries and other research reports. You can research both in the library and online.

Question your sources. To make sure that your information is current, correct, and balanced, follow these guidelines:

- Check publication dates to make sure information is current.

- Sometimes you might see a difference in the information given by two sources. If this happens, check the facts in a third source. If three or more sources disagree, talk about the disagreement in your paper.

- Whenever possible, cross-check your information with other sources.

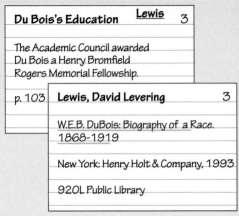

Du Bois's Education   **Lewis**   3

The Academic Council awarded
Du Bois a Henry Bromfield
Rogers Memorial Fellowship.

p. 103 | **Lewis, David Levering**   3

W.E.B. DuBois: Biography of a Race.
1868-1919

New York: Henry Holt & Company, 1993

920L Public Library

Taking Notes

Use source cards and note cards. When you find information related to your topic, take detailed notes on index cards.

- Create a source card for each book, article, Web site, or person you interviewed.

- As you take notes, write one idea on each card. Be sure to write the information in your own words.

- On each card, write a keyword that links to the full information on the source card.

- Use quotation marks whenever you copy words exactly. Write neatly so you can read it. Make sure to spell words correctly.

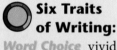

Six Traits of Writing:

Word Choice vivid words that "show, not tell"

Writing Your Draft

Shaping Your Writing

Define your thesis. Sum up the point of your paper in a sentence, called a thesis statement. Use your thesis statement to guide what you write.

Make an outline. Before you start to write, make an outline. Make sure every point on your outline supports your thesis.

Six Traits of Writing:

Organization order, ideas tied together

Revising

Revising Your Overall Structure

Check for unity. All the parts of your report should fit together in a complete, self-contained whole.

1. Make sure that every paragraph develops your thesis statement. Take out those that do not, or revise for a stronger connection.

2. Identify the main idea of each paragraph. If a paragraph does not contain a topic sentence, consider adding one.

3. In each paragraph, delete sentences that do not support or explain the topic sentence or main idea.

Revising Your Word Choice

Use vivid action verbs. Use action verbs to bring life to your writing. They can help you to share exactly what you learned in your research.

Circle action verbs in your draft—ignore being verbs such as *be, am, is, are, was,* and *were.* Change some non-action verbs to action verbs.

Editing and Proofreading

Proofread your research report and correct errors in grammar.

Focus on Citations: Review your draft against your notes. Be sure you have correctly quoted your sources. In addition, check that numbers, dates, and page references are correct.

Six Traits of Writing:
Conventions correct grammar, spelling, and mechanics

Publishing and Presenting

Consider one of these ways to share your writing:

Share your report with a large audience. Find out which organizations (historical societies, fan clubs, or other groups) might be interested in your topic. Submit your report for publication in a newsletter or on a Web site.

Deliver an impromptu speech. Describe your beginning questions, your thesis, and what you found out from research. After you finish, answer questions from your classmates.

Reflecting on Your Writing

Writer's Journal Jot down a few notes about writing a research report. Begin by answering these questions:

- What was the most interesting thing you learned about your topic? Why?

- Which plan for prewriting or drafting might you suggest to a friend? Why?

Farmer Sowing Seeds
Larry Moore

The United States has a rich oral tradition of literature. It includes myths, folktales, and tall tales about heroes. *Oral* means that these myths and tales were first spoken, and not written down until a later time. People told these stories to make each other laugh and cry. They passed down myths that explained aspects of nature like why it rains. They recalled their greatest heroes, or invented new ones. Every region of the country and every ethnic group has its own oral tradition. The literature of the people is a storehouse of memory and entertainment.

"I cannot tell how the truth may be, I say the tale as 'twas said to me."

—Sir Walter Scott,
The Lay of the Last Minstrel, 1805

Unit 6 About Themes in American Stories

The American Folk Tradition

The American folk tradition is a rich collection of literature that grew out of the **oral tradition.** The oral tradition is stories originally told at festivals and around campfires, rather than shared in print. Here are some characteristics of the oral tradition:

- **Theme** is the main idea of a literary work and often contains a message or lesson. Sometimes a theme is called universal. This means that the theme is found in stories of different cultures and throughout many different time periods.

- **Heroes** and **heroines** are the leading characters in a story, novel, play, or film. Heroes often show values and actions that are celebrated in stories from the oral tradition.

Storytelling Techniques Before stories were written down, they were told orally. To make the stories more exciting, storytellers used different types of figurative language.

- A **hyperbole** is an overstatement or exaggeration to show that something is important.

- **Personification** is giving characters such as animals or objects the characteristics or qualities of humans.

- An **idiom** is a phrase that has a different meaning than its words really mean. For example, *It is raining cats and dogs!* does not really mean that cats and dogs are falling from the sky. It means it is raining very hard. Idioms often develop among a language, region, community, or class of people.

American folk literature is a living tradition that is constantly being updated and adapted. Many of its subjects and heroes are present in modern American movies, sports heroes, and even politics.

Reprinted with permission. All rights reserved.

The American Folk Tradition in Print

Although stories in the oral tradition have similar characteristics, the genre can be divided into categories. These categories are based on purposes and styles.

- **Myths** are important stories that explain how the world came to be or why natural events happen. Myths usually include gods, goddesses, or unusually powerful human beings. Every culture has its own collection of myths, or **mythology.**

- **Fables** are short stories or poems with a moral, or lesson about life. The characters in fables are often animals who act like humans.

- **Tall tales** are stories from the past that feature enlarged characters who have unreal adventures. These tales often involve a hero who performs impossible acts. Tall tales are a form of **legend.** A legend is a story from folklore that features characters who actually lived, or real events or places.

- **Epics** are long poems written in verse. In epics, heroes go on dangerous journeys that are important to the history of a nation or culture.

In the second half of this unit, you will read about a different type of American folk hero. These are everyday heroes such as firefighters, civil rights workers, and American Indian children. These heroes rise above difficult situations to take their place beside the earlier heroes of the American landscape.

Part 1

Reading Strategy:
Summarizing

You learned about Summarizing strategies in Unit 3. Continue to use those strategies as you read the selections in this unit. Ask yourself:

■ Who or what is this about?

■ What is the main thing being said about this topic?

If you are having trouble identifying the main idea, try rereading the text.

Literary Terms

myth an important story, often part of a culture's religion, that explains how the world came to be or why natural events happen; usually including gods, goddesses, or unusually powerful human beings

theme the main idea of a literary work

mythology a collection of myths

folktale a story that has been handed down from one generation to another

oral literature stories that were first told, rather than being written down

dialect the speech of a particular part of the country, or of a certain group of people

hero the leading male character in a story, novel, play, or film

personification giving characters such as animals or objects the characteristics or qualities of humans

ballad a form of poetry, passed from person to person, often as a simple song

legend a story from folklore that features characters who actually lived or real places or events

tall tale a story from the past that features enlarged characters who have unreal adventures

humor literature created to be funny or to amuse

exaggeration the use of words to make something seem more than it is; stretching the truth to a great extent

hyperbole using gross exaggeration to show that something is important

Coyote Steals the Sun and Moon   retold by Erdoes and Ortiz

About the Authors

Richard Erdoes and Alfonso Ortiz grew up worlds apart
from one another. A shared love of American Indian culture
brought them together. They worked together on several
collections of American Indian stories. Their stories "were
jotted down at powwows, around campfires, even inside a
moving car."

Richard Erdoes
1912–

Richard Erdoes was born in Frankfurt, Germany. He was
educated in Vienna, Austria; Berlin, Germany; and Paris,
France. As a young boy, he became interested in American
Indian culture. In 1940, he moved to the United States to
escape Nazi rule. Erdoes became a well-known author,
photographer, and illustrator. He wrote several books on
American Indians and the American West.

Alfonso Ortiz, a Tewa Pueblo, was born in New Mexico. He
became a professor of anthropology at the University of New
Mexico. He was also a leading expert on Pueblo culture.

About the Selection

"Coyote Steals the Sun and Moon" is a Zuni myth. The Zuni
belong to a group of Indians known as the Pueblos. They
live in the southwest United States. Early Spanish explorers
called them by this name because *pueblo* is the Spanish word
for "town." The small Zuni towns, built around open plazas,
looked just like Spanish towns.

Alfonso Ortiz
1939–1997

The Zuni believe that the Great Spirit guided them to their
homelands. The Great Spirit taught them to plant corn and to
live in peace together. Zuni myths often involve the sun and
the moon. Coyote, who is usually full of mischief, is a popular
character in Zuni myths. "Coyote Steals the Sun and Moon"
tells about how Coyote brought winter into the world.

Objectives

◆ To read and
understand a myth
and mythology

◆ To recognize the
theme in a myth

◆ To summarize
main events and
ideas in a myth

Before Reading continued on next page

Coyote Steals the Sun and Moon   *retold by Erdoes and Ortiz*

myth an important story, often part of a culture's religion, that explains how the world came to be or why natural events happen

theme the main idea of a literary work

mythology a collection of myths

Literary Terms A **myth** is an important story that is often part of a culture's religion. Myths explain how the world came to be or why natural events happen. Myths usually include gods, goddesses, or unusually powerful humans. Some myths feature animal characters with human qualities. A myth often has a **theme,** or main idea, that teaches a lesson. Every culture has its own **mythology,** or collection of myths.

Reading on Your Own A summary includes the most important ideas and information of a text. Because of this, a summary is much shorter than the original work. Summarizing helps you remember what you have read by focusing on the main ideas. Follow these steps to summarize a text:

• Write down the main events and ideas in a story.

• Cross out minor details that are not important to the overall meaning.

• Restate the major events or ideas in as few words as possible.

Writing on Your Own People in every culture have used myths to explain the world around them. Write a paragraph to explain why people might try to understand the natural world through myths.

Vocabulary Focus The myth you will read on the following pages contains some words that come from a different language. Use a dictionary to look up the definition and origin of *pueblo* and *kachina*. Then talk with a partner about why you think these words might be used in the myth.

Think Before You Read Why do you think Coyote would want to steal the sun and moon? Write your prediction. Then read the selection to see if your prediction is correct.

Coyote Steals the Sun and Moon

Cosmic Canine,
John Nieto

Coyote is a bad hunter who never kills anything. Once he watched Eagle hunting rabbits, catching one after another—more rabbits than he could eat. Coyote thought, "I'll team up with Eagle so I can have enough meat." Coyote is always up to something.

"Friend," Coyote said to Eagle, "we should hunt together. Two can catch more than one."

"Why not?" Eagle said, and so they began to hunt in partnership. Eagle caught many rabbits, but all Coyote caught was some little bugs.

At this time the world was still dark; the sun and moon had not yet been put in the sky. "Friend," Coyote said to Eagle, "no wonder I can't catch anything; I can't see. Do you know where we can get some light?"

"You're right, friend, there should be some light," Eagle said. "I think there's a little toward the west. Let's try and find it."

And so they went looking for the sun and moon. They came to a big river, which Eagle flew over. Coyote swam, and swallowed so much water that he almost drowned. He crawled out with his fur full of mud, and Eagle asked, "Why don't you fly like me?"

"You have wings; I just have hair," Coyote said. "I can't fly without feathers."

> Many American Indian myths describe a world that is not yet finished. In this myth, the sun and moon are not yet in the sky.

> **Reading Strategy: Summarizing**
>
> How did Coyote and Eagle cross the river?

Kachinas are beings that serve as links between Earth and the spirit world. Colorful Kachina dances take place every year. Dancers wear masks that represent the different Kachinas. Every year, they dance to pray for a good harvest and good fortune.

At last they came to a **pueblo,** where the Kachinas happened to be dancing. The people invited Eagle and Coyote to sit down and have something to eat while they watched the **sacred** dances. Seeing the power of the Kachinas, Eagle said, "I believe these are the people who have light."

Coyote, who had been looking all around, pointed out two boxes, one large and one small, that the people opened whenever they wanted light. To produce a lot of light, they opened the lid of the big box, which contained the sun. For less light they opened the small box, which held the moon.

Coyote nudged Eagle. "Friend, did you see that? They have all the light we need in the big box. Let's steal it."

"You always want to steal and rob. I say we should just borrow it."

"They won't lend it to us."

"You may be right," said Eagle. "Let's wait till they finish dancing and then steal it."

After a while the Kachinas went home to sleep, and Eagle scooped up the large box and flew off. Coyote ran along trying to keep up, panting, his tongue hanging out. Soon he yelled up to Eagle, "Ho, friend, let me carry the box a little way."

"No, no," said Eagle, "you never do anything right."

He flew on, and Coyote ran after him. After a while Coyote shouted again: "Friend, you're my chief, and it's not right for you to carry the box; people will call me lazy. Let me have it."

"No, no, you always mess everything up." And Eagle flew on and Coyote ran along.

So it went for a stretch, and then Coyote started again. "Ho, friend, it isn't right for you to do this. What will people think of you and me?"

"I don't care what people think. I'm going to carry this box."

pueblo an American Indian village of homes grouped together to form a large building several stories high

sacred holy

Again Eagle flew on and again Coyote ran after him. Finally Coyote begged for the fourth time: "Let me carry it. You're the chief, and I'm just Coyote. Let me carry it."

Eagle couldn't stand any more **pestering.** Also, Coyote had asked him four times, and if someone asks four times, you'd better give him what he wants. Eagle said, "Since you won't let up on me, go ahead and carry the box for a while. But promise not to open it."

"Oh, sure, oh yes, I promise." They went on as before, but now Coyote had the box. Soon Eagle was far ahead, and Coyote lagged behind a hill where Eagle couldn't see him. "I wonder what the light looks like, inside there," he said to himself. "Why shouldn't I take a peek? Probably there's something extra in the box, something good that Eagle wants to keep to himself."

> What human qualities does Coyote show here?

And Coyote opened the lid. Now, not only was the sun inside, but the moon also. Eagle had put them both together, thinking that it would be easier to carry one box than two.

> **Reading Strategy: Summarizing**
> What happens when Coyote opens the box?

As soon as Coyote opened the lid, the moon escaped, flying high into the sky. At once all the plants **shriveled** up and turned brown. Just as quickly, all the leaves fell off the trees, and it was winter. Trying to catch the moon and put it back in the box, Coyote ran in **pursuit** as it skipped away from him. Meanwhile the sun flew out and rose into the sky. It drifted far away, and the peaches, squashes, and melons shriveled up with cold.

Eagle turned and flew back to see what had delayed Coyote. "You fool! Look what you've done!" he said. "You let the sun and moon escape, and now it's cold." Indeed, it began to snow, and Coyote shivered. "Now your teeth are chattering," Eagle said, "and it's your fault that cold has come into the world."

It's true. If it weren't for Coyote's curiosity and mischief making, we wouldn't have winter; we could enjoy summer all the time.

> Notice the theme of the myth— human failings like curiosity lead to trouble.

---

pestering bothering   **shriveled** dried up; shrank and wrinkled   **pursuit** the act of chasing

Coyote Steals the Sun and Moon   retold by Erdoes and Ortiz

Directions Choose the letter of the best answer or write the answer using complete sentences.

Comprehension: Identifying Facts

1. Why does Coyote want to team up with Eagle?
  A to catch more food to eat
  B to steal the sun and moon
  C to learn to fly
  D to find the Kachinas

2. Why do Eagle and Coyote want the Kachinas' box?

3. Why does Eagle give the box to Coyote?

Comprehension: Putting Ideas Together

4. Which word best describes Coyote?
  A lazy
  B clever
  C clumsy
  D mean

5. Why does Eagle refuse to give Coyote the box at first?

6. Why does Coyote want to carry the box for Eagle?

Understanding Literature: Mythology

A myth is a story that explains how the world came to be or why events in nature take place. Many myths feature animals that talk or beings with magical powers. Each character often has one main character trait, such as curiosity or jealousy. Many cultures have a collection of myths, called mythology, that reflects the beliefs of its people.

7. In what ways do the animals in this myth act like people?

8. What part of nature does this myth explain? What lesson does this myth teach?

Critical Thinking

9. Which character, Eagle or Coyote, did you like better? Explain.

Thinking Creatively

10. Why do you think people continue to tell stories about Coyote?

Grammar Check

There are four basic sentence structures:

- A <u>simple sentence</u> has one independent clause and at least one subject and verb. *Example:* The cat sleeps on the chair.

- A <u>compound sentence</u> has two or more independent clauses usually joined by a comma and a conjunction.
  Example: The cat sleeps on the chair, and the dog sleeps in the basket.

- A <u>complex sentence</u> has one independent clause and one or more subordinate clauses.
  Example: The cat, which belongs to my aunt, sleeps on the chair.

- A <u>compound-complex sentence</u> has two or more independent clauses and one or more subordinate clauses.
  Example: During the exam, Carol remembered she had to pick up food for her cat, but she wanted to finish writing first.

Change each simple sentence to the type of sentence in parentheses. Write your new sentences on a sheet of paper.

1 Carmelo read the story. (compound)
2 Gretel skated away. (compound)
3 Tasha worked hard. (complex)
4 Mechal gazed outside. (compound-complex)

 Vocabulary Builder

The prefixes *dis-* and *non-* mean "not." Adding *dis-* or *non-* to a word creates its antonym, or opposite. *Non-* often appears with nouns and *dis-* with verbs.

please/displease   to make happy/angry
fiction/nonfiction   imaginary/true

Add the prefix *dis-* or *non-* to each word below. Then write each new word in a sentence.

1 prove   **3** believe
2 sense   **4** obey

 Writing on Your Own

Choose one part of nature (for example, a rainbow, the seasons, or certain animal behaviors). Write your own myth that explains this part of nature.

 Listening and Speaking

Use the library or Internet to research Zuni culture. Look for ways in which history and tradition influence the Zuni today. Then present your findings in an oral presentation.

 Research and Technology

Find another myth that explains an event in the natural world. Then find out how science explains the same event. Write a summary of the myth and how science explains it.

Business Letters

In this unit, you have been using the strategy of summarizing to tell about the main ideas in a story. You can also use summarizing when you read a letter. This will help you figure out the reason for writing the letter.

About Business Letters

People write business letters for many different reasons. At some point in your life, you may need to write a business letter or read a business letter that is sent to you. It is important to know the seven main parts of a business letter:

1. Return address—the address of the person writing the letter

2. Date—the month, day, and year when the letter was written

3. Inside address—the person or company receiving the letter

4. Salutation—a formal greeting, followed by a colon

5. Body—information that tells why the person is writing

6. Complimentary close—a polite ending followed by a comma

7. Signature—the handwritten name of the person writing the letter

Reading Skill

When you read a business letter, it is important to find the main idea. The main idea is the letter's most important piece of information. Most people state the main idea in the opening sentence of the body of the letter. When you find the main idea, you know what the writer wants to tell you. This makes it much easier to write a helpful and useful answer.

This chart shows some common reasons why people write business letters.

A person writes to a company—	• to order a product • to apply for a job • to complain about service • to ask a question
A company writes to a person—	• to inform a customer about an order • to invite someone for an interview • to answer a question • to resolve a complaint • to collect an overdue bill

On the next two pages are examples of business letters.

4326 Arden Avenue
Houston, TX 77013
September 30, 2007

Ms. Esther Fine
Mighty Fine Company
4511 Leeds Road
Houston, TX 77013

Dear Ms. Fine:

I am writing in answer to your ad for a file clerk that
appeared in yesterday's *Daily Report*.

> The first sentence
> states why Ms. Levy
> is writing the letter.

I have worked at Bell, Inc. for three years as a file clerk. I have always
received very high job-performance ratings. However, Bell, Inc. is closing
and I am looking for another job.

I would like to come in for an interview. Please call me at (832) 555-3255
to set up an appointment.

Yours very truly,

Lillian S. Levy

Lillian S. Levy

47 Winslow Drive
Cedar Rapids, IA 52401
December 12, 2007

This letter is being sent to Aldo Carducci.

Mr. Aldo Carducci
1230 Grand Drive
Houston, TX 77013

Dear Mr. Carducci:

Thank you for ordering our special digital watch. This popular item is currently sold out. It will be three weeks before we can send you the watch you ordered.

We hope this delay will not cause you any inconvenience. We know you will be glad you waited!

Sincerely,

Isabel Diaz

Isabel Diaz
Mail Order Division

Isabel Diaz wrote this letter.

Monitor Your Progress

Directions Choose the letter of the best answer or write the answer using complete sentences.

1. Who wrote the business letter asking for an interview with the Mighty Fine Company?
   A Esther Fine
   B Lillian S. Levy
   C Aldo Carducci
   D Isabel Diaz

2. What is the main idea of the letter written by Isabel Diaz?
   A to apply for a job with the company
   B to apologize for a delay in sending a product
   C to thank the company for sending the watch
   D to assure the customer that he will like the watch

3. What is the main idea of the letter to the Mighty Fine Company?
   A The writer is applying for a job.
   B The writer is about to lose a job.
   C The writer has three years' work experience.
   D The writer saw an ad in the *Daily Report*.

4. Why is it important to include a salutation and a complimentary close?

5. Why should you state the main idea of a business letter in the first sentence?

Writing on Your Own

Look through the want ads in your local newspaper. Find a job that interests you. Write a business letter applying for the job. Be sure to include all of the parts of a business letter.

Brer Possum's Dilemma   by Jackie Torrence | John Henry

Jackie Torrence
1944–2004

Objectives

◆ To read and understand a folktale and a ballad

◆ To recognize dialect in oral tradition literature

◆ To explain how hero and personification are important in folk literature

About the Author

Jackie Torrence was one of America's best-known and best-loved storytellers. Torrence was born in Chicago and grew up on a North Carolina farming settlement. She learned the "Brer Rabbit" tales from her grandparents. They also taught her other tales that had been passed along by enslaved Africans in the South.

Torrence began telling stories in 1972 at the library where she worked. Soon large audiences were coming to hear the "Story Lady." Her humor, lively language, hisses, and shrieks brought the stories to life. Torrence told classic ghost stories and her own tales, along with traditional **folktales.** Her collected stories appear in *The Accidental Angel, My Grandmother's Treasure*, and other books.

About the Selections

"Brer Rabbit," by Jackie Torrence, and other animal tales show a part of history and record the way slaves spoke on southern plantations. Torrence says, "If it had not been for storytelling, the black family would not have survived." In the selection that follows, Brer Possum has to make a choice when Brer Snake asks him for help.

John Henry is part of the American folklore, just like Paul Bunyan and Pecos Bill. There have been many songs and stories written about John Henry. In most stories, he is shown as an African American man, but he served as a hero for all workers. In this selection, John Henry, a steel driver, challenges a steam drill to a race. John Henry digs farther and faster than the drill, but he dies from the effort.

Literary Terms **Oral literature** is the stories that were first told, rather than being written down. Because these stories were spoken, they are often written in **dialect.** Dialect is the speech of a particular part of the country or of a certain group of people. In folktales, the **hero** is the leading male character. The hero is often bigger, faster, stronger, smarter, or braver than everyone else. Animal characters with human traits are common in folktales, as you will see in "Brer Possum's Dilemma." Giving characters such as animals or objects the characteristics or qualities of humans is called **personification.** "John Henry" is an example of a **ballad**—a form of poetry, passed from person to person, often as a simple song.

Reading on Your Own Previewing a selection can help to prepare you for reading. Look at the titles of the two selections you are about to read. Glance through the pages and look at the illustrations. Have you ever heard of Brer Possum or John Henry? Read the selections to find out more about these two characters.

Writing on Your Own Folktales have been retold throughout many years. Write a paragraph to explain why you think people continue to tell each other these stories. Also tell whether you think it is important that these stories have been written down.

Vocabulary Focus Language written in dialect is spelled how it sounds. Because of this, words are often spelled wrong. Letters or word endings also are often missing from words written in dialect. As you read "Brer Possum's Dilemma" and "John Henry," notice how dialect is used. On a sheet of paper, write at least 10 words that are written in dialect. Then write the correct spelling and the meaning of each word.

Think Before You Read Would you help an animal that was in trouble? Would it depend on the type of animal? Explain your answer.

folktale a story that has been handed down from one generation to another

oral literature stories that were first told, rather than being written down

dialect the speech of a particular part of the country, or of a certain group of people

hero the leading male character in a story, novel, play, or film

personification giving characters such as animals or objects the characteristics or qualities of humans

ballad a form of poetry, passed from person to person, often as a simple song

Brer Possum's Dilemma

As you read, try reading the story aloud. This may help you understand the dialect better.

Brer means brother. It is used before a person's name, like Mr. or Dr. *Critters* is dialect for creatures, or small animals.

Notice how the dialect sounds like common everyday speech. It shows that this tale was first told rather than written down.

Back in the days when the animals could talk, there lived ol' Brer Possum. He was a fine feller. Why, he never liked to see no critters in trouble. He was always helpin' out, a-doin' somethin' for others.

Ever' night, ol' Brer Possum climbed into a persimmon tree, hung by his tail, and slept all night long. And each mornin', he climbed outa the tree and walked down the road to sun 'imself.

One mornin', as he walked, he come to a big hole in the middle of the road. Now, ol' Brer Possum was kind and gentle, but he was also nosy, so he went over to the hole and looked in. All at once, he stepped back, 'cause layin' in the bottom of that hole was ol' Brer Snake with a brick on his back.

Brer Possum said to 'imself, "I best git on outa here, 'cause ol' Brer Snake is mean and evil and lowdown, and if I git to stayin' around 'im, he jist might git to bitin' me."

So Brer Possum went on down the road.

But Brer Snake had seen Brer Possum, and he **commenced** to callin' for 'im.

"Help me, Brer Possum."

---

commenced began or started

Brer Possum stopped and turned around. He said to 'imself, "That's ol' Brer Snake a-callin' me. What do you **reckon** he wants?"

Well, ol' Brer Possum was kindhearted, so he went back down the road to the hole, stood at the edge, and looked down at Brer Snake.

"Was that you a-callin' me? What do you want?"

Brer Snake looked up and said, "I've been down here in this hole for a mighty long time with this brick on my back. Won't you help git it offa me?"

Brer Possum thought.

"Now listen here, Brer Snake. I knows you. You's mean and evil and lowdown, and if'n I was to git down in that hole and git to liftin' that brick offa your back, you wouldn't do nothin' but bite me."

Ol' Brer Snake just hissed.

"Maybe not. Maybe not. Maaaaaaaybe not."

Brer Possum said, "I ain't sure 'bout you at all. I jist don't know. You're a-goin' to have to let me think about it."

So ol' Brer Possum thought—he thought high, and he thought low—and jist as he was thinkin', he looked up into a tree and saw a dead limb a-hangin' down. He climbed into the tree, broke off the limb, and with that ol' stick, pushed that brick offa Brer Snake's back. Then he took off down the road.

Brer Possum thought he was away from ol' Brer Snake when all at once he heard somethin'.

"Help me, Brer Possum."

Brer Possum said, "Oh, no, that's him agin."

But bein' so kindhearted, Brer Possum turned around, went back to the hole, and stood at the edge.

"Brer Snake, was that you a-callin' me? What do you want now?"

Ol' Brer Snake looked up outa the hole and hissed.

Reading Strategy:
Summarizing
What kind of character is Brer Snake?

reckon to think

"I've been down here for a mighty long time, and I've gotten a little weak, and the sides of this ol' hole are too slick for me to climb. Do you think you can lift me outa here?"

Brer Possum thought.

"Now, you jist wait a minute. If'n I was to git down into that hole and lift you outa there, you wouldn't do nothin' but bite me."

Brer Snake hissed.

"Maybe not. Maybe not. Maaaaaaaybe not."

Brer Possum said, "I jist don't know. You're a-goin' to have to give me time to think about this."

So ol' Brer Possum thought.

And as he thought, he jist happened to look down there in that hole and see that ol' dead limb. So he pushed the limb underneath ol' Brer Snake and he lifted 'im outa the hole, way up into the air, and throwed 'im into the high grass.

Brer Possum took off a-runnin' down the road.

Well, he thought he was away from ol' Brer Snake when all at once he heard somethin'.

"Help me, Brer Possum."

Brer Possum thought, "That's him agin."

But bein' so kindhearted, he turned around, went back to the hole, and stood there a-lookin' for Brer Snake. Brer Snake crawled outa the high grass just as slow as he could, stretched 'imself out across the road, rared up, and looked at ol' Brer Possum.

Then he hissed. "I've been down there in that ol' hole for a mighty long time, and I've gotten a little cold 'cause the sun didn't shine. Do you think you could put me in your pocket and git me warm?"

Brer Snake keeps repeating the same answer. How does this affect the story?

Rared up means reared up. Brer Snake raised his head and the front part of his body high off the ground.

Brer Possum said, "Now you listen here, Brer Snake. I knows you. You's mean and evil and lowdown, and if'n I put you in my pocket you wouldn't do nothin' but bite me."

Brer Snake hissed.

"Maybe not. Maybe not. Maaaaaaaybe not."

"No sireee. Brer Snake. I knows you. I jist ain't a-goin' to do it."

But jist as Brer Possum was talkin' to Brer Snake, he happened to git a real good look at 'im. He was a-layin' there lookin' so **pitiful**, and Brer Possum's great big heart began to feel sorry for ol' Brer Snake.

"All right," said Brer Possum. "You must be cold. So jist this once I'm a-goin' to put you in my pocket."

So ol' Brer Snake **coiled** up jist as little as he could, and Brer Possum picked 'im up and put 'im in his pocket.

Brer Snake laid quiet and still—so quiet and still that Brer Possum even forgot that he was a-carryin' 'im around. But all of a sudden, Brer Snake commenced to crawlin' out, and he turned and faced Brer Possum and hissed.

"I'm a-goin' to bite you."

But Brer Possum said, "Now wait a minute. Why are you a-goin' to bite me? I done took that brick offa your back, I got you outa that hole, and I put you in my pocket to git you warm. Why are you a-goin' to bite me?"

Brer Snake hissed.

"You knowed I was a snake before you put me in you pocket."

And when you're mindin' your own business and you spot trouble, don't never trouble trouble 'til trouble troubles you.

Reading Strategy: Summarizing

How has Brer Possum helped Brer Snake?

pitiful causing others to feel pity   **coiled** curled up

JOHN HENRY

Ten Pound Hammer,
Thomas Hart
Benton

© Christie's Images / CORBIS All Rights Reserved. © Thomas Hart Benton and Rita P. Benton Testamentary Trusts / VAGA, New York

As you read, notice the songlike tone of the ballad.

C. & O. road stands for Chesapeake & Ohio Railroad. The C&O's Big Bend Tunnel was built in the 1870s. It goes through a West Virginia mountain.

Many years have passed. In the first stanza, John Henry was a baby. In the second stanza, he is a grown man.

John Henry was a lil baby,
Sittin' on his mama's knee,
Said: 'The Big Bend Tunnel on the C. & O. road
Gonna cause the death of me,
5 Lawd, Lawd, gonna cause the death of me.'

Cap'n says to John Henry,
'Gonna bring me a steam drill 'round,
Gonna take that steam drill out on the job,
Gonna whop that steel on down,
10 Lawd, Lawd, gonna whop that steel on down.'

John Henry tol' his cap'n,
Lightnin' was in his eye:
'Cap'n, bet yo' las, red cent on me,
Fo' I'll beat it to the bottom or I'll die,
15 Lawd, Lawd, I'll beat it to the bottom or I'll die.'

Sun shine hot an' burnin',
Wer'n't no breeze a-tall,
Sweat ran down like water down a hill,
That day John Henry let his hammer fall,
20 Lawd, Lawd, that day John Henry let his hammer fall.

John Henry went to the tunnel,
An' they put him in the lead to drive,
The rock so tall an' John Henry so small,
That he lied down his hammer an' he cried,
25 Lawd, Lawd, that he lied down his hammer an' he cried.

John Henry started on the right hand,
The steam drill started on the lef'—
'Before I'd let this steam drill beat me down,
I'd hammer my fool self to death,
30 Lawd, Lawd, I'd hammer my fool self to death.'

John Henry had a lil woman,
Her name were Polly Ann,
John Henry took sick an' had to go to bed,
Polly Ann drove steel like a man,
35 Lawd, Lawd, Polly Ann drove steel like a man.

John Henry said to his shaker,
'Shaker, why don' you sing?
I'm throwin' twelve poun's from my hips on down,
Jes' listen to the col' steel ring,
40 Lawd, Lawd, jes' listen to the col' steel ring.'

Oh, the captain said to John Henry,
'I b'lieve this mountain's sinkin' in.'
John Henry said to his captain, oh my!
'Ain' nothin' but my hammer suckin' win',
45 Lawd, Lawd, ain' nothin' but my hammer suckin' win'.'

John Henry tol' his shaker,
'Shaker, you better pray,
For, if I miss this six-foot steel,
Tomorrow'll be yo' buryin' day,
50 Lawd, Lawd, tomorrow'll be yo' buryin' day.'

Reading Strategy:
Summarizing
What key events have happened up to this point?

Do you think John Henry can beat the steam drill? Why or why not?

The shaker sets the spikes and places the drills for a steel-driver to hammer.

John Henry tol' his captain,
'Look yonder what I see—
Yo' drill's done broke an' yo' hole's done choke,
An' you cain' drive steel like me,
55 Lawd, Lawd, an' you cain' drive steel like me.'

The man that invented the steam drill,
Thought he was mighty fine.
John Henry drove his fifteen feet,
An' the steam drill only made nine,
60 Lawd, Lawd, an' the steam drill only made nine.

The hammer that John Henry swung,
It weighed over nine pound;
He broke a rib in his lef'-han' side,
An' his intrels fell on the groun',
65 Lawd, Lawd, an' his intrels fell on the groun'.

Intrels is dialect meaning entrails, or insides.

All the womens in the Wes',
When they heared of John Henry's death,
Stood in the rain, flagged the eas'-boun' train,
Goin' where John Henry fell dead,
70 Lawd, Lawd, goin' where John Henry fell dead.

John Henry's lil mother,
She was all dressed in red,
She jumped in bed, covered up her head,
Said she didn' know her son was dead,
75 Lawd, Lawd, didn' know her son was dead.

Dey took John Henry to the graveyard,
An' they buried him in the san',
An' every locomotive come roarin' by,
Says, 'There lays a steel-drivin' man,
80 Lawd, Lawd, there lays a steel-drivin' man.'

In a machine age, why would people look up to John Henry as a folk hero?

Directions Choose the letter of the best answer or write the answer using complete sentences.

Comprehension: Identifying Facts

1. Which word best describes Brer Possum?
   - **A** kind
   - **B** silly
   - **C** clever
   - **D** mean

2. Why is Brer Possum not eager to help Brer Snake?
   - **A** He is in a hurry to go lie in the sun.
   - **B** He does not trust Brer Snake.
   - **C** Brer Snake has never helped him.
   - **D** He never helps anyone in trouble.

3. Why does Brer Possum decide to trust Brer Snake?

4. Why does Brer Snake want to bite Brer Possum?

5. What lesson does "Brer Possum's Dilemma" teach?

6. What does John Henry's captain plan to do?

7. How does Polly Ann help John Henry?

8. What happens to the steam drill?

9. What happens after John Henry wins the race?

10. How do the people react when John Henry dies?

Comprehension: Putting Ideas Together

11. Why does Brer Snake ask Brer Possum for help?
    - **A** Brer Possum is kind and always helps those in trouble.
    - **B** Brer Possum has always helped him in the past.
    - **C** Brer Possum is very clever.
    - **D** Brer Possum is very strong.

12. Why does John Henry's captain want to use the steam drill?
    - **A** to see if John Henry can beat its pace
    - **B** to get the job done faster
    - **C** so he can get rid of John Henry
    - **D** so he can retire from the job

13. What three favors does Brer Snake ask for?

14. What is Brer Possum's dilemma (problem)?

15. Who is smarter, Brer Snake or Brer Possum? Explain.

16. Why does John Henry challenge the steam drill?

17. What kind of person is John Henry? Which details from the selection support your answer?

After Reading continued on next page

Brer Possum's Dilemma *by Jackie Torrence* | *John Henry*

18. What can you infer, or guess, about John Henry's marriage to Polly Ann? Explain.

19. Which details in "John Henry" hint at its ending?

20. Which details help you picture the race between John Henry and the steam drill?

Understanding Literature: Oral Tradition

The oral tradition is a collection of tales that were spread by word of mouth before they were written down. Sometimes the hero is an animal that talks and acts like a person. This is an example of personification. Folktales often give great powers to their heroes. Many folktales are written in dialect that sounds like actual speech.

21. How is John Henry like most folk heroes? How is he different?

22. Is Brer Possum a hero? Is Polly Ann a hero? Why or why not?

23. How would these stories be different if they were not told in dialect?

24. How are Brer Possum and Brer Snake personified?

25. Which features of both tales show that they belong to the oral tradition?

Critical Thinking

26. Does the author of "Brer Possum's Dilemma" want you to think Brer Possum is foolish? Explain.

27. Why does Brer Snake suggest that he may not bite Brer Possum?

28. What might have happened to Brer Snake if Brer Possum had not agreed to help him?

29. Do you think John Henry would be remembered if he had not died after winning the race?

Thinking Creatively

30. Which character from the two tales do you admire most? Why?

Grammar Check

A comma signals a pause in a sentence. Here are some common uses for commas:

- before the conjunction in a compound sentence
  Example: Paul Bunyan was a logger, and Davy Crockett was a hunter.

- between items in a series
  Example: John Henry was a big, strong, husky man.

- to set off appositives, participial phrases, or adjective clauses
  Example: Brer Possum, who sleeps at night, basks in the sun all day.

Rewrite each sentence, inserting the commas where they belong.

1 The Nile River which flows through Egypt provides water for farming.

2 The long flat dry stretches of land were bare of any plants.

 Vocabulary Builder

Dialect is sometimes very difficult to understand. Work with a partner to figure out what Standard English words these dialect words stand for. Write the Standard English words on a sheet of paper.

1 lil		**5** brer
2 gonna		**6** outa
3 yo'		**7** jist
4 jes'		**8** throwed

 Writing on Your Own

Most folk literature is written in informal language. It often uses dialect and sayings. Write a short essay explaining how language can affect the tone and mood in folk literature. Give specific examples from folktales you have read.

 Listening and Speaking

Work with a small group to organize a storytelling workshop. First, create a tip sheet for storytellers. Encourage them to make eye contact, create the action, and use dialect as they tell their stories. Next, select different folktales to perform. Practice the storytelling several times, and then present the story to the class.

 Research and Technology

Use a library resource to gather a collection of folktales. Find at least three tales that could be easily made into movie versions. For each title, write an introduction that describes its historical or cultural background. Explain why each tale you chose would make a good movie.

Davy Crockett's Dream   by Davy Crockett

Davy Crockett
1786–1836

Objectives

◆ To compare and contrast a tall tale and a folk ballad

◆ To recognize humor, exaggeration, and hyperbole in literature

About the Author

Davy Crockett was a real person whose tales about himself made his story a **legend.** (A legend is a story from folklore that features characters who actually lived or real places or events.) Crockett represented Tennessee in Congress and joined the fight for Texas independence. Crockett was killed at the battle of the Alamo in 1836. The 1950s television show *Davy Crockett* brought his legend to life. Millions tuned in, sparking a nationwide fad for Crockett-style coonskin caps.

About the Selection

In "Davy Crockett's Dream," Crockett goes out into the icy weather to hunt for food. He finds shelter and decides to take a nap. He has a strange, lifelike dream about a neighbor called Oak Wing.

As you read "Davy Crockett's Dream," recall the "John Henry" selection that you read earlier in this unit. Think about how it compares to "Davy Crockett's Dream" and how the two heroes are similar and different.

Literary Terms "Davy Crockett" and "John Henry" are examples of **tall tales.** A tall tale is a story from the past that features enlarged characters who have unreal adventures. Tall tales often contain **humor** and **exaggeration.** Humor is literature created to be funny or to amuse. Exaggeration is the use of words to make something seem more than it is. In a tall tale, the hero is bigger and stronger than a real person could ever be. This kind of exaggeration of the characters and events is called **hyperbole,** or exaggeration to show that something is important.

Reading on Your Own Think about whether you would use the term "tall tale" to describe "John Henry." Which parts of "John Henry" are like a tall tale? Which are not like a tall tale? Keep "John Henry" in mind as you read "Davy Crockett's Dream."

Writing on Your Own "John Henry" is a ballad, and "Davy Crockett's Dream" is a prose tale. Think about the difference between telling a story in verse and telling it in prose. Write a short paragraph comparing the effect of verse and prose on the reader.

Vocabulary Focus You can use prefixes to form antonyms, or opposites. The prefix *un-* makes a word mean its opposite. Use the prefixes to create antonyms for these words: *necessary, interesting, lock, known,* and *popular.* Write a sentence using each new word correctly.

Think Before You Read Do dreams often make good or exciting stories? Explain why or why not.

---

legend a story from folklore that features characters who actually lived or real places or events

tall tale a story from the past that features enlarged characters who have unreal adventures

humor literature created to be funny or to amuse

exaggeration the use of words to make something seem more than it is

hyperbole using gross exaggeration to show that something is important

DAVY CROCKETT'S DREAM

One day when it was so cold that I was afeard to open my mouth, lest I should freeze my tongue, I took my little dog named Grizzle and cut out for Salt River Bay to kill something for dinner. I got a good ways from home afore I knowed where I was, and as I had swetted some before I left the house my hat froze fast to my head, and I like to have put my neck out of joint in trying to pull it off. When I sneezed the icicles crackled all up and down the inside of my nose, like when you walk over a bog in winter time. The **varmints** was so scarce that I couldn't find one, and so when I come to an old log hut that had belonged to some **squatter** that had ben reformed out by the nabors, I stood my rifle up agin one of the door posts and went in. I **kindled** up a little fire and told Grizzle I was going to take a nap. I piled up a heap of chestnut burs for a pillow and straitened myself out on the ground, for I can curl closer than a rattlesnake and lay straiter than a log. I laid with the back of my head agin the hearth, and my eyes looking up chimney so that I could see when it was noon by the sun, for Mrs. Crockett was always rantankerous when I staid out over the time. I got to sleep before Grizzle had

As you read, notice the exaggeration. Here, Crockett says his tongue would freeze if he simply opened his mouth.

Rantankerous means bad-tempered. Mrs. Crockett becomes upset with Davy when he comes home too late.

varmints creatures such as rats or mice	**squatter** a person living in a building that the person does not own or rent	**kindled** built a fire

done warming the eend of his nose, and I had swallowed so much cold wind that it laid hard on my stomach, and as I laid gulping and belching the wind went out of me and roared up chimney like a young whirlwind. So I had a pesky dream, and kinder thought, till I waked up, that I was floating down the Massassippy in a holler tree, and I hadn't room to stir my legs and arms no more than they were withed together with young saplings. While I was there and want able to help myself a feller called Oak Wing that lived about twenty miles off, and that I had give a most almighty licking once, cum and looked in with his blind eye that I had **gouged** out five years before, and I saw him looking in one end of the hollow log, and he axed me if I wanted to get out. I told him to tie a rope to one of my legs and draw me out as soon as God would let him and as much sooner as he was a mind to. But he said he wouldn't do it that way, he would ram me out with a pole. So he took a long pole and rammed it down agin my head as if he was ramming home the cattridge in a cannon. This didn't make me budge an inch, but it pounded my head down in between my shoulders till I look'd like a turcle with his head drawn in. This started my temper a **trifle,** and I ript and swore till the breath boiled out of the end of the log like the steam out of the funnel pipe of a steemboat. Jest then I woke up, and seed my wife pulling my leg, for it was enermost sundown and she had cum arter me. There was a long icicle hanging to her nose, and when she tried to kiss me, she run it right into my eye. I telled her my dreem, and sed I would have revenge on Oak Wing for pounding my head. She said it was all a dreem and that Oak was not to blame; but I had a very diffrent idee of the matter. So I went and talked to him, and telled him what he had done to me in a dreem, and it was settled that he should make me an apology in his next dreem, and that wood make us square, for I don't like to be run upon when I'm asleep, any more than I do when I'm awake.

The *Massassippy* is Davy's name for the Mississippi River. *Mississippi* is an Indian word meaning big river.

Here, Crockett is saying "I did not have room to move my legs and arms any more than I could have had they been tied up."

Cattridge is dialect for cartridge or bullets.

Reading Strategy
Summarizing
What happens in Davy Crockett's dream?

Make us square means make us even.

gouged dug out   **trifle** a small amount

Davy Crockett's Dream   by Davy Crockett

Directions Choose the letter of the best answer or write the answer using complete sentences.

Comprehension: Identifying Facts

1. Who is Grizzle?
   A Davy Crockett's neighbor
   B Davy Crockett's dog
   C Davy Crockett's wife
   D Davy Crockett's son

2. What makes Davy wake up from his dream?

3. What does Oak Wing agree to do at the end of the tale?

Comprehension: Putting Ideas Together

4. What do John Henry and Davy Crockett have in common?
   A They are both clever hunters.
   B They both like to tell tall stories.
   C They both have wives who yell at them.
   D They are both strong and tough.

5. Describe the main challenges John Henry and Davy Crockett face. How are they alike? How are they different?

6. What is the theme of "Davy Crockett's Dream"? How is it different from the theme of "John Henry"?

Understanding Literature: Tall Tale

A tall tale is a story full of what Mark Twain once called "stretchers." Everything in a tall tale is exaggerated. Heroes are bigger and stronger than other people. They brag more, they talk louder, and they have more amazing skills. Storytellers use exaggeration, or hyperbole, to make tall tales funnier and more memorable.

7. Does "John Henry" qualify as a tall tale? Why or why not?

8. Identify at least three details that make "Davy Crockett's Dream" a tall tale.

Critical Thinking

9. Which do you think is more of a hero, John Henry or Davy Crockett? Why do you think so?

Thinking Creatively

10. Which would make a better movie, "John Henry" or "Davy Crockett's Dream"? Explain.

Grammar Check

An apostrophe is a punctuation mark used to replace missing letters. Use an apostrophe in these situations:

- in a contraction; *Examples:* can't, won't, doesn't
- to show possession; *Examples:* Becky's letter, Mi Won's exam, Carlos's sneakers
- to replace missing letters in a dialect word; *Examples:* runnin', 'imself, ol', a-goin'

Insert apostrophes in the correct places in each sentence.

1 I is askin you, is the steamboat a-comin?

2 I dont know. Cant you see around the river bend?

3 I tripped over Nancys skates and couldnt save myself from falling.

 Vocabulary Builder

Review each group of words. Decide whether the boldfaced word from "Davy Crockett's Dream" belongs with the other two words. Explain why or why not.

1 **squatter,** renter, owner

2 **kindled,** watered, dampened

3 **trifle,** little, small

4 **gouged,** fixed, filled

 Writing on Your Own

Write a short essay comparing the heroes John Henry and Davy Crockett. How does each tale present its hero? Consider these questions:

- How does each tale use exaggeration? What is the effect?
- How important is humor in each tale?
- Why have these characters become part of America's oral tradition?

 Listening and Speaking

Retell either "John Henry" or "Davy Crockett's Dream" to someone who has not read the story. Use dialect and try to keep the tone of the original tale.

 Media and Viewing

Look at several images of John Henry and Davy Crockett. Start with the illustrations in your textbook. Then go online and to the library to find other images. With a partner, discuss the way actors and artists have portrayed these two folk heroes.

The organization of a text helps readers figure out which parts are most important. Readers can also use text structure to help identify a purpose for reading. Two of the main reasons for reading a text are for entertainment and for information. As you read, ask yourself what is the purpose of the reading. Read each selection carefully so that you remember the information.

Literary Terms

simile a figure of speech that makes a comparison using the words *like* or *as*

imagery the pictures created by words that appeal to the five senses

dialogue the conversation among characters in a story

address another term for a speech; a written work meant to be read aloud

author's influences the people, experiences, and works of literature and art that affect a writer's choices

fiction writing that is imaginative and designed to entertain

nonfiction writing about real people and events

theme the main idea of a literary work

universal theme a main idea that appears in many times, places, and cultures

BEFORE READING THE SELECTION | Build Understanding

Mose   by Mary Pope Osborne

About the Author

Mary Pope Osborne's father was an army officer. She grew
up on military bases with her brother and her sister. Osborne
worked and acted at the local community theater. She studied
religion and mythology in college. One day, she wrote a story
about a small girl, like herself as a child. This became her first
novel. Since then, Osborne has written dozens of books for
young readers. She is best known for the "Magic Tree House"
series. In these books, the characters travel through time and
have many adventures.

Mary Pope Osborne
1949–

About the Selection

"Mose" is a legend about Mose Humphreys, a real volunteer
fireman of old New York. In 1848, B.A. Baker wrote a
Broadway play about him. The play, *A Glance at New York,*
was a big hit, and Mose became a folk hero. He was featured
in newspaper stories and more plays. In Osborne's story,
Mose puts out fires and rescues people in danger. Everyone
cheers him as a hero. When steam-powered fire engines
appear, Mose realizes there is no place for him anymore at
the firehouse.

Before Reading continued on next page

Objectives

◆ To read and
understand a
legend

◆ To recognize the
use of dialogue in
literature

◆ To identify
examples of simile
and imagery in a
story

Mose   by Mary Pope Osborne

simile a figure of speech that makes a comparison using the words *like* or *as*

imagery the pictures created by words that appeal to the five senses

dialogue the conversation among characters in a story

Literary Terms As you learned in Part 1, a legend is a story from folklore that features characters who actually lived. Legends often use hyperbole, or great exaggeration. **Similes** and **imagery** are sometimes used to help create this exaggeration. A simile is a figure of speech that makes a comparison using the words *like* or *as*. Imagery is the pictures created by words that appeal to the five senses. "Mose" also contains **dialogue,** the conversation among characters in a story. Readers can better picture a character's feelings and thoughts through the use of imagery and dialogue.

Reading on Your Own "Mose" is a legend about a real person. As you read, ask questions about the story. Ask yourself: Could Mose really have done this? Which details are true and which ones are imaginary?

Writing on Your Own To become a legend, a person must have been a true hero in real life. Write a paragraph describing the qualities you think make a hero into a legend. Are there any people living today who you think could become legends?

Vocabulary Focus Legends are often set in the past. They may include words that describe everyday items from long ago. Use a dictionary to find the meaning of each word or phrase from "Mose:" *stovepipe hat, tenement, soup house, cobblestones, liveries.*

On a sheet of paper, write the definition. Then write a sentence using each word or phrase correctly.

Think Before You Read Why do you think a firefighter might be a good subject for a legend?

BURNING OF THE NEW YORK CRYSTAL PALACE.

MOSE

As you read, think about why the author chose to exaggerate certain details. Notice the simile "as large as Virginia hams" in the third sentence.

   "Afternoon, Mac!" Mose Humphreys tipped his stovepipe hat, revealing his flaming red hair. Puffing a huge cigar, he **swaggered** toward his special table at the Paradise Soup House on the Bowery. Mose was eight feet tall and had hands as large as Virginia hams. His arms were so long that he could scratch his kneecaps without bending his back.

   "Hi, Mose! What'll it be?" shouted Mac, one of the soup house waiters.

The Bowery is a New York City neighborhood east of Broadway and below 14th Street. Today this neighborhood is called the Lower East Side or the East Village.

swaggered walked in a way meant to show off

Reading Strategy: Text Structure
Describe the structure of the story. How does the text structure help determine your purpose for reading?

Mose sat down in the big chair made especially for him and said, "Bring me a plate of pork and beans, Mac."

But just then cries came from outside—"Fire! Fire! Turn out! Turn out!"—and the fire-alarm bell jangled from the City Hall tower.

A newsboy burst into the soup house, shouting, "Front Street **tenement** on fire! Spreading fast!"

Mose bounded out of the soup house. As an **eerie** glow lit up the evening sky of New York City, he hurried to his fire station. Other volunteer firemen rushed out of workshops, ballrooms, shipyards, and factories, until soon twenty-nine **brawny** men had joined Mose at the station house.

They all pulled on their bright-red shirts and rainbow suspenders. Then they rolled out their old fire machine, *Lady Washington*. The machine was hardly more than a pump. She had no engine or horses to move her along, so Mose and his men grabbed the old pumper by her two wooden bars and began lugging her through the streets to the fire.

As Mose and the other volunteers clattered over the cobblestoned streets of old New York City, they ran past the steamboat pier.

They ran past horse liveries and wooden shanties.

They ran past soup houses, pigsties, roosters, and ragmen.

They ran past newsboys crying, "Papers, one cent!"

They ran past oystermen lowering their traps into the Hudson River.

They ran past chimney sweeps, and women shouting, "Apples for sale!" and nurserymaids pushing carriages.

But suddenly the firemen came to a halt. A horse-drawn trolley was stopped in the middle of the road, blocking their path.

Suspenders are straps that button or clip to the back of a waistband on a pair of pants. They go up over the shoulders and fasten again in the front.

Cobblestones are round stones a little smaller than tennis balls. They were once used for paving streets. Cobblestoned streets were bumpy, which is why the engine "clattered."

Liveries are places where people can hire horses and carriages. A *shanty* is a roughly built hut or cabin.

tenement a cheaply made building divided into apartments	**eerie** creepy, ghostly, spooky	**brawny** big, strong, and muscular

"Move! Fire!" Mose cried.

"I can't! She's stuck!" the trolley driver shouted. "One of her wheels is caught between the tracks!"

"I'll take care of it, boys!" Mose shouted to his men. He quickly unhooked the horses from the trolley car. Then he rolled up his sleeves and placed his huge hands under the trolley. Grunting and groaning, Mose lifted the crowded car slowly into the air—until he held it with just one long arm over his head, like a waiter carrying a tray.

As the trolley passengers screamed, Mose staggered across the street, then slowly set the trolley car down. After he dusted off his hands, he returned to his fire machine. Once again the group of volunteer firemen took off, racing through the streets of old New York toward the black clouds of smoke billowing into the sky.

Hundreds had gathered on Front Street to watch the burning tenement building. As soon as Mose's fire company arrived, he shouted, "Move out of the way!" The crowd quickly parted as the volunteers lugged their pumper to a **hydrant.**

> Identify examples of imagery that help to show this story is a legend.

After Mose hooked up the hose, a team of sixteen men began pumping the long handles on either side of the machine, to build up pressure to form a jet of water.

But suddenly a woman ran toward the volunteers, screaming, "My baby's on the third floor!"

"Hold the **nozzle,** boys," Mose said, handing the hose to his men. He grabbed his fire ladder. But when he threw it against the tenement, he discovered it wasn't long enough to reach the third-floor window.

"Bring me a whiskey barrel!" he cried.

When someone brought him the barrel, Mose set the ladder on top of it, then started to climb. The crowd screamed as the ladder swayed left and right.

> This sentence is an example of dialogue. The words in quotation marks show exactly what Mose said.

hydrant an upright pipe with a valve for drawing water

nozzle a tip on a hose where the water comes out

Mose climbed to a window on the third floor. Then, using his ax, he hacked the wood to make room to wedge his giant body inside. Just as he disappeared into the smoke and flames, the roof of the building began to cave in.

"Nobody can escape now!" someone cried.

Moments later Mose reappeared at the hacked-out window, coughing and covered with soot.

"He's alone!" the mother screamed. "Where's my baby?"

Flames **engulfed** the tenement as Mose held his stovepipe hat to his chest and started down the ladder. When the ladder caught fire too, Mose leaped into the air, still holding his hat.

Mose landed on the ground, jumped up, and moved quickly out of the way as the tenement **collapsed.**

The crowd rushed toward him, but Mose pushed them back and shouted, "Where's the baby's mother?"

When the sobbing woman stumbled over, Mose reached into his big hat and pulled out a tiny, crying infant.

"Oh, thank you!" the woman cried as she hugged her child.

"Just doing my duty, ma'am," Mose said.

The volunteers returned *Lady Washington* to the fire station, and when she was safely put away, Mose **resumed** his seat across the street at the Paradise Soup House.

"Don't forget about that plate of pork and beans, Mac," he said. "Make it a large piece of pork, and don't stop to count the beans."

Mose Humphreys was famous all over New York City. Boys and girls would follow him everywhere. He could cross the Hudson River with two breaststrokes, and with six he could swim all the way around the island of Manhattan.

Mose's laughter caused the tenement buildings to sway as if in a storm. And when he was angry, his shouting sounded like a trolley car rumbling over the rails. If his old neighborhood gang, the Bowery Boys, got into a scrape with

Why do people look up to Mose as a hero?

Reading Strategy:
Text Structure

How does the text structure change at this point in the story?

| **engulfed** swallowed up | **collapsed** fell | **resumed** began again |

their rivals, the Dead Rabbits, Mose immediately came to the rescue. Once, when the Dead Rabbits wrecked the Bowery Boys' headquarters, Mose ran after the **vandals,** hurling huge paving blocks from the sidewalk. He even hurled lampposts before his anger cooled.

But most of all Mose was known as the city's most **valiant** volunteer fireman. He and his men lugged *Lady Washington* to fires all over the city—in shanties, **mansions**, theaters, horse stables, soup houses, and butcher shops. He walked through flames as if he were made of bricks, rescuing bankers, bakers, shoemakers, dressmakers, parlormaids, politicians, gamblers, actors, and tiny little babies.

THE AMERICAN FIREMAN,
Facing the Enemy

Though Mose was never paid for his work, the city took good care of him. Soup houses fed him barrels of milk and coffee, **bushels** of oysters and potatoes, and huge amounts of pork and beans. Ragmen gave him their best garments. Bowery shoeshine boys shined his gigantic hobnailed boots for free.

But one day, quite suddenly, Mose Humphreys discovered that his city didn't need him as much as it once had.

He was playing cards and smoking his cigar at the station house when the city alarm bell started going off.

"Fire! Fire! Turn out! Turn out!"

Hobnails are short nails with large heads. They were used to stud the soles of shoes and boots.

---

vandals people who destroy or damage things on purpose

valiant brave

mansions large houses

bushels units of volume equal to about 32 quarts

"She's at the docks, boys!" Mose shouted to his men. He could tell the location of the fire by the number of bell strokes.

Mose and the other volunteers pulled on their suspenders and bright-red shirts. Then they grabbed *Lady Washington*'s wooden bars and started hauling the pumper through the streets.

When they arrived at the docks at the end of Houston Street, they found a huge crowd cheering and screaming. Above the crowd a great arc of water was **cascading** down onto a burning warehouse.

"Get out of our way!" Mose shouted as his men tried to push through the crowd to a fire hydrant.

But the **hordes** of people didn't pay much attention to Mose and his men. They were too busy cheering the shiny new horse-drawn steam fire engine that was rapidly putting out the fire.

"Look at that!" a newsboy shouted. "It takes only six men to work her!"

As Mose peered over the heads of the crowd, he saw that indeed the boy was right. One firefighter was stoking the steamer's shiny brass chamber with coal, one was tending to her elegant black horses, and the other four were aiming her mighty hose at the roaring flames.

"Out of my way!" Mose shouted.

"Don't worry, Mose, she's under control," an apple seller called to him cheerfully. "Your old pumper's no match for that machine."

Mose was so angry, he began pacing back and forth, huffing and puffing. As he paced, he listened to the newsboys and fruit sellers.

"The mayor says they'll be all over the city soon."

"Yep. He's hiring professional trained firemen to run those fancy machines."

Stoking means stirring up and feeding fuel to a fire. This kept the fire going at a constant rate.

cascading falling in waves

hordes large crowds

"Say good-bye to the old pumpers."

"Yeah, and the volunteers, too. Hey, look, the steamer's put out the fire!"

"Things are changin' in this city."

As Mose listened to the newsboys, he started pounding his giant fist into the palm of his hand. He began rocking back and forth with rage. Then suddenly he grabbed the wooden handles of *Lady Washington* and began pushing her toward the river.

"Chief, what are you doing?" one of his men cried.

"Wait!" shouted the others. "Wait!"

But there was no stopping Mose as he picked up speed and started running toward the end of the dock. He gave one last push, sending the old pumper over the edge of the dock.

The crowd heard a huge *splash!* as *Lady Washington* crashed into the Hudson River. Everyone was silent as Mose slowly turned around. He stared at his fellow volunteers with dazed eyes, then staggered away alone.

Mose disappeared from his old haunts after that. Nobody knew for sure what had happened to him. For years folks **speculated** on his whereabouts. In soup houses, on steamboat piers, in stale barrooms, they asked, "Heard anything about Mose?"

Sometimes folks answered, "Oh, didn't you hear? He went west and made a fortune in the California gold rush."

"Oh, didn't you hear? He's driving a mule team in the Dakota territory."

"He's leading a wagon train across the country."

"He's part of the pony express."

"He's working for President Lincoln."

The Gold Rush began in 1849 when gold was discovered at Sutter's Mill, California. When the news spread, thousands of people went west in search of riches.

speculated wondered

The Pony Express mail service ran from St. Joseph, Missouri to Sacramento, California. Young boys carried the mail on horseback at top speed. Riding for the Pony Express was very dangerous. The Pony Express service began in 1860 and ended about 18 months later.

But one evening, one of the old fire volunteers, playing checkers on a worn bench near the old station house on the Bowery, had this to say: "If you want to know the truth about Mose, pay attention to me. He's among us still. I seen him hanging around lampposts on cold winter nights. I seen him sleeping in burned-out old tenements. I seen him walking along the foggy wharfs.

"You could say Mose is the spirit of old New York. And when all them shiny new machines decide to break down, and when the city fire-alarm bell starts to ring again, watch out. Because by then, you know, that fireman will have grown to be at least twenty feet tall."

Mose   by Mary Pope Osborne

Directions Choose the letter of the best answer or write the answer using complete sentences.

Comprehension: Identifying Facts

1. What is Mose's volunteer job?
   A waiter **C** firefighter
   B hero **D** gang leader

2. Who are the Bowery Boys?
   A Mose's firefighting crew
   B Mose's old gang
   C Mose's fan club
   D Mose's neighbors

3. What does Mose look like?

4. What happens when the fire-alarm bell rings?

5. What does Mose do when the trolley gets stuck on the tracks?

6. How does Mose rescue the baby from the fire?

7. How do people repay Mose for his hard work fighting fires?

8. Why does Mose get angry when he sees the steam fire engine?

9. Where do people think Mose went after he disappears?

10. Where does the old volunteer see Mose?

Comprehension: Putting Ideas Together

11. Whom does Mose rescue from the tenement fire?
    A a mother **C** an actor
    B a baby **D** a waiter

12. Which of these does **not** describe Mose?
    A unfriendly hero
    B brave firefighter
    C good swimmer
    D big eater

13. How do Mose and his team fight fires?

14. What makes Mose more heroic than the rest of his crew?

15. What kind of person is Mose? Which details support your answer?

16. Why do people choose the steam fire engine over Mose and his crew?

17. Why does Mose shove *Lady Washington* into the river?

18. Why does Mose disappear from New York City?

19. Which details help you picture New York City during Mose's lifetime?

20. Why does the old volunteer say that "Mose is the spirit of old New York"?

After Reading continued on next page

Mose　　*by Mary Pope Osborne*

Understanding Literature: Simile and Imagery

A simile is a figure of speech that makes a comparison using the words *like* or *as.* Examples: *The house is as big as a castle* and *Her smile shone like the sun.* Similes help to add to the description of a story. In folk literature, similes can be used to exaggerate details to make the characters and events seem more unreal. Imagery is the use of words that appeal to the five senses. Imagery helps to paint the picture of the people and events in a story.

21. Identify at least two similes from "Mose."

22. How do similes help to create imagery in a story?

23. How can you tell that some of the details in "Mose" are exaggerated?

24. Recall the events of the story. Write a simile of your own to describe Mose.

25. How do you think "Mose" might be different if similes and imagery were not used?

Critical Thinking

26. What does Mary Pope Osborne want readers to think of Mose? Explain.

27. What do you think happened to Mose after he disappeared? Why do you think this?

28. Do you think the old volunteer really sees Mose again?

29. Do you agree that Mose is a hero? Why or why not?

Thinking Creatively

30. If you were Mose, what would you have done when you saw the steam engine? Explain.

Grammar Check

Correct writing contains subjects and verbs that agree. Subject-verb agreement means that the verb form matches the subject. A singular subject takes a singular verb. A plural subject takes a plural verb.

Examples:

She talks so loudly that my ears hurt.
  (singular subject, singular verb)

They talk on the phone every Saturday.
  (plural subject, plural verb)

Rewrite each sentence using the correct verb in parentheses.

1 I (want, wants) to have pie for dessert.

2 Keisha (like, likes) to have a snack after school.

3 Carmit (stand, stands) at a tall desk while writing.

4 Brenda and Eddie (work, works) at the diner on weekends.

 Vocabulary Builder

Synonyms are words that mean the same thing. Find a synonym for each of these words from "Mose." Write each original word and its synonym on a sheet of paper.

1 brawny   **4** eerie

2 mansion   **5** valiant

3 vandal   **6** collapsed

 Writing on Your Own

Write your own legend about a real person whom you admire. This person can be alive today or can be someone from history. Focus on the heroic actions of this person. Entertain your readers with vivid details and exaggeration.

 Listening and Speaking

Write and deliver a speech urging New York to honor Mose Humphreys with a statue. Include the following in your speech:

• Explain what Mose gave to New York.

• Use persuasive language, writing that urges people to think like you.

• Mention specific details that support your opinion.

 Media and Viewing

Look online and in your library for images of New York City in the 1840s and 1850s. Prepare a short talk for your classmates about what the city was like when Mose was alive. Use the images you find to illustrate your presentation.

Choice: A Tribute to Martin Luther King, Jr.   *by Alice Walker*

Alice Walker
1944–

Objectives

◆ To read and
   understand an
   address
◆ To identify
   influences on an
   author's writing

About the Author

Alice Walker's childhood in the rural South had a lasting effect on her writing. Walker's parents loved to tell her stories. She later called her mother "a walking history of our community."

As a college student, Walker became involved in the civil rights movement. She took part in marches and voter-registration drives. By the end of the 1960s, Walker had started her writing career. Since then, she has written essays, novels, and poems. Many of Walker's stories examine the lives of rural African American women. Her novel *The Color Purple* won both a Pulitzer Prize and a National Book Award. It was made into a major motion picture directed by Steven Spielberg.

About the Selection

Martin Luther King, Jr. was an important leader of the civil rights movement. He believed in using peaceful ways for African Americans to gain equal rights.

In "Choice: A Tribute to Martin Luther King, Jr." Alice Walker describes Dr. King's leadership during the civil rights movement. She also argues that he helped African Americans appreciate the history of their people.

Literary Terms "Choice: A Tribute to Martin Luther King, Jr." is an **address.** This is another term for a speech, which is a written work meant to be read aloud. In "Choice," the author Alice Walker was affected by the words and actions of Martin Luther King, Jr. An **author's influences** are the people, experiences, and works of literature and art that affect a writer's choices. As you read, note details in the work that show the author's values or attitudes. Also pay attention to cultural influences that might have shaped the author's viewpoints.

address another term for a speech; a written work meant to be read aloud

author's influences the people, experiences, and works of literature and art that affect a writer's choices

Reading on Your Own When you set a purpose for reading, you determine your focus before reading. Once you have set a purpose, adjust your reading rate according to that goal. When you read to learn new information, read slowly and carefully. Take time to think about what you have just read. Reread the passage, if necessary. When you read for entertainment, you can read more quickly. You may still choose to reread certain passages to understand them better.

Writing on Your Own Walker describes watching a television broadcast of Dr. King being arrested. You probably have seen or read about many news events in your life. Write a paragraph to explain one news event and how it affected you.

Vocabulary Focus In her address, Walker uses the titles *Jr.* and *Dr.* Like many titles, these are abbreviations. These shortened titles are capitalized and followed by a period. Identify the full words these titles come from: *Dr., Jr., Mr., Mrs.,* and *Esq.* Use a dictionary for help if you need to. Then write each title and its full word on a sheet of paper.

Think Before You Read Why do you think Martin Luther King, Jr. is considered a hero by many people?

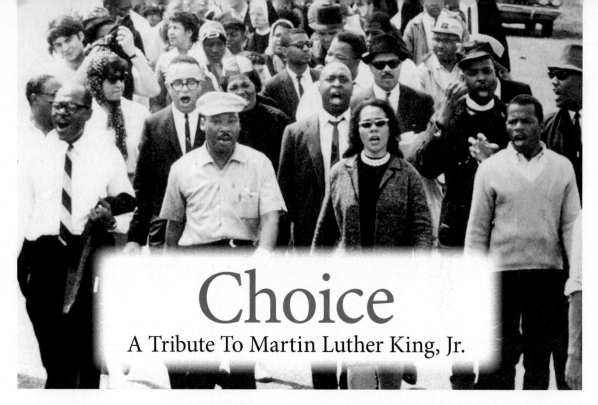

Choice

A Tribute To Martin Luther King, Jr.

This address was made in 1973 at a Jackson, Mississippi, restaurant that had refused to serve people of color until forced to do so by the civil rights movement a few years before.

As you read, think about how Walker's family history has influenced her writing.

My great-great-great-grandmother walked as a slave from Virginia to Eatonton, Georgia—which passes for the Walker **ancestral** home—with two babies on her hips. She lived to be a hundred and twenty-five years old and my own father knew her as a boy. (It is in memory of this walk that I choose to keep and to embrace my "maiden" name, Walker.)

There is a cemetery near our family church where she is buried; but because her marker was made of wood and rotted years ago, it is impossible to tell exactly where her body lies. In the same cemetery are most of my mother's people, who have lived in Georgia for so long nobody even remembers when they came. And all of my great-aunts and -uncles are there, and my grandfather and grandmother, and, very recently, my own father.

ancestral relating to a person's own family

If it is true that land does not belong to anyone until they have buried a body in it, then the land of my birthplace belongs to me, dozens of times over. Yet the history of my family, like that of all black Southerners, is a history of **dispossession.** We loved the land and worked the land, but we never owned it; and even if we bought land, as my great-grandfather did after the Civil War, it was always in danger of being taken away, as his was, during the period following Reconstruction.

My father **inherited** nothing of material value from his father, and when I came of age in the early sixties I awoke to the bitter knowledge that in order just to continue to love the land of my birth, I was expected to leave it. For black people— including my parents—had learned a long time ago that to stay willingly in a beloved but **brutal** place is to risk losing the love and being forced to **acknowledge** only the brutality.

It is a part of the black Southern **sensibility** that we treasure memories; for such a long time, that is all of our homeland those of us who at one time or another were forced away from it have been allowed to have.

I watched my brothers, one by one, leave our home and leave the South. I watched my sisters do the same. This was not unusual; abandonment, except for memories, was the common thing, except for those who "could not do any better," or those whose strength or stubbornness was so **colossal** they took the risk that others could not bear.

In 1960, my mother bought a television set, and each day after school I watched Hamilton Holmes and Charlayne Hunter as they struggled to **integrate**—fair-skinned as they were—the University of Georgia. And then, one day, there appeared the face of Dr. Martin Luther King, Jr. What a funny

Reconstruction means rebuilding. This is the name given to the period right after the Civil War. Southern cities, railroads, and homes had been destroyed during the war and had to be rebuilt. By 1877, Reconstruction had come to an end.

In 1961, Holmes and Hunter became the University of Georgia's first African-American students.

dispossession something that has been given up or is no longer owned	**brutal** cruel	**colossal** huge
	acknowledge to admit to be true	**integrate** to make public places available to people of all races
inherited received something after the former owner dies	**sensibility** a way of thinking and feeling about the world	

name, I thought. At the moment I first saw him, he was being handcuffed and shoved into a police truck. He had dared to claim his rights as a native son, and had been arrested. He displayed no fear, but seemed calm and **serene,** unaware of his own extraordinary courage. His whole body, like his **conscience,** was at peace.

At the moment I saw his resistance I knew I would never be able to live in this country without resisting everything that sought to **disinherit** me, and I would never be forced away from the land of my birth without a fight.

He was The One, The Hero, The One Fearless Person for whom we had waited. I hadn't even realized before that we had been waiting for Martin Luther King, Jr., but we *had.* And I knew it for sure when my mother added his name to the list of people she prayed for every night.

I sometimes think that it was **literally** the prayers of people like my mother and father, who had bowed down in the struggle for such a long time, that kept Dr. King alive until five years ago. For years we went to bed praying for his life, and awoke with the question "Is the 'Lord' still here?"

The public acts of Dr. King you know. They are visible all around you. His voice you would recognize sooner than any other voice you have heard in this century—this in spite of the fact that certain **municipal** libraries, like the one in downtown Jackson, do not carry recordings of his speeches, and the librarians chuckle cruelly when asked why they do not.

You know, if you have read his books, that his is a complex and **revolutionary philosophy** that few people are capable of understanding fully or have the patience to **embody** in themselves. Which is our weakness, which is our loss.

Reading Strategy:
Text Structure

How do the images on these pages help your understanding of the story?

In 1965, King organized a peaceful march from Selma to Montgomery, Alabama. White policemen tried to stop the marchers. After this, friends told King to give up the fight. Instead, he organized another march. He left Selma with 3,200 people. Four days and 50 miles later, they arrived in Montgomery, 25,000 people strong. Five months later, President Lyndon Johnson signed the Voting Rights Act.

---

serene calm

conscience a sense of right and wrong

disinherit to take away from

literally word for word without exaggeration

municipal public; belonging to a town or city

revolutionary bringing or causing great changes to society

philosophy a system of thoughts and ideas

embody to stand for; to be a symbol of

And if you know anything about good Baptist preaching, you can imagine what you missed if you never had a chance to hear Martin Luther King, Jr., preach at Ebeneezer Baptist Church.

You know of the prizes and awards that he tended to think very little of. And you know of his concern for the disinherited: the American Indian, the Mexican-American, and the poor American white—for whom he cared much.

You know that this very room, in this very restaurant, was closed to people of color not more than five years ago. And that we eat here together tonight largely through his efforts and his blood. We accept the common pleasures of life, **assuredly,** in his name.

But add to all of these things the one thing that seems to me second to none in importance: He gave us back our **heritage**. He gave us back our homeland; the bones and dust of our ancestors, who may now sleep within our caring *and* our hearing. He gave us the blueness of the Georgia sky in autumn as in summer; the colors of the Southern winter as well as glimpses of the green of vacation-time spring. Those of our relatives we used to invite for a visit we now can ask to stay. . . . He gave us full-time use of our woods, and **restored** our memories to those of us who were forced to run away, as realities we might each day enjoy and leave for our children.

He gave us **continuity** of place, without which community is **ephemeral.** He gave us home.

1973

> Why does Walker call Dr. King a hero on page 556? What did he do that made him heroic?

> *Reading Strategy:*
> **Text Structure**
>
> How does the text structure show the importance of Dr. King to people like Walker?

assuredly certainly; confidently

heritage what is handed down from one generation to the next

restored brought back

continuity the act of going on without stopping

ephemeral lasting for a very short time

Choice: A Tribute to Martin Luther King, Jr.   by Alice Walker

Directions Choose the letter of the best answer or write the answer using complete sentences.

Comprehension: Identifying Facts

1. Where did Walker first see Dr. King?
   A in church
   B in a restaurant
   C on television
   D at a protest march

2. Why did Walker keep her "maiden" name?

3. Why was King being arrested when Walker first saw him?

Comprehension: Putting Ideas Together

4. Where is Walker making this address?
   A in a church
   B in a restaurant
   C in a library
   D in a theater

5. According to Walker, why do many African Americans feel the need to leave their birthplace?

6. What important things did Dr. King give to all African Americans?

Understanding Literature: Author's Influences

Many things influence the choices a writer makes. Influences include important events, people they know or admire, and works of art. Every life experience a person has can affect what he or she writes about. These experiences become part of a writer's memory. Many writers agree that their best work is about what they know. They use their influences and experience to create true works of literature.

7. How did King's example influence Walker as a person and a writer?

8. How did Walker's parents influence her writing?

Critical Thinking

9. Given the African-American experience in the South, why does Walker describe it as "homeland"?

Thinking Creatively

10. What do you think is Walker's most important message? Restate this message in your own words.

Grammar Check

There are many different reasons to use capital letters. Capitalize a word if it:

- begins a sentence
  Example: <u>E</u>veryone admires a hero.

- is a proper noun
  Example: <u>M</u>artin <u>L</u>uther <u>K</u>ing, Jr. fought for civil rights.

- is the pronoun <u>I</u>
  Example: Tomorrow <u>I</u> will read it and give you my answer.

- is a person's title
  Example: Does <u>M</u>r. <u>V</u>argas ever call on you in class?

On a sheet of paper, rewrite each sentence using the correct capitalization.

1 i enjoyed reading that legend.

2 that's a question i have to ask captain schultz.

3 can we travel to london with miss fitch?

 Vocabulary Builder

"Choice: A Tribute to Martin Luther King, Jr." includes the words *inherited, disinherit,* and *heritage.* These words all come from the same Latin root *heri-,* which means *yesterday.* The English language contains many examples of such "word families."

Look up each root word listed below and read its definition. Then, on a sheet of paper, write two new words that contain the root word.

1 sens

2 script

3 gram

4 cycle

 Writing on Your Own

Write a speech for the dedication of a monument to Dr. King. The speech should celebrate King's leadership in the struggle for civil rights. Explain why King's ideas are still important today.

 Listening and Speaking

In pairs, role-play an interview with a civil rights marcher who followed Dr. King. One person should play the interviewer and the other should play the marcher. Prepare by reading first-person accounts of King's participation in historic events. Then practice the role-play and present it to your class.

 Media and Viewing

Prepare a photo essay about Martin Luther King, Jr. Research King's role in the civil rights movement and the difficulties he faced. Use both your words and your images to show why people still view King as a hero today.

Word Choice

In this unit, you have read selections that are part of the oral tradition. As these stories were told, the storytellers and authors chose their words carefully so that people would want to keep listening.

About Word Choice

American writer Mark Twain once wrote, "Use the right word, not its second cousin." Twain was referring to the importance of word choice. Writers must make choices every time they sit down to work. They know how important it is to choose the words that say what they mean.

A writer's first job is to make you want to know more about what they have to say. This means writers have to think carefully about the words they choose. They want to make their writing interesting and vivid. They want it to be dramatic and colorful.

Reading Skill

When you read stories, you analyze word choice. Writers of real and imaginary stories try to appeal to all five senses. They want to bring new and unfamiliar worlds to life for you. As you read, look at the descriptive details. Note the nouns and vivid adjectives that help draw you into a story.

This chart shows some examples of strong and poor word choice.

Poor Word Choice	Why It's Poor	Strong Word Choice
It was very cold.	too vague and too general; does not give a specific idea of how cold it is	I could see my breath like smoke in the frosty air.
I was very thirsty.	dull sentence; use of the vague word *very*	My throat was as dry as sandpaper.
He was really happy to see me.	vague words; does not show how the person truly feels	His eyes lit up like stars in the sky when I walked through the door.
This job is as easy as pie.	popular saying; boring	This job is so simple my little brother could do it.

The examples on the following pages show the same story. One example is written with dull, everyday language. The other has a more descriptive use of words. Read each piece to see if you can decide which has the stronger word choice.

A Snowy Morning

Stan opened his eyes and blinked sleepily. Something seemed different. Where were all the familiar street noises—the wagon wheels trundling on the cobbled streets, and the peddlers selling their wares?

Stan wriggled out of his cocoon of blankets and padded over to the window. He pushed back the rough, thick drapes and stared out at an unfamiliar world. Yesterday the soft snowflakes had floated lazily through the air like white dandelion seeds. Today, the street was buried under a heavy blanket of white.

Stan cracked his hairbrush against the ice in the basin. The icy water on his face woke him up. He dressed hastily and burst into the kitchen.

Mama poured him a cup of steaming tea. Stan cradled the thick white china in both hands and sipped. Mama smiled at him. "The bread didn't come today," she apologized. "No one can get through this snow."

Stan gulped the rest of his tea and rose. "I can get through!" he asserted.

Stan hauled his sled down the street, sliding along on the hard-packed snow. The scent of fresh bread wafted tantalizingly toward him along the street.

Stan tugged open the bakery door. Dozens of fresh loaves confronted him. They were piled on the counter like building blocks. Mr. Rindelaub shuffled in from the back. His tired eyes lit up at the sight of a customer.

"You are the only brave one in the neighborhood!" he told Stan. "And what will happen to all the day's bread?"

"I'll deliver it for you, since no one has come out in the snow! Just tell me who gets which loaves," said Stan. "I can deliver it all."

A Snowy Morning

Stan woke up. Something seemed different. Where were all the familiar street noises? He couldn't hear anything coming from outside.

Stan got out of bed and went over to the window. He moved the drapes and stared out at an unfamiliar world. It had begun to snow yesterday, but not hard. But it must have snowed a lot during the night. Today, the street was buried under a heavy fall of snow.

Stan broke the ice in the basin of water so that he could wash his face. He dressed quickly and went into the kitchen for his tea and toast.

Mama quickly poured him a cup of tea. Stan held the cup in both hands and sipped. Mama smiled at him. "The bread didn't come today," she apologized. "I think no one can get through this snow."

Stan drank the rest of his tea and got up from the table. "I can get through!" he said.

Stan got out his sled and left the building. He walked carefully along the surface of the hard-packed snow. It was a little hard to keep his balance. He could smell the fresh bread from a block away. He walked toward the source of the good smell.

Stan opened the bakery door. Dozens of fresh loaves were piled on the counter. Mr. Rindelaub walked in from the back. He was pleased to see Stan.

"You are the only brave one in the neighborhood!" he told him. "I don't know what will happen to all of today's bread. It will go stale if no one comes for it. My delivery boy could not get here today."

"I'll deliver it for you, since no one has come out in the snow! Just tell me who gets which loaves," said Stan. "I can deliver it all."

Monitor Your Progress

Directions Choose the letter of the best answer or write the answer using complete sentences.

1. Which detail gives a sense of the time period in which this story is set?
   A "wagon wheels trundling on cobbled streets"
   B "snowflakes floated lazily through the air"
   C "Mama quickly poured him a cup of tea."
   D "He could smell the fresh bread from a block away."

2. Which type of figurative language appears only in the first example?
   A similes
   B allusions
   C characterization
   D nonfiction

3. Which story gives you a better sense of the characters? Why?

4. Contrast the two versions of the story. Point out at least three differences in the story details.

5. Which version of the story did you enjoy more? Explain your answer.

Writing on Your Own

Write a short story about a special or unusual morning that you remember. Use nouns and vivid adjectives to show the right mood.

COMPARING LITERARY WORKS | Build Understanding

The Deserted Children   by Gros Ventre Indians of Montana

Objectives

◆ To read and understand a legend

◆ To compare and contrast a legend and an address

◆ To compare and contrast themes in fiction and nonfiction

About the Authors

The Gros Ventre tribe has close ties to the Arapaho Indians and Cheyenne Indians. These Northern Plains Indians first came from the Saskatchewan River area of Canada. They moved to the area that is now Montana around the end of the 1700s. The Gros Ventre settled on the Fort Belknap Reservation in Montana. Today they still celebrate two traditional ceremonies, the Feathered Pipe and the Flat Pipe.

About the Selection

In "The Deserted Children," an American Indian tribe moves on, leaving two children behind. The children discover that they have magic powers. They find food and build a comfortable tepee. They then take revenge on the tribe that abandoned them.

"The Deserted Children" is a legend and is **fiction.** "Choice: A Tribute to Martin Luther King, Jr." is a **nonfiction** address that recalls memories of a real-life hero. In both selections, characters deal with cruel actions by others. Look back at "Choice" on page 554. Think about how African Americans had to deal with being treated in an awful way. As you read "The Deserted Children," notice how the brother and sister respond to cruel actions as well.

Literary Terms A **theme** is the main idea of a literary work. A theme is often an important lesson about life that the author wants readers to remember. A **universal theme** appears in many times, places, and cultures.

Reading on Your Own Recall the selection "Choice: A Tribute to Martin Luther King, Jr." that you read earlier in this unit. How would you describe the important theme or themes of that selection? As you read "The Deserted Children," think about its theme or themes. Compare them to the themes found in "Choice."

Writing on Your Own "Choice" is about a real person. "The Deserted Children" is an American Indian tale that is fiction. Think about the differences between fiction and nonfiction. Write a short paragraph explaining how fiction and nonfiction can be part of the oral tradition.

Vocabulary Focus Study the boldfaced vocabulary words before you read the story. Work with a partner as you study these words. Read each word and its definition out loud. Also write each word correctly on a sheet of paper. Reviewing the vocabulary words ahead of time will help you as you read the selection.

Think Before You Read In "The Deserted Children," the children want to take revenge on, or get back at, their parents. Is revenge always the best choice? Explain.

fiction writing that is imaginative and designed to entertain

nonfiction writing about real people and events

theme the main idea of a literary work

universal theme a main idea that appears in many times, places, and cultures

The Deserted Children

As you read, think about the themes that are present in the story.

Indians sewed animal hides together and draped them over poles to make a tepee. A tepee looks very much like a tent. Plains tribes, like the Gros Ventre, often moved from place to place. The tepee was a good type of housing for them because it was easy to move.

One day a little boy and his sister, returning from play, found only **smoldering** campfires where their village had been. Deep in the distance the people could still be seen, traveling farther and farther away. As they hurried to catch up, the children found a tepee pole that had been dropped by their parents. "Mother!" they shouted. "Here is one of your poles!" But the parents were moving to a new camp and had left the children on purpose, not caring for them, and from far away came the **faint** answer, "Never mind, you are not my child!"

The sister kept stopping to help her little brother, who was too young to keep going, and the two were soon left far behind. She led him to a **thicket** and, making him a bed of **boughs,** left him there to rest while she cut brush and built a small shelter. From then on they lived in this shelter, eating berries and roots gathered by the child-mother. Many summers passed. The children grew older.

One day, as the girl was looking out of their little lodge, she saw a herd of elk going by, and she exclaimed, "Brother, look at the elk! So many!"

smoldering burning and smoking without flames

thicket bushes or small trees growing close together

boughs branches from a tree

faint not clear, dim

Homeward Bound, E. Martin Hennings, ca. 1933–1934

The boy was sitting with his head bowed. His eyes were cast downward, because he was now old enough to feel ashamed of living alone with his sister, and without looking up he replied, "Sister, it will do us no good if I look at them."

But she **insisted.** Then the boy raised his head and looked at the elk, and they all fell dead in their tracks.

insisted refused to give in

Reading Strategy:
Text Structure

How is text structure used to keep you interested in the story?

Reading Strategy:
Text Structure

What is the effect of the repeating events in the story?

The girl went out, skinned and butchered the elk, and carried the flesh and hides into the lodge. Looking at the pile of meat, she said, "I wish this meat were dried," and no sooner were the words out of her mouth than it was all perfectly dried. Lifting a hide and shaking it, she said, "I wish these hides were tanned," and so they were. She spread a number of them on the ground and murmured to herself, "I wish these were sewn into a tepee cover," and behold! there was a fine large tepee cover lying where the unsewn skins had been. Later the same day a herd of buffalo appeared, and she cried, "Brother! Look at the buffalo!"

"Why do you want me to look at those buffalo?" he protested **peevishly.** But she insisted, and when at last he raised his head, they too fell dead. Then she skinned them and brought the hides into the brush lodge, where she spread out a few and said, "I wish these hides were tanned into fine robes." Immediately they became what she wished. Then to the other skins she addressed the same magic words, and they became soft robes decorated with paintings. Now that she had everything she needed, she built and arranged her tepee.

One day the girl saw a raven flying by, and she called out, "Raven, take this piece of buffalo fat and go to the camp of my tribe, and when you fly over, drop it in the center of the camp circle and say, 'There is plenty to eat at the old campsite!'"

The raven took the fat and flew to the faraway camp. There he saw all the young men playing the wheel game, and dropping his burden, he croaked, "There is plenty to eat at the old campsite!" It happened that at this time there was a **famine** in the village, and when the words of the raven were heard, the head chief ordered some young men to go to the old camp to see what they could find. The scouts set forth, and where the old camp had been they saw a fine elk-skin lodge with racks of meat swinging in the wind and buffalo grazing

---

peevishly very cross or upset

famine a lack of food that causes much starvation

on the surrounding hills. When the chief heard their report, he immediately told his crier to give the order to break camp.

When a new camp had been made near the elk-skin tepee, the father and the mother of the girl quickly discovered that it belonged to their daughter, and they went to her, calling, "My daughter! My daughter!" But she answered, "Keep back! You are not my father, and you are not my mother, for when I found the lodge poles and cried out to you not to leave me, you went on, saying that I was no daughter of yours!"

After a while, however, she seemed to forgive them, and calling all the people around her, she divided among them a large quantity of boiled buffalo tongues. She asked her parents to sit by her side. Meanwhile, her brother had been sitting with his head bowed.

Suddenly the girl cried, "Brother, look at these people! They are the ones who **deserted** us!"

She repeated her words twice, but the boy would not look up. At the fourth command he raised his head slowly, and as he looked around, the people fell lifeless.

Then the girl said, "Let a few of the men and women return to life, so that the tribe may grow again, but let their characters be changed. Let the people be better than they were." Immediately some of them came to life, and the tribe increased, and their hearts were good.

deserted left behind
or abandoned

The Deserted Children   by Gros Ventre Indians of Montana

Directions Choose the letter of the best answer or write the answer using complete sentences.

Comprehension: Identifying Facts

1. What magic power does the girl in this story have?
   A A look from her eyes can kill.
   B Whatever she wishes for comes true.
   C She can take care of her brother.
   D She can understand the speech of animals.

2. What powers does the boy have?

3. What does the girl tell the raven to do?

Comprehension: Putting Ideas Together

4. Why are the two children left behind?
   A They were away from camp when the tribe began to move.
   B The little brother cannot walk fast enough.
   C They stop to pick up their mother's tepee pole.
   D They cannot see where the rest of the tribe went.

5. Both the girl in this story and Alice Walker deal with troubles at home. How are their situations alike and different?

6. Describe the difference in the girl's actions and the actions taken by Dr. King in "Choice." Which do you admire more? Why?

Understanding Literature: Theme

Theme is a part of both fiction and nonfiction writing. A story's theme is the most important message the writer wants the reader to understand. Sometimes the theme of a story is universal. This means that the same message is found across time periods and in different cultures.

7. How do the characters and actions of the children affect the story's theme?

8. Are the themes in "The Deserted Children" and "Choice" universal? Explain.

Critical Thinking

9. Identify one lesson taught in "The Deserted Children." Do you agree with this lesson? Explain.

Thinking Creatively

10. How do you think Dr. King would react to the lesson in "The Deserted Children"? Explain.

Grammar Check

Writers use quotation marks for many different reasons. Three of the uses for quotation marks are listed below:

- to set off a speaker's exact words
  Example: "Come along, then!" she said.

- around the title of a short poem, short story, or work of art
  Example: "The Raven" "Jingle Bells"

- to set off a title or quotation within a quotation (use single quotation marks for the inside title or quotation)
  Example: "She said 'There is plenty to eat at the old campsite!'" croaked the raven.

On a sheet of paper, rewrite each sentence using quotation marks correctly.

1 I don't understand you at all, I said angrily.

2 I have to recite The Bells in class tomorrow, said Tommy.

Vocabulary Builder

It is a good idea to review new vocabulary words. This will help you to better remember the meanings of these words. Review the definition of each word below from "The Deserted Children." On a sheet of paper, write a paragraph containing all of the words. Be sure to use each word correctly.

1 smoldering
2 peevishly
3 famine
4 insisted
5 thicket

Writing on Your Own

The girl in "The Deserted Children" takes revenge on her tribe. How did Dr. King feel about taking revenge on those who hurt his people? Write a short essay to compare and contrast the attitudes of the girl and of Dr. King. Then explain whose point of view you agree with more.

Listening and Speaking

Read "The Deserted Children" aloud to a group of younger students. Change the tone and volume of your voice for dramatic effect as you read. When you are finished reading, encourage students to ask questions about the story.

Research and Technology

Use your library to find another story or fairy tale about children who are left behind. Read the story. Then write an e-mail message to your teacher. Explain how "The Deserted Children" and the story you found are similar and different.

In many words, the vowel sound in one or more syllables is not clear. These unclear vowel sounds can cause spelling problems.

How Do You Spell "Uh"?

Words like *dislocate* do not often cause spelling problems—you can clearly hear the vowel in each syllable. However, the vowel sound "uh" can be spelled with any vowel. For example, the *a* in *obstacle* sounds like the *i* in *hesitate*.

Notice the unstressed syllables in the words on the list. Then notice which vowels are used in spelling them.

Practice

Add the correct letters to complete each word. Write each word on a sheet of paper. Then, use each word in a sentence.

1. hes__tate
2. ben__factor
3. pleas__nt
4. ep__logue
5. barg__n
6. buoy__nt
7. syll__ble
8. __djourn
9. p__rsue
10. __non__m__s

Word List
adjourn
anonymous
bargain
benefactor
buoyant
epilogue
hesitate
pleasant
pursue
syllable

obstacle hesitate

I always hesitate when spelling the uh sound.

yeah that uh sound is a real obstacle for me too.

In Unit 6, you read a number of folktales. "Folk" is from the German word for "people." Folktales, legends, and myths are the literature of the people. These are stories that people have told and retold through the generations. Each time the story is told, it changes just a little. This is an important part of the oral tradition.

Folktales often feature folk heroes. Sometimes these heroes are real people. "Mose" is an example of a folk hero who was a real person. Martin Luther King, Jr., the subject in "Choice," is also a hero. He is a real-life hero, not a folk hero.

Exaggeration, or hyperbole, is common in folktales. People want their stories to be entertaining. Therefore, they often stretch the facts to make the story more exciting. This makes the heroes look braver and their deeds more amazing.

Selections

■ "Coyote Steals the Sun and Moon," retold by Richard Erdoes and Alfonso Ortiz, is a Zuni myth. It explains how the winter season came to be.

■ "Brer Possum's Dilemma" by Jackie Torrence is a folktale where Brer Possum comes across Brer Snake. It cautions readers not to go looking for trouble.

■ "John Henry" is a folktale in ballad form. It tells the story of a hero who challenged a machine.

■ "Davy Crockett's Dream" by Davy Crockett is a tall tale. When he goes hunting, Crockett has a vivid dream.

■ "Mose" by Mary Pope Osborne is a legend. It recounts the life of New York City firefighter Mose Humphreys.

■ "Choice: A Tribute to Martin Luther King, Jr." by Alice Walker is an address. Walker describes how Martin Luther King, Jr.'s actions influenced her life.

■ "The Deserted Children" is an American Indian legend about children who are left behind by their parents.

Directions Choose the letter of the best answer or write the answer using complete sentences.

Comprehension: Identifying Facts

1. Which selection is a myth?
 A "Brer Possum's Dilemma"
 B "Mose"
 C "John Henry"
 D "Coyote Steals the Sun and Moon"

2. In "Coyote Steals the Sun and Moon," what does Eagle tell Coyote when he gives him the box to carry?

3. In "Brer Possum's Dilemma" why does Brer Snake ask Brer Possum to put him in his pocket?

4. Why does the steam drill in "John Henry" lose the race?

5. Why is the brother in "The Deserted Children" ashamed?

Comprehension: Putting Ideas Together

6. Which does Coyote **not** ask Eagle to do?
 A go hunting with him
 B give him the box to carry
 C help him find a light source
 D help him out of a hole

7. Name one important way in which Brer Possum and Brer Snake are alike.

8. What happens to Davy Crockett in his dream?

9. Why does Alice Walker admire Martin Luther King, Jr.?

10. Why does the sister in "The Deserted Children" send the raven to bring the tribe back?

Understanding Literature: Oral Tradition

The oral tradition includes works that were told and retold before being written down. Many of these stories include big, strong heroes or animals that can talk. These stories often are written in dialect and sound the way people actually speak. Tales from the oral tradition usually are entertaining and have an important message. Myths, part of the oral tradition, explain how the world came to be. Folktales and legends tell stories of heroes who are larger than life.

11. How are "Coyote Steals the Sun and Moon" and "Brer Possum's Dilemma" alike? How are they different?

12. Identify two selections from this unit that contain dialect. How would the stories be different without dialect?

13. Give examples of repeated words and phrases in "John Henry." What effect does the repetition have on the ballad?

14. Is Davy Crockett a hero? Explain.

15. Explain why Martin Luther King, Jr. might be considered a folk hero.

Critical Thinking

16. Do you think the lesson in "Brer Possum's Dilemma" is important today? Explain.

17. Do you think the characters of Mose and John Henry could trade places in their stories? Why or why not?

18. Why do you think the children want to get back at their parents in "The Deserted Children"?

Thinking Creatively

19. Which hero in this unit did you admire the most? Explain.

20. Which character from this unit would you ask for help if you were in trouble? Why?

Speak and Listen

Choose a main character from one of the selections in this unit. Make up a new tale about this character. Make sure that the events of your tale fit the character. For example, any tale about Mose should include actions needing great strength. When you finish your tale, share the story with your class.

Writing on Your Own

Write a research report about any of the major characters from the unit. There are many tales about John Henry and Coyote. Davy Crockett and Mose were real people. Find out more about your subject's place in folk literature. Identify other tales and the regions they come from.

Beyond Words

Create illustrations to go along with any of the selections in this unit. Go online or look through collections in the library for ideas.

Test-Taking Tip

After you have completed a test, reread each question and answer. Ask yourself: Have I answered the question that was asked? Have I answered it completely?

Exposition: Cause-and-Effect Essay

Almost anything that happens involves causes and effects. A cause-and-effect essay analyzes why something happened and considers its results. Follow the steps outlined in this workshop to write your own cause-and-effect essay.

Assignment Write a cause-and-effect essay about a question that interests you.

What to Include Your essay should feature the following parts:

- a clear and appropriate organization

- an explanation of how one or more events or situations resulted in another event or situation

- a thorough presentation of facts and details that support the explanation presented

- an effective conclusion

- error-free grammar, including properly punctuated quotations

Prewriting
Choosing Your Topic
Self-interview To find topics that interest you, ask yourself questions such as these:

- What is my favorite book? What natural or historical events are important to the story?

- What interesting facts have I learned in science class?

- Which political leader do I admire most? What was happening in the world when he or she was in office?

- What invention am I most grateful for?

Review your answers to choose a topic.

Using the Form
You may use parts of this form in these types of writing:
- historical essays
- news reports
- science reports

Six Traits of Writing:
Ideas message, details, and purpose

Narrowing Your Topic

Make sure your topic is narrow enough for you to cover in depth. Take time to jot down subtopics for your broad topic. Continue this process until you pinpoint a subject for your writing.

Sample Topic: NASA technology

   Subtopic: Satellites

      Subtopic: Benefit to average citizen

         Subtopic: Improvement to cell phone communication

Gathering Details

Conduct research. Gather facts, examples, and details that will illustrate cause-and-effect relationships. A K-W-L Chart like the one shown is an excellent tool for planning and guiding your research.

K-W-L Chart		
What I **K**now	What I **W**ant to Know	What I **L**earned
• Air pollution is increasing and dangerous. • Pollution smells bad. • Cars and factories cause it. • It hurts people and animals.	• How can it be reduced? • What causes it besides cars and factories? • Which countries or cities are the worst? • How can we stop it? • What does it do to people? To animals?	

Writing Your Draft

Shaping Your Writing

Focus and organize your ideas. Review your research, and circle the main causes and effects. Identify which description below best fits your topic. Then, organize your information accordingly.

Six Traits of Writing:
Organization order, ideas tied together

Providing Elaboration

Prove the connection. Convince your audience that causes and effects are not coincidence. Add details to elaborate on the link you are showing.

Weak connection: The stores were crowded the weekend before the holiday.

Cause-and-effect connection: With the pressure of last-minute shopping, the stores were crowded before the holiday.

Include personal experiences. Interview people who have experience related to your subject. Use their comments to help explain your ideas. Their stories can provide an interesting slant to facts or studies you may mention.

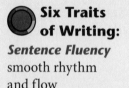

Six Traits of Writing:
Sentence Fluency
smooth rhythm and flow

Revising

Revising Your Paragraphs

Use transitions to show connections. Your goal is to prove the link between a cause and its effects. Transition words can help make the relationship between cause and effect obvious to your readers. Use transition words and phrases like these to clarify connections:

Introducing Causes: *since, if, because, as soon as, until*

Introducing Effects: *therefore, as a result, subsequently, then*

Revising Your Word Choice

Define key terms for your audience. Make sure you have expressed your ideas clearly. Follow these steps:

1. Reread your essay, circling any terms that your audience may not know.

2. Provide more background information or definitions where necessary. Review your research notes or reference materials as needed.

Editing and Proofreading

Check grammar, usage, and mechanics to make sure that your final draft is error-free.

Focus on Prepositions: Whenever possible, avoid ending a sentence with a preposition.

Draft: Which friend are you traveling **with?**

Revised: **With** which friend are you traveling? OR Who is traveling **with** you?

Publishing and Presenting

Consider one of the following ways to share your writing:

- **Present a speech.** Offer to speak to classes or clubs that can benefit from your work.

- **Publish a feature article.** Submit your essay to your local or school newspaper. Explain to the editor why the issue you address is important to readers.

Reflecting on Your Writing

Writer's Journal Jot down your thoughts on writing a cause-and-effect essay. Begin by answering these questions:

- Did learning about the causes and effects of your topic encourage you to take any action?

- What tips have you used that will help you improve your writing?

Six Traits of Writing:
Conventions correct grammar, spelling, and mechanics

Appendix A: Graphic Organizers

Graphic organizers are like maps. They help guide you through literature. They can also help you plan or "map out" your own stories, research, or presentations.

1. Character Analysis Guide

This graphic organizer helps you learn more about a character in a selection.

To use: Choose a character. List four traits of that character. Write down an event from the selection that shows each character trait.

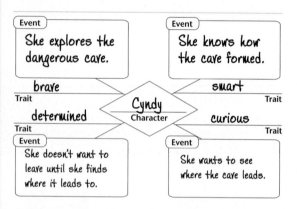

2. Story Map

This graphic organizer helps you summarize a story that you have read or plan your own story.

To use: List the title, setting, and characters. Describe the main problem of the story and the events that explain the problem. Then write how the problem is solved.

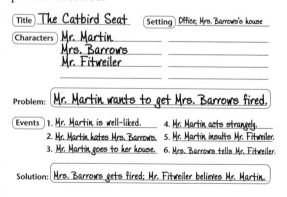

3. Main Idea Graphic (Umbrella)

This graphic organizer helps you determine the main idea of a selection or of a paragraph in the selection.

To use: List the main idea of a selection. Then, write the details that show or support the main idea of the story.

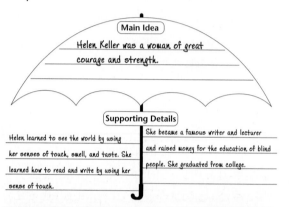

4. Main Idea Graphic (Table)

This graphic organizer is another way to determine the main idea of a selection or of a paragraph in the selection. Just like a table is held up by four strong legs, a main idea is held up or supported by many details.

To use: Write the main idea of a selection or paragraph on the tabletop. Then, write the details that show or support the main idea of the selection or paragraph on the table legs.

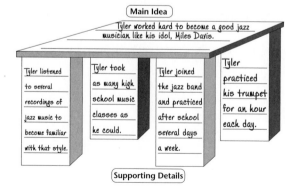

5. Main Idea Graphic (Details)

This graphic organizer is also a way to determine the main idea of a selection or of a paragraph in the selection. If the main idea of a selection or paragraph is not clear, add the details together to find it.

To use: First, list the supporting details of the selection or paragraph. Then, write one sentence that summarizes all the events. That is the main idea of the story.

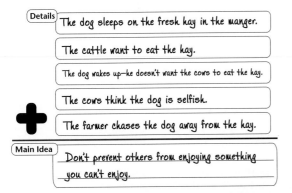

6. Venn Diagram

This graphic organizer can help you compare and contrast two stories, characters, events, or topics.

To use: List the things that are common to both stories, events, characters, and so on in the "similarities" area between the circles. List the differences on the parts that do not overlap.

What is being compared? _____

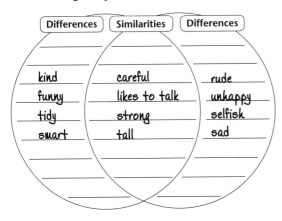

7. Sequence Chain

This graphic organizer outlines a series of events in the order in which they happen. This is helpful when summarizing the plot of a story. This graphic organizer may also help you plan your own story.

To use: Fill in the box at the top with the title of the story. Then, in the boxes below, record the events in the order in which they happen in the story. Write a short sentence in each box and only include the major events of the story.

Sequence Chain for: ___Cinderella___

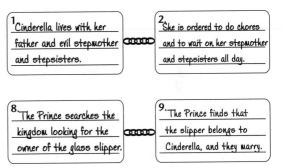

8. Concept Map

This graphic organizer helps you to organize supporting details for a story or research topic.

To use: Write the topic in the center of the graphic organizer. List ideas that support the topic on the lines. Group similar ideas and details together.

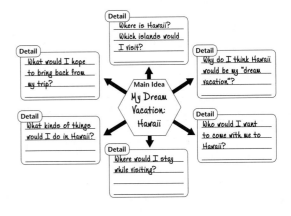

9. Plot Mountain

This graphic organizer helps you organize the events of a story or plot. There are five parts in a story's plot: the exposition, the rising action, the climax, the falling action, and the resolution (or denouement). These parts represent the beginning, middle, and end of the selection.

To use:

- Write the exposition, or how the selection starts, at the left base of the mountain. What is the setting? Who are the characters?
- Then, write the rising action, or the events that lead to the climax, on the left side of the mountain. Start at the base and list the events in time order going up the left side.
- At the top of the mountain, write the climax, or the highest point of interest or suspense. All events in the rising action lead up to this one main event or turning point.
- Write the events that happen after the climax, or falling action, on the right side of the mountain. Start at the top of the mountain, or climax, and put the events in time order going down the right-hand side.
- Finally, write the resolution, or denouement, at the right base of the mountain. The resolution explains how the problem, or conflict, in the story is solved or how the story ends.

10. Structured Overview

This graphic organizer shows you how a main idea branches out in a selection.

To use: Write the main idea of a selection in the top box. Then, branch out and list events and details that support the main idea. Continue to branch off more boxes as needed to fill in the details of the story.

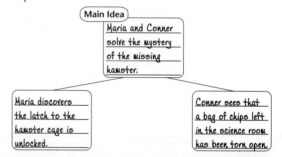

11. Semantic Table

This graphic organizer can help you understand the differences among words that have similar meanings.

To use: Choose a topic. List nouns for that topic in the top row. Put adjectives that describe your topic in the first column. Then, fill in the rest of the grid by checking those adjectives that are appropriate for the nouns. That way, in your writing, you can use words that make sense for your story.

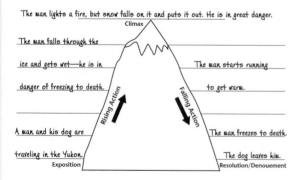

Topic: **Homes**

Adjectives ↓ Nouns→	apartment	4-bedroom home	cabin
large	—	✔	—
expensive	—	✔	—
quiet	—	✔	✔

12. Prediction Guide

This graphic organizer can be used to predict, or try to figure out, how a selection might end. Before finishing a selection, fill in this guide.

To use: List the time, place, and characters in the selection. Write what the problem, or conflict, is in the story. Then, try to predict possible endings or solutions. Compare your predictions with others.

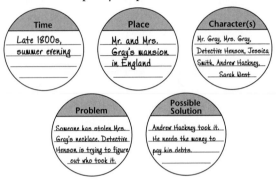

13. Semantic Line

This graphic organizer can help you think of synonyms for words that are used too often in writing.

To use: At the end of each line, write two overused words that mean the opposite. Then, fill in the lines with words of similar meaning. In the example below, the opposite words are *beautiful* and *ugly*. Words that are closer in meaning to beautiful are at the top. Words that are closer in meaning to ugly are at the bottom. The word *plain* falls in the middle.

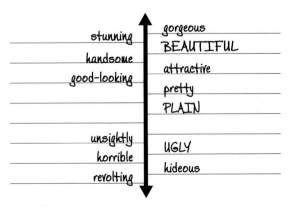

14. KWL Chart

This graphic organizer can help you learn about a topic before you start reading a selection or conducting research.

To use: Before you start reading a selection or conducting research, fill in the organizer. Write the topic on the line. In the first column, write what you already *know* (K) about your topic. Next, list what you *want* (W) to know about your topic in the next column. Then, as you start reading a selection or conducting research, write down what you *learn* (L) in the last column.

Topic: __Mount Everest__

K What I Know	W What I Want to Know	L What I Have Learned
It's a tall mountain in Asia. People may have tried to climb it. It's part of a larger mountain chain. It's one of the most famous mountains in the world.	How tall is it? Is it the tallest? What mountain chain is it part of?	It is the tallest in the world. It is part of the Himalayas. People have climbed it before. Some people have died trying.

Appendix B: Grammar

Parts of Speech

Adjectives

- Adjectives describe nouns and pronouns. They answer *What kind? Which one? How many?* or *How much?* Example: The *new* book costs *five* dollars.

- Comparative adjectives compare two nouns and usually end in *–er*. Example: *newer*

- Superlative adjectives compare three or more nouns and usually end in *–est*. Example: *newest*

Adverbs

- Adverbs modify verbs, adjectives, and other adverbs. They answer *When? How? How often?* and *How long?* Many adverbs end in *–ly*. Example: She laughed *loudly*.

Conjunctions

- Conjunctions connect parts of a sentence.

- Coordinating conjunctions connect two equal parts of a sentence using words like *and, but, nor, or, for, yet, so,* and *as well as.* Example: Do you want milk *or* water?

- Correlative conjunctions are used in pairs and connect equal parts of a sentence. Correlative conjunctions are *both/and, neither/nor, either/or, but/also.* Example: The teenagers had *neither* the time *nor* the money.

- Subordinating conjunctions connect two unequal parts of a sentence using words like *after, although, before, because, since, if, unless, while.* Example: *Since* you are arriving late, we will eat dinner at 7 p.m.

Interjections

- Interjections are words or phrases that show strong feeling, often followed by exclamation points. Examples: Wow! Ouch! Oops!

Nouns

- A noun names a person, place, thing, or idea.

- Proper nouns are names that are capitalized. Examples: Susan, New York

Prepositions

- Prepositions relate nouns and pronouns to other words in a sentence. Examples: above, from, with

Pronouns

- Pronouns replace nouns. Antecedents are the nouns that the pronouns replace. Example: Jorge takes karate lessons, and *he* practices every week.

- Demonstrative pronouns identify particular nouns: *this* hat, *those* shoes

- Indefinite pronouns do not refer to particular nouns. Examples: all, everyone, none

- Interrogative pronouns begin questions. Examples: who, which, what

- Personal pronouns refer to people or things. Examples: I, me, you, it, he, she, we, us, they, him, her, them

- Possessive pronouns show ownership. Examples: my, mine, his, hers, its, our, yours, their, ours, theirs

- Reflexive pronouns follow a verb or preposition and refer to the noun or pronoun that comes before. Examples: myself, themselves, himself, herself

- Relative pronouns introduce a subordinate clause. Examples: who, whom, whose, which, that, what

Verbs

- Verbs show action or express states of being.

- If the verbs are *transitive*, they link the action to something or someone. Example: John *hit* the ball. Action verbs that are *intransitive* do not link the action to something or someone. Example: The ball *flew*.

- Linking verbs connect a subject with a word or words that describe it. Some linking verbs are *am, are, was, were, is,* and *be.* Example: Susan *is* student council president.

Grammar Glossary

Active and Passive Voice

- Active voice is when the subject is *doing* the action. A sentence written in active voice is often shorter and easier to understand. Example: Jane drove the car to school.

- Passive voice is when the subject *receives* the action. A sentence written in passive voice can be awkward. Use a passive sentence only when the doer is unknown or unnecessary. Example: The car was driven by Jane.

Antecedent

- An antecedent is the noun or pronoun that a pronoun refers to in a sentence. Example: *Kevin* ran for Student Council so that *he* could help improve the school. *Kevin* is the antecedent for the pronoun *he.*

Appositives

- An appositive is a noun or pronoun that follows another noun or pronoun. An appositive renames or adds detail about the word. Example: Mr. Smith, *our principal*, is a great leader.

Clauses

- A clause is a group of words that contains a subject and a verb. There are independent and dependent clauses.

- An independent clause can stand alone because it expresses a complete thought. Example: Our dog eats twice a day. She also walks two miles a day. Two independent clauses can also be joined to form one sentence by using a comma and a coordinating conjunction, such as *and, but, nor, or, for, yet, so,* and *as well as.* Example: Our dog eats twice a day, *and* she walks two miles a day.

- A dependent clause cannot stand alone because it does not express a complete thought. Example: Because exercise is good for pets. This is a fragment or incomplete sentence. To fix this, combine a dependent clause with an independent clause. Example: Our dog walks two miles a day because exercise is good for pets.

Complements

- A complement completes the meaning of a verb. There are three types of complements: direct objects, indirect objects, and subject complements.

- A direct object is a word or group of words that receives the action of the verb. Example: Jane set the table. (*The table* is the complement or direct object of the verb *set.*)

- An indirect object is a word or group of words that follow the verb and tell for whom or what the action is done. An indirect object always comes before a direct object in a sentence. Example: Setting the table saved her mother some time. (*Her mother* is the complement or indirect object of the verb *saved.*)

- A subject complement is a word or group of words that further identify the subject of a sentence. A subject complement always follows a linking verb. Example: Buddy is the best dog. (The word *dog* is the complement of the subject *Buddy.*)

Contractions

- A contraction is two words made into one by replacing one or more letters with an apostrophe. Examples: *didn't* (did not), *you're* (you are)

Double Negatives

- A double negative is the use of two negative words, such as *no* or *not*, in a sentence. To fix a double negative, make one word positive. **Incorrect:** She *did not* get *no* dessert after dinner. **Correct:** She did not get *any* dessert after dinner.

Fragments

- A fragment is not a complete sentence. It may have a subject and verb, but it does not express a complete thought. **Incorrect:** The leaves that fell in the yard. **Correct:** The leaves that fell in the yard needed to be raked.

Gerunds

- A gerund is a verb with an *-ing* ending. It is used as a noun. Example: *Golfing* is fun! Here, *golfing* is a noun and the subject of the sentence.

Infinitives

- An infinitive is the word *to* plus the present tense of a verb. An infinitive can be a noun, adjective, or adverb in a sentence. Example: *To write* was her dream job. Here, *To write* is the infinitive, and it serves as a noun.

Modifiers

- A modifier is a word or group of words that change the meanings of other words in the sentence. Adjectives and adverbs are modifiers.

- A dangling or misplaced modifier is a group of descriptive words that is not near the word it modifies. This confuses the reader. **Incorrect:** Tucked up in the closet, Sarah found her grandma's photographs. *Tucked up in the closet* modifies Sarah. However, the photographs, not Sarah, are tucked up in the closet! **Correct:** Sarah found her grandma's photographs tucked up in the closet.

Parallel Structure

- Parallel structure is the use of words to balance ideas that are equally important. **Incorrect:** In the winter, I love to skate, snowmen, and to ski. **Correct:** In the winter, I love *to skate*, *to make* snowmen, and *to ski*.

Phrases

- A phrase is a group of words that does not have both a subject and a verb. Types of phrases include gerund phrases, infinitive phrases, and participial phrases.

- A gerund phrase has a gerund plus any modifiers and complements. The entire phrase serves as a noun. Example: Playing basketball with his friends was Trevor's favorite pastime. *Playing basketball with his friends* is the gerund phrase.

- An infinitive phrase has an infinitive plus any modifiers and complements. The entire phrase serves as a noun, adjective, or adverb in a sentence. Example: My mother liked to bake cookies on the weekend. *To bake cookies on the weekend* is the infinitive phrase.

- A participial phrase has a participle (a verb in its present form *[-ing]* or past form *[-ed or -en]*) plus all of its modifiers and complements. The entire phrase serves as an adjective in a sentence. Example: Wearing the robes of a king, Luis read his lines perfectly during play tryouts. *Wearing the robes of a king* is the participial phrase, and it modifies or describes the subject, Luis.

Plural Nouns

- A plural shows more than one of a particular noun. Use the following rules to create the plural form. Remember that there are exceptions to many spelling rules that you must simply memorize.

- Add –*s* to most singular nouns. Example: table/tables

- Add –*es* to a noun if it ends in –*ch*, –*sh*, –*s*, –*x*, and –*z*. Example: chu<u>ch</u>/churches

- If a noun ends with a vowel and a –*y*, add an –*s* to make the plural. Example: donk<u>ey</u>/donkeys

- If a noun ends with a consonant and a –*y*, drop the –*y* and add an –*ies* to make the plural. Example: pupp<u>y</u>/puppies

- If a noun ends in an –*f* or –*fe*, change the –*f* or –*fe* to a *v* and add –*es*. Example: kni<u>fe</u>/knives

- If a noun ends in an –*o*, sometimes you add –*es* and sometimes you add –*s*. Look in a dictionary to find out. Examples: potat<u>o</u>/potatoes, radi<u>o</u>/radios

Possessives

- A possessive noun shows ownership of an object, action, or idea. A possessive noun ends in 's. Example: Susan's book

- A possessive pronoun also shows ownership of an object, action, or idea. Example: his glove

Pronoun–Antecedent Agreement

- Pronoun-antecedent agreement occurs when the pronoun matches the antecedent (the word it refers to) in gender and number.

- To agree in gender:
  –Replace the name of a male person with a masculine pronoun. Example: *Jake* ran down the field, and *he* scored.

  –Replace the name of a female person with a feminine pronoun. Example: *Ana* read "The Most Dangerous Game," and *she* loved it.

  –Replace singular names with *it* or *its*. Example: The *kitten* ran through the room, and *it* pounced on the ball.

  –Replace plural names with *they*, *them*, or *their*. Example: The *tenth graders* came into the gym, and *they* played volleyball.

- To agree in number:

  –Make the pronoun singular if its antecedent is singular. Example: *Michael* told *himself* that he did the right thing.

  –Make the pronoun plural if its antecedent is plural. Example: The hungry *teenagers* ordered sandwiches for *themselves*.

Run-on Sentences

- A run-on sentence is the combination of two or more sentences without proper punctuation.

- To correct a run-on sentence, you can break it into two or more sentences by using capital letters and periods. Incorrect: The house was built in 1960 it needs new windows. Correct: The house was built in 1960. It needs new windows.

- You can also correct a run-on sentence by adding a comma and a coordinating conjunction to separate the sentences. Correct: The house was built in 1960, *so* it needs new windows.

- Another way to correct a run-on sentence is by adding a semicolon between the sentences. A semicolon should stand alone and should not have a coordinating conjunction after it. Correct: The house was built in 1960; it needs new windows.

Sentence Construction

- A simple sentence has one independent clause that includes a subject and a predicate. Example: The afternoon was warm and sunny.

- A compound sentence has two or more independent clauses joined by a comma and a coordinating conjunction or joined by a semicolon. Example: The afternoon was warm and sunny, so we decided to drive to the beach.

- A complex sentence has one independent clause and one or more dependent clauses. Example: We are going to the beach if you want to come along.

- A compound–complex sentence has two or more independent clauses joined by a comma and a coordinating conjunction. It has at least one dependent clause. Example: Although the morning was cold and damp, the afternoon was warm and sunny, so we decided to drive to the beach.

Sentence Types

- You can use a declarative sentence, an exclamatory sentence, an imperative sentence, or an interrogative sentence in writing.

- A declarative sentence tells us something about a person, place, or thing. This type of sentence ends with a period. Example: Martin Luther King Jr. fought for civil rights.

- An exclamatory sentence shows strong feeling or surprise. This type of sentence ends with an exclamation point. Example: I can't believe the price of gasoline!

- An imperative sentence gives commands. This type of sentence ends with a period. (Note: The subject of an imperative sentence is the implied "you.") Example: Please read chapter two by next Monday.

- An interrogative sentence asks a question. This type of sentence ends with a question mark. Example: Will you join us for dinner?

Subjects and Predicates

- The subject of a sentence names the person or thing doing the action. The subject contains a noun or a pronoun. Example: The students created posters and brochures. The subject of this sentence is *The students*. The predicate of this sentence (see definition below) is *created posters and brochures*.

- The predicate of a sentence tells what the person or thing is doing. The predicate contains a verb. Example: The fans waited for the hockey game to begin. The predicate of this sentence is *waited for the hockey game to begin*. The subject of this sentence is *The fans*.

Punctuation Guidelines

Apostrophe

- Shows ownership (possessive nouns): Kelly's backpack

- Shows plural possessive nouns: The five students' success was due to hard work.

- Shows missing letters in contractions: that's (that is)

Colon

- Introduces a list after a complete sentence: We learned about planets: Mars, Venus, and Jupiter.

- Adds or explains more about a complete sentence: Lunch was one option: pizza.

- Follows the salutation in a formal letter or in a business letter: Dear Mr. Jackson:
- Separates the hour and the minute: 2:15
- Introduces a long quotation: Lincoln wrote: "Four score and seven years ago . . ."

Comma

- Separates three or more items in a series: We planted corn, squash, and tomatoes.
- Joins two independent clauses when used with a coordinating conjunction: Sam and Raul did their homework, and then they left.
- Separates a city and state: Los Angeles, California
- Separates a day and year: October 15, 2006
- Follows the salutation and closing in a friendly letter: Dear Shanice, Love always,
- Follows the closing in a business letter: Sincerely,
- Sets off a restrictive phrase clause: Angela, the youngest runner, won the race.
- Sets off an introductory phrase or clause: Before he started the experiment, Jason put on safety glasses.

Dash

- Sets off an explanation in a sentence: The three poets—Langston Hughes, Robert Frost, and William Carlos Williams—are modernist poets.
- Shows a pause or break in thought: After years away, I returned—and found lots had changed.

Ellipses

- Show that words have been left out of a text: Our dog dove into the lake . . . and swam to shore.

Exclamation Point

- Shows emotion: Our team won!

Hyphen

- Divides a word at the end of a line: We enjoyed the beaches.
- Separates a compound adjective before a noun to make its meaning clearer: much-loved book
- Separates a compound number: thirty-three.
- Separates a fraction when used as an adjective: two-thirds full

Period

- Marks the end of a statement or command: July is the warmest month.
- Follows most abbreviations: Mrs., Dr., Inc., Jr.

Question Mark

- Marks the end of a question: How many eggs are left?

Quotation Marks

- Enclose the exact words of a speaker: He said, "I'll buy that book."
- Enclose the titles of short works: "Dover Beach," "America the Beautiful"

Semicolon

- Separates items in a series when commas are within the items: We went to Sioux Falls, South Dakota; Des Moines, Iowa; and Kansas City, Kansas.
- Joins two independent clauses that are closely related: We went to the movie; they came with us.

Capitalization Guidelines

Capitalize:

- the first word of a sentence: The teacher asked her students to read.

- the first word and any important words in a title: *To Kill a Mockingbird*

- all proper nouns: Marlon Smith, Atlanta, March

- the pronoun *I*

- languages: English, French

- abbreviations: Mrs., Sgt., FDR, EST

Commonly Confused Words

accept, except

- *Accept* (verb) means "to receive." Example: The children will *accept* ice cream.

- *Except* (preposition) means "leaving out." Example: The children enjoyed all flavors *except* strawberry.

affect, effect

- *Affect* (verb) means "to have an effect on." Example: This storm will *affect* our town.

- *Effect* (noun) means "a result or an outcome." Example: The *effect* was a struggling local economy.

its, it's

- *Its* (adjective) is the possessive form of "it." Example: Our hamster liked to run on the wheel inside *its* cage.

- *It's* is a contraction for "it is." Example: *It's* a long time before lunch.

lie, lay

- *Lie* (verb) means "to rest." Example: Jenny had a headache, so she needed to *lie* down.

- *Lay* (verb) means "to place." Example: Jamal went to *lay* his baseball glove on the bench.

lose, loose

- *Lose* (verb) means "to misplace or not find something." Example: I always *lose* my sunglasses when I go to the beach.

- *Loose* (adjective) means "free or without limits." Example: Someone let Sparky *loose* from his leash.

than, then

- *Than* (conjunction) shows a comparison. Example: You are older *than* I am.

- *Then* (adverb) means "at that time." Example: Will turned the doorknob and *then* slowly opened the door.

their, there, they're

- *Their* (pronoun) shows possession. Example: This is *their* house.

- *There* (adverb) means "place." Example: Sit over *there*.

- *They're* is a contraction for "they are." Example: *They're* coming over for dinner.

to, too, two

- *To* (preposition) shows purpose, movement, or connection. Example: We drove *to* the store.

- *Too* (adverb) means "also or more than wanted." Example: I, *too*, felt it was *too* hot to go outside.

- *Two* is a number. Example: Ava has *two* more years of high school.

your, you're

- *Your* (adjective) shows possession and means "belonging to you." Example: Take off *your* hat, please.

- *You're* is a contraction for "you are." Example: *You're* the best artist in the school.

Appendix C: Writing

Types of Writing

Before you can begin the writing process, you need to understand the types, purposes, and formats of different types of writing.

Descriptive Writing

Descriptive writing covers all writing genres. Description can be used to tell a story, to analyze and explain research, or to persuade. Descriptive writing uses images and colorful details to "paint a picture" for the reader.

Five Senses in Descriptive Writing

Consider the five senses in your descriptive writing: sight, smell, touch, sound, and taste. Using your senses to help describe an object, place, or person makes your writing more interesting. Before you begin, ask yourself the following:

- How does something look? Describe the color, size, and/or shape. What is it like?

- What smell or smells are present? Describe any pleasant or unpleasant smells. Compare the smells to other smells you know.

- How does something feel? Think about textures. Also think about emotions or feelings that result from the touching.

- What sounds do you hear? Describe the volume and the pitch. Are the sounds loud and shrill, or quiet and peaceful? What do the sounds remind you of?

- What does something taste like? Compare it to a taste you know, good or bad.

Expository Writing

Expository writing explains and informs through essays, articles, reports, and instructions. Like descriptive writing, it covers all writing genres. The purpose of this type of writing is to give more information about a subject. This can be done in many ways. The two most common formats in the study of literature are the compare and contrast paper and the cause and effect paper.

- Compare and Contrast Paper—This paper shows the similarities and differences of two or more characters, objects, settings, situations, writing styles, problems, or ideas.

- Cause and Effect Paper—This paper explains why certain things happen or how specific actions led to a result. A cause and effect paper can be set up by writing about the result (effect) first, followed by the events that led up to it (causes). Or, the paper can trace the events (causes), in order, that lead up to the result (effect).

Narrative Writing

Narrative writing tells a story. The story can be true (nonfiction) or made up (fiction). Narratives entertain or inform readers about a series of events. Poetry, stories, diaries, letters, biographies, and autobiographies are all types of narrative writing.

Key Elements in Narrative Writing

Think about the type of narrative you want to write and these key elements of your story:

- Characters: Who are the major and minor characters in the story? What do they look like? How do they act?

- Dialogue: What conversations take place among the characters? How does the dialogue show the reader something about the personalities of the characters?

- Setting: Where and when do the events take place? How does the setting affect the plot?

- Plot: What events happen in the story? In what order do the events occur? What is the problem that the main character is struggling with? How is the problem solved?

There are two common ways to set up your narrative paper. You can start at the beginning and tell your story in chronological order, or in the order in which the events happened. Or, you can start at the ending of your story and, through a flashback, tell what events led up to the present time.

Persuasive Writing

Persuasive writing is used when you want to convince your reader that your opinion on a topic is the right one. The goal of this paper is to have your reader agree with what you say. To do this, you need to know your topic well, and you need to give lots of reasons and supporting details. Editorials (opinion writing) in the newspaper, advertisements, and book reviews are all types of persuasive writing.

Key Elements of Persuasive Writing

Choosing a topic that you know well and that you feel strongly about is important for persuasive writing. The feelings or emotions that you have about the topic will come through in your paper and make a stronger argument. Also, be sure that you have a good balance between appealing to the reader's mind (using facts, statistics, experts, and so on) and appealing to the reader's heart (using

words that make them feel angry, sad, and so on). Think about these key elements:

- Topic: Is your topic a good one for your audience? Do you know a lot about your topic? Is your topic narrow enough so that you can cover it in a paper?

- Opinion: Is your opinion clear? Do you know enough about the opposite side of your opinion to get rid of those arguments in your paper?

- Reasons: Do you have at least three reasons that explain why you feel the way you do? Are these reasons logical?

- Supporting details or evidence: Do you have facts, statistics, experts, or personal experience that can support each reason?

- Opposing arguments: Can you address the opposite side and get rid of their arguments?

- Conclusion: Can you offer a solution or recommendation to the reader?

- Word choice: Can you find words that set the tone for your opinion? Will these words affect your readers emotionally?

There are two common ways to set up this paper. The first format is a six-paragraph paper: one paragraph for your introduction, three paragraphs for each of your three reasons, one paragraph for the opposing arguments and your responses to them, and one paragraph for your conclusion. Or you can write a five-paragraph paper where you place the opposing arguments and responses to each of your three reasons within the same paragraphs.

Research Report

A research report is an in-depth study of a topic. This type of writing has many uses in all subjects. It involves digging for information in many sources, including books, magazines, newspapers, the Internet, almanacs, encyclopedias, and other places of data. There are many key elements in writing a research report. Choosing a thesis statement, finding support or evidence for that thesis, and citing where you found your information are all important.

There are several uses of a research report in literature. You can explore a writer's life, a particular writing movement, or a certain writer's style. You could also write about a selection.

Business Writing

Business writing has many forms: memos, meeting minutes, brochures, manuals, reports, job applications, contracts, college essays. No matter what the format, the goal of business writing is clear communication. Keep the following key elements in mind when you are doing business writing:

- Format: What type of writing are you doing?

- Purpose: What is the purpose of your writing? Is the purpose clear in your introduction?

- Audience: Are your words and ideas appropriate for your audience?

- Organization: Are your ideas well-organized and easy to follow?

- Style: Are your ideas clearly written and to the point?

The Writing Process

The writing process is a little different for each writer and for each writing assignment. However, the goals of writing never change: Writers want to:

- have a purpose for their writing

- get their readers' attention and keep it

- present their ideas clearly

- choose their words carefully

To meet these goals, writers need to move through a writing process. This process allows them to explore, organize, write, revise, and share their ideas. There are five steps to this writing process: prewriting; drafting; revising; editing and proofreading; and publishing and evaluating.

Use the following steps for any writing assignment:

Step 1: Prewriting

Prewriting is where you explore ideas and decide what to write about. Here are some approaches.

Brainstorming

Brainstorming is fast, fun, and full of ideas. Start by stating a topic. Then write down everything you can think of about that topic. Ask questions about the topic. If you are in a group, have one person write everything down. Think of as many words and ideas as you can in a short time. Don't worry about neatness, spelling, or grammar. When you are finished, group words that are similar. These groups may become your supporting ideas.

Graphic Organizers

Graphic organizers are maps that can lead you through your prewriting. They provide pictures or charts that you fill in. Read the descriptions of these organizers in Appendix A, and choose the ones that will help you organize your ideas.

Outline

An outline can help you organize your information. Write your main ideas next to each Roman numeral. Write your supporting details next to the letters under each Roman numeral. Keep your ideas brief and to the point. Here's an example to follow:

Topic for persuasive paper: Lincoln High School should have a swimming pool.

I. Health benefits for students

    A. Weight control

    B. Good exercise

II. Water safety benefits for students

    A. Learn-to-swim programs

    B. Water safety measures to help others

III. School benefits

    A. Swim team

    B. Added rotation for gym class

IV. Community benefits

    A. More physically fit community members

    B. More jobs for community members

Narrowing Your Topic

Narrowing your topic means to focus your ideas on a specific area. You may be interested in writing about Edgar Allan Poe, but that is a broad topic. What about Poe interests you? Think about your purpose for writing. Is your goal to persuade, to explain, or to compare? Narrowing your scope and knowing your purpose will keep you focused.

Note-Taking and Research

Refer to the "How to Use This Book" section at the beginning of this textbook and Appendix D for help with note-taking and research skills.

Planning Your Voice

Your voice is your special way of using language in your writing. Readers can get to know your personality and thoughts by your sentence structure, word choice, and tone. How will your writing tell what you want to say in your own way? How will it be different from the way others write?

Step 2: Drafting

In the drafting step, you will write your paper. Use your brainstorming notes, outline, and graphic organizers from your prewriting stage as your guide. Your paper will need to include an introduction, a body, and a conclusion.

Introduction

The introduction states your topic and purpose. It includes a *thesis statement,* which is a sentence that tells the main idea of your entire paper. The last line of your introduction is a good place for your thesis statement. That way, your reader has a clear idea of the purpose of your paper before starting to read your points.

Your introduction should make people want to read more. Think about what your audience might like. Try one of these methods:

- asking a question
- sharing a brief story
- describing something
- giving a surprising fact
- using an important quotation

When you begin drafting, just write your introduction. Do not try to make it perfect the first time. You can always change it later.

Body

The body of your paper is made up of several paragraphs. Each paragraph also has a topic sentence, supporting details, and a concluding statement or summary. Remember, too, that each paragraph needs to support your thesis statement in your introduction.

- The topic sentence is usually the first sentence of a paragraph. It lets the reader know what your paragraph is going to be about.

- The supporting details of a paragraph are the sentences that support or tell more about your topic sentence. They can include facts, explanations, examples, statistics, and/or experts' ideas.

- The last sentence of your paragraph is a concluding statement or summary. A concluding statement is a judgment. It is based on the facts that you presented in your paragraph. A summary briefly repeats the main ideas of your paragraph. It repeats your idea or ideas in slightly different words. It does not add new information.

Conclusion

The conclusion ties together the main ideas of the paper. If you asked a question in your introduction, the conclusion answers it. If you outlined a problem, your conclusion offers solutions. The conclusion should not simply restate your thesis and supporting points.

Title of the Paper

Make sure to title your paper. Use a title that is interesting, but relates well to your topic.

Step 3: Revising

Now that you've explored ideas and put them into a draft, it's time to revise. During this step, you will rewrite parts or sections of your paper. All good writing goes through many drafts. To help you make the necessary changes, use the checklists below to review your paper.

Overall Paper

- ☑ Do I have an interesting title that draws readers in?
- ☑ Does the title tell my audience what my paper is about?
- ☑ Do I have an introduction, body, and conclusion?
- ☑ Is my paper the correct length?

Introduction

- ☑ Have I used a method to interest my readers?
- ☑ Do I have a thesis statement that tells the main idea of my paper?
- ☑ Is my thesis statement clearly stated?

Body

- ☑ Do I start every paragraph on a new line?
- ☑ Is the first line of every paragraph indented?
- ☑ Does the first sentence (topic sentence) in every paragraph explain the main idea of the paragraph? Does it attract my readers' attention?
- ☑ Do I include facts, explanations, examples, statistics, and/or experts' ideas that support the topic sentence?
- ☑ Do I need to take out any sentences that do not relate to the topic sentence?
- ☑ Do the paragraphs flow in a logical order? Does each point build on the last one?
- ☑ Do good transition words lead readers from one paragraph to the next?

Conclusion

- ☑ Does the conclusion tie together the main ideas of my paper?
- ☑ Does it offer a solution, make a suggestion, or answer any questions that the readers might have?

Writing Style

- ☑ Do I use words and concepts that my audience understands?
- ☑ Is the tone too formal or informal for my audience?
- ☑ Are my sentences the right length for my audience?
- ☑ Do I have good sentence variety and word choice?

Step 4: Editing and Proofreading

During the editing and proofreading step, check your paper or another student's paper for errors in grammar, punctuation, capitalization, and spelling. Use the following checklists to help guide you. Read and focus on one sentence at a time. Cover up everything but the sentence you are reading. Reading from the end of the paper backward also works for some students. Note changes using the proofreader marks shown on the following page. Check a dictionary or style manual when you're not sure about something.

Grammar

- ☑ Is there a subject and a verb in every sentence?
- ☑ Do the subject and verb agree in every sentence?
- ☑ Is the verb tense logical in every sentence?
- ☑ Is the verb tense consistent in every sentence?
- ☑ Have you used interesting, lively verbs?
- ☑ Do all pronouns have clear antecedents?
- ☑ Can repeated or unnecessary words be left out?
- ☑ Are there any run-on sentences that need to be corrected?
- ☑ Does sentence length vary with long and short sentences?

Punctuation

☑ Does every sentence end with the correct punctuation mark?

☑ Are all direct quotations punctuated correctly?

☑ Do commas separate words in a series?

☑ Is there a comma and a coordinating conjunction separating each compound sentence?

☑ Is there a comma after an introductory phrase or clause?

☑ Are apostrophes used correctly in contractions and possessive nouns?

Capitalization

☑ Is the first word of every sentence capitalized?

☑ Are all proper nouns and adjectives capitalized?

☑ Are the important words in the title of the paper capitalized?

Spelling

☑ Are words that sound alike spelled correctly (such as *to, too,* and *two*)?

☑ Is every plural noun spelled correctly?

☑ Are words with *ie* or *ei* spelled correctly?

☑ Is the silent *e* dropped before adding an ending that starts with a vowel?

☑ Is the consonant doubling rule used correctly?

If the paper was typed, make any necessary changes and run the spell-check and grammar-check programs one more time.

Proofreading Marks

Below are some common proofreading marks. Print out your paper and use these marks to correct errors.

Symbol	Meaning
¶	Start new paragraph
◯	Close up
#	Add a space
⋒	Switch words or letters
=	Capitalize this letter
/	Lowercase this letter
ℰ	Omit space, letter, mark, or word
∧	Insert space, mark, or word
⊙	Insert a period
⋏	Insert a comma
◯ sp	Spell out
· · · · stet	Leave as is (write dots under words)

Step 5: Publishing and Presenting

Once you have made the final text changes, make sure that the overall format of your paper is correct. Follow the guidelines that were set up by your teacher. Here are some general guidelines that are commonly used.

Readability

■ Double space all text.

■ Use an easy-to-read font such as Times Roman, Comic Sans, Ariel, or New York.

■ Use a 12-point type size.

■ Make sure that you have met any word, paragraph, or page count guidelines.

Format

- Make at least a one-inch margin around each page.

- Place the title of the paper, your name, your class period, and the date according to your teacher's guidelines. If you need a title page, make sure that you have a separate page with this information. If you do not need a title page, place your name, class period, and date in the upper right-hand corner of the first page. Center the title below that.

- Check to see if your pages need to be numbered. If so, number them in the upper right-hand corner or according to your teacher's guidelines.

- Label any charts and graphics as needed.

- Check that your title and any subheads are in boldface print.

- Check that your paragraphs are indented.

Citations

- Cite direct quotations, paraphrases, and summaries properly. Refer to the Modern Language Association (MLA) or American Psychological Association (APA) rules.

- Punctuate all citations properly. Refer to MLA or APA rules.

Bibliographies

- Include a list of books and other materials you reviewed during your research. This is a reference list only. Below are examples of how you would list a book, magazine article, and Web site using MLA style:

Book:
Author's Last Name, Author's First Name. *Book Title*. Publisher's City: Publisher's Name, Year.

London, Jack. *The Call of the Wild*. New York: Scholastic, 2001.

Magazine:
Author's Last Name, Author's First Name. "Article Title." Magazine Title. Volume Date: Page numbers.

Young, Diane. "At the High End of the River." *Southern Living*. June 2000: 126–131.

Web Site:
Article Title. Date accessed. URL

Circle of Stories. 25 Jan. 2006. <http://www.pbs.org/circleofstories/>

Six Traits of Writing

Good writing is not a miracle. It is not an accident either. Good writing is part science and part art. It is the result of careful thinking and choices. To write well, you need to know about six different traits that determine the quality of writing.

 **Six Traits of Writing:**

Ideas message, details, and purpose

What message do you want to get across? What details are important to get your message across clearly? Ideas are the heart of any writing. So begin the writing process by developing strong, clear ideas. Set off your ideas with details that stand out and catch attention.

 **Six Traits of Writing:**

Word Choice vivid words that "show, not tell"

Choose your words so that they are clear and interesting. Name things exactly. Use strong action verbs and specific adjectives. Good word choice helps you say exactly what you want to say. It helps your readers create a mental picture of what you want them to understand.

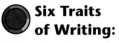 **Six Traits of Writing:**

Organization order, ideas tied together

A piece of writing has a structure or pattern, just like a building. Organize your ideas into a structure that makes sense and fits the ideas well. For example, you may tell about events or steps in order. You may compare two things or explain a solution or an effect. Organization holds writing together and gives shape to ideas.

Six Traits of Writing:

Sentence Fluency smooth rhythm and flow

Well-made sentences make your writing easy to read. Aim for sentences that have the natural rhythms of speech. Vary sentence length and style. Then your sentences will flow. They will move your readers through your writing with ease.

 **Six Traits of Writing:**

Voice the writer's own language

Your writing should "sound like you." It should capture your thoughts and your point of view. This is your "voice." In writing, your voice shows that you are interested in and understand the subject. Your voice also gives a personal tone to your writing that is yours alone.

Six Traits of Writing:

Conventions correct grammar, spelling, and mechanics

Once you have written something, ask yourself: Could this be published in a newspaper? Make sure your writing is free from mistakes in spelling, grammar, and mechanics. Mechanics includes things such as correct capitalization and punctuation.

Appendix D: Research

Planning and Writing a Research Report

⬇ *Use the following steps to guide you in writing a research report.*

Step 1: Planning the Report

Choose a subject. Then narrow your topic. You may be interested in the poetry of Robert Frost, but that subject is too broad. Narrow your focus. The graphic organizers in Appendix A may help you narrow your topic and identify supporting details.

Step 2: Finding Useful Information

Go to the library and browse the card catalog for books. Check almanacs, encyclopedias, atlases, and other sources in the reference section. Also review *The Reader's Guide to Periodical Literature* for magazines.

Draw from primary sources. Primary sources are first-hand accounts of information, such as speeches, observations, research results, and interviews. Secondary sources interpret and analyze primary sources.

Use the Internet to further explore your topic. Be careful; some Internet sources are not reliable. Avoid chat rooms, news groups, and personal Web sites. Check the credibility of sites by reviewing the site name and sponsor. Web sites whose URL ends with .org, .gov, and .edu are typically good sources.

Step 3: Logging Information

Use index cards to take notes. Include this information for each source:

- name of author or editor
- title of book or title of article and magazine
- page numbers
- volume numbers
- date of publication
- name of publishing company
- Web site information for Internet sources
- relevant information or direct quotations

Step 4: Getting Organized

Group your cards by similar details and organize them into categories. Find a system that works for you in organizing your cards. You can color-code them, use different-colored index cards for different sections, label them, and so on. Do not use any note cards that do not fit the categories that you have set up. Make conclusions about your research. Write a final topic outline.

Step 5: Writing Your Report

Follow the writing process in Appendix C to write your report. Use your own words to write the ideas you found in your sources (paraphrase). Do not plagiarize—steal and pass off another's words as your own. Write an author's exact words for direct quotations, and name the author or source.

Step 6: Preparing a Bibliography or Works Cited Page

Use the information on your note cards to write a bibliography or works cited page. If you are writing a bibliography, put your note cards in alphabetical order by *title*. If you are writing a works cited page, put your note cards in alphabetical order by *author*.

See *Bibliographies* in Appendix C.

Research Tools

Almanac
An annual publication containing data and tables on politics, religion, education, sports, and more

American Psychological Association (APA) Style
A guide to proper citation to avoid plagiarism in research papers for the social sciences

Atlas
A bound collection of maps of cities, states, regions, and countries including statistics and illustrations

Audio Recording
Recordings of speeches, debates, public proceedings, interviews, etc.

The Chicago Manual of Style
Writing, editing, proofreading, and revising guidelines for the publishing industry

Database
A large collection of data stored electronically and able to be searched

Dictionary
A reference book of words, spellings, pronunciations, meanings, parts of speech, and word origins

Experiment
A series of tests to prove or disprove something

Field Study
Observation, data collection, and interpretation done outside of a laboratory

Glossary
A collection of terms and their meanings

Government Publications
A report of a government action, bill, handbook, or census data usually provided by the Government Printing Office

Grammar Reference
Explanation and examples of parts of speech, sentence structure, and word usage

History
A chronological record that explains past events

Information Services
A stored collection of information organized for easy searching

Internet/World Wide Web
A worldwide network of connected computers that share information

Interview
A dialogue between a subject and a reporter or investigator to gather information

Journal
A type of magazine offering current information on certain subjects such as medicine, the economy, and current events

Microfiche
Historical, printed materials saved to small, thin sheets of film for organization, storage, and use

Modern Language Association (MLA) Handbook
A guide to proper citation to avoid plagiarism in research papers for the humanities

News Source
A newspaper or a radio, television, satellite, or World Wide Web sending of current events and issues presented in a timely manner

Periodical
A magazine, newspaper, or journal

The Reader's Guide to Periodical Literature
A searchable, organized database of magazines, newspapers, and journals used for research

Speech
A public address to inform and to explain

Technical Document
A proposal, instruction manual, training manual, report, chart, table, or other document that provides information

Thesaurus
A book of words and their synonyms, or words that have almost the same meanings

Vertical File
A storage file of original documents or copies of original documents

Appendix E: Speaking

Types of Public Speaking

Public speaking offers a way to inform, to explain, and to entertain. Here are some common types of public speaking:

Debate

A debate is a formal event where two or more people share opposing arguments in response to questions. Often, someone wins by answering questions with solid information.

Descriptive Speech

A descriptive speech uses the five senses of sight, smell, touch, taste, and sound to give vivid details.

Entertaining Speech

An entertaining speech relies on humor through jokes, stories, wit, or making fun of oneself. The humor must be appropriate for the audience and purpose of the speech.

Expository Speech

An expository speech provides more detailed information about a subject. This can be done through classification, analysis, definition, cause and effect, or compare and contrast.

Group Discussion

A group discussion allows the sharing of ideas among three or more people. A group discussion may be impromptu (without being planned) or may include a set topic and list of questions.

Impromptu Speech

An impromptu speech happens at a moment's notice without being planned. The speaker is given a random topic to discuss within a given time period.

Interview

An interview is a dialogue between a subject and a reporter or investigator. An interview draws out information using a question-and-answer format.

Literature Recitation

A literature recitation is the act of presenting a memorized speech, poem, story, or scene in its entire form or with chosen excerpts.

Literature Response

A literature response can serve many purposes. A speaker can compare and contrast plots or characters. An analysis of the work of one author can be presented. Writing style, genre, or period can also be shared.

Narrative

A narrative is a fiction or nonfiction story told with descriptive detail. The speaker also must use voice variation if acting out character dialogue.

Reflective Speech

A reflective speech provides thoughtful analysis of ideas, current events, and processes.

Role Playing

Role playing is when two or more people act out roles to show an idea or practice a character in a story. Role playing can be an effective tool for learning.

Preparing Your Speech

⬇ *Use the following steps to prepare your speech:*

Step 1: Defining Your Purpose

Ask yourself:

- Do I want to inform?
- Do I want to explain something?
- Do I want to entertain?
- Do I want to involve the audience through group discussion, role playing, or debate?
- Do I want to get the audience to act on a subject or an issue?

Step 2: Knowing Your Audience

Ask yourself:

- What information does my audience already know about the topic?
- What questions, concerns, or opinions do they have about the topic?
- How formal or informal does my presentation need to be?
- What words are familiar to my audience? What needs explanation?
- How does my audience prefer to get information? Do they like visuals, audience participation, or lecture?

Step 3: Knowing Your Setting

Ask yourself:

- Who is my audience?
- Is the room large enough to need a microphone and a projector?

- How is the room set up? Am I on stage with a podium or can I interact with the audience?
- Will other noises or activity distract the audience?

Step 4: Narrowing Your Topic

Ask yourself:

- What topic is right for the event? Is it timely? Will it match the mood of the event?
- Is there enough time to share it?
- What topic is right for me to present? Is it something I know and enjoy? Is it something people want to hear from me?

Step 5: Prewriting

Ask yourself:

- What examples, statistics, stories, or descriptions will help me get across my point?
- If telling a story, do I have a sequence of events that includes a beginning, middle, and end?

Step 6: Drafting Your Speech

Your speech will include an introduction, a body, and a conclusion.

The introduction states your topic and purpose. It includes a thesis statement that tells your position. Your introduction should also establish your credibility. Share why you are the right person to give that speech based on your experiences. Lastly, your introduction needs to get people's attention so they want to listen. At the top of the next page are some possible ways to start your speech.

- Ask a question.
- Share a story.
- Describe something.
- Give a surprising fact.
- Share a meaningful quotation.
- Make a memorable, purposeful entrance.

The body of your speech tells more about your main idea and tries to prevent listener misunderstandings. It should include any of the following supporting evidence:

- facts
- details
- explanations
- reasons
- examples
- personal stories or experiences
- experts
- literary devices and images

The conclusion of your speech ties your speech together. If you asked a question in your introduction, the conclusion answers it. If you outlined a problem, your conclusion offers solutions. If you told a story, revisit that story. You may even want to ask your audience to get involved, take action, or become more informed on your topic.

Step 7: Selecting Visuals

Ask yourself:

- Is a visual aid needed for the audience to better understand my topic?
- What visual aids work best for my topic?
- Do I have access to the right technology?

The size of your audience and the setting for your speech will also impact what you select. Remember that a projection screen and overhead speakers are necessary for large groups. If you plan on giving handouts to audience members, have handouts ready for pickup by the entrance of the room. A slide show or a video presentation will need a darkened room. Be sure that you have someone available to help you with the lights.

Practicing and Delivering Your Speech

Giving a speech is about more than simply talking. You want to look comfortable and confident.

Practice how you move, how you sound, and how you work with visuals and the audience.

Know Your Script

Every speaker is afraid of forgetting his or her speech. Each handles this fear in a different way. Choose the device that works for you.

- Memorization: Know your speech by heart. Say it often so you sound natural.
- Word-for-word scripts: Highlight key phrases to keep you on track. Keep the script on a podium, so you are not waving sheets of paper around as you talk. Be careful not to read from your script. The audience wants to see your eyes.
- Outlines: Write a sentence outline of your main points and supporting details that you want to say in a specific way. Transitions and other words can be spoken impromptu (without being planned).

- Key words: Write down key words that will remind you what to say, like "Tell story about the dog."

- Put your entire speech, outline, or key words on note cards to stay on track. They are small and not as obvious as paper. Number them in case they get out of order.

Know Yourself

Your voice and appearance are the two most powerful things you bring to a speech. Practice the following, so you are comfortable, confident, and convincing:

- Body language: Stand tall. Keep your feet shoulder-width apart. Don't cross your arms or bury your hands in your pockets. Use gestures to make a point. For example, hold up two fingers when you say, "My second point is . . ." Try to relax; that way, you will be in better control of your body.

- Eye contact: Look at your audience. Spend a minute or two looking at every side of the room and not just the front row. The audience will feel as if you are talking to them.

- Voice strategies: Clearly pronounce your words. Speak at a comfortable rate and loud enough for everyone to hear you. Vary your volume, rate, and pitch when you are trying to emphasize something. For example, you could say, "I have a secret. . . ." Then, you could lean toward the audience and speak in a loud, clear whisper as if you are telling them a secret. This adds dramatic effect and engages the audience.

- Repetition of key phrases or words: Repetition is one way to help people remember your point. If something is important, say it twice. Use transitions such as, "This is so important it is worth repeating" or "As I said before, we must act now."

Appendix F: Listening

Listening Strategy Checklist

Here are some ways you can ensure that you are a good listener.

Be an Active Listener

☑ Complete reading assignments that are due prior to the presentation.

☑ Focus on what is being said.

☑ Ask for definitions of unfamiliar terms.

☑ Ask questions to clarify what you heard.

☑ Ask the speaker to recommend other readings or resources.

Be a Critical Listener

☑ Identify the thesis or main idea of the speech.

☑ Try to predict what the speaker is going to say based on what you already know.

☑ Determine the speaker's purpose of the speech.

☑ Note supporting facts, statistics, examples, and other details.

☑ Determine if supporting detail is relevant, factual, and appropriate.

☑ Form your conclusions about the presentation.

Be an Appreciative Listener

☑ Relax.

☑ Enjoy the listening experience.

☑ Welcome the opportunity to laugh and learn.

Be a Thoughtful and Feeling Listener

☑ Understand the experiences of the speaker.

☑ Value the emotion he or she brings to the subject.

☑ Summarize or paraphrase what you believe the speaker just said.

☑ Tell the speaker that you understand his or her feelings.

Be an Alert Listener

☑ Sit up straight.

☑ Sit near the speaker and face the speaker directly.

☑ Make eye contact and nod to show you are listening.

☑ Open your arms so you are open to receiving information.

Analyze the Speaker

☑ Does the speaker have the experiences and knowledge to speak on the topic?

☑ Is the speaker prepared?

☑ Does the speaker appear confident?

☑ Is the speaker's body language appropriate?

☑ What do the speaker's tone, volume, and word choices show?

Identify the Details

☑ Listen for the tendency of the speaker to favor or oppose something without real cause.

☑ Be aware of propaganda—someone forcing an opinion on you.

☑ Don't be swayed by the clever way the speaker presents something.

☑ After the speech ask about words that you don't know.

Identify Fallacies of Logic

A fallacy is a false idea intended to trick someone. Here are some common fallacies:

- *Ad hominem*: This type of fallacy attacks a person's character, lifestyle, or beliefs. Example: Joe should not be on the school board because he skipped classes in college.

- False causality: This type of fallacy gives a cause–effect relationship that is not logical. This fallacy assumes that something caused something else only because it came before the consequence. Example: Ever since that new family moved into the neighborhood, our kids are getting into trouble.

- Red herring: This type of fallacy uses distractions to take attention away from the main issue. Example: Since more than half of our nation's people are overweight, we should not open a fast-food restaurant in our town.

- Overgeneralization: This type of fallacy uses words such as *every, always*, or *never*. Claims do not allow for exceptions to be made. Example: People who make more than a million dollars a year never pay their fair share of taxes.

- Bandwagon effect: This type of fallacy appeals to one's desire to be a part of the crowd. It is based on popular opinion and not on evidence. Example: Anyone who believes that our town is a great place to live should vote for the local tax increase.

Take Notes

- Write down key messages and phrases, not everything that is said.

- Abbreviate words.

- Listen for cues that identify important details, like "Here's an example" or "To illustrate what I mean."

- Draw graphs, charts, and diagrams for future reference.

- Draw arrows, stars, and circles to highlight information or group information.

- Highlight or circle anything that needs to be clarified or explained.

- Use the note-taking strategies explained in "How to Use This Book" at the beginning of this textbook.

Appendix G: Viewing

Visual aids can help communicate information and ideas. The following checklist gives pointers for viewing and interpreting visual aids.

Design Elements

Colors

☑ What colors stand out?

☑ What feelings do they make you think of?

☑ What do they symbolize or represent?

☑ Are colors used realistically or for emphasis?

Shapes

☑ What shapes are created by space or enclosed in lines?

☑ What is important about the shapes? What are they meant to symbolize or represent?

Lines

☑ What direction do the lines lead you?

☑ Which objects are you meant to focus on?

☑ What is the importance of the lines?

☑ Do lines divide or segment areas? Why do you think this is?

Textures

☑ What textures are used?

☑ What emotions or moods are they meant to affect?

Point of View

Point of view shows the artist's feelings toward the subject. Analyze this point of view:

☑ What point of view is the artist taking?

☑ Do you agree with this point of view?

☑ Is the artist successful in communicating this point of view?

Graphics

Line Graphs

Line graphs show changes in numbers over time.

☑ What numbers and time frame are represented?

☑ Does the information represent appropriate changes?

Pie Graphs

Pie graphs represent parts of a whole.

☑ What total number does the pie represent?

☑ Do the numbers represent an appropriate-sized sample?

Bar Graphs

Bar graphs compare amounts.

☑ What amounts are represented?

☑ Are the amounts appropriate?

Charts and Tables

Charts and tables organize information for easy comparison.

☑ What is being presented?

☑ Do columns and rows give equal data to compare and contrast?

Maps

☑ What land formations are shown?

☑ What boundaries are shown?

☑ Are there any keys or symbols on the map? What do they mean?

Appendix H: Media and Technology

Forms of Media

Television, movies, and music are some common forms of media that you know a lot about. Here are some others.

Advertisement

An advertisement selling a product or a service can be placed in a newspaper or magazine, on the Internet, or on television or radio.

Broadcast News

Broadcast news is offered on a 24-hour cycle through nightly newscasts, all-day news channels, and the Internet.

Documentary

A documentary shares information about people's lives, historic events, objects, or places. It is based on facts and evidence.

Internet and World Wide Web

This worldwide computer network offers audio and video clips, news, reference materials, research, and graphics.

Journal

A journal records experiences, current research, or ideas about a topic for a target audience.

Magazine

A magazine includes articles, stories, photos, and graphics of general interest.

Newspaper

A newspaper most often is printed daily or weekly.

Photography

Traditionally, photography has been the art or process of producing images on a film surface using light. Today, digital images are often used.

The Media and You

The media's role is to entertain, to inform, and to advertise. Media can help raise people's awareness about current issues. Media also can give clues about the needs and beliefs of the people.

Use a critical eye and ear to sort through the thousands of messages presented to you daily. Be aware of the media's use of oversimplified ideas about people, decent and acceptable language, and appropriate messages. Consider these questions:

- Who is being shown and why?
- What is being said? Is it based on fact?
- How do I feel about what and how it is said?

Technology and You

Technology can improve communication. Consider the following when selecting technology for research or presentations:

Audio/Sound

Speeches, music, sound effects, and other elements can set a mood or reinforce an idea.

Computers

- Desktop publishing programs offer tools for making newsletters and posters.
- Software programs are available for designing publications, Web sites, databases, and more.
- Word processing programs feature dictionaries, grammar-check and spell-check programs, and templates for memos, reports, letters, and more.

Multimedia

Slide shows, movies, and other electronic media can help the learning process.

Visual Aids

Charts, tables, maps, props, drawings, and graphs provide visual representation of information.

Handbook of Literary Terms

A

act (akt) the major unit of action in a play
(p. 410)

adaptation (ad ap tā′ shən) a work that has
been changed to fit a different form, usually
by leaving out some parts of the original
work (p. 401)

address (ə dres′) another term for a speech; a
written work meant to be read aloud (p. 553)

alliteration (ə lit ə rā′ shən) repeating sounds
by using words whose beginning sounds are
the same (p. 314)

analogy (ə nal′ ə jē) a comparison between
two otherwise different things that share the
same characteristics (p. 365)

antagonist (an tag′ ə nist) the person or animal
who struggles against the main character of
a story (p. 194)

author's influences (ó′ thərs in′ flü ən səz) the
people, experiences, and works of literature
and art that affect a writer's choices (p. 553)

author's purpose (ó′ thərs pėr′ pəs) the reason
for which an author writes: to entertain, to
inform, to express opinions, or to persuade
(p. 234)

autobiographical essay (ô tə bī ə graf′ ə kəl es′ ā)
an essay about true events in the author's life
(p. 241)

autobiography (ó tə bī og′ rə fē) a person's life
story, written by that person (p. 67)

B

ballad (bal′ əd) a form of poetry, passed from
person to person, often as a simple song
(p. 521)

biographical essay (bī ə graf′ ə kəl es′ ā) an
essay about true events in a person's life
(p. 241)

C

cause-and-effect order (kôz and ə fekt′ ôr′dər)
showing the relationship among events
(p. 257)

character (kar′ ik tər) a person or animal in a
story, poem, or play (pp. 6, 106)

character trait (kar′ ik tər trāt) a character's
way of thinking, behaving, or speaking
(p. 122)

chronological order (kron′ ə loj′ ə kəl ôr′dər)
moving a plot forward in the order of time
(p. 257)

climax (klī′ maks) the highest point of interest
or suspense in a story or play (p. 46)

comparison and contrast order (kəm par′ ə
sən and kon′ trast ôr′dər) showing the
ways in which two or more subjects are
similar and different (p. 257)

conflict (kon′ flikt) the struggle of the main
character against himself or herself, another
person, or nature (pp. 6, 122)

D

description (di skrip′ shən) a written picture of
the characters, setting, and events of a work
of literature (p. 194)

dialect (dī′ ə lekt) the speech of a particular
part of the country, or of a certain group of
people (pp. 138, 521)

dialogue (dī′ ə lôg) the conversation among
characters in a story (pp. 106, 384, 540)

drama (drä′ mə) a story told through the
words and actions of a character; a play
(p. 384)

dynamic character (dī nam′ ik kar′ ik tər)
a character who develops and learns because
of events in the story (p. 138)

E

end rhyme (end rīm) a feature of a poem or song in which the last words of two lines rhyme (p. 349)

essay (es´ā) a written work that shows a writer's opinions on some basic or current issue (p. 234)

exaggeration (eg zaj ə rā´ shən) the use of words to make something seem more than it is; stretching the truth to a great extent (p. 533)

excerpt (ek´ sėrpt) a short passage from a longer piece of writing (pp. 257, 485)

exposition (ek spə zish´ ən) the first stage of plot where the characters and setting are introduced (p. 46)

external conflict (ek stėr´ nl kon´ flikt) a character's struggle against an outside force such as another character, nature, or some part of society (p. 22)

F

falling action (fȯl´ ing ak´ shən) the events that follow the climax in a story (p. 46)

fantasy (fan´ tə sē) a kind of fiction writing that often has strange settings and characters (p. 485)

fiction (fik´ shən) writing that is imaginative and designed to entertain; the author creates the events and characters (pp. 6, 565)

figurative language (fig´ yər ə tiv lang´ gwij) writing or speech not meant to be understood exactly as it is written (p. 325)

first person (fėrst pėr´ sən) a point of view where the narrator is also a character, using the pronouns *I* and *we* (pp. 46, 152)

flat character (flat kar´ ik tər) a character that is based on a single trait or quality and is not well developed (p. 122)

folktale (fōk´ tāl) a story that has been handed down from one generation to another (p. 521)

foreshadowing (fôr shad´ ō ing) hints that a writer gives about something that has not yet happened (p. 34)

free verse (frē vėrs) poetry that does not have a strict rhyming pattern or regular line length and uses actual speech patterns for the rhythms of sound (p. 349)

H

hero (hir´ ō) the leading male character in a story, novel, play, or film (p. 521)

humor (hyü´ mər) literature created to be funny or to amuse (pp. 333, 533)

humorous essay (hyü´ mər əs es´ ā) a written work created to be funny or to amuse (p. 288)

hyperbole (hī pėr´ bə lē) using gross exaggeration to show that something is important (p. 533)

I

idiom (id´ ē əm) a phrase that has a different meaning that its words really mean (p. 234)

imagery (im´ ij rē) the pictures created by words that appeal to the five senses (pp. 333, 540)

internal conflict (in tėr´ nl kon´ flikt) a character's struggle against an inside force such as personal feelings or beliefs (p. 22)

irony (ī´ rə nē) the difference between what is expected to happen in a story and what does happen (p. 152)

J

journal (jėr´ nl) writing that gives an author's feelings or first impressions about a subject (p. 152)

a	hat	e	let	ī	ice	ȯ	order	u̇	put	sh	she	ə	a in about
ā	age	ē	equal	o	hot	oi	oil	ü	rule	th	thin		e in taken
ä	far	ėr	term	ō	open	ou	out	ch	child	ᵺ	then		i in pencil
â	care	i	it	ȯ	saw	u	cup	ng	long	zh	measure		o in lemon
													u in circus

L

legend (lej´ ənd) a story from folklore that features characters who actually lived or real places or events (p. 533)

letter (let´ ər) impressions or feelings written to a specific person (p. 277)

lyric poem (lir´ ik pō´ əm) a short poem that expresses a person's emotions or feelings (p. 340)

M

metaphor (met´ ə fôr) a figure of speech that makes a comparison but does not use *like* or *as* (p. 325)

mood (müd) the feeling that writing creates (pp. 46, 106)

moral (môr´ əl) a lesson or message about life told in a story (p. 456)

mystery (mis´ tər ē) a story about a crime that is solved (p. 46)

myth (mith) an important story, often part of a culture's religion, that explains how the world came to be or why natural events happen, usually including gods, goddesses, or unusually powerful human beings (p. 510)

mythology (mi thol´ ə jē) a collection of myths (p. 510)

N

narrative (nar´ ə tiv) a story, usually told in chronological order (p. 34)

narrative essay (nar´ ə tiv es´ ā) a short nonfiction work involving real events, people, and settings (p. 234)

narrative poem (nar´ ə tiv pō´ əm) a poem that tells a story (p. 340)

narrator (nar´ ā tər) one who tells a story (pp. 46, 122)

nonfiction (non fik´ shən) writing about real people and events (pp. 67, 234, 565)

novel (nov´ əl) fiction that is book-length and has more plot and character details than a short story (p. 485)

O

onomatopoeia (on ə mat ə pē´ ə) using words that sound like their meaning (p. 314)

oral literature (ôr´ əl lit´ ər ə chủr) stories that were first told, rather than being written down (p. 521)

P

personification (pər son ə fə kā´ shən) giving characters such as animals or objects the characteristics or qualities of humans (p. 257, 325, 521)

persuasive essay (pər swā´ siv es´ ā) a short work that is meant to influence the reader (p. 268)

playwright (plā´ rīt) an author of a play (p. 384)

plot (plot) the series of events in a story (pp. 6, 122)

poetry (pō´ i trē) literature in verse form that usually has rhythm and paints powerful or beautiful impressions with words (p. 314)

point of view (point ov vyü) the position from which the author or storyteller tells the story (pp. 22, 152)

props (propz) pieces of equipment used on stage during a play (p. 410)

protagonist (prō tag´ ə nist) the main character of a story (p. 194)

R

refrain (ri frān´) a repeated line in a poem or song that creates mood or gives importance to something (p. 340)

repetition (rep ə tish´ ən) using a word, phrase, or image more than once, for emphasis (p. 268, 325)

resolution (rez ə lü´ shən) the act of solving conflict in a story (p. 22)

rhetorical questions (ri tôr´ ə kəl kwes´ chənz) questions asked for effect and not for information (p. 268)

rhyme (rīm) words that end with the same or similar sounds (p. 314)

rhythm (riŦH´ əm) a pattern created by the stressed and unstressed syllables in a line of poetry (p. 314)

rising action (rīz´ ing ak´ shən) the buildup of excitement in the story (p. 46)

round character (round kar´ ik tər) a well-developed character possessing a variety of traits (p. 122)

S

scene (sēn) a unit of action that takes place in one setting in a play (p. 410)

science fiction (sī´ əns fik´ shən) fiction based on real or imagined facts of science (p. 106)

script (skript) the written text of a play, used in production or performance (p. 410)

setting (set´ ing) the time and place of a story (pp. 6, 106, 384)

short story (shôrt stôr´ ē) a brief work of prose fiction that includes plot, setting, characters, point of view, and theme (pp. 22, 401)

simile (sim´ ə lē) a figure of speech that makes a comparison using the words *like* or *as* (pp. 325, 540)

stage directions (stāj də rek´ shəns) notes by playwrights describing such things as setting, lighting, sound effects, and how the actors are to look, behave, move, and speak (p. 384)

stanza (stan´ zə) a group of lines that forms a unit in a poem (p. 314)

static character (stat´ ik kar´ ik tər) a character who does not change (p. 138)

style (stīl) an author's way of writing (pp. 67, 257, 401)

suspense (sə spens´) a quality in a story that makes the reader uncertain or nervous about what will happen next (p. 122)

symbol (sim´ bəl) something that represents something else (p. 207)

T

tall tale (tȯl tāl) a story from the past that features enlarged characters who have unreal adventures (p. 533)

theme (thēm) the main idea of a literary work (pp. 22, 194, 510, 565)

third person (thėrd pėr´ sən) a point of view where the narrator is not a character, and refers to characters as *he* or *she* (pp. 81, 152)

tone (tōn) the attitude an author takes toward a subject (p. 288)

U

universal theme (yü nə vėr´ səl thēm) a main idea that appears in many times, places, and cultures (p. 656)

a	hat	e	let	ī	ice	ô	order	u̇	put	sh	she	ə	a in about
ā	age	ē	equal	o	hot	oi	oil	ü	rule	th	thin		e in taken
ä	far	ėr	term	ō	open	ou	out	ch	child	ŦH	then		i in pencil
â	care	i	it	ȯ	saw	u	cup	ng	long	zh	measure		o in lemon
													u in circus

Glossary

A

abide (ə bīd´) to stay or remain (p. 317)

abiding (ə bī´ ding) permanent (p. 278)

abject (ab´ jekt) hopeless or miserable (p. 117)

abruptly (ə brupt´ lē) suddenly (p. 458)

abruptness (ə brupt´ ness) suddenness (p. 87)

accelerated (ak sel´ ə rā tid) increased (p. 182)

accordance (ə kôrd´ ns) agreement (p. 139)

account (ə kount´) a bill for work done (p. 402)

acknowledge (ak nol´ ij) to show an awareness of (p. 470); to admit to be true (p. 555)

acquainted (ə kwān´ tid) made aware; informed (p. 144)

acquired (ə kwī´ rd) gained (p. 181)

acquiring (ə kwīr´ ing) getting (p. 280)

actuated (ak´ chü ā təd) put into action (p. 141)

acute (ə kyüt´) sharp (p. 123)

adamant (ad´ ə mənt) not willing to give in (p. 212)

adaptation (ad ap tā´ shən) a development of characteristics to survive (p. 260)

advise (ad vīz´) to give an opinion about what should be done (p. 172)

affectionate (ə fək´ shə nit) having a fondness for something (p. 35)

agitation (aj ə tā´ shən) strong emotion; disturbance (p. 48)

allotted (ə lot´ tid) allowed (p. 270)

amnesia (am nē´ zhə) a loss of memory (p. 182)

anachronism (ə nak´ rə niz əm) something outside of its proper place in history (p. 271)

ancestral (an ses´ trəl) relating to a person's own family (p. 554)

anonymously (ə non´ ə məs lē) without being named (p. 244); without being known (p. 444)

antithesis (an tith´ ə sis) opposite (p. 422)

apologized (ə pol´ ə jīzd) said one was sorry for something (p. 404)

apologizing (ə pol´ ə jīz ing) saying you are sorry (p. 8)

appendix (ə pen´ diks) added information at the end of a book or document (p. 181)

appends (ə pendz´) adds to a larger thing (p. 210)

applicability (ap lə kə bil´ ə tē) use (p. 182)

aptly (apt´ lē) correctly (p. 271)

architects (är´ kə tektz) people who design and construct buildings (p. 243)

ardor (är´ dər) love (p. 294)

aristocratic (ə ris tə krat´ ik) of high social class (p. 50)

ark (ärk) a shelter or safe place (p. 315)

aromas (ə rō´ məz) smells (p. 345)

Artillery (är til´ ər ē) branch of the military armed with large guns (p. 51)

artisan (är´ tə zən) a person skilled at a craft (p. 210)

ascend (ə send´) go up (p. 110)

ascent (ə sent´) upward climb; rise (p. 88)

ashen (ash´ ən) pale (p. 342)

assembly (ə sem´ blē) a gathering of people for some purpose (p. 436)

assortment (ə sôrt´ mənt) a collection of different kinds of things (p. 487)

assume (ə süm´) to take for granted without proof (p. 385)

assuredly (ə shür´ id lē) certainly; confidently (p. 557)

astonishing (ə ston´ i shing) very surprising; amazing (p. 243)

asylum (ə sī´ ləm) a place where mentally ill people receive care (p. 472)

atrocious (ə trō´ shəs) very bad or unpleasant (p. 411)

audacity (ô das′ ə tē) boldness (p. 128)

authentic (ô then′ tik) real (p. 419)

authorized (ô′ thə rīzd) gave permission to do something (p. 242)

averted (ə vėr′ təd) looked away (p. 50)

B

babble (bab′ əl) to talk without making sense (p. 452)

bade (bād) told (p. 72)

bafflement (baf′ əl mənt) confusion (p. 392)

balked (bôkd) stopped (p. 84)

ballerina (bal ə rē′ nə) a kind of dancer (p. 430)

barren (bar′ ən) without any growing thing (p. 88); unattractive; dull (p. 199)

bequeathed (bi kwē ᴛʜd′) gave to, as in a will (p. 51); left to after death (p. 270)

berserk (bėr′ sėrk) to be carried away by madness (p. 110)

bestowed (bi stōd′) given (p. 73)

bestows (bi stōz′) presents (p. 260)

bevy (bev′ ē) a group (p. 73)

blanched (blanchd) turned pale (p. 55)

blunt (blunt) straightforward; without kindness (p. 392)

bologna (bə lō′ nē) a type of sandwich meat (p. 464)

bongos (bong′ gōz) small drums (p. 13)

borne (bôrn) carried (p. 353)

bosom (bùz′ əm) chest (p. 125)

boughs (bouz) branches from a tree (p. 566)

boundaries (boun′ dər ēz) limits or borders (p. 26)

brambles (bram′ bəlz) wild, untrimmed bushes (p. 411)

brawny (brô′ nē) big, strong, and muscular (p. 542)

brigand (brig′ ənd) thief (p. 71)

brink (bringk) edge (p. 71)

broached (brōchd) brought up (p. 25)

brutal (brü′ tl) cruel (p. 555)

brutality (brü tal′ ə tē) violence or cruelty (p. 212)

bugged (bugd) bothered (p. 17)

burlap (bėr′ lap) rough fabric, often used for bags (p. 38)

bushels (bùsh′ əl) a unit of volume equal to about 32 quarts (p. 545)

buttressed (but′ trisd) supported (p. 85)

C

calculate (kal′ kyə lāt) to figure out (p. 269)

capricious (kə prish′ əs) flighty (p. 262)

carnal (kär′ nl) focused on the body (p. 261)

cascading (ka skā′ ding) falling in waves (p. 546)

casements (kās′ məntz) windows that open out like doors (p. 316)

casualties (ka′ zhəl tēz) victims (p. 213)

ceased (sēst) stopped (p. 127)

cemented (sə mən′ təd) held in place with cement (p. 432)

chaperones (shap′ ə rōnz) persons responsible for one's behavior (p. 416)

chasm (kaz′ əm) a deep opening or crack in the earth (p. 84)

chassis (chas′ ē) the frame, wheels, and machinery of a motor vehicle that supports the body (p. 112)

chef (shef) a head cook (p. 342)

chiffon (shi fon′) sheer fabric (p. 294)

a	hat	e	let	ī	ice	ô	order	ù	put	sh	she	ə	a	in about
ā	age	ē	equal	o	hot	oi	oil	ü	rule	th	thin		e	in taken
ä	far	ėr	term	ō	open	ou	out	ch	child	ᴛʜ	then		i	in pencil
â	care	i	it	ȯ	saw	u	cup	ng	long	zh	measure		o	in lemon
													u	in circus

chlorophyll (klôr´ ə fil) the green pigment found in plant cells (p. 259)

circulating (sėr kyə lā´ ting) flowing (p. 85)

circumstances (sėr´ kəm stan səz) conditions (p. 291)

clamoring (klam´ ər ing) yelling (p. 73)

client (klī´ ənt) a customer; a person for whom one does a professional service (p. 47)

coherence (kō hir´ əns) a quality of fitting together in a way that is easily understood (p. 271)

coiled (koild) wound around in a circular shape (p. 35); curled up (p. 525)

collapsed (kə lapsd´) fell (p. 544)

colossal (kə los´ əl) huge (p. 555)

commenced (kə mensd´) began or started (p. 522)

compensation (kom pən sā´ shən) pay; something given to make up for something else (p. 141)

competition (kom pə tish´ ən) a contest (p. 243)

complacently (kəm plā´ snt lē) doing what is asked graciously (p. 111)

complexity (kəm plek´ sə tē) complication (p. 271)

complicate (kom´ plə kāt) to make difficult (p. 236)

comprehensive (kom pri hen´ siv) knowing (p. 48)

compulsory (kəm pul´ sər ē) required (p. 139)

conceived (kən sēvd´) thought of (p. 123)

conception (kən sep´ shən) a creative idea (p. 248)

concepts (kon´ septz) ideas (p. 176)

conclusions (kən klü´ zhənz) decisions or opinions reached by reasoning (p. 440)

condensed milk (kən densd´ milk) a thick, sweetened, canned milk (p. 342)

confidence (kon´ fə dəns) firm belief or trust (p. 68)

confidentially (kon fə dən´ shəl lē) secretly (p. 210)

confiscate (kon´ fə skāt) to seize or take (p. 211)

conscience (kon´ shəns) a sense of right and wrong (p. 556)

consequence (kon´ sə kwens) importance (p. 54)

constructive (kən struk´ tiv) positive (p. 269)

contact (kon´ takt) a touching together (p. 176)

contemplating (kon´ təm plāt ing) thinking about; considering (p. 87)

contemptuous (kən temp´ chü əs) scornful (p. 73)

continuity (kon tə nü´ ə tē) uninterrupted flow (p. 244); the act of going on without stopping (p. 557)

contrary (kon´ trer ē) completely different; opposite (p. 175)

contrasts (kon´ trastz) shows differences (p. 470)

convulsed (kən vulsd´) shaken or pulled with a jerk (p. 55)

convulsively (kən vul´ siv) having twitching in muscle spasms (p. 84)

copperhead (kop´ ər hed) a kind of poisonous snake found in the eastern United States (p. 40)

cordons (kôrd´ nz) lines or cords that prevent free movement (p. 317)

coroner (kôr´ ə nər) the official who decides the cause of death (p. 57)

corporate (kôr´ pər it) having to do with a business or a company (p. 430)

corpse (kôrps) a dead body (p. 127)

corsages (kôr säzh´ əz) small bunches of flowers worn on a blouse or jacket (p. 12)

covaledictorian (kō val ə dik tôr´ ē ən) a student who delivers a graduation speech with another student (p. 246)

cowered (kou´ ərd) bent in fear (p. 177)

cranny (kran´ ē) a small break or split (p. 83)

crevice (krev´ is) a crack (p. 115)

criteria (krī tir´ ē ə) standards by which something is judged (p. 244)

critical (krit´ ə kəl) using judgment (p. 491)

crouch (krouch) to lower the body by bending the legs (p. 15)

crusade (krü sād´) cause (p. 280)

cryptic (krip´ tik) having a hidden meaning (p. 214)

cumbrously (kum´ brəs lē) clumsily; hard to manage (p. 116)

curtsies (kėrt´ sēz) bends the knees and lowers the body to bow in respect, done by a girl or woman (p. 385)

D

darling (där´ ling) a person or animal very dear to another (p. 39)

daunted (dôn´ təd) bothered (p. 463)

dean (dēn) the head of a department at a university (p. 246)

debris (də brē´) scattered parts (p. 112)

decade (dek´ ād) a period of ten years (p. 269)

deduct (di dukt´) to take away; to subtract (p. 388)

deduction (di duk´ shən) conclusion (p. 109)

deductions (di duk´ shənz) answers found by reasoning (p. 47)

defensive (di fen´ siv) on one's guard (p. 412)

deficiency (di fish´ ən sē) a lack of something needed (p. 111)

defied (di fīd´) avoided (p. 82)

definitive (di fin´ ə tiv) trustworthy (p. 290)

definitiveness (di fin´ ə tiv nəss) an exact form (p. 129)

defray (di frā´) pay the costs (p. 49)

delicate (del´ ə kit) pleasing to taste or smell (p. 36); of fine quality (p. 357)

delicately (del´ ə kit lē) done with great skill (p. 487)

delouse (dē lous´) to remove lice (p. 422)

demented (di men´ tid) insane (p. 434)

denizen (den´ ə zən) a person or animal that lives in a place (p. 139)

deprives (di prīvz´) prevents someone from having something (p. 292)

deputed (di pyüt´ id) sent out (p. 128)

derision (di rizh´ ən) laughter or ridicule (pp. 129, 145)

descendants (di sen´ dəntz) those born of a certain family or group (p. 26)

descent (di sent´) fall, drop (p. 70); downward climb (p. 88)

desecration (des´ ə krā shən) ruin (p. 73)

deserted (di zer´tid) left behind or abandoned (p. 569)

desolate (des´ ə lit) deserted (p. 117)

despised (di spīzd´) hated (p. 174)

detected (di tekt´ id) found out (p. 76)

deteriorating (di tir´ ē ər ā ting) falling apart (p. 411)

deterioration (di tir´ ē ər ā shən) a lowering of quality or value (p. 182)

development (di vel´ əp mənt) a change; progress (p. 437)

devices (di vī´ sez) techniques or means for working things out (p. 235)

dexterity (dek ster´ ə tē) skill in using the hands, body, or mind (p. 112)

diminutive (də min´ yə tiv) very small or tiny (p. 215); a suffix that shows smallness; a childhood nickname (p. 341)

diplomatic (dip lə mat´ ik) having skill in dealing with others (p. 143)

disarray (dis ə rā´) disorder (p. 460)

a	hat	e	let	ī	ice	ô	order	ù	put	sh	she		ə	a	in about
ā	age	ē	equal	o	hot	oi	oil	ü	rule	th	thin			e	in taken
ä	far	ėr	term	ō	open	ou	out	ch	child	̄ᴛн	then			i	in pencil
â	care	i	it	ȯ	saw	u	cup	ng	long	zh	measure			o	in lemon
														u	in circus

discharged (dis chärjd´) fired; dismissed from a job (p. 389)

discrepancies (dis krep´ ən sēz) differences; results that do not match the facts or agreed-upon points (p. 386)

disinherit (dis in her´ it) to take away from (p. 556)

disintegration (dis in tə grā´ shən) breakup (p. 261)

dismembered (dis mem´ bərd) cut apart (p. 128)

dispel (dis pel´) to make disappear (p. 58)

dispossession (dis pə zesh´ ən) something that has been given up or is no longer owned (p. 555)

disproportionately (dis prə pôr´ shə nət lē) in a way that is out of proportion; in an unlike way (p. 356)

dissemble (di sem´ bəl) to hide real feelings; to disguise (p. 129)

dissimulation (di sim´ yə lāt shən) the hiding of feelings or of the truth (p. 124)

dissolute (dis´ ə lüt) wicked; of bad character (p. 50)

dissolving (di zol´ ving) ending as if by breaking up (p. 491)

distinction (dis tingk´ shən) difference (p. 109)

distinctness (dis tingkt´ ness) awareness of detail (p. 126)

dithery (diŧH´ ə rē) nervous and confused (p. 315)

diversion (də vėr´ zhən) a change of attention (p. 272)

dock (dok) to subtract part of one's salary or wages (p. 403)

documentation (dok yə men tā´ shən) a written record (p. 426)

doggedly (dô´ gid lē) without giving up (p. 278)

dormitory (dôr´ mə tôr ē) a building with many rooms for sleeping in (p. 73)

dubbed (dubd) gave a title, name, or nickname to (p. 75)

E

earshot (ir´ shot) at a distance close enough to be heard (p. 488)

edicts (ē´ diktz) commands (p. 258)

eerie (ir´ ē) creepy, ghostly, spooky (p. 542)

ejected (i jek´ təd) sent out (p. 108)

elapsed (i lapsd´) went by (p. 110)

elected (i lek´ təd) chose; decided (p. 88)

eloquent (el´ ə kwənt) vividly expressive (p. 245)

emancipation (i man´ sə pā shən) freedom (p. 278)

embarrass (em bar´ əs) to make uneasy and ashamed (p. 199)

embody (em bod´ ē) to stand for; to be a symbol of (p. 556)

embroidered (em broi´ dərd) made a pattern using stitches in cloth (p. 208)

encamp (en kamp´) set up camp (p. 52)

enchanted (en chan´ təd) charming, magical (p. 72)

encircled (en sėr´ kəld) made a circle around (p. 317)

enclosed (en klōzd´) surrounded; shut in on all sides (p. 356)

endurance (en dùr´ əns) power to last and withstand hard wear (p. 145)

enfeebled (en fē bəld) weakened (p. 279)

engaged (en gājd) hired (p. 388)

engulfed (en gulfd´) swallowed up (p. 544)

enormity (i nôr mə tē) enormousness; hugeness or difficulty (p. 463)

entreaty (en trē´ tē) a prayer (p. 113)

enveloped (in ve´ ləpd) surrounded (p. 86)

environment (en vī´ rən mənt) surroundings (p. 246)

ephemeral (i fem´ ər əl) lasting for a very short time (p. 557)

equipped (i kwip´ pəd) prepared; ready (p. 179)

ere (er) before (p. 83)

erect (i rekt´) straight (p. 85)

erosion (i rō´ zhən) the wearing away of land by glaciers, water, or wind (p. 115)

erupted (i rup´ təd) exploded (p. 236)

eschew (es chü´) avoid (p. 293)

espoused (e spouzd´) adopted (p. 279)

esteemed (e stēmd´) honored, respected (p. 68)

etiquette (et´ ə ket) rules of correct behavior (p. 289)

evaded (i vād´ əd) avoided (p. 236)

excelled (ek seld´) did very well (p. 386)

excursion (ek skėr´ zhən) a trip (p. 68)

exertion (eg zėr´ shən) effort (p. 86)

expanse (ek spans´) a wide area of land (p. 237)

expectant (ek spek´ tənt) eager, hopeful (p. 73); thinking something will come or happen (p. 210)

expectations (ek spek tā´ shən) hopes (p. 76)

extensive (ek sten´ siv) far-reaching; large (p. 115)

extinct (ek stingkt´) no longer alive or active (p. 113)

exulting (eg zul´ ting) rejoicing (p. 366)

F

faint (fānt) not clear, dim (p. 566)

fallow (fal´ ō) unplanted (p. 107)

familial (fə mil´ yəl) having to do with the family (p. 215)

famine (fam´ ən) a lack of food that causes much starvation (p. 568)

fantasy (fan´ tə sē) a picture existing only in the mind; a daydream (p. 8)

fawning (fôn ing) trying to win favor by flattery or other insincere behavior (p. 215)

feigning (fān ing) fake (p. 343)

fetishes (fet´ ə shiz) unusually strong feelings (p. 296)

figments (fig´ məntz) creations of the imagination (p. 261)

financial (fə nan´ shəl) having to do with money (p. 388)

flanks (flangkz) the sides of an animal or person (p. 110)

flatterer (flat´ ər ər) one who praises insincerely to win approval (p. 315)

flickered (flik´ ərd) twinkled (p. 492)

fluently (flü´ ənt lē) easily and accurately (p. 269)

footfuls (fut´ fulz) large amounts grabbed by the feet; like fistfuls (p. 16)

foraging (fôr´ ij ing) hunting for (p. 292)

forebodings (fôr bō´ dingz) feelings that something bad is going to happen (p. 294)

foresight (fôr´ sīt) the ability to see what is likely to happen and prepare for it (p. 124)

forthright (fôrth´ rīt) straightforward (p. 245)

fortnight (fôrt´ nīt) a period of two weeks (p. 52)

fragile (fraj´ əl) easily broken (p. 208, 423)

frequent (frē´ kwənt) often (p. 141)

fruitless (früt´ lis) unsuccessful (p. 216)

furrow (fėr´ ō) a deep, long row in the soil (p. 107)

a	hat	e	let	ī	ice	ȯ	order	u̇	put	sh	she	ə	a	in about
ā	age	ē	equal	o	hot	oi	oil	ü	rule	th	thin		e	in taken
ä	far	ėr	term	ō	open	ou	out	ch	child	ᵺ	then		i	in pencil
â	care	i	it	ȯ	saw	u	cup	ng	long	zh	measure		o	in lemon
													u	in circus

G

garments (gär′ məntz) pieces of clothing (p. 488)

gaunt (gônt) very thin and bony (p. 487)

gazelle (gə zəl′) a small, quick, deer-like animal found in Asia or Africa (p. 23)

generous (jen′ ər əs) willing to share with others (p. 26)

gesticulations (je stik′ yə lā′ shənz) a lively or excited movement of the body (p. 129)

gesture (jes′ chər) movement of any part of the body to help express an idea or feeling (p. 13)

glockenspiels (glok′ ən spēlz) musical instruments with metal bars that make bell-like tones when struck with small hammers (p. 13)

gnarled (närld) twisted; crooked (p. 23, 76)

gouged (goujd) dug out (p. 535)

governess (guv′ ər nis) a woman hired to care for and teach children in a private home (p. 385)

grandeur (gran′ jər) the quality or state of being grand (p. 74)

gratification (grat′ ə fə kā′ shən) satisfaction (p. 269)

gravel (grav′ əl) pebbles and pieces of rock in larger pieces than sand (p. 15)

gravitate (grav′ ə tāt) to move gradually (p. 289)

grim (grim) horrible or frightful (p. 492)

groundhogs (ground′ hôgz) woodchucks (p. 38)

grove (grōv) a group of trees standing together (p. 36)

guardian (gär′ dē ən) someone who takes care of another (p. 71)

guileless (gīl′ lis) without deceit or trickery; innocent (p. 392)

gullies (gul′ lēz) narrow valleys that are steep and rocky (p. 83)

H

haggard (hag′ ərd) looking worn because of worry (p. 48)

hammock (ham′ ək) a hanging bed or couch made of canvas cord (p. 354)

haphazard (hap haz′ ərd) unplanned (p. 260)

harmony (här mə nē) an orderly or pleasing arrangement of parts (p. 244)

hayloft (hā′ lôft) a place in a barn for storing hay (p. 38)

hearken (här′ kən) listen (p. 123)

heirloom (er′ lüm) a precious object that has been in a family a long time (p. 389)

herculean (hėr kyü′ lē ən) nearly impossible (p. 85)

heritage (her′ ə tij) what is handed down from one generation to the next (p. 557)

heroine (her′ ō ən) a woman or girl admired for bravery (p. 76)

hie (hī) to fly swiftly (p. 353)

hollering (hol′ ər ing) yelling (p. 14)

hordes (hôrdz) large crowds (p. 546)

horizon (hə rī′ zn) the line where the earth and sky seem to meet (p. 70)

hospitality (hos pə tal′ ə tē) the friendly treatment of guests (p. 52)

humid (hyü′ mid) hot and damp weather (p. 39)

humiliation (hyü mil ē ā′ shən) shame (p. 76)

humus (hyü′ məs) rich soil (p. 262)

hustling (hu′ səl ing) getting or selling in a hurried, rough, or illegal way (p. 7)

hydrant (hī′ drənt) a large, upright pipe with a valve for drawing water (pp. 8, 447, 543)

hypothesis (hī poth′ ə sis) a theory (p. 183)

I

idiotic (id ē ot´ ik) crazy (p. 296)

idle (ī dl) doing nothing; not busy (p. 237)

idly (ī dlē) lazily; not busy (p. 107)

ignorance (ig´ nər əns) a lack of knowledge or awareness (p. 237)

ill-fitting (il fit´ ing) not fitting very well (p. 488)

illiteracy (i lit´ ər ə sē) inability to read (p. 179)

immense (i mens´) huge (p. 112)

immensity (i men´ sə tē) grandness; hugeness (p. 317)

immoral (i môr´ əl) bad (p. 279)

impatient (im pā´ shənt) not able to wait; eager (p. 179)

impending (im pen´ ding) about to happen (p. 54)

implores (im plôrz) begs (p. 278)

impressed (im presd´) affected deeply (p. 54)

impressive (im pres´ iv) amazing (p. 437)

imprisoned (im priz´ ənd) put into prison (p. 212)

inactive (in ak´ tiv) not active (p. 107)

inadequate (in ad´ ə kwit) not good enough (p. 279)

inalienable (in ā´ lyə nə bəl) protected by law (p. 272)

incident (in´ sə dənt) an event; something that happens (p. 177)

incoherence (in kō hir´ əns) the state of being impossible to understand (p. 294)

incorrigible (in kôr´ ə jə bəl) too firmly fixed in bad ways to be changed (p. 139)

indio (in´ dē ō) American Indian (p. 344)

inferior (in fir´ ē ər) lower in status or rank (p. 386)

inflict (in flikt´) to cause (p. 293)

influence (in´ flü əns) the power to act on others and have an effect without using force (p. 269)

infuriated (in fyür´ ē ā təd) made very angry (p. 178)

ingratitude (in grat´ ə tüd) a lack of thankfulness (p. 343)

inhale (in hāl´) to breathe air in (p. 434)

inherent (in hir´ ənt) a natural part of (p. 270)

inherited (in her´ i təd) received something after the former owner dies (p. 555)

innate (i nāt´) natural (p. 292)

innocent (in´ ə sənt) free from sin or wrong; not guilty (p. 290)

innumerable (i nü´ mər ə bəl) too many to count (p. 23)

inordinately (in ôr´ dən ət lē) very great or excessive (p. 143)

inquiries (in´ kwər ēz) requests for information (p. 243)

insecure (in si kyür´) fearful; not sure of doing well (p. 294)

insisted (in sist´ əd) refused to give in (p. 567)

instability (in stə bil´ ə tē) unsteadiness (p. 183)

instilling (in stil´ ing) gradually teaching (p. 290)

instinct (in´ stingkt) a natural feeling, knowledge, or ability that guides animals (p. 139)

insulted (in sult´ əd) said or did something mean or rude (p. 24)

integrate (in´ tə grāt) to make public places available to people of all races (p. 555)

intelligent (in tel´ ə jent) smart; able to learn (p. 107)

a	hat	e	let	ī	ice	ô	order	ù	put	sh	she	ə	a	in about
ā	age	ē	equal	o	hot	oi	oil	ü	rule	th	thin		e	in taken
ä	far	ér	term	ō	open	ou	out	ch	child	ŦH	then		i	in pencil
â	care	i	it	ȯ	saw	u	cup	ng	long	zh	measure		o	in lemon
													u	in circus

intemperate (in tem´ pər it) severe (p. 292)

intensification (in ten sə fə kā´ shən) strengthening (p. 182)

intensified (in ten´ sə fīd) became stronger (p. 51)

interfere (in tər fir´) to get in the way of (p. 83)

internal (in tėr´ nl) inside (p. 108)

introspective (in trə spek´ tiv) thoughtful; examining one's own thoughts and feelings (p. 183)

intuitions (in tü ish´ ənz) ways of knowing without proof (p. 47)

invariably (in ver´ ē ə blē) having no change (p. 177)

inviolability (in vī ə lə bil´ ə tē) state of security (p. 296)

irritable (ir´ ə tə bəl) easily bothered (p. 183)

irritation (ir ə tā shən) an ongoing bother (p. 489)

J

jaunty (jôn´ tə) smartly placed (p. 487)

justified (jus´ tə fīd) gave a good reason for (p. 175)

jutting (jut´ ting) sticking out (p. 15)

K

keel (kēl) a main beam that extends along the bottom of a ship and supports the frame (p. 366)

keen (kēn) sharp (p. 258)

kin (kin) family members or relatives (p. 23)

kindled (kin´ dləd) built a fire (p. 534)

L

lax (laks) lazy (p. 390)

legacy (leg´ ə sē) anything handed down from an ancestor (p. 344)

liable (lī´ ə bəl) likely (p. 10)

literally (lit´ ər ə lē) word for word without exaggeration (p. 556)

livery (liv´ ər ē) a stable for housing horses (p. 140)

loam (lōm) rich, dark soil (p. 353)

loathing (lō´ ᴛʜing) intense dislike (p. 56)

loathsome (lōᴛʜ´ səm) disgusting (p. 57)

logical (loj´ ə kəl) reasonable (p. 47)

loudspeaker (loud´ spē´ kər) a device that helps sound to travel long distances (p. 16)

lullaby (lul´ ə bī) a soothing song usually sung to a baby (p. 213)

lumbering (lum´ bər ing) slow and heavy (p. 428)

M

macabre (mə kä´ brə) grim (p. 258)

machete (mə shet´ ē) a broad, heavy knife (p. 356)

mahouts (mə houtz´) elephant drivers or keepers in India and the East Indies (p. 327)

maneuver (mə nü´ vər) a series of planned steps (p. 88); a controlled movement (p. 262)

mania (mā´ nē ə) an intense, almost insane, excitement (p. 51)

manifestly (man´ ə fest lē) clearly (p. 84)

manifold (man´ ə fōld) of many kinds (p. 50)

mannerly (man´ ər lē) polite (p. 292)

manor (man´ ər) the main house on an estate (p. 53)

mansions (man´ shənz) large houses (p. 545)

maroon (mə rün´) a dark brownish red color (p. 144)

marquee (mär kē´) a large lighted sign (p. 260)

marrow (mar´ ō) the most important part (p. 126)

marveling (mär´ vəl ing) saying something is wonderful (p. 237)

mayhem (mā´ hem) chaos (p. 296)

meager (mē´ gər) poor (p. 141)

membrane (mem´ brān) a thin skin (p. 354)

mere (mir) plain; simple (p. 343)

merit (mer´ it) value (p. 244)

meticulous (mə tik´ yə ləs) very careful (p. 210)

metropolis (mə trop´ ə lis) a city (p. 47)

mingled (ming´ gəld) mixed (p. 70)

miraculous (mə rak´ yə ləs) extraordinary (p. 295)

mistrusted (mis trus´ təd) doubted (p. 199)

mockery (mok´ ər ē) the act of making fun of something (p. 129)

momentarily (mō´ mən ter e lē) for an instant (p. 438)

morose (mə rōs´) gloomy (p. 51)

mortar (môr´ tər) a thick mixture (p. 262)

mortification (môr tə fə kā´ shən) embarrassment (p. 76)

mortified (môr´ tə fīd) embarrassed or humiliated (p. 214)

muck (muk) wet, muddy dirt (p. 327)

mummified (mum´ ə fīd) shriveled (p. 261)

municipal (myü nis´ ə pəl) public; belonging to a town or city (p. 556)

mushed (mushd) drove a dogsled team (p. 82)

mute (myüt) understated (p. 261)

mutely (myüt´ lē) silently; without sound (p. 213)

mutilated (myü´ tl ā təd) injured by removing parts (p. 280)

N

naïvete (nä ē və tā´) having little understanding of how things really are (p. 179)

nape (nāp) the back of the neck (p. 208)

narcotic (när kot´ ik) a drug that dulls the senses (p. 270)

nausea (nò´ zē ə) unsettled stomach (p. 87)

neglected (ni glek´ tid) gave too little care or attention (p. 176)

negotiation (ni gō´ shē ā shən) the act or process of arranging for something (p. 23)

niceties (nī´ sə tēz) fine points; details (p. 290)

nigh (nī) near (p. 343)

ninny (nin´ ē) a simple or foolish person (p. 404)

notion (nō´ shən) an idea (p. 246)

nozzle (noz´ əl) a tip on a hose where the water comes out (p. 543)

nuclear (nü´ klē ər) of or about atoms or atomic energy (p. 107)

nucleus (nü´ klē əs) center (p. 86)

nutrients (nü´ trē əntz) substances that can be turned into energy and build tissue (p. 259)

O

obdurate (ob´ dər it) stubborn (p. 142)

obligations (ob lə gā´ shənz) things that must be done (p. 215)

obscure (əb skyür´) to hide (p. 182)

obviously (ob´ vē əs lē) very clear to the eye or mind (p. 17)

occupant (ok´ yə pənt) a person who lives or stays in a certain place (p. 57)

occurred (ə kėrd´) happened or made known (pp. 16, 38)

onslaught (ôn´ slôt) attack (p. 213)

oppressor (ə pres´ ər) bully (p. 293)

opulence (op´ yə ləns) wealth (p. 437)

organdy (ôr´ gən dē) a very fine, stiff fabric (p. 12)

ornate (ôr nāt´) fancy (p. 214)

outcropping (out´ krop ing) an area of a rock that sticks out above the ground (p. 86)

a	hat	e	let	ī	ice	ô	order	ù	put	sh	she	⎧ a	in about
ā	age	ē	equal	o	hot	oi	oil	ü	rule	th	thin	ə e	in taken
ä	far	ėr	term	ō	open	ou	out	ch	child	ᴛʜ	then	i	in pencil
â	care	i	it	ò	saw	u	cup	ng	long	zh	measure	⎩ o	in lemon
												u	in circus

outfits (out´ fitz) groups that work as a team (p. 82)

outset (out´ set) the beginning (p. 47)

overacuteness (ō ver ə kyüt´ nis) too sharp or severe (p. 126)

overtly (ō´ vėr lē) openly; for show (p. 431)

P

paddocks (pad´ əkz) an enclosed area near a stable where horses are exercised (p. 140)

pageant (paj´ ənt) a public entertainment that represents scenes from history, legend, and the like (p. 12)

palpable (pal´ pə bəl) physical; capable of being touched (p. 356)

palsy (pôl´ zē) a paralysis with trembling and muscular weakness (p. 87)

pantaloons (pan tl ünz´) pants (p. 71)

parapet (par´ ə pet) a railing along the edge of a roof or wall (p. 52)

parenthetical (par ən thet´ ə kəl) explanatory (p. 293)

parkas (pär´ kəz) heavy waterproof coats with a hood (p. 350)

parochial (pə rō´ kē əl) of or in a district that has its own church and clergy (p. 235)

parsonage (pär´ sə nij) a house where a church minister lives (p. 56)

partition (pär tish´ ən) a wall or screen between rooms (p. 39)

passion (pash´ ən) strong feelings (p. 123)

passions (pash´ ənz) intense emotions or feelings (p. 243)

patrons (pā´ trənz) customers (p. 292)

peculiar (pi kyü´ lyər) strange or odd (pp. 71, 143)

peevishly (pē´ vish lē) very cross or upset (p. 568)

penitent (pen´ ə tənt) sorry for doing wrong (p. 74)

perceived (pər sēvd´) seen, sensed (p. 272)

perilous (per´ ə ləs) full of danger (p. 86)

periscope (per´ ə skōp) part of a submarine that allows those inside to view the surface (p. 13)

perished (per´ ishd) died (p. 83)

perpendicular (pėr pən dik´ yə lər) straight up (p. 83)

perpetrated (pėr´ pə trā tid) carried out (p. 51)

perpetuation (pər pech´ ü ā shən) continuation (p. 279)

perspiration (pėr spə rā´ shən) sweat (p. 404)

pervading (pər vād´ ing) spreading throughout (p. 270)

perverting (pər vėrt´ ing) worsening (p. 279)

pestering (pes´ tər ing) bothering (p. 513)

pesticide (pes´ tə sīd) a chemical used to kill insects (p. 415)

petition (pə tish´ ən) a written request for a right or privilege, often signed by many people (p. 173)

pharmacy (fär´ mə sē) a place where medicines are prepared and sold (p. 444)

philosophical (fil ə sof´ ə kəl) thoughtful (p. 291)

philosophy (fə los´ ə fē) a system of thoughts and ideas (p. 556)

phony (fō´ nē) fake (p. 17)

photosynthesis (fō tō sin´ thə sis) the chemical process by which green plants use energy from the sun to turn water and carbon dioxide into food (p. 259)

pigment (pig´ mənt) coloring (p. 259)

pitiable (pit´ ē ə bəl) causing a feeling of pity (p. 48)

pitiful (pit´ i fəl) causing others to feel pity (p. 525)

pleaded (ple´ dəd) begged or argued (p. 26)

pneumonia (nü mō´ nyə) a lung infection that causes fever and cough (p. 141)

poised (poizd) balanced a certain way (p. 88)

pollen (pol´ ən) a powder made in flowers that helps a plant form seeds (p. 353)

ponderous (pon´ dər əs) very heavy (p. 327)

practicable (prak´ tə kə bəl) possible to put into practice (p. 280)

precipitate (pri sip´ ə tāt) sudden and forceful (p. 88)

precipitous (pri sip´ ə təs) steep, dangerous (p. 70)

predatory (pred´ ə tôr ē) living by robbery or other crime (p. 417)

predicament (pri dik´ ə mənt) dilemma; problem (p. 85)

predisposed (prē dis pōzd´) willing (p. 260)

prefer (pri fėr´) to like better; to choose or wish (p. 11)

preliminary (pri lim´ ə ner ē) leading up to something important (p. 25)

premature (prē mə chùr´) earlier than expected (p. 48)

premises (prem´ is əz) a house or building with its grounds (p. 128)

premonition (prē mə nish´ ən) warning, hunch (p. 72)

prescription (pri skrip´ shən) an order from a doctor for medicine (p. 444)

presentable (pri zen´ tə bəl) fit to be seen (p. 198)

previous (prē´ vē əs) coming before (p. 70)

proclaims (prə klāmz´) makes known publicly (p. 342)

prodigy (prod´ ə jē) a person with amazing talent (p. 10)

profound (prə found´) deeply felt or very great (p. 215)

prominent (prom´ ə nənt) well-known or important (pp. 68, 212); important, socially respected (p. 246)

protein (prō´ tēn) a necessary part of a human diet provided by foods like meat and nuts (p. 421)

protruding (prō trüd´ ing) sticking out (p. 56)

psyching (sīk´ ing) outsmarting or making nervous (p. 14)

pueblo (pweb´ lō) an American Indian village of homes grouped together to form a large building several stories high (p. 512)

pueblos (pweb´ lōz) American Indian towns in central and northern New Mexico (p. 345)

punctures (pungk´ chərz) small holes caused by a sharp object (p. 57)

purgatory (pėr´ gə tôr ē) a place of temporary punishment (p. 115)

pursue (pər sü´) follow (p. 280)

pursuit (pər süt´) the act of chasing (p. 513)

puttering (put´ ər ing) doing unimportant things (p. 445)

Q

quaint (kwānt) strange or odd in an interesting way (p. 23)

quake (kwāk) to tremble or shake (p. 328)

quakes (kwākz) shakes or trembles (p. 428)

R

rack (rak) destruction or ruin (p. 366)

radiate (rā´ dē āt) to spread out from the center (p. 262)

radiator (rā´ dē ā tər) a heating device made of a set of pipes through which steam or hot water travels (p. 351)

random (ran´ dəm) by chance; with no plan (p. 108); without a pattern (p. 290)

rapidity (rə pid´ ə tē) speed (p. 57)

rapture (rap´ chər) joy; delight (p. 317)

a	hat	e	let	ī	ice	ô	order	ù	put	sh	she		a	in about
ā	age	ē	equal	o	hot	oi	oil	ü	rule	th	thin	ə	e	in taken
ä	far	ėr	term	ō	open	ou	out	ch	child	ŦH	then		i	in pencil
â	care	i	it	ȯ	saw	u	cup	ng	long	zh	measure		o	in lemon
													u	in circus

realm (relm) a region or area (p. 75)

recall (ri kôl´) to call back; remember (p. 58)

recede (ri sēd´) to move away (p. 353)

recite (ri sīt´) to say over; repeat (p. 75)

reckon (rek´ ən) to think (p. 523)

recognition (rek əg nish´ ən) appreciation (p. 242)

rectory (rek´ tər ē) a house provided for priests (p. 235)

reflection (ri flek´ shən) thought (p. 245)

reflectively (ri flek´ tiv lē) thoughtfully (p. 113)

refrained (ri frānd´) held back (p. 127)

refute (ri fyüt´) prove false (p. 176)

registrants (rej´ ə strəntz) people who sign up (p. 244)

regression (ri gresh´ ən) a return to an earlier stage or condition (p. 181)

regulated (reg´ yə lā təd) controlled by rule or system (p. 208)

reliance (ri lī´ əns) help, dependence (p. 73)

reluctantly (ri luk´ tənt lē) unwillingly (p. 209); hesitantly, not wanting to do something (p. 390)

rendezvous (rän´ də vü) meeting (p. 68)

repellent (ri pel´ ənt) disgusting (pj. 291)

repentance (ri pen´ təns) sorrow, regret (p. 74)

reposed (ri pōzd´) rested (p. 128)

reprehensible (rep ri hen´ sə bəl) totally unacceptable (p. 295)

reputation (rep yə tā´ shən) what people think and say about a person's character (p. 10); fame or good name (p. 246)

requisitions (rek wə zish´ ənz) demands or takes by authority (p. 211)

resembled (ri zem´ bəld) looked similar to (p. 123)

residence (rez´ ə dəns) a place where one lives (p. 76)

resistant (ri zis´ tənt) acting against (p. 216)

resolution (rez ə lü´ shən) determination (p. 141); the power of holding firmly to a purpose (p. 345)

respectively (ri spek´ tiv lē) in the same order (p. 109)

restored (ri stôrd´) brought back (p. 557)

resumed (ri zümd´) began again (p. 544)

retaliation (ri tal ē ā´ shən) getting even (p. 293)

retire (ri tīr´) to give up a job (p. 16)

retorted (ri tôrtd´) replied with anger (p. 47)

retractable (ri trakt´ ā bl) able to go back inside (p. 110)

retracted (ri trak´ təd) withdrew; took back (p. 145)

retrieving (ri trēv´ ing) bringing back (p. 292)

reveal (ri vēl´) show (p. 418)

revealed (ri vēld´) showed (p. 58); made known (p. 112)

reveals (ri vēlz´) makes known (p. 259)

reverie (rev´ ər ē) daydream (p. 290)

revolutionary (rev ə lü´ shə ner ē) bringing or causing great changes (p. 114, 556)

righteous (rī´ chəs) fair and just (p. 209)

rituals (rich´ ü əlz) customs or ceremonies (p. 214)

rivulets (riv´ yə litz) gullies; ditches (p. 344)

robustly (rō bust´ lē) strongly (p. 259)

rotate (rō´ tāt) to go through a cycle (p. 235)

rowdier (rou´ dē ər) noisier (p. 178)

rudiments (rü´ də məntz) basic elements (p. 280)

ruthless (rüth´ lis) cruel (p. 57)

S

sacred (sā′ krid) holy (p. 512)

sagacity (sə gas′ ə tē) wisdom or sound judgment (p. 125)

salary (sal′ ər ē) a fixed sum of money paid for work done (p. 403)

salvation (sal vā′ shən) saved from sin (p. 74)

sanity (san′ ə tē) the state of good mental health (p. 290)

sarcastically (sär kas′ tik lē) in a mocking way (p. 412)

sasses (sas′ əz) speaks rudely (p. 11)

satisfactory (sat i sfak′ tər ē) good enough (p. 389)

scanty (skan′ tē) very little (p. 141)

scarce (skers) few (p. 39)

scheme (skēm) a plan (p. 235)

scorched (skôrchd) burned slightly (p. 142)

sculpted (skulp′ təd) shaped (p. 418)

sculptors (skulp′ tərz) artists who create solid, three-dimensional works (p. 243)

seared (sird) burned (p. 53)

sector (sek′ tər) a section or zone (p. 111)

security (si kyur′ ə tē) safety (p. 54)

seditious (si dish′ əs) stirring up discontent or rebellion (p. 211)

seldom (sel′ dəm) not often (p. 177)

sensibility (sen sə bil′ ə tē) feeling or emotion (p. 178); a way of thinking and feeling about the world (p. 555)

sensitive (sen′ sə tiv) easily disturbed (p. 390)

sentiment (sen′ tə mənt) feeling (p. 279)

serene (sə rēn′) calm (p. 556)

shamefacedly (shām′ fāst lē) embarrassingly; shyly (p. 142)

shelled (sheld) separated the kernels an ear of corn (p. 37)

shoon (shün) an old-fashioned word for "shoes" (p. 316)

shortchanging (shôrt chānj′ ing) not taking all that is due (p. 390)

shrew (shrü) a mouselike mammal with a long snout and brownish fur (p. 171)

shriveled (shriv′ əld) dried up; shrank and wrinkled (p. 513)

shush (shush) to hush or make quiet (p. 16)

sickening (sik′ ə ning) able to cause a sickness (p. 442)

sidekicks (sīd′ kikz) friends (p. 10)

significantly (sig nif′ ə kənt lē) importantly (p. 490)

signify (sig′ nə fī) to make known by signs, words, or actions (p. 11)

simmering (sim′ ər ing) boiling for a long time at a low temperature (p. 355)

simpleton (sim′ pəl tən) a foolish or silly person (p. 392)

skeptically (skep′ tə kəl lē) doubtfully (p. 272)

skirted (skėrtd) went around (p. 115)

slouch (slouch) droopy (p. 71)

smoldering (smōl′ dər ing) burning and smoking without flames (p. 566)

sociable (sō′ shə bəl) friendly (p. 39)

soggy (sog′ ē) damp and mushy (p. 355)

sonorous (sə nôr′ əs) giving or having a deep, loud sound (p. 140)

soothe (süᴛʜ) to calm (p. 243)

a	hat	e	let	ī	ice	ô	order	u̇	put	sh	she	ə	a	in about
ā	age	ē	equal	o	hot	oi	oil	ü	rule	th	thin		e	in taken
ä	far	ėr	term	ō	open	ou	out	ch	child	ᴛʜ	then		i	in pencil
â	care	i	it	ȯ	saw	u	cup	ng	long	zh	measure		o	in lemon
													u	in circus

spattered (spat´ ərd) splashed (p. 49)

specialization (spesh´ ə līz ā shən) the pursuit of a special type of study or work (p. 175)

spectacular (spek tak´ yə lər) making a great display (pp. 247, 259)

specter (spek´ tər) something that causes fear or dread (p. 175)

speculated (spek´ yə lāt) wondered (p. 547)

speculation (spek yə lā´ shən) consideration (p. 295)

speculatively (spek´ yə lā tiv lē) thoughtfully (p. 110)

speedily (spē´ dl ē) quickly (p. 57)

spitfire (spit´ fīr) someone who is easily excited or angered (p. 315)

squatter (skwot´ tər) a person living in a building that the person does not own or rent (p. 534)

static (stat´ ik) a crackly noise that blocks radio or television reception (p. 14)

statistics (stə tis´ tikz) facts (p. 295)

stealth (stelth) secretive behavior (p. 258)

steed (stēd) a high-spirited horse (p. 145)

stifled (stī´ fəld) held back (p. 125)

stilts (stiltz) tall sticks that people can walk on (p. 13)

stimulates (stim´ yə lātz) excites (p. 126)

stimulation (stim´ yə lā shən) cause for excitement (p. 271)

stimulus (stim´ yə ləs) something that excites (p. 270)

stoic (stō´ ik) calm in the face of suffering (p. 345)

stricken (strik´ ən) struck; strongly affected (p. 55)

sturdily (stėr´ də lē) in a strong, solid way (p. 488)

suavity (swä´ və tē) politeness (p. 128)

subdue (səb dü´) to overcome or take control of (p. 140)

subdued (səb düd´) quieted (p. 470)

submitted (səb mit´ təd) handed in (p. 244)

successive (sək ses´ iv) following (p. 50)

suede (swād) leather with a soft, velvety surface (p. 197)

sufficient (sə fish´ ənt) having enough (pp. 87, 124)

supple (sup´ əl) capable of moving easily (p. 345)

suppositions (sup ə zish´ ənz) beliefs; opinions (p. 126)

suppressed (sə presd´) held back (p. 208)

supremacy (sə prem´ ə sē) the state of being most powerful (p. 278)

surged (sėrjd) rose and fell like waves (p. 70)

surveyor (sər vā´ ər) a person who examines the land (p. 24)

suspicion (sə spish´ ən) a belief, feeling, or thought (p. 169)

suspiciously (sə spish´ əs lē) not believing something (p. 487)

swaggered (swag´ ərd) walked in a way meant to show off (p. 541)

swarthy (swôr´ ᵺē) dark (p. 71)

swiped (swīpd) taken (p. 464)

sympathizing (sim´ pə thīz ing) sharing another's sorrows or troubles (p. 443)

symphonic (sim fon´ ik) having a harmony of colors (p. 260)

systematic (sis tə mat´ ik) orderly (p. 209)

T

tangible (tan´ jə bəl) able to be touched or felt (p. 175)

temporarily (tem´ pə rer ə lē) for a short time (p. 420)

tendency (ten´ dən sē) a natural urge to do something (p. 85)

tenders (ten´ dərz) people who care for animals (p. 327)

tenement (ten´ ə mənt) a cheaply made building divided into apartments (p. 542)

tension (ten´ shən) worry; strain (p. 86)

tentacle (ten´ tə kəl) a feeler used to touch, hold, or move (p. 112)

thatch (thach) a roof made of straw or other plant material (p. 316)

theological (thē ə loj´ ə kəl) religious (p. 75)

thermos (thėr´ məs) a container for keeping liquids hot or cold (p. 415)

thicket (thik´ it) bushes or small trees growing close together (p. 566)

thoroughly (thėr´ ō lē) completely; fully (p. 83)

tiara (tē ər´ ə) a small crown (p. 49)

tightrope (tīt´ rōp) a rope or wire on which acrobats perform (p. 8)

timidly (tim´ id lē) in a shy or fearful manner (p. 404)

tolerance (tol´ ər əns) endurance (p. 272)

tolerant (tol´ ər ənt) willing to put up with something or someone (p. 431)

tourist (tùr´ ist) a person traveling for pleasure (p. 334)

trace (trās) a path, trail, or road (p. 40)

transparent (tran sper´ ənt) able to be seen through; clear (p. 335)

traumatic (trô mat´ ik) shocking (p. 459)

treacherous (trech´ ər əs) dangerous (p. 84)

treadmill (tred´ mil) a wearisome routine of daily life (p. 74)

trellis (trel´ is) a frame to support a growing vine (p. 457)

trifle (trī´ fəl) a small amount (p. 535)

trills (trilz) makes a fluttering sound (p. 366)

trimmings (trim´ ingz) decorations on clothing, such as buttons or lace (p. 402)

trivial (triv´ ē əl) not important (p. 50)

trough (trôf) a long, deep, narrow bin (p. 327)

tuition (tü ish´ ən) money paid for instruction (p. 75)

U

unanimous (yü nan´ ə məs) in complete agreement (p. 245)

unanimously (yü nan´ ə məs lē) all together (p. 75)

unattainable (un ə tā´ nə bəl) impossible to achieve (p. 272)

undergraduate (un dər graj´ ü it) a college student (p. 245)

unforeseen (un fôr sēn) not expected (p. 182)

unfurling (un fėrl´ ing) unrolling (p. 296)

uniquely (yü nēk´ lē) in a special, one-of-a-kind way (p. 245)

unison (yü´ nə sən) at the same time (p. 114)

unjust (un just´) unfair (p. 392)

unperceived (un pər sēvd´) not aware or understood (p. 126)

unprecedented (un pres´ ə den tid) never done before (p. 109)

unruly (un rü´ lē) hard to rule or control (p. 261)

unsanitary (un san´ ə ter ē) dirty (p. 279)

uptight (up´ tīt) very upset, angry, or worried (p. 9)

urban (ėr´ bən) of or about cities or towns (p. 327)

usurps (yü zėrpz´) uses without permission (p. 270)

utterly (ut´ ər lē) totally, completely (p. 70)

uttermost (ut´ ər mōst) furthest; greatest (p. 317)

a	hat	e	let	ī	ice	ô	order	ù	put	sh	she		a	in about
ā	age	ē	equal	o	hot	oi	oil	ü	rule	th	thin	ə	e	in taken
ä	far	ėr	term	ō	open	ou	out	ch	child	ŦH	then		i	in pencil
â	care	i	it	ȯ	saw	u	cup	ng	long	zh	measure		o	in lemon
													u	in circus

V

vacant (vā′ kənt) empty; not filled (p. 178)

vacate (vā′ kāt) leave (p. 211)

vacillate (vas′ ə lāt) sway (p. 292)

vacuous (vak′ yü əs) empty (p. 178)

vagabonds (vag′ ə bond) homeless people who wander from place to place (p. 52)

vague (vāg) not clear (p. 70)

valiant (val′ yənt) brave (p. 545)

vandals (van′ dlz) people who destroy or damage things on purpose (p. 545)

variegated (ver′ ē ə gā tid) varied; marked with different colors (p. 108)

varmints (vär′ məntz) creatures such as rats or mice (p. 534)

vehemently (vē′ ə mənt lē) strongly (p. 129)

ventilator (ven′ tl ā tər) a passage in a house that air is blown through (p. 56)

verge (vėrj) the point at which something begins (p. 84)

verified (ver′ ə fīd) proved to be true (p. 181)

veterans (vet′ ər ənz) people who have served in the Armed Forces (p. 242)

vexed (veksd) angered or annoyed (p. 125)

vice versa (vī′ sə vėr′ sə) Latin for "the other way around" (p. 294)

vicious (vish′ əs) very violent or cruel (p. 180)

victor (vik′ tər) winner (p. 367)

vigilant (vij′ ə lənt) watchful; alert (p. 216)

violation (vī′ ə lā′ shən) disobedience (p. 74); breaking the law (p. 280)

virtually (vėr′ chü əl lē) almost (p. 272)

vitiated (vish′ ē ā təd) destroyed the legal force of something (p. 107)

vouch (vouch) to guarantee as true (p. 212)

W

warp (wôrp) to change the shape of; to twist (p. 343)

wary (wer′ ē) careful or cautious (p. 128, 208)

welfare (wel′ fer) well-being (p. 278)

well-manicured (wel′ man′ ə kyürd) trimmed and tidy (p. 411)

well-tended (wel′ ten′ dəd) carefully cared for (p. 490)

withdraw (wiŧH drô′) to retreat; to fall back (p. 353)

wizened (wiz′ nd) dried up; shriveled (p. 117)

woven (wō′ vən) threads or strips of cloth made into fabric (p. 40)

wretched (rech′ id) poor and miserable (pp. 23, 214); worthless, seen with scorn (p. 54)

writhed (rīŧHd) twisted as in pain (p. 55)

Y

yearningly (yėr′ ning lē) longingly (p. 111)

Index of Authors and Titles

Index

Exaggeration, 534, 541. *See also* Hyperbole
  defined, 530
Excerpt, defined, 257, 485
Exclamation points,
  punctuation guidelines
  for, 589
Exposition, 102
  defined, 46
Expository speeches, 602
Expository writing, 591
  defined, 231
External conflict, 102
  defined, 22

F

Fables, 507
  defined, xi
Fact, opinion *vs.*, 268, 302
Falling action, 17, 102
  defined, 46
False causality, defined, 607
Fantasy, defined, 485
Farjeon, Eleanor, 313
Fiction, 2, 3, 6, 81, 221.
  defined, xi, 2, 6, 565
  elements of, 2
  historical, 2
  nonfiction *vs.*, 67, 81, 94
  novellas, 2
  novels, 2
  short stories, 2
  types of, 2
Figurative language, 310, 325, 330
  defined, 325
"Finish of Patsy Barnes, The," 137–49
First-person, 2, 47, 60, 103, 154, 164, 183, 191
  defined, 46, 152
  narrator, 46, 47
  pronouns, 191

Flashback, 103
Flat character, 129, 131
  defined, 122
"Flowers for Algernon," 151–92
Folk heroes, 573
Folktales, 573
  defined, xi, 521
Foreshadowing, 36, 103
  defined, 34
Forums, panels, 307
Fragments, 586
Free verse poetry, 311, 353
  defined, 349

G

García, Lionel G., 233
García, Richard, 324
Generalization, defined, 396
Genre definitions, xi
"Gentleman of Río en Medio," 21–28
Gerunds, 586
"Go to Boarding School," 66–79
Governess, The, 383–95
Grammar
  active and passive voice, 585
  adjectives, 219, 239, 265, 319, 584
  adverbs, 251, 265, 584
  antecedents, 91, 585, 587
  appositives, 585
  clauses, 585
  common *vs.* proper, 20
  complements, 585
  conjunctions, 275, 584
  contractions, 586
  double negatives, 307, 586
  fragments, 586
  gerunds, 586
  infinitives, 359, 586

interjections, 369, 584
  irregular plural, 496
  modifiers, 586
  nouns, 20, 98, 496, 584
  nouns, plural, 79, 496, 587
  parallel structure, 586
  phrases, 586
  possessive nouns, 79, 587
  prepositions, 282, 347, 584
  pronoun-antecedent agreement, 91, 587
  pronouns, 60, 61, 191, 319, 584
  pronouns, antecedents, 91, 587
  pronouns, possessive, 61, 587
  run-on sentences, 587
  sentence construction, 588
  sentence types, 515, 588
  subjects and predicates, 588
  verbs, 98, 359, 395, 455, 551, 584–86
  verbs of action, 120, 503
  verbs, tenses of, 132, 146, 192, 201
Graphic organizers, xv, 594
  Character Analysis Guide, 239, 580
  Concept Map, 20, 581
  KWL Chart, 577, 583
  Main Idea Graphic (Details), 581
  Main Idea Graphic (Table), 265, 580
  Main Idea Graphic (Umbrella), 580
  Plot Mountain, 225, 582
  Prediction Guide, 583
  Semantic Line, 583
  Semantic Table, 582
  Sequence Chain, 22, 91, 581

Acknowledgments

Grateful acknowledgment is made to the following for copyrighted material:

Pages 7–17: "Raymond's Run" by Toni Cade Bambara from *Gorilla, My Love*. Copyright © 1971 by Toni Cade Bambara. Used by permission of Random House, Inc.

Pages 23–26: "Gentleman of Río en Medio" by Juan A.A. Sedillo from *The New Mexico Quarterly, A Regional Review, Volume Ix, August, 1939, Number 3*.

Pages 35–40: "Old Ben" by Jesse Stuart from *Dawn of Remembered Spring*. Copyright © 1955, 1972 Jesse Stuart. Copyright © Renewed 1983 by The Jesse Stuart Foundation. Reprinted by permission of Marian Reiner, Literary Agent.

Pages 47–58: "The Adventure of the Speckled Band" by Sir Arthur Conan Doyle from *The Adventure Of The Speckled Band*. Copyright © 1996 Sir Arthur Conan Doyle Copyright Holders. Reprinted by kind permission of Jonathan Clowes Ltd., London on behalf of Andrea Plunket, the Administrator of the Sir Arthur Conan Doyle Copyrights.

Pages 107–117: "Who Can Replace a Man?" by Brian W. Aldiss from *Masterpieces: The Best Science Fiction Of The Century*. Copyright © 1965 by Brian Aldiss. Reproduced with permission of Curtis Brown Group, Ltd., London on behalf of Brian Aldiss.

Pages 123–129: "The Tell-Tale Heart" edited by Thomas Ollive Mabbott from *Collected Works of Edgar Allan Poe: Volume III—Tales and Sketches 1843–1849*, pp. 789–798, Cambridge, Mass.: Harvard University Press. Copyright © 1978 by the President and Fellows of Harvard College. Reprinted by permission of Harvard University Press.

Pages 153–189: "Flowers for Algernon" (short story version edited for this edition) by Daniel Keyes. Copyright © 1959 by Daniel Keyes. Reprinted by permission of William Morris Agency, LLC on behalf of the Author.

Pages 195–199: "Thank You, M'am" by Langston Hughes from *Short Stories*. Copyright © 1996 by Ramona Bass and Arnold Rampersad. Used by permission of Hill and Wang, a division of Farrar, Straus and Giroux, LLC.

Pages 208–216: "A Moving Day" by Susan Nunes. Reprinted from Silvia Watanabe and Carol Bruchac (eds.), *Asian American Women's Fiction*, and Scott Walker (ed.) *The Graywolf Annual Seven: Stories from the American Mosaic*. Reprinted by permission of Susan Nunes.

Pages 235–237: "Baseball" by Lionel G. García from *I Can Hear the Cowbells Ring* (Houston: Arte Publico Press—University of Houston, 1994). Reprinted by permission of Arte Público Press.

Pages 242–248: "Always to Remember: The Vision of Maya Ying Lin" by Brent Ashabranner from *Always to Remember*. Copyright © 1988. Reprinted by permission of Brent Ashabranner.

Pages 253–254: "The War in Vietnam" by Dr. James West Davidson and Dr. Michael B. Stoff from *The American Nation*. Copyright © 2003 by Pearson Education, Inc., publishing as Prentice Hall. Used by permission.

Pages 258–262: "Why Leaves Turn Color in the Fall" by Diane Ackerman from *A Natural History Of The Senses*. Copyright © 1990 by Diane Ackerman. Used by permission of Random House, Inc.

Pages 269–272: "The Trouble with Television" by Robert MacNeil condensed from a *Speech, November 1984 at President Leadership Forum, SUNY*. Copyright © 1985 by Reader's Digest and Robert MacNeil. Reprinted by permission of Robert MacNeil.

Pages 289–296: "A Child's Garden of Manners" by Jean Kerr from THE SNAKE HAS ALL THE LINES, copyright © 1960 by Jean Kerr. Used by permission of Doubleday, a division of Random House.

Page 315: "Cat!" by Eleanor Farjeon from *Poems For Children*. Copyright © 1938 by Eleanor Farjeon. Copyright © renewed 1966 by Gervase Farjeon. Used by permission of Harold Ober Associates Incorporated.

Page 316: "Silver" by Walter de la Mare from *The Complete Poems of Walter de la Mare 1901–1918*. Reprinted by permission of The Literary Trustees of Walter de la Mare and the Society of Authors as their representative.

Page 317: "Your World" by Georgia Douglas Johnson from *American Negro Poetry*.

Page 327: "Concrete Mixers" by Patricia Hubbell from *8 A.M. Shadows*. Copyright © 1965, 1993 by Patricia Hubbell. Reprinted by permission of Marian Reiner, Literary Agent.

Page 328: "The City is So Big" by Richard Garcia.

Page 329: "Harlem Night Song" by Langston Hughes from *The Collected Poems of Langston Hughes*, copyright © 1994 by The Estate of Langston Hughes. Used by permission of Alfred A. Knopf, an imprint of Random House Children's Books, a division of Random House, Inc.

Pages 334–335: "Southbound on the Freeway" by May Swenson from *The Complete Poems to Solve*. Reprinted by permission of The Literary Estate of May Swenson.

Pages 341–342: "Pig Roast" by Sandra Castillo from *Cool Salsa: Bilingual Poems on Growing Up Latino in the United States.* Copyright © by Sandra Castillo. Reprinted by permission of Sandra Castillo.

Pages 344–345: "Old Man" by Ricardo Sánchez from *Selected Poems.* Used by permission of Maria Teresa Sánchez.

Pages 350–351: "January" by John Updike from *A Child's Calendar.* Text copyright © 1965, 1999 by John Updike. All rights reserved. Reprinted by permission of Holiday House, Inc.

Pages 352–353: "New World" by N. Scott Momaday from *The Gourd Dancer.* Reprinted with the permission of Navarre Scott Momaday.

Pages 354–357: "Easter: Wahiawa, 1959" by Cathy Song from *Picture Bride.* Copyright © 1983 by Cathy Song. Reprinted by permission of Yale University Press.

Pages 385–392: "The Governess" by Neil Simon from *The Good Doctor.* Copyright © 1974 by Neil Simon. Copyright © renewed 2002 by Neil Simon. Professionals and amateurs are hereby warned that THE GOOD DOCTOR is fully protected under the Berne Convention and the Universal Copyright Convention and is subject to royalty. All rights, including without limitation professional, amateur, motion picture, television, radio, recitation, lecturing, public reading and foreign translation rights, computer media rights and the right of reproduction, and electronic storage or retrieval, in whole or part and in any form, are strictly reserved and none of these rights can be exercised or used without written permission from the copyright owner. Inquiries for stock and amateur performances should be addressed to Samuel French, Inc., 45 West 25th Street, New York, NY 10010. All other inquiries should be addressed to Gary N. DaSilva, 111 N. Sepulveda Blvd., Suite 250, Manhattan Beach, CA 90266-6850. Used by permission of Gary N. DaSilva.

Pages 402–404: "The Ninny" by Anton Chekhov from *The Image of Chekhov,* translated by Robert Payne, copyright © 1963 and renewed 1991 by Alfred A. Knopf, Inc. Used by permission of Alfred A. Knopf, an imprint of Random House Children's Books, a division of Random House, Inc.

Pages 411–452 and Pages 457–476: "Afternoon of the Elves" by Y York from Afternoon of the Elves. Copyright © by Y York. All inquiries regarding performance rights should be addressed to The Dramatic Publishing Company, 311 Washington Street, P.O. Box 129, Woodstock, IL 60098; Phone 815-338-7170; Fax 815-338-8981. Used by permission of The Dramatic Publishing Company.

Pages 486–492: "from Afternoon of the Elves" by Janet Taylor Lisle from *Afternoon Of The Elves.* Scholastic Inc./Orchard Books. Copyright © 1989 by Janet Taylor Lisle. Reprint by permission of Scholastic, Inc. /Orchard Books.

Pages 511–513: "Coyote Steals the Sun and Moon" by Richard Erdoes and Alfonso Ortiz from *American Indian Myths and Legends,* copyright © 1984 by Richard Erdoes and Alfonso Ortiz. Used by permission of Pantheon Books, a division of Random House, Inc.

Pages 522–525: "Brer Possum's Dilemma" Retold by Jackie Torrence from *Homespun: Tales From America's Favorite Storytellers.* Copyright © 1988 by Jackie Torrence, published in Homespun: Tales from America's Favorite Storytellers by Jimmy Neil Smith. Used by permission of the Estate of Jackie Torrence.

Pages 541–548: "Mose" by Mary Pope Osborne from AMERICAN TALL TALES, copyright © 1991 by Mary Pope Osborne. Used by permission of Alfred A. Knopf, an imprint of Random House Children's Books, a division of Random House, Inc.

Pages 554–557: "Choice: A Tribute to Martin Luther King, Jr." by Alice Walker from *In Search Of Our Mother's Gardens: Womanist Prose.* Copyright © 1983 by Alice Walker, reprinted by permission of Harcourt, Inc.

Pages 566–569: "The Deserted Children" by John Bierhorst and Edward S. Curtis from *The Girl Who Married a Ghost and Other Tales from North American Indians.* Copyright © 1978 by John Bierhorst. Reprinted by permission of John Bierhorst.

Note: Every effort has been made to locate the copyright owner of material reproduced in this component. Omissions brought to our attention will be corrected in subsequent editions.

Photo Credits

Cover image © Digital Vision/Getty Images; page x middle, © Andres Rodriguez/Shutterstock; page x bottom, © Anna Chelnokova/Shutterstock; page xx top, © PhotoDisc Volumes Education 2 41307; page xx middle, © Blend Images/SuperStock; page xxiv, © Andrew Judd/Masterfile; page 3, © Cartoonist Group; page 9, © Jeff Greenberg/PhotoEdit Inc; page 14, © Tony Freeman/PhotoEdit, Inc.; page 21, Courtesy of Raul A. Sedillo; page 23, Paul Burlin, "The Sacristan of Trampas," 1918, oil on canvas, 24 x 20 inches. Collection of the Museum of Fine Arts, New Mexico. Museum purchase, before 1922; page 25, *Springtime.* c. 1928–29, oil on canvas, 24 x 20 inches. Private collection, photo courtesy of the Gerald Peters Gallery, Santa Fe, NM; page 33, © Ed Clark/Time Life Pictures/Getty Images; page 35, © M.P. Kahl/Photo Researchers, Inc; page 45, © Keystone/Getty Images Inc.—Hulton Archive Photos; pages 48, 52, 54, 57, © Prentice Hall School Division; page 66, © Eugene S. Hill/Minnesota Historical Society; page 69, © Roger Viollet/Getty Images; page 74, © Underwood Photo Archives/SuperStock; page 80, © Brown Brothers, Sterling, PA; page 82, © Museum of History and Industry/CORBIS; page 87, © University of Washington Libraries, Special Collections, Hegg 3209; page 100, © Superstock, Inc.; page 103, © Bob Taves. All rights reserved. Reprinted with permission.; page 105, © Sophie Bassoul/CORBIS SYGMA; page 107, © PhotoDisc Volumes U.S. Landmarks and Travel 16247; page 116, © Yann Arthus-Bertrand/CORBIS; page 121, © CORBIS/Bettmann; pages 123, 124, 127, © Culver Pictures, Inc.; page 134, © Curt Pickens/Shutterstock; page 137, © The Ohio Historical Society; page 139, © Clark Atlanta University Art Collections; page 143, © Alan D. Carey/Photo Researchers,Inc., page 151, © Miriam Berkley; pages 157, 158, © Photofest; page161, © Martin Barraud/Stone/Getty Images; pages 162, 170, 174, 184, © Photofest; page 193, © Art Resource/The New York Public Library, Rare Book Division; page 195, © National Museum of American Art, Washington, DC/Art Resource, NY; page 198, © Tom Christopher, "Empire State." Courtesy of the artist.; page 206, © Susan Nunes; page 208, © Craig Hansen/Shutterstock; page 211, © Bettmann/CORBIS All Rights Reserved.; page 213, © Rosa & Rosa/CORBIS; page 214, © Michael Maslan Historic Photographs/CORBIS; page 228, © Jim Dandy/Images.com; page 231, www.CartoonStock.com; page 233, © HOUSTON CHRONICLE; page 236, © Jana Leon/Images.com; page 240, © Brent Ashabranner; page 242, © Catherine Ursillo/Photo Researchers, Inc.; page 247, © Rick Fatica at Ohio University; page 256, © Eye on Books; page 258, © PhotoDisc Volume 006 Nature and Environment 6328; page 267, © Robert Maass/CORBIS; page 271, © Jon Feingersh/CORBIS; page 276, © CORBIS All Rights Reserved; pages 278–279, © Bettmann/CORBIS All Rights Reserved; page 287, © Bettmann/CORBIS All Rights Reserved; pages 289, 291, 295, Marilee Harrald-Pilz; page 308, © Gilbert Mayers/SuperStock; page 311, © 'BIG TOP' 2003 Rob Harrell. Dist. By UNIVERSAL PRESS SYNDICATE. Reprinted with permission. All rights reserved.; page 313 top left, © Getty Images, Inc.; page 313 top right, © Hulton-Deutsch/CORBIS; page 313 middle, © Schomburg Center for Research in Black Culture, Art and Artifacts Division, The New York Public Library, Astor, Lenox and Tilden Foundations. Courtesy of Art Resource.; page 315, © Gary Nugent/Shutterstock; page 316, Edward Munch, "A Summer Night on the Beach". © 2003 The Munch Museum/The Munch-Ellingsen Group/Artists Rights Society (ARS), New York/ADAGP, Paris. Erich Lessing/Art Resource, NY; page 317, © PhotoDisc Volumes 044 Nature, Wildlife, and the Environment 2 44131; page 324 top left, Photo courtesy of Lee & Low Books; page 324 top right, © Prentice Hall High School; page 324 middle, © Art Resource/The New York Public Library, Rare Book Division; page 326, © Robert Pernell/Shutterstock; pages 328–329, © Roy Ooms/Masterfile Corporation; page 332, © Photo by Dorothy Alexander; page 334, *Where to? What For? #3* © 1998 Nancie B. Warner; page 339 top left, © Sandra M. Castillo; page 339 top right, © National Portrait Gallery, London/SuperStock.; page 339 middle, Photo of Ricardo Sanchez is reprinted with permission from the publisher—APP Archive Files (Houston: Arte Publico Press—University of Houston ©); page 341, © Barnes Foundation/SuperStock; page 343, © Andrey Khrolenok/Shutterstock; page 344, *El Pan Nuestro (Our Daily Bread)*, Ramon Frade, c.1905, oil on canvas, 60 1/4" x 38 3/4", Instituto de Cultura Puertorriquena; page 348 top left, © Michael Brennan/CORBIS; page 348 top right, © Sophie Bassouls/Corbis/Sygma; page 348 middle, From "School Figures," by Cathy Song, © 1994. Reprinted by permission of the University of Pittsburgh Press.; pages 350–351, Claude Monet, *The Magpie*, 1869, oil on canvas, 89 x 130. Herve Lewandowski, Reunion des Musees Nationaux/Art Resource, NY; page 352, Stephen W. Harley (Oregon, 1927–1928), *Wallowa Lake,* oil on canvas. Abby Aldrich Rockefeller Folk Art Museum, The Colonial Williamsburg Foundation, Williamsburg, VA; page 355, © David Muench/CORBIS All Rights Reserved.; page 357, © M.L. Campbell/SuperStock; page 364, © Corbis/Bettmann; page 367, © CORBIS All Rights Reserved.; page 378, © Freshman Brown/SuperStock; page 381, Mother Goose and Grimm ©2005 Grimmy, Inc. All rights reserved. Used with the permission of Grimmy, Inc. in conjunction with the Cartoonist Group.; page 383, © AP Wide World Photos; page 385, © Photofest; pages 387, 391,

© Everett Collection; pages 397, 398, © Bettmann/CORBIS All Rights Reserved; page 400, © Bettmann/CORBIS; page 402, © Jeffrey Coolidge/Getty Images Inc.–Image Bank; page 403, Courtesy of the artist Richard Solomon; page 409, © Dramatic Publishing Company; 419, © Envision/CORBIS All Rights Reserved; page 424, © Stapleton Collection/CORBIS; page 439, © Stewart Cohen/Images.com; page 451, © Leigh Beisch/Images.com; page 458, © Frank Paul/Alamy; page 471, © Bridget Zawitoski/Shutterstock; page 475, © Andrew Bordwin/Images.com; page 484, © Penguin Young Readers Group; pages 486, 490, 491, Judy King; page 504, © Images.com/CORBIS; page 507, © Cartoonist Group/Reprinted with permission. All rights reserved.; page 509 top, © Sophie Bassouls/CORBIS Sygma; page 509 middle, © AP/Wide World Photos; page 511, Cosmic Canine, John Nieto, Courtesy of the artist; page 512, © Ray Manley/SuperStock; page 520, © Irene Young; page 522, © DLILLC/CORBIS; page 524, © Casey K. Bishop/Shutterstock; page 526, Thomas Hart Benton, "Ten Pound Hammer" © Christie's Images/CORBIS All Rights Reserved. © Thomas Hart Benton and Rita P. Benton Testamentary Trusts/VAGA, New York; page 532, © Burstein Collection/CORBIS; page 534, © Corbis/Bettmann; page 539, © Getty Images, Inc.; pages 541, 545, © Museum of the City of New York/CORBIS All Rights Reserved; page 552, © AP Wide World Photos; page 554, © Bettmann/CORBIS All Rights Reserved; page 557, © Corbis/Bettmann; page 564, © Newberry Library/SuperStock; page 567, © Smithsonian Institution/CORBIS All Rights Reserved.

Staff Credits

Rosalyn Arcilla, Melania Benzinger, Carol Bowling, Laura Chadwick, Kazuko Collins, Nancy Condon, Barbara Drewlo, Kerry Dunn, Marti Erding, Sara Freund, Sue Gulsvig, Daren Hastings, Laura Henrichsen, Brian Holl, Bev Johnson, Julie Johnston, Patrick Keithahn, Marie Mattson, Daniel Milowski, Stephanie Morstad, Carrie O'Connor, Jeffrey Sculthorp, Julie Theisen, LeAnn Velde, Daniela Velez, Amber Wegwerth, Charmaine Whitman, Sue Will